ENVIRONMENTAL PROTECTION AND THE LAW

ENVIRONMENTAL PROTECTION AND THE LAW

N. K. CHAKRABORTI

ASHISH PUBLISHING HOUSE
8/81, Punjabi Bagh,
New Delhi - 110 026

Published by:

S.B. Nangia
for **Ashish Publishing House**
8/81, Punjabi Bagh
New Delhi - 110 026
Tel : 500581, 5410924

Showroom:
5, Ansari Road,
New Delhi - 110 002
Phone : 3274050

ISBN 81-7024-642-3

1994

Composed by:

S.S. Graphics
UG-8, Ansal Chambers II,
6, Bhikaji Cama Place,
New Delhi - 110 066
Tel : 6881521

Printed at:
Efficient Offset Printers
215, Shahzada Bagh Indl. Complex,
Phase-II, Phone : 533736, 533762
Delhi - 110 035

This book is dedicated
to
my wife Smt Enakshi Chakrabarti
and
my daughter Miss Poulomi Chakrabarti
who willingly gave up
their claim to the time
which would have been theirs
in order that this book
may be written.

Preface

"We shall have not another Earth
If this one were dead".

Thus environmental protection is a topic which has been at the forefront of the social concern during last two decades in both national and international level. But most of this concern has been directed towards the study of impact of environmental pollution to human health, natural fauna and flora, bio-sphere and developing a preventive technology. Therefore this book on "Environmental Protection and the Law" will be very much helpful for adopting regulatory mechanisms to protect human environment through law.

A national seminar of law teachers and scholars at Punjab University in February, 1984 recommended for adopting environmental law as an optional subject in the law curriculum and as a compulsory subject in due course. The seminar also felt urgent need for : (1) a compilation of environmental legislation; (2) a compendium of cases and materials; and (3) a text of environmental law. Thereafter the Curriculum Development Committee of University Grants Commission on Law in 1990 also recommended environmental law as a compulsory paper in both LL.B. and LL.M. levels. This book has been designed to meet the aforesaid needs and to add the currently available materials on environmental law particularly to make a complete volume of environmental legislations in India.

I would take this opportunity to acknowledge my deep gratitude to Dr. Chhatrapati Singh for his encouragement in writing this book. I am also indebted to Shri Biswajit Mukherjee, Law Officer, West Bengal Pollution Control Board for his co-operation to collect source materials and information in many aspects. My thanks are also due to Shri Benimadhav

Chatterjee, Part-time Lecturer of my Department who constantly helped me in collecting materials and preparation of the manuscripts who has done his LL.M. Term Paper on Environmental Law.

Last but not the least, I have to express my gratitude to M/s. Ashish Publishing House for publishing another academic book on Environment in an excellent manner.

Bankim Kanan, P.O. Chuchura R.S.
Hooghly-712102 **Dr. N.K. Chakrabarti**

CONTENTS

Appendices

Abbreviations

AIR	...	All India Reporter
CCNNR	...	Convention of Conservation of Nature and Natural Resources
DDT	...	Dichloro-Diphenyl Trichloro-ethane
ECE	...	Economic Commission for Europe
FAO	...	Food and Agricultural Association
IGF	...	Inspector General of Forest
IMCO	...	International Maritime Consultative Organisation
MAB	...	Man And Biosphere
MIC	...	Methyl isocyanate
NEER	...	National Environmental Engineering Research Institute
UK	...	United Kingdom
UNCHE	...	United Nations Conference on Human Environment
UNDP	...	United Nations Development Programme
UNESCO	...	United Nations Educational, Scientific and Cultural Organisation
UN (O)	...	United Nations Organisation
USA	...	United States of America
USSR	...	Union of Soviet Socialist Republics
WCED	...	World Commission on Environment and Development
WHO	...	World Health Organisation
WWF	...	World Wild Convention

Table of Cases

Table of Statutes

1. AMERICA

(1) Noise Pollution and Abatement Act, 1970

(2) Oil Pollution Control Act, 1924 (U.S.A)

(3) Public Health Services Act, 1912 (U.S.A)

(4) Rivers and Harbours Act, 1899 (U.S.A)

(5) Water Duality Act, 1965 (U.S.A)

(6) Water Pollution Control Act, 1948, (U.S.A) 1970

2. AUSTRALIA

(1) Biological Control Act, 1984 (Australia)

(2) Environmental Planning and Assessment Act, 1979.

(3) Fisheries Act, 1952 (Australia).

(4) Environment Protection (Alligator Rivers Region) Act, 1978 (Australia).

(5) Environment Protection (Impact of Proposals) Act, 1974, (Australia).

(6) Environment Protection (Sea Dumping) Act, 1981 (Australia)

(7) Environment Protection (Northern Territory Supreme Court) Act, 1978 (Australia).

(8) Environment Protection (Nuclear Code) Act, 1978 (Aus.)

(9) Protection of Sea (Civil Liability) Act, 1981 (Aus.)

(10) Protection of the Sea (Prevention of Pollution for Ships) Act, 1983 (Australia).

3. ENGLAND

(1) Clean River (Estuaries and Tidal Water) Act, 1962 (E)

(2) Fish Water Fisheries Act, 1923 (England)

(3) Public Health Act, 1936 (England)

(4) Public Health (Drainage of Trade Premises) Act, 1937 (E)

(5) Rivers (Prevention of Pollution) Act, 1951 (E)

(6) Smoke Nuisance Law, 1273 (England)

(7) Water Resources Act, 1963 (England)

4. USSR

(1) Principles of Land Use, 1948

(2) Principles of Mineral Legislation, 1975

(3) Principles of Forestry Legislation 1977

(4) Principles of Mineral Legislation 1975

(5) Punishment of Environmental Pollution Crimes relating to Human Act, 1970

(6) Laws on Air Quality, 1981

(7) Laws on Animal World, 1980

OTHER COUNTRIES

1. Basic Law of Environment Pollution Control, 1971 (Japan)
2. Environmental Public Health Act, 1968 (Singapore).
3. Environmental Pollution Law, 1969 (Sweden).

INDIA

1. Air (Prevention and Control of Pollution) Act, 1981.
2. Ancient Monument And Archaeological Sights and Remains Act, 1958.
3. Atomic Energy Act, 1962.
4. Bengal Smoke Nuisance Act, 1905.
5. Environment (Protection) Act, 1986.
6. Explosives Act, 1884.
7. Factories Act, 1948.

8. Forest (Conservation) Act, 1980.
9. Indian Penal Code, 1860.
10. Indian Easement Act, 1982.
11. Indian Fisheries Act, 1897.
12. Indian Ports Act, 1908.
13. Inland Stream Vessels Act, 1917.
14. Indian Forest Act, 1927.
15. Indian Boilers Act, 1923.
16. Industries (Development & Regulation) Act, 1951.
17. Insecticides Act, 1968.
18. Motor Vehicles Act, 1939.
19. Mines and Minerals (Regulation & Development) Act 1947
20. Merchant Shipping (Amendment) Act, 1983.
21. Northern India Canal and Drainage Act, 1873.
22. Obstruction in Fairways Act, 1881.
23. Orient Gas Company Act 1857.
24. Poison Act, 1919.
25. Prevention of Food Adulteration Act, 1954.
26. Rivers Boards Act, 1956.
27. Serais Act, 1867.
28. Shore Nuisance (Bombay and Kolba) Act, 1853.
29. Water (Prevention and Control of Pollution) Act, 1974
30. Water (Prevention & Control of Pollution) Cess Act, 1977
31. Wild Life (Protection) Act, 1972.
32. West Bengal Panchayat Act, 1973.

Bibliography

S.No.	Author's Name	Name of the books
1.	Agarwal, S.L	*Legal Control of Environmental Pollution,* Indian Law Institute Publication, N.M. Tripathi Pvt. Ltd. Bombay, 1980.
2.	Bates, G.M.	*Environmental Law in Australia,* Butterworths, Australia, 1987.
3.	Baxi, Upendra (ed.)	*Environmental Protection Act: An Agenda For Implementation,* Indian Law Institute Publication, N.M. Tripathi Pvt. Ltd., Bombay, 1987.
4.	Gupta,	Kautilyan Jurisprudence, 1987.
5.	Government of West Bengal	*Compendium of Environmental Guidelines,* Department of Environment, Calcutta, 1987.
6.	Government of West Bengal	*The State of Environment in West Bengal,* Department of Environment, 1989
7.	Iyer, Krishna V.R.	*Environmental Pollution And The Law,* Vedpal Law House, Bhopal, 1984.
8.	Iyer, Krishna V.R.	*Law and Social Change, An Indian Overview,* Punjab University, 1987.
9.	Karpagam, M.	*Environmental Economics,* Sterling Publisher Private Limited, New Delhi, 1991.

10. Khanna, Gopesh Nath — *Environmental Problems And The United Nations,* Ashish Publishing House, New Delhi, 1990.

11. Leelakrishnan P. — *Law and Environment,* Eastern Book Company, Lucknow, 1992.

12. Manivasakam N. — *Environmental Pollution,* National Book Trust, India, New Delhi, 1989.

13. Oakes, Judge — *The Judicial Role in Environmental Law,* New York, 1977.

14. Rosencranz, Armin Divan, Shyam Noble — *Environmental Law and Policy in India Cases, Materials and Statutes,* Tripathi, Bombay, 1991.

15. Thapar, A — *Asoka and the Decline of the Mauryas* (2nd Ed.) 1973.

REPORTS

1. Human Development Report 1991, published for the United Nations Development Programme (UNDP) by Oxford University Press, Oxford, 1991.
2. International Law Association, Calcutta Seminar 24-27, 1991 Seminar Papers on "Implementing the Right to Development".
3. Planning Commission, 6th Plan, (1981), New Delhi.
4. Royal Commission on Environmental Pollution: First Report 1971.
5. World Commission on Environment and Development 95 (1987)
6. Government of W.B. Management of Hazardous Chemicals and Plant safety in some selected Industries in W.B., Department of Environment (year not mentioned).

ARTICLES

1. Buch, M.N. "Restoring Rural Ecological Balance Some Suggestions", In *Yojana.*

2. Dick, Thompson, "The Greening of the USSR" in *Time* Jan, 2, 1989 p. 44-45.
3. Divan, Shyam A. "Making Indian Bureaucracies Think: Suggestions For Environment Impact Analysis in India Based on The American Experience" in *Journal of the Indian Law Institute*, Vol. 30, No. 3, July-September 1988 pp. 263-292.
4. Fossyth, J. "The Highlands of Central India" in *Yojana*, August 15, 1990. Vol-34, No. 14-15.
5. Gowda, M.V. Srinivasa. "Social Factors of Economic Development", *Employment News* 28th March, 3rd, April, 1992, p.1.
6. Guha, "Forestry in British and Post British India: A historical Analysis" in *Economic and Political Weekly*, October, 29, 1983.
7. Harald Hopmann. "Environmental Implications of the Principle of Sustainable Development", ILA, Calcutta Seminar Paper, 1991.
8. Jacob, Alice: "Responsible Development and Ecological Balance" in *Journal of the ILI*, Vol. 27, No. 3, 1985, pp. 483-486.
9. Jain: "Poverty, Environment, Development: A View From Gandhi's Windows", *The Economic and Political Weekly*, Feb. 13, 1988, p. 311.
10. Khosboo, T.N.: "Deraded Lands For Agro-eco-systems: Some Policy Issues", in *Yojana*, New Delhi, Vol. 35, No. 1 & 2, 1991, p. 22.
11. Ogolla, Bondi D.: "Role of Environmental Law in Development" in *Journal of the Indian Law Institute*, Vol. 29, No. 2, April 1987, June 1987, pp. 186-200.
12. L.N. Mathur: "A Federal Legislative History of Control of Water Pollution in India", in Agarwal (ed.) *Legal Control of Environmental Pollution*, ILI Publication, pp. 86-94.
13. Kulshrestra: "Noise Pollution—Emerging Challenges and Regulation" in Agarwal (ed.), *Supra*, pp. 188-198.
14. Asit Kumar Bose: "Legal Control of Water Pollution in India" in Agarwal (Ed.), *Supra*, pp. 118-125.
15. Pal, Chandra: "Towards Better Management of Environment Law and Policy", in Central India Law Quarterly, Jabalpur, Vol. III, April-June, 1990, pp. 177-201.

16. Raina, S.M.N. (J): "Environmental Pollution by Use of Pesticides in Central India Law Quarterly, Vol. II, Part-IV, Oct.-December, 1989, pp. 455-465.

17. Sripada, Sumitra: "The Multinational Corporations and Environmental Issue" in the *Journal of ILI*, Vol. 31, No. 4, October-December, 1989, pp. 534-552.

18. Swaminathan, M.S.: "Science and Agriculture", in *Yojana*, Vol. 35, No. 1-2, 1991, p.8.

JOURNALS AND PERIODICALS

1. All India Reporter (Nagpur)
2. Central India Law Quarterly (Jabalpur)
3. Competition Master (Ambala)
4. Economic and Political Weekly
5. Employment News (New Delhi)
6. Journal of the Indian Law Institute (New Delhi)
7. Judgment Today (New Delhi)
8. Supreme Court Cases (New Delhi)
9. The Gazette of India (New Delhi)
10. The Calcutta Gazette (Calcutta)
11. Year Book of the United Nations (N.Y.)
12. Yojana, (New Delhi)

NEWSPAPERS

1. Ananda Bazar Patrika (Bengali)
2. Bartaman (Bengali)
3. Amrita Bazar Patrika.

CHAPTER - I

Introduction and Methodology

"The world is finite, resources are scarce
Things are bad and will be worse,
coal is burned and gas exploded
Forests out and soil eroded.
Well are dry and air polluted
Dust is blowing, trees uprooted
Oil is going, Ores depleted,
Drains receive what is excreted.
Land is sinking, seas are rising,
Man is far too enterprising,
Fire will rage with man to fan it,
Soon will have a plundered planet."

KENNETH BOULDING'S poem "A Conservationists"

A Background Study

The environmental pollution is now assuming a dangerous proportion throughout the world and a growing awareness is discernible to maintain ecological balance for the future generations. Throughout the last quarter of this century a global concern to protect environment is witnessed to preserve our inalienable right to life. Environmental pollution is said to be the gift of modern technological development, rapid growth of industrialisation and urbanization. Paul Harrison has put the point pithily:

> "The rape of the earth has been central to the past progress of Western industrialism: the plunder and waste of irreplaceable resources, the poisoning or destruction of fragile ecosystems, the belief that man can mould nature with no need to take account

> of nature's reactions to such a violation. Disdain for traditional cultures and social systems was a fundamental characteristic of all modern European empires, and this attitude spread to the new ruling elites who had adopted Western ways"[1].

A Soviet pamphlet also tells us the following facts:

> "It has been estimated that every year 16,000 million tons of oxygen ore burned up and that between 21,000 and 24,000 million tons of carbon dioxide are discharged into the atmosphere. The pollution of rivers, lakes, seas and oceans has reached a dangerous level with about 50 per cent of all the pollution of the biosphere being caused by the United States, which has less than six per cent of the world population"[2].

In the language of Martin Luther King Jr :

> "The means by which we live have out-distanced the ends for which we live. Our scientific power has out turn our spiritual power. We have guided missiles and misguided men"[3].

According to an author:

> "The vast use of energy and new materials effluents, urbanization and conjunction of pollutant elements are leading man on a course which can alter natural system of the planets geopardising mere existence of human civilization"[4].

The Bergen Ministerial Declaration on Sustainable Development in the ECE Region has pointed out:

> "Today destruction of the biosphere and its ecosystems, environmental degradation, population pressures, depletion of resources, and extinction of species threatened the quality of human life as well as human health and many of the earth's biological systems. Unsustainable patterns of production and consumption, particularly in industrialized countries, are at the root of numerous environmental problems, notably foreclosing options for future generations by depletion of the resource base"[5].

To comment upon the situation N. Manivasakam observed:

> "The Industrial revolution and our modern civilization turns the air we breath into a waste basket in which dust, noxious fumes, toxic gases, mist, odour and smoke are thrown"[6].

A World Health Organization Report says :

> "One hospital bed out of four in the world is occupied by a patient who is ill because of polluted water. Provision of a safe and convenient water supply is the single most important activity that could be undertaken to improve the health of people living in rural areas of the developing world"[7].

Environmental degradation is a global concern, and people everywhere should accept that the preservation of ecological balance is a responsibility of all. The Human Development Report 1991 of the United Nations observed :

> "It is ironic that significant environmental degradation is usually caused by poverty in the South and affluence in the North. ....
>
> Everyone has to share the same environmental space, requiring equity in the use of the environment within, and between, generations. Rich countries will have to consider cutting back consumption to allow developing countries to achieve their full potential. But both industrial and developing countries must also increase their energy efficiency and develop new and renewable sources of energy"[8].

To comment upon the effect of such environmental degradation particularly Developing Countries in the South the said Report also observed :

> "Three-quarters of the poor people in the South live in ecologically fragile zones, and around 14 million have become environmental refugees— driven from their homes by ecological degradation"[9].

Thus another question crops up in the present day society — Development or Environmental Protection? Thus environmental economists gradually assumes importance of environment in the question of development. According to Karpagam :

> "Environmental economics mainly builds its theoretical foundation on welfare economics. Through environmental pollution society incurs significant costs by reducing the assimilative capacity of the environment. These costs are external costs because the individuals and firms that use the waste assimilative

capabilities of the environment, are not charged for this use. They are in essence, using a scarce good at a zero price, at the expense of the rest of the society. Such external costs are also called as spill over cost. It is in this sense that pollution becomes an externality"[10].

He further observed :

"Environmental degradation has been considered by economists as a particular instance of 'market failure' because of the external costs it imposes on the society. This means that externalities like pollution disrupt the smooth functioning of the market system. The external costs imposed on the society and not accounted for by the firms are not reflected in relative market price"[11].

One Indian economist Dr. M.V. Srinivasa Gowda is of the opinion that :

"Development must not be at the cost of nation's life supporting ecosystem comprising soil, water, flora, fauna and other natural resources. Environment Protection is thus a new dimension of development which cannot be overlooked"[12].

This becomes so vital an issue that the United Nations is going to next International Earth Summit on Environment Protection at Riode Jeneiro in Brazil last June, 1992 to discuss many such controversial problems and the conference is entitled by the UNO as— "United Nations Conference on Environment and Development" (UNCED). In fact after the Stockholm conference on Human Environment in 1972, i.e. after twenty years this is the second big international conference on Environmental problem.

The conflict between development and protection of environment is also a burning issue in India today. On 18th March, 1992, some MPs in both Houses of the Parliament draw the attention of the Government about reconsideration of construction of the Tehri Dam in Garhwal, Uttar Pradesh and Mr. Sundarlal Bahuguna's (the leader of famous Chipko movement) three weeks old fast on this issue.

Responding to the MPs concern the Environment Minister Mr. Kamal Nath stated that the Union Government (which had earlier cleared the Tehri Dam Project in July 1990) was now actively considering withdrawing the clearance because of the failure of the Uttar Pradesh Government to fulfil secured conditions attached to the Union Government's clearance.[13] Incidentally it may be mentioned that the demand of withdrawal of the project was strengthen due to the earthquake occurred in the Garhwal in last Oct. 1991.

Prof. Suresh Srivastava also writes:

> "A recent survey reveals that every day millions of gallons of trade wastes and effluents are discharged into the rivers, streams, lake and sea etc. Indiscriminate water pollution is a problem all over this world but is now acute in closely populated industrial cities, India is no exception to this"[14].

Justice Sodhi has pointed out briefly the present state of affairs of India's environmental degradation thus :

1. With only two per cent of the world's land mass, India possess around five per cent of the known living organisms on earth.
2. Today a significant portion of 15,000 plant species and 75,000 animal species found in India are threatened by the pressure of human activity on land forests.
3. A little over 10% of India's flora faces extinction; many species may be lost even before possible value is known to society"[15].

He further reports :

> "Pollution levels in major cities of India like Bombay and Calcutta are going up and pollution of the atmosphere today poses a great threat to human health and life. One of India's Premier Pollution Research Institutes has reported that 60% of Calcutta's residents suffer from respiratory diseases because of air pollution"[16].

According to Dr. T.N. Khosboo,

> "The root-cause of poverty of India's teeming millions can be traced to land degradation, which assumes critical importance on account of the fact that agriculture, animal husbandry and other landbased rural vocations are unable to generate and support employment for subsistence and landless farmers in the rural areas"[17].

Environmental scientists have warned about water problems in India. S.N. Jain reports:

"Water technology experts have estimated that large parts of India will go without water by the years 2025 AD."[18]

The Centre for Science and Environment (CSE), India's premier NGO operating in the field of environmental activism, reports on the state of India's environment in the following ways:[19]

Between 100 million to 150 million hectares of India's land areas are rapidly turning barren and 1 million hectares of croplands and grazing lands are badly affected. Official figures claim current afforestation rates of about 1.5 million hectares. But real afforestation may not even be a third of that.

On an average, every hectare loses 20 tonnes of top soil a year. Every six months, more top soil gets washed away than has been used to build all the brick houses across the country.

Four million hectares have already been swallowed up by ravines. In the famous Chambal Valley more than 10 per cent of the villages are completely depopulated.

More than half the national mining comes from 40 contiguous districts of central and eastern India, the tribal heartland of the country. Several million hectares of good crops and forest lands have been destroyed in this tract by mining operations and hundreds of villages have been depopulated.

The Green Revolution pulls out more plant nutrients from the soil than it puts back. Ludhiana district records the highest deficiencies of plant micronutrients in its soil. Many farmers have already started applying zinc, iron, copper and manganese deficiencies are not far behind.

Seventy per cent of all the water available in India is polluted. Even the high altitude lakes are dying because of pollution. In many places the ground water table is going down leaving the poor person's dugwell high and dry. In many other places, the water table is going up creating serious problems of water-logging.

Between a quarter to half of the lands brought under irrigation can go out of cultivation permanently because of soil salinity and waterlogging.

The flood-prone area has doubled over the last ten years 20 million to 40 million hectares. And millions of people have been displaced and uprooted."

Justice Krishna Iyer's comments is worth mentioning in this regard:

"The unconscionable industrialization, the unpardonable deforestation and the inhuman extermination of living species betray an exploitative brutality and anti-social appetite for profit and pleasure incompatible with humanism and conservationism. Today a bath in the Yamuna and Ganga is a sin against bodily health, not a salvation for the soul—so polluted and noxious are these Holly waters now"[20].

The World Watch Institute's Report 1990 by Lester Brown and John Young estimate :

"That the world could be losing 14 million additional tonnes of grain output due to land degradation and crop damage caused by factors such as flooding and pollution. According to them, environmental damage could led to the net gain in global food output remaining at about 1 per cent per year, while population growth will be close to 2 per cent. Hence, they conclude that the food supply position will be tight and prices will rise in the coming year"[21].

The present state of affairs of the environmental pollution in this world has sarcastically described by Justice V.R. Krishna Iyer in the following words :

"Our century, before it expires, has a choice to make. It faces a Hamletian dilemma. To be, or not to be: that is the question — if we care or dare at least to frame the question and face the problem. I mean here not the nuclear terror in the hands of some of whom one holds mankind to horrendous ransom. Human survival is menaced by another equally homicidal missile eupher-mistically described as environmental pollution. If dehumanized industrialization, with all its profit-hungry vulgarity and its ecological insensitivity, invades Nature without enlightened resistance from society and poisons or depletes all the resources of land, water and air, the crucifixion of humanity is a certainty and the basurrection of the race a lost possibility unless we begin

> the battle for human values against barbarity incorporated, right now. Today is late; Tomorrow may be too late"[22].

Hence a study on Environment Protection and the Law is much significant in the present society not only for our country but for the world at large because law is regarded as one of the control machanisms to protect our environment. So, Prof. C.K. Chaturvedi has rightly observed:

> "Law is a means to an end. The primary end is assurance of human survival and so the first change on the legal system is elimination of pollution of those vital sources without which life on earth may prove impossible"[23].

Similarly, Bondi D. Ogolla rightly observed :

> "Environmental law has an important role to play in the development process. Through the creation of institutional and normative structures for environmental management, it ensures, **first,** that the utilisation and development of natural resources proceeds on ecologically acceptable lines; and **second,** that environmental considerations are incorporated in development planning"[24].

Framework of the Study

The events of last 50 years or so have demonstrated that the world is a small space in which all important events transient national and international concern due to massive development of technology in the communication system. The United Nation is deeply committed on the proposition that all nations should be able to enjoy to the benefit of the experience of all other nations. Thus, the UNEP Draft Principles of Conduct in the field of Environment for the Guidance of States in the conservation and harmonious utilization of Natural Resources 1978 postulates:

> "Since most natural resources are international, an isolated eco-management of a single State is senseless. Therefore International co-operation is necessary in the case of a shared natural resources"[25].

Therefore to a study of environmental protection and law, we have to take international perspective because we all need to know the experiences of other countries and more due to the fact that this is a global problem. Thus, in this study attempt has been made to look into the subject both national and international aspects though in matters of empirical study experiences in India, particularly, in West Bengal, has given emphasised.

Environmental pollution is a vast subject and the legal development during last 50 years, or so is so vast that detail description in this Macro level Research paper could not be possible. Hence, along with the International perspectives, focus of the study is mainly on the Indian Laws, regulation, Govt. policy and judicial role to protect human environment.

Though there is no acceptable clear cut definition of environmental pollution we may describe it as the unfavourable alteration of our surroundings and it occurs mainly because of actions of man. The environmental poilution may take place through changes in energy patterns, radiation levels, chemical and physical constitutions and abundances of organism[26]. Thus, pollution includes *inter-alia:*

i) release of materials into atmosphere which making air unsuitable for breathing;
ii) harm the quality of water by any release materials;
iii) harm the quality of soil and land by run-off and release materials;
iv) give out substances which damage the health of human beings, plants and animals;
v) odour and noise which may cause danger to health.

Methodology Adopted for the Study

The traditional research method is divided into two parts, one is basic research or theoretical research and other is applied research. Towards the end of this Century most of the Social Science researches are based on applied research, methodology. Since, law is one of the social sciences, so, the most appropriate approach to legal research should be applied research. This applied legal research is commonly termed as Socio-legal research. The study of "Environment Protection and Law" is in fact the problem of present life and law. Therefore, for a meaningful study it must be conducted in the applied research methodology. The model of research adopted in this study is the model developed by famous English jurists Bentham and his followers. Applied research may be undertaken in any of the following methods:

i) Historical;

ii) Experimental;

iii) Speculative;

iv) Descriptive.

Among the above methods the descriptive method will be applied in the study. The descriptive methods will be further developed by adopting the following modes of the study:

i) Armed-Chair study of the available materials,

ii) such as books, reports, journals etc.;

iii) Survey and field study;

iv) Reported as well as unreported case studies and current flow of informations on the subject.

Sources of Informations and Elements of Study

The sampling frame of this study is the world at large but, the ultimate analysis is based on the informations available in India specially in West Bengal has been relied on. The main sources of informations are taken primarily from West Bengal Pollution Control Board and Environment Department at Calcutta and secondly from current Journals, Law Reports and Books. In the macro as well as micro level study following elements are dealt with in this research paper:

a) What and why — environmental pollutions.

b) Need for control of environmental pollutions.

c) Various types of environmental pollutions.

d) Legislative provisions and its development, national and international level.

e) Court and problems of environmental pollutions.

f) Legal control mechanism to combat with pollution in West Bengal.

g) An appraisal of the legal process and suggestions for improvement.

The Research design of this study may be shown in the following diagram:-

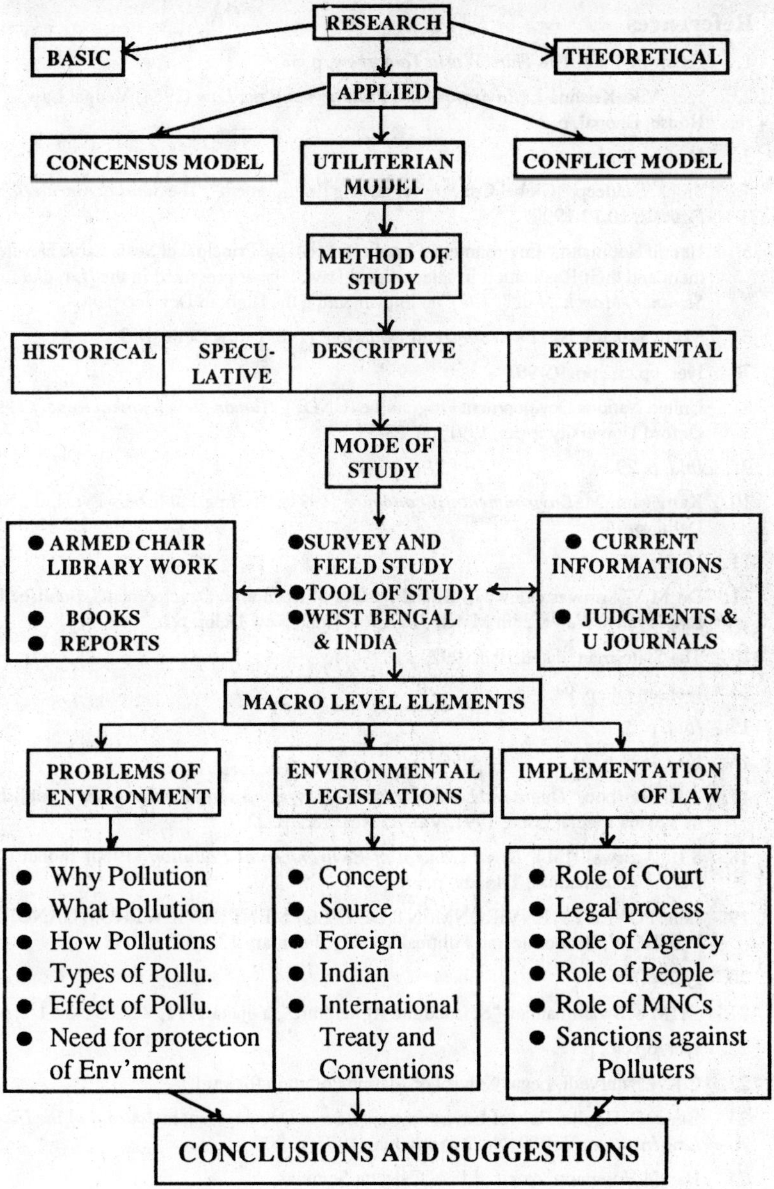
RESEARCH
BASIC
THEORETICAL
APPLIED
CONCENSUS MODEL
UTILITERIAN MODEL
CONFLICT MODEL
METHOD OF STUDY
HISTORICAL
SPECU-LATIVE
DESCRIPTIVE
EXPERIMENTAL
MODE OF STUDY
● ARMED CHAIR LIBRARY WORK
● BOOKS
● REPORTS
●SURVEY AND FIELD STUDY
●TOOL OF STUDY
●WEST BENGAL & INDIA
● CURRENT INFORMATIONS
● JUDGMENTS & U JOURNALS
MACRO LEVEL ELEMENTS
PROBLEMS OF ENVIRONMENT
ENVIRONMENTAL LEGISLATIONS
IMPLEMENTATION OF LAW
● Why Pollution
● What Pollution
● How Pollutions
● Types of Pollu.
● Effect of Pollu.
● Need for protection of Env'ment
● Concept
● Source
● Foreign
● Indian
● International Treaty and Conventions
● Role of Court
● Legal process
● Role of Agency
● Role of People
● Role of MNCs
● Sanctions against Polluters
CONCLUSIONS AND SUGGESTIONS

References

1. Harrison, Paul: *The Third World Tomorrow*, p. 38.
2. Iyer, V.R. Krishna J.: *Environmental Pollution and the Law* (1984) Vedpal Law House, Bhopal, p. 3.
3. *Ibid.* p. 95.
4. Sinha, Sandeep, "Global Concern for Saving Environment", The *Sunday Amrita Bazar Patrika*, 10.12.1990.
5. Harald Hopmann, "Environmental Implications of the Principle of Sustainable Development and their Realization in International Law." Paper presented in the *ILA, Calcutta Seminar, March 24-.27, 1991* on Implementing the Right to Development.
6. Manivasakam, N.: *Environmental Pollution,* (1989) New Delhi, p. 3.
7. Iyer, op.cit., pp. 95-96.
8. United Nations Development Programme (UNDP), *Human Development Report 1991*, Oxford University Press, 1991, pp. 28-29.
9. *Ibid.* p. 29.
10. Karpagam, M. *Environmental Economics* (1991), Sterling Publishers Pvt. Ltd., New Delhi, p. 14.
11. *Ibid.* p. 15.
12. Dr. M.V. Srinivasa Gowda, "Social Factors of Economic Development", published in *Employment News,* 28th March 3rd April, 1992, New Delhi. p.1.
13. The Statesman, dated 19.3.1992.
14. Iyer. op.cit., p. 94.
15. *Ibid.* p. 3.
16. Iyer, *Ibid.* p. 94.
17. T.N. Khosboo, "*Degraded Lands for agro-eco-systems some Policy issues*". published in Yojana special Issue, 1991, Vol. 35 Nos. 1&2 p. 22.
18. S.L. Agarwal (Ed.), *Legal Control of Environmental Pollution* (1980) Indian Law Institute Publication, Tripathi, p. iii.
19. Jain : POVERTY, ENVIRONMENT, DEVELOPMENT : A VIEW FROM GANDHI'S WINDOW, Economic and Political Weekly, February 13, 1988. p. 311.
20. Iyer. p. 95.
21. Dr. M.S. Swaminathan: "Science and Agriculture", Yojana 1991, Vol. 35 Nos. 1-2, p. 8.
22. Iyer, op.cit., p.1.
23. C.K. Chaturvedi, Legal Control of Marine Pollution forward.
24. Bondi D. Ogolla, Role of Environmental Law in Development in *Journal of the Indian Law Institute,* Vol-29. No-2. April-June 1987. p. 200.
25. Harald Hopmann, *op.cit.*, I L A, Calcutta Seminar.

CHAPTER - II

Problems of Environmental Pollution and Need for Protection

"Environmental Problems are really social problems. .... They begin with people as the cause, and end with people as victims".

— Sir Edmund Hillary

Environment Problem — What and Why

Conservation and preservation of environmental quality is the cry of the day. During last few centuries with the growth of population the environment has been subject to a harsh treatment by various human activities based on development of scientific knowledge. Be it capitalistic or socialistic mode of production and development all types are exploiting the world's common natural resources. We know that natural resources will be the ultimate supply factor to sustain growth. The capitalist capitalises nature, converting it into "inorganic body" of profit and treats nature as a means of multiplying cash-profit, capital and not man's essential forces and creative capabilities. Capitalist's exploitative consumption nature develop a negative attitude to ecological consequences[1]. The United States of America for example — with its affluence and industrial might, is by far the most profitable offender. It is reported that each year Americans throws away sixteen billion disposable diapers, 1.6 millions pens, 2 billion razors and blades, 220 million tyres. The carbon emissions from fossil fuels in 1224 million tonnes in 1987 as compared to affairs of 8783.7 million tonnes in 1960.

Although, U.S. accounts for less than 5% of the world population, yet it generated 15% of world's so, emissions and 25% of nitrogen oxides and carbon dioxide[2]. On the contrary a communist country like USSR is also facing problem of environment pollution. In U.S.S.R. in 1965 almost all the fish in the Oka river were killed because of uncontrolled dumping of effluent from chemical plant. Factories along major rivers such as Volga, Ob, Yenesei, Ural and Northern Dorina have committed similar offences and these rivers are considered as drighly polluted. Sixty per cent of all the factories in the Soviet Russia discharge their waste without treating. The shores of Baltic, Black and Caspian Seas are coated with oil. The Aral and Caspian seas have been gradually disappearing due to construction of dams across rivers[3]. The most recent example of misuse of water resources in USSR is of Lake Baikal. It is reported that the Baikal pulp factory produces 2,00,000 tonnes of cellulose fibres a year and its effluent discharged directly into the lake, has created a polluted zone; 23 mills wide. Clouds of yellowish smoke belching from the factory's smokestacks has settled over 770 sq. miles of Siberian wilderness and have killed an estimated 86,000 fir trees[4].

The present state of human affairs relation to environment led many philosophers, economists, sociologists, scientists and environmentalists to express their unhappiness of unnecessary destruction of earth's resources with horror. Philosophers like Prof. Jay Forrester, Barry Commoner, Paul and Anne Ehrlich and D.H. Meadows have predicted that if the present course of environmental degradation continue then it will destroy the capability of the environment to support a reasonably civilised human society[5]. Similarly the economist like John Stuart Mill in his Principles of Political Economy expressed a same view most eloquently:

> "If the earth must lose that great portion of its pleasantness which it owes to things that the unlimited increase of wealth and population would extirpate from it for the mere purpose of enabling to support a larger but not a better or a happier population, sincerely hope, for the sake of posterity, that they will be content to be stationary, long before necessity compels them to it"[6].

It is said that in 1800 A.D. the population of the world was only 100 crore. This number became double in 1930. Again that number became double in 1975. It is estimated that by 2025 world population will be around 1000 crores[7]. So the questions are how to get the required food, shelter, and other basic needs of human being in this world?

Prof. Jay Forrester has predicted a deterioration in the quality of life in future. He has been supported by many biologists and scientists like

Barry Commoner, Paul and Anne Ehrlich and predicted violent collapse of the world ecological system on the basis of two studies — 1. The "World Dynamics" headed by Forrester and 2. The "Limits of Growth" prepared by club of Rome under the leadership of Meadows[8].

Dr. S. Dillon Ripley said at a seminar in Delhi that in India :

> "Massive exposure of land, the soil and water and the air to the fruits of technological advance and development without regard for essential biological precepts can only hasten the degradation of what has been a fair land and a marvellous one for all manner of life"[9].

A recent study of the Doon Valley indicates that the once beautiful area is now becoming an ecological disaster. The region's 2,000 mm rainfall has percolated into its limestone-belt — a vital cog in the ecological cycle of hills. Thoughtless limestone mining over the past 20 years has resulted in a 50 per cent drop in agriculture productivity and the drying up of several perennial streams which once watered the land. Very few commercial concerns have benefited from the "rape of the land" but thousands of residents continue to suffer[10]. The Supreme Court observed in Doon Valley case :

> "This is the first case of its kind in the country involving issues relating to environment and ecological balance and the questions arising for consideration are of grave moment and significance not only to the people residing in the Mussoories Hill range forming part of the Himalayas but also in their implications to the welfare of the generality of people living in the country"[11].

Now to get answer why we are facing the present environmental crisis there are some Reports which are relevant to this issue and merit reproduction. First, Royal Commission on Environmental Pollution. First Report (1971): *Why there is a Pollution Problem.*

It may well be asked why it is that there should be a growing conflict between economic and technological advance on the one hand, and the quality of the environment on the other. There are two main reasons. One is rooted in a basic law of nature : it is impossible to add to the material resources with which the world is endowed and impracticable to dispose of waste materials outside the world and its envelope of air. Industry transforms natural resources and in doing so depletes some of them and spoils other — for example, our water resources — as a result of the undesirable accumulation of waste products. The second reason for the growing conflict is largely economics. Little can be done about the first reason, for even the most powerful legislatures cannot change the laws of nature; but many things can be done about the second. Governments can protect the environment through legal and institutional arrangements.

This characteristic of pollution has three main consequences:

i) Output of goods and services which give rise to pollution tends to be pushed beyond the socially optimum point. Also, expenditure to reduce pollution will often be inadequate. This is true not only for private firms or individuals : it is true also for public authorities.

ii) There is generally not enough incentive to reduce the amount of pollution per unit of output of the goods and services responsible, so that not enough resources and efforts are devoted to this objective.

iii) In so far as pollution costs are not borne by those who cause pollution or by the purchasers of their products, but by people who happen to be victims of the pollution, some of the total welfare resulting from the economic activity of the community is being redistributed away from the victims of pollution in favour of other groups in the community[12].

The second is the Report of the World Commission on Environment and Development (1985) : *Our Common Future :*

> In 1985, some million people were added to a world population of 4.8 billion. Each year the number of human beings increases, but the amount of natural resources with which to sustain this population, to improve the quality of human lives, and to eliminate mass poverty remains finite. On the other hand, expanding knowledge increases the productivity of resources.
>
> Present rates of population growth cannot continue. They already compromise many Governments' abilities to provide education, health care, and food security for people, much less their abilities to raise living standards. This gap between numbers and resources is all the more compelling because so much of the population growth is concentrated in low income countries, ecologically disadvantaged regions, and poor households.

> Thus, many Governments must work on several fronts — to limit population growth; to control the impact of such growth on resources and, with increasing knowledge, enlarge their range and improve their productivity; to realize human potential so that people can better husband and use resources; and to provide people with forms of social security other than large numbers of children. The means of accomplishing these goals will vary from country to country, but all should keep in mind that sustainable economic growth and equitable access to resources are two of the more certain routes towards lower fertility rates[13].

Similarly the Bergen Ministerial Declaration on Sustainable Development in the ECE Region declared :

> "In order to achieve sustainable development, policies must be based on the precautionary principle, environmental measures must anticipate, prevent and attack the causes of environmental degradation. Where these are threats of serious or irreversible damage, lack of full scientific certainty should not be used as a reason for postponing measures to prevent environmental degradation"[14].

With these background Government of India formulated its policy statement for Abatement of Pollution 1992 issued on 26th, February 1992 by Ministry of Environment & Forests which deserved reproduction:

> There is an increasing trend in environmental pollution. Water is polluted by four kinds of substances : traditional organic waste, waste generated from industrial processes, chemical agents for fertilisers and pesticides for crop protection and silt from degraded catchments. While it is estimated that three-fourths by volume of the waste water generated is from municipal sources, industrial waste, though small in volume, contributes over one-half of the total pollutant load, and the major portion of this is coming from large and medium industries. For class-I cities of the country, less than five per cent of the total waste water generated is collected and less than one-fourth of this is treated.
>
> Ambient air quality trends in the major cities indicate that levels of suspended particulate matter are higher than the prescribed standards or limits, especially in summer months. Levels of

nitrogen dioxide are increasing in urban centres with growing vehicle emissions.

Environmental problems are becoming larger in scale. The chemical industry generates an increasing quantity of substances every year, adversely affecting essential aspects of the composition of the atmosphere, soil and water. In the industrial high density areas, in addition to the effects on local health and impact on nature, we are confronted with damage to the social and economic functions of the environment.

With restrictions on releases to air and waste water, hazardous chemical wastes are getting diverted to land for their disposal. Earlier concerns with pollution that was visible and degradable are giving way to new types of pollution with very small quantities of synthetic chemicals that are not so visible and are injurious to health and damage the environment because of widespread use, persistence and toxicity. Reducing the hazards from toxic chemicals is now a primary public concern.

Human activities are also influencing the composition of the atmosphere. Despite uncertainties and insufficient knowledge, political and scientific decisions concerning environmental change will increasingly be necessary.

The state of the environment continues to deteriorate. The growth in scientific and technical knowledge has made it possible to use an ever increasing quantum of natural resources. The increase in population is further enhancing the pressure on the environment. The depletion of forests has been accompanied by increasing amount of pollution affecting atmosphere, soil and water. Some of the damage is irreversible. In seeking a higher quality of life while developed countries need to focus on changing the composition of their processes and products, developing countries will need to obtain the benefits of economic growth. The policy statement on Abatement of Pollution thus complements the Forest Policy Statement. The Government seeks to ensure that its policies in every sector are based on a set of principles that harmonise economic development and environmental imperatives".[15]

Let us now therefore discuss various types of environmental pollution resulted from development process affecting human health, plant, animal life and upset our ecosystems.

Various Types of Environmental Pollution

Precisely it may be said that rapid growth of population, industrialization, increase in the number of motor and other vehicles, various solid wastes burn in air dumping of raw wastes, the run-off fertiliser, pesticides in the agricultural lands, thermal pollution cause various environmental pollution. We may divide pollution in the following categories : (i) air pollution, (ii) water pollution (iii) soil and land pollution, (iv) thermal pollution (v) noise pollution and (vi) deforestation.

Air Pollution

Air pollution may be described as imbalance, inquality of air which causes ill effect in the nature. In the natural air various types of pollutants are continuously produced in the atmosphere and are continually removed by self-purification process of air. Hence, when the self-purifying capacity decrease in the Hermosphern the serfus Public Health problems may be developed due to accommodation of air pollutants. Though there are natural pollutants, such as forest fires, but we are concern with man-made pollutants which may be classified into two main roots: (i) gaseous pollutants and (ii) particulate pollutants.

(i) Gaseous Pollutants : These pollutants are substance which are gaseous in nature and most common of them are carbon monoxide, oxides of sulpher, hydrogen oxide, hydro-carbon, oxides of nitrogen, ozon and other oxides.

> **Carbon mono-oxide :** It is released in the atmosphere mainly from the automobile exhaust and it is said to be the most abundant pollutant and present in the urban atmosphere and it's density depends upon the Motor Traffic.
>
> **Sulpher di Oxide :** Sulpher di oxide is one of the most important contaminants of air originated from the combastion of sulpher fossil, and fuels. The presence of sulpher di oxide may be found in the appreciable quantity in the air surrounding the Thermal Power Plant. However it is also released in the air forms smelters where sulpher bearing ore is rosted such as copper and zinc, organic smelting Industries. Significant amount of sulphur di

oxide give out from Oil Refineries, Sulfuric Acid manufacture Industries, Fertilizer Industries, Paper and Pulp Industries and reported to cause heavy damage to agricultural and forest areas.

Hydrogen sulfide and Organic sulfide : Sulfides generally caused odour nuisance in the locality and they are present in very low concentration also affects the atmosphere. Hydrogen sulfide generally released from the production process of natural gas refining, manufacture of coke, paper manufacture distilition of Tar, Petroleum and manufacture of Rayon.

Hydrogen Floride : Hydrogen and other Florides are considered to be serious pollutants even when presents in concentration of 0.001 p.p.m. by volume. These Florides are generally released from Alluminium Smelting Industries, Phosphate Fertiliser, Ceramics and some of the Foundry operation. Hydrogen floride accumulates leaves of plants and thereby causes animal flourosis.

Hydrogen Chloride : The concentration Hydrogen chloride in the atmosphere are found to be less but if its concentration is higher then it will cause damage to vegetation, and also to properties.

Oxides of Nitrogen : Nitrogen Oxide are produced from automobile exhaust and also produced as by products of some Chemical Industries such as manufacture of Nitric Acid, Sulphuric Acid, Nylon intermediates, Oxides of Nitrogen are reported to be the second most abundant atmospheric pollutants and extremely dangerous to human health.

Secondary Pollutants : The aforesaid gaseous pollutants, are known as primary pollutants. In contrast to the primary pollutants there are secondary pollutants which are formed in the atmosphere. From the experiment it has been indicated that secondary pollutants, such as Nitrogen Oxide, produced in the combastion of Petroleum and other fuels emitted to the atmosphere yield ozon in the presence of sunlight. Many attempts have been made to reduce the level of ozon in the atmosphere but it has not reduced.

Air pollution affects on human health, animals, plants, materials and on atmosphere. Though the direct causes and effect relationship of Air pollution is not our concern but it may be said that it affects the human health and particularly respiratory system. Lungs Cancer, Bronchitis, Emphysema (enlargement of air vesicles of the lungs) and Asthma are some of the Chronic diseases caused due to exposure to polluted air. The effects of air pollution on domestic animals are similar to those observing man. The effects on plant primarily concern to agriculture. The effects of the Sulpher di Oxide are proved clearly beyond doubt. The gas is set to be absorbed through the Stomata into the Mesophel of the leaves. Florides seem to interfere with the photosynthesis and respiration of plants. Air pollutants also caused damage to property and materials to increased combastion of fossil, fuels and oil increase the carbon dioxide concentration of the atmosphere in recent years. Carbon dioxide absorbs heat strongly and the Radio active cooling effect of the Earth is thus decreased. Calculation and predication show that present amount of carbon dioxide will be double in the future resulting in an increase in the temperature of the Earth surface by about 1.30.[16]

Water pollution affecting agricultural atmosphere

Due to scientific and technological development new chemicals and techniques are applied in agriculture which contributed to environmental pollution, particularly to water pollution. Problems of water pollution are associated with agriculture and Industries. So we may discuss the problem in two heads. The agricultural water pollution may be caused from various sources, such as (i) Fertilizers, (ii) Pesticides and Insecticides, (iii) farm animal wastes and (iv) Sediments which enter water ways as run-off from agricultural lands.

i) **Fertilizers** : It has already been mentioned that use of fertilizers increased to a large extent. It is generally known that the agricultural fertilizers contain one or more of the plant nutrients — Nitrogen, Phosphorus and Potassium. Excessive application rates of such fertilizers causes pollution problems. These fertilizers may be easily transmitted to grown water by leaching, and to surface water by natural drainage and run-off. Nitrates are of the most pollutant elements since the presence of it in drinking water may cause methemoglobinemia in infants ("Blue-Babies"). The nitrates are reported to be reduced to nitrates in the stomach of the babies which has a great affinity for hemoglobin of the blood and consequently it forms methemoglobin. By the same process live stock are also affected by nitrate poisoning. The plant nutrients also contribute to eutrophication. It is also reported that plant-nutrients, nitrogen and phosphorus stimulate the growth of algae and other aquatic plants. Excessive growth of these plants interfere water uses and ultimately decay evil odours with the resultant increase in bio-chemical oxygen demand.

ii) **Pesticides** : Pesticides can be classified as insecticides, herbicides, fungicides, rodenticides, algaecides, molluscicides, acaricides and nematocides. Almost all the pesticides used in agriculture are toxic to human beings and animals. It is also reported that large quantity of D.D.T., Aldrin, Minex endrin etc. are capable of inducing rumors in mice as well as producing Chromosomal aberrations in plants. Besides there are hazards of occupational exposure of these pesticides which cause impotency in man. Moreover, pesticides affect reproductive abilities of fish and birds. So, it is said that the use of pesticides are the main reason for the decline of population of several birds and fishes.

iii) **Farm animal wastes** : One of the most important sources of soil fertility is farm animals wastes. But today they pose serious problems of odour and water pollution. Animal wastes are a major problem since they are permitted to enter water supplies when run-off carries the wastes into water courses, control of animal wastes is a problem of utmost importance but municipal sewage system are not applicable to farm animal wastes.

iv) **Sediments** : Sediments are soil and mineral particles washed from the land by storms and flood waters, from crop-lands and overgrazed pastures. Sediments cause many ill-effects. They also blanket fish nests, spawn and food supplies and thus reduce fish and shell-fish populations. It is estimated that the amount of suspended solids from surface run-off is always greater than that of sewage discharge[17].

Water pollution industrial : Industrial activities generate a wide variety of waste products which are generally discharged into water courses. Some of these wastes are poisonous and the effects of others are obscures. As the technology develop newer types of wastes are formed.

The principal industries affecting environment in all countries are paper and pulp industries, textile industries, food processing industries, chemical industries, metal industries and petroleum industries. The effects of the pollutants from the effluents of these industries are described briefly hereunder :

Paper and Pulp Industries:

These industries not only cause air pollution but also cause a great amount of water pollution. The effluents contains stray wood chips, bits of bark, cellulose fibres and dissolved lining in addition to a complex mixture of chemicals. The effluent may also contain methyl mercaptan, pentachlorophenol and sodium pentachlorophenate which are considered to be highly poisonous to fish. It also interfere with the aquatic photosynthesis.

Textile Industries :

The effluents from textile industries are alkaline in nature and they have a higher demand for oxygen. The effluents result from the cooking and desizing of the fibres. It is reported that the treatment procedures are tedious and the cost of the treatment is also high.

Food Processing Industries :

The wastes from the food processing industries such as dairy, breweries, distilleries, meat packing industries are principally organic in nature and they are putrescible. Hence, the receiving waters may be depleted of oxygen. Sugar industries, breweries and distilleries discharge wastes containing nitrogen, sugar, proteins, fermented starches.

Chemical Industries:

This category of industry including, acid manufacturing industries, alkali manufacturing industries, fertilizer industries, pesticides industries, and many other industries that manufacture organic and inorganic chemicals. Many of the industrial effluents contain acids. These wastes should be neutralized before discharge. Rayon manufacturing industries and D.D.T. manufacturing industries have a higher proportion of acids which have corrosive effects.

Petroleum Industries:

Oil refineries and petro-chemical plants produce a mixture of wastes containing hydrocarbons, phenolic compounds and numerous organic and inorganic sulphur compounds. They impart objectionable tastes and odours to the receiving waters.

Other Industries :

Other industries which are producing water pollutants are tanneries, soap and detergent industries, glass industries, electroplating industries etc.[18]

Thermal Pollution

Thermal Pollution means the impairment of the quality of environmental air or water by raising its temperature. To meet the tremendous need of electricity the generating power of the installations is required to be raised which need a larger proportion of stream flow. Thermal pollution is mainly due to "cooling waters" from power generating stations. This results in the raise of steam temperature to a level out of which natural dissipation of heat will be insufficient. During generation of hydroelectronic power sometimes negative thermal loading also occurs. Another contributor of thermal pollution is municipal sewage. The temperature of water is considered to be the major factor of environment problems since it may affect the concentration of dissolved oxygen, the rate of bio-chemical reactions and the physical activity of aquatic animals particularly to fish. Moreover due to defective technology burned coal ashes are flown from the thermal plant in the surrounding areas affecting plants and human health. As to cope with the development project we need more and more electricity. So it is obvious that the problem of thermal pollution will grow at a sharp rate because of increase in the electric power productions.

Noise Pollution

Noise may be defined us unwarranted sound which is caused by the vibration of molecules and is the periodic mechanical disturbances in fluids and solids. Man-made noise arises primarily from industry and transport though sometimes it may transmitted through amplifiers. In our present society we create more and more noise and it has become a major environmental pollution. Today number of motor vehicles has increased enormously and noise from these vehicles is most annoying form of noise.

Noise has its ill-effect on bodily functions such as cardiovascular system. Prolonged exposure to loud and uncomfortably sound will lead to temporary or permanent damage to the hear cells in the ear causing hearing loss.

Radio-active Pollution

Radio-active pollution may be two types (i) naturally occurring radiations and (ii) man-made radiation. Other man-made radiations developed from use of radio-active materials such as Radio-nuclides are used for production of nuclear fuel, nuclear weapons and production of electricity. The ill-effects due to Radio-active pollution are numerous. In short we may note that it can cause cancers, abnormal births and mutations in man and common to plants and animals.

Soil or Land Pollution

About one hundred years back in 1889 J. Forsyth, one of the earliest conservationists of Madhya Pradesh in India observed :

> "Our strong and equitable rule so greatly encouraged the arts of peace that population soon began to press upon the immediately available land, and this circumstance, together with the moderation and certainty of land taxation, soon bestowed on property in land a value it had never possessed. The culturable waste were becoming much in demand by enterprising settlers. The forest question also became urgent. A fear arose of the impending exhaustion of the whole forests of the country."[19]

The problem of soil and land pollution today assume great importance in the background of huge population growth. It results from (i) the disposal of solid and semi-solid waters from agricultural practices, (ii) insanitary habits and (iii) fall out from atmospheric pollution. Year after year the solid wastes are increasing at the same time rapid urbanisation with the increase of buildings has resulted reduction of lands of dispose of these wastes. Dumping of industrial and municipal wastes causes toxic materials to be leached and seep into the soil which affects the ground water course. Introduction of pesticides, fertilizers and manuers for agricultural contamination. Apart from these, direct pollution of the land by pathogenic organism causing diseases such as dysentery, diarrohea, etc. is a major problem of soil pollution. The soil pollution occurs in the following ways :

i) soil pollution by industrial and urban wastes,

ii) soil pollution by agricultural practices,

iii) soil pollution by Radio-active materials,

iv) soil pollution by biological agents.

Thus soil or land is heavily polluted day by day and as a consequence hazardous materials and micro-organisms enter in the food chain or water and ingested by man.

Problems of Deforestation

Forest is regarded as one of the main resources of a country and linked with all sectors of economy. But due to large scale industrial interest forests have been used as the source of raw materials for paper, pulp and rayon mills. Export of timber_products generates foreign revenue. Forest land is now being used for development projects such as dams. Moreover to the rural people forests are used as source of fuel, fodder, building material and minor forest products. On the other hand some industrial strip mining on forested land destroys the integrity of forest ecosystems and soil stability is lost. As a result of these soil erosion, run-off flooding and siltation of water are caused. For this continuous demand on the forests the problem of deforestation has gained much attention for its conservation. Due to deforestation the amount of carbon dioxide is estimated as 2 thousand ton and as a result the temperature of this world is increasing. The scientists estimated that from 1880 to 1990 all the seven highest temperature observed during last one decade. The average temperature in 1980 was 0.6 degree greater than that of in 1880 and in 1990 it is 0.7 degree centigrade higher the 1880. If such things continue the average temperature of this world will increase about 4 degree centigrade[20]. Moreover new development projects of construction of dams, irrigation and hydroelectric power creating problems of conflict between citizens and the State as we have seen in India regarding Silent Valley in Kerala and on going Tehri Dam in Uttar Pradesh. M.N. Bach observed :

> "After independence the hold of the vested interests was slightly loosened, though it is these very people who became the main instruments of destruction of the village forests and encroachment on common land. The State on its part, adopted a weak-kneed policy of tolerating encroachment and destruction and

allowed the delicate balance of land use in villages to be severely disturbed"[21].

About various environment pollution the Planning Commission Govt. of India described the present state of affairs in its **Sixth Five Year Plan** (1980-85)[22] which is worth mentioning : "Pollution refers essentially to a process by which a resource (natural or man-made) is rendered unfit for some beneficial use due to physical, chemical or biological factors. Of the various kinds of pollution (air, water, land, noise, radiation and odour) that affect the quality of life in India, water pollution is by far the most serious in its implications for the health and well-being of our citizens.

Water Pollution

The 14 major rivers in India carry, among themselves, 85 per cent of the surface run-off, cover 83 per cent of the country within their drainage basins and house about 80 per cent of the population in their basin area. Together with other medium and minor rivers, lakes, tanks, etc., they provide for our fresh water needs. For India's large and growing population, water courses must satisfy various domestic demands besides those for agriculture, industry, fisheries, navigation and power generation as well as be a receptacle for community, industrial and agricultural wastes. There is now a wealth of documented evidence of the adverse effects of water pollution from all over the country. These range from the transmittal of waterborne diseases like cholera, jaundice, typhoid and dysentery to fish kills and loss of agricultural productivity through the use of polluted water. From the Dal Lake in the North, to the Periyar and Chaliyar rivers in the South, from the Damodar and Hooghly in the East to the Thana Creek in the West, the picture of water pollution is uniformly gloomy. Even our large perennial rivers like the Ganga are today heavily polluted. Investigations by the Central and State Boards for the Prevention and Control of Water Pollution show that the major sources of pollution of our natural water courses including coastal waters are the discharge of community wastes from human settlements. Most of the community and industrial waste waters go straight into water courses rendering them unfit for most uses, least of all as drinking water sources. According to the Central Board for

Water Pollution only 8 cities in India are provided with complete sewerâge and sewage treatment facilities. They are Ahmedabad, Bangalore, Bijapur, Sangli, Nanded, Nasik, Thana and Durgapur. In a report on a detailed study of the seriousness of water pollution in the Yamuna caused by the discharge of Delhi's waste, the Board state :

> "What is depicted in this report is a replica of what may be seen at Ludhiana in Punjab, Srinagar in Jammu and Kashmir, Varanasi in U.P., Patna in Bihar, Calcutta in West Bengal, Gauhati in Assam, Cuttack in Orissa, Visakhapatnam in Andhra, Indore in Madhya Pradesh and Madras in Tamil Nadu. The daily discharge of waste water.... is threatening the natural water bodies like rivers, estuaries and coastal waters".

The water pollution Boards in the Central and State have not yet been given adequate support to tackle these massive problems. Far greater priority than hitherto must be given to this special sector.

Air Pollution

Air pollution is usually associated with industrial growth and urbanisation. However, in many towns and cities of India domestic sources which burn coal, cowdung, firewood or trash can be a significant source of pollution particularly under conditions of stagnant air in winter months. Fortunately, Indian coal is low in Sulphur content, the number of automobiles is relatively small and the rainy season is an effective scrubber for mitigating air pollution. Despite these advantages problems of air pollution are becoming severe in major cities like Calcutta, Bombay and Delhi. A high background dust level during certain times of the year aggravates the problem. Studies conducted by the National Environmental Engineering Research Institute (NEER) confirm that levels of sulphur dioxide and particulate matter in certain major cities exceed permissible limits set by organization like WHO. The high incidence of problems such as asthma, bronchitis, cough, breathlessness, sneezing and nasal blocks among people living in the Chembur area in Bombay is attributed to constant exposure to the high levels of air pollutants.

Studies by the Banaras Hindu University and the Tamil Nadu Agriculture University have established the adverse impact of industrial and transportation emissions on crop productivity. Fears have been expressed about the effect of power plant and refinery emissions on targets ranging from lungs to ancient monuments. With the Air Pollution Control Legislation soon to be enacted a strong and well-equipped enforcement authority will be required if the problem is to be checked in its relatively early stages.

Land Pollution

Pollution of Land results largely from the insanitary disposal of solid wastes. In India open dumping of such wastes (of municipal and industrial origin) on low lying land is a common phenomenon. This serves as a breeding ground for pests and disease carrying vectors.

Noise

Noise in our major cities and towns is a growing menace. Studies by the National Physical Laboratory, the All India Institute of Medical Science, the National Institute of Occupational Health, and the Madras Medical College have indicated the growing threat to our physiological and mental well-being from community noise in the occupational environment. While there are desperate bits of legislation (municipal bye-laws) that attempt to control noise, these have inadequate and there is now a clear need for a comprehensive legislation to curb noise pollution.

Among large sections of our population there is an inadequate perception of the extent of, and potential hazards from pollution problems in India. This sometimes leads to statements about pollution being primarily a problem of the advanced nations and therefore of no consequence to India. Such trends must be countered vigorously through appropriate methods of environmental education before the magnitude of our response to the challenge of pollution in India can bear a reasonable relationship to what is warranted by its actual dimensions.

Need for Environment Protection

The discussion of various types of pollution discloses the fact that mankind alter the characteristic feature of the earth of surface and surroundings. It has also been noted the detrimental and severe effect of man-made changes in nature. Therefore there is strong need to protect and preserve nature. It is said that God has given us this beautiful earth without its blue print and that does not mean we can use it to fulfil our own greed disregarding the need of the future generations. So, Mahatma Gandhi said : "There is enough in this world for every body's needs but not for everybody's greed"[23]. Almost same attitude revealed Mrs. Indira Gandhi while she was addressing the Stockholm Conference on Human Environment in June, 1972, she said :

> "The natural resources of the earth, including the air, water, land, flora and fauna .... must be safeguarded for the benefit of the present and future generations through careful planning or management. Nature conservation including wild life must therefore receive importance in planning for eco-development"[24].

She also asserted the need for attention of the Government to pollution problems in developing countries and said (1980):

> "The interest in conservation is not a sentimental one but rediscovery of the truth well-known to our ancient sages. The Indian traditilon teaches us that all form of life — human, animal and plant — are so closely interlinked that disturbance in one gives rise to imbalance to the others"[25].

Pollution is to be with us in same form or other since all production involves pollution in one form or another. Zero pollution can be thought only with zero production. Therefore what is needed is a policy to protect our environment by regulating pollutant elements, their ecological and sociological effects and to confine their ill effect to the minimum levels which are safe and appropriate for the quality of life expected today. That is why Prof. M.A. Markov observed:

> "It is become a recognised fact that civilised society is still intensively working on transforming our plan ...., into a desert, annihilating life. Everyone understands that it is time to stop this disruptive process, but we are hurrying with the decisive initiatives"[26].

Preservation of environmental quality is now the major challenge facing the world just as what we observed the labour and social questions in the classical period of economics. We should think in the long run to make a balance between planet's capacity and a sustainable growth in our agenda for progress. With this end in view some economist postulated introduction of the cost benefit analysis with the problems of environment[27].

In their draft convention on environmental protection and sustainable development, the legal experts of the W C E D drafted the following Article 7 para 1 :

> "States shall ensure that the conservation of natural resources and the environment is treated as an integral part of the planning and implementation of development activities. Particular attention shall be paid to environmental problems arising in developing countries and to the need to incorporate environmental considerations in all development assistance programmes"[28].

The Planning Commission of Government of India in its 6th Five Year Plan considered environment as a crucial guiding dimension for plans and programmes and environmental protection was understood in its proper context. The Planning Commission observed :

Environmental problems in India can be classified into two broad categories:

i) Those arising from conditions of poverty and underdevelopment.

ii) Those arising as negative effects of the very process of development.

The first category has to do with the impact on the health and integrity of our natural resources (land, soil, water, forest, wildlife, etc.) as a result of poverty and the inadequate availability, for a large section of our population, of the means to fulfil basic human needs (food, fuel, shelter, employment, etc.). The second category has to do with the unintended side effects of efforts to achieve rapid economic growth and development. In this latter category would fall the distortions imposed on national resources from poorly planned development projects and programmes, as well as from lack of attention to long-term concerns by commercial and vested interests. Thus, it is clear that a concern for environment is essentially a desire to see that national development proceeds along rational sustainable lines. Environmental conservation is, in fact, the very basis of all development[29]. Alongwith the tremendous growth of technology this world already witnessed three major catastrophe either due to little mistake as in Bhopal Gas tragedy or due to envy and greed for war recklessly as we have seen in the last Gulf War and these disasters caused thousands of death and at least ten lakhs of people are suffering various health hazards. In 1984 on the night of 3rd December about 42 tonnes of Mythile Iso Cyanide (MIC) gas was leaked from Union Carbide Plant at Bhopal which caused death to about 2,500 people and about 18,000 become permanently disabled. The Delhi Science Forum reported that at least one man is dying each day still now as a consequence of Bhopal tragedy. The legal battle between the Union Carbide and the Govt. of India is still going on Bhopal is bearing the dark side of modern industrial society. Within two years on 28th April, 1986 another disaster occurred in the Soviet Union at Chernobil within Ucrane due to leakage from one of the Atomic Power Unit. It is reported that at least two thousand people died as a result of the disaster and about 60 sq. km. within the radium of Chernobil the soil, water, plant affected seriously and the place is being now called as "Death Place". The effect of Gulf War 1991 is still effecting our environment as fire in all the Oil refineries could not be extinguished till today. Due to the Gulf War black smoke is covered surrounding the area on the sea water now following oil and the ecological balance had been suffered a lot.

Aforesaid incidences led us to think of environment protection at the International level also.

Professor Robert Seidman has articulated what is relevant in this context for our country in a working paper on Law and Development. He says :

> "By Law and Development, we mean something more precise and more professionally oriented. Every development programme proposed by economists, political scientists, public administration scholars, sociologists, agriculturists and other invokes law and the State as principal instruments to initiate the processes of change. The world around, it has not worked very well, Gunnar Myrdal has labelled the phenomenon 'soft development'. Our domain of study is the causes — and hopefully — the solutions for soft development"[30].

Therefore, the legal experts of the W C E D drafted the following Article 2 and Article 3 of their draft agreement :

> "State shall ensure that the environment and natural resources are conserved and used for the benefit of present and future generations (Article 2).
>
> State shall observe in the exploitation of living natural resources and ecosystems, the principle of optimum sustainable yield" (Article 3)[31].

Thus from the foregoing discussion it becomes very clear that in the name of development and civilisation we have plundered this earth and now facing its ill effects and imminent danger of human environment. Environment itself is not a crisis or problem but we have made this environment polluted by our irrational and selfish conduct. So all these environmental problems and crisis have to be analysed and judged in this context to evolve a preventive mechanism for controlling human conduct.

Hence development of legislations are required to protect our environment.

References

1. Karpagam M. *Environmental Economics* (1991) Sterling Publishers : New Delhi. p. 35.
2. Katyal, Timmy and Prof. M. Satakei : "*Environmental Pollution*", Anmol Publications, New Delhi. Cited in Karpagam, *op.cit.,* p. 35-39.
3. Karpagam, *op.cit.,* p. 38-39.
4. Thompson, Dick : "The Greening of the USSR", in Time, Jan. 2, 1989. p. 44-45.
5. Karpagam, *op. cit.,* p. 161.
6. *Ibid.* pp. 160-161.
7. Pathik Guha in *Ananda Bazar Patrika,* 29th, April, 1991.
8. Karpagam, *op.cit.,* p. 165.
9. Dr. S. Dillon Ripley, reproduced in *Competition Master* Dec. 1986 p. 348.
10. *Ibid* p. 349.
11. Rural Litigation and Entitlement Kendra, *Dehradun* v. *State of U.P.* 1985 SC 408.
12. Royal Commission on Environmental Pollution : First Report (1971) 4 reproduced in Rosencranze, *op.cit.,*
13. World Commission on Environment and Development, 95 (1987).
14. Harald Hopmann, University of Frankfrut, Germany, *op.cit.* ILA Seminar at Calcutta. p. 206.

15. Govt. of India Notification No. H 11013(2)/90 CPW dt. 26th. February, 1992 of the Ministry of Environment and Forests, New Delhi, pp. 2-4.

16. Manivasakam, *op.cit.*, pp. 20-23.

17. Manivasakam, *op.cit.*, pp. 70-73.

18. Manivasakam, *op.cit.*, pp. 63-65.

19. J. Forsyth in "The Highlands of Central India", (1989) cited by M.N. Buch in *YOJANA* August 15, 1990. p. 43.

20. Pathik Guha, Ananda Bazar Patrika, dt. 29.4.1992.

21. M.N. Buch: "Restoring Rural Ecological Balance — some suggestions", in *YOJANA*, August 15, 1990, vol. 34, Nos. 14-15 p.45.

22. Planning Commission, Govt. of India, 6th. Plan (1981) (1980-85) p. 343.

23. Karpagam, *op.cit.*, p. 79.

24. Karpagam, *op.cit.*, p. 243.

25. Harold Hopmann, *op.cit.*, ILA, Calcutta Seminar, p.193.

26. *Ibid.* p. 185.

27. Karpagam, *op.cit.*, p. 147.

28. Experts Group on Environmental Law of the World Commission on Environment and Development, Graham & Toofman, 1987, p. 65.

29. V.R. Krishna Iyer : *Law and Social Change. An Indian Overview* (1978) Punjab University. p. 60.

30. *Government of India.* Planning Commission, Sixth Five Year Plan 1980-1985, 343 (1981).

31. Experts Group on Environmental Law of the World Commission on Environment and Development, Munro. *Environmental Protection and Sustainable Development — Legal Principles and Recommendations,* London, Graham & Trofman, 1987, p. 28.

CHAPTER - III

Legislative Development of Environmental Law

"Remember, law must keep promises by reversing the self-destructive, over-indulgence of commercial exploitation of nature, burying up the tribal innocence and raping virgin earth, bleeding to death tomorrow for today's profit and in the process, blinding degrading ecosystem and distabilising the flow of progress".

—Justice Krishna Iyer

The Concept of Environmental Law

It is difficult to define precisely the boundaries of Environmental Law in the same way as we define Law of Contract or Law of Tort. The traditional legal subjects like Tort or contract are well developed by our long experience and precedent whereas the Environmental Law is said to be still in its infancy. However, attention is now increasingly focussed on the rationalization and streamlining of existing measures rather than the development of substantial Law. In the general sense Environmental Law means rules or regulations governing human conduct likely to affect our environment.

The term Environment when used in the statute may be construed according to the context in which it is used and the concerns of the person using the term. For example, Environment means the natural living and non-living surroundings of a person but not the built environment. To a planner it means man-made structures and surroundings in which human beings live and work.

To a social worker Environment relate to peoples, among themselves to Government and Bureaucracy, while a health and safety workers concern more on the protection of employees in the working places and so on. The notion of Environmental Law may encompass all or any of these Environmental question. Therefore to set boundaries of the Environmental Law it is quite difficult and complex matter. However, there is an accepted boundaries of Environmental Law which is in a state of flux. However, the accepted view of current definition of the Environmental Law is that which reflects the Legislative measures, the Administrative and Judicial structure to protect the Environment. Therefore, in this study under the various facets of environment the definition of Environmental Law does not generally cover health and safety work but that control over pollutants and Environmental contaminants. Current Legislations in India and abroad seems to acknowledge this concept of Environmental Law with all aspects of surroundings of man whether affecting him as a individual or in his social groupings.

To draw the boundaries of the Environmental Laws the first thing we should note that man seems to occupy the central place and it's affects on man of his or her environment which is the concern of Environmental Legislation. It may appears that the man is concerned largely with its own self-preservation, and there is no reason why environmental law should not be more wide. Therefore, legislation may be made to control human activities on natural ecosystem and living things. For example, legislation prohibiting cruelty to animals may be thought to be benefited only to the animals protected but it involves also the human dignity and morality. The practices of ecosystem are interrelated and the destruction of any habited or animal species which may not have any obvious physical repercussion and the surroundings of man may well have a mental effect on those closed to it. Boer has pointed out that environmental dispute is a touch-point of human feelings. "His feelings do not necessarily depend on any physical proximity or financial connection, and can be experienced simply by hearing about an environmental problem"[1].

The categorisation of environmental legislation reflects basically 3 stages of Governmental reaction to the problems of environment expectation, protection and managerial. Fowler has recently identified and developed 4 components of environmental law on the basis of Governmental intervention : developmental legislation, legislation relating to the disposition of natural resources, conservation of natural and cultural resources, and environmental planning and protectionist legislation[2]. Broadly speaking the environmental laws are intended to counter balance the application of developmental and resources exploitative legislation.

However Fishery has suggested 3 category of environmental legislation namely : resources legislation, (relates to development, exploitation or use of natural resources); conservation of specific elements (such a scenic features, wild life etc. and environmental plan) but basically we accept Fowler's classification of legislation which may be reproduced in Table 1:

In the past there has been a controversy whether natural resources law should be regarded as part of environmental law. The development and exploitation of natural resources always raised environmental question ranging from whether the development ought to be permitted at all, through the assessment of environmental impact, on two conditions governing reservation and regeneration of affected areas and the protection of the environment. Accordingly the environmental impact of resource development is treated as part of environmental law though the substantive law relating to other aspect reserve and development is not taken as environmental law. The environmental aspect of urban or town and rural planning have been included within the area of environmental law because comprehensive land use planning over a wide area will have environmental repercussion and party because at a more regular level decision taken to permit development may leave to environmental problems such as pollution, soil erosion or lands unique habitats. However, substantive law relating to urban planning are excluded. Thus we can described environmental law as any legislation or regulation or common law which affects the natural environment per se; which declares the rights or duties of any person to take action to development or protect the environment; or which may be affected the scenic historical, artistic or cultural beauty or appropriation of human efforts to harmonise the people and natural environment.

In practice, when we come to deal with problems of environment within the recognised legal framework we have two different types of law on this point — common law and statute law. Environment protection controlled under common law is concerned on recognised rights which are generally known in law as torts. Under statute law, on the other hand, environmental protection or control is concerned on public rights and interests. Yet, environmental law is more than just enforcing the statute law in the interest of people in general to protect the environment in both present and future generation. It is a recognition by the public and the Government to achieve a balance between development and protection of

Table 1

CLASSIFICATION OF ENVIRONMENTAL LEGISLATIONS

Development Legislation	Resource Allocation Legislation	Conservation Legislation	Planning and Protection Legislation
Public Development Indenture Fast Track Legislation	Mining Forestry Fisheries Rights to- Water Land Air etc.	National Parks, Reservation of- Fauna Flora Cultural and Natural heritage	Land use Planning Environmental Impact Assessment Pollution Control Waste Disposal Environmental Contaminants etc.

environment with a view to achieve quality of life on the basis of non-economic factors which is called "ecological ethnic".

Sources of Environmental Law

We have already noted that protection of environment were admitted through common law as well as by statute law. The common law is that body of law which has been developed by the courts of England since 1066 A.D. and Indian courts since the date of the reception of English law into British India from 1858. But today the main source of environmental law, as we understand now, is mainly statute law or legislation. So environmental law is almost a product of legislation and falls largely within the category of public law rather than private law. For centuries the common law was concerned with the protection of private, individual rights rather than with matters of public concern. This simply reflects the nature of the legal system that resembles 'mountain' and the courts must waits for 'Mohammed' in the person for a litigation to appear before them, otherwise they cannot pronounced on an issue relating to environmental problems. The litigants were generally appeared before the court under common law because of some private injury they have suffered, rather than out of any sense of public grievance. Consequently, only private environmental rights can be enforced at common law, such as escape of sewage and other contaminants, the pollution of water occurs the release of harmful agents (smoke) into the air and excessive noise or vibration. Any further rights beyond individual property will have to be derived from the modern legislation on environmental problems and not from common law. Consequently parliamentary activities on the control and protection of environment has been increased considerably particularly in the last quarter of this century. In one sense these legislations are also regarded as social welfare legislation creating a vast administrative structure to apply those environmental legislations. Though, environmental laws may be termed as social legislations yet, it does create any individual rights in the same way that welfare legislation does. Partly within and partly without the normal distinction between the common law and legislation, there is the existence of Tribunal or quasi judicial body dissolving disputes relating to environmental laws, such as, in relation to licences and permissions granted in respect of polluting effluents. Such Tribunals are established by statute and are generally entrusted the task of the court of law. These Tribunals are maned by both lawyer and non-layer members such as engineers and other experts.

Legislative Development in International Level

First attempt of International Concern for protection of Environment began with the formation of the American Fisheries Society in 1870. This society was extended in 1902 and renamed as International Association of Game, Fish and Conservation Commission. But it was a Joint Venture of U.S.A. and Canada and fail to extent its impact on other countries. The North-American migratory Bodies Treaty of 1960, demanded the Legislation in that country and as a consequences and Institutional structure was developed. In this way the things were going on.

In 1933, a global awareness was failed relying to preservation of Fauna and Flora in their natural States and raised question of International Co-operation to prevent environmental pollution and to develop Legislation. This lead to the Convention of 1938, which was signed by more than 60 states in London under the auspices of League of Nations. Following this Convention another Multi-National Venture took place for the protection and preservation of nature and wild life on Western hemisphere and was signed in Washington.[3]

In 1962, the first World Conference on Natural Park was held at Scattle in Switzerland. Following this Conference in the same year another Conference to preserve wild life of the indigenous states of the world was held at Gland in Switzerland which established World Wild Convention (W.W.F.) to care for nature. In 1963, the Council of Europe decided to set up a European Committee for the Convention of Conservation of Nature and Natural Resources (CCNNR) as a specialised body of Experts to assist the member States in their environmental problems. This must be said to be the first inter Governmental co-ordination to protect the environment[4].

In 1968, the biosphere Conference of UNESCO held in Paris on the basis of success of the previous attempt in the regional Conferences. However, the problem of Environmental protection and conservation have been dealt with by this Convention and Conferences not only a fragmentary amendment[5].

Other Treaties and Conventions to protect the environment pollution which deserve mention in this connection are as follows :-

The Nuclear Weapon Test Ban Treaty of 1963, Treaty of the Principles Governing the Activities of States on the Exploration and Use of Outer Space, 1967; Trȩaty for the Prohibition of Nuclear Weapons in

Latin America, 1968; Treaty on the Non-Proliferation of Nuclear Weapons, 1968; two Brussels Conventions, 1969; relating to intervention in the high seas in the case of oil pollution the Convention on wetlands of International importance and the Convention concerning protection of the world cultural and natural heritage 1972[6].

The U.N. Concern to the Problems of Environment

The U.N. concern for control of human environment was manifested in 1946 for the regulation and control of atomic energy ultimately led to the establishment of an International Atomic Energy (I A E A) in Viena in 1957. In 1949, a scientific Conference on conservation and utilization of natural resources was organised by the U.N. wherein it was declared: "The Nature's plentifulness is a heritage not to be squandered with impurity, it must be conserved for the future generations or its bankruptcy will extinguished us all"[7].

Under Article 22 of the U.N. charter the General Assembly has established a number of specialized agencies and launched many programmes, conferences and projects to fulfil the objective of Article 55 for a higher standard of living and social progress and to solve the health and related problems. Similarly U.N. Region Commissions help in formulating and co-ordinating and establishing organizations and Institutions to curb environmental problems as pointed out by the Bishop and Munro: "That merely all the Economic Commissions are, in one way or other, engaged in major studies or co-operative programme soon the environmental-problem resulting from the industrial and other activities in their respective field"[8].

The role of U.N. Secretariat is very important in this respect and it involves the following units for the environmental protection :—

1. *Office of Science and Technology* — to deal with the subjects such as developmental and utilization of natural resources, the identification and control of pollutants.
2. *The Social Development Division* — to deal with research and training Programme for Regional Planning and Development and utilisation human resources which includes studies of the social aspects of Industrialisation and Urbanization.
3. *The Centre for Housing, Building and Planning* — to deal with the development of measures designed to prevent deterioration of the human environment due to urban sprawl over-crowding, noise, air, and water pollution, traffic congest, congestion etc.

4. *Resources and Transport Division* — to deal with the integrated development of whole river begins involving the need for difficult Trade - offs, and the pollution free transportation in the internal water basin.

5. *The Public Administration Division* — to deal with the environmental questions through such activities as a comparative study of administrative aspects of code and territorial ecosystem[9].

But all this divisions of the U.N. Secretariat deals with the environment problem in fragmented way. This led to establish specialised U.N. agencies to deal with problems of environmental pollution.

Specialised U.N. Agencies

The following specialised Agencies of the U.N. are also dealing with environmental problems and collaborating in finding out the global problem to protect the environment. Some of the important activities of these Agencies are briefly stated below[10] :

United Nation Development Programme (U N D P) : This Agency helps to finance large number of resource conservation project related to conservation such as afforestation and legislation recallment, study of ecological changes and trading programme of different Training Institute e.g. forestry and water state management Training Institute (Argentina), Forestry Training Institute (Philippines) which gives training for the records Application of an Environmental approach to the decision-makers in the economic development.

International Labour Organization (ILO) : It was established in 1919, and since then it is concern of occupational Health and Hazards specially over the labour. It is also concern for prevention of dust in mining and Air Pollution control in the Industries. It is a subsidiary Organization namely International Governmental safety and health Information Centre in Jeneva which distribute materials dealing with problems of Air Pollution. At present it is more than 30 such Centres in different countries for distribution of such information.

Food and Agriculture Association (FAO) : This agency is mainly concern in conservation of soil, forest and territorial water. It has laid down certain norms which are to be followed by the member States. This norms are relating to water quality criteria for Fish, Integrated Pest control techniques, Pulp and Paper Mills effluents and use of sewage effluents for agriculture, forests and fisheries. It has organised various conferences and established various Commissions and launched Organization for the protection of living resources of earth such as Technical Aspect of Marine pollution, 1970 in Rome; International Plan Protection Association, Commission for Control of Food and Mouth diseases etc. are some examples in this regard :

UNESCO : It has been deeply involved with research on natural resources and related problems such as Arid-Zones Research and Humid Tropics Research. It had also launched an International Hydrological Decade in 1958 need banner of Inter governmental Oceanography Commission for monitoring ocean environment. It has also launched an integrated global ocean station system with World Meteorological Organization. In 1968 it has launched a programme on "Man and Biosphere" (M A B) to supplement a social-science programme and environment design for living which began in 1966. The Report of the Secretary General has highly appreciated the works done by the UNESCO. To quote "UNESCO has particular obligations in this field because it is becoming increasingly clear that development programme must be structured on the basis of the signed ecological principles and that there is no rationalization use without conservation"[11].

World Health Organization (WHO) : The traditional concern of WHO have been focussed on following 3 aspects —

a. Definition of environmental standard for the human to various stress factors concern.

b. The identification environmental hazards such as Air, Water, Oil and Food pollution, the effect besides, this it is vector the abuse of drug.

c. The study affected induced changes with environment such as rapid pollution changes, massive migration, urbanization rapid industrialisation, construction, irrigation brand and man-made lacks.

Besides the aforesaid specified areas UNESCO has also developed other projects of related interests. These are for example :-

The International Maritime Consultative Organization (IMCO): It was the repository of 1954 International convention for the prevention of pollution of the sea by Oil it is developed new methods and techniques to control marine pollution by new techniques of remove oil from sea protecting coastal area from pollution and detention and penalisation of violator of deliberate marine pollution.

The World Bank took a policy in 1970 to apply environmental criteria on major economic development, industrial project to the evoluent of development goals and strategy taking proper construction for the ecological factors. In November 1970, then the President of World Bank Robert McMamara made it clear in his report to the ECOSOC that Bank has established a Unit to foresee the environmental consequences of proposed development projects[12].

All the two aforesaid agencies involved in the fragmented way to the environmental problems. There is no integration and cooperation between various programmes and Associations. There was urgent need to harmonious these various functions in one body and thereby to prevent the impairment of human environment. Ultimately by General Assembly resolution No. 1346 of 1968 of the Economic and Social Council initiated by Swedish representative a cohesive action was taken on the economy of the environmental problems in its different aspects for proper solution by all nations both at the national and international level. This ultimately led the General Assembly by a resolution dated 20th December 1971 to held the U.N. Conference on Human Environment (UNCHE) in Stockholm from 5th to 10th June, 1972.

Stockholm Declaration

The most comprehensive law on Environmental Pollution in the International level is the United Nations Declaration on the Human Environment, Stockholm, June 1972, some of the important aspects of the declaration is given below:

"Having considered the need for a common outlook and for common principles to inspire and guide the people of the World in the preservation and enhancement of the human environment,

i) Proclaims that: man is both creature and molder of his environment, which gives him physical sustenance and affords the opportunity or intellectual moral, social and spiritual growth. In the long and tortious revolution of the human race in this Planet a stage has been reached when, through the rapid acceleration of Science and Technology, man has acquired the power to transform his environment in quountless ways and on a unprecedented scale. Both aspects of man's environment, the natural and the man-made, are essential to his well-being and to the enjoyment of basic human rights even the right to live itself. The protection and improvement of the human environment is a major issue which affects the well-being of peoples and economic development throughout the world, it is the urgent desire of the peoples of the whole world and the duty of all Government.

ii) The natural resources of the earth, including the air, water, land, flora and fauna and especially representative samples of natural ecosystems, must be safeguarded for the benefit of present and future generations through careful planning or management as appropriate.

iii) The capacity of the earth to produce vital renewable resources must be maintained and wherever practicable restored or improved.

iv) Man has a special responsibility to safeguard and wisely manage the heritage of wildlife and its habitat which are now gravely imperilled by a combination of adverse factors. Nature conservation including wildlife must therefore receive importance in planning for economic development.

v) The non-renewable resources of the earth must be employed in such a way as to guard against the danger of their future exhaustion and to ensure that benefits from such employment are shared by all mankind.

vi) Appropriate national institutions must be entrusted with the task of planning, managing or controlling the environmental resources of States with the view to enhancing environmental quality.

vii) Science and technology, as part of their contribution to economic and social developmental must be applied to the identification, avoidance and control of environmental risks and the solution of environmental problems and for the common good of mankind"[13].

Legislative Development in the National Level

England :

In England legislative measures to protect environment began in 1273 with the Smoke Nuisance Law. The next comprehensive legislation in the field of water pollution was Salmon and Fresh Water Fisheries Act, 1923. Thereafter a series of environmental legislations were passed by the British Parliament. They are—The Public Health Act, 1936; The Public Health (Drainage of Trade Premises) Act, 1937; The Rivers (Prevention of Pollution) Act, 1951; The Clean Rivers (Estuaries and Tidal Waters) Act, 1960; and Water Resources Act, 1963[14].

American Federal Legislations:

The earliest federal legislation in the United States in the field of Environmental laws was the Rivers and Harbours Act of 1899 for the abatement of water pollution. It prohibited the discharge of any effluents other than drainage waters from the streets and sewers into the navigable waters in U.S.A. Thereafter we get the Public Health Services Act, 1912 by which organizations are required to conduct research concerning the Health aspects of water pollution. Later on in 1924, the Oil Pollution Control Act was passed prohibiting the dumping of oil into navigable waters except in life threatening emergencies or unavoidable accidents. The first bold step towards control of water pollution in U.S.A. was a temporary legislation namely Water Pollution Control Act 1948 to expire after five years. This statute later on extended in 1952, 1956, 1961, 1965 and 1970. This was in fact their present national water control campaign providing fund for realising the objectives of the Act. In 1965 an administrative set-up was proposed by Water Duality Act 1965 creating Federal Water Pollution Control Administration (F.W.P.C.A.) in the Department of Health Education and Welfare. Following the recommendations of the International Convention for the Prevention of the Pollution of the Sea by Oil 1954, the Oil Pollution Act 1961 was passed by the

U.S. Congress which prohibited any discharge of oil or oily mixture by a tanker into defined zones.[15]

As regards sound pollution the first comprehensive law was passed in 1970 namely U.S. Noise Pollution and Abatement at under which every person is entitled to take action against noise pollution which is detrimental to his life and health. To control the special problems of big cities Local Law No. 5706 the city of New York, New York Noise Control Code[16] was made which says that the creation of any unreasonably loud, disturbing and unnecessary noise is prohibited. The National Environmental Policy for maximum attainable recycling of national resources.

Australia :

In Australia there are Environment Protection (Alligator Rivers Region) Act, 1978, Environment Protection (Impact of Proposals) Act 1974, Environment Protection (Nuclear Code) Act 1978, Environment Protection (Sea Dumping) Act 1981, Environment Protection (Northern Territory Supreme Court) Act 1978 etc. There are also Biological Control Act 1984, Fisheries Act 1952; Protection of the Sea (Civil Liability) Act 1981, Protection of the Sea (Prevention of Pollution for Ships) Act 1983, Environmental Planning and Assessment Act 1979. Environmental Protection (Penalties) Act 1982 etc.[17]

Soviet Russia :

In U.S.S.R. by a 1961 Regulation the water courses were divided in two categories according to their use. They are :

1. Water used for centralised and decentralised domestic drinking water supplies and also for water supplies for the food Industries.
2. Water used for bathing, sport and recreation and also bodies of water within the boundaries of inhabited areas.

The discharge of effluents into these two types of water courses were also prescribed in that law.

At least six major environmental laws have been passed in USSR during 1968 to 1988, such as in Principles of Water Legislation 1979, Principles of Land use 1968, Principles of Mineral Legislation 1975, Principles of Forestry Legislation 1977, Laws on Air Quality 1981 and the Animal World 1980[18]. The trend of various environmental legislations to control pollution can also observed in other countries also. Thus, we get in the Singapore Environmental Public Health Act, 1968, the Environmental Protection Law 1969 of Sweden, the Basic Law of

Environmental Pollution. Control of Japan 1971, the Punishment of Environmental Pollution Crimes relating to Human Act 1970.

Development of Environmental Regulation in India

Ancient India

The most detailed policy and provisions regarding environment can be found in Kautilya's **Arthashastra** written between 321 to 300 B.C. during the reign of Chandragupta Maurya. Most of those provisions are in Book Two (Arthashastra is divided into 14 books) though some **shlokas** may be found elsewhere. These provisions, in brief, are :

> "**State to maintain forests :** The ruler shall not only protect produce-forests, elephant-forests, but also set up new ones.
>
> **Cutting and selling of trees :** For cutting the tender sprouts of trees in the city parks that bear flowers or fruits or yield shade the fine shall be six **panas,** for cutting small branches twelve **panas;** for cutting stout branches twenty four **panas;** for destroying trunks the fine shall be the first **amercement;** for uprooting the tree the middlemost amercement.
>
> **Damaging forests:** The officer of forest-produce shall cause forest produce to be brought in by guards in the produce-forests. He shall fix adequate fines and compensations to be levied on those who cause any damage to productive forests except in calamities.
>
> **Forest Reserves for Wild animals:** On the borders of the Kingdom or in any other suitable locality, animal forests shall be established where all animals are welcomed as guests and given full protection.
>
> **Protection to wild life :** The superintendent of slaughter-house shall punish with the highest amercement, a person for entrapping, killing or injuring deer, bison, birds or fish which are declared to be under state protection or who are kept in reserved parks; the middle amercement on householders for these offences in reserved park enclosures. For entrapping, killing or injuring fish and birds whose killing is forbidden, he shall impose a fine of twenty-six **panas** and three quarters, for entrapping deer and beasts, double that. One-sixth of live animals and birds shall be let off in forests under state's

protection. Sea-fishes and also other birds and deers shall be protected from all dangers of injury; for transgression of this rule, the fine shall be the first amercement"[19].

Similarly, in 5th Pillar Edict of Asoka we get the following informations :

"Thus speaks the Beloved of the Gods, the King Piyadassi when I had been concentrated for twenty-six years I forbade the killing of the following species of animals, namely: parrots, mainas, red-headed ducks, cakravaka-geese, swans, nandi-mukhas, pigeons, bats, ants, tortoises, boneless fish, vedaveyakas, pupu-tas of the Goanges (fish?), skate, porcupines, squirrels, deer, lizards, domesticated animals, rhinoceroses, white pigeons, domestic pigeons, and all quadrupeds which are of no utility and are not eaten. She goats, ewes and sows which are with young or aggrieving suck are not to be killed, neither are their young up to the age of six months. Capons must not be made. Chalf which contains living things must not be set on fire. Forests must not be burned in order to kill living things or without any good reason. An animal must not be fed with another animal.

On the first full moon days of the three four-monthly sessions, and for three days when the full moon falls on the star, Tisya, and the fourteenth and fifteenth of the bright fortnight, and the first of the dark, and regularly on past days, fish are not to be caught or sold. And on these same days in the elephant park and fisheries, other classes of animals likewise must not be killed. On the eighth, fourteenth, and fifteenth days of the fortnight, on the days of the star Tisya and Punarvasu, on the three first full moons of the four-monthly seasons, and on festival days, bulls, goats, rams, boars, and other animals which it is customary to castrate are not to be castrated. On the days of the stars Tisya and Punarvasu, on the first full moon days of the four-monthly sessions, and on the fortnights following them, cattle and horses are not to be branded. In the period from my conservation to the anniversaries on which I had been conservated twenty-six years, twenty-five releases of prisoners have been made[20].

Forestry in Colonial and Post-Colonial India

Based on the writings of the colonial administrators and official had book of Forest Department R. Guha reports :

> Among Britain's colonies, "India stood pre-eminent by reason of its vastness, the density of the population, and seemingly immeasurable extent of its natural resources. The early days of British rule were characterised by a total indifference to the needs of forest conservancy indeed, upto the middle of the nineteenth century, the Raj saw a "fierce onslaught on India's forests". .... The first show of interest in forestry — the reservation of teak in Malabar in 1806 was predictably dictated by imperialists considerations. By the sixteenth century, much of Western Europe had been deforested, and Northern Europe was supplying Britain with large quantities of wood. .... This was the period of fierce competition between the colonial powers, and Indian teak, the most durable of shipbuilding timbers, saved England during the war with Napoleon and the later maritime expansion. Ships were built in dockyards in Goa and on the Malabar coast, as well as from teak imported into England. The first attempt that asserting state monopoly right was through the Indian Forest Act of 1865, which was replaced by a much more comprehensive piece of legislation 13 years later by the Forest Act 1878. The provisions of the 1878 Act ensured that the state could demarcate 'valuable' tracts of forests, needed specially for railway purposes, and retain enough flexibility over the remaining extent of forest land to revise its policy from time to time.

The continuity between colonial and post-colonial forest policy is provided by two official documents: the post-war scheme enumerated by the then IGF in 1944 and the national forest policy of 1952. The 1952 statement affirms that the 1894 policy "constitutes the basis for the forest policy of India upto this day, and this new policy shares with its predecessor certain other important features. Thus, as late as in 1978, the then IGF could blandly state :

> "His (Lord Dalhousie in 1855) proclamation laid down the ruling principle of management of 'state forest' namely, that timber standing on a state forest was state property to which individuals had no rights or claims"[21].

Development in British India

a. Common Law Provisions

The seeds of legal control of pollution in India may be traced in the common law remedies introduced by the establishment of Mayor Courts at three presidency towns in India, namely, Calcutta, 1661; Madras on 13th, December 1687 and Bombay, March 25th 1718. Subsequently these Mayor Courts were superseded by establishment of High Courts in pursuance of letters Patent Act of 1861. The High Court's at Calcutta, Madras and Bombay having original jurisdiction may decide on environment pollution matters in pursuance of common law remedies available in England. As regards other courts in India there is no express provision for the administration of the English Common Law. These courts have been established by Acts almost all local and the Acts establishing them contain each a section which requires them in the absence of any specific law or usage, to act according to "equity and good conscience". The expression "equity and good conscience" means the rules of English law so far as they are applicable to Indian society and circumstances.

The common law controls of environmental pollution under law of torts can be classified into three groups, (a) liability for the escape of noxious objects; (b) the careless use of noxious articles or pollutants; and (c) the infringment of property rights.

a) Liability for escape of noxious object

The liability for escape of any dangerous or noxious things brought by a person on his own land which is not naturally there can be found in the famous rule of *Rylands* v. *Fletcher*. While delivering judgment on behalf of the court of eschequers Justice Blackburn made the following well known statement : "We think that the true rule of law is that the person who for his own purposes brings on his lands and collects and keeps there anything likely to do mischief if it escapes, must keep it in at his peril and if he does not do so in *primafacie* answerable for all the damage which is the natural consequence of its escape. He can excuse himself by showing that the escape was owing to the plaintiff's default; or, perhaps, that the escape was the consequence of vis-major or the act of God; but as nothing of the sort exists here, it is unnecessary to inquire what excuse would be sufficient. The person whose grass or corn is eaten down by the escaping cattle of his neighbour, or whose mine is flooded by the water from his neighbour's reservoir, or whose cellar is invaded by the filt of his neighbour's privy, or whose habitation is made unhealthy by the fumes and noisome vaporous of his neighbour's alkali works, is damnified without any fault of his own, and it seems but reasonable and just that the neighbour who has brought something on his own property which was not naturally there, harmless to others so long as it is confined to his own property, but which he knows to be mischievous if it gets on his neighbour's should be obliged to make good the damage which ensures if he does not succeed in confining it to his own property. But for his act in bringing it there no mischief could have occurred, and it seems but just that he should at his peril keep it there so that no mischief may occur or answer for the natural and anticipated consequences. And upon authority, this we think is established to be the law whether the things so brought be beasts, or water, or filth, or stanches"[22].

The above rule in law of torts is popularly known as strict or absolute liability, it means if anyone collects or brings a dangerous or noxious objects on his land, such as explosive chemicals, and he allows it to escape, then he is liable for the consequences absolutely. The importance of this rule is so significant that even after more than hundred years of the decision of the aforesaid famous case we still invoke the rule for disposal of tort cases in India. The glaring example of application of this rule is the famous Bhopal case in India, which clearly shows the inadequacy of Indian statutory tort law. In fact the Bhopal mass disaster of 3rd December 1984 led Indian parliament to pass comprehensive Environment Protection Act, 1986. It would be pertinent to question here whether pesticide used by a farmer for the improvement of his crop would be tantamount to an abnormal use of land under the rule of *Rylands* v. *Fletcher*.

b) Careless use of noxious articles of pollutants

Under the common law the careless use of noxious objects which are dangerous things and affects the person or property of another will give rise to an action in the law of Negligence. In the law of torts negligence has two aspects, (i) it may be an element indetermining liability for many torts (a nuisance may be caused intentionally or negligently) or (ii) It is in itself and independent tort — It is a relevant question here what is careless use of noxious or dangerous things and what is the test of liability for use of such articles or things? Professor Asit Kumar Bose observed:

"Probably it may be correct to say that anything is dangerous object if it used in a dangerous manner. By applying this test a view may be held that the pesticides that we used in our country are dangerous and if an assessable injury can be proved as a result of careless use of pesticides, an action in negligence is very likely to lie"[23].

c) The infringment of property rights in water

Every reparian owner enjoyed a natural night to the natural flow of water in his stream, substantially unaffected in quality and undeminised in quantity in *Wood* v. *Wand*. It was held "a riparian proprietor has a right to the natural stream of water flowing through the land in its natural estates; and if the Water be polluted by a proprietor higher up the stream, so as to occasion damage in law, though not in fact, to the first mentioned proprietor, it gives him a good cause of action against the upper proprietor unless the later has gained a right by long enjoyment or grant".

Thus the common law has set a standard in respect of water pollution which may appear to be higher than the Helsinki Rules.

B. Specific Legal Provision

As it has been already noted that comprehensive environmental law is of recent origin so to find out the scattered legal provisions relating to pollutions in India various enactments in British India. Let us point out Chronologically the various Acts and its provisions in brief, relating to control of pollutions:

(i) The Shore Nuisance (Bombay and Kolba) Act, 1853

This is the 1st enactment passed by the legislature in the year of 1853 relating to control of water pollution. This Act empowered the collector of land Revenue, Bombay to give notice to an offending party for removal of any nuisance anywhere below the high-water in the Bombay harbour. It also provided to authorised the collector of land Revenue, Bombay to remove the nuisance if the party violates the provision after one month notice.

(ii) The Orient Gas Company Act, 1857

This is the Second enactment passed in the year of 1857 related to thwart water pollution such as that concerned the Company. Section 15 of the said Act relating to water pollutions provided as follows :

If the said company shall at any time cause or suffer to be brought, or to flow into any Stream, Reservoir, aqueduct, pond or place of water, or into any drain communicating therewith, any washing or other substance produced in making or supplying Gas or shall wilfully do any act connected with the making or supplying of Gas, whereby the water in any such stream, reservoir, aqueduct, pond, or place for water, shall be fouled, the said company shall forfeit for every such offence a sum not exceeding one thousand rupees, and they shall forfeit an additional sum not exceeding five hundred rupees for each day during which such washing or other substance shall be brought or shall flow, or the act by which such water shall be fouled shall continue, after the expiration of twenty-four hours from the time when notice of the offence shall have been served on the said company, by the person into whose water such washing or other substances shall be brought or shall flow, or whose water shall be fouled, and such penalties shall be paid to such last mentioned person.

Section 17 of the same Act further provided that :

Whenever any water shall be fouled by the Gas of the said company, they shall forfeit to the person whose water shall be so fouled for every such offence a sum not exceeding two hundred rupees, and a further sum, not exceeding two hundred rupees, and a further sum, not exceeding one hundred rupees, for each day during which the offence shall continue, after the expiration of twenty four hours form the service of notice of such sum.

Section 18 of the said Act authorised a person to dig up the grounds and examine pipes and conducts of the gas Company for the purpose of ascertaining any leakage causing water pollution.

(iii) The Indian Penal Code, 1860

In the Indian Penal Code there are some sections dealing with control of pollution. They are :

Section 277: Whoever voluntarily corrupts or fouls the water of any public spring or reservoir, so as to render it less fir for the purposes for which it is ordinarily used, shall be punished with imprisonment of either description for a term which may extend to three months, or with fine which may extend to five hundred rupees, or with both. In this regard Justice V.R. Krishna Iyer observed:

> "This provision is extremely limited in scope. It applies only to a public spring or reservoir. It has been held that the term public spring does not includes a public river or water flowing in a continuous stream in a river bed. On the same analogy a canal or any other running water will not be covered by the term. A well, however, in a spring. A reservoir may be natural or artificial. A lake will be covered by the term reservoir"[24].

Section 284: Whoever, does, with any poisonous substance, any act in a manner so rash or negligent as to endanger human life, or to be likely to cause hurt or injury to any person, or knowingly or negligently omits to take such order with any poisonous substance in his possession as is sufficient to guard against any probable danger to human life from such poisonous substance.

Shall be punished with imprisonment of either description for a term which may extend to six months, or with fine which may extend to one thousand rupees, or with both.

Section 425: Whoever with intent to cause, or knowing that he is likely to cause, wrongful loss or damage to the public or to any person, causes the destruction of any property, or any such change in any property or in the situation thereof as destroys or diminishes its value or utility or affects it injuriously, commits "mischief".

Explanation 1 : It is not essential to the offence of mischief that the offender intended to cause loss or damage to the owner of the property injured or destroyed. It is sufficient if the intends to cause, or knows that he is likely to cause, wrongful loss or damage to any person by injuring any property, whether it belongs to that person or not.

Explanation 2 : Mischief may be committed by an act affecting property belonging to the person who commits the act, or to that person and others jointly causing dimunition of water supply has been treated as mischief in Section 430 of the code and the possible direct cause may also be pollution. Adulterating of food or drink so as to make it noxious has also been made punishable.

(iv) **The Serais Act, 1867**

This Act imposed a duty upon a keeper of a serai or and in to keep a certain quality of water fit for consumption by persons and animals using it to the satisfaction of the District Magistrate or his nominees and failure to observe it entailed a liability of rupees twenty only.

(v) **The Northern India Canal and Drainage Act, 1873.**

The Act of 1873 in Section 70, sub-clause (3) and (5) provided that any interference with or alteration in the flow of water in any river or stream, so as to endanger, damage or render less useful for the purpose for which it is ordinarily used would be an offence. The prescribed punishment for this offence would be imprisonment not exceeding one month or fine not exceeding fifty rupees or both.

(vi) **The Obstruction in Fairways Act, 1881.**

Section 8 of this Act empowered the central Government to make suitable rules for regulating or prohibiting the throwing of rubbish in any fairway leading to a port causing or likely to give rise to a bank. The punishment for violation of this provision was fine of not more than rupees five hundred or imprisonment of a maximum term of six months or with both.

(vii) **Indian Easement Act, 1882.**

There is also germs of water pollution control under the Indian Easement Act Section 7 Illustration-F provides: "The right of every owner of land that, within his own limits, the water are natural pass of percolations by, over or through his land shall not before so passing or percolating, be unreasonably polluted by other persons". Thus, though the section contemplates the rights of riparian owners yet, what is reasonable pollution has not been clarified and to be interpreted according to circumstances of our case.

Similarly, Illustration-H of Section 7 provides that "the right every owners of land that the water of every natural stream which passes by, through or over his land in a defined natural channel shall be allowed by other persons to flow within such owners limits, without interruption and without 'material alteration' in quantity, direction, forces or temperature; the right of every owner of land abutting on a natural lake or pond into or out of which a natural stream flows that the water of such lake or pond shall be allowed by other persons to remain within such owners limits without 'material alteration' in a quantity or temperature". Again, Illustration-J to Section 7, deals with the "right of every owner of land abutting on a natural stream, lake or pond — to use and consumed the water for irrigating such land and for the purpose of any manufactory situated thereon; provided that he does not there by against material injury to other like owners". Thus, in case of 'material alteration' or 'material injury' the persons affected has the righ· · ›relief from the hazards by way of injunction against the pollution for damages.

Explanation (vi) to section 15 of Easements Act provides, in the case of an Easement to pollute water, this said period of 20 years begins when the pollution, prejudice, perceptably the conservation heritage". However, for property own by the period is 60 years, Section 2 of the same Act empowered the Government "to regulate the collection, retention and distribution of water of rivers and stream flowing in natural channels and of natural lakes and ponds......".

Regarding prescriptive right to pollute air or water Section 28(d) provides : "the extent of the prescriptive right to pollute air or water is the extent of the pollution at the commencement of the period of user on completion of which the right arose". But there should not be a statutory recognition of the prescriptive right to pollute air or water. Therefore disprovision is to be amended to connect specifically that no right to pollute Air or Water can be acquired by prescription.

(viii) **The Indian Fisheries Act, 1897**

The fisheries Act provides in Section 5 :

If any person puts any poison, lime or noxious material into any water with intent thereby to catch or destroy any fish, he shall be punishable with imprisonment which may extend to two months, or with fine which may extend to two hundred rupees. The Act also prohibited destruction of fish by explosive in inland water or coasts and use of donamite in water.

(ix) **The Indian Ports Act, 1908**

By this water pollution by oil had been regulated. Section 6 of this Act empowered the Government to make necessary rules for the purpose of "regulating the manner in which oil or water mixed with oil shall be discharged in any such port and for the disposal of the same". Section 21 of the said Act further prohibited throwing of rubbish blust or oil or water mixed with oil or any other thing likely to form a bank or shoal detrimental to navigation.

Punishment for violation of this provision was a fine which may extend to rupees five hundred and for continuation of this offence, the offender is liable to a maximum of two months imprisonment.

(x) **The Inland Stream Vessels Act, 1917**

This Act provided a mandatory Rule of fresh water for the use of passengers.

(xi) **The Indian Forest Act, 1927**

The Indian forest Act provided control of water in the forest area. Whoever, poisons water of a forest area shall be liable to be punished by the State Government.

(xii) **The Factories Act, 1948**

Sections 11 of the Factories Act directs every factory to keep premises clean and free from effluent arising from any drain privy or other nuisance.

Section 12 of this said Act prescribed DISPOSAL OF WATERS AND EFFLUENTS :- (1) Effective arrangements shall be made in every factory for the disposal of wastes and effluents due to the manufacturing process carried on therein.

(2) The State Government may make rules prescribing the arrangement to be made under sub-section (1) or requiring that the arrangements made in accordance with sub-section (1) shall be approved by such authority as may be prescribed.

Section 92 of the Act prescribed the general penalty for non-observance or noncompliance with the requirement of Section 12. It provides that "the occupier and manager of the Factory shall each be guilty of an offence and punishable with imprisonment for a term which may extend to Rs. 500 or with both and if the contravention is continued after condition, with a further fine which may extent to Rs. 75 for each day on which the contravention is so continued". Section 105 of the Act also provides: no Courts shall take cognizance of any offence under this Act except on a complaint by or with the previous sanction of an Inspector.

But factories Rules are framed in persuance of the Factories Act by various states in India such as Tamil Nadu 1950, West Bengal 1958, Maharashtra 1963 and Mysore 1969. West Bengal Factories Rules 1958, in rule 19 of chapter (iii) (Health) provided identical rules with rule 22 of Maharashtra Factories Rule relating to disposal of Trade wastes and effluents, Rule 34(3) states: "any pond well of reservoir from which drinking water is derived shall be so situated and protected as not to be liable to a pollution by organic matter of other impurity". Rule 17(4) says that "the area around any place where drinking water is supplied to the workers shall be maintained in a clean and drained condition". Mysore Factories Rules 1952, deals with the construction and maintenance of drains carrying Trade wastes and sulage water. The rules provided that they "shall be constructed in masonary or other impermixable material and shall be regularly flusts the effluent disposed of by connecting such drain with a suitable drainage line". This provision intact to prevent pollution of underground stream from becoming polluted by the industrial effluents of Trade wastes permitting to the ground.

The Rule 52 of the Mysore Factories Rule further provided that "where there is no such drainage line, the effluents shall be deodorised and rendered and innocuous and then disposed of in a suitable manner to the satisfaction of the Health Officer".

Similarly Rule 22 of the Maharashtra Factories Rule provides guidelines regarding disposal of Industrial wastes and effluents. It provides : "(i) in the case of Factory where the drainage system is to be connected to the public sewerage prior approval of arrangement made shall be obtained from the local Authority; (ii) in the case of Factories other than those mentioned shall sub-Rule (1) from approval of the arrangement made for the disposal of Trade wastes and effluents shall be obtained from the Health Officer".

Rule 74 of the said Rule provided washing facilities to the employees and states : "the facilities shall be conveniently accessively and shall be kept in section and orderly conditions and shall not be located in the vicinity of latrines and urinals". Rule 9 of schedule (vi) of Maharashtra Factories Rule deals with manufacture and treatment of lead and certain components lead and prohibits any into or drink being brought into a work room in order to preventing such food or drink from getting polluted.

The Tamil Nadu Factories Rule provided in Rule 17(1) or (2) provided similar rule of Mysore Factories Rules. However Rule 17(3) is quite significant and different it provides: "in the case of a Factory where their rivers or fisheries at any other water resources in the vicinity, *including territorial water of the sea* and this water sources likely to be affected by the arrangement made for the disposal of Trade wastes and effluents, prior approval shall be obtained from the Director of fisheries or such authority as the State Government may appoint in this behalf". Rule 37 which was prescribed under said Section (iv) of Section 18 of the Factories Act provides : (i) drinking water shall not be supplied from any pond, well or reservoir unless it is so constructed, situated, protected and maintained as to be free from the *possibilities of pollution* by chemical or bacterial and extraneous impurities".

Motor Vehicle Act, 1939

In India there is no comprehensive legislation to control noise pollution. Though for the common law, private individual could seek redress of problem of noise pollution under law of torts. However under the Motor Vehicle Act 1939 there are certain restrictions on trucks regarding the use of double sirens while passing through certain localities, violation of which leads to prosecution. The Act originally does not make any provisions to control emission of smoke for the vehicles and diesel engines.

Bengal Smoke Nuisance Act 1905

The seeds of air pollution clause can be tested out in the provincial legislation in India in the two provinces namely Bombay and Bengal in passing of Bengal Smoke Nuisance Act 1905 and Bombay Smoke Nuisance Act 1912 in order to provide measures for controlling air pollution. The Act 1905 was enacted to provide a machinery "for the abolition of the nuisance arisen from the smoke of furnace or fire-places". But it should be noted here that when the act originally passed it had limited application in terms of territorial area as well as nuisance it admitted to abate. For example, when it was first came into force it was extended only at Calcutta and Howrah and only in 1953 the Act extends to whole of West Bengal. As regards abatement of nuisance the definition of furnace as amended in 1916 includes furnace or fire-places used for working engines by steam or for any other purposes whatsoever (Section 3). However, certain types of furnace were exempted from the operation of the Act such as no furnace or fire-place used for operating of the or in private use for benefit of the domestic purposes shall be deemed to be furnace or fire-places within the meaning of the Act. The Act was first applied by notification of the State Government to prohibit the erection or use of kilnes or furnace or the manufacture of cock in specified areas and contravention of the aforesaid prohibition were made punishable with fine. The cases involving manufacturing to cock in contravention of the prohibition attract higher penalty likewise the owner or occupier of a building or land who loss any person to make cock thereon any contravention of such prohibition is liable to fine and the cock so made is liable to seiser by the Inspector pending order of the Magistrate (Section 6). The Act provided for the constitution of the commission and also for the appointment of chief and assistant Inspector of commission nuisance to carry out the purposes of the Act. The Act also provided that no furnace or chimney shall be erected of the existing furnace flew or chimney, shall be re-erected, water was added too otherwise than in regards with plans approved by the commission (Section 8).

Post Independent Legislation in India

Provisions in *The Indian Constitution* and the environment:-

At the time of the Constitution of India came into force there was no specific provisions on environmental protection. However, environmental protection and improvement were incorporated into the Constitution by the Constitution (Forty second Amendment) Act of 1976. Article 48 A was added to the Directive Principles of State policy. It declares:

> "The state shall endeavour to protect and improve the environment and to safeguard the forests and wild life of the country".

Similarly a new Chapter entitled 'Fundamental Duties', added under Article 51A (g) and imposes responsibility on every citizen:-

> "to protect and improve the natural environment including forests, lakes, rivers and wild life, and to have compassion for living creatures. ...."

This in several cases the Courts in India have been guided by the provisions of Article 48A and 51A (g). In *Sachidanand Pandey* v. *State of West Bengal*[25] the Supreme Court has held:

> "Whenever a problem of ecology is brought before the Court, the Court is bound to bear in mind Article 48A of the Constitution.... and Article 51A (g).... When the Court is called upon to give effect to the Directive Principle and the fundamental duty, the Court is not to shrug its shoulders and say priorities are a matter of policy and so it is a matter for the policy making authority. The least that the Court may do is to examine whether appropriate considerations are borne in mind and irrelevancies excluded. In appropriate cases, the Court may go further, but how much further will depend on the circumstances of the case. The Court may always give necessary directions. However the Court will not attempt to nicely balanced relevant considerations. When the question involves the nice balancing of relevant considerations the Court may feel justifies in resigning itself to acceptance of the decision of the concerned authority".

In the process of interpretation of fundamental right to life guranteed in Article 21 was expanded by the Court to include environmental protection. Article 21 states:

> "No person shall be deprived of his life or personal liberty except according to procedure established by law".

The Supreme Court in Dehradun quarrying case[26] indicated the right of the citizen to a wholesome environment may be traced in Article 21. At least four High Courts namely Andhra Pradesh[27], Rajasthan[28], Kerala[29], and Himachal Pradesh[30], have observed that environmental degradation violates the Governmental right to life. How the Court stretched the interpretation of Article 21 has been explained beautifully by the Andhra Pradesh High Court while considering a writ petition to enjoin the Life Insurance Corporation and the Income Tax Department from building residential houses in a recreational zone, the Court held:

> "It would be reasonable to hold that the enjoyment of life and its attainment and fulfilment guaranteed by Article 21 of the Constitution embraces the protection and preservation of nature's gifts without (which) life cannot be enjoyed. There can be no reason why practice of violent extinguishment of life alone should be regarded a violative of Article 21 of the Constitution. The slow poisoning by the polluted atmosphere caused environmental pollution and spoilation should also be regarded as amounting to violation of Article 21 of the Constitution. In R.L. & E. Kendra, *Dehradun* v. *State of U.P.*, AIR 1985 SC 652, the Supreme Court has entertained environmental complaints alleging that the operations of limestone quarries in the Himalayan range of Mussoorie resulted in the depredation of the environment affecting ecological balance..... The Supreme Court in an application under Article 32 has ordered the closure of some of these quarries on the ground that their operations were upsetting ecological balance. Although Article 21, is not referred to in these judgments of the Supreme Court, those judgments can only be understood on the basis that the Supreme Court entertained these environmental complaints under Article 32 of the Constitution as involving violation of Article 21's right to life.
>
> It, therefore, becomes the legitimate duty of Courts as the enforcing organs of Constitutional objectives to forbid all action of the State and the citizen from upsetting the environmental balance. In this case the very purpose of preparing and publishing the development plan is to maintain such an environmental

balance. The object of reserving certain area as a recreational zone would be utterly defeated if private owners of the land in that area are permitted to build residential houses. It must, therefore, be held that the attempt of the Life Insurance Corporation of India and the Income-tax Department to build housed in this area is contrary to law and also contrary to Article 21 of the Constitution".

Rivers Boards Act, 1956

Certain states passed special laws to combat with the problem of pollution of their water resources. Firstly, the state of Orissa passed the Orissa River Pollution Prevention Act 1953. Then Maharashtra, one of the India's most industrialised and one of densely populated states, passed the Maharashtra Prevention of Water Pollution Act, 1969. This Act unlike the Orissa Act not extends to rivers but also extends water courses, inland water, ocean streams, and tidal waters to such point as the State Government may specify in this behalf. The Central Government ultimately passed Rivers Boards Act, 1956 for the prevention of pollution of the water of the inter-state rivers.

The Atomic Energy Act, 1962

To control radio-active pollution in India the Atomic Energy Act 1962 was passed. Thus regulation of nuclear energy and radio-active substances in India is now governed under this Act. Thus statutory obligation imposed upon the Central Government to prevent radiation hazards, guarantee public safety and the safety of workers handling radio-active substances and the safe disposal of radio-active wastes. The Central Government is also required to control the manufacture and transport of radio-active substance and the production and supply of atomic energy and nuclear-generated electricity.

The Insecticides Act, 1968

The Insecticides Act was passed by the Parliament to implement the recommendation of the Kerala and Madras Food Poisoning cases enquiry Commission. The Act provided establishment of a Central Insecticides Board to advise the Centre and the State on technical aspects of the Act. The manufacture and distribution of insecticides are now regulated through licensing under this Act and violation of which lead to prosecution and penalties.

The Wild Life (Protection) Act, 1972

Parliament enacted the Wild Life Act 1972 pursuant to the enabling resolutions of 11 states under Article 252(1) of the Constitution. The Act provides for establishment of State Wild Life advisory board, regulation for hunting wild animals and birds, developing sanctuaries and national parks and regulations for trade in wild animals, animal products. An amendment to the Act in 1962 introduced provisions permitting the capture and transportation of wild animals for the scientific management of animal populations.

The Water (Prevention and Control) of Pollution Act of 1974

In 1974, the Parliament came out for the first time with a comprehensive legislation for controlling water pollution by enacting the Water (Prevention and Control of Pollution) Act. The Act was passed with the object of prevention and control of water pollution and of restoring the wholesomeness of water quality. The Act provides for the constitution of a Central Board for the prevention and control of water pollution. The Act also provides for the constitution of State Boards for the prevention and control of water pollution in states.

The statute is aimed to promote cleanliness of streams and walls in different areas of the states. The Board's function includes advise to Central Government concerning the prevention and control of water pollution through co-ordination of efforts by State Boards, giving of technical assistance and guidance to states, sponsoring of research and training of persons engaged in the field of water pollution. A Central Board coordinates activities among the states and performs same function.

The Boards control sewage and industrial effluent discharge by approving, rejecting or conditioning applications for consent to discharge. The State Boards applications State Governments on approving sites for new industry. The Act was amended in 1988 to strengthen the Acts implementation provisions. Now, a board is competent to close a defaulting industrial plant or withdraw its supply of power or water by an administrative order and a citizen's suit provision bolsters the enforcement machinery.

The Water (Prevention and Control of Pollution) Cess Act of 1977

The water Cess Act was passed to augment the resources of the Central and State Water Boards. The Act envisaged incentives for adopting pollution control and authorised government to impose Cess (Tax) for water consumption. The Central Government after deducting the expenses of collection, distribute the amount among Central and State Boards as it deems fit to enforce the Water Act.

The Forest (Conservation) Act, 1980

To stop the growing deforestation and the resulting environmental degradation the Parliament enacted the Forest (Conservation) Act in 1980. The Act was again amended in 1988. Now under the Forest Act as amended in 1988 a prior approval is essential for any state to "dereserves" a reserved forest, use forest land for non-forest purposes, assigns forest land to a private person or corporation, or clears forest land for the purpose of reforestation. There is an Advisory Committee constituted under the Act to advise the Centre for these approvals.

The Air (Prevention and Control of Pollution) Act 1981

To oblige the U.N. Conference on the Human Environment held at Stockholm in June 1972 our Parliament enacted the Air (Prevention and Control of Pollution) Act 1981. The framework of the Act is almost in the line of Water Act 1974. Under the Air Act, all industries operating within designated air pollution control areas shall have to obtain a permit or 'consent' from the respective state Board. The states are required to prescribe emission standards for industry and automobiles in consultation with the Central Board.

The Air Act was amended in 1987 to strengthen the enforcement machinery and prescribing stiffer penalties. Under the 1987 Amendment Act the State Boards may close down a defaulting industrial plant or may stop its supply of electricity or water and also may move to a competent court to restrain emissions that exceeds prescribed standards.

Environment (Protection) Act 1986

The Bhopal Gas mass disaster on 3rd December 1984 led the Govt. of India to enact the Environment (Protection) Act 1986 under Article 253 of the Constitution.

'The Act' is according to Rosencranz,

> "The 'umbrella' legislation designed to provide a framework for Central Government Coordination of the activities the various Central and State authorities established under previous laws, such as Water Act and Air Act"[31].

The Act of 1986 is a broad based environment legislation. Environment under Section 2(a) of the Act means and includes water, air, land and the interrelationships among water, air, land and human beings and other living creatures, plants, micro-organizations and property. Section 3(1) of the Act empowers the Centre "to take all such measures as it deems necessary or expedient for the purpose of protecting and improving the quality of the environment and preventing, controlling and abating environmental pollution". Thus under this Act the Central Government is authorised to develop new national standards for the quality of the environment; to regulate cites of big industries, to prescribe procedure for manufacturing hazards for preventing accidents, and to collect and disseminate information regarding environmental pollution.

Environment related other legislations

There are some other legislations which may not be called as environmental laws but they are related to environment protection though main object of these laws are not to prevent environment pollution. These are mentioned below:

1. The Merchant Shipping (Amendment) Act, 1983.
2. Indian Boilers Act, 1923.
3. The Mines and Minerals (Regulation & Development) Act 1947.
4. The Industries (Development & Regulation) Act, 1951.
5. The Poison Act, 1919.
6. Insecticides Act, 1948.
7. The Prevention of Food Adulteration Act, 1954.
8. Ancient Monuments & Archaeological Sights and Remains Act, 1958.
9. Explosives Act, 1884.
10. Urban Land (Ceiling & Regulations) Act, 1976.

11. The Calcutta Municipal Act, 1951.
12. West Bengal Town and Country Planning Act.
13. The West Bengal Cattle Licensing Act.
14. The West Bengal Panchayat Act, 1973.

Thus from the discussion of development of environmental legislations particularly in the national level it is revealed that particularly during last two decades specific laws on environment protection have been passed by the legislatures of different countries, though the seeds of environmental law can be traced in various laws made more than a century ago. In the International level also the growth is discernable. Thus it can be said now that there is no dearth of environmental legislations but there is need for proper implementation of those legislations.

References

1. Boer, *The Social College and Environmental Law* (1984), 1 EPLG 233.
2. G.M. Bates. *Environmental Law in Australia* (1987) Butterwroths.
3. Gopesh Nath Khana, *Environment Problems and the United Nations*, (1990) New Delhi, p. 3.
4. *Ibid.* p. 3.
5. *Ibid.* p. 4.
6. *Ibid.* p. 4.
7. See. Year Book of the United Nations, 1949, p. 329.
8. G.N. Khanna, *op.cit.*, p. 5.
9. *Ibid.* p. 6.
10. *Ibid.* p. 8.
11. *Ibid.* p. 8.
12. *Ibid.* p. 9.
13. Krishna Iyer, *op.cit.*, p. 17-18.
14. L.N. Mathur, "A Federal Legislative History of Control of Water Pollution in India", in Agarwal, *op.cit.*, p. 87.
15. *Ibid.* pp. 87-88.
16. V.D. Kulshreshtra, "Noise Pollution: Emerging Challenges and Regulation", in Agarwal, *op.cit.*, p. 196.
17. See Bates. *op. cit.*

18. See : Karpagam, *op.cit.*, Environmental Economics.
19. See. Gupta: Kautilyan Jurisprudence (1987). p. 155-156.
20. Thapar: Asoka and the Decline of the Mauryas, (2nd. Ed.) 1973, p. 264.
21. Guha : Forestry in British and Post-British India : A historical analysis, *Economic and Political Weekly*, October 29, 1983. p. 1882.
22. R.F.V. Heuston (ed.) *Salmond on the Law of Torts* (1957) 12th Edn., Sweet and Maxwell, London, pp. 554-555.
23. Asit Kumar Bose. "Legal Control of Water Pollution in India" in the *Legal Control of Environmental Pollution*. S.L. Agarwal (ed). by Indian Law Institute, New Delhi. p. 121.
24. Iyer, *op.cit.*, p. 20.
25. AIR 1987 SC 1109.
26. AIR 1988 SC 2187.
27. T. Damodar Rao v. The Special Officer, Municipal Corporation of Hyderabad, AIR 1987 AP 171, 181.
28. L.K. Koolural v. State of Rajasthan, AIR 1988 RAJ 2, 4.
29. Madhavi v. Tilakan 1988 (2) KER L.T. 730.
30. Kinkri Devi v. State of Himachal Pradesh, AIR 1988 HP 4, 9.
31. Rosencranz, *op.cit.*, p. 68.

CHAPTER - IV

Implementation of Environmental Laws

"It (Environment Laws) should not be a cobra with fangs having no venom but be a king cobra, the sight of which itself will be a terror. Wisdom of the legislative draftsmanship or administrative rule-making expertise is certainly to be widened by an interaction with environmentalists academics and research institutions".

—*N.S. Chandrasekharan*

An Overview

In the previous chapter we have noted the growth of environmental laws and the present trends of rapid environmental legislations in India as well as in other countries. Even in International level a growing concern is discernable to evolve an international control mechanism to protect human environment. Now we will examine the process of implementation of various environmental laws in Indian perspective though whenever possible a comparison may be made with other countries. The main concentration here will be on the results expected, results achieved and results not achieved in the field of legal control of environmental pollution.

Enforcement of law is a problem all over the world. It is said that we have no dearth of laws we have want of implementation of laws. Though generally the task of implementation of laws is on the Executives of the Government yet other organs of the State and people's acceptance and participation in the implementing process are also necessary especially in the vast and vital matters like prevention of pollution. Prof. Upendra Baxi has rightly observed :

> "No specialist bureaucracy by itself, especially where the regulatory domains are so vast and vital can hope to establish monopoly or hegemony of information access necessary and sufficient to establish either adequate implementation or enforcement, even when it is assumed, contrary to any law of probabilities, that the enforcement and implementation processes will be:
>
> — incorruptible
>
> — immune from capture or seizure by dominant or vested interests
>
> — immune from partisan political interference
>
> — autonomous to a point where the aspiration to achievc major dominant objectives of the legislation provide sole legitimoative for bureaucratic/technocratic divisions.
>
> — accountable in socially significant sense to affected communities and people at large.
>
> — capable of cumulative learning and unlearning, without significant levels of public participation
>
> — so intimately connected with the production cycles as to be aware, without warning (signals of impending disasters, breakdowns or catastrophe), enumerating from workers, NGOs, investigative journalists"[1].

For implementation of environmental laws a view was also expressed by some sociologists that the mobilisation of public opinion on concrete issues of environmental pollution and degradation was far more effective than general environmental laws. Again a view was expressed that in the absence of effective political will to enforce them, the laws merely create illusions and mystifications[2].

Moreover today it is not possible to pass a law in details by the legislature. So the legislature prescribes the skeleton of a law laying down the main principles of the respective legislation and the details necessary to implement the law is normally delegated to some subordinate authority. Hence proper delegated legislations are one of the important factors for implementation of law. So we have to examine the Rules, Regulations and procedural laws framed under various environmental legislations.

Above all there is Court to say final words in matters of disputes and to apply laws in practice, as presumed by Realist School of law which postulated that law is what the court says. Therefore, in the matters of implementation of environmental laws we will also examine the role of Court particularly our Supreme Court and High Courts having power of Judicial review of Administrative actions and even laws passed by legislature.

Thus to study implementation of the environmental laws we will discuss the issues on the following heads:

1. Role of the Court
2. Procedural Laws
3. Administrative Policy and Process
4. Role of the people
5. Legal Control of Multinational Corporations
6. Role of the U.N.O.
7. Sanctions against Polluters.

1. Role of the Court

The controversy regarding desirability of dissolving administrative dispute in the Courts instead of tribunals is a matter of great public debate. On the one hand, the critics argued that the substantive review of mathematical and scientific evidence of technical matters judges are unreliable and therefore we should concentrate our efforts on administrative adjudication. On the other hand, as Sax has pointed out, the courts are frequently called upon to decide cases where evidence of technical experts is crucial to the outcome. At the same time Justice Oakes is of the view that conscientious judges can with study become sufficiently conversant in technical fields to allow them to make determinations of arbitrariness or irrationality. Therefore, Judge Oakes talked the notion that Judges are ill-equipped to deal with technical matters in the following words :

> "The criticism that judges are legal generalists who cannot intelligently analyse technical, non-legal issues appears to contain two partially false assumptions, that judges are simply generalists and that generalist review is necessarily bad. On the first point, it is simply not true that judges are altogether incapable of mastering scientific concepts and terminology. ...... While a court may never understand a specific problem as well as a

> scientist or the EPA administrator, such depth of understanding is not necessary to decide the lesser question whether an agency has acted arbitrarily or capriciously. When, as is so often the case in environmental litigation, briefs are submitted by three sides — agency, industry and public interest group — no judge genuinely interested in the issue can fail to get a modicum of education adequate for the problem at hand. In the end, much depends, at other levels in the system, upon the individual traits of agency officials or laboratory scientists. .... Even if all judges were pure generalists lacking the means to understand legal issues posed in technical language, such generalist review would not necessarily be harmful or inappropriate. When experts talk only to each other, they tend to forget for whom the decisions are being made. When they are forced to explain their decisions in terms a judge can understand, it is more likely that the public also will understand. This, then, is a key benefit from generalist court review : it makes environmental decisions more comprehensible to those who must ultimately pay the costs of implementation"[3].

Now to examine the role of our Supreme Court in the matter of interference we may note two cases. In the First Case popularly known as *Silent Valley case*[4] the Supreme Court not entered into the question of whether there will be an ecological upset or not and only examined whether there is any arbitrariness or matter disregard of existing norms to launch any project. The case deserved reproduction below :-

Extract from the Judgment by Hon'ble Mr. Justice V.P. Gopalan Nambiar in the Silent Valley Case:

> 1. There is, in the Palghat District of this State (Kerala), 45 km. to the north of Mannarghadu, stretch of forest, nearly 8952 hectares in extent, known as the "Silent Valley". The name is apparently derived from the peace, quiet and serenity of the place. But paradoxically enough, as was once remarked in the far past in the Madras Legislature, the Valley has been creasking and squeaking loudly on many occasions. The present noise and bustle are over the hydroelectric project sought to be built in this Valley. These writ petitions, broadly stated, seek to forbid the State from proceeding with the project. As representatives of the arguments advanced, we may refer to O.P. No. 2949 of 1979.

The Government of Kerala is proposing to deforest the Silent Valley and to construct a dam for .... a hydroelectric project for power generation and supply of electricity. It is said that the dam is to generate 120M. Watts higherm. This venture has been represented as fraught with adverse consequences deleterious to the public. Experts have warned against the proposed construction of the dam and processing of the project. Scientists and technologists have joined the chorus of denunciation of the project.

2. The adverse effects from the conversion of the Silent Valley into a hydroelectric project were listed thus ; *first*, the deforestation was bound to affect the climatic conditions in the state and even outside, by depriving the state of its legitimate share of rain during the Monsoon, *second,* that the preservation of the forests was needed for conducting research in medicine, pest control, breeding of economic plants and a variety of purposes, and *third* that deforestation was bound to interfere with the balance of nature, as between the forest land on the one side and arable and other types of lands on the other.

3. The argument stressed that a project like the hydroelectric project, if sanctioned and set up would have its impact on environment, and this has to be carefully considered. Copious citations were made from various treatises, reports and publications, to show the importance of the environmental factor in industrial planning.

4. The learned Advocate-General stressed the fact that the project was sanctioned on 11.4.1973 by the Planning Commission, and that administrative sanction was given to it in 1976. The question of ecological upset likely to result from the execution of the project was raised. This was considered. Paragraph 4 of the counter-affidavit which has detailed the nature of the project, and its potentialities and has stressed that the location is ideal for a hydroelectric project, which would produce considerable amount of power at the cheapest rate, Paragraph 5 refers to revised working plan and the details therein regarding the silent valley reserve. Paragraph 20 of the counter-affidavit has referred to the report of the Task Force for sociological planning in the Western Ghats. It has recommended that

policy decision should be taken on seventeen recommendations prior to commencing the project work, if the Government felt that the work cannot be abandoned for any reason. It is pointed out that the Legislature of Kerala was of the unanimous view that the project was crucial importance to the State. A resolution was unanimously adopted on 22.8.1978 expressing anxiety on the continuing delay. An all-party delegation from Kerala visited the Prime Minister on 7.4.1978. The various steps and developments of a similar nature are detailed in Paragraph 20. They show clearly that the Government's mind was addressed to the question of the ecological aspects involved in the execution of the project and its impact upon the same. We were taken through copious extracts from various works, reports and other materials regarding the technical feasibility of the project and the importance of ecological considerations in assessing the worth and utility of a proposed project. But in this region we cannot substitute our judgment for that of the Government, on the question as to whether a national asset is to be more conveniently utilised as a hydroelectric project with prospects of greater power generation, or retained in its pristine glory for preservation of forests deleterious effects on the community. The scope for interference with such policy decision of the Government should, in the nature of things be limited. A wealth of material was cited and placed before us on the technical feasibility of the project and the impolitic decision to destroy the forest.

5. In O.P. No. 2949 of 1979 it was objected that the petitioner was mere *pro bono publico*, having no *locus standi* to maintain the application. The decision in the *Rann of Cutch case* (AIR 1969 S.C. 1306) were cited. We do not think it necessary to deal finally with this aspect of the case, as we are satisfied that on the merits the petition must fail.

6. Counsel for the petitioner stressed the national importance of forests as having been responsible for certain amendments in the Constitution. Reference was made to Article 48-A of the Constitution where by the preservation of forests and wildlife is one of the directive principles of State policy Article 49 was also stressed giving obligation to protect every monument or place or object of artistic or historic interest, declared by Parliament to be of national importance from destruction, removal etc.

7. Rich and worthy material of a variegated nature was placed before us in regard to the national policy and environmental considerations. We are by no means satisfied that these aspects have not been borne in mind by the Government in planning and processing the project. We are also not satisfied that the assessment of these considerations made by the Government and the policy decisions taken thereafter are liable to be reviewed by this Court in these proceedings. Even if they be open to review no grounds for such review have been disclosed.

8. As against the argument that .... the Prime Minister of India had recommended that the project should be abandoned, it was argued that the counter-affidavit of the State had detailed the necessity for more electricity for the State, it is not as if a veto once by the Prime Minister, or an advice from the same high source once to drop the project, will arrest its development for all time.

9. There was then an argument that the Silent Valley project conflicts with the Wild Life Preservation Act. It was also argued that the petitioners have the legal right to breathe pure air and drink pure water etc. and that these would be vitally affected by the proposed deforestation of the Silent Valley. These were the arguments developed in O.P. No. 3025 of 1979. The protection of environment granted by various countries such as America, England etc., was stressed and reference was made to the Endangered Species Act 1973 and the National Environmental Policy Act 1969 in America; the Control of Pollution Act 1974, the Country Side Act 1968, and the Clean Air Act 1956 in England. The learned Advocate General relied on Article 37 that it shall be the duty of the State to apply the directive of principles in making laws. He referred to Ext. R3 filed with the original counter-affidavit which shows the various reserved forests in the State. It was pointed out that there was no planning as to environmental pollution or the danger resulting from the execution of the project. Administrative sanction was accorded to the project in 1973 before the 42nd Amendment and the work also started before the said Amendment.

10. As for the danger of extinction of the lion-tailed monkey, the matter is dealt with in paragraph 8 of the counter-affidavit. We

do not think it necessary to cover the entire gamut of the material — whether scientific, technical, technological or ecological — placed before us in great detail. It is not for us to evaluate these considerations again as against the evaluation already done by the Government. It is enough to state that we are satisfied that the relevant matters have received attention before the Government decided to launch the project. There has been no non-advertence of the mind to the salient aspects of the project. We are not to substitute our opinion and notions on these matters for those of the Govt. We find no reason to interfere. We dismiss these applications with no order as to costs.

The second case is *Sachidananda Pandey* v. *State of West Bengal*[5] where the Court justified in resigning itself to acceptance of the decision of the concerned authority is granting the lease of 'Begumbari' land adjacent to Calcutta Zoo to the Taj Group of Hotels for construction of a Five Star Hotel. The arguments forwarded by the court may be stated below:-

Chinnappa Reddy, J :- Todays society's interaction with nature is so extensive that the environmental question has assumed proportions affecting all humanity. * * *

In India, as elsewhere in the world, uncontrolled growth and the consequent environmental deterioration are fast assuming menacing proportions and all Indian cities are afflicted with this problem. The once Imperial City of Calcutta is no exception. The question raised in the present case is whether the Government of West Bengal has shown such lack of awareness of the problem of environment in making an allotment of land for the construction of a Five Star Hotel at the expense of the Zoological garden that it warrants interference by this court. Obviously, if the Government is alive to the various considerations requiring thought and deliberation and has arrived at a conscious decision after taking them into account, it may not be for this court to interfere in the absence of *mala fides*.

On the other hand, if relevant considerations are not borne in mind and irrelevant considerations influence the decision, the court may interfere in order to prevent a likelihood of prejudice to the public. Whenever a problem of ecology is brought before the court, the court is bound to bear in mind Article 48-A of the

Constitution, Directive Principle which enjoins that "The State shall endeavour to protect and improve the environment and to safeguard the forests and wild-life of the Country," and Article 51-A(g) which proclaims it to be the fundamental duty of every citizen of India "to protect and improve the natural environment including forests, lakes, rivers and wild life, and to have compassion for living creatures. "When the court is called upon to give effect to the Directive Principle and fundamental duty, the court is not to shrug its shoulders and say that priorities are a matter of policy and so it is a matter for the policy making authority. The least that the court may do is to examine whether appropriate considerations are borne in mind and irrelevancies are excluded. In appropriate cases, the court may go further, but how much further, but how much further must depend on the circumstances of the case. The court may always give necessary directions. However the court will not attempt to nicely balance relevant considerations. When the question involves the nice balancing of relevant considerations, the court may feel justified in resigning itself to acceptance of the decision of the concerned authority.

Bearing in mind the proper approach that we have to make when questions of ecology and environment are raised, an approach which we have mentioned at the outset, we are satisfied that the facts and circumstances brought out by the appellants do not justify an inference that the construction of the proposed hotel in the Begumbari land would interfere in any manner with the animals in the Zoo and the birds arriving at the 400 or otherwise disturb the ecology. The proposed hotel is a garden-hotel and there is perhaps every chance of the ecology and environment improving as a result of planting numerous trees all around the proposed hotel and the removal of the burial ground and dumping ground for rubbish.

On a consideration of all the facts and circumstances of the case we are satisfied that the Government of West Bengal acted perfectly *bona fide* in granting the lease of Begumbari land to the Taj Group of Hotels for the construction of a Five Star Hotel in Calcutta. The Government of West Bengal did not fail to take into account any relevant considerations. Its action was not against the interests of the Zoological Garden or not in the best interests of the animal inmates of the zoo or migrant birds visiting the zoo. The financial interests of the State were in no way sacrificed either by not inviting tenders or holding a public auction or by adopting the 'net sales' method. In the result, the judgments of the learned single Judge and the Division Bench of the Calcutta High Court are affirmed and the appeal is dismissed. In the circumstances of the case, we do not desire to award any costs.

Public Interest Litigation as an Instrument of Environmental Protection

The innovation of Public Interest Litigation[6] by the Supreme Court of India in judicial system is now contributing much influence in the protection of environment. Dr. Alice Jacob observed : "Social action litigation or Public interest litigation has come of age in India and the higher judiciary is doing a yeoman service in enforcing the rights of the Indian populace in socio-economic and environmental matters in the face of executive apathy and indifference. The process the Supreme Court has established in resolving these matters in commendable. The Court seeks the help of experts in the field through the constitution of Committees and decides the relevant issues on the basis of technical reported data"[7].

The PIL cases are filed in the Indian Courts in the following areas of Environmental Problems:

Environment and Fundamental Right

The Supreme Court in *Rural Litigation and Entitlement Kendra* v. *State of U.P.*[8] the court held that it could interfere the mining rights already given and to lesses by the Government on the ground of ecological disturbance and the traditional rule of *locus standi* did not stand in the way in cases of environmental questions in the interest of the general public. According to the court the hardship caused to the lessees is:

"a price that has to be paid for protecting and safeguarding the right of the people to live in healthy environment with minimal disturbance of ecological balance and without avoidable hazard to them and to their cattle, house and agricultural land and without undue affectation of air, water and environment"[9]. But in this case popularly known as *Doon Valley* case or the

Mussoorie case the Supreme Court by its order dated 11 August 1983 appointed an expert committee known as the Bhargav Committee to advise the bench on technical issues.

In *Kinkri Devi* v. *State*[10] on similar facts, the High Court of Himachal Pradesh followed the observation of the Supreme Court in Rural Litigation Kendra and pointed out that if a just balance is not struck between development through tapping of natural resources and the Protection of ecology and environment, there will be violation of fundamental rights conferred by Articles 14 and 21 of the Constitution.

Court against Industrial Pollution

M.C. Mehta a social activist lawyer filed a series of PIL cases in Supreme Court of India under the title *M.C. Mehta* v. *Union of India*[11]. In the first M.C. Mehta case[12] popularly known as Olevum gas leak case raised 'some seminal questions concerning the true scope and ambit of Articles 21 and 32 of the Constitution' and the Court adopted an approach of balancing values of environment with those of development. The Court observed:

"When science and technology are increasingly employed in producing goods and services calculated to improve the quality of life, there is certain element of hazard or risk inherent in the very use of science and technology and it is not possible to totally eliminate such hazard or risk altogether. We cannot possibly adopt a policy of not having any chemical or other hazardous industries merely because they pose hazard or risk to the community .... such industries even if hazardous have to be set up since they are essential for economic development and advancement of well-being of the people"[13].

The *second M.C. Mehta case*[14] modified some of the conditions which were laid down by the Supreme Court in the first M.C. Mehta case which the hazardous industry of the nature in question (Shree Ram Fertilizers Ltd.) be permitted to function.

The *third M.C. Mehta case*[15] made further extension of the scope of the right to life under Article 21 of the Constitution and held that read with remedies available under Article 32 including issuance of directions for enforcement, the right to life contains the right to claim compensation to victims of pollution hazards. The *fourth M.C. Mehta case*[16] was relating to pollution of the river Ganga by a group of tanneries. The Supreme Court issued directions to those tanneries to set up affluent treatment plants within a period of six months and also directed the Central Government, Pollution Control Board and the District Magistrate to oversee the work. In the *fifth M.C. Mehta case*[17] the Court held that a citizen of India interested in protecting lives of the people who make use of the water flowing in the river Ganga has the right to move in the Supreme Court.

The High Courts have been interfered in the environmental problems under Article 21 and a judicial trend is now firmly set. In *Damodhar Rao* v. *S.O., Municipal Corporation, Hyderabad*[18] *Attakoya Thangal* v. *Union of India*[19] reiterated. Justice Sankaran Nair in the later case observed:

"The right to life is much more than the right to animal existence and its attributes are manifold as life itself. A prioritisation of human needs and a new value system has been recognised in these areas. The right to sweet water and the right to free air, are attributes of the right to life, for these are the basic elements which sustain life itself"[20]. By invoking jurisdiction under Article 225 the High Courts contributed much to the development of PIL in environmental cases. Thus in *N.S. Subba Rao v. Government of A.P.*[21] the High Court of Andhra Pradesh gave relief to the residence of a particular locality who were aggrieved by emission of pungent smell from a bone factory.

In *L.K. Koolwal* v. *State of Rajasthan*[22] the High Court of Rajasthan allowed a petition for the preservation of sanitation in the city of Jaipur. Again in *Kinkri Devi* v. *State of Himachal Pradesh*[23] the High Court directed the closure of mining activities affecting the environment.

Court against Public Nuisance

In India the provision of class actions against public nuisance can be brought under Section 91 of the C.P.C. or Section 133 of the Cr.P.C. Thus in *Municipal Council Ratlam* v. *Vardhichand*[24] a group of residents in a locality and in *Krishnan Gopal* v. *State of M.P.*[25] a single residents had been permitted to move under Section 133 of the Cr.P.C. for removal of public nuisance. This dormant provision was revitalised by the Supreme Court in *Gobind Singh* v. *Shanti Sarup*[26] where a chimney constructed for the business of the respondent by an oven bakes created public nuisance. The Supreme Court held :

> "We are of the opinion that in a matter of this nature where what is involved is not merely the right of a private individual but the health, safety and convenience of the public at large, the safer course would be to accept the view of the learned Magistrate who saw for himself the hazard resulting from the working of the bakery"[27].

I similar view was expressed in *Municipal Council, Ratlam* v. *Vardhichand*[28] and the Court held that if a public nuisance created in a locality due to open drains and harp of dirt, the Magistrate could direct the municipality under Section 133 Cr.P.C.: to discharge its responsibilities. The Court said :

> "Although these two codes (the other being the code of Civil Procedure) are of an ancient vintage the new social justice orientation imparted to them by the constitution of India makes it a remedial weapon of versatile use. The social justice is due to the people and therefore, the people must be able to trigger off the jurisdiction vested for their benefit in any public functionary like a Magistrate under Section 133 Cr.P.C."[29].

In *Krishna Gopal* v. *State of M.P.*[30] a lady complained that her husband, a heart patient had been disturbed in his sleep every night due to the booming noise produced by the boiler in the factory. The Court observed :

> "It is not the intent of law that the community as a whole or large number of complainants come forward to lodge their complaint or protest against the nuisance, that does not require any particular number of complaints. A mere reading of Section 133(1) would go to show that the jurisdiction of Sub-Divisional Magistrate can be invoked on receiving a report of a Police-Officer or other information and on taking such evidence if any as he thinks fit"[31].

In *Ajeet Mehta* v. *State of Rajasthan*[32] the Rajasthan High Court confirmed the order of the Magistrate under Section 133 Cr.P.C. directing the removal of a business enterprise from a residential locality. According to the petitioners, the business involves loading unloading and stocking of fodder had become serious health hazard to the residents and the whole atmosphere was polluted on account of time dust particles of the fodder. Similar to *Krishna Gopal* and *Ajeet Mehta* there was a case of *Madhavi* v. *Thilakan*[33] where the Kerala High Court had to examine the nuisance created by an automobile workshop in a residential area. Allowing removal of the Health hazard the Court said:

> "We recognise every man's home to be his castle which cannot be invaded by toxic fumes, or tormenting sounds. This principle expressed through law and culture, consistent with nature's ground rules for existence has been recognized in Section 133(1)(6). The conduct of any trade or occupation, or keeping of any goods or merchandise injurious to health or physical comfort of community could be regulated or prohibited under the Section[34].

On the question of pollution of water and air the Kerala High Court and the Madhya Pradesh High Court had an opposite view of the scope of Section 133 after enactment of special laws of 'Water and Air' Act. In *Tata Tea Ltd.* v. *State of Kerala*[35] the Court held :

> "While under Section 133 of the code it is open to a citizen to directly approach an Executive Magistrate under the provisions of the Water Act. But, that would make no difference since under the provisions of the Act, it is open to the citizen concerned to approach the State Board with his grievance and it is open to the State Board to take such measures as are contemplated in the Act including filing petition before a Judicial Magistrate. All remedies which could be provided by an Executive Magistrate under Section 133 could certainly be provided by authorities contemplated under the Act"[36].

On the other hand the Madhya Pradesh High Court in *Abdul Hamid* v. *Gwalior Rayon Silk Mfg. (Wvg.) Co. Ltd.*[37] stressed heavily on the sanctioning power of the Board under the Water and Air Acts and held that "the special statutes on pollution of water and air have to prevail over Section 133 of the Code of Criminal Procedure and the Provisions of the Indian Penal Code"[38].

Court and Conservation of Forest

The role of Courts in conservation of Forest after notable feature in the present context after passing of the Forest (Conservation) Act 1980. In *Yaswant* v. *State of U.P.*[39] in *Banshi Ram Modi*[40] in *Hyderabad*

Abrasives and Minerals v. *Government of Andhra Pradesh*[41], in *Anupama Minerals* v. *Union of India*[42] and in *Ambica Quarry Works* v. *State of Gujarat*[43] the Supreme Court and the High Courts dissolved disputes developed from the Act of 1980 and took the conservative attitudes. The Supreme Court in *Ambica Quarry Works* v. *State of Gujarat* observed :

> "What is to be remembered is that the Act is an Act in recognition of the awareness that afforestation and ecological imbalances as a result of deforestation have become social menaces and further deforestation and ecological imbalances should be prevented. That was the primary purpose writ large in the Act. Therefore, the concept that power coupled with duty enjoined upon the authorities to renew the lease stands eroded by the mandate of the legislation"[44].

Therefore it has been extracted from the discussion of the aforesaid cases it is revealed that in evolving a new environmental jurisprudence in India the Supreme Court and High Courts used some unused provisions (Section 133 Cr.P.C.) of law as significant tools in the protection of environment, developed environmental law through public interest litigation, highlights the vigilance of the judiciary against violation of special laws on environment helping growth of law relating to liability of hazardous and inherently dangerous industry and unfolds the constitutional dimensions of the right to environment under Article 21 of our Constitution. Therefore, it has rightly been observed that :

> "In its attempt to formulate legal principles for environmental protection the Indian Judiciary rejected inadequate and outmoded doctrines and introduced new strategies ..... Undoubtedly, the Indian judiciary has played an activist creative role in evolving and indigenous environmental jurisprudence for the land"[45].

2. Procedural Laws

Implementation of any law much depends upon the sound and proper rules and regulations. The procedural law deals with the functional aspect of that law. The procedural laws mainly aimed at to provide preventive and remedial measures to enforce a law naturally two things are involved with the procedural laws — one *who* will perform the statutory obligations or duties under the parent law and *how* they will perform these duties. Thus the procedural laws may be discussed, from two angles —

one the persons or authorities (who) implementing the laws and the other is the Rules and Regulations (how) to implement the laws. So the procedural laws may be discussed under two heads (1) Role of Agency and (2) Delegated Legislations.

Role of Agency

The implementation of environmental laws are entrusted to the Pollution Control Boards constituted under the provisions of the Water or Air Act. The chief personal entrusted to implement the environmental laws are not free from bureaucratic aggrandisement. Thus too much arrogant attitude to implement the environmental laws disregarding the practical problems of sustainable development of problem may cause much hardship and develop legal battle between the Agency and the Industries creating pollutions. Thus in *Tanya Pulverising Industry* v. *Karnataka State Pollution Control Board*[46] unpractical attitude of the Board to implement Rules proved under Air Pollution Act clearly brings out this inherent defective attitudes of the implementing agency. For a clear understanding of the problem let us go through the case in details reproduced below from the Order of the Karnataka High Court.

> **"Order:-** Petitioner, a Small Scale Industry, carrying on the business of pulverising Dolomite stones, has filed this petition challenging the order of the Karnataka State Pollution Control Board (hereinafter referred to as 'Board') dated 4th December, 1985, by which, he is prohibited from operating his industry and directing him to obtain clearance certificate before establishing the same in any other place. This writ petition could have been avoided, if only, the petitioner on his part and the Officers of the Board on their part had adopted a purposeful attitude and were more pragmatic problems is not without solution.
>
> The Air (Prevention and Control of Pollution) Act, 1981 (hereinafter called as the "Act") came into force on 16th May, 1981. The Board constituted under Section 4 of the Water (Prevention and Control of Pollution) Act, 1974 is deemed to be the Board for purposes of Prevention of Air Pollution Act. Section 19 requires the State Government, after consulting the Board, to declare certain areas as "Air Pollution Control Area", for purposes of Air Pollution Act. The State Government has framed Rules which came into force on 18th, November 1983. Rule 19 in Chapter VI of the Rules require such declaration to be published

in the Official Gazette and at least in two local newspapers having wide circulation in that area. The declaration was published in the Gazette on 30th, January, 1984, in "Kannada Prabha" and on 26th June 1983 in "Deccan Harald". It was declared that Area bounded by respective boundaries of the industries specified in the Schedule as Air Pollution Control Area. Item 13 in the Schedule refers to "Ores/minerals processing industries including beneficiation, pelletization etc." The effect of the declaration was that the area, where the petitioner's industry is situated, comes under Air Pollution Control Area. While the notification in original was published in the Gazette, what was published in the newspaper was information regarding the publication of the notification and the requirement of obtaining consent. Since there is a criticism to the effect that there is no compliance with Rule 19, it is necessary to reproduce the contents of the notification:-

Notification (Decean Herald, dt. 26.6.1984) "Karnataka State Pollution Control Board, Bangalore.

Notification : Attention of all the Industrialists and Industries in the State of Karnataka is drawn to the provisions of the Air (Prevention and Control of Pollution) Act, 1981 which is in force in the state of Karnataka. In terms of the provisions of the Act, the Government vice their notification No. Dec. 205 ENV 83, dated 28.1.1984 published in the Gazette Extraordinary Dated : Monday 30th January, 1984 have declared the area bounded by the respective industries specified in the schedule appended to the Act as Air Pollution Control Areas in the state of Karnataka. It is also a statutory obligation on the part of all the industries specified in the Gazette to apply for and obtain a consent for emissions/continuation of emissions from industrial plants under Section 21 of the Act, for which purpose, they have to make an application to the Board in the prescribed form to be accompanied with the prescribed fees.

Government have also, vide Notification No. Dec. 42 ENV 84, dated 3.3.1984 published in the Gazette Extraordinary dated : Tuesday, March 6th 1984, specified 31st July, 1984 as the date on or before which the consent application shall be made by the industries listed in the Schedule situated in the area declared as

Air Pollution Control Area in the State of Karnataka.

Prescribed consent application forms can be had from the Board office on payment of Rs. 10/- by M.O./D.D./P.O., payable in the name of Member Secretary of the Board.

It is necessary for all industries specified in the Schedule to apply for and obtain the consent of the Board, for which necessary immediate action may be taken. In case of any further clarifications required, the Board Office may be contacted.

Sd/-

For Member Secretary
Karnataka State Pollution Control Board,
M.G. Road, Bangalore - 1."

The Kannada version of the above notification was published on 25th June, 1984 in "Kannada Prabha".

Section 21(1) of the Act requires the Industrialist to obtain prior consent for operating any industrial plant; proviso to Section 21(1) requires the existing industry owners to apply for consent of the Board, the said proviso reads thus :-

"21. (1) ....

(2) ....

Provided that where any person, immediately before the declaration of any area as an air pollution control area, operates in such area any industrial plant for the purpose of any industry specified in the Schedule, such person shall make the application under this sub-section within such period (being not less than three months from the date of such declaration) as may be prescribed and where such person makes such application, he shall be deemed to be operating such industrial plant with the consent of the State Board until the consent applied for has been refused".

This provision makes it obligatory to prescribe a date, within which an application for consent has to be made and on the making of the application, the consent is deemed to have been given, until the same is refused by the Board. After filing such application for consent, the Industry can be operated and such operation shall be deemed to be with the consent of the Board. By notification dated 3rd March, 1984 published in Karnataka Gazette dated 6th March, 1984 the Government prescribed 31st July, 1984 as the last date for filing applications for consent. The notification extracted above included this information also. On 11th January, 1985 the Board issued a circular asking the Industrialists to file applications for consent; the relevant directions read thus:

"You are therefore hereby required to comply with the following:

1) Apply for the consent of the Board in the prescribed form available on application to the Member-Secretary, Karnataka State Pollution Control Board, No. 25, 6th, 7th and 8th Floors, Public Utility Building, M.G. Road, Bangalore-1, on payment of Rs. 10/- and if the forms are required by registered post, an additional Rs. 6.50 may please be sent.

2) It will be necessary in order to make the application for consent, to monitor the emissions as existing from the various sources of emission within the area declared as Air Pollution Control applicable to your industry and furnish the details in the prescribed application form, together with detailed information on any air pollution control equipment currently installed with full technical details of the same.

On receipt of your consent application form containing full details of the nature and sources of emissions, relevant emission standards will be intimated, together with time within which the control equipment will have to be installed.

Each consent application will have to be accompanied by the scale of fees prescribed as per the details furnished in the Annexure Circular".

These being the provisions of law and steps taken by the Authorities, the *facts of the case* are as follows:

On 8th January, 1985 the Regional Officer (APC) inspected petitioner's Factory; it was noticed that the buildings and fields surrounding the Factory were covered with white dust; which according to the officer was due to dust emissions from the

Factory. Factory had not been provided with Air Pollution Control devices; the people in the area were complaining about the dust emissions. On 16th January 1985, a show cause notice was issued, pointing out the above facts and asking the petitioner to show cause as to why actions should not be initiated under Sections 37(1) and (2) of the Act, and, for violating the provisions of the Act, in that he has failed to apply for and obtain consent of the Board. Show cause notice is filed as Annexure-B. On 22nd January 1985, petitioner filed his reply. He contended that he had provided for dust collector; and had planned to install efficient dust collector. In this regard he had placed order with M/s. Nagdevi Machine Industries, Bangalore. Along with the reply he sent a postal order of Rs. 10/- towards the cost of application form, for consent. He requested for better suggestion for collecting dust. On 17th October, 1985; the Advocate for the Board, gave notice to the petitioner, alleging that he has not applied for consent and has paid requisite consent fee. The petitioner promptly gave a reply on 30th October, 1985. He stated that on two occasions the Board had sent the application form prescribed for consent under Water Pollution Act, instead of the form prescribed under the Act. The fact is admitted, but the defence was justification on the first occasion, but it cannot be accepted for the second one. It appears from Annexure-II filed by respondent, that Capt. S. Raja Rao, Member Secretary inspected the Factory on 18th and 19th October, 1985 and had discussions with the petitioner. It was specifically stated that on two occasions wrong forms were sent. The measures suggested are :

1) Ask the industry to have low key operation and at the same time establish the control equipment already procured to give relief to the affected people. At the same time a committed programme from the industry will have to be obtained for shifting the industry to its new location in about three to four months' time. The industry should here this time limit irrespective of their commitment.

2) Alternatively the industry should be prohibited from operation as they have not yet applied for consent and also as the complaint from the public is persisting, action in terms of

Section 23(2) may have to be initiated against the industry which will force the industry to shift to its new location".

Again the factory was inspected on 26.12.1985; it was noted that:

"8..... The industry has installed the bag filters, even then it was observed the surrounding area was affected by air pollution, sufficient draft is not provided to seek the dust into cyclone and bag filters, connected machineries are not provided and all the required bag filters are not provided."

Before this inspection, Annexure-F was issued to the petitioner on 4.12.1985; the petitioner was prohibited from operating the industry; hence this petition. The impugned order is purported to have been issued under Section 23 of the Act, which reads thus:

"23(1) where in any air pollution control area the emission of any air pollutant into the atmosphere in excess of the standards laid down by the state board occurs or is apprehended to occur due to accident or other unforeseen Act or event, the person in charge of the premises from where such emission occurs or is apprehended to occur shall forthwith intimate the fact of such occurrence or the apprehension of such occurrence to the State Board and to such authorities or agencies as may be prescribed.

2) On receipt of information with respect to the fact or the apprehension of any occurrence of the nature referred to in sub-section (1) whether through intimation under that sub-section or otherwise, the State Board and the authorities or agencies shall, as early as practicable, cause such remedial measures to be taken as are necessary to mitigate the emission of such air pollutants.

3) Expenses, if any, incurred by the State Board, authority or agency with respect to the remedial measures referred to in sub-section (2) together with interest (at such reasonable rate, as the State Government may, by order, fix) from the date when a demand for the expenses is made until it is paid may be recovered by that Board, authority or agency from the person concerned, as arrears of a land revenue, or of public demand".

Sections 37 and 38, which are referred to in the show cause notice deal with the penalties and imposition of sentence on conviction. The contravention and violation, contemplated by these sections, are failure to comply with conditions stipulated under sub-section (5) of Section 21 after obtaining consent; causing or discharging emission in excess of the standard laid down by the State Board or any order or directions given by the State under the Act.

On behalf of the petitioner it was urged that :

i) The action of the Board was illegal, as it had no power to prohibit the operation of the Factory;

ii) The Board having not complied with Rule 19 had no authority to take any action; the contention was while the declaration u/s. 19 was published in Karnataka Gazette on 30th January 1984, there was no simultaneous publication of the notification in two local newspapers having wide circulation;

iii) The date under sub-section (2) of Section 21 has to be prescribed by Rules and not by notification in the form of an Executive order; Rules being silent regarding the period within which such application shall be made, as provided in clause (1) of Section 54(2) of the Act, there is no violation.

iv) "Remedial Measures" contemplated by Section 23(2) does not include "Closing down" of the Factory;

v) While the petitioner was willing to obtain 'Consent' the same was frustrated by the Board by sending erroneous Forms".

Counsel for the Board, supporting the action of the Board, contended that the petitioner had an alternate remedy by appeal under Section 31 of the Act and therefore this petition is liable to be rejected. In the statement of objections, the non-obtaining of consent has been very much highlighted and it is stressed in more places than one.

The point raised as preliminary objection is not stated in the statement of objections. While both the Advocated did not mention as to who is constituted as appellate authority, it appears to me that the orders now challenged is not an order made by the Board under the Act. Annexure-F is sent of the Board. The transactions of the Board are required to be con-

ducted as per Rule 8 to 14. The statement of objections is silent regarding the proceedings of the Board. It neither refers to Minute Book nor to any resolution of the Board. Copy of Agenda is not furnished to find out whether this subject was included in it and was placed before the meeting of the Board. In fairness, if there had been such a resolution, the communication at Annexure-F, should have made a reference to that, Secondly, Annexure-F requires the petitioner to close the industry, which in my view is not an order contemplated by Section 23. Neither in form nor in spirit can it be construed as an order of the Board under the Act. Hence, I reject the preliminary objection.

The Act is designed to prevent, control and abatement of air pollution, the provisions relate to preservation of quality of air and control of pollution. Keeping in view these objects the Act has provided for measures, which are preventive in nature, in the cases of industries to be established; and in the case of industries already established, they are remedial. In the case of established industries, it insists on obtaining consent of Board, making the industry amenable to the administrative control of the Board. Once a consent is given, the Board can issue orders, directions etc., which are to be complied with by the Industry. Precisely for this reason, the industry, which has given consent, is required to comply with certain conditions, enumerated in sub-section (5) of Section 21. Non-compliance of these conditions is made punishable under Section 37. The primary responsibility of controlling the Air Pollution is on the Board. Sub-section (2) of Section 23 casts a duty on the Board to cause such remedial measures as are necessary to mitigate the emission of air pollutants, and the expenses that are incurred can be recovered from the person concerned as arrears of land revenue.

Viewed in this background the direction to close down the Factory, solely because it has not obtained consent of the Board is clearly illegal. If the Board thinks that the petitioner has failed to comply with its order it may take action under Section 37, as proposed in the show cause notice; but that would not justify the passing of a prohibitory order which apart from causing loss to the owner has a serious consequence of paralysing the industry affecting the livelihood of employed persons; the consequences

> may be more hazardous than the air pollution. Therefore the "remedial measures" contemplated must be understood as such measures which mitigate the emission of air pollutants. Therefore, the harsh step of prohibiting the working of the Factory is neither warranted nor has it the legal sanctity.

The above conclusion is sufficient to dispose of the petition.

However, against the drawbacks preventive regulations in Australia some jurist recommended Diagnostic regulations for implementation of environmental legislations. They observed :

> "Diagnostic inspection recognizes both the importance of specific regulations and the limits of the better of the law. The most important enforcement activity is directed at companies which fail to have or abide by plans by law, at companies which fail to meet a performance standard after the inspector has shown management how the standard is attainable by recognising the workplace or work routines. The diagnostic inspector spends less time at work-places with solid management systems for monitoring and compliance internally, more time with companies who think a safety engineer, a company safety inspector and union management safety committee are a waste of money.
>
> Diagostic regulation requires inspectors who have experience of the relevant industry, an understanding of technical systems and how to change them, an appreciation of management systems and how to change them"[47]. Therefore, against the background of the case we may think to revise our procedural rules in the line of diagnostic regulations as per as practicable.

ii) Delegated Legislations and Quasi-laws

Today it is not possible for the Parliament or the legislatures to make laws complete in all respects. Therefore the legislature only gives the principles of the respective law and the details rules and regulations are prescribed by subordinate authorities authorised for the purpose by the Parent law. In the field of environmental legislation this type of laws are very essential as the subject requires consideration of technical matters and many policy issues. Thus, environmental legislations in India naturally delegated such power to the Central and State Government to formulate such subordinate legislations. In pursuance of those powers conferred upon the Central Government and each State Government a

huge list of rules and regulations have been developed in our country. The notable of which are mentioned below:

i) Rules framed under the Water (Prevention and Control of Pollution) Act, 1974:-

In pursuance of the power conferred by sub-section (1) and in particular by claused (a) and (e) of sub-section (2) of Section 64 of the Water (Prevention and Control of Pollution) Act 1974 (6 of 1974) every State Government framed Rules for implementation of Water Act. Thus, by a Notification dated 20th September 1974 West Bengal Prevention and Control of Water Pollution Rules 1974[48].

ii) Rules framed under the Water (Prevention and Control of Pollution) Cess Act, 1977:-

In exercise of the powers conferred by Section 17 of the Water (Prevention and Control of Pollution) Cess Act, 1977 (36 of 1977) the Government of India framed the Water (Prevention and Control of Pollution) Cess Rules 1978[49].

iii) Rules framed under the Air (Prevention and Control of Pollution) Act, 1981:-

In exercise of the powers conferred by Section 54 of the Air (Prevention and Control of Pollution) Act, 1981 every State Government framed their Rules for the respective state. Thus we get West Bengal Air (Prevention and Control of Pollution Rules, 1983[50] substituted again on 1st February 1984 and 16th August 1985.

iv) Rules framed under the Environment (Protection) Act, 1986:-

In exercise of the powers conferred by Sections 6 and 25 of the Environment Protection Act, 1986 (29 of 1986) the Government of India formulated the Environment (Protection) Rules 1986 with effect from November 19, 1986[51].

Besides the aforesaid existing delegated legislations in the environmental field framed under the parent Acts there are various Quasi administrative regulations and guidelines for implementation of Environmental laws. These are :

(i) Emission standard as per Section 17(1)(g) of the Air (Prevention & Control of Pollution) Act, 1981[52]. (Annexure-I)

(ii) Emission Standards for Automobiles for prevention and Control of Pollution[53]. (Annexure-II)

(iii) Indian Standard Institute (ISI) specifications for Standard Tollerance Limits for Industrial and Sewage effluents followed by West Bengal Pollution Control Board[54]. (Annexure-III)

(iv) Standard for Emission of Air Pollutants into the Atmosphere from Industrial Plants[55]. (Annexure-IV)

(v) Guidelines for diversion of forest lands for non-purposes under the Forest (Conservation) Act 1980[56]. (Annexure-V)

(vi) Guidelines for Environmental Impact Assessment[57].(Annexure-VI)

(vii) Guidelines for Environmental Appraisal of Industrial Projects[58]. (Annexure-VII)

(viii) Guidelines for Integrating Environmental Concerns with Exploitation of Mineral Resources[59]. (Annexure-VIII)

(ix) Environmental Guidelines for Formulation of River Valley Projects[60]. (Annexure-IX)

(x) Environmental Guidelines for Development of Beaches[61]. (Annexure-X)

(xi) Environmental Guidelines for Thermal Power Plants[62].

(xii) Guidelines for Environmental Impact Assessment of Shipping and Harbour Projects[63]. (Annexure-XII)

(xiii) Prevention of Hazards from Industrial Units: Government of India's Instructions[64]. (Annexure-XIII)

(xiv) Environmental Clearance of Industrial Licence—Conditions of Letter of Intent/Industrial Licence[65]. (Annexure-XIV)

(xv) Safety and Health Accident Reduction Action Plan (SAHARA)[66]. (Annexure-XV)

(xvi) Guidelines for Dereservation of Reserved Forests or Diversion of Forest land to any Non-Forest use[67]. (Annexure-XVI)

(xvii) Guidelines for Massive Tree Plantation for Abatement of Air Pollution caused by Industries[68]. (Annexure - XVII)

(xviii) Decision of the Cabinet on Amendment of the Rules of Business of effecting the Guidelines of the Department of Environment[69].

(Annexure-XVIII)

(xix) Incentives to Industries for Prevention and Control of Pollution and for Conservation of Resources[70]. (Annexure - XIX)

(xx) Environmental Guidclincs for Siting of Industry. (Annexure - XX)

In formulating these procedural rules and regulations under the Parent laws relating to environment the authorities are not able to foresee all the resultant situation and practical difficulties. So, conflicts may arise from those delegated legislations and the existing usage and normal development process. And we have already noted that there is an unnecessary proliferation of legislation and the working of the environmental laws exacerbates the already deplorable record of implementation of environmental management legislation.

Court in Practice

The survey of working of environmental laws in West Bengal also reveals this deplorable situations. From the starting of its function the West Bengal Pollution Control Board instituted various suits as show in Table - 2 under various environmental legislations but not a single case yet been decided by the court and not a single polluter being punished in the State of West Bengal[71].

The difficulty in implementing environmental legislation is perhaps, a common problem of the developing countries. Bondi D. Ogalla, a Kenyan environmentalist writes:

> "The brief survey of the Kenyan experience in incorporating environmental management considerations into the development process through the instrumentality of law, however reveals that although legislation is important it may not be the only critical factor for protection of the environment in developing countries. The dominant postulate of rapid economic growth undermines the political will to formulate and implement what is environmentally vital. The resultant regulatory machinery is therefore truncated, inadequate innumerative content and functionally ineffective"[72].

Table 2

Cases filed against the Industries under the water (Prevention & Control of Pollution) Act 1974.

	Name of the Industries & Address	Date of filing and the name of the Court
1.	M/s. Everest Paper Mills Ltd., Barasat, North-24 Pgs (Paper Mill).	1.1.80 in the Court SDJM at Barasat.
2.	M/s. Eastern Paper Industries Ltd., Bansberia, Hooghly, (Paper)	2.8.1980 in the SDJM court Chinsurah. Now appeal filed before District Judge at Chinsurah No. 179/88.
3.	Organic Dyes & Intermediated Mfg.Co. Ltd., D.H. Road, Calcutta (Chemical).	6.7.1985 in the SDJM court at Alipore.
4.	M/s. Serampore Distillery, Serampore, Dist. Hooghly. (Distillery)	1.8.1985 in the SDJM court at Serampore.
5.	M/s. Carew & Co. Asansol, Burdwan (Distillery).	11.10.1985 in the SDJM court at Asansol.
6.	M/s. Kesoram Rayon, Bansberia, Hooghly (Chemical).	18.1.1986 in the court of SDJM at Chinsurah.
7.	M/s. Aceto Chemicals, B.L. Shah Road, Calcutta-55 (Chemical).	19.2.1986 in the court of SDJM at Alipore.
8.	M/s. Bowreah Cotton Mills, Bowreah, Howrah (Cotton Ind.)	1.3.1986 in the court of SDJM at Uluberia.
9.	M/s. Kesoram Industries & Cotton Mills, Garden Reach, Calcutta (Cotton Ind.).	6.12.1986 in the court of at Alipore.
10.	M/s. Usha Automobiles, R.G. Ghosh Road, Calcutta-2 (Engg. Industry)	6.12.1986 in the court of CJM court at Alipore.

11.	M/s. Greaves Foseco. Taratalla Road, Calcutta-88. (Chemical).	6.12.1986 in the court of CJM at Alipore.
12.	M/s. Farmentation Industries, Kalyani, Nadia (Distillery Industry).	17.2.1987 in the court of SDJM at Kalyani.
13.	M/s. Dunbar Mills Ltd., Garulia Shyambazar, 24-Pgs (N).	29.4.1987 in the court of SDJM at Kalyani.
14.	M/s. Vegetable Products Ltd., Balghoria, Calcutta-56 (Dil).	7.7.1987 in the court of SDJM at Barrackpore.
15.	M/s. Prakash Distillery, Siliguri, Dist. Darjeeling (Distillery).	29.6.1987 in the court of SDJM at Siliguri.
16.	M/s. Bharatiya Chemical, Lalbunglow, Rupnarayanpur, PO. Rupnarayan. Dist. Burdwan, W.B.	8.9.1990 in the court of ACJM of Asansol.
17.	M/s. Eastern Gelatins (P) Ltd. Chandmarimore, Gayeshpur, Kalyani.	16.1.1991 in the court of SDJM at Kalyani.
18.	M/s. Mahaluxmi Cotton Mills. P.O. Bengal Enamel, Palta, 24 Pgs (N).	19.1.1991 in the court of Ld. SDJM at Barrackpore.
19.	M/s. Bharat Battery Mfg.Co. Pvt. Ltd., 56, Bondel Road, Calcutta-19.	22.1.1991 in the court of Ld. CJM at Alipore.
20.	M/s. Rosol Ltd (Vanaspati Divn) 1, Station Road, New Alipore, Calcutta-53.	22.1.1991 in the court of Ld. CJM at Alipore.
21.	M/s. Cycle Corporation of India, Asansol, Burdwan, W.B.	2.2.1991 in the court of ACJM at Asansol.
22.	M/s. Reckit and Colman of Ltd. Asansol, Burdwan, W.B.	2.2.1991 in the court of ACJM at Asansol.

Table 2 (Cont.)

Cases Filed by the W.B. Pollution Control Board under The Provision of Environment (Protection) Act 1986.

	Name of the Industry	No.	Date filing and name of Court.
1.	M/s. Aceto Chemicals 124, B.L. Saha Road, Calcutta - 53.	C/1008/90	21.12.1990 in the court of Ld. CJM at Alipore.
	Under the provision of Manufacture, Storage and Import of Hazardous Chemical Rules 1989 and Hazardous waste (Management and Handling)		
1.	Rupantar & Co. & Ors. 290, Kalighat Road, Calcutta-26.	C/245/90	21.2.1990 in the court Ld. CJM at Alipore.
2.	Nirmalendu Basu & Ors. 46, Mahim Halder Street Calcutta-26.	0/286/90	9.3.1990 in the court of Ld. CJM at Alipore.
3.	M/s. Hydro Carbon & Chemicals & Ors. 25, Chanditala Main Road, Calcutta-53.	C/1009/90	21.12.1990 in the court of Ld. CJM at Alipore
4.	M/s. Lubricating Oil Co. & Ors. 35/2/2 Chanditala Main Road, Calcutta-53.	C/1007/90	21.12.1990 in the court of Ld. CJM at Alipore.

The same things are happening in West Bengal and other States in India. There is lack of political will to enforce the environmental regulations with strong hand. The procedural laws in India are called soft regulation with which such a vital controversial law like environmental legislations cannot be implemented properly.

3. Administrative Policy and Process

It is true that the philosophy of environmental protection is still very largely a political rather than a legal issue. The enforcement of legislative

principle and position of environmental statutes are concerned largely to facilitate the implementation of Government Policy not to create enforceable legal rights. That is why much of the environmental legislation are drafted in rather, vague terms, leaving the application of the legislation to ministerial discretion which is difficult to challenge in the courts of law. Therefore we can say the administration has not only the task of implementing environmental policy but also the responsibility of enforcing environmental legislation.

National Policy on Environment

Thus there should be a clear policy and planning of the Government for implementation of environmental legislation. As such the Government of India formulated its National Policy Statement For Abatement of Pollution on 1.9.1992, the main strategies of which are reproduced below:

3. **Future Directions And Objectives**

3.1 It is not enough for the Government to notify laws which are to be complied with. A positive attitude on the part of everyone in society is essential for the prevention of pollution and wide consultation has been held with those who will ultimately implement the policy.

3.2 A comprehensive approach is taken to integrate environmental and economic aspects in development planning stress is laid on preventive aspects for pollution abatement and promotion of technological inputs to reduce industrial pollutants; and through reliance upon public cooperation in securing a clean environment to respond to the coming challenges.

3.3 The objective is to integrate environmental considerations into decision-making at all levels. To achieve this, steps have to be taken to:

Prevent pollution at source;

encourage, develop and apply the best available practicable technical solutions;

ensure that the polluter pays for the pollution and control arrangements;

focus protection on heavily polluted areas and river stretches; and

involve the public in decision-making.

4. **Critically Polluted Areas**

4.1 Mechanisms will be involved to reduce local concentration of pollutants in complex industrial sites. Strategies will be developed for areas with high pollution loads where the accumulative effect of the various types of pollutants would be taken into account including pollution of ground water. Existing units in these areas will be targeted for effective action. New units in these areas will be required to comply with location specific standards for stringent environmental quality objectives. These will include matching waste generators with waste buyers, with the objective of solving waste disposal.

4.2 Setting up of industrial estates, and clusters of small industrial units in rural areas, will include pollution abatement measures as an essential component of infrastructure. In the past, the absence of adequate provision of space for installing treatment facilities and arrangements for disposal of wastes has led to severe pollution of agricultural land and rivers.

4.3 There has been a steady increase in the amount of waste water produced from urban communities and industries. In the coming years, due to rapid growth in population, urbanisation, industrial development and better water supply, the amount of waste water may increase manifold. Generally, these waters are discharged into lagoons or dumped on low lying areas without any pre-treatment, thereby creating sewage polls, contaminating ground waters, salinizing good quality lands around cities, acting as a source of foul smell and breeding grounds for mosquitoes and other pathogens. At many places this waste water is discharged into drains and rivers causing serious water pollution. However, awareness has now grown and more attention is being paid to develop systems to treat sewage waters. For a country like India, conventional treatment plants are costly. In fact, these are beyond the financial means of many small towns. Biological waste water treatment, on land disposal using suitable vegetative cover and resource recovery technologies cannot only be an attractive alternative, but also economical, safe and socially acceptable.

4.4 Mining operations will not ordinarily be taken up in ecologically gragile areas. Every mining project shall be accompanied by a mining plan, including an environmental management plan and time bound reclamation programme for controlling the environmental damage and for restoration of mined areas.

5. Assistance for Adoption of Clean Technologies by Small Scale Industries.

5.1 Small scale industries are a special feature of our economy. Government are implementing a scheme for providing assistance for promoting combined facilities for treatment of effluents and solid wastes generated in clusters of small scale units. This scheme will be extended to provide necessary technical support as well.

5.2 While the large and medium industrial units will remain totally responsible for control of their pollution, assistance will be provided to small-scale industrial units, particularly those located in rural areas, to aid the implementation of pollution control measures. This will be achieved by promoting development and adoption of cleaner technologies, including environmentally friendly biotechnology.

6. Standards

6.1 The present standards are based on the concentration of pollutants in effluents and in emissions. The norms will be revised to lay down mass-based standards, which will set specific limits to encourage the minimisation of waste, promote recycling and reuse of materials, as well as conservation of natural resources, particularly water. Since the standards will be source related, they will require for the most polluting industrial processes, particularly those using toxic substances, application of the best available technological solutions, and also be an instrument for technological upgradation.

6.2 To act against potential problems in the future, new units will have to conform to stricter standards. They will need to select technologies that produce no or low quantities of wastes and recycle or reuse waste products. Progressively, more strict vehicle emission standards will also be evolved to deal with environmental hazards caused by vehicular traffic.

6.3 Standards will not merely be a regulatory tool but will be mechanism to promote technological upgradation to prevent pollution, conserve resources and regulate waste. For this purpose codes of practice and guidelines will be evolved for specific processes.

6.4 The environmental effects, from production to disposal of products that are hazardous and toxic will be taken into account in the regulations. Chemicals will be reviewed according to the level of risk, and where safer alternatives have become available, restrictions will be imposed. Regulations for liability and compensation for damages will supplement standards to promote greater care and caution, particularly in the management of hazardous waste and remedial action in case of contamination of soil and ground water.

7. **Fiscal Measures**

7.1 While regulatory measures remain essential for the effectiveness of the policy, new approaches for considering market choices will be introduced. The aim is to give industries and consumers clear signals about the cost of using environmental and natural resources. The expectation is that market-oriented price mechanisms will influence behaviour to avoid excessive use of natural resources.

7.2 There are at present several fiscal incentives for installation of pollution control equipment and for shifting polluting industries from congested areas. The items for which excise and customs rebate are allowed will be reviewed. This will stimulate the advancement of abatement technologies and create increased demands for the products.

7.3 Economic instruments will be investigated to encourage the shift from curative to preventive measures, internalise the costs of pollution and conserve resources, particularly water. A direct economic signal is offered by an effluent charge based on the nature and volume of release to the environment. The level will be based on the cost of treatment and the flow discharged, in order to provide and incentive to set-up treatment plants. The scope of the charges will also be extended to emissions and solid waste. Charges provide a continuing incentive towards optimal releases.

7.4 These instruments will also have a distributive effect as the revenues will be used for enforcement, collective treatment facilities, research and promoting new investment.

7.5 The precise choice of economic instruments adopted will be determined by the ease with which releases can be measured, as well as perspective changes in technology and market structures. To deal with the range of pollution problems a mix of regulatory and economic measures will be adopted.

8. **Integration**

8.1 Critical policy areas for control of pollution come under different departments and levels of Government. Sectoral Ministries, State Governments, local bodies and agencies responsible for planning and implementation of development projects will be required to integrate environmental concerns more effectively in all policy areas. Local authorities play a key role in abatement of pollution and environmental concerns need to be built into the way they operate. Steps will have to be taken to strengthen governmental and institutional structures dealing with environmental management, especially within the ministries dealing with the sectors of energy, industry, water resources, transport and agriculture and who would develop specific programmes in regard to pollution prevention.

8.2 Policy making, legislation and law enforcement influence each other. The increase in the number of regulations increases difficulties in enforcement. Legislation regulating particular activities will be amended to incorporate and eliminate clashes with environmental criteria. Traditional instruments for monitoring of compliance and investigation of offences are becoming over-burdened. An integrated overview and organisational structure for decentralised environment impact assessments and environmental law, enforcement based on cooperation with local authorities will be sought.

8.3 While pollution from specific sources including towns and industries have been addressed, non-point pollution from run-off of agricultural inputs such as pesticides, insecticides, fertilisers, etc. has not been dealt with. This is gaining increasing proportions, which is polluting not only our water bodies but even sub-soil water resources and would affect the health of human beings. A long-term policy for pesticides use, including the introduction of environmentally acceptable pesticides, particularly biopesticides and non-persistent bio-degradable ones, and integrated pest management together with the phasing out of the proven harmful toxic and persistent ones, would be formulated in collaboration with the concerned Ministries and infrastructure involved for its effective implementation. A similar policy for fertiliser use will also need to be formulated.

8.4 Plant and vegetation in general play a vital role in controlling pollution by regulating the climate and atmospheric equilibrium, protecting the soil and maintaining the hydrological regime. Hence, existing forests and natural vegetation should be fully protected. The forest and vegetal cover should be restored and increased wherever possible, specially on hill slopes, in catchment areas of rivers, lakes and reservoirs, ocean shores, semi-arid and arid tracts, in around urban centres and industrial establishments. It is necessary to encourage the planting of trees alongside roads, rail lines, canals and on other unutilised lands under State/corporate, institutional or private ownership. Green belts should be raised in urban and industrial areas as well as in arid tracts. Such a programme will also check erosion decertification as well as improve the micro-climate.

8.5 The Annual Administration Reports of the Ministries will include a chapter on the action taken to follow up the policy statement, and other environmental initiatives they have taken or are proposing.

9. **Environmental Audit**

9.1 Industrial concerns and local bodies should feel that they have a responsibility for abatement of pollution. The procedure of an environmental statement will be introduced in local bodies, statutory authorities and public limited companies to evaluate the effect of their policies, operations and activities on the environment, particularly compliance with standards and the generation and recycling of waste. An annual statement will

> help in identifying and focussing attention on areas of concern, practices that need to be changed and plans to deal with adverse effects. This will be extended to an environmental audit. The measures will provide better information to the public".[73]

For implementation of laws and the policy there is necessity of administrative authorities and structure. In India, for example, in the first comprehensive environmental legislation, namely Water (Prevention of Pollution) Act 1974 provisions were made for establishment of a Central Water Pollution Control Board and similar Boards in each state. In pursuance of that Act a Central Board and State Boards were set-up the Government. Thereafter when the Air (Prevention of Pollution) Act, 1981 was passed the authorities under Water Act were entrusted with the power to implement Air Act also. The Environment Protection Act 1986, however envisaged only a Central authority which may delegate its power to any State Board. Now all the State Boards are named as Pollution Control Board of the respective state.

As regards structures required for the authorities under Environmental laws the Central Government set-up a Committee which is known as Beliappa Committee[74]. As per recommendations of the Beliappa Committee the structure required for proper implementation of environmental laws have been accepted by the Government but its full implementation is not yet been materialised. As for example in West Bengal the present Administrative structure is far short of Beliappa Committee Report. The constitution of the State Board under Water or Air Act need to be changed because at present out of 17 persons only two needs knowledge and experience in pollution control. Moreover Chairman of the Board can be a part-timer engaged in some other responsibilities.

To comment upon the problem of implementation of environmental legislation Shyam A Divan, an American scholar in the field observed:

> "Perhaps the most potent threat to the adoption of such a scheme is the probable response for the entrenched bureaucracy. India has a fairly long tradition of powerful bureaucrats. The Moghal fouzaders or subadars weilded considerable power and British rule strengthened the tradition. The suggested scheme with its provisions for citizen participation, judicial over sight and access to information will loosen the grip of the bureaucrat, and is promised on a thinly-concealed disrespect for bureaucratic

> 'expertise'. For this reasons absent strong political backing, the proposed reform is unlikely to receive bureaucratic endorsement"[75].

How the bureaucratic power hungry attitudes interfered and created problems in India as been clearly ascertained from the case of *Chaitanya Pulverising Industry* v. *Karnataka State Pollution Control Board*[76]. So members of the Central and State Boards should be experts in environmental protection and related areas to avoid unnecessary disputes.

Policy Conflict-Deviance v. *Development*

We have already noted in Chapter-I that there lies a conflict between sustainable development policy and the programme of environment protection. Justice S.M.N. Raina with a very common example unavailed the issue very beautifully in the following words:

> "What worries me, however is that pollution due to spraying of pesticides and other uses of pesticides in pursuance of the policy of government to increase agricultural production is almost completely ignored. I have a feeling that this is deliberate because pesticides are badly needed for green revolution to meet the requirements of rapidly growing population of the country and it is apprehended that too much talk about the harmful effects of pollution due to pesticide may give rise to reluctance of the farmers to make use of them"[77].

Thus in a developing country like India industrialisation or sustainable development projects as to be harmonised with environmental protection.

Role of the People

About the role of the people in protection of our environment a commentator observe the Indian scene, though to some extent extravagant or eloquent, in the following words:

> "Two elections from today, people will vote for those who understand and promise to protect the land, not exploit it. A powerful mass movement is poised to spring. Politics and environment have a common destiny"[78].

But the environmental legislations including Environment Protection Act 1986 do not provide any express provisions recognising the role of public participation in enforcement implementation of law relating to pollution of environment. Such public participations through Non-Government Organization (NGOs) as been recognised in some progressive legislation in India since 1985, (e.g. The Child Labour Act 1986, The Juvenile Justice Act 1986). The Consumer Protection Act 1986. A meeting of Experts to consider the ways in which the Environmental Protection Act 1986 (EPA) may be effectively implemented was concerned by the Consumer Education and Research Centre (CERC) and the Indian Law Institute (ILI) on August 22-24, 1986 and said meeting recommended the following Rules for Public participation in implementing EPA:

> **"Rule 1:**
>
> Where under any law relating to pollution of environment, including the Environment Protection Act, 1986, the consent license or permission of the State (as interpreted under Article 12 of the Constitution of India) is required by law, any member of the public shall have a right to inspect free of cost any document that might have been filed by the applicant for such consent, etc.
>
> **Rule 2:**
>
> Where a person complains to the competent officer that water, soil or air is polluted in any particular place or source, such authority shall take appropriate steps for sealing the sample(s) so that sample(s) analysed and sealed may be made available as evidence in subsequent legal proceedings.
>
> **Rule 3:**
>
> Under Section 3(2) (x) empowering inspection of any premises, plant, equipment, machinery, manufacturing or other process, the concerned authorities, shall authorise in addition to officers other persons including public citizen of the area and relevant non-governmental organizations (NGOs) to carry out joint inspections.
>
> **Rule 4:**
>
> Public citizen and non-governmental organizations (NGOs) authorised to conduct joint inspections under Rule 3 above or a person who provides samples under Rule 2 above shall be deemed to be an officer of the Government or any other authority under Section 18 and a public servant under Section 21 of the EP Act 1986"[79].

However these recommendations were not accepted by the Government. On the contrary Section 19(d) of the EP Act imposed restriction on powers of courts to take cognisance of any offence under the Act unless a person complaining of an alleged offence under the Act as given a notice of sixty days, of his intention to make a complaints to the Central Govt. or a designated authority or officer. The hegemony of the governmental power to institute suit against alleged polluters "military comprehensively against public participation in the enforcement of the salutary provisions of the EPA"[80]. The rational of such provision in the EPA and other environmental legislation in doubtful and criticised by many environmentalised. This scholar is also of the view that this restriction should be withdrawn.

Inspite of this fact the citizens of India in some occasions come forward with demand to abandon development project if it affect heavily on the environment. Such a recent project is the controversial Tehri Hydro Power Project and Teri Dam in Uttar Pradesh. Teri Band Virodi Sangars Samiti thereafter filed a case in the Supreme Court under Article 32 of the Constitution[81]. The Supreme Court in this case also opined that Government of India paid adequate attention through Environmental Appraisal Committee and High Level Committee of Experts and clearance was given only after consideration of the reports of the Committee. Hence the court dismissed the petition. In the meantime an unprecedented earthquake occurred in this hill area which led the people's movement more vigorous. Ultimately the project had to be withheld by the Government due to strong public protection in the leadership of Sundarlal Bahuguna which we have already noted in the introduction. Thus from the foregoing discussion we have seen that if people become environmental conscious and mass movements gather momentum, then it would be more effective than legal control. Hence people's participation in the environment protection programme should be incorporated within the legal framework.

The Policy Statement for Abatement of Pollution of our Government, therefore, rightly postulated the following:

"PUBLIC PARTNERSHIP

11.1 The public must be made aware in order to be able to make informed choices. A high governmental priority will be to educate citizens about environmental risks, the economic and health dangers of resource degradation and the real cost of natural resources. Information about the environment will be published periodically. Affected citizens and non-governmental organisations play a role in environmental monitoring and therefore allowing them to supplement the regulatory system and recognising their expertise were such exists and their commitments and vigilance, will also be cost effective. Access to information to enable public monitoring of environmental concerns, will be provided for.

11.2 Public interest litigation as successfully demonstrated that responsible non-governmental organisations and public spirited individuals can bring about significant pressure on polluting units for adopting abatement measures. This commitment and expertise will be encouraged and their practical work supported.

11.3 Householders, as consumers, make large number of relatively small individual contributions, whose cumulative effect is considerable. A system of certification of goods that are "environmentally friendly" will be set up to make available information to encourage environmental consciousness amongst consumers. This advice will also encourage manufacturers to produce goods that are environmentally more friendly as well as encourage recycling and adequate waste management. Consumer awareness would also be encouraged by involvement of consumer organisations in cooperative testing, and dissemination of information relating to environmental friendliness of these products.

11.4 As the present system of jurisprudence does not provide for compensation to individuals for environmental damage, including effects on health and environmental damage caused by pollution, it is proposed to set up special legal institutions to redress this deficiency and also make adequate arrangements for interim relief.

11.5 Greater emphasis will be placed on promoting awareness, undertaking and competence in schools, colleges, and training institutions. Professional and non-governmental bodies will be encouraged to be more active in environmental training and building awareness.

11.6 Society as accepted many practices which cause pollution. Reckless use of loudspeakers, dumping in water bodies, and scattering of wastes are common. Noise nuisance requires specific devices as well as greater consideration for neighbours and there is growing concern that litter has increased in recent years. Social action in these matters by voluntary organisations and individuals will be promoted through knowledge, education, training camps and public information campaigns.[82]

5. Legal Control of Multinational Corporations

A discourse on environmental law particularly in India would be incomplete unless we discuss the Bhopal disaster which took place just after midnight in December 3, 1984. In the Bhopal case about 40 tones of MIC (Methyle isocyanate) gas which had been manufactured and stored in Union Carbide's chemical plant in Bhopal escaped into the atmosphere and killed over 2,500 people and as many as 2,00,000 persons were injured. Thereafter the Government of India firstly made an Ordinance on February 20, 1985 to ensure the claims arising out of the disaster against the Union Carbide, a multinational corporation. The Ordinance was replaced in March, 1985 by enactment of the Bhopal Gas Leak Disaster (Processing of Claims) Act 1985 which conferred an exclusive right on the Government of India to represent all claimants.

In the first suit against the U. Carbide filed in the United States District Court[83], Southern District of New York, the Government of India pleaded in their Plaint the Multinational Liability in the following way :

> "Multinational corporations by virtue of their global purpose, structure, organization, technology, finances and resources have it within their power to make decisions and take actions that can result in industrial disasters of catastrophe proportion and magnitude. This is particularly true with respect to those activities of the multinationals which are ultra hazardous or inherently dangerous.
>
> Key management personnel of multinational exercise a closely held power which is neither restricted by national boundaries nor effectively controlled by international law. The complex corporate structure of the multinational with networks of subsidiaries and divisions, makes it exceedingly difficult or even impossible to pinpoint responsibility for the damage caused by

the enterprise to discrete corporate units or individuals.

A multinational corporation as a primary, absolute and non-delegable duty to the persons and country in which it has in any manner caused to be undertaken any ultra hazardous or inherently dangerous activity. This includes a duty to provide that all ultra hazardous or inherently dangerous activities be conducted with the highest standard of safety and to provide all necessary information and warnings regarding the activity involved.

Defendant multinational Union Çarbide breached this primary absolute and non-delegable duty through its undertakings of an ultra hazardous and inherently dangerous activity causing unacceptable risks at its plant in Bopal and the resultant escape of lethal MIC from that plant. Defendant Union Carbide is primarily and absolutely liable for any and all damages caused or contributed to by the escape of lethal MIC from its Bopal plant"[84].

The American Court, however declined to try the case for want of appropriate forum and in Sept. 1986, about two years after the tragedy, the Indian Government filed a tort case against the Union Carbide in the court of District Judge, Bhopal for Rs. 3,900 crores (US $ 3 billion) damages. This case ultimately reached to the Supreme Court through the separate appeals of Union Carbide and Government of India against the judgment of the Madhya Pradesh High Court[85]. After a long battle astonishingly on February 14, 1989 the Supreme Court suggested to the India Government and Union Carbide for an overall settlement of the claims arising from the Bhopal tragedy. Thus a settlement was reached whereby the Union Carbide paid US $ 470 million to India Government on behalf of all the Bhopal victims in full and final settlement of all past, present and future claims arising for the Bhopal disaster. But the decision could not satisfy all section of the people and when the National Front Government came into power a review petition was filed in the Supreme Court. So the Bopal disaster raised the complex legal question on Multinational Corporations (MNCs) liability.

But Justice Bhagwati said that in the Bhopal case the multinational as won and the people of India have lost. He observed :

"It was difficult to understand how a landmark judgment disposing of the case for compensation was suddenly delivered by the

Supreme Court when it was only an appeal against the interim order which was being argued and even in this appeal, the arguments had not concluded. It defies one's credulity as to how the proposal for settlement made by the Chief Justice of India on behalf of the Constitution bench and its prompt acceptance by the parties could be described as a judgment or verdict of the Supreme Court. The persistent effort by the Government, its lawyers and Doordarsan to describe the settlement as a judgment shows that the Government did not want to own responsibility for striking a deal plainly against the interest of the victims. It used the judiciary to disguise what was really a settlement. Unfortunately, the Court fell a victim to this strategy"[86].

On the contrary Divan and Rosen Cranz, the American scholars opined :

"The Bhopal settlement is welcome because it obtains compensation efficiently. Future litigation costs have been secured within five years of the disaster a short time by Indian standards. Frequently, the compensation secured in mass tort cases is dwarbed by the transaction costs of the litigation. Attorney's fees may eat into more than one third of the total award. For example, one study of the asbestos trials in the United States concluded that litigation expenses consumed 63% of the recovery, leaving only 37% for victim relief. The Bhopal settlement both contains transaction costs and cuts long years of expensive litigation. At the sluggish pace at which the Indian Government was proceeding in the case it might have been 15 more years before the victims saw the colour of their money. By that time, the compensation — so urgently required by the impoverished and displaced victims would have been meaningless. With the settlement, the victims should begin receiving compensation in a few months time"[87].

The complexity and controversy is yet to be dissolved. Sumitra Sripada observed :

"There still remains complex questions of resolution of disputes in the matters of environmental harm between the MNCs and the host states. There are no international courts that can exercise jurisdiction in such cases at the MNCs have not yet been recognised as full subject of international law. The municipal courts of the hosts states may not be fully trusted for the possibility that the court is sympathetic towards the victims of a disaster or accident especially when they are nationals of the state of forum. Moreover the environmental disputes are so technical a nature that a regular court may not be the most appropriate forum. Hence a third party settlement may provide a good alternative. Compulsory reference to arbitration may be advised in such cases, wherein both the parties will have an equal right of participation"[88].

6. Role of the U.N.O.

We have already noted in the previous chapter UN's concern to the problem of human environment and the first international conference on human environment in 1972 at Stockholm. Here an attempt will be made to discuss briefly the role of UN's through the establishment of a full-fledged environmental programme (UNEP) and promotion of other international governmental as well as non-governmental organizations against the pragmatic reality of a world composed of different sovereign states.

The institutional mechanism of the UN Environment Programme during last two decades as implemented various recommendation of. Action plan envisaged in the Stockholm Declaration on Human Environment to protect and preserve the natural quality of mother earth. In pursuance of UNEP objectives the world Conservation Strategy was formulated —

i) to maintain ecological process and life support system;

ii) to preserve the genetic diversity;

iii) to ensure the sustainable utilization of species and economic systems[89].

In 1975 UNEP and UNESCO as jointly established an ongoing global International Environmental Education Programme (IEEP) as a major programme designed to develop an overall framework and direction for the environmental education at all levels.

In 1984 an International Notification Scheme for Dangerous Chemicals was launched as a significant step towards increasing safeguard of health and environment, specially in the developing countries. This is also known as "Earth Watch" Programme.

The UN Council and Secretariate along with their auxiliaries as-made medium potential use of existing machinery and resources, both within and outside the UN system. The highest priorities were given to the need for coordination and rationalisation of international environmental activities.

However, the UNEP Executive Director's report 1982 admitted that in environmental issues they achieve limited success. It has been said that much of what ought to be donc was not donc to help the developing countries in their domestic environmental programmes[90]. Despite some shortcomings and impediments the achievements of UNEP are numerous. These are mainly (i) attitudinal changes in the developing countries, (ii) the catalytic role of the UNEP for environmental management and (iii) review of Stratospheric Zone for protection of human life from the ultra violate rays of sun be secured.

The UNEP also includes coordination among nations for realising various conventions and Treaty obligations. The major treaties and agreement to which India also is a party[91] are mentioned below:

1. Convention Relating to the Preservation of Fauna and Flora in their Natural State (London, 1936)
2. International Convention for the Regulation of Whaling (Washington, 1946).
3. The International Plant Protection Convention (Rome 1951).
4. The Antartic Treaty (Washington, 1959).
5. Convention Concerning the Protection of Workers Against Ionizing Radiations (Geneva, 1960).
6. Treaty Banning Nuclear Weapon Tests in the Atmosphere, in Outer Space and Under Water (Moscow, 1963).
7. International Convention on Civil Liability for Oil Pollution Damage (Brussels, 1975).
8. Convention on Wetlands of International Importance, Especially as Waterfowl Habitat (Ramsar, 1971).
9. Convention on the Prohibition of the Development, Production, and Stockpiling of Bacteriological (Biological) and Toxin Weapons and on their Destruction (London, Moscow, Washington, 1972).

10. Convention Concerning the Protection of the World Cultural and Natural heritage (Paris, 1972).
11. Convention on International Trade in Endangered Species of Wild Fauna and Flora (Washington, DC, 1973).
12. Protocol of 1978 Relating to the International Convention for the Prevention of Pollution from ships, 1973 (London, 1978).
13. Convention on the Conservation of Migratory Species of Wild Animals (Bonn, 1979).
14. Convention on the Conservation of Antarctic Marine Living Resources (Canberra, 1980).
15. United Nations Convention on the Law of the Sea (Montego Bay, 1982).
16. International Tropical Timber Agreement (Geneva, 1983).
17. Convention on Early Notification of a Nuclear Accident (Viena, 1986).
18. Convention on Assistance in the case of a Nuclear Accident or Radiological Emergency (Viena, 1986).

But the widening gap between developed and developing countries have to be reconciliated in the light of healthy formula for 'protective development' devised to respect environmental ethics and needs of humanity. In this respect ideological differences etc. has to be harmonised to give a way for survival of humanity : for future can't be sacrificed for the gratification of present. This question again arises in the just concluded Earth Summit 1992 at Reo de Zenero in Brazil. The conflict between developed and developing countries concentrated on signing of Bio-diversity Agreement to save unnumerable fauna and flora of this earth. The U.S.A. President Bush openly declared that he will not sign any agreement which affect the businessmen and industrialists of his country.

Earth Summit - 1992

The Earth Summit 1992 is the biggest International Conference organised by the U.N.O. attended by 166 countries with about 3,500 delegates. All the countries principally accepted the proposed 'Agenda 21' for an environment programme in the twenty first century and signed two agreements. But on two vital matters no decision could be reached. These are firstly, to lessen the emission of carbon dioxide and other greenhouse gases in the Atmosphere by the year 2000 and secondly to contribute 0.75 G.N.P. of the developed countries for implementation of UNEP. The developed countries not shown any interest to transfer new pollution free technology on easy terms and conditions. That is why Prof. R.P. Anand observed long ago:

> "Governments no longer posed the problems as environment v/s. development, but as environment and developed, where the former is regarded as proceeding to the later"[92].

Perhaps the Executive Director of UNEP realised this situation and rightly warned the world in one of his famous statement:

> "In the year 2071 AD, the world is wreaked with anarchy and civil strife, (as a result of the failure) of the governments to deal effectively with the environmental crisis"[93].

A summary of the documents of the Earth Summit 1992 produced below:-

THE EARTH SUMMIT - 1992 produced a vast documents relating to *two* conferences on environment and development. The first was the formal 12 day conference of government delegations called the United Nations Conference on Environment and Development (UNCED). The other one was a large gathering of Non-governmental Organisations (NGOs) held in Flamengo Park 40 kilometers from the site of Rio Centro conference under the title of Global Forum. Te formal UNCED yielded following five documents signed by heads of participated states. These are :

(i) The Rio Declaration
(ii) Treaties on Climate Change
(iii) Convention on Biodiversity
(iv) Forest Principles; and
(v) Agenda 21.

(i) The Rio Declaration

The Rio Declaration was originally conceived of as an 'Earth Charter', a statement of environmental principles for national behaviour. During Preparatory Committee meetings develop in countries insisted that a balance be established between environmental principles and those relating to development. Although the resultant compromise declaration is less inspiring and coherent than its original proponents had hoped, its 27 principles include key elements of the political agendas of both industrialized and developing countries. Principles in the document include a state's sovereign right to exploit its own resources in accordance with its own policies, without arming the environment elsewhere (principle 2); the right to development (principle 3); environmental protection as an integral part of development (principle 4); sustainable development that requires reducing unsustainable patterns of production and consumption, and that promotes "appropriate demographic policies" (principle 8); access to information and citizen participation 9 (principle 10); the precautionary principle (principle 15); the polluter pays principle, including the internalization of costs and the use of economic instruments (principle 16).

The strongest U.S. objection was to principle 23, which called for protection of the environmental and natural resources of "people under oppression, domination, and occupation." In a late compromise involving the United States, Israel, and the Arab states, this phrase was retained in the declaration but all references to people under occupation were removed from Agenda 21. The United States accommodated its other objections by issuing a statement of its reservations to several principles, including the right to development, which it said could be used to justify human-rights violations, and the principle of "differentiated responsibilities."

(ii) Convention on Climate Change

Because of UNCED's political prominence, many other international environmental debates were merged into the process, such as those of conventions on climate change and biodiversity, which was not negotiated at UNCED or in the Prep-Com meetings but were signed in Rio following separate negotiations. In 1988 the Intergovernmental Panel on Climate Change (IPCC), an advisory body of scientists and officials that assessed comprehensively climate science, was established. Thereafter the UN General Assembly passed a resolution in December 1990 that established the Intergovernmental Negotiating Committee (INC). After five negotiating sessions, however, discussion stalled between the United States and other industrial countries, particularly the European Community, which asserted that the convention should contain specific commitments to limit emissions of carbon dioxide to 1990 levels by 2000.

INC chairman Jean Ripert of France broke the deadlock by drafting a compromise document that requires industrialised countries to develop national emission limits and emission inventories and to report periodically on their progress without target dates. All the major participants finalized on 9 May 1992 the convention to sign in Rio which contains a very strong objective: "stabilization of greenhouse-gas concentrations in the atmosphere at a level that would prevent dangerous anthropogenic interference with the climate system.... within a time frame sufficient to allow ecosystem to adopt naturally."

The convention establishes a financial assistance mechanism to support its implementation in developing countries, to be administered by the Global Environmental Facility on an interim basis. The convention also established institutional mechanisms for periodic review and an update of commitments, including the scheduling of regular conferences. Finally, two new subsidiary bodies were established by the treaty, one on science and technology and one on implementation. Like IPCC but unlike the Montreal Protocol, membership in these bodies is restricted to government representatives. Representatives from 153 countries signed the climate convention in Rio, though only 50 ratifications were needed.

(iii) Convention on Biodiversity

Discussions for a convention on biological diversity, or biodiversity, which concluded on 22 May 1992 in Nairobi, were initiated in 1988 by the United Nations Environment Programme's (UNEP) Governing Council. The issues of biodiversity and biotechnology were originally treated by separate working groups, but were merged to be handled by a single intergovernmental negotiating committee in 1991, over the objections of the United States and other nations. The treaty has three goals: the conservation and sustainable use of biological diversity, and the fair sharing of product made from genestocks. To advance these goals, the signatories must develop plans for protecting habitat and species; provide funds and technology to help developing countries provide protection; ensure commercial access to biological resources for development and share revenues fairly among source countries and developers; and establish safety regulations and accept liability for risks associated with biotechnology development. Financial assistance, initially set at $ 200 million, will ultimately be channelled through some mechanism under the control of the signatories but will be administered by the Global Environmental Facility on an interim basis.

The negotiations were plagued by conflict over the financial mechanism, the sharing of benefits and biotechnology regulation. France originally threatened not to sign the treaty because it did not include a list of global biodiversity-rich regions; Japan threatened not to sign because it feared biotechnology regulation. At last moment only the United States refused to sign because it fears that the financial mechanism represented an open-ended commitment with insufficient oversight and control; that the benefit-sharing provisions were incompatible with existing international regimes for intellectual property rights; and that the requirement to regulate the bio-technology industry be stifle innovation. Although only 30 ratification were needed for it to enter into force, 153 nations signed the Biodiversity Convention in Rio.

(iv) Forest Principles

When an early attempt to negotiate a treaty on the protection of global forests failed, the Preparatory Committee of UNCED added a legally nonbinding declaration of forest principles to its own agenda. The UN Food and Agriculture Organisation (FAO) had discussed for a forest treaty before the UNCED and recommended in November 1990 that a treaty be concluded in time for UNCED. But the possibility of a forest treat were inhibited by strong differences between industrialized countries, which wanted a treaty focusing on tropical rain forests, and developing countries which insisted on the inclusion of temperate and boreal forests.

However at last a statement of 17 nonbinding principles negotiated in Rio explicitly includes all types of forests. Although some delegation advocated adding a statement to the forest principles that either explicitly called for or excluded a future treaty, the final document merely commits governments to keeping the principles "under assessment for their adequacy with regard to future international cooperation on forest issues".

(v) Agenda 21

Agenda 21 is the only document signed at UNCED that attempts to embrace the entire environment and development agenda. It is also the largest product of UNCED, comprising 40 chapters and 800 pages and states goals and priorities regarding a dozen major resource, environmental, social, legal, financial, and institutional issues. Each chapter contains a description of a programme and its cost estimate. Agenda 21 is not a legally binding document but a "work plan", or "agenda for action", with a political commitment to pursue a set of goals. It may become "soft law", if, as is likely, the UN General Assembly adopts it as a resolution. Agenda 21 includes estimates of the annual costs of its programs in developing countries from 1993 to 2000, of which about $125 billion per year will come from the industrialized countries. Although it may be only soft law, the contentious negotiation of many parts of Agenda 21 underscores its importance to the signatories. The chapters of Agenda 21 are divided into four major headings including a preamble. The divisions are :

Section I	:	Social and Economic Dimensions;
Section II	:	Conservation and Management of Resources for Development;
Section III	:	Strengthening the Role of Major Groups;
Section IV	:	Means of Implementation.

Products of NGOs

An enormous volume of information, too vast to catalog, was produced by NGOs at both UNCED and the Global Forum. Following is a list of treaties that were completed in the Global Forum:

(a) ● Earth Charter;

(b) ● NGO Cooperation and Institution-Building Cluster;

(c) ● Alternative Economic Issues Cluster;

(d) ● Major Environmental Issues Cluster;

(e) ● Food Production Cluster; and

(f) ● Cross-Sectorial Issues Cluster

7. Sanctions in Environmental Law in India

The primary object of punishment in the prevention of crime. With that end in view the offenders of environmental laws are treated under criminal justice system though there are criminologists who preferred to use the term 'deviance' in cases of violation of environmental laws and regulations. However in India from ancient time punishment was inflicted to an offender destroying trees, animals or for polluting waters as mentioned in our sacred classical books such as Manu Samhita, Brihat Parasar Samhita, Narad Samhita, Brihaspati Samhita etc. Now to examine the present punishments prescribed in three major environmental legislations a comparative study of these offences and punishment may be made.

Comparative study of offences and punishments of Environmental Laws

Offences	Punishments
Under the Water (Prevention and Control) of Pollution Act, 1974.	
i) Whoever fails to comply with any direction given by the State Board for the prevention and control of Water Pollution under Section 20 (2) (3) or orders issued under Section 32(1)(c).	on conviction, shall be punishable with imprisonment for a term which may extend to *three months* or with fine which may extend to *five thousand* rupees or with both and in case the failure continues, with an additional fine which may extend to *one thousand* rupees for every day etc.
ii) Whoever destroys, pulls down, removes, injures or defaces any piller, post or stake .... put up, inscribed or placed by or under authority of the Board etc. .... or in giving any information knowingly or will fully makes a statement which is false in any material particular.	shall be punishable with imprisonment for a term which may extend to *three months* or with fine which may extend to *one thousand* rupees or with both. (Section 42 of sub-sec. (1).
iii) Where for grant of a consent in pursuance of the provisions of Sections 25, 26 ..... any person who knowingly or wilfully alters or interferes with that device (e.g. metre or gauge) so as to prevent it from monitoring or measuring correctly.	shall be punishable with imprisonment for a term which may extend to *three months* or with fine which may extend to *one thousand rupees* or with both.
iv) Whoever knowingly cause or permit any poisonous, noxious or polluting matter to enter into stream or well or without the previous consent of the State Board, bring into use any new or altered outlet for the discharge of sewage or trade effluent into a stream or well and thereby contravenes the provisions of **Sections 24 or 25** (Sections **43/44**)	shall be punishable with imprisonment for a term which shall not be less than *six months* but which may extend to *six years* and with fine. But for the second and on every subsequent conviction, be punishable with imprisonment for a term which shall not be *less than one year* but which may extend to *seven years* and with fine.

2. The Air (Prevention and Control of Pollution) Act, 1981

i)	Whoever fails to comply with the provisions of sub-section (5) of Section 21 or Section 22 and operate any industrial plant for the purpose of any industry specified in the Schedule in an air pollution control area. (Section 37)	shall be punishable with imprisonment for a term which may extend to *three months* or with fine which may extend to *ten thousand rupees* or with both. For continuation of offence additional fine of *rupees one hundred* for every day after conviction for first time.
ii)	Whoever destroys, pulls down removes etc. any post or stake fixed ... by or under authority of the Board or fails to furnish informations required by the Board or make a statement which is false in any material particular etc. for obtaining any consent u/ s. 21 of the Act.	shall be punishable with imprisonment for a term which may extend to *three months* or with fine which may extend to *five hundred rupees* or with both. (Section 38)
iii)	Whoever contravenes any provisions of this Act such as standards for emission from automobiles etc. (Section 39)	shall be punishable with fine which may extend to *five thousand rupees* and for continuation of the offence Rs.100/- for everyday after conviction.

3. The Environment (Protection) Act, 1986

Whoever fails to comply with or contravenes any of the provisions of this Act, or the rules made or orders or directions issued thereunder such as failure to prevent or mitigate the environmental pollutant in excess of the prescribed standards or is apprehended to occur due to any accident or other unforeseen Act or Event etc.	shall, in respect of each such failure or contravention, be punishable with imprisonment for *a term* which may extend to *five years* or with fine which may extend *to one lakh rupees*, or with both and continuation of the offence additional fine of Rs. 5,000/- for everyday after first conviction. (Section 15)

In this connection it may also be mentioned that where any offence under any of the aforesaid Acts *has been committed by a company, every person who*, at the time the offence was committed was *directly in charge* of, and was responsible to, the company for the conduct of the business of the company, as well as the company, shall be deemed to be guilty of the offence and shall be liable to be proceeded against and punished accordingly :

Provided that nothing contained in the above section shall render any such person liable to any punishment provided in the Act, if he proves that the offence was committed *without his knowledge* or that he *exercised all due diligence* to prevent the commission of such offence.

Critical Appraisal of the punishments

To begin our discussion on the efficacy of the punishments prescribed in the aforesaid environmental laws we may mention here the Rule 1 of the proportion between punishments and offences as enunciated by Bentham as follows: "The value of the punishment must not be less in any case than what is sufficient to outweigh that of the profit of the offence"[94].

Bentham also observed the following three rules by way of supplement and explanation to Rule 1 :

Rule 7 : To enable the value of the punishment to outweigh that of the profit of the offence, it must be increased, in point of magnitude, in proportion as it falls short in point of certainty.

Rule 8 : Punishment must be further increased in point of magnitude, in proportion as it falls short in point of proximity.

Rule 9 : Where the Act is conclusively indicative of a habit if such an increase must be given to the punishment as may enable it to outweigh the profit not only of the individual offence, but of such other like offences as are likely to have been committed with impurity by the same offender[95].

The tendency of the above Rules is to dictate an augmentation in the punishment, particularly where the punishment proposed is of such a nature as to be well calculated to answer the purpose of a moral lesson. In the words of Bentham "A punishment may be said to be calculated to answer the purpose of a moral lession, when, by reason of the ignomy it stamps upon the offence, it is calculated to inspire the public with sentiments of aversion towards those pernicious habits and dispositions"[96]. Now if we raise the question what should be the objectives or principles of punishments the answer may come from the above principles of punishments as propounded by Jeremy Bentham in his An Introduction to The Principles of Morals and Legislations in 1780. The objectives of punishments in the environmental laws may be *inter alia.*

a) To award punitive damage to the victim as exemplary to others;

b) To award substantial compensation to the victims;

c) To outweigh the gains by committing the offence;

d) To give a moral lesson to the public in general;

e) To give wide discretion to the courts to fit the punishment according to the circumstances of the case;

f) To incapacitate the offenders to repeat the offence.

Now if we look into the prescribed punishments in the three major laws to prevent environmental pollution we will observe the following phenomena :

Firstly, in most of the cases the prescribed term of imprisonment may extend to only three months only. The author is of the view that this prescription was blindly borrowed from the prescribed punishment in Section 336 of Indian Penal Code 1860 for doing any act which endangers human life or the personal safety of others where punishment will be imprisonment for 3 months or fine of Rs. 250/- or both. The other offences of I.P.C. where 3 months imprisonment were prescribed are—(i) Section 186 Obstructing public servant when bound by law to give such assistance; (ii) Section 352 Assault or use of Criminal force otherwise than on grave provocation; (iii) Section 426 Mischief and (iv) Section 447 Criminal Trespass etc. Naturally the question that will come to one's mind is that whether the offences of environmental pollution can be equated with that of mischief, criminal trespass, assault or obstructing public servant and not to give assistance when bound by law. Moreover the punishment as prescribed in the year 1860 for doing any Act which endangers human life of the personal safety was made when the movement against environment pollution not started in this world.

Therefore in the present context we should not prescribe the quantum of punishment as contemplated about more than one hundred thirty years back. In considering the pressing need of prevention of environmental pollution the punishment for committing offences against environment should be more deterrent and there must be some minimum hursh punishment.

Secondly, the prescription of minimal limit of fine in cases of environmental pollution is against the principles of such type of tortious liability whether it is five/ten thousand or one lakh rupees as prescribed in the Indian laws. There may be a minimum fine for the offence but the maximum limits be left to the discretion of the court depending upon the circumstances of each case. The Supreme Court of India has, however, formulated the appropriate standards for the measures of damages. The measure of damages must be "correlated to the magnitude and capacity of the enterprise because such compensation must have a deterrent effect". The Supreme Court Observes : "The larger and more prosperous the enterprise the greater must be the amount of compensation payable by it for the harm caused on account of accident in the carrying on of the hazardous or inherently dangerous activity by the enterprise"[97].

Thirdly, the conditions of liability of inflict punishment under our environmental laws are faulty. For example, as provided in Sections 24-25 of Water (P & C Pollution) Act a person or a company will be liable for the Act if it is committed "knowingly or wilfully" and in the Environment (Protection) Act it is provided that a person or a company will not be liable if he proves that the offence was committed without his knowledge or that he exercised all the diligence to prevent the Commission of such offence. But we know that in these types of offences the principle of absolute or strict liability shall be applicable. Our Supreme Court of India in the Oleum Leakage case[98], held that : "an enterprise which is engaged in a hazardous or inherently dangerous industry which poses a threat to the health and safety of the persons working in the factory and residing in the surrounding areas owes an absolute and non-delegable duty to the community to insure that no harm results to anyone on account of hazardous or inherently dangerous nature of activity it has undertaken". Furthermore, such an enterprise "must be conducted with the highest standard of safety and if any harm results, the enterprise must be absolutely liable to compensate for such harm and it should be no answer for the enterprise to say that it had taken all reasonable care and that the harm occurred without any negligence on its part"[99].

Fourthly, as regards certainty of punishment regarding violations of environmental laws an emperical study had been undertaken in West Bengal. In that study it was revealed that since starting of its function the West Bengal Pollution Control Board initiated proceedings against about 40 Factories in the State but not a single case yet been finalised and none has been penalised under those cases[100]. As such due to want of certainty the magnitude of punishment should be increased in the Environmental laws.

From the above discussion and without being exhaustive it can easily be said that the traditional method of punishments or sanctions for violation of environmental laws is no longer an adequate way of controlling the problems of environmental damage and degradation. Therefore, innovation approaches have to be evolved such as the compulsory requirement of compensatory arrangements, ecological restitution, compulsory equity participation in the share capital of the company by potential victims of employment in the company among the victims and side by side more deterrent punishments should be prescribed in the respective laws by necessary amendments as soon as possible.

References

1. Upendra Baxi, *Environment Protection Act: An Agenda for Implementation* (1987) Indian Law Institute, New Delhi, (p. 37).
2. *Ibid.* p.1.
3. Judge Oakes, *The Judicial Role in Environmental Law,* 1977 52 NYUR 498-499.
4. Society for Protection of Silent Valley v. Union of India (unreported) cited in Rosencranz, *op.cit.* pp-285-287.
5. A.I.R. 1987 S.C. 1109.
6. Alice Jacob: "Responsible Development and Ecological Balance in *Journal of the ILI,* Vol-27, July, Sept. 1985, No-3, p. 485.
7. The Public Interest Litigation (PIL) is a devise innovated by the Chief Justice P.N. Bhagawati in Asiad Case whereby even a letter by Post Card may be taken as Writ Petition by the Supreme Court. It is also called Social Action Litigation by some Jurist.
8. A.I.R. 1985 S.C. 652.
9. *Ibid.* p. 656.
10. AIR 1988 H.P. 4 at p. 9.
11. (1986) 2 SCC 176: 1986 Sec. (Cri.) 122: A.I.R. 1987 S.C. 965; (1986) 2 SCC 325: A.I.R. 1987 SC 982; (1987) 1 Sec. 395 : 1987 Sec. (L&S) 137: A.I.R. 1987 S.C. 1086; (1987) 4 SCC 463: A.I.R. 1988 SC 1037 and (1988) 1 Sec. 471: 1988 SCC (Cri.) 141 : A.I.R. 1988 S.C. 1115.
12. A.I.R. 1987 S.C. 965.
13. *Ibid.* p. 981.
14. A.I.R. 1987 SC 982.
15. A.I.R. 1987 SC 1086.
16. A.I.R. 1988 SC 1037.
17. A.I.R. 1988 SC 1115.
18. A.I.R. 1987 AP 171.

19. 1990 KLT 580.
20. *Ibid.*
21. A.I.R. 1968 A.P. 98.
22. A.I.R. 1988 Raj. 2.
23. A.I.R. 1988 HP 4.
24. (1980) 4 Sec. 162.
25. 1986 Cri. L.J. 396.
26. A.I.R. 1979 SC 143.
27. *Ibid.* p. 145.
28. A.I.R. 1980 SC 1622 : (1980) 4 SCC 162.
29. *Ibid* pp. 1628-1629; per Krishna Iyer, J.
30. 1986 Cri. L.J. 396 M.P.
31. *Ibid* at p. 399. per V.D. Gyani J.
32. 1990 Cri. L.J. 1596.
33. 1989 Cri. L.J. 499.
34. *Ibid* at p. 501.
35. 1984 KLT 645, per U&L. Bhat, J.
36. *Ibid.* at p. 648.
37. 1989 Cri. L.J. 2013.
38. *Ibid.* p. 2015.
39. A.I.R. 1988 All 121.
40. A.I.R. 1985 S.C. 814.
41. - ——- - -
42. - - - ——- -
43. A.I.R. 1987 S.C. 1073.
44. *Ibid* at p. 1076.
45. P. Leelakrishnan, N.S. Chandrasekheran, G. Sadasivan Nair and K.V. Ramana Murthy: "Evolving Environmental Jurisprudence: The Role Played by the Judiciary" in P. Leelakrishnan ed. *Law and Environment* (1992) Eastern Bank Co. Lucknow p. 152.
46. A.I.R. 1987 Karn 82.
47. John Braithwaite and Peter Grabosky : *Occupational Health and Safety Environment in Australia* (1985), Australian Institute of Criminology, pp. 82-83 in Upendra Baxi *op.cit.*, p. 43.
48. See Calcutta Gazette, Notification No. P.H./2409/2R-11/74 dt. 20.9.1974 of Government of West Bengal.
49. See India Gazette, Extraordinary Notification No. G.S.R. 378 (E) dated 24th July, 1978.
50. ————

51. The Gazette of India, Extraordinary: Ministry of Environment and Forests, Notification No. S.O. 844(E) dt. 19th Nov. 1986.
52. See West Bengal Pollution Control Board Publication *Environmental Protection Laws* (1987) p. 226-29.
53. *Ibid.* p. 230.
54. See *Government of West Bengal:* Compendium of Environmental Guidelines (1987) p. 227.
55. *Ibid.* p. 231.
56. *Ibid.* pp. 300-311.
57. *Ibid.* pp. 1-6. Vide Govt. of West Bengal Notification No. 4987 & 4898 A.R. dt. 8th December 1986.
58. *Ibid.* pp. 7-18.
59. *Ibid.* pp. 30-47.
60. *Ibid.* pp. 48-54.
61. *Ibid.* pp. 62-83.
62. *Ibid.* pp. 55-61.
63. *Ibid.* pp. 84-112.
64. *Ibid.* pp. 113-115.
65. *Ibid.* p. 116.
66. *Ibid.* pp. 117-142.
67. *Ibid.* pp. 143-146.
68. *Ibid.* pp. 156-159.
69. *Ibid.* p. 160.
70. *Ibid.* pp. 188-189.
71. Source: West Bengal Pollution Control Board, Cammac Street, Calcutta-16.
72. Bondi D Ogolla: "Role of Environmental Law in Development" 1987, No. 2, p. 200.
73. Government of India, Ministry of Environment and Forests, Resolution No. H. 11013(2)/90-CPW dt. 26th February, 1992.
74. The Committee to Strengthen the Infrastructure Facilities of the Central and State Pollution Control Boards, constituted by Deptt. of Environment, Govt. of India, Report submitted on 30th June, 1984.
75. Shyam A Divan: "Making Indian Bureaucracies Think: *The Journal of Indian Law Institute* Vol. 30, July-Sept. 1988 No. 3. p. 292.
76. A.I.R. 1987 Karn. 82.
77. Justice S.M.M. Raina: "Environmental Pollution by use of pesticides", in *Central India Law Quarterly*, vol-11, Oct-Dec. 1988. Part-iv.
78. Sahagal: "If the Dams Come can the Deluge be Far Behind?"

The Times of India (18th Oct. 1987, Bombay Ed.).

79. Upendra Baxi ed. Environment Protection Act, An Agenda For Implementation, *op. cit.*, p. 38.

80. *Ibid.* p. 39.

81. Judgment Today 1990(4) SC 519.

82. *Government of India*, Ministry of Environment & Forests, New Delhi, POLICY STATEMENT FOR ABATEMENT OF POLLUTION, 1992.

83. This reveals that Government of India had lack of confidence on India's Tort law and was doubtful whether Carbide would submit to the jurisdiction of Indian Court.

84. See Rosencranz, Divan and Noble, *op.cit.*, pp. 351-352.

85. *Union Carbide Corporation* v. *Union of India*. Civil Revision No. 26 of 1988 dt. 4th April, 1988.

86. *India Today*, March 15, 1989, p. 45.

87. Rosencranz and Divan: "The Bhopal Settlement", *Environmental Policy and Law*, 19 (1989) p. 166.

88. Sumitra Sripada: "The Multinational Corporation and Environmental Issues", *Journal of the Indian Law Institute*, Vol-31 Oct-Dec. 1989 No. 4, p. 551.

89. G.N. Khanna, *op.cit.*, p. 162.

90. *Ibid.* p. 164-65.

91. United Nations Environment Programme. *Register of International Treaties and Other Agreements in the Field of the Environment* (1989).

92. R.P. Anand, "Development and Environment: The case of the developing countries", *Indian Journal of International Law*, Vol-20 (1980) pp. 1-19.

93. UNEP Press Release - 82/87 cited in G.N. Khanna, *op.cit.*, p. 169.

94. Burns, J.H. and Hart, H.L.A. Edited The Collected Work of Jeremy Bentham — *An Introduction to The Principles of Morals and Legislation* (1970) University of London.

95. *Ibid.*

96. *Ibid.*

97. Baxi, Upendra Ed. *Environment Protection Act, An Agenda for Implementation* (1987) I.L.I. publication, N.M. Tripathi, Bombay. p. 48.

98. *M.C. Mehta* v. *Union of India & Other* W.P. (Civil No. 12739 of 1985) cited in Baxi, Supra, p. 47.

99. *Ibid.*

100. See Table - 2 at page 146-148.

CHAPTER - V

Conclusions and Suggestions

"Whatever makes the past, the distant or the future, predominate over the present, advances us in the dignity of thinking beings".

—Samuel Johnson

In the previous chapters of this study on "Environmental Protection and the Law" attempt has been made to examine the various problems of environmental pollution and need for protection of human environment, the growth of environmental legislations both substantive and procedural and implementation of those environmental laws in India. However the position of environmental law in other countries and under international law have been referred whatever information available here. This study is based on enthnographic research and in general does not deal with questions of impact (what works?) but rather with questions of process (How does it work?). Thus in our discourses naturally we had to resort to find out how environmental pollutions affect our life, how various legislations developed in national and international levels and finally tried to evaluate the various implementation process in perspective of India. On the basis of this studies following conclusions and observations can be made by way of suggestions for improvement.

Conclusions

1. The problem of environmental pollution is now assuming a dangerous proposition throughout the world and global concern is discernible to protect environment.

2. Today is late; Tomorrow may be too late. Therefore an earnest effort to change the present trends of dehumanised process of industrialisation, and man's invasions in the Nature with hungry vulgarity for profit and development should immediately be checked to prevent 'crucifixion of humanity'.
3. Law is regarded as a means of controlling human conduct. So first charge on the legal system is to eliminate or control sources of pollution for human survival.
4. It is said that Capitalist's exploitative consumption of nature develop ecological problems. But socialist country like USSR is also facing problem of environmental pollution. Hence it is global problem.
5. The present state of human affairs in relation to environment led many philosophers, economists, sociologists, scientists and jurists express their unhappiness of unnecessary destruction of earth's resources and predicted that if the present rate of environmental degradations continue then it will destroy the capability of the environment to support human society.
6. On the question of What and Why environmental pollution the environmentalists characterised pollution in various types, such as — Air Pollution, Water Pollution, Soil Pollution, Green house Pollution, Biosphere Pollution etc.
7. As pollution are various so legislations are also varied to combat different types of pollutions. However environmental laws have been classified into three or four component such as developmental legislation (controlling development), legislation relation to the disposition of natural resources, conservation of natural resources, and environmental planning protectionist legislation.
8. The growth of environmental laws may be divided into two periods — early stage prior to Stockholm Conference 1972 and present stage post Stockholm Conference. In the early stage the environmental regulations were mostly enshrined with many other legislations main object of which is not to protect environment. But after Stockholm Conference many countries concluding India passed specific legislations to protect our environment.

9. U.N. Concern for control of human environment which began with organisation of Scientific Conference on Conservation and Utilisation of natural resources in 1949 through Stockholm Conference 1972 till end of Earth Summit, in Brazil in the month of June 1992 reveals that all nations agreed that immediate steps should be taken to protect our environment.
10. In India after Stockholm Conference 1972 three major environmental legislations namely Water Act 1974, Air Act 1981 and Environment Protection Act 1986 have been passed by our Parliament as a means of legal control of environmental Pollution.
11. In implementing environmental laws besides legal mechanisms other means are necessary such proper administrative policy and process, public participation, international cooperation.
12. There is a very vital question on the role of court in implementation of environmental laws. There is criticism that judges are generalists who cannot intelligently analyse technical issues as a scientists such as Environment Impact Assessment. But if we look into the various cases decided by our Supreme Court it will be seen that without much going in the technical aspect of a case the judges decide the cases on the question whether an agency has acted arbitrarily or capriciously.
13. Right to life guaranteed in Indian Constitution has been extended in the protection of environment by the Supreme Court through Public Interest Litigations. But its scope is very limited.
14. Though there are plethora of procedural rules and regulations for applications of environmental legislations but from the survey of its application in West Bengal it reveals that enforcement is very poor and almost negative in the legal field. After establishment of West Bengal Pollution Control Board no suit has yet been completed successfully punishing any polluter.
15. Administrative set up and infrastructure as recommended by expert Committee could not be fully materialised by the Government for want of sufficient fund though at last Government of India declared its Policy Statement for Protection of Environment in 1992 setting clear objectives, standards and various strategies for protection of environment.

16. Gradually public awareness on environment protection is increasing and encouraged by the Government. In India on the strong public demand Government of India had to postpone Tehri Dam Project in Uttar Pradesh.
17. There is an inherent conflict between development and environmental pollution. But development and growth cannot be ignored altogether. Hence a balance should be made between sustainable development and deviances of environmental regulations.
18. Among the Industrial polluters control of multinational corporations is a very difficult and complex question of legal battles as has been revealed in Bhopal Gas (MIC) tragedy. The law in this respect either in national or in international levels is in primary stage.
19. The U.N.O.'s attempt to control and protect human environment through UNEP failed to achieve expected results due to conflict between North-South or Developed and Developing countries. That is even Reo-De-Zenero Earth Summit could not resolve this dispute particularly on the question of Bio-diversity and share of contribution of developed countries for the environment protection programme.
20. Polluters and violators under various environment laws are offenders (some say deviants) and provisions for sanctions have been made on deterrent theory of punishment under criminal justice administration. But the retributive values of the punishments fail to deter polluters because there is a total disparity between retribution and the economic benefits of non-compliance.

Suggestions

1. Legal Control of environmental pollution is a remedial measure to protect environment. So more emphasis be given to the preventive measure, specially by strict observance of Environment Impact Assessment for new Industries and development projects.
2. The environmental litigations should be dissolved through administrative adjudication by establishment of Tribunals as Courts are over burdened and disposals of a case in the ordinary

court of law requires lengthy procedure. However power of judicial review and Public Interest Litigation under Article 32 and 226, of the Indian Constitution shall be continued.

3. Public participation in the implementation of environmental legislations is to be encouraged by giving legal recognition and financial assistance to the voluntary non-governmental agencies. To make public partnership more meaningful right to information is required to be extended.
4. To enforce legal control of environmental pollution meaningful the people are to be educated about causes of pollutions, various legal provisions and their rights and duties. Environmental agencies and educational institutions may take the duty to educate the people.
5. As there is lack of certainty of conviction for violation of environmental laws so the prescribed punishment should be more deterrent and unlimited in the line of tortious liability which should prescribe minimum punishment and not the maximum punishment.
6. As most of the environmental litigations involve economical development so there should be a time limit within which litigations should be disposed off for which simple and effective procedure be development.
7. The legal provisions of closure of industries manufacturing hazardous substances shall be reconciled with the question of sustainable development and cost-benefit analysis.
8. The present set up of the Pollution Control Agencies shall be made more strong. An inquisitorial system of adjudication by the Board may be introduced for first hearing of any case in the line of Income Tax Act so as to make the cost of violation more than the cost of law observance.
9. A new jurisprudence of estoppel in its broader sense may be developed within environmental laws so that the government agencies and municipalities can be held responsible for breach of trust — the duties given to them for implementation of environmental programme.

10. Above all continuous protection of human environment requires proper perception, economic strength and research along with legal principles and administrative structure.

This discourse begins with the words such as — 'The world is finite, resources are scarce, things are bad and will be worse, ... soon will have a plundered planet'. These words uttered about a century ago. Now I conclude with the words with which the biggest Earth Summit 1992 begins by General Mon's Strong, the Secretary General of United Nations Conference on Environment and Development — "If we do not stop our invasion on environment then this environment will destroy the human civilisation build up with man's hard work through thousands of years and that fearful day is not far away"[1].

Reference

1. *Bartaman* (Bengali) reported by Debjani Gangopadhyaya on 5th June, 1992.

ANNEXURE I

MINAS (MINIMAL NATIONAL STANDARDS) AND EMISSION STANDARDS

For the purpose of grant of consent conditions for the different industries, the MINAS and Emission Standards prescribed by the Central Board in consultation with the State Boards be followed (Please refer to Annexure A).

Annexure A

INDUSTRIES FOR WHICH MINAS AND EMISSION STANDARDS HAVE BEEN PRESCRIBED BY THE CENTRAL BOARD IN CONSULTATION WITH THE STATE BOARDS.

1. Man-made Fibre Industry

Reference — Central Board Publication.

'Minimal National Standard for Man-made Fibre Industry'.

(a) The general parameters of pollution relevant to man-made fibre industries:

temperature

pH

total suspended solids

total dissolved solids

Biochemical Oxygen Demand (BOD)

Chemical Oxygen Demand (COD)

Oil and grease.

(b) Special pollution parameters that may be relevant in stated specific situations are :

Zinc in viscose spinning bath and washing section effluent.

Cyanides in case of acrylonitrile manufacture.

Mercury in case of captive caustic soda plant (Mercury cell).

Ammonical Nitrogen in case nitrates are used in nitration process in acrylonitrile manufacture.

Hexavalent chromium in cooling water discharge.

(c) Minimal National Standards for Synthetic Fibre Industry:

Parameter	Concentration, mg/1 not to exceed
pH	5.5 to 9
Suspended solids	100
Biochemical Oxygen Demand 20^{0}C, 5 days	30

(d) Minimal National Standards for Semi-Synthetic Fibre Industry :

Parameter	Concentration, mg/1 not to exceed
pH	5.5 to 9
Suspended solids	100
Biochemical Oxygen Demand 20^0 C, 5 days	30
Zinc	1

2. Caustic Soda (Mercury Cell) Industry

(a) Minimal National Standards for Caustic Soda (Mercury Cell) Industry:

(i) Parameter	Concentration, not to exceed, mg/1
pH	5.5 to 9
Total suspended solids (Non-mercuric)	100
Total residual chlorine	1
Mercury in all forms	0.01

The concentrations should not be exceeded in the combined effluent and from:

(a) Cell house, (b) brine plant, (c) Chlorine handling section, (d) hydrochloric acid plant and (e) hydrogen handling.

(ii) The combined effluent from the above cited five sections shall not exceed 10 kilolitre/tonne of caustic soda produced. The units which are producing less volume of waste should be encouraged to continue that good practice.

(b) Permissible Limits (Water) :

Limits specified in I.S. 2490 (Part-1 : General limits) : 1981 Tolerance limits for industrial effluents discharged into inland surface waters — should be adopted for all inland units. For all units located near sea coasts, limits specified in I.S. 7968 : 1976. Tolerance limits for industrial effluents discharged into marine coastal areas should be prescribed as the standard. The following limits should be strictly adhered to :

(i) pH	5.5 to 9
(ii) Total suspended solids, mg/litre	100
(iii) Total residual chlorine mg/litre	1.0
(iv) Mercury in all forms, mg/ltr.	0.01
(v) Nickel, mg/litre	3.0
(vi) Standardised Bio-assay test	Must Pass

(c) Permissible Limits (Air):

	Cell room	
	Within	outside
(i) Mercury, mg/cu.m of air	0.05	0.015
(ii) Chlorine mg/cu.m of air	5	3

If any Indian standard is published, the same may be adopted without relaxing the limits for Mercury and Chlorine.

(d) Permissible Limits for workmen's health:

For	per	Micro-gram, Mercury
Blood	100 ml	3.5
Urine	1000 ml	150
Hair	1000 ml	less than 50

The check should be conducted every six months. The medical man should look for specific and non-specific symptoms. The new entrants should undergo an initial check up.

3. Minimal National Standards for Oil Refineries

(a) It is considered that Refineries having once through cooling should not dispose of the pollutants under the deceptive dilution offered by the cooling water. Therefore, Minas are stipulated both in terms of concentration and quantum of pollutants worked out on the basis of waste water generation of 700 kilo litre per 1000 tonne of crude refined.

MINIMAL NATIONAL STANDARDS FOR OIL REFINERIES

Parameter	Maximum Permissible Concentration in mg/1	Maximum Permissible Quantum in kg/1000 tonnes of Crude processed
Oil and grease	10	7
Phenol	1	0.7
Sulphide	0.5	0.35
Biochemical Oxygen Demand	15	10.5
Suspended solids	20	14
pH	between 6 and 8.5	

(b) The above parameters should be determined daily for the final effluent and every alternate day at the three stages of treatment:

(i) Primary Oil Separation

(ii) Secondary Oil separation

(iii) Biological treatment.

ANNEXURE II

STATUTORY PROVISIONS FOR PREVENTION & CONTROL OF AUTOMOBILE POLLUTION

RULE 258 OF THE WEST BENGAL MOTOR VEHICLES RULES, 1989

Rule 258. (1) Emission standard for motor vehicles — (a) For every diesel driven motor vehicle, the smoke density shall not exceed the levels laid down below:

Motor Vehicle, Produced for registration for the first time (Zero Kilometre run) 60 HSU or 4.3 BSU	Motor Vehicle already used upon road 70 HSU or 4.9 BSU

(b) For petrol driven motor vehicles, the following carbon monoxide limits (per cent by volume) under idling shall apply:

	Motor vehicles produced for registration for the first time	Motor vehicles already used upon road
(i) Two-wheeler and three-wheeler with engine displacement of less than 50 cm	5%	5%
(ii) Two-wheeler and three-wheeler, other than those mentioned in (i) above	4.5%	4.5%
(iii) Four-wheeler	3.5%	4%

(c) The permissible emission level for all other pollutants present in vehicular exhaust (like hydro-carbons, oxides of nitrogen, etc.) shall be such as may be laid down by the State Government from time to time.

(2) Test for smoke emission level and other pollutant level for motor vehicles —

(a) Any Officer not below the rank of Sub-Inspector of Police or Police Sergeant or any Motor Vehicles Inspector or Assistant Director (Technical), Public Vehicles Department, Calcutta, who has reason to believe that a motor vehicle driven on or used upon public road is, by virtue of smoke or other pollutants emitted from it, is likely to cause environmental pollution endangering the health or safety of any other user of the road or the public, may direct the driver or any person in-charge of the vehicle to undergo test to measure the standard of black smoke or other pollutants emitted from the vehicles.

(b) The driver or any person in-charge of the vehicle shall, upon demand by any officer under clause (a) of this sub-rule, allow the vehicle to be tested for the purpose of measuring the standard of smoke or level of other pollutants or both.

(c) The measurement of standard smoke shall be done with a smoke metre of a type approved by the State Government. The measurement of other pollutants shall be done with the help of instruments of a type approved by the State government.

(d) The officer conducting the test shall prepare a notice, in duplicate, containing among other things, the reading of the metre or his level of pollutants, as the case may be, and direct the driver or the owner in-charge of the vehicle to produce the vehicle for re-test within such period, not being later than 14 days, as may be specified in the notice, with defects duly rectified.

(e) In the event of the driver or the owner of the vehicle failing to produce the vehicle within the specified period for re-test of the vehicle or the vehicle, on re-test, shows the level of smoke or other pollutants being, more than that permissible under these rules, the Registering Authority or other prescribed Authority may suspend the certificate of registration of the vehicle under section 53 of the Act.

(3) Pollution under Control Certificate —

(a) Every motor vehicle will have to obtain a "Pollution under Control" certificate showing that the smoke emission level from that vehicle is within the limit prescribed hereinbefore. A "Pollution under Control" Certificate will remain valid for a period of six months from the date of its issue.

(b) A "Pollution under Control" Certificate issued only by a State Government Department or an agency authorised by the State Government to test smoke emission level in the Form prescribed in this behalf will be accepted for the purpose of these rules.

(c) Notwithstanding the provisions contained in caluse (a), the authority if it so thinks fit, may direct a vehicle to be tested in spite of its having a valid "Pollution under Control" certificate.

(d) Agencies authorised by the state Government to test smoke emission level will charge such fees for different categories of vehicles as will be prescribed by the Government by order from time to time.

(e) The State Government may, by issue of an order delegate the power to the Director, Public Vehicles Department, for the city of Calcutta, or to the District Magistrates for their respective districts or to any other officer subordinate to them as the State Government may think it, to authorise an agency to test smoke emission level.

(4) Horns —

(a) Every motor vehicle shall be fitted with a horn or other approved device available for immediate use by the driver of the vehicle and capable of giving audible and sufficient warning of the approach or position of the vehicle.

(b) No motor vehicle shall be fitted with any multitioned horn giving a succession of different notes or with any other sound-producing device giving an unduly harash, shrill, loud or alarming noise.

(c) Nothing contained in clause (b) shall prevent the use on vehicle, used as ambulances or for fire fighting or salvage purposes or on vehicle used by Police Officers in the course of their duties, or on other similar vehicles, of such sound signals as may be approved by the Registering Authority.

(d) Every transport vehicle shall be fitted with a bulb horn.

(e) No air horn shall be fitted or used in any transport vehicle in Calcutta (including suburbs) or in the districts of 24 Paraganas. Howrah and Hooghly and no air horn or multitioned horn shall be blown within a vicinity of 100 meters of any Hospital or Health Centre.

ANNEXURE III

INDUSTRIES FOR WHICH I.S.I SPECIFICATIONS WOULD BE FOLLOWED BY THE WEST BENGAL POLLUTION CONTROL BOARD

Indian Standard Tolerance Limits for

A. Industrial Effluents discharged into inland Surface Waters.
IS: 2490 (Part-1) —1974

B. Industrial Effluents discharged on Land for irrigation purposes.
IS: 3307 — 1965

C. Industrial Effluents discharged into Public Sewers.
IS: 3306 — 1974

D. Inland Surface Waters subject to pollution.
IS: 2296 — 1974

E. Sewage Effluents discharged into inland Surface Waters.
IS: 4764 — 1973

This standard prescribes [the tolerance limits for inland surface waters (rivers), estuaries, streams, lakes and reservoirs, including rivers liable to seasonal drying] subject to pollution which are used for the following purposes:

(a) Raw Water for public water supply.

(b) Bathing GHATS,

(c) Fish culture, and

(d) Irrigation.

These tolerance limits are shown in Table-1.

+, These requirements shall apply only when, after treatment, the sewage effluents is disposed of for irrigation and on land.

–, Not required.

(a) Tolerance limits for colour and odour of 'A' have not been prescribed in this Standard but it is recommended that as far as practicable, colour and unpleasent odours should not be present in the industrial effluent.

(b) Tolerance limits for odour of 'E' have not been prescribed but it is for recommended that as far as practicable, unpleasant odours should not be present in the sewage effluent. Further, while not limit have been laid down in this Standard for pathogenic bacteria it is expected that adherence to limits for total suspended solid and BOD will reduce the bacterial load of the effluent.

When the sewage also carries industrial effluent the sewage effluents also satisfy the tolerance limit for industrial effluents as given in 'A'.

(c) The disposal of solids, such as ash, cinder, and tar, hair, rag, metal shavings and garbage into public sewers from industries is also considered inadmissible.

Table 1

Sl. No.	Characteristic	A	B	C	Tolerance limits for D (a)	D (b)	D (c)	D (d)	E
1.	Total suspended solids, mg/1, Max	100	—	600 , relaxable to 750 by the local authority	—	—	—	—	30
2.	Particle size of total suspended solids	Shall pass 850 micron is sieve	—	—	—	—	—	—	—
3.	Total dissolved solids (inorganic), mg/1, Max	—	21,00	21,00	—	—	—	21,00	—
4.	pH	5.51 to 9.0	5.5 to 9.0	5.5 to 9.0	6.0 to 9.0	6.0 to 9.0	6.0 to 9.0	5.5 to 9.0	—
5.	Electrical conductance at 25° C, Max.	—	—	—	—	—	1000x 10-6 mhos	3,000x 10-6 mhos	—
6.	Temperature	Shall not exceed 40°C in any section of the stream within 15 meters down stream from the effluent outlet	—	45°C Max	—	—	—	—	—
7.	B.O.D. (5 days at 20° C) mg/1, Max	80	500	500, subject to relaxation or right ending by the local authority	3	3	—	—	28

Table 1 (Contd.)

Sl. No.	Characteristic	A	B	C	Tolerance limits for D (a)	D (b)	D (c)	D (d)	E
8.	C.O.D. mg/1, Max	250	—	—	—	—	—	—	—
9.	Dissolved Oxygen, Min	—	—	—	40% Saturation value or 3mg/1 whichever is higher	40% Saturation value or 3 mg/1 whichever is higher	40% Saturation value or 3 mg/1 whichever is higher	—	—
10.	Oils and grease, mg/1, Max	10	30	100	0.1	0.1	0.1	—	—
11.	Phenolic Compounds, mg/1, Max (as C_5H_6OH)	1.0	—	5, relaxable to 50 by the local authority when secondary treatment of the sewage is carried out	0.005	0.005	—	—	—
12.	Fluorides (as F), Mg/1, Max	2.0	—	—	1.5	1.5	—	—	—
13.	Chlorides (as Cl), Mg/1, Max	—	600	600	600	600	—	600	—
14.	Total residual Chlorine, mg/1,	1.0	—	—	—	—	—	—	—
15.	Cyanides (as CN), mg/1, Max	0.2	—	2.0	0.01	0.01	—	—	—

Table 1 (Contd.)

Sl. No.	Characteristic	A	B	C	Tolerance limits for D (a)	D (b)	D (c)	D (d)	E
16.	Sulphides (as S), mg/1, Max	2.0	—	—	—	—	—	—	—
17.	Sulphates (as SO_4), mg/1, Max	—	1,000	1,000†	—	—	—	1,000	—
18.	Nitrates (as NO_3), mg/1, Max	—	—	—	50	50	—	—	—
19.	Ammonical nitrogen, mg/1, Max	50	—	50	—	—	1.2	—	—
20.	Arsenic (as As), mg/1, Max	0.2	—	—	0.2	0.2	—	—	—
21.	Lead (as Pb), mg/1, Max	0.1	—	1.0	0.1	0.1	—	—	—
22.	Mercury (as Hg), mg/1, Max	0.01	—	—	—	—	—	—	—
23.	Copper (as Cu), mg/1,	3.0	—	3.0	—	—	—	—	—
24.	Cadmium (as Cd), mg/1, Max	2.0	—	—	—	—	—	—	—
25.	Zinc (as Zn), mg/1, Max	5.0	—	15	—	—	—	—	—
26.	Total Chromium (as Cr), mg/1, Max	—	—	—	0.05	0.05	—	—	—
27.	Hexavalent chromium (as Cr),	0.1	—	2.0	—	—	—	—	—
28.	Nickel (as Ni), mg/1, Max	3.0	—	2.0	—	—	—	—	—

Table 1 (Contd.)

Sl. No.	Characteristic	A	B	C	Tolerance limits for D (a)	D (b)	D (c)	D (d)	E
29.	Selenium (as Se), mg/1,	0.05	—	—	0.05	0.05	—	—	—
30.	Percent Sodium, Max	—	60	60 †	—	—	—	60	—
31.	Boron (as B), mg/1, Max	—	2.0	2.0 †	—	—	—	2.0	—
32.	Free Carbon dioxide (as Co_2), mg/1, Max	—	—	—	—	—	6.0	—	—
33.	Insecticides	Absent	—	—	Absent	Absent	—	—	—
34.	Radioactive materials								
	(a) Alpha emitters, µC/ml, Max	10^{-7}	10^{-9}	10^{-7}	10^{-9}	10^{-9}	10^{-9}	10^{-9}	—
	b) Beta emitters, µC/ml, Max	10^{-6}	10^{-8}	10^{-6}	10^{-8}	10^{-8}	10^{-8}	10^{-8}	—
35.	Coliform organism (Monthly average MPH per 100 ml.)	—	—	—	Not 5×10^3 with 5% of the samples with value 20×10^3 and 20% of the samples with value 5×10^3	—	—	—	—

ANNEXURE IV

STANDARDS FOR EMISSION OF AIR POLLUTANTS INTO THE ATMOSPHERE FROM INDUSTRIAL PLANTS

In accordance with the Air (Prevention & Control of Pollution) Act, 1981, the standard for the following categories of industries have been laid down by the Board :

1. Cement
2. Thermal power plant
3. Iron & Steel industry
4. Calcium Carbide manufacture
5. Copper, Lead and Zinc smelting/refining industry
6. Carbon black industry
7. Fertilizer industry
8. Aluminium manufacturing industry/Aluminium and its allied and processing industry
9. Oil refineries
10. Industrial boilers for electrical energy or steam
11. Furnace
12. Paper and pulp industry
13. Sulphur acid manufacture
14. Sulphuric acid manufacture
15. Nitric acid manufacture
16. Glass manufacture
17. General standards for emission wherever applicable from any industry

In addition to this, the Board is also adopting the MINAS (Minimal National Standard) as and when formulated by the Central Board for the Prevention & Control of Water Pollution.

1. Cement

Standard for particulate matter emission

Capacity	Protected area	Other area
200 tpd and less	250 mg/Nm^3	400 mg/Nm^3
Greater than 200 tpd	150 mg/Nm^3	250 mg/Nm^3

Note: A protected area is one that is already polluted from being in a metropolitan/industrial location or the area is sensitive because of its proximity to national parks, forests, historical monuments and health resorts.

2. **Thermal Power**

(a) Standard for particulate matter emission

Boiler size	Protected area	Other area: Old (before 1979)	Other area: New (after 1979)
Less than 200 MW	150 mg/Nm^3	600 mg/Nm	350 mg/Nm^3
200 MW and above	150 mg/Nm^3	—	150 mg/Nm^3

(b) Standard for sulphur dioxide control (through stack height)

Boiler size	Stack height
Less than 200 MW	$H = 14 (Q)^{0.3}$
200 MW to less than 500 MW	220 metres
500 MW and more	275 metres

Q = Sulphur dioxide emission in kg/hr.
H = Stack height in metres.

3. **Iron & Steel**

Standard for particulate matter.

Process		Emission limits
Sintering plant		150 mg/Nm^3
Coke oven		—
Blast furnace		—
Steel making	During normal operation	150 mg/Nm^3
	During oxygen lancing	400 mg/Nm^3

4. **Fertilizer (Urea)**

Standard for particulate matter emission.

Process	Emission limit
Prilling Tower	50 mg/Nm^3

5. **Nitric Acid**

Standard for oxides of nitrogen, NO_x

3 kg of NO_x per tonne of weak acid (before concentration) produced

6. **Sulphuric Acid**

Standard for sulphur dioxide and acid mist emission.

Process	Sulphur dioxide emission	Acid mist emission
Single conversion Single absorption	— 10 kg/tonne of concentrated (100%) acid produced	50 mg/Nm^3
Double Conversion Double absorption	— 4 kg/tonne of concentrated (100%) acid produced	50 mg/Nm^3

ANNEXURE V

GOVERNMENT OF INDIA
MINISTRY OF ENVIRONMENT & FORESTS

Department of Environment, Forests & Wildlife

No. 2-3/86-FC New Delhi, Dated 31 July 1986

To

The Chief Secretary,

(All States & UTs)

Subject: Guidelines for diversion of forest lands for non-forest purposes under the Forest (Conservation) Act, 1980.

Sir,

Detailed guidelines for submission of proposals for diversion of forest lands for non-forest purposes under the Forest (Conservation) Act, 1980 were issued vide Ministry of Agriculture's circular letters of even number dated 25.2.1983 and 3.9.1983. In addition various circulars were issued from time to time either to resolve some difficulties, clarify certain points, or to cope up with new situations. These circulars are chronologically listed below:

Sl. No.	No.	Date	Subject
(i)	8-4/80-FRY (Coord)	26.12.1980	Proforma for submission of proposals.
(ii)	8-4/80-FRY (Coord)	5.6.1981	General lacunae in the proposal.
(iii)	25-6/81-FRY(Coord)	16.6.1981	Working of Private forests—Guidelines regarding.
(iv)	8-22/81-FRY(Coord)	24.9.1981	Investigations and surveys for laying of transmission lines.
(v)	11021/25/76-FRY(Coord)	26.10.1981	Grant and renewal of mining leases in forest areas.
(vi)	8-4/80-FRY (Coord)	19.12.1981	Laying down of specific time limits for disposal of cases at various levels.

Sl. No.	No.	Date	Subject
(vii)	5-2/82-FRY (Cons)	11.1.1982	Preservation of beaches—instructions of Prime Minister.
(viii)	11021/25/76-FRY	15.1.1982	Mining in forest areas.
(ix)	8-4/82-FRY (Cons)	5.2.1982	Ex-post facto approval will not be granted.
(x)	8-22/81-FRY (Coord)	11.3.1982	Laying of transmission lines.
(xi)	2-1/82-FRY (Cons)	26.3.1982	Definition of term 'forest land' grant of renewal of mining lease, specific orders for dereservation or diversion of forest land, anticipatory action by State Governments.
(xii)	2-1/82-FRY (Cons)	5.5.1982	Growing of cash crops in forest areas.
(xiii)	8-22/81-FRY (Cons)	12.5.1982	Survey and investigations in forest areas in connection with hydro-electrical projects.
(xiv)	8-22/81-FRY (Coord)	16.9.1982	Simplified procedure for submitting proposals for laying of transmission lines, pipelines etc. where no tree felling is involved.
(xv)	11-8/83-FRY (Cons)	10.4.1984	Simplification of procedure for clearance of proposals.
(xvi)	9-9/84-FRY (Cons)	28.6.1984	Use of forest land for afforestation by individuals, institutions etc.
(xvii)	8-98/85-FC	19.11.1985	Contravention of the provisions of the Act— anticipatory action by the State Authorities.
(xviii)	2-2/85-FC	21.11.1985	Compensatory afforestation.
(xix)	11-8/83-FRY (Cons)	30.12.1985	Exploratory drilling for prospective oil.
(xx)	11-61/85-FRY (Cons)	13.1.1986	Cost-benefit analysis.
(xxi)	2-2/85-FC	2.4.1986	Compensatory afforestation.
(xxii)	11021/25/76-FRY (Coord)	2.4.1986	Mining activities on forest lands.
(xxiii)	11-28/86-FRY (Cons)	8.5.1986	Surveys for oil explorations.
(xxiv)	1-1/86-FC	6.6.1986	Release of forest lands for mining purposes.

2. This circular is intended to be a compendium of what has been laid down before and not modified, and what is decided to lay down now by the Government of India in regard to formulation of proposals for dereservation or diversion of forest lands or non-forest use under the Forest (Conservation) Act, 1980, and implementation of the Act. In other words, in addition to prescribing some new norms and guidelines the circular contains all that is still valid in previous circulars.

3. Application of the Forest (Conservation) Act, 1980

(i) The term 'forest land' mentioned in Section 2 of the Act refers to reserved forests, protected forests or any area recorded as forest in the government records. All proposals for diversion of such areas to any non-forest purpose, even if the area is privately owned, would require the prior approval of the Central Government under the forest (Conservation) Act, 1980.

(ii) Since mining is a non-forest activity prior approval of the Central Government is essential before a mining lease is granted in respect of any forest area. Renewal of an existing mining lease in a forest area also requires the prior approval of the Central Government.

The advice of the Ministry of Law, Government of India regard to the Supreme Court Orders in Civil Appeals No. 2349 of 1984 dated 7.5.1985 are at Annexure V.

(iii) Cases in which specific orders dereservation or diversion of forest areas in connection with any project were issued by the State Government prior to 25.10.1980, need not be referred to the Central Government. However, in cases where only administrative approval for the Project was issued without specific orders regarding dereservation and/or deforestation of forest lands, prior approval of the Central Government would be necessary under the aforesaid Act.

(iv) Growing of fodder grasses, legumes etc. which grow naturally in a particular region in barren forest areas, without removal of existing tree growth, should not require prior approval of the Central Government under the Forest (Conservation) Act, 1980. However lease of such areas to private parties may have large implications and such cases should be referred to the Central Government for prior approval under the Forest (Conservation) Act, 1980.

(v) Use of forest areas for growing commercial crops such as rubber, palm oil, tea, coffee, cardamom etc. amounts to use of forest areas for non-forest purposes and will consequently attract the provisions of the Forest (Conservation) Act, 1980.

(vi) Lease of forest areas to private parties for raising plantations of bamboo or other tree species required as industrial raw material would also have larger implications and may create environmental problems. Such cases therefore, will also require prior approval of the Central Government under Forest (Conservation) Act, 1980.

(vii) The use of forest lands for afforestation purposes even by individuals, institutions etc. under different schemes will attract the provisions of the Forest (Conservation) Act, 1980 and hence would require prior approval of the Central Government in each case.

(viii) Raising horticultural crops in erstwhile shifting cultivation areas and other forest areas will attract provisions of the Forest (Conservation) Act, 1980. Similar Schemes for permanent settlement of shifting cultivators in forest areas will attract provisions of the Forest (Conservation) Act, 1980.

(ix) Investigation and surveys:

(a) Transmission Lines — Investigation and surveys carried out in connection with the laying of transmission lines in forest areas will not attract the provisions of the Forest (Conservation) Act, 1980, if no felling of tree is involved. The work of construction and laying of transmission lines, however, fully attracts the provisions of the aforesaid Act and the prior permission of the Central Government must be obtained before this is allowed in forest areas.

(b) Hydro-electrical projects—Investigations and surveys carried out in connection with hydro-electric projects will not attract the provisions of the Forest (Conservation) Act, 1980 so long as these surveys do not involve any clearing of forest or cutting of trees and operations are restricted to clearing of bushes and lopping of tree branches for purposes of sightings. In such cases, survey work may be allowed by the State Governments. A reference need be made to the Central Government under Section 2 of the aforesaid Act only if it involves any clearing of forest area or felling of trees.

(c) The cases relating to seismic surveys and explorations for oil drilling as well as prospecting licences for mining need not be referred Central Government for prior approval provided these do not involved cutting trees or clearance of forests.

(d) It should be however be made clear in each case that the permission to survey, explore or prospect does not imply commitment on the part of the Central Government for any subsequent use of the forest land.

(e) It is specifically stated that surveys, investigations and explorations should not be carried out in wildlife sanctuaries, national parks, preservation and sample plots demarcated by Forest Department.

4. Use of forest lands for raising plantations by forest-based industries

As far as possible, afforestation/plantations on forest lands should be taken up by the Forest Departments of States/UTs. Where the Forest Departments are not in a position to take up such work because of paucity of funds, other reasons, they should involve the Forest Corporations for this purpose. However, degraded forest lands and wastelands not likely to be taken up by the Forest Departments and/or Forest Corporations, in the near future, may be considered for raising plantations by the forest-based industries on selective basis and as pilot projects, after ensuring that the legal status of such lands is not charged and possession remains with the concerned Forest Departments and the management is through joint participation.

The Forest Departments should carry out survey of such degraded areas and then select areas suitable for raising industrial plantations with great care and with advertance to the considerations mentioned above. However in each such cases prior approval of the Central Government should be taken, as laid down in para 3(vi) above and should not involve clear-felling of existing forests.

5. Submission of proposals

Rule (4) of the Forest (Conservation) Rules, 1981 (Annexure II) prescribes the procedures for submission of proposals regarding dereservation of reserved forests or use of forest land for non-forest purpose. The annexure (Annexure III) to the Rules specifies the particulars to be furnished with the proposals.

5.1 A brief note giving essential details of the project for which forest land is required should be furnished as per item No. 1 of the proforma prescribed under the Rules. This should include (a) cost and outlay (b) justification for locating the project in the forest areas giving alternatives that were examined and reasons for their rejection, (c) financial and social benefits, (d) total population benefited, (e) employment generated etc. A comprehensive land use plan of the area required should be attached if land is required for more than one purpose. The building plan should invariably be attached, if the area is required for construction purposes.

5.2 Adverse recommendations of subordinate officers in the proforma or in the documents attached with the proforma should be invariably commented upon by the CCF. Similarly, adverse remarks of the CCF should be commented upon by the State Government so that it may be clear that a conscious decision has been taken in the case.

5.3 All hydel projects, major irrigation projects and mining projects require clearance from environmental angle as well. (Irrigation project having command area over 10,000 hectares are called Major Projects.) Therefore, all hydel projects, major irrigation projects and mining projects should be referred to the Environment Wing of the Department of Environment and Forests for environmental clearance simultaneously with the proposal for forest clearance.

5.4 It is note that area, length, breadth and other measurement are not often given in metric units and various units like acre, bigha, kanal, muthi, yard etc. are used. All measurements must be given in metric units.

5.5 A map showing location of the area to be deforested viz. the boundary of the surrounding forest block is an essential requirement. It has been represented that maps on 1:50,000 scale are sometimes not available. Maps on 1:50,000 scale have been published for the entire country and should be obtained from the Surveyor of India. In the meantime, if maps on 1:50,000 scale are not available maps may be submitted on 1" = 1 mile or 1" = 4 miles or any other suitable scale according to the size of the area demanded. If the area is too small an index may be submitted showing forest boundaries and a location map on a larger scale showing land use of the area required.

5.6 Specieswise and diameter classwise list of trees to be felled is an essential requirement for a meaningful appraisal of the proposal. It has been represented that in larger areas this takes a lot of time. It has, therefore been decided that total enumeration may be carried out only up to 10.0 ha. For larger areas specieswise and diameter classwise list may be computed either from the working plans or by standard sampling methods. Further, this information may be given only for the area asked for in item 3 of the proforma and not for various levels in case of irrigation projects which can be estimated proportionately.

5.7 Proposals for dereservation of reserved forest should be viewed with extreme caution and should be sent only in exceptional cases.

5.8 *Irrigation and Hydel Projects:* When the forest land is required for irrigation and hydel projects, the following details are necessary.

(a) Total catchment area

(b) Total command area

(c) Full reservoir level

(d) High flood Level

(e) Minimum Drawal level

(f) Total catchment area of the Dam (in hectares) and its break-up : Forest land: Cultivated land, pasture land, human cultivation and others.

(g) Details as per item (g) above for the area coming under submergence.

(i) Total number of families and population affected. Scheduled Caste and Scheduled Tribe families to be displaced should be separately indicated.

(j) Proposals for the rehabilitation of the affected persons.

(k) Comprehensive land use plan for area required outside submergence is buildings, roads and other ancillary facilities.

5.8.1 It has been observed that water hardly stands all the year round up to FRL. Trees can definitely stand in water for one to three months and therefore, submergence should be calculated 2-4 m below FRL. For this the following should be given for forest areas involved:

(i) Area of submergence at HFL (High Flood Level)

(ii) Area of submergence at FRL (Full Reservoir Level)

(iii) Area of submergence 2 m below FRL

(iv) Area of submergence at 4 m below FRL (for medium and major irrigation projects only)

(v) Area of submergence at Minimum Drawal Level (MDDL).

5.9 *Roads and Railway Lines.* The land for road project is generally asked piecemeal of land needed immediately is asked for. Before any sanction is given, it is necessary to examine the entire project and a note on the present and future requirement should be submitted. The following information should be submitted alongwith the proposals:

(a) A map on 1:50,000 scale forest areas, forest boundaries and road alignment.

(b) Length and width of the strip required and forest area required.

(c) Total length of the road as per final project, or as per alignment already surveyed.

(d) Length of the road already constructed.

(e) Total length of the road passing through the torest out of the length given under (c) above.

(f) Was an alternative alignment avoiding the forest land explored? If so, why it was rejected.

(g) Similar details may be given for new railway lines.

5.10 Reacting to a representation that use of forest areas for laying of transmissions lines should be exempted from the provisions of the Forest (Conservation) Act, 1980, the late Prime Minister had observed:

> "Where laying of transmission lines involved cutting trees we should find feasible alternatives."

5.10.1 It is, therefore, asserted that while determining the alignment of any transmission line, forest areas should be avoided so far as possible. Use of forest land for this purpose should be allowed only if absolutely unavoidable and after obtaining the prior approval of the Central Government under Section 2 of the Forest (Conservation) Act, 1980.

5.10.2 Width of the strip of forest land required for various kinds of transmission lines should be strictly in accordance with the ISI specifications. Further, clearance of forest should be done only for the purpose of erection of towers and laying of conductors. Elsewhere the trees should only be lopped when necessary. The total strip area required for towers and the area required for three 2-metre wide corridors, one below each conductor, should be given separately. Specieswise and diameter classwise list of trees, standing on the entire strip should be furnished.

5.10.3 Special guidelines in regard to laying of transmission lines in forest areas are Annexure IV.

5.11 *Mining*—In regard to proposals for diversion of forest lands for mining, in addition to the particulars specified for submission vide annuxure to the rule 4 of the Forest (Conservation) Rules, 1981, the following information should be given:

1. Total mining lease area and forest area required.
2. Period of mining lease proposed.
*3. Estimated reserve of each mineral/ore in the forest area and in the non-forest area adjoining.
4. Annual estimated production of mineral/ore.
5. Nature of mining operations (opencast/underground)
6. Plans for rehabilitation of the area after mining.
7. Gradient of the area where mining would be undertaken.
8. *Fore renewals* — Was forest Department consulted at the time of proposing present renewal of mining lease or present grant of surface right? Copies of the concerned lease deed should be attached.
9. Average number of persons to be employed everyday.
10. Area of forest land required for :
    (a) Mining
    (b) Storing mineral/ore
    (c) Dumping of overburden
    (d) Storing tools and machinery.
    (e) Construction of buildings, power stations, workshops etc.
    (f) Township/housing colony.
    (g) Construction of road/ropeway/railway lines.
    (h) Full land use plan for forest area required.
11. Reasons why forest landtasked for any of the activities under the project cited cannot be located outside forest area.

---

* The overburden should not be heaped in forests other than in those released for the project.

12. The extend of damage that would be caused in terms of number of trees affected on account of mining and related activities.

**13. Distance of the mining area from perennial water-courses, national and state highways, national park, sanctuaries and biosphere reserves.

14. Procedure for stocking of the topsoil for reuse.

15. Phased reclamation programme concurrently with the mining operation.

16. Extend of subsidence expected in underground mining operations and its impact on water, forest and other vegetation.

5.11.1 While proposing the grant/renewal of mining leases in forest areas, care should be taken to ensure that as far as possible no forest area is included, unless unavoidable. This may kindly be kept in view while sending proposals to the Central Government for permission under the Forest (Conservation) Act, 1980.

5.11.2 *Proposals for renewal of mining leases* — The State Government would send the proposal for renewal of mining lease at least three months prior to the date of expiry of the earlier lease, to this Ministry for consideration. Additional information or clarification asked for by this Ministry from the State Government, should be furnished within a maximum time limit of 3 weeks. This Ministry will, then dispose of proposals which are received in all respects, prior to the expiry of the lease period.

6. **Proposals for laying of transmission lines, pipes for drinking water supply and exploratory drillings for perspective oil which do not involve any felling or cutting of trees.**

In cases containing proposals for laying of transmission lines or pipes for drinking water supply and exploratory drilling for perspective oil which do not involve any felling or cutting of trees, it would not be necessary for the State Government or other authority to submit the proposals in the prescribed proforma. In order to expedite disposal of such cases, proposals of this type may be sent to the Central Government with the following particulars :

(i) Purpose for which forest land is required to be used.

(ii) Extent of forest land.

(iii) Status of forest land (i.e. whether reserved forest or any other class of forests).

(iv) Whether the forest land forms part of any national park, wildlife sanctuary, biosphere reserve or forms part of the habitat of any endangered or threatened species of flora and fauna?

** Major mining operations would not be permitted within one kilometer of National and State highways.

(v) Whether no alternative alignment is possible to avoid or minimise use of the forest land and whether the required area is the minimum needed for the purpose? A certificate in this regard furnished by the concerned Divisional Forest Officer after an inspection of the spot must be submitted along with the proposal.

6.1 Cases involving small forest area up to 2 ha. in extent, which are devoid of tree cover or which have scanty tree growth may also be dealt with as per simplified procedure.

6.2 It is to be noted that this procedure would apply to only such proposals for laying of transmission lines or pipes for drinking water supply which do not involve cutting or felling of any trees. The covering letter should clearly indicate that no cutting or felling of trees is involved. In all other cases, the normal procedure laid down in the Forest (Conservation) Rules would continue to apply.

7. Anticipatory action by State Authorities — Violation of the provisions of the Forest (Conservation) Act, 1980.

Cases have come to the notice of the Central Government in which permissions for diversion of forest lands was accorded by the concerned State Government in anticipation of the approval of the Central Government under the Act. Such anticipatory action is neither proper nor permissible under the Act, which clearly provides for prior approval of the Central Government in all cases. No proposal seeking the ex-post-facto approval of the Central Government under the Act, will be entertained from any State Government. The Central Government do not accord to any project on which work has been commenced without prior approval under the Act.

8. Steps to compensate for loss of forest area — Compensatory afforestation

Item No. 6 of the Annexure to the Forest (Conservation) Rules, 1981 prescribes that steps proposed to be taken to compensate for the loss of forest area should be specified while making proposals for dereservation or diversion of forest land to non-forest use Compensatory afforestation is one of the most important condition stipulated by the Government of India in approving proposals for dereservation or diversion of forest land to non-forest use. Therefore, it would be essential that with all the proposal for dereservation or diversion of forest land for non-forest use, a comprehensive scheme to compensatory afforestation is formulated and submitted to the Government of India.

8.1 *Land for compensatory afforestation :* The following norms are laid down for compensatory afforestation :

(i) Where non-forest lands are available, compensatory afforestation be raised over equivalent area of non-forest land.

(ii) Where non-forest lands are not available compensatory plantations be raised over degraded forests twice in extent to the area being diverted.

(iii) Where, non-forest land available is less in extent to the forest land being diverted in addition to compensatory afforestation on available non-forest land plantation be raised in degraded forest twice in extent to the difference between forest land being diverted and available non-forest land.

It should, however, be made clear that non-availability of non-forest lands for compensatory afforestation would be accepted by the Government of India only on a certificate to that effect from the Chief Secretary of the State /UT Government.

8.2 Compensatory afforestation will not be insisted upon in the following cases:

(a) In cases of diversion of forest lands for laying of power transmission lines.

(b) In cases of renewal of mining leases which were either under operation in the forest land prior to enactment of forest (Conservation) Act, 1980 or were renewed after the enactment with the prior approval of Central Government but were not having compensatory plantations as a pre-condition.

(c) In cases of diversion of forest land in small areas of less than 1 ha. in extent, unless specifically asked for, by the Department.

8.3 *Elements of schemes for compensatory afforestation:* The scheme for compensatory afforestation should contain the following details:

(i) Details of equivalent non-forest or degraded forest land identified for raising compensatory afforestation.

(ii) Delineation of proposed area on suitable map.

(iii) Agency responsible for afforestation.

(iv) Details of Work Schedule proposed for compensatory afforestation.

(v) Provision of funds and the mechanism to ensure that the funds will be utilised for raising afforestation.

(vi) Details of proposed monitoring mechanism.

8.4 *Lands identified for compensatory afforestation to be transferred to the Forest Department:*

(i) Equivalent non-forest land identified for the purpose are to be transferred to the control of the State Forest Department, so that the plantation raised can be maintained permanently. The transfer must take place prior to the commencement of project.

(ii) Non-forest lands identified for compensatory afforestation should be declared Protected Forests to ensure their safety from biological interference.

(iii) The afforestation should be specifically identifiable as related to the project. It should be adjacent to another forest area and should be clearly an additional plantation activity and not a diversion of a part of the annual plantation programme.

8.5 *Special Fund:* The State/UT Governments should create a special fund to which the individual user agency will make their deposits for compensatory afforestation. The Forest Department or any other agency which is assigned the job of compensatory afforestation should be able to fully draw this fund for the afforestation activity envisaged.

9. Cost-benefit analysis:

In considering proposals for dereservation or diversion of forest lands for non-forest use, it is essential ecological and environmental losses and sufference caused to the people who are displaced, are weighted against economic and social gains.

9.1 Annexure VI(a) details the types of cases on which a cost-benefit will be required. Annexure VI(b) lists the parameters according to which the cost aspect will be determined, while Annexure VI(c) gives the parameters for assessing the benefits accruing.

9.2 A cost-benefit analysis as above should accompany the proposals sent to the Central Government for clearance under the Forest (Conservation) Act, 1980.

10. Plan for rehabilitation of Oustees:

Suffering caused to people, who are displaced on account of a project cannot be over-stated. It is, therefore essential that a proposal for dereservation or diversion of forest land, if it involves displacement of people it should be accompanied by a satisfactory plan for their rehabilitation. Scheduled Tribe and Scheduled Caste populations should be separately considered, and a plan for their rehabilitation should be in consonance with their socio-economic cultural and emotional life-structure.

10.1 It is a stated that the Government of India do not allow diversion of forest land for rehabilitation of people. Non-forest land must therefore, be identified for rehabilitation.

11. Diversion for construction of houses :

On a proposal for construction of houses, the late Prime Minister had observed:

"Destruction of our forests has already caused great damage to our environment. Therefore, I am not at all in favour of use forest land for construction of houses. The State Govt. should find other land for such purposes.

The Government of India will not entertain any proposal for diversion of forest lands for construction of houses.

11.1 Diversion of forest lands for construction of other buildings also will not be normally considered.

12. **Preservation of beaches:**

Degradation misutilisation of beaches in coastal States by building construction and other activity should be totally avoided. The letter dated 27.11.1981 from the late Prime Minister is at annexure VII. Proposals for diversion of beaches will not be entertained by the Government of India.

13. **Other matters relating to formulation of proposals:**

13.1 *Opinion of Chief Conservator of Forests:* The opinion of the Chief Conservator of Forests has been often found to be very lacking in material. In some cases it is difficult to know if the Forest Department was consulted at all.

13.1.1 The forest authority must get the area inspected by a responsible officer depending on the sensitivity and potential value of the forest involved. For instance if the area is very important from the forestry angle, the territorial conservator should inspect the area and give complete information relating to the forest. Scientific names of important timber species should be given while describing composition of the forest crop. If the area is relatively less important, then the Divisional Forest Officer should see the area himself. The Inspecting Officers should record item 7 of the proforma very clearly if they have noticed any anticipatory activities such as tree-felling, land-breaking etc. in that area. In case the recommendation of the Chief Conservator of Forests should be categorical and specific.

13.2 *Specific time limits :* To ensure speedy of proposals under the Act, specific time limits have been laid down for disposal of such references at various levels. Efforts should be made to dispose of a case at the State Government level within a maximum period of two months. In simple cases, a lesser time limit should be laid down. Specific instructions may be issued in this regard to officers at all levels.

13.3 *Complete Details:* While forwarding the proposals to the Central Government, complete details of all aspects of the case should be given. It has been decided that incomplete and deficient proposals will not be considered and will be returned to the State Government in original.

13.4 *Clarifications or additional information — treating of a case as closed:* In cases in which the State Government is requested to furnish clarifications or additional information relating to a proposal, a reply should be sent within a maximum time limit of three weeks. If the required clarification information is not given within this period, it will be presumed that the State Government is not interested in pursuing the proposal and the case will be closed by the Government of India. The case may, however, be reopened on receipt of the required clarification and/or additional information with justification for delay in submission thereof.

13.5 *Separate cell for dealing forest conservation cases:* Separate cells for dealing with forest conservation cases should be opened at the State Government and Forest Department levels. A wholetime senior officer not below the rank of Conservator of Forests should head the Cell at the Forest Department level, who should be designate as the Nodal Officer.

13.6 *Nodal Officer:* The Nodal Officer should receive cases from other Government Departments and entertain all correspondence from them. The Nodal Officer should scrutinise and process the case and after obtaining views/ certificate of the CCF, should put up the case to State Government besides office staff, the Nodal officer should also be given sufficient field so that the cases are processed at the State level within the stipulated time of two months. The State Governments while forwarding cases to the Central will endorse copies to the CCF and the Nodal officer. The Central Government also while corresponding with State Government will send copies to the Nodal Officer. The Nodal Officer will also obtain all additional information required by the Centre about the cases from the concerned authorities directly and send the same to the Central Government through the State Government endorsing a copy directly to the Central Government.

14. **Observance of stipulated conditions :**

While approving a proposal for diversion of forest lands for non-forest purposes, the government of India stipulates certain conditions to reduce environmental damage on account of forest loss. The reports from the State reveal that in regard to the cases approved so far, by and large the conditions stipulated by the Government of India have not been observed by the States and Union Territories. The major difficulties faced by the States/UTs are:

(i) Non-forest lands for compensatory afforestation are not available.

(ii) Funds for compensatory afforestation which are realised from the user agency, are remitted as revenue in the State Exchequer and are not subsequently available to the planting agency.

14.1 With a view to resolve these difficulties and ensure to satisfactory implementation of stipulated conditions in future, it is proposed that the State/ UTs be requested to take following steps:

(i) As indicated earlier in para 8.5 above the State/UT Governments should create a special fund to which the individual user agency will make their deposits for compensatory afforestation. The money from this fund should be made readily available to the Forest Department or any other agency which is assigned the job of compensatory afforestation.

(ii) In each case where the afforestation target is over 200 hectares, a Monitoring Committee will be established with a nominee of the Department of Environment & Forests, to oversee that the stipulation, including those pertaining to compensatory plantations are carried out.

(iii) The Nodal Officer should monitor the implementation of the conditions of compensatory afforestation and the survival ratio of the seedings planted.

(iv) In the case of large projects the user agency be asked to establish fuelwood depots, and the fuelwood be provided to construction labour and staff free of cost by user agency or its cost deducted from the salaries and wages to be paid to staff and labour.

(v) In cases of open cast mining, it should be ensured that the mined area is reclaimed as per the approved Environmental Management Plan within the stipulated time-frame. It should be the responsibility of the Nodal Officer and his staff to ensure that all necessary inputs like creation of nursery, storage of top soil for reuse and methodology for its restoration, choice of species etc. are so planned and implemented that the mined area is fully afforested by the time mining operations are completed.

(vi) In all cases the states will submit quarterly reports regarding the implementation of the stipulations laid down by the Government of India while approving the project, and future clearance of projects of the States and Union Territories concerned will depend upon the reporting of the fulfilment of the stipulations.

15. **Projects involving forest as well as non-forest lands:**

In accordance with Section 2 of the Forest (Conservation) Act, 1980 prior approval of the Central Government is required for diversion of forest land for non-forest purposes. Some projects involve use of forest land as well as non-forest land. It has come to the notice of the Government of India that in some projects which involve use of forest as well as non-forest lands, the concerned Government have started work on non-forest lands in anticipation of the approval of the Central Government for release of the forest lands required for the projects. Though provisions of the Forest (Conservation) Act, 1980 may not have been violated by starting of work on forest lands, expenditure incurred on works on non-forest lands may prove to be infructuous in diversion of forest land involved is not approved under the Forest (Conservation) Act, 1980. It has, therefore, been decided that if a project involves forest as well as non-forest land, work should not be started on non-forest land till the approval of the Central Government for release of forest land under the Forest (Conservation) Act has been given.

Yours faithfully,

Dr. M.K. Ranjitsinh

Joint Secretary to the Government of India

ANNEXURE VI

GUIDELINES FOR ENVIRONMENTAL IMPACT ASSESSMENT

1. Since most development activities have an impact on the environment, the procedure for assessing such impact and for ensuring appropriate environment safeguards has been engaging the attention of the Government for some time. While the Government attaches high priority to the formulation and timely execution of development activities consistent with the socio-economic objectives of State Policy, Government also consider it essential that such development does not result in indiscriminate and destructive uses of natural and other resources; nor should it lead to adverse environmental consequences, Government have considered the various guidelines for Environmental Impact Assessment that the Government of India have issued so far in respect of some departmental activities. The State Department of Environment has already consulted several other departments about the scope of these guidelines and the manner in which they could be effectively followed. The government accordingly resolves that the following should henceforth be the procedure for co-ordination between the Departments and Agencies of the State Government in respect of Programmes, Projects and Activities relating to environment.

2. The Programmes, Projects and Activities will mainly be of three categories as follows:

(a) Where no separate Environmental Impact Assessment is called for. An indicative list is furnished in Schedule -1.

(b) Those where a separate Environmental Impact Assessment will have to be made by the Agency or the Department sponsoring the Project and the views of the Environment Department on the assessment made will be obtained and revisions made, as necessary, before the projects are approved of funded. An indicative list is contained in Schedule -II.

(c) Where the Environment Department itself will be associated along with the sectoral department concerned in the formation and finalisation of the programme (Schedule-III).

3. In respect of the activities mentioned in Schedule-I, attention of the Department and Agencies concerned are drawn to the provisions of the Water (Prevention and Control of Pollution) Act, 1974, the Air (Prevention and Control

of Pollution) Act, 1981, the Factories Act, 1948, the Bengal Municipal Act and similar acts containing stipulations and procedures for treatment and discharge of wastes and effluent and emission, for control of dusts and fumes in factories and workshops, for standards of safety, for maintenance of the surrounding areas etc. It will be the responsibility of the Administrative Department concerned to ensure that the activities falling within Schedule -I comply with the various provisions and furnish such periodical reports as may sought by the Environment Department.

4. In regard to activities contained in Schedule II, which require separate Environmental Impact Assessment, some guidelines have been formulated by the Government of India and different Technical Agencies concerned. Such guidelines in respect of power and river projects, extraction of minerals, development of new industries etc. have been circulated to concerned departments by the Environment Department.

5. The Agency or the department sponsoring the activities as indicated in Schedule-II ensure that Environmental Impact Assessment according to guidelines approved by Department of Environment is carried out. The expenditure involved in carrying out which assessment should be charged to the project or activity concerned or provided otherwise by the Sponsoring Agency or the Department. Upon completion of the Assessment, a draft Environmental Impact Assessment Report should be furnished to the Department of Environment for its views which would be incorporated before finalizing the same. The activities/projects should be placed before the Finance Department for funding and sanction only after the E.I.A incorporating views of the Environment Department.

6. In respect of activities identified in Schedule - III, the Department of Environment should be fully associated in the finalization of the plans and programmes.

SCHEDULE - I

INDICATIVE LIST OF SCHEMES AND ACTIVITIES WHICH MAY NOT REQUIRE A SEPARATE ENVIRONMENTAL IMPACT ASSESSMENT

1. **Department of Cottage & Small Scale Industries**
   - Small Scale Industries with an investment of Rs. 25 lakhs or below;
   - Handicrafts, cottage industries etc. provided (a) selection of siting of factories has been approved under the acts in force: (b) appropriate consent has been obtained under the Water (Prevention and Control of Pollution) Act, 1974, the Air (Prevention and Control of Pollution) Act, 1981 and the Bengal Smoke Nuisances Act, 1905.

2. Department of Agriculture/Minor Irrigation

— Minor Irrigation Scheme with command area of less than 2,000 hectares executed by a State agency or approved for execution on the basis of availability of ground water as vertified by State Ground Water Inspectorate.

— Reclamation, Soil Conservation and Drainage Schemes with command area of less than 2,000 hectares.

3. Local Government & Urban Development Department

— Issue of licences for all trading and non-trading activities by the Municipalities, Corporations, Notified Area Authorities and Town Committees under the Bengal Municipal Act, Calcutta Corporation Act etc. subject to conformity with the provision of the Water (Prevention and Control of Pollution) Act, 1974, the Air (Prevention and Control of Pollution) Act, 1981, Bengal Smoke Nuisances Act, 1905.

— Water Supply, Drainage and Sewarage Schemes for population of less than 50,000 subject to provisions of the Water (Prevention and Control of Pollution) Act, 1974.

— Disposal of Solid Wastes in towns of less than 50,000.

4. Public Health Engineering Department

— Water Supply Schemes below Gallons per day subject to the guidelines of the State Ground Water Inspectorate where ground water is the source.

— Sewerage and Drainage Scheme in towns of less than 50,000 population subject to observation of the provisions of the Water (Prevention and Control of Pollution) Act, 1974.

SCHEDULE - II

INDICATIVE LIST OF PROJECTS/ACTIVITIES WHERE A SEPARATE ENVIRONMENTAL IMPACT ASSESSMENT REQUIRED TO BE DONE BY THE AGENCY OR ADMINISTRATIVE DEPARTMENT CONCERNED BEFORE THE PROJECT IS APPROVED OR FUNDED

1. Animal Husbandry & Veterinary Services Department

— Location of cattle settlements dairies and abattoire.

2. Department of Irrigation

— Irrigation, Drainage, Reclamation or multi-purpose, large or medium with a command area of 2,000 hectares or more.

3. **Department of Agriculture**

— Soil Conservation Schemes with a command area of 2,000 hectares or more.

— Introduction of new fertilisers, pesticides and insecticides.

4. **Department of Commerce & Industries/Land Reforms Department**

— New industrial units in the large and medium sectors.

— Extraction of major and minor minerals.

— Production and distribution of natural and other gases.

— Regulation and development of oil fields and mineral oil resources.

5. **Department of Power**

— Thermal and Hydro Electric Power Stations.

— Regulations and procedures for the approval of power generating sets.

6. **Public Works Department**

— Construction of major Public Buildings in areas for which an approved development plan under the West Bengal Town and Country Planning Act is not available.

— Construction of Highways and major bridges.

7. **Housing Department**

— Mechanised brick production units.

— Housing Estates of 100 dwellings or more and land acquisition and development schemes in areas for which approved development plans under the West Bengal Town and Country Planning Act are not available.

— Development of new towns or L.A.D. Scheme of more than 100 hectares.

8. **Home (Transport) Department**

— Inland Waterways Harbours.

— Goods and Passenger Transport Terminals in areas where approved development plans under the West Bengal and Country Planning Act are not available.

9. **Health and Family Welfare Department**

— Location of hospitals, sanatories or nursing homes with more than 50 beds.

— Location of morgues.

— Water Supply Schemes above 2 million gallons per day.

— Sewerage and Drainage Schemes for town with population above 50,000.

10. Department of Education

— Location of new universities.

11. Department of Fisheries

— Government Fish Farms

— Deep sea Fishing Projects.

12. Department of Cottage & Small Scale Industries

— Industrial Estates carrying more than 20 units or employing more than 200 people.

SCHEDULE - III

INDICATIVE LIST OF PROJECTS/ACTIVITIES IN WHICH THE ENVIRONMENT DEPARTMENT IS TO BE ASSOCIATED PRIOR TO APPROVAL

1. Town and Country Planning Branch of Development and Planning Department

— Outline and Development Plans under the Town and Country Planning Act.

— Major changes in land uses in areas for which approved outline and development plans under the T. & C.P. Act are not available.

2. Metropolitan Development Department

— Outline and detailed development plans for the C.M.D. under the T. & C.P. Act.

— Major changes in land uses in areas for which approved outline and development plans under the T. & C.P. Act are not available.

3. Forest Deparment

— Statewide or Regional Afforestation Plans.

— Forest Working Plans.

— Creation or relocation of sanctuaries.

— National Parks and Biosphere Reserves.

4. Land Reforms Department

— Rules and procedures relating to conversion or acquisition of agricultural and into non-agricultural purposes.

— Procedures relating to licensing extraction of major and minor minerals.

5. Fisheries Department

— Rules, procedure, guidelines relating to conversion of agricultural land into fisheries and conversion of fisheries into other purposes.

6. Minor Irrigation Department

— State ground water abstraction/availability plans.

ORDER

Ordered that the resolution be communicated to all Administrative Departments of Government.

Ordered also the resolution be published in the Calcutta Gazette.

By order of the Governor

Secy. to the Govt. of West Bengal

GOVERNMENT OF WEST BENGAL
HOME DEPARTMENT
CONSTITUTION AND ELECTIONS
NOTIFICATION

No. 4897-A.R Calcutta, the 8th December, 1986

In exercise of the power conferred by Clause (3) of Article 166 of the Constitution of India, the Governor is pleased hereby to make the following amendment in the West Bengal Rules of Business, as subsequently (hereinafter referred to as the said rules):

Amendment

In the said rules, under the heading "Part I — Allocation and disposal business", after rule 10, insert the following rule:—

"10A (1) No department shall without the previous consultation with, and without the concurrence of, the Department of Environment, accord administrative approval to any scheme or project other than the schemes or project specifically exempted from such consultation and concurrence by the Department of Environment. Every order according the administrative approval a scheme or project shall indicate the concurrence of the Department of Environment, where necessary.

(2) No proposal for any project of scheme which requires the previous consultation with the Department of Environment under this rule, but in which the Department of Environment has not concurred may be proceeded with unless a decision to that effect has been taken by the Cabinet."

By order of the Governor
Sd/-R.N. Sengupta
Chief Secretary to the Govt. of West Bengal

ANNEXURE VII

GUIDELINES FOR ENVIRONMENTAL APPRAISAL OF INDUSTRIAL PROJECTS

— A. POLICY APPROACH

1. Introduction

1.1 The techniques of Environmental Impact Assessment (EIA) has been evolved in the last decade in the developed countries. Particularly the USA, and have become an essential tool for environmental planning and management. This kind of analysis when built into the economic analysis of the project costs and benefits, help the decision makers to perceive more or less objectively some of the major environmental concerns arising of the project. While such analyses do not always yield precise quantitative optima on all environmental issues, they do focus attention on the major ones and thus help in examining alternative options before choosing an environmentally acceptable course of action.

1.2 Of all development projects, industrial projects have a profound influence on society and environment, both in the positive and negative directions. Industries mean more jobs, generation of goods and services and some observable rise in a standard of living as positive impacts. But they bring in their make the associated ills of environmental pollution, resources depletion overcrowing, health effects, corrosion of structures buildings and monuments, loss of yield of crops and animals including wild life, descreation of forests and often aesthetic plight. EIA procedure can help to anticipate such fallouts of industries and thereby help to decide on alternative technology and resetting. It also makes possible anticipatory pre-planning and implementation of adequate environmental safeguards, especially for pollution abatement and even undertaking simultaneously environmental improvement programmes. Thus EIA is a most efficient and effective aid to planners of industrial development in any country or setting.

1.3 It is to be fully realised that development goals and environmental aspirations have to be reconciled without conflict. It is believed that environmental safeguards built into the development projects at the planning stage and implemented during pre-and-post-execution stages, would reinforce and enhance the benefits derived from the development process. In India, all round development is essential not only for meeting the basic minimum needs of the people but also enhancing the quality of life in the country. However, such development must take place along right lines in consonance and in harmony with the environmental and ecological conditions. For this, it is necessary to conserve and indeed develop natural resources, adopt energy-efficient means of production and reduce, if not avoid, wasteful pollution.

1.4 The task of Environmental Appraisal of all development projects in India is an enormous one for a single agency to attempt. Therefore, it is planned to permit internal environmental assessment by the ministry or agency administratively responsible for the development programme. Such ministers and agencies interfacing with the environment are to have Environment Advisors and cells, functioning under the overall guidance of the Department of Environment. The Department of Environment has to provide guidelines and procedures for such environmental impact assessment, but has to have the right to observe or modify these assessment where necessary or provide a final opinion in critical cases.

1.5 Though easily stated environmental scrutiny of projects is not all that easy or straightforward. The necessary expertise, documented information on the environmental status in the project area, the appropriate methodology for assessment the criteria for decision-making and the institutional infrastructure for according environmental clearance have all to be built from scratch in India. What is to be assessed, when, how and by whom are question that have to be clearly laid down.

2. Environmental Appraisal Procedure

2.1 Environmental Appraisal is the term used in India to differentiate the procedure from the more exacting environmental impact assessment techniques. The method is somewhat more rigorous than the preliminary environmental impact assessment lead for screening in several countries. A two-stage assessment methodology is implied here also. Such development projects which call for a complete and comprehensive environmental impact assessments are screened out by the appraisal for investigation by specially constituted task forces.

2.2 The environmental parameters that are included in the appraisal procedure in the vicinity of industrial or other development projects are listed. For industries the vicinity is arbitrarily taken as the encompassed by a 20 kms. radius circle. The parameters include both physical features, population characteristics, ecological status and socio-economic consideration. Some of the items are quantifiable, but some obviously, can be answered in descriptive terms only.

2.3 It is the intention in fact the practice, to require the project proponent to submit the environmental information at the earliest stage in the planning of the project. The detailed project feasibility reports for power generation projects invariably include an environment section, though the information included is often far from adequate for environmental clearance. As a result, the appropriate Environment Appraisal Committee has to arrange for collecting relevant information by sending a special team to the project site, or otherwise help the project proponent to collect the necessary information and data.

2.4 It is obvious that projects like mining hydroelectricity dams, harbours etc. are site-specific, giving in almost all cases no choice of site. On the other hand, industrial projects and thermal power stations are not site-specific, at least theoretically. However coal-based thermal power projects are being built. Industries are also not always site-independent, considering their infrastructural needs for power, water, raw materials, land skilled of labour, waste disposal sites, and proximity to market. The Government of India has adopted an Industrial Policy Resolution three years ago, with the view to dispersing industries to backward and undeveloped areas decisions, large industries are not to be located in or near metropolitan cities; industries sited in backward areas receive several kinds of financial and other incentives and concessions, like relief from excise duty, raw material allocation, import facility etc. Industrial siting, especially when it concerns large public sector and other non-economic and non-environmental considerations. Environmental considerations have only began to be taken into account in site selection. Subsequent to the controversy about the location of the refinery at Mathura and gas-based fertilizer plants near Bombay, this sector invariably includes environmental pollution specialists in their site-selection teams. The culture it is expected would spread to other industrial sectors. However, it has been made amply clear that association of environmental specialists in the site-selection process would not exempt the project from the environmental appraisal process.

2.5 The Environmental Appraisal Committee (EAC) invariably include environmental and ecology specialists, to ecology experts, representatives of the sponsoring ministry or agency, State Government representatives, and officers of the Department of Environment. In addition, they include one or more public men with a commitment to the cause of environment. For example, the Industrial Environmental Appraisal Committee is composed of a reputed, retired environmental scientist as Chairman, Director of Department, Director of National Environmental Engineering Research Institute (NEERI) or his nominee, the Chairman of the Central Board for the Prevention and Control of Water Pollution or his nominee, representative of the India Meteoriological Department, representatives of the State Government where the industry is proposed to be located who could be from the industries department and pollution control authority, an ecologist, a physical planning expert and a public man, with an officer of department as member secretary. The EAC may induct other specialists as necessary. The EAC is charged with the responsibility of scrutinizing the project from the environmental angle and recommend one of the following course of actions:

(a) rejection of the project on substantive environmental grounds;

(b) relocation of the project on substantive environmental grounds;

(c) according environmental clearance to the project without any attached conditions;

(d) according environmental clearance subject to the incorporation of the specific and/or general environmental safeguards; or

(e) deferring clearance till a comprehensive environmental impact assessment is made.

The EAC may call for additional data on process details, environmental status of the project site or other relevant information from the proponent hold discussions with the project authorities, make site visits or order specific studies to be carried out.

2.6 Separate environmental questionnaries are to be filled for different site for the same project. Each site is considered on its environmental merits by the EAC. Very often, the EAC is asked to choose from several sites for an industrial projects. The EAC however, restricts its role to the best choice available on environmental grounds and does its role to the best choice does not include in site hunting. Sometimes it raids sites in some order of preference from the environmental point of view, for obviously no site offered can be ideal from all environmental considerations. The recommentations of the EAC in regard to site selections and environmental safeguards are at best advice rendered for environmental management and are not clearly obligatory conditions for setting up the industry. However, such advice is more often not needed by the administrative ministry.

2.7 Once environmental clearance is accorded with attached conditions the monitoring of the implementation of the environmental safeguards is now left to the administrative ministry, though EAC may require periodical reports to be submitted to it. This aspect does require further strengthening for a number of reasons. For example, there may be a subsequent change in the process technology, which if major would require reassessment of environmental safeguards or in the final site for the plant. Further, the administrative ministry is not always fully geared to perform this task of monitoring, at least at present. It is obvious that for the success of the environmental arrangement of industrial projects, strict vigilance on the implemention of the environment protection measures at every stage of the execution of the project and thereafter during the operational stage is essential. Unless this is ensured, the environmental appraisal excise may become only a farse.

2.8 However, in respect of liquid effluents from industry, there is at present a final check from the State Water Pollution Control Board, whose 'consent' is to be obtained before discharge are allowed into the environment. This has also become operative for air emissions now that the Air Pollution Control Act is enacted.

3. Limitations of the Environmental Appraisal Procedure

3.1 The environmental appraisal procedure is a limited approach to incorporate environmental considerations in industrial project planning, as would have become apparent from the previous section. For one thing the EAC is dependent on the proponent to provide the information of environmental relevance. Such information is not always readily available, for example, factual data on flora and fauna or on specific ecological impacts. Another constraint is with regard to the time available for environmental analysis. Obviously, environmental appraisal should not be a time consuming of delaying exercise, lest development is impeded; this would make environmental appraisal a self-defeating procedural exercise. However, the most important defect at present in the matter of environmental appraisal of industrial projects is in regard to objective criteria for deciding, whether the project needs a detailed EIA, criteria for waiving EIA, criteria on standards of environmental quality which have to be achieved and so on.

3.2 Other issues and biases are concerned with the subjectiveness of impact identification the need to include an inter-disciplinary appraisal team with varying or conflicting interests and value judgments, inability to quantify several components of environmental imapcts like human suffering, cultural and social value deterioration foreclosing of options by wrong assessments and so on. These are of course common and recognised constraints for all types of EIA methodologies at present and only further experience and research can lead to their resolution.

3.3 We have very special problem, due to its vastness and variety, climate, culture and customs are greatly diversified and as a consequence, lifestyles, agricultural practices, nature of terrain, agroclimate, domesticated animals, flora, fauna wild life-hydrological regime, all very considerably in different parts of the country. No reliable environmental information base for the entire country is existent. Such data base and environmental statistics has to be quickly built up if we are to undertake comprehensive EIA's and make ecologically sound decisions. The department is proposing to take steps to fill this void.

3.4 In a similar fashion, expertise for EIA is also very limited. Inter-disciplinary teams have to be trained and given necessary experience quickly for meeting the requirements of EIA in the future. International cooperation in this effort to train EIA experts would be most welcome. The Department plans to organise a National Training Seminar on EIA in order to sensitise decision makers in industries departments of Governments. Industrial Development Corporations, private sector undertaking, consultants for industrial projects and industry or manufacturer's associations.

3.5 The political and public acceptance to impact assessment is the next hierarchical level of concern. Public acceptance can often be extremely prejudiced from fear of adverse impacts and from aspirations for development equally. Public hearing for resolving the environmental issues of a development project is not resorted to in India. Public involvement is, of course, desirable in environmental matters, provided the public is an informed one. More often than not under the existing situation in India, the environmental budget is taken up by a few sensitive groups and invariably leads to a confrontation. This is to be avoided at any cost. A well prepared objective EIA can and should be the means and basis for resolving such confrontations.

3.6 There is a subtle interface of technological, social, economic, political and ecological facets implied in environmental impact assessments. These interfaces unfortunately are in a constant ever-changing dynamical flux, and makes the laying down of boundary conditions and criteria a task fraught with complications. This is bound to continue for some time in a developing country, till at least a level of development has been achieved, when environmental aspirations begin to transcend urgent development needs.

4. Suggestions and Recommendations

4.1 Inconsistencies in government policies relating to economic development planning and environmental goals, such as energy needs and air pollutions or ecological security, industrial decentralization and pollution containment, irrigation requirements, and land conservation, forest-based industry and forest management etc. have to be resolved at the earliest throught inter-departmental consultations.

4.2 Preliminary environmental appraisal should be mandatory for all development projects. A more comprehensive EIA should be invariably be carried out for all industrial projects falling in the following categories:

(a) Where investment exceeds Rs. 10 million;

(b) Producing or handling materials of hazardous nature:

(c) Located in sensitive areas such as highly industrialized or urbanized areas, areas having cultural, historical, aesthetic or tourist importance or near Biosphere Reserves, Sanctuaries, National Parks.

4.3 Professional expertise for EIA has to be created, special training programmes for "Environment Managers" have to be started. Environment Managers are ultimately needed at various levels, from the industrial site for dealing with day to day problems to the decision-making levels. They have to be broad-based enough in their knowledge and aptitude to deal with most environmental problems. Preferably environmental managers should be rooted in the technology concerned and trained in environmental management subsequently.

4.4 Environmental data-base information systems are essential for implementing the EIA procedure adequately and efficiently. A national environmental information system with suitable regional network is to be established.

4.5 The following steps in environmental impact assessment are suggested for adoption.

(a) Project description—constituent activities from land acquisition to development to operational aspects and alternatives.

(b) Site description—present socio-economic and environmental status and site requirements for project implementation.

(c) Enumeration of impact—physical, chemical, health, ecology, socio-economic, both adverse and beneficial.

(d) Evaluation of impacts in quantitative or qualitative terms.

(e) Aggregation of impacts on environmental components (land, water, air forest, flora, fauna, settlements, health, etc).

(f) Forecast short and long-term environmental changes—identification or modifications and safeguards to protect the environment, including resting and process alternatives.

(g) Recommendation of alternatives, environmental safeguards, monitoring process for feedstock on compliance and performance in the operational phase.

(h) Review and assessment in the post-completion phase.

5. Conclusion

5.1 The purpose of environmental impact assessment is to determine as precisely as possible within the present constraints of knowledge and expertise, the likely environmental impacts of a planned industrial development activity. It is desirable that this exercise is undertaken early enough in the planning stage so that adequate and appropriate prevention measures can be incorporated into the project at least cost. EIA would help understand the physical and ecological effects on social, cultural and aesthetic concerns, if it involves multidisciplinary expertise in identifying critically evaluating and interpreting the potential impacts. EIA can help in identifying alternatives to siting, technology or to plan and incorporate the required measures for ensuring protection of the environment to the extent possible.

B. PROCEDURES

1. Stages at which EIA is required to be carried out and reviewed are:

(a) Strategic Planning	Preliminary assessment
(b) Feasibility Studies	Full EIA, if necessary
(c) Design & Construction	Incorporation of EIA recommendations
(d) Project Operation	Implementation of recommendations and Monitoring performance.

2. Control actions should be possible

(a) Stop development as proposed at the site chosen

(b) Regulate manufacturing processes, size of project

(c) Restrict capacity or period when plant can be operated

(d) Specify or exclude transport routes and methods for movement of raw materials or finished products

(e) Enforce waste treatment—disposal requirements specify plants to be installed and standards to be achieved

(f) Recommend specific precautionary measures during construction phase

3. Project brief should include

(a) Name of developer

(b) List of products and annual capacity

(c) Type of processes, including methods of waste treatment

(d) Options for siting and reasons for choosing them. Any special constraints/advantages

(e) Timing of construction and initial operation. Expected life of project

(f) Sources, quantities of raw materials and supplies methods of transport

(g) Possible new infrastructure requirements (power, water supply, housing, transport, labour etc).

(h) Expected employment opportunities.

4. Preliminary Stages for EIA

Developer Submits Project Brief

Review if data are adequate for screening

No — Request further data from developer

Yes — Developer Submits Preliminary EIA

Preliminary Environmental Assessment

Apply Screening Tests

No further study required

Communicate decision recommendation

Decide terms of reference and study team for full EIA

Call for full EIA

Review full EIA

Communicate decision

5. Screening Test — Examples

(a) Are there potential physical or health hazards associated with the project?

(b) Will existing community/society be significantly disturbed ?

(c) Is there potential conflict with other economic interests ? (Eg. Agriculture/forestry/fisheries)

(d) What is size of new employment opportunities compared to existing level ?

(e) Will major development of infrastructure be needed ?

(f) What would be the increased demand on social and community services? How will it be met ?

(g) Is the location suitable for industrial siting ?

6. Public Communication

As far as is possible EIS should be published and public reaction invited. During the EIA, the study team should endeavour to seek the views of the community near the site and gauge public opinion about the proposed project. A system to establish a channel of communication with public bodies and other concerned interests should be evolved.

7. DOEn's functions include

(a) Assist the conduct of preliminary environmental assessments and recommend further steps;

(b) Call for additional data/information from developer;

(c) Decide on terms of reference for full EIA, composition of study team, scope of EIA and time frame for completion;

(d) Ensure compliance of full EIA with specified terms of reference review and seek clarifications;

(e) Receive completed full EIA, with additional supporting documents, review and recommend measures;

(f) Maintain records of completed EIA's and such other data/information relevant to environmental studies;

(g) Serve as a forum for exchange of information on environmental matters, baseline data, environmental regulations pollution abatement technology etc. for industrial developers.

8. Full Assessment of Environmental Impacts

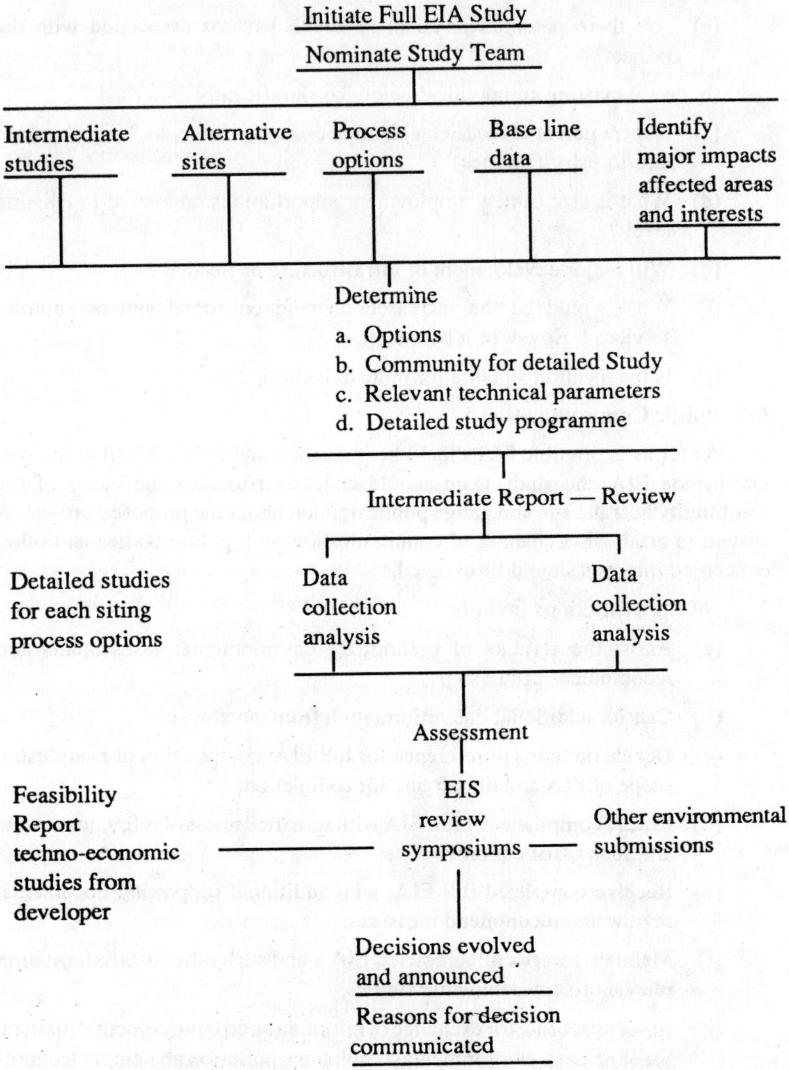

B. Population shifts population structure
Housing demand
Educational facilities
Medical facilities

C. Wage structure
Income distribution
Entrepreneurial opportunity
Commercial services
Local resource development

D. Land use effects
Agricultural crops.
Farm livestock
Transport services
Property values

E. Air quality
River/Surface water quality
Ground water quality
Coastal effects
Gaseous effects
Gaseous emissions
Effluent loads
Solid waste disposal

F. Effects on fauna
Effects on flora
Recreational resources
Noise and vibration
Visual amenity.

9. Study Team

The following areas must be included in all study team other specialised areas, such as forestry, archaeology etc. may be added as necessary—

— Process

— Pollution Control Specialist

— Toxicologist—Health Specialist

— Ecologist

— Natural Resource Specialist

— Socio-economics Specialist.

10. Criteria and Parameters

Major headings are—

(a) Health and safety or population on the area

(b) Ecological concerns (flora, fauna, soil, etc.)

(c) Employment

(d) Economic effects

(e) Cultural effects

(f) Aesthetic concerns.

These are not mutually exclusive. Several parameters fall into several criteria. A toxic pollutant may also stink badly and affect (a), (b) and (f) criteria.

11. Checklist

Checklists are useful tools for quick review and reminders on items likely to be overlooked.

Environmental Checklist for Industrial Projects — An Example

A. Employment opportunities
Diversity of employment
Development of skills
Technical training opportunities
Technology transfer

12. Environmental Impact and Social Cost-Benefit Analysis is a useful tool for decision-making

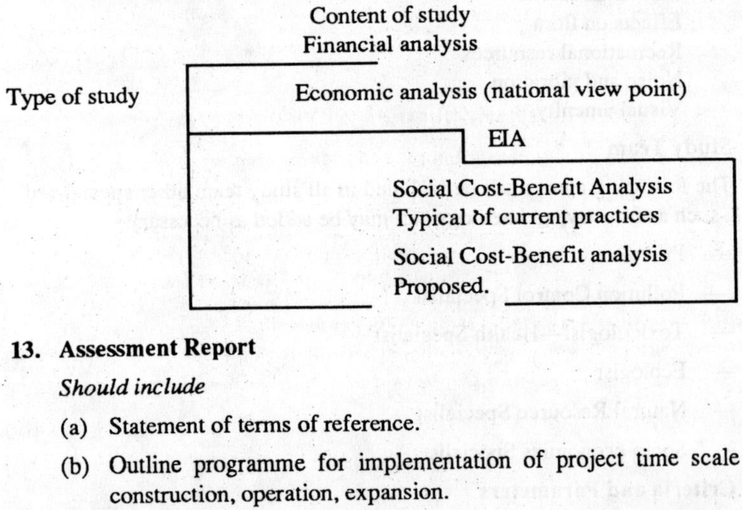

13. Assessment Report

Should include

(a) Statement of terms of reference.

(b) Outline programme for implementation of project time scale for construction, operation, expansion.

(c) Outline description of industrial process, flow charts, potential pollution sources, type & magnitude.

(d) Listing of pollution abatement technology, estimates of costs — competitiveness of plant with various procedures.

(e) Definitions of environmental assessment criteria and parameters. Express impact in terms of effect upon potential use of environmental resources.

(f) History of alternative sites — Preferred options.

(g) Results of baseline studies for each sites.

(h) Description of environmental effects of projects at each site.

(i) Comparison of sites for ability to assimilate environmental impacts.

(j) Groups environmental resources affected.

14. Guide to Assessment Procedure for Proposed Development

Step	Procedure
Preliminary Assessment	1. Identify Problems and specify alternatives — State Problems and requirements. — Nature and extent of each alternative. 2. Assemble available data — Collect data relevant to each site/process/operation alternative. — Reference to national/international lists of priority chemicals. 3. Assessed Staff Competence — In-house sufficiency of external experts.
	4. Initial Impact Assessment — Review sites/processes in relation to available environmental data. 5. Preliminary Assessment — Apply screening tests — are there potential impacts of significance caused by project. —/O — No further Assessment MES — Proceed to full EIA 6. Preparation and Execution of detailed baselines and process studies — Define terms of reference, appoint study team of appropriate specialists. — Data collection and analysis. 7. Identification/Confirmation of Environment Impacts — On existing environment — Consideration of constraints during construction and operational phases.

8. Impact Assessment
    — Assessment of Impacts of project activities in term of exposure, reversibility, directness and cumulative and synergistic effects.
    — Corrective measures — Environmental safeguards to minimise impacts.
9. Summary and Presentation of
    — Summary sheet.
    — Provisions of follow up and monitoring.

15. Accidents/Hazards

Potential for accidents/hazards should be reviewed from comparable previous experience.

16. Waste Disposal/Control

Should be fully detailed with costs (capital and operating), back up systems in case of future, performance criteria, standards achieved — Waste recovery/recycling schemes.

17. Monitoring

Environmental monitoring/management improvement schemes should be detailed.

18. Impact Assessment Methodologies

— Practical—relevant to problem under consideration and ability to implement

— Accurate—ability to portray objectively all impacts

— Repeatable — ability to be used by different teams repeatably

— Feasible—reasonableness of demand for time and facilities

— Comprehensible—ability to be understood by persons of different backgrounds and view points.

19. Evaluation

In terms of —

— exposure (extent, intensity, duration)

— Nature of the effect

— Directness (primary/secondary)

— Accumulative of additive effects.

20. Assessment of Socio-Economics Impacts

A. *Direct Impacts—An Example*

INPUT

Labour required Skills/numbers

Compare with

Existing labour Employed/ Unemployed skilled/ Unskilled etc.

Assess Impact in terms of in migration, retraining transfer from existing in job etc.

Proposed development

OUTPUT

Income generation

General demand for local goods & services

Compare with

Existing characteristics of local economy

Assess Impact on local economy

B. Indirect Impact—An Example

Requirement for well drained land

Loss of shelfish yields increased stress in existing in shore fishing

Assess in socio-economics terms

Proposed development

Flouride Emissions

Reduced agricultural productivity — loss of farmers income

Assess in soco-economic terms

ANNEXURE VIII

GUIDELINES FOR INTEGRATING ENVIRONMENTAL CONCERNS WITH EXPLOITATION OF MINERAL RESOURCES

Introduction

These guidelines attempt to identify some of the vital aspects relevant to environmental protection in context of mineral exploitation. Accordingly, they include the problems related to: (i) water pollution; (ii) solid waste management; (iii) land degradation; (iv) air pollution; (v) noises & vibration; (vi) subsidences & landslides; (vii) human settlements; (viii) impact of mining on the water regime.

These guidelines highlight the salient aspects of the various problems and briefly indicate some of the steps that need to be incorporated during the planning phase and various stages of the mining operations. The need for evolving certain tolerance standards/limits by the appropriate agencies, has also been emphasised. It is hoped that these guidelines will not only be of practical use to the Government and mining industry but also help in creating an awareness of the essentiality of incorporating environmental protection measures in the mining sector in our country.

These guidelines cover mining and mineral beneficiation operations on land only and do not apply to exploitation of minerals in the oceanic region or oil exploration and drilling.

1.0 Water Pollution

1.1 *Liquid effluents*

1.1.1 The major sources of liquid effluents include:

(a) Mine water pumped out during drainage operations;

(b) Spent water from handling plants, dust extraction and dust suppression systems;

(c) Effluents from preparation and beneficiation plants;

(d) Leacheates/washoffs from waste/trailings dumps.

1.2 Efforts should be made to preclude or reduce the discharge of toxic and objectionable effluents into Surface water bodies, ground water aquifers or usable lands to a minimum. Wherever possible, reuse of waste water should be practised.

1.3 Effluents should be treated to conform to the standards laid down by the Central & State Boards for Prevention and Control of Water Pollution before discharge. Parameters to be covered by environmental quality standards for liquid effluents have been listed in Schedule-I.

1.4 While laying down environmental quality standards for liquid effluents, due consideration to local conditions should be given with a view to possible reuse.

1.5 The Central Board for the Prevention and Control of Water Pollution should prepare guidelines for treatment of liquid effluents for different mineral industries on the basis of problems specific to the particular industry, characteristics of effluents, ambient soil and water quality and other relevant factors.

1.6 Wherever practicable, the mine water should be utilised for irrigation of the plantations raised to stabilize the mine waste dumps.

1.7 *Acid mine drainage*

1.7.1 Acid mine drainage is produced wherever a mine of any type in permeable formations interacts with the water table, aquifer, perched water body, or where surface water finds its way into a mine in terrains where sulphides (particularly pyrites) are present in the ore or country rock.

1.7.2. Among objectionable features of acid mine drainage are low pH and high levels of sulphates, iron and total dissolved solids. These deplete oxygen level in water, increase toxicity by rendering heavy metals soluable and create corrosion problems.

1.7.3 The following classification of mine drainage has been formulated by the USEPA:

Parameter	Class 1 Acid Drainage	Class 2 Partially Oxidised and/or neutralised	Class 3 Oxidised and neutralised and/or alkaline	Class 4 Neutralised and not oxidised
pH	2-4.5	3.5-6.6	6.5-8.5	6.5-8.5
Acidity (mg/litre $CaCo_3$)	1000-15000	0-1000	0	0
Ferrous iron (mg/litre)	500-1000	0-500	0	50-1000
Ferric iron (mg/litre)	0	0-1000	0	0
Aluminium (mg/litre)	0-2000	0-20	0	0
Sulphate (mg/litre)	1000-20000	500-10000	500-10000	500-10000

It is suggested that the above classification along with similar classifications from other sources may be reviewed in order to adopt an appropriate classification for Indian conditions.

1.7.4 Available techniques, as categorised hereunder, should be used to control acid mine drainage, according to the prevalent situation:

(i) To prevent the formation of acid mine drainage at source. The techniques include modified mining methods; sealing of mine of part after closure; surface reclamation; water diversion; and control of groundwater flow system by well fields or other methods to prevent the exposure of groundwater to sulphides in a mine coating sources with gels.

(ii) To control the acid mine drainage, the techniques include deep well injection, subsurface dams and grout curtains.

(iii) To dilute acid mine drainage to an acceptable effluent quality.

(iv) To employ standard waste water treatment methods for neutralisation and removal of dissolved solids. The techniques include lime or limestone treatment accompanied by aeration or oxidation process to convert ferrous iron to ferric iron; neutralisation with soda ash, caustic soda and anhydrous ammonia; reverse osmosis; ion exchange; electrodialysis; evaporation; ozone oxidation; desulfating; sulfide iron removal; microbiological control; and permanent iron removal.

2.0 Solid Waste Management

2.1 *Overburden and mine waste disposal*

2.1.1 The following factors are of crucial importance in selecting a site for disposal of overburden and mines wastes:

(i) Proper area for disposal should be identified at the planning stage:

(ii) The sites should always be located on a secure and impervious base (solid rock if possible)

(iii) Their location and building up should ensure minimum leaching effects due to natural precipitation.

(iv) The sites should be as far away as possible from natural water courses, shallow aquifers etc. Where this is not feasible; uncontaminated fresh water streams etc., should be diverted from such waste storage areas.

(v) Wastes with abnormally high concentrations of iron sulphides or other undesirable reactive elements should be disposed off in sanitary landfills.

(vi) Such dumps and piles must not be permitted to become a major visual feature of the local landscape. The height of the dump should preferably not exceed the mature tree top level in the area. The type and characteristics of the waste rock is also important in determining the height of the dump. Low height dumping of pyritical material minimises oxidation and leaching. While low height coal dumps reduce the risk of spontaneous combustion.

2.1.2 The various techniques for waste disposal include:

(i) Utilization of the overburden and mine waste by back filling to help in reclamation, restoration and rehabilitation of the terrain, without affecting the drainage and water regimes.

(ii) Dumping the overburden and wastes in available low lying areas accompanied by levelling and providing soil cover to utilise the land profitably.

(iii) If considered suitable, the wastes may be used as road metal of construction aggregates, after crushing to proper size.

(iv) The dump must be properly graded and terraced with contour drainage as necessary.

(v) Terracing of dumps must be accompanied by stabilisation of the slopes and terraces using proper vegetation.

2.2 *Tailings disposal*

The following general principles should be followed for disposal of tailings:

2.2.1 Mine/Mill waste water should be recycled to the maximum practicable extent.

2.2.2 Wherever practicable, land disposal of tailings should be adopted in preference to disposal into surface waters.

2.2.3 Devegetation of tailings disposal areas should be phased to synchronise with the disposal schedule.

2.2.4 Tailing area decant ponds must be adequately deep to provide a quiscent settling zone for the particles. Wind and wave action would prevent settling if the pond is too shallow.

2.2.5 The water in a decant pond should not come into direct contact with the tailings dam. In such an eventuality, the water depth should be minimal with protection against wave action provided.

2.2.6 Tailing dams should be designed to provide for storm water runoff.

2.2.7 Decant tunnels (within a tailing mass) should be kept as short as possible.

2.2.8 Wherever practicable, tailings, should be used for filling in the mine workings.

2.2.9 The important methods available for tailings disposal are:

(i) disposal in deep water;

(ii) land water disposal; and

(iii) dry land disposal.

2.2.9.1 *Deep water tailings disposal* involves the direct discharge of tailings, at depth into a relatively large body of water. In India, general non-availability of large natural lakes of reservoirs in mining belts preclude the use of this method. However, in the case of mining operations near the sea coast, tailings may be discharged into the sea after ensuring that the discharge point is sufficiently deep and the quality of effluents is within the limits of tolerance of equatic life/planktons.

2.2.9.2 *Land water tailings disposal* uses the principles of tailings disposal into shallow waters. Usually a dam is built across a lake, stream or the mouth of a Bay with the impounded area upstream on the dam utilised for disposal. With the accumulation of tailings, this area is converted to dry or relatively dry land. As far as possible tailings disposal in rich forests, sanctuaries, and reservoir catchments should be avoided. The hills slopes in the foreshores and catchments of the tailing dams require dense afforestations, with contour trenching above the high flood level, to preclude the discharge of monsoon water into the tailing reservoir and agitation of the tailings. The borrow areas around the tailings dams also need to be revegetated. The following restrictive measures are necessary for the use of such disposal sites:

(i) Tailings with significant quantities of releasable substances, such as ammonia arsenic, asbestos (Chrysolite and/or amphibole), cadmium, copper cyanide, lead, mercury, nickel, zinc, radioactive material, and toxic compounds and substances, that tend to bio-accumulate and are harmful to all forms of life and flora may be disposed only if the dam is impervious and the decant serving the tailings area is directed to a 'downstream' facility (preferably on land) for any required chemical and or physical treatment;

(ii) Tailings containing slime fractions should not be deposited in land-water sites without provisions for effective desliming;

(iii) The tailings area should be revegetated before being abandoned.

2.2.9.3 *In dry land disposal method*, the tailings are disposed in a tailing pond constructed in a low area unconnected with the natural drainage system of the area. After deposition of the tailings, the water decants off by means of suitable provisions for the purpose and the area remains dry. For such a disposal system, the following measures should be adopted.

(i) Adequate provision should be provided for drainage of water discharged with the tailings to decantation wells or other systems;

(ii) A site having the least permeability should be chosen to preclude contamination of groundwater;

(iii) In case the area is surrounded by hills, the site should have a minimum storm water catchment area. However, proper arrangements for the storm water drainage should also be provided;

(iv) Peripheral plantations should be raised as wind belts to minimise the dry tailings being airborne. Once a tailings dam is abandoned it should be revegetated with suitable species to bring it into harmony with the environment.

2.2.10 *Tailing dams*

2.2.10.1 *Considerations for selections of sites*

(i) A site underlain by maximum available thickness of unsaturated material (deep water table) should be selected;

(ii) A site underlaine by material with lowest permeability should be chosen;

(iii) The site should not be underlain by shallow unconfined aquifers;

(iv) Sites adjacent to streams, where the contaminated seepage or leacheate and groundwater may discharge into them, must not be selected;

(v) If such locations are not available, the designs should provide for minimum seepage. Out off zones beneath dams, impermeable lines and segregation of mill tailings are important design parameters to ensure this.

2.2.10.2 Tailings dams for landwater disposal should be constructed to their final weights before mailing commences; all downstream slopes of tailing dams should be vegetated as quickly as possible.

2.2.10.3 The use of classified mill tailings for the construction of perimeter (external) tailing dams should be avoided to the extent practicable.

2.2.10.4 Tailing dams should be impervious so as not to allow to leakage of contaminated fluids. Seepage should be tested and appropriately treated.

2.2.10.5 Tailings areas, tailing ams, waste rock dumps and mill sites etc. should be revegetated.

3.0 Land Use Planning

Land use plans for the mining areas must be prepared along with the project report for exploitation of a particular mineral deposit in the area. Even in case the existing mines, the mining agencies shall prepare the land use plans for their lease areas. Such a land use plan is aimed to achieve the minimisation of adverse environmental impacts, and also the economic and effective rehabilitation of the closed mine site to a productive after use (restoration or enhancement of land surface values).

3.1 The land use plan should be prepared to encompass preoperational, operational and post-operational phases of a mine. It should clearly indicate the planned post-operational land use for the area, with details of the measure required to achieve survey the intended purpose. The preparation of land use plan should be based on general survey and collection of relevant information during which the main features of the plan may emerge, followed by detailed planning.

3.1.1 The general survey must take into account not only the broad feature of the actual proposed mining operations, but also the surrounding terrain conditions. The most important components on such a survey include:

(i) Present land use pattern in the area:

(ii) Main features of the human settlements in the area:

(iii) Characteristics of local eco-system:

(iv) Climate in the area:

(v) Relevant terrain information that will help in waste dumping, tailings disposal, etc. with least effects on the local land water system. For this, exploration should interalia, include:

(a) Geomorphological analysis (topography and draomage)

(b) Geological analysis (structural features: including lineaments, fractures, faults, joints etc.)

(c) Hydrogeological analysis (disposition of permeable formations, surface, ground water links, hydraulic parameter determination, etc.):

(d) Analysis of the natural soil and water to assess pollutant absorption capacity:

(e) Availability and distribution of top soil:

(vi) Communications and transport:

(vii) Details concerning the mining plans:

(a) Minerals to be worked;

(b) Method of working

(c) Details of fixed plants;

(d) Nature and quantity of wastes and disposal facilities required for them;

(e) Possibilities subsidence and landslides;

(f) Transportation facilities needed;

(g) Services to be installed.

3.1.2 An action plan for minimizing adverse environmental impacts from the proposed mining activity should be prepared. This shall also include rehabilitation of the mining area. The important aspects to be taken into consideration during various phases are as below:

3.1.2.1 *Pre-operational phase*

(i) Vegetational barriers shall be raised along the contours in the hilly areas for the prevention of soil erosion and for arresting mine wash.

(ii) Steps should be taken to construct check dams, either of rubble or brush wood, across small gullies and streams on the ore body to contain soil wash. These check dams shall be stabilized by vegetation.

(iii) The banks of streams in the mining area should be intensively vegetated to prevent the discharge of sediments into the streams.

3.1.2.2 *Operational phase*

(i) For open working, screens or banks of soil and overburden shall be constructed in the peripheral zone.

(ii) Vegetation barriers shall also be constructed along the periphery of a mining areas on either side of mines/service roads and between other locations. The various advantages of these tree/soil screens include top soil preservation, lessening of adverse visual impact, noise-baffling, dust absorption etc.

(iii) Clearance of vegetation should be restricted to the minimum necessary for mining operations and planned in advance.

(iv) Backfilling should synchronise with mining operations as far as practicable.

3.1.2.3 *Post-operational phase*

Once the mining operations are over, the land should be rehabilitated for productive uses like agriculture, foresty, pasturage, pisciculture recreation, setting up of wild life habitats/sancturies, etc.

4.0 Air Pollution

Air pollution is defined as the presence in the atmosphere of substances or radiations which adversely affect living organisms or their habitats.

4.1 *Pollution due to mining and mineral beneficiation activities:*

4.1.1 *Pollution due to mining:*

Air pollution caused by mining and associated activities can be classified into the following categories:

(i) Gaseous pollutants (Sulphur dioxide, Nitrogen oxides, Carbon monoxide and Hydrocarbons etc.);

(ii) Suspended Particulate Matter (Selica, Fluorides, Asbestos and Metallic Mineral Fumes).

4.1.2 *Pollution due to mineral beneficiation:*

4.1.2.1 Soft cake making, prevalent in the coalfields, is a major source of pollution of localised areas.

4.1.2.2 Guidelines for control of emissions of flume gases from beehive coke oven plants or regular coke even plants and processing plants within acceptable limits should be drawn up.

4.2 *Prevention and control of suspended particulate matter:*

4.2.1 Transportation of minerals from mines to plant and ports is the main source of dust. To prevent dust from being air borne, transport equipment (trucks and railway wagons etc.) should be leak proof and properly covered. Alternatively, suitable chemicals may be sprayed on the top to prevent such effects.

4.2.2 Adequate dust suppression and extraction facilities must be provided at the coal/ore handling plants, crushing and screening units.

4.2.3 The haul roads in the opencast mines/quarries need to be adequately water sprayed.

4.2.4 Roadside plantation of dense belts of trees serves as dust arresters (one hectare of trees can arrest 30-50 tonnes of dust).

4.2.5 To minimise dust pollution, measures such as adoption of hoods at transfer points, proper design of chutes, vulcanising of conveyor belt joints, under belt cleaning devices apart from installation of dust suppression and/or dust extraction system for conveyors should be introduced.

4.2.6 In the case of surface mines and allied operational units, dust concentration standards should be specified.

5.0 Noise and Vibration Problems

5.1 *Source*

Several mining and mineral processing activities generate abnoxious levels of noise and vibrations. In underground mines these constitute occupational health problems. In above ground operations, these may also cause noise pollution in neighbouring communities and damage to structures in the vicinity. Blasting, drilling, underground mining equipment and ventilation fans are sources of noise and vibration underground. Heavy earth moving machinery, drills, dumpers, material handling, crushing and cleaning equipment are prominent sources above ground. In benefication plants noise and vibration are primarily occupational health problems.

5.2 Ambient noise level limits during day and night time should be specified. These ambient noise level limits could be specified in the following format.

	Ambient noise level limits in B	
Zone Characterisation*	Day/Evening (6 a.m. to 10 p.m.)	Night (10 p.m. to 6 a.m.)
Underground mine		
Opencast mine premises		
Material handling and loading point		
Mineral preparation/benefication plant		
Predominantly residential zones		
Hospital areas		

*(Illustrative: not exhaustive)

5.3 *Noise abatement and control*

5.3.1 Noise is best abated at source by choosing machinery and equipment suitably, by proper mounting of equipment and ventilation systems and by providing noise insulating enclosures or padding where practicable.

5.3.2 Residential colonies and township should be located reasonable away from the mining premises.

5.3.3 Boundary walls (baffle walls), waste banks and dense belt of tree should be erected to act as acoustic barriers. A 50 m. wide belt of trees of different heights is specially useful to act as a noise absorbant in the mining areas.

5.3.4 In existing mines it is suggested that a noise survey should be conducted by an expert to identify sources of excessive noise and to design and implement appropriate control measures.

5.3.5 In new mines anticipatory measures for noise reduction should be incorporated at the planning stage in consultation with an expert.

5.4 *Vibration abatement*

5.4.1 Ground vibrations are caused by blasting operations, subsidence due to mining operations, deployment of mobile equipment, rock, bursts and rock bumps. Blasting also generates air vibration waves (airblasts). Vibration may cause structural damages, which depend upon the periodical acceleration due to vibration. Air blasts can damage structurally unsound buildings and cause window glass failure. Vibration can also be a cause of annoyance to human beings.

5.4.2 Control of ground movement due to vibration can be achieved by avoiding over-charing, use of delays and improved blasting technology. Due regard must be paid to vibration transmission properties of geological formations and terrain stability (tectonism, seismicity etc.)

5.4.3 Buildings likely to be affected due to vibrations should be identified and protected by trenching or other appropriate measures to minimise vibration effects.

5.4.4 Vibrations due to mobile plants and equipment can be minimised by modernisation and proper maintenance.

5.4.5 Norms for permissible limits of vibration for various zones should be prescribed.

6.0 Subsidence Problems

6.1 Surface subsidence causes extensive degradation of the natural environment and damages to man-made structures. It affects the groundwater regime, surface drainage pattern and usable land. Highways, buildings, bridges, water and gas mains may also be sheared, twisted or broken by strains and slope changes.

The environmental significance of subsidence is related to three main factors:

(i) surface area affected;

(ii) nature of the land in the affected areas; and

(iii) the type and magnitude of ground movement.

6.2 The alleviation of subsidence damage can be undertaken either by precautionary measures on surface to protect installations, or by appropriate modification of the mining methods so as to minimise deformation of the surface.

6.2.1 The following structural precautions should be taken into consideration while designing new structures in mining areas:

(i) The site should be away from areas of natural geological discontinuities/weaknesses (faults, trusts, fractures etc.);

(ii) The structures should be designed (factor of rigidity, flexibility etc.) with due consideration for the subsidence possibilities and geotechnical setting.

6.2.2 The following precautions and methodology should be adopted for the mining operations to minimise and control subsidence:

(i) The mining operations should be planned to permit controlled subsidence, with the entire overlying ground subsiding uniformly e.g. by adopting Harmonic Mining;

(ii) Adequate support should be provided in the underground workings to avoid subsidence, where necessary;

(iii) The worked-out areas particularly for steeply dippling metalliferous ore bodies should be filled with sand or other suitable packing material.

7.0 Landslide Problems

7.1 A landslide can be defined as the 'Downward' lipping of a mass of rock or unconsolidated material of any size-moving as a unit or as several subsidiary units. Landslides are often caused by inherent weakness, instability of the geological formations, unsystematic mining and human interference in the slope regions.

7.2 Care should be taken to maintain slopes at proper gradients during the mining operations. For slops steeper than the natural angle of repose of material, artificial supports with seepage and storm water drains should be provided.

7.3 The Himalayan and other tectonically active regions, where ground is comparatively weak and unsuitable, special care shall be taken while designing the mines. A complete study of geotechnical features in respect of the mines in such regions has to be undertaken. Similar care should be taken in the layout of roads and other facilities.

7.4 The slopes be stabilized by planting them adequately with trees or other soil binding vegetation.

7.5 The water courses along the slopes should be diverted in such a manner that minimum water flows the higher slopes towards mine openings.

7.6 The water courses in landslide-prone areas must be protected from landslides triggered by dumping of mines by careful selection of sites for such purposes.

8.0 Human Settlement Problems

8.1 The mining activities are mostly confined to remote areas which are sparsely populated. Though the population affected by these activities is very small and the problem is not so acute, measures for rehabilitation of the people displaced by the mining operations should be taken.

8.2 While initiating rehabilitation measures care should be taken to ensure, to the extend possible that the traditional life style of the people is not disturbed. The local population should get the maximum benefit accruing due to development of the mineral deposit. Adequate facilities for health care, education, recreation, employment etc. should be provided.

8.3 Since these are located in remote areas the township is an essential component of mining activities. These townships shall be properly planned according to normal town planning practices and should not be allowed to grow indiscriminately. Adequate infrastructure should be developed so as to avoid straining infrastructural facilities of the nearby settlements.

8.4 The township shall be provided with safe drinking water supply and sanitary system for collection, treatment and disposal of sewage and garbage. Possibilities of reuse of treated effluent water for sewage farming and pisciculture shall be seriously considered.

8.5 Adequate space for recreational activities and parks.

8.6 Tree plantation shall be taken up in a systematic manner in the township.

8.7 Adequate arrangements for grazing of cattle should be made. Care should be taken to avoid cattle grazing in areas near streams which may be contaminated by pollution.

8.8 To prevent indiscriminate foraging for fuel, fuel depots should be opened.

8.9 All care should be taken to avoid growth of slums and temporary settlement.

9.0 Impact of Mining on Water Regime

9.1 *Surface water*

9.1.1 Streams traversing the proposed mining area may often need to be diverted. Measures for diversion of such streams will have to take note of the conditions in the catchment and downstream areas so as not to affect the regime and downstream users.

9.1.2 Apart from providing adequate channel capacity of the diversion section with due regard to maximum flood intensity, area of command catchment etc., it would also be necessary to consider the bed slope and coefficient of rugosity of the water course and other hydraulic parameters.

9.1.3 The exact course of diversion should be determined not only on the basis of surface topography but also the hydrological aspects, calling for hydrological model studies, if necessary.

9.1.4 Diversion of water course would also have an effect on flora and fauna resulting in ecological invalance to some extent. The measures proposed for changing the water course should ensure the rehabilitation of flora/fauna.

9.1.5 Mining operations apart from changing the water course, may also cause drastic changes in the drainage pattern, which must be studied and avoided to the extent possible.

9.1.6 Influx of fines and wastes (solid) from mining operations may lead to excessive aggradation of stream courses, leading to several adverse effects including overspilling and creating artificial barriers in the channel - such situations need to be avoided.

9.1.7 Withdrawal of surface water for mining/colony requirements upstream reduce the flow and adversely affect the pollution absorption/dilution capacity of the stream. Efforts should be made to obtain water supplies from a separate source.

9.2 *Ground water*

9.2.1 Artificial lowering of the groundwater table and depletion of aquifers that are tapped by underground mining operations may lead to the following problems:

(i) adverse effects on wells, tanks and even effluent reaches of streams/ rivers:

(ii) enhancing drawdowns in pump wells in alluvial/sedimentary areas (coal/sand mining operations).

(iii) changes in the hydrodynamic conditions of river/underground recharge basins;

(iv) reduction in volume of subsurface discharge to rivers, depending on the hydrogeological conditions.

9.2.2 In many cases where there are permeable strata near the surface, introduction of fines through leaching and percolation may reduce the effective transmissibility of the aquifers and their water yielding properties.

9.2.3 Adverse hydrochemical alteration will be caused by chemical pollution from mining wastes.

9.3 *Control measures*

Considering the local geological, geomorphological and hydrogeological setting, various measures may be incorporated into the overall plan for mining operations to minimise the adverse effects on the water regimes.

Amongst such steps are:

(a) Settling ponds and coagulant aids prior to discharge of wastes into water bodies, to reduce influx of fines;

(b) Sealing of shafts against aquifer zones;

(c) Filling up of mined/stoped zones.

(d) Controlled subsidence;

(e) Properly located tailings/waste disposal sites away from water bodies etc.

10.0 Protection of sites of Cultural, Historical and Scenic importance

Mining activities which are likely to cause damage to such sites should be undertaken only after sufficient safeguards are built into the system.

SCHEDULE - I

PARAMETERS TO BE COVERED BY ENVIRONMENTAL QUALITY STANDARDS FOR LIQUID EFFLUENTS

1. Substances relating to protection of human health

Toxic Substances —

Cadmium and its compounds (as Cd)
Cyanide compounds (as CN)
Organic phosphorous compounds
(Parathion, methyl parathion, methyl dematon and EPN only)
Chromium and its compounds (as Cr)
Selenium (as Se)
Arsenic and its compounds (as As)
Total mercury (as Hg)
Alkyl mercury compounds.

2. Items Relating to Preservation of Living Environment

pH
Dissolved Oxygen
Biochemical Oxygen Demand BOD (5 days at 20^0 C)
Chemical Oxygen Demand (COD)
Total Dissolved Solids (TDS)
Total Suspended Solids (TSS)
N-hexane extracts

Phenols
Copper (as Cu)
Zinc (as Zn)
Dissolved Iron (as Fe)
Dissolved Manganese (as Mn)
Chrome
Fluorides (as F)
Chlorides (as Cl)
Sulphates (SO_4)
Phenolic compounds
Nitrates (as NO_3)
Oils and grease
Free Carbon dioxide (as CO_2)
Free Ammonia (as N)
Electrical conductance at 25^0 C Max.
Alpha emitters (uc/ml.)
Beta emitters (uc/ml.)
Coliform organisms
(monthly average MPN per 100 ml)

Note. 1 Categorisation based on purpose of utilisation

(A) Raw Water for Public Water supply

(B) Bathing ghats

(C) Fish culture

(D) Irrigation

Tolerance limits in respect of parameters as listed should be furnished for each of the above category.

*As laid down by Central Board for Prevention and Control of Water Pollution.

Method of test as stipulated in the relevant IS code shall be furnished against each parameter. Following IS codes would be relevant:

IS 1622—1964	Method of sampling and test (physical and chemical) for water used in industry
IS 5025—1964	Method of sampling and test for microbiological examination of water used in industry.
IS 2499 (pt. I) —1966	Method of sampling and test for industrial effluents.
IS 2488 (pt. III) —1968	-do-
IS 6582—1971	Bioassay methods for evaluating acute toxicity of industrial effluents and waste water.

QUESTIONNAIRE FOR ENVIRONMENTAL APPRAISAL OF MINING OPERATIONS

To Be Completed By Mining Companies

Questionnaire

1. This questionnaire seeks to elicit preliminary information which would indicate some of the major environmental impacts of mining and ancillary operations. Additional information for a mere detailed assessment, would be sought throught a more elaborate questionnaire and/or inspection visits.

2. Please provide only information specific to the activities in your mine. Answer "Does not apply" to Questions not relevant to your mine. All data should be in appropriate metric units.

3. Additional information relevant to the impact on the environment from the siting and operation of the mines if such is available for example reports of surveys of mine environment, pollution data or health survey data, etc., may be appended.

4. The completed questionnaire may please be submitted in triplicate. If the space provided in the questionnaire for answering any particular item is not sufficient, additional sheets or tabular statements may be appended, with due reference in the questionnaire.

5. Please note that the information provided would be kept strictly confidential. Any publication based on the information would not identify the Companies completing this Questionnaire.

Note:

On satisfactory completion and submission of the Questionnaire a follow-up questionnaire specifically designed for the mining project proposal would issue. Alternatively the proponent would be requested to submit a detailed environmental impact statement or environmental management plan which would include also the proposed environmental protection measures incorporated in the project report.

ENVIRONMENTAL IMPACTS OF MINING OPERATIONS

Questionnaire: Preliminary Information

PART A: GENERAL INFORMATION ABOUT MINING OPERATIONS

1. General

1.1 Name and address of the Mines — Place..................................
Distt..................................
State..................................

1.2 Name and address of owner:

1.3 Date of opening of Mines:

2. Mineral Exploitation Detail:

2.1 Reserves (Proved and Estimated) in the above location of such mineral/ore (in tonnes)

Sl. No.	Mineral/ Ore	Av. daily Reserve
		Proved
		Estimated

2.2 Average daily production of various minerals:

Sl. No.	Mineral/ Ore	Av. daily Production

If it is less than the planned production, time phasing for achieving full production capacity.

2.3 Nature of Mining Operations (Check the appropriate box):
1. Opencast ☐
2. Undergound ☐

2.4 For opencast mines only

2.4.1 Stripping Ratio (Overburden to Ore/Mineral ratio). Please attach a typical vertical section of the working showing the lithology);

2.4.2 Details of machinery used:

(i) Excavation/Removal of overburden:

(ii) Loading of mineral/ore at face;

(iii) Transportation of Overburden/Ore:

2.5 For underground mines only

2.5.1 Depth of the workings, (Please attach a typical vertical section of the working showing the lithology).

2.5.2 Mode of Entry (by Shaft, Adit or Incline).

2.5.3 Details of machinery used: Surface/Underground

(i) At face

(ii) For transportation

(iii) Any other purposes

2.5.4 Type of stopes (in case of Metalliferous Mines only):

1. Open Stopes
2. Timbered Stopes
3. Filled Stopes
4. Shrinkage Stopes
5. Caving Method
6. Combined Method

2.5.5 For Underground Coal Mines:

2.5.5.1 Method of Mining (Check the appropriate box):

1. Board & Pillar ☐
2. Longwall ☐

If longwall, whether advancing or retreating longwall.

2.5.5.2 Method of Depillaring (Check the appropriate box):

1. Caving ☐
2. Stowing ☐

2.6 Are you carrying out ancillary operations for processing of the minerals/ ore mined. (If yes, please specify).

PART B : ENVIRONMENTAL CONSIDERATIONS

1. General

1.1 *Location*

1.1.1 Total lease area (in hectares):

1.1.2 Elevation above mean sea level:

1.1.3 Indicate general topography of the level (Check the appropriate box):

1. Rolling ground ☐
2. Rocky ☐
3. Plain ☐
4. Hilly ☐
5. River basin ☐
6. Coastal ☐
7. Other, specify. ☐

1.1.4 Area based for mining (in hectares): (Attach map of the mineable land showing area phasing programme of mining, if any).

1.1.5 What of the following features exist within 10 kms. of the site ? Human Settlements (specify population), Agricultural (specify crops), Grazing land, Nallahs/Streams/Rivers, Ponds/ Lakes/Dams, Estuary/Sea, Fisheries, Industries (specify), Hills/ Mountains, Forests/Sanctuary/National Park/Tourist Spots/Monuments, National/State/District Highway.

1.2 *Climate*

1.2.1 (a) Yearly average
(b) Range

1.3 *Manpower Employed*

1.3.1 Average No. of persons employed every day:

Below Ground	Above Ground
Opencast otherwise	Plant workings

1.3.2 Population of the township/ housing colony for the employees.

2. Population

2.1 *Water*

Public Supply/Ground/ River/Lake

2.1.1 Source of Water:

2.1.2 Average daily quantity of water consumed:

2.1.3 Waste Water discharges per day from:

(i) Mines
(ii) Township
(iii) Total

2.1.4 Point of final discharge: Fallow land/Agricultural land/ River/Lake/Bay/Estuary/Sea.

2.1.5 Do you treat waste water before discharging ? If yes, specify treatment method.

2.1.6 Characteristics of the discharged water (colour, pH, Hardness, Total suspended solids, Total dissolved solids, Chemical Oxygen Demand etc.)

2.2 *Solid Wastes*

2.2.1 Quantities of solid wastes, e.g. Overburden. Waste rocks, Tailings, etc., from mining and ore-processing operations per day.

2.2.2 Nature of Solid Wastes: Lumps/Granules Dust/Slurry/Sludge

2.2.3 Waste Disposal method practised like land filling. dumping etc.

2.2.4 Are there any problems of pollution of air, water or land at the place of disposal of solid wastes ?

If yes, indicate nature of pollution and abatement measures used.

2.3 *Air*

2.3.1 Are there any emissions of dust or gases (CO, CO_2 SO_2 NO_x CH_4 etc.) from your mining/ore-processing operations into the atmosphere ?

If yes, specify nature and concentration and steps to control/abate such Air-Pollution.

2.4 *Health Hazard:*

2.4.1 Is there any potential health hazard from dust or gases in the underground mine atmosphere ?

If yes, specify nature of such hazards and measures to prevent exposure of workers.

2.5 *Other types of Pollution*

2.5.1 Do various operations in mines/plant cause, Noise Pollution or any other type of pollution ? If yes, what measures are taken to control it.

2.6 *Management*

2.6.1 Have you had your mine/ore-processing Plant monitored for environmental pollution/hazards at any time ?
If yes, give details.

2.6.2 Do you propose to reclaim excavated/ subsided area after completion of mining operations ?
If yes, indicate general features of the scheme.

Date:

Signature...
Name...
Designation.......................................
Address...
Telephone...
Telex...

Law Department's advice in regard to Mining Leases

(i) In respect of the mining operations being carried on forest lands leased before the commencement of the Forest (Conservation) Act, 1980 during the continuance of the lease period, the approval of the Central Government under Section 2 of the said Act is not required.

(ii) A renewal of a lease is really the grant of a fresh lease. *(See Delhi Development Authority v. Durga Chand Kausish, AIR 1973 SC 2609.)* The prior approval of the Central Government in terms of section 2 of the Forest (Conservation) Act, 1980 would be required when a mining lease granted before the commencement of the said Act is renewed after its coming into force.

(iii) As held by the Supreme Court in *State of Bihar* v. *Banshi Ram Modi (supra)* prior approval of the Central Government in terms of section 2 of the Forest (Conservation) Act, 1980 would not be required for mining and winning any new mineral from a forest land leased for mining before the commencement of the said Act during the lease period originally granted, if the said land is already broken up or cleared before the commencement of the Act. Otherwise, the prior approval of the Central Government under Section 2 of the said Act would be required.

ANNEXURE VI (A)

Category of proposals for which cost-benefit analysis is applicable

Sl. No.	Nature of Proposal	Applicable/ Not applicable	Remarks
(1)	(2)	(3)	(4)
1.	All category of proposals involving forest land less than 5 ha. in plains and less than 2 ha. in hills.	Not applicable	These proposals are to be considered on case by case basis and value judgment.
2.	Proposals for defence installation purposes and oil prospecting. (Prospecting only)	Not applicable	In view of National Priority accorded to these sectors, the proposals would be critically assessed to help ascertain that the utmost minimum forest land above is diverted for non-forest use.
3.	Habitation, Establishment of Industrial units, tourist lodges/complex and other buildings construction.	Not applicable	These activities being detrimental to protection and conservation of forests, as a matter of policy, such proposals would be rarely entertained.
4.	All other proposals involving forest land more than 5 ha. in plains and more than 2 ha. in hills including roads, transmission lines, minor, medium and major irrigation projects, hydel projects mining activity, railway lines, location specific installations like micro-wave stations auto repeater centres, T.V. towers etc.	Applicable	These are cases where a cost-benefit analysis is necessary to determine whether diverting the forest land to non-forest use is in the overall public interest.
5.	Environmental Losses; Soil erosion, effect on hydrological cycle, wildlife habitat, microclimate upsetting of ecological balance.		Though technical judgement would be primarily applied in determining the losses, as a thumb rule the environmental value of one hectare of fully stocked forest (density 1.0) would be taken as Rs. 125.74 lakhs to

Sl No.	Nature of Proposal	Applicable/ Not applicable	Remarks
(1)	(2)	(3)	(4)
			accrue over a period of 50 years. The value will reduce with density, for example if density is 0.4 the value will work out at Rs. 50.696 lakhs. So, if a project which requires deforestation of 1 ha. of forest of density 0.4 gives monetary returns worth over Rs. 50.696 lakhs over a period of 50 years, may be considered to give a positive cost-benefit ratio. The figure of assumed environment at value will change if there is an increase in bank rate; the change will be proportional to percentage increase in the bank rate.
6.	Suffering to oustees.		The social cost of rehabilitation of an outsee (in addition to the cost likely to be incurred in providing residence, occupation and social services to him) be worked out as 1.5 times of what he should have earned is two years had he been not shifted.

ANNEXURE VI (b)

Parameters for evaluation of loss of forests

Sl. No.	Parameters	Nature of proposals		
		Roads, transport and railway lines	Minor irrigation projects, quarrying of stones/metals	Medium and major Irrigation, hydro electric, large mining and other misc. projects
(1)	(2)	(3)	(4)	(5)
1.	Loss of value of timber, fuelwood and minor forest produce on an annual basis including loss of manhours per annum of people who derived livelihood and wages from the harvest of these commodities.	To be quantified and expressed in monetary terms	To be quantified and expressed in monetary terms	To be quantified and expressed in monetary terms
2.	Loss of animal husbandry productivity, including loss of fodder.	- do -	- do -	- do-
3.	Cost of human resettlement	- do -	- do -	- do -
4.	Loss of public facilities and administration infrastructure (roads, buildings, schools, dispensaries, electric lines, railways etc.) on forest land, or which would require forest land if these facilities were diverted due to the project.	- do -	- do -	- do -

ANNEXURE VI (c)

Parameters for Evaluation of Benefit, Notwithstanding Loss of Forests

Sl. No.	Parameters	Nature of proposals		
		Roads, tr. lines and railway lines	Minor projects	Irrigation/Hydel projects and others
(1)	(2)	(3)	(4)	(5)
1.	Increase in productivity attributable to the specific project	To be quantified and expressed in monetary terms	To be quantified and expressed in monetary terms	To be quantified and expressed in monetary terms
2.	Benefits to economy	Value judgement	- do -	- do -
3.	No. of population benefited	- do -	Value judgement	Value judgement
4.	Employment potential	- do-	- do -	- do -
5.	Cost of acquisition of facility on non-forest wherever feasible	To be quantified and expressed in monetary terms	To be quantified and expressed in monetary terms	To be quantified and expressed in monetary terms
6.	Loss of (a) agricultural and (b) animal husbandry production due to diversion of forest land	- do -	- do -	- do -
7.	Cost of rehabilitating the displaced persons as different from compensatory amounts given for displacement	- do -	- do -	- do -
8.	Cost of supply of free fuel-wood to workers residing in or near forest area during the period of construction	- do -	- do -	- do -

ANNEXURE IX

ENVIRONMENTAL GUIDELINES FOR FORMULATION OF RIVER VALLEY PROJECTS

While preparing feasibility reports of the River Valley Multipurpose Projects, the following guidelines may be observed:

1. Locational Aspects

The site selection must incorporate environmental considerations in addition the normal techno-economic ones. Expertise should be sought to incorporate the environmental aspects of hydrology, geology, seismology, topography and meteorology etc. in the criteria for site selection. Major environmental components that need to be kept in view during site selection include:

— immediate and long-term impact on population in the surrounding human settlements, both in the inundated and watershed areas;

— impact on flora and fauna (wildlife) in the vicinity;

— impact on national parks & sanctuaries—both existing and potential;

— impact on wildlife (including birds) breeding area/feeding area/migration route;

— impact on sites & monuments of historical, cultural and religious significance;

— impact on forests; agriculture, fishery & recreation etc.

Requisite data for impact assessment, if not already available, may be generated through such Field-Surveys as:

— census of flora and fauna in submergence areas, particularly rare and endangered species;

— census of animal population and available grazing areas;

— land use pattern in the area with details of extent & type of forest in catchment and submergence areas;

— pre-impoundment survey of fish habitat and nutrients levels;

— groundwater levels, quality and existing water use pattern;

— mineral resources in the impoundment;

— living conditions of affected tribals/aboriginals; etc.

2. Physical Aspects

The impoundment will create altered surface water patterns that may have for reaching impact on underground aquifers and their recharge. Major aspects to be considered included:

— siltation or sedimentation expected in the reservoir and adoption of watershed management practices to retard siltation process;

— potential groundwater recharge or other groundwater changes due to impoundment;

— expected water quality (salinity) changes over time and their effect on overine ecosystem both in impoundment and downstream;

— landuses patterns and practices in the vicinity of waterspread that would affect acquatic vegetation growth patterns;

— potential seismic impact of reservoir loading.

3. Resource Linkages Aspects

Creation of an impoundment caused considerable disruption and results personably in the adoption of alternative landuses. Careful evaluation of the impact should be undertaken of factors as:

— resource trade-off such as loss of optional land uses due to impoundment, mineral deposit loss, forest reserve diminish monuments inundated, recreational facilities lost, dislocation of existing settlements because of submergence etc;

— compatibility of dam's presence and operation, including the important, with present or planned development of the region;

— effect on resident and migrating fish and other acoustic wildlife and assessment of new fishing potential.

4. Socio-cultural Aspects

Since, relocation may strain/disrupt the social fabric affected population effects should be directed towards enchancing their quality of life and preserving to the extent possible, the special characteristics of their life-style:

— population relocation requirements in inundated as well as watershed areas. This aspect has special bearing on the relocation of Tribunals and Address etc.

— resettlement area planning for housing and other amenities of community life (water supply sanitation, schools, health services etc.) to be provided at resettlement sites.

5. Public Health Aspects

— new health problems or vector patterns that may due to changes in water velocities, temperature, quality or other physical change factors caused by water impoundment;

— adequate public health planning to create facilities for migrant construction workers and immigrant influx. Possibility of disease aggravation or new public health problems introduced due to changes in population density and distribution should be looked into.

Also measures should be drawn up to control pesticides and fertilizer contamination of surface and ground-water due to irrigation water or rainfall run off.

6. Cost -Benefit Analysis

The cost of proposed remedial and mitigative measures. If any to protect the environment must be included in the project costs. Mitigative measures may include:

— compensatory afforestation;

— restoration of land in construction areas by filling, grading etc. to prevent further erosion;

— control of aquatic weeds in submerged areas to provide improved habitat for aquatic life;

— measures to salvage/rehabilitate any rare or endangered species of flora and fauna in the affected area;

— measures to salvage monuments from inundation and their relocation;

— enforcement of anti-poaching laws;

— measures to prevent forest fires; over-grazing etc;

— establishment of fuel depots etc. to meet fuel requirements of labour force to prevent indiscriminate felling of trees;

— public health measures to control spread of water and soil-borne diseases. Also should be included the cost of;

— Field Surveys and Studies undertaken to create the environment database;

— technical and administrative measures to effectively MONITOR the observance of suggested safeguards and mitigative measures etc.

DEPARTMENT OF ENVIRONMENT ECOLOGICAL ASPECTS OF RIVER VALLEY HYDRO-ELECTRIC PROJECTS

1. Detailed Basic Information Affecting the Environment

1.01 Predominant existing land-use pattern (agricultural land/Reserve and other Forests etc.) in project area and up to 100 Kms. upstream.

1.02 Break-up of submerged area:

Total submerged area:

Forest land...............% (hectares). Cultivated land.........% (hectares).

Shrubs & Fallow................Rockey outcrop...........% Wetland............

Open water............Other uses..................

1.03 (a) Forest type in catchment and submerged areas:

(Indicate the type of trees, whether, sparse or thickly wooded and other details.)

(b) Extent and nature of forest to be cut for the construction of roads, colony and other appurtenant works.

1.04 Duration of project's construction stage..

1.05 Estimated Peak Labour strength...........Skilled...........unskilled...........

Labour to be recruited from affected population........................ skilled.......................unskilled..................

1.06 Population density in the area per sq. km.

1.07 Number of villages and population to be displaced:

Displaced: ....

Size of affected villages: ....

Affected families in each village...........ST.........SC........Others.......

Occupation:.........................Agriculture.................................. Industrial Labour............Artisans............Forest based.............Others..........

Owner— Cultivators by size of	Marginal ( )-1-0 Hect.	Small (1.0 - 2-5) Hect.	Medium (2.5-5-0) Hect.	Big (Over 5.0) Hect.
Land-Holdings:				

1.08 Resettlement:

Is a Rehabilitation Committee being constituted?...............................

Existing Guidelines, if any, for compensation?..................................

Level of compensation in cash and kind:

---

1. Contact Forest Department

Number of oustee families likely to be settled in new settlements.................

Size of proposed new settlements...

Layout plans/Master plans for new settlements:...

Distance of new settlements from the present habitat:........................

1.09 Number and type of facilities (e.g. school, post offices, bank, panchayat ghar, police station, approach road, drainage, and water supply etc.) proposed to be provided:..

1.10 Is the affected area covered by development programmes like IRD, SFD, drought-prone area, tribal development etc..............................

Any proposals to provide/create employment for oustees:........................

Nature and quantum employment to be provided:...........................

Vocational training programmes envisaged, if any:..................................

1.11 What is the expected rate of siltation ?..

Details of how the siltation problem is proposed to be handled.

1.12 Is downstream area subject to flooding ?..

1.13 Wind rose at Dam site: ....

(Diagram giving statistical information concerning the direction and speed of the wind at the site.)

1.14 Hurricane, tornadoes, cyclones : Frequency of occurrence:

Wind velocity: Average...........................Maximum...........................

1.15 Plan of areas, on the reservoir perphery, subject to erosion, slides and slips:..

1.16 The depth of groundwater table maximum..........minimum..................

Quality of groundwater: potable/non-potable fit for irrigation/industry:

1.17 Present groundwater use pattern in the command:

Area under irrigation....................................surface..........................

Groundwater:..

1.18 Based on the experience of similar projects in the area, specify the interaction between the altered surface patterns and underground aquifers and their recharge.

2. Environmental Status

2.01 (a) Indicate known pollution source in the region:

(Indicate the industrial like—chemicals, textiles and others: thermal power units; mining operations etc.)

2. Contact IMD

(b) Indicate the industrial and other development projects likely to be taken up in the area during the next five to ten years:

2.02 (a) Does the area support economically viable aquatic like — fish, crocodiles? Please give details :

(b) Are there any fish/crocodile breeding grounds in the river/tributaries in the submergence area:[3]

2.03 Does the site contain a wild-life (including birds) habitat.........breeding area/feeding area..................migration route..................indicate the number of wild-life available in the area:[4,5]

2.04 Is the site a potential wild-life sanctuary ?

2.05 Specify any rare or endangered species of flora and fauna in the affected area alongwith their approximate number and measures to salvage/rehabilitate them.[5-7]

2.06 Is the area a tourist resort ?

2.07 Are any monuments/sites of cultural, historical, religious, archeological or recreational importance including wild-life sanctuaries and national parks etc. likely to be affected by the proposed project ? If so, details thereof.

2.08 Does the proposed area suffer from endemic health problems due to water/soil-borne disease ?[6]
If yes, specify the problem(s) and give details.

3. Environmental Impacts

3.01 What measures are planned to develop the site to enhance its aesthetic aspects ? (i.e. recreation and water sport facilities, and picnic sites etc.)

3.02 Will the project help in flood control reduction on even eradication of flood havoc downstream ?

3.03 Are any changes in water salinity expected ? If yes, give details of proposed measures to counteract this.

3.04 Are problems of waterlogging envisaged in the command area ? If so, give details of proposed steps to combat the problem.

3.05 Will the reservoir be used for fisheries development (fish culture as well as fish breeding), crocodile farming etc. ? If yes, give details thereof.

3.06 Will fish ladders/lifts and like arrangements be provided to allow movement of important migratory fish population ?

---

3. Contact Fisheries Department
4. Contact ZSI
5. Contact Wild-life Department
6. Contact Health Department

3.07 Measures proposed to prevent grazing and cultivation on reservoir slopes to avoid erosion and pre-mature silting-up of the impoundment.

3.08 Will any important natural resources (minerals, commercial timber etc.) be lost of their use precluded because of the presence or operation of the project? If yes, specify the resource and the magnitude of the estimated loss.

3.09 What is potential loss in aquatic production on site, up-and down-stream? (Fish and other useful aquatic animals and plants).

3.10 Will the formation and use of the water body result in the introduction or enhancement of water borne disease?

3.11 Will the impounded reservoir lead to :

(i) Noxious aquatic weeds like salvinia, water hyacinth etc. ?[7]

(ii) Intermittent host (vectors) like snails, mosquitoes etc.

3.12 How will aquatic weeds be controlled in submerged areas so as to provide an improved habitat for fishery exploitations. [8]

3.13 Will the project induce adverse climatological changes (regarding temperature, humidity, wind and precipitation including modifications to micro and macro climate) ?

3.14 What impact is expected on geological factors (e.g. seismic impact of reservoir leading) ?

3.15 Indicate the magnitude of impact due to population pressure on:

(i) felling of trees for firewood;

(ii) forest fires;

(iii) over-grazing leading to depletion of the pastures; and

(iv) visual pollution and damages to scenic values.

3.16 What arrangements are being made:

(i) to meet fuel requirements of the labour force during construction period to prevent indiscriminate felling of trees for firewood ?

(ii) for compensatory afforestation ?

(iii) to enforce anti-poaching laws ?

(iv) to control flow of sediments and pollutants due to fertilizer and pesticide run-off for cultivated areas ?

(v) for restoration of land in construction areas (filling, grading, and reforesting etc. to prevent erosion and to erase the scars) ? and

(vi) for soil conservation in the catchment ?

---

7. Contact BSI
8. Contact GSI

4. Cost of Environmental Studies, Project Management and Monitoring

4.01 Provision for environmental studies/surveys need for this project.

4.02 Cost of proposed remedial and mitigative measures, if any, to protect the environment.

4.03 Has the cost of environmental studies/protection measures been considered in the cost-benefit analysis of the project ?

ANNEXURE X

ENVIRONMENTAL GUIDELINES FOR DEVELOPMENT OF BEACHES

INTRODUCTION

1.1 The coastal areas of the country are in the midst of economic development of increased proportions. All these developments are the life line for a sizeable portion of the country's population. There is much variety of fauna and flora in these areas, mineral and oil resources for utilisation and development. But the coastal areas are highly complex and dynamic eco-systems, sensitive to development pressures. The traditional use of sea water as a dump site for our land-derived wastes have increased the pollution loads of sea and reduced its development potentials including the economic support it provides to the people living nearby. With the growth of cities, towns, ports industrial establishments and other developments great expenses of the coasts have been altered to an extent which little resembles the original. Degradation and misutilisation of beaches are affecting the aesthetic and environmental values including considerable economic and recreational loss. These could be avoided through prudent coastal development and management based on assessment of ecological values and potential damages from coastal developments. Environmental impact assessments, therefore, should precede all coastal developments to conserve these precious heritage areas.

1.2 This environmental management guideline is designed to provide environmental impact assessments for activities related to coastal area developments. The guidelines are in reference to the potential impact assessments of activities which have "direct impact" on coastal land-sea interface area and its hinterland. The guidelines list the major activities or sub-activities that might characterise development pressures. The decision maker will be able to identify which of these are present in the project under consideration. The environmental impact of such activities and their severity in terms of magnitude, and importance on aesthetic, ecological and cultural values etc. could then be determined by further indepth scrutiny or classification etc. Measures which may control the environmental impacts could then be completed by referring to the management guidelines to ensure that appropriate measures have been incorporated the project design.

1.3 By informing the decision-maker (or entrepreneurs) of the different aspects of environmental management, it is hoped that necessary corrective or control measures are incorporated in the project design in the initial stages itself. For environmental management in existing areas these guidelines will help in the assessment of environmental degradation. These will ensure that appropriate remedial measures are taken by the concerned authorities after carefully considering the socio-economic cost benefits involved.

1.4 By definition 'beach' is the shore especially of sea between high and low water mark. Of late this has been further enlarged to include river or lake systems —that part of the sea or of a large river or a lake which is washed by tide or wave. From these considerations beaches could be interpreted as that land-sea interface or the coasts along the country. Therefore, for the purpose of these guidelines the word 'beach' has been interpreted as the 'coast' and these words are used interchangeably in the guidelines.

II. PREAMBLES

2.1 The coastal areas in the country are subject to a varied mixture of uses comprising that of ports, cities, industrial establishments, rural regions with fisherman villages etc. Depending on the regional attributes of overall development and urbanisation, the problems of coastal area in terms of development, population content, pollution and pollutant loads vary :

(i) In some of them tourism and extractive industrial form the economic base of the region. The historic, cultural scenic heritage values complement the physical attractiveness of the area.

(ii) In others, the high density of population in coastal areas, fisherman villages and sea erosion problems necessitate different management issues.

(iii) Location of salt industries along the coast, mangroves, mining of sand and corals, and development of religious-cum-tourist spots are primary issues in several other areas. Development of vast stretches of beaches as part of tourism development in conjunction with the cultural attractions of the region are equally significant pressures.

(iv) In few areas it is off-shore oil prospecting, high density metropolitan cities other coastal towns, and salt water intrusions in the subsoil waters.

These development linked environmental management problems are illustrative and of exhaustive. These varied issues involve not only scientific and administrative aspects but local spatial aspects such as adoption of coastal areas for town and country planning techniques and legislations.

2.2 The country with its, 6,000 kilometres of coastal land has indeed a great scope for development with its abundance of natural endowments, geographic attractions of natural beauty, the dominant cultural and historical heritage etc. The stresses and pressures of high populations growth, non-restrained development, lack of adequate infrastructure facilities (or life support systems) for the resident population have become responsible for the decline in environmental quality in these areas. Serious shortcomings are also becoming apparent in the matter of resource planning and environmental management of coastal areas.

2.3 Concerned with this deficiency in planning and development the Prime Minister had issued directives to the coastal states in November, 1981. In her letter to the Chief Ministers of the States she had mentioned that "the degradation and misutilisation of beaches in the coastal States is worrying as the beaches have aesthetic and environmental value as well as other values. They have to be kept clear of all activities at least up to 500 meters from the water at the maximum high tide. If the area is vulnerable to erosion, suitable trees and plants have to be planted on the beach sands without marring their beauty. Beaches must be kept free from all kinds of artificial development. Pollution from industrial and town wastes must also be avoided totally."

2.4 In view of this directive several aspects of development and control, and management of different uses along the coastal land, both within the said 500 metres from the High Tide Line (HTL) and outside it, becomes significant and needed immediate attention. In the beaches and urban areas of the coastal states, development control and management of existing developed areas became immediate issues due to the freezing of activities in the area. There was the imperative need to preserve the beauty of beaches as a national heritage, and for their aesthetic and environmental values. Appropriate management of these areas therefore became significant.

2.5 Amongst the many development activities in the coastal areas tourism development is a significant one as it directly depends on natural environment, aesthetic and environmental quality of the resource. But it has the heavy dependency on the socio-cultural environment in the areas for its development. It can have negative or adverse impacts on the local eco-system. Haphazard developments of coastal areas for tourism development can lead, in the long-term, to the destruction of the very characteristics which make them attractive and cause irreversible damage or destruction of the natural resources of the area. There are several existing developed beaches on both the eastern and the western coasts of the country, and several others are under consideration for tourism development. The location of the beaches, their accessibility and quality have a key role in beach development for tourism purposes. A Consultant Report commissioned by the

Central Department of Tourism (prepared by Harris, Kerr, Forster and Company : Belt, Collins and Associates, Ltd, New York, U.S.A.) has clearly established the attraction of Indian beaches for touristic developments and beach resorts both for domestic and International tourism. But every coast is not fit for tourism development, as it is dependent on water quality, scenic beauty and accessibility of the area for such developments.

2.6 In view of these facts as well as the need for understanding the current status of the beaches, the Department of Environment has been advising the concerned States to prepare a status report of 500 metres area and then follow it up with a master plan for development and control along with a compatible development beyond the limits in the hinterland areas. The Working Group reiterated the requirement of such master plan for development and control specially considering the facts that there exists already developed areas within the 500 metres limits and beyond. In such areas the development and control be exercised on merits after careful Environmental Impact Assessment. As development and planning and land are within the domain of state subjects, it is essential to provide a set of guidelines for development and management of beaches and the said coastal areas to ensure their environmental compatibility in the ecologically sensitive area of the interface of land and sea.

2.7 The main objectives of these guidelines is to identify environmental parameters for management and derive a set of indices for assessment of environmental and ecological values and the potential damage from coastal developments. The guidelines put forward a methodology for Environmental Impact Assessment (EIA) and environmental management. It would be difficult to evolve a standard guidelines uniformaly applicable to all beaches. The physical characteristics like the width of the beach, the vegetative cover, sand and beach-dune environment, the terrain and subsoil conditions, other chemical and biological factors determine the sensitivity of the beach. Impact assessments of development activities, therefore have to study all these factors. The main trust of the guidelines is therefore the assessment of the "direct impact" of development activities on this land-sea interface. It would be seen that the direct impacts are related to the activities and depend on the local spatial characteristics. Thus adverse "direct impact" is possible within 500 metres from the high water mark or beyond two kilometres from it. For example mining of laterite in coastal areas can alter the sub-terranean water quality (and flow) causing salt water intrusion well beyond two kilometres from the shores as has happened in some parts of the country. Sand dunes and vegetation clearing high density construction etc, along the coast can alter the ecological system of the area.

2.8 The "direct impact" of activities are to be understood by careful analysis of environmental factors for potential negative or adverse effects. Environmental impact assessments of the activity to be basically on merits, regardless of the distance of the activity from the high water mark. It would not be prudent to restrict the EIA to activities located within a particular distance from the high water mark without considering the impact of activities developed beyond that distance and which may cause grave damages in the coastal eco-system. A good example of such an impact is "mining" in the coastal interiors. This affects the water quality through dumps of mine tailings, leachates, and overburden washing down into the coastal waters. A case in point is the iron ore mining operations in the district of Goa. The EIA with reference to the direct impact of proposed activities is therefore not limited to any physical limits of distance by metres or kilometres. For the purpose of these guidelines the assessment of direct impact is based on a full analysis of all the potential adverse impacts.

2.9 These guidelines are most effectively employed for EIA before development projects get underway, to serve the decision-maker with adequate insight about environmental quality and safeguards. Application of guidelines to already developed area is rather difficult for reasons that — (i) future landuse options are foreclosed (ii) present use patterns may be irreversible for several reasons. Nevertheless the guidelines would be useful in repairing the past damage or ensuring additional safeguards. Furthermore such post-mortem exercises help bridging knowledge gap in understanding the impacts of activities on the environment.

III. COASTAL AREA MANAGEMENT PARAMETERS

Definition

3.1 Beach by definition is the shore especially of sea between high and low water mark. All considerations dealing with beaches therefore have to consider the beach-dune environment. This environment is shaped, controlled and dominated by strong physical forces—such as high winds, salt spray, storm waves and the resulting patterns of erosion and sand deposition. Thus along the 6,000 kilometres of coastline of the country there exists many types of beaches and a great range of conditions which effect them. For the purpose of our consideration two types of beaches need consideration:

> The first beach is narrow, steep and most important usually lies, adjacent to high ground. Wave energy on this type of beach is concentrated in a narrow zone and has minimal impact on land due to rise in elevation.
>
> The second type of beach, which is broad and has a low profile, functions in a more complicated manner and presents more difficulties for management and wise utilisation. A combination of factors such as sea level fluctuation, sand movement on and off-shore, long-shore currents and the patterns of seasonal storms dominate the variables which shape this type of beach.
>
> The important point in respect of the type of beach is that the beach with its associated dunes is a transitional environment. It is the transitional area between land eco-system and marine eco-system.

3.2 The bio-physical and socio-economic are the primary components of the coastal area, especially for relaxation, leisure and recreation in relation to the water environment with additional attractions for a multitude of activities to carryout leisure pursuits. Beach development therefore includes variety of accommodations, housing, shopping and entertainment activities, with hinterland commercial recreational and public and tourist functions. The environmental setting for beach development therefore has major components of scenic, natural and aesthetic values.

3.3 The management of beaches therefore encompasses a multiplicity of interface environments of land, sea, human population and the flora and fauna of the area. These are important factors for environmental management apart from the aesthetic values such as the natural beauty, scenic grandeur and landscape. However, the significant aspect of beach management is that it is dependent on one resource that is the beach itself, and which is easily liable to overuse and misuse, wastage and eventual disappearance if some of its ecological and environmental functions are not clearly understood and managed. For example, the construction of a protecting wall for the shore temple at Mahabalipuram, while serving the limited purpose, resulted in erosion of a large chunk of beach north of the shore temple wiping out a fishing village and seven cottages built for Touristic activities (ITDC complex). The straight shoreline also changed to a curved bay thereby altering the topography of coastline at Mahabalipuram. In yet another case the denudation of mangrove forests along the Digha coast (West Bengal) has resulted in extensive erosion of beaches.

Parameters for Management

3.4 The element and principles which need to be considered in development of coastal areas and the management process are several. But the coastal area is subject to the structure and interaction of two systems namely :

(a) the ecological system that relates man and his environment,

(b) the spatial system that relates the coastal area with other regions in a complex exchange of economic, social, and cultural flow.

3.5 The scenic and recreational aspects are the primary components of beach development. But the aesthetic value and the health and environmental issues are critical conditions of the process—i.e. that of the beach development programme. Planning and management of beaches are extremely complex processes. This complexify is derived not from the process itself but from the elements to be managed and diverse influences that underlie the process. The first of them is the physical environment. Since beach is a transitional area of interfaces among the land, the sea and the atmosphere, unique and distinct phenomena and processes are present that severally influence (and limit) the utilisation of the coastal resources.

In terms of spatial management, beach is a significant area whose relative importance is for recreational framework; and that will have considerable importance to environmental health and aesthetic value.

As a complex environment, coastal area (and beaches) comprise of many closely related eco-systems. It is constantly under stress due to natural actions and human activities. It is a limited resource area facing unlimited demand.

For development and sound management of beaches, environmental assessment study is essential. This has to specify the nature and degree of interaction between economic activity and its physical environment.

3.6 There are nine major areas of concern in beach development and management:

1. The Sea
2. Tourism and Recreational Value
3. Human Settlements and Habitat
4. Natural Resources and Eco-systems
5. Level of Economic Development and Social Environment
6. Environmental Health
7. Industry and Technology
8. Natural/Aesthetic Potential
9. Energy

These are interrelated to each other in a delicate and intricate manner.

3.7 The sea-land interface which is a transitional environment is sensitive to the developmental pressures. The natural resources and aesthetic value of this interface area (beach area) are direct inputs to the development activities in the form of human settlements, tourism or industrial establishments. The negative or positive impacts of these activities on economic and social development and environmental health often result in depletion of (local) resources or ultimately in changes in the eco-systems or environmental changes. This change when it is irreversible may result in eventual disappearance of some of the ecological and environmental values of the beach itself.

3.8 In a beach development programme, the first priority will be the improvement of the capabilities of the beach area to provide the requisite development and recreational value.* But the developmental activities are governed by the general legal framework that exists at the specific location. These relate to administration and laws relating to landuse, town and country planning and resource exploitation.

3.9 An integrated management programme for beaches should aim at protection of beaches or shorelines, environmental health, natural resources, and special plan for critical sections of coastal or urban areas. Along with this the management plan should have an inbuilt environmental monitoring system to provide the feedback, and watch for any environmental or ecological changes or contribution due to the tourism or recreational activities.

* Urban and tourism developments, industrial establishments or others can change the equilibrium of the interface area due to improvement activities, pollutant loads or by overuse.

IV. MANAGEMENT GUIDELINES FOR ENVIRONMENTAL IMPACT ASSESSMENT

4.1 Coastal areas are complex and dynamic zones with large number of potentially conflicting uses. The physical, sedimentary, chemical and biological aspects of coasts area are all interrelated and constitute the complex and dynamic eco-system. The proximity of the sea in coastal areas gives rise to their peculiar multifaceted development. It influences the climate and rainfall in the coastal regions; and coastal waters are the most productive than deep oceans. Utilising these natural endowments, sea-trade, port facilities, large scale industrial and urban developments, tourism development, off-shore and on-shore recovery of hydro-carbon resources etc., become the paradigms of coastal developments.

4.2 A characteristic feature of the coastal areas is the current landuse and other practices that cause environmental problems. By utilising coastal waters as convenient places to get rid of waste materials we do not want on land we have increased the pollutant loads far outweighing the utility of sea for its development potentials and that economic support it provides to the resident population which inhabit these areas. Any coastal development and management plan, therefore, has to have an assessment of the ecological values and the potential damage from coastal development.

4.3 Coastal developments encompass the multiplicity of qualities related to natural environmental components, man-made environments such as human settlements, heritage areas etc., and socio-cultural environment like system values, general life-styles etc. However for environmental management purposes these developments are restricted to critical land-use activities that pose such issues affected by "adverse impacts". For subsequent discussions on Environmental Impact Assessment (EIA) and management guidelines six major areas have been identified which require integrated management. These are:

(i) Tourism Development

4.4 Beach tourism utilises the aesthetic and environmental values of the beach such as beautiful natural scenery, water quality (water should be clear and devoid of undertow and other currents, the gradient should be gentle), adequate size of the beach to avoid overcrowding absence of rocks and coral debris along the beach etc. Beach tourism activities combine water and land resource usage. Water usage comprises swimming, surfing and other water sports. Landuse activities incorporate construction of different types of accommodation (hotels, cottages, villas, camping sites, trailer parks) recreational areas (parks, play-grounds, golf courses, club houses, amusement parks), car and bus parking areas entertainment and shopping commercial areas, access roads and transportation networks. Other activities may include visits to tourist attractions the vicinity of beach areas. The development and management issues of beach tourism are thus several. A beach resort for example needs to be developed as an integrated complex to function as a self-contained community. Environment control also needs to be exercised over the style, form, height, use of construction material, colour etc. buildings and structures as related to their surroundings. Environmental management of beach tourism should also take into consideration the road systems to encourage : cluster type rather than the linear development, the arterial road running well alway from the coast and providing access points to coastal or beach areas. Environmental management should also ensure the availability of necessary infrastructure in the immediate hinterland to the coastal region in support of the development on the coast so as to maintain its eco-system. The environmental management of beach tourism development is thus vitally dependent upon the physical, chemical, biological characteristics of the land-sea interface area and the local spatial conditions.

(ii) Industrial Development

4.5 Industrial establishments may be located as part of urban settlements, ports, harbours or otherwise. But they affect the aesthetic and environmental values of the coastal areas in many ways. These depend upon the performance characteristics, technology and resources used in the manufacturing processes, effluent and waste disposals, emissions, dust, odour and noise issues. These require adequate abatement, control and management techniques. Transportation of raw materials and finished goods over land or marine surfaces affect directly the environmental and aesthetic value of the beaches.

(iii) Urban Development

4.6 Urban development and human settlement activities require greater environmental, management concerns as compared to other types of developments. All the urban landuse activities require critical assessments for their environmental impacts. Disposal of town and other wastes, construction activities and structures, water resource management, denudation of vegetation or introduction of exotic flora and fauna, pollution etc., are some of the important aspects which require environmental management and safeguards. Environmental health issues related to lack of management and sanitary condition affect the water quality and the land-sea interface eco-system critically.

(iv) Fishing Villages and Rural Areas

4.7 Fishing villages and rural areas present a different scale of development pressures than urban settlements. Environmental health issues, introduction of exotic flora and fauna, agricultural production and farm technology, mining and quarrying activities, leachates from pesticides and fertilizers are some of the environmental management concerns. Other development pressures include the denudation of vegetation and tree covers, location of industrial establishments associated with fisheries and others, cultural and religious heritage areas which attract huge congregations during particular periods or seasons.

(v) Special Areas (mangroves, scenic areas, coral reefs, and oceanic islands

4.8 Environmental management requirements of special areas are related to their local spatial eco-system attributes and the maintenance of the equilibrium and natural quality, tidal fluctuations, indiscriminate cutting and denudation of vegetal covers and other factors. Scenic areas require control and check from urban and industrial development pressures for preservation of their aesthetic and environmental values. Coral reefs are sensitive to water quality changes and turbidity and dredging, diking and other alterations which affect the aquatic system. Oceanic islands encompass a multiplicity of qualities of island eco-systems. They are sensitive to insular landuse activity such as tourism, introduction of exotic flora and fauna, human settlement development pressures and others. They, therefore, require specific environmental management techniques.

(vi) Communication and Transportation Network (rail, road and water)

4.9 Major highway and railway systems improve the accessibility of the beaches to hinterland areas. But they affect the aesthetic value and the terrain characteristics due to their physical design structures and development. In addition, the introduction of vehicular movements increase and the environmental impacts from noise, vibration and emissions drips etc. In airports the exposure to aircraft noise and the extensive nature of the land requirements for such ports have greater impact on the beach areas and its aesthetic value. Water conveyance system such as channels and other structures disturb the equilibrium due to the terrain and structural alterations that accompany their development. Besides the introduction of water environment may result in perpetuation of certain species of flora and fauna not indigenous to the area.

4.10 The relationship between these activities and effects from the background for environmental management guidelines under this report. The identified major activities are not mutually exclusive nor are absolute. They mirror the current priorities for such assessments, but the list can be expanded depending upon the importance of other development activities and their likely adverse impacts. This, however has to be made for location, specific situations by concerned agencies by taking into account the environmental impacts to be experienced and devising a framework for their assessment on similar lines.

A : Broad Classification of Coastal Areas for Ecological Values

4.11 A broad classification of coastal areas can provide a basis for a crude assessment of ecological values and the potential damage from coastal development. They can be as below:

(i) Exposure of coast to open sea

(ii) Production of renewable living sources (near, shore, inland......)

(iii) Configuration of coastline (straight, bayformation, lagoons, estuarine etc.)

(iv) Freshwater runoff characteristics
(v) Topography (steepness and breadth of inter-tidal area)
(vi) Substrate characteristics (rock, gravel, sand, mud, cobbles, etc.)
(vii) Character and dynamics of sedimentary materials
(viii) Vegetation (type, density, distance from shoreline etc.)
(ix) Fauna

Further breakdowns can be had and indices developed in the classification for evaluation of physical, biological or chemical aspects at detailed specific areas.

B : Landuse Activities and Adverse Impacts

4.12 The landuse practices that currently cause environmental problems can be identified for their adverse impacts on aesthetic, cultural and environmental values or for implication on resource management. Table 1 lists some of the major activities and sub-activities that characterise the development pressure for the six identified areas.

4.13 The environmental issues can be identified in the table by combining selected major activities in Column II with relevant sub-activities listed in Column III. Fir example:

"A:20:37" refers to "Tourism development: associated with water recreation and beach resorts and hotels."

"C:1:10" refers to "Urban development associated with housing and sewerage and septic tanks."

"E:17:33" refers to "Preservation of special areas namely scenic areas from associated introduction of exotic species."

"F:6:35" refer to "Communication and transport network system associated with airports having runways, aprons and helped."

"D:21:29" refers to "Fishing villages and rural areas needing waste disposal associated with fishing vessels, offals and other waste disposal problems."

4.14 These examples are illustrative but their environmental impacts have to be further assessed for their significance. For this purpose each can be considered indepth by constituting to measure of impact's severity, scale etc. These inevitably involves one degree of subjective evaluation, but will help in arriving at an informed basis for decision-making weighing the environmental impacts for their adverse or negative potentials.

4.15 In order to illustrate the process of such impact assessment a few examples of the many activities are discussed in the following paragraphs. Not all of the major or sub-activities mentioned in the table are included in the illustrative matrix, although their reference number according to the table are given.

A : Activities that affect Ecological Values

Only some selected activities are listed. For activity combinations reference is made to table 1.

(i) 12:20 Mining : blasting-terristrial and underwater.
(ii) 2:3 Highways and roads : embankments, cutting
(iii) 10:12 Pipelines (terrestrial and marine) : fuel and oil spills discharges
(iv) 0:31 Excavation and earth moving
(v) 0:39 Dredging
(vi) 14:19 Reclaiming land through submerged landfill
(vii) 15:5 Forestry and vegetation clearing
(viii) 0:9 Sewage discharges: outfalls
and
0:10 Sewerage by septic tanks
(ix) 0:23 Collecting marine flora and fauna
and
0:25 Collecting terrestrial flora and fauna
(x) 0:40 Population increase, overcrowding, insanitary conditions.
(xi) 26:27 Pesticides/fertilizers and leachates from them.

B : Activities that affect Aesthetic Values

(i) 21:7 Waste disposal through landfills
or
22:8 Offshore dumping of effluents and wastes into the sea
(ii) 12:21 Terrestrial mining for rock crushing and ore treatment etc.
(iii) 13:22 Marine mining for sand or corals
(iv) 1:1 Residential: structures or constructions
or
9:1 Constructions for commercial (or trade) purposes
(v) 0:2 Demolition of structures, neglected maintenance
(vi) 11:17 Power generation (locally) with stack emissions and transmission lines
(vii) 8:12 Oil refining and storage, petro-chemicals with fuel oil spills and discharges
(viii) 22:11 Sea dumping of waste water
(ix) 5:16 Ports, terminals with noise or vibration
or
5:13 Ports, terminals with ships and tankers
(x) 7:15 Industries, vehicles and emissions
(xi) 0:32 Brick making and kilns

C : Activities that affect Cultural Values

(i) A:0 Tourism development
(ii) 0:2 Demolition of structures, and neglected maintenance

(iii) 0:24 Collecting artistic and historic objects
(iv) 0:31 Excavating and earth moving
(v) B:0 Industrial development
(vi) 7:40 Industries: population increase, overcrowding and insanitary conditions
(vii) 0:23 Collecting marine flora and fauna
or
0:25 Collecting terrestrial fauna and flora
(viii) 16:0 Deep sea fishing
(ix) 0:40 Population increase, overcrowding and insanitary conditions.

4.16 This matrix is general in scope. But other functional matrices can be readily derived from the table (no. 1) to cover specific development or resource use situations. The environmental impacts can then be assessed for both their magnitude and significance by constituting suitable evaluative measures (or indices). The magnitude refers to the severity or degree, and gross scale of the impact. The significance refers to consequences of the impact (which is a subjective evaluation) and therefore requires assumption of some measurement values. For example magnitude can be classified into judgement categories such as severe, moderate and low. Similarly the significance can be based on a relative scale of "adverse" environmental impacts profound (severe), moderate and low.

4.17 To help decision-makers understand environmental impact assessments it can be presented in the form of a statement on a standard format. This Environmental impact statement (EIS) would provide the "brief" to decision-makers by quantifying the impacts under different categories of environmental parameters. Annexure 'A' presents the format and its organisation. The extent of details to be included in the EIS will depend on the size and nature of the project and its location. Preparation of EIA generally involves considerable exercise from a number of specialised field such as physical and social sciences, ecology and engineering etc. Thus the EIS technology is inter-disciplinary in nature. It would therefore, be desirable to obtain expert consultants from the public and private sectors to assist in preparing the EIA and the EIS. With a view to promote capabilities of consultants in the area of EIA (and EIS) technology and to prevent and control proliferation of pseudo-experts in the area the Departments of Environment, both at the Centre and States, may undertake requisite measures including preparation of panel of experts and their periodic review in the form of post-mortem examination of existing developments and new development etc. The Departments may recognise or derecognise panelled expert consultant(s) based on such reviews.

V. MANAGEMENT GUIDELINES

5.1 By combining the knowledge of environmental impacts derived from the assessments suggested in the previous sections with practical management experiences, it is possible to outline a series of management guidelines. These are presented in this section for a range of potential problems which might arise and which can be avoided. These guidelines ensure that the adverse impacts (or costs) that can be generated, are critically evaluated and decisions are taken avoiding such negative or adverse impacts (or costs).

A. Protection and Wise Utilisation of Valuable Ecosystems

1. Is recreational land or beaches going to be lost ? Do sufficient alternate areas exist for projected populations in the future ?
2. Will features with unusual aesthetic value be degraded or destroyed ? Are these important to an existing tourist industry ?
3. Will the proposed development or alternation result in the loss of productive farmland ? Is this land highly productive or only of marginal quality ? Are there nearby areas of comparable quality available for farming ? Will there be enough food produced in the region to support the human population without depending upon costly imports ?
4. Will important wildlife habitat be damaged or lost ? Critical areas include: (a) spawning and breeding grounds; (b) nesting and nursery areas; (c) dry or wet season refuge areas; and (d) feeding areas.
5. Are there endangered species dependent upon the area to be developed? Can they be protected by preserving features which are necessary for their survival ? Should they be protected directly from exploitation ?
6. Will animals or plants which from links in foodwebs be properly protected ? A good example of such a link is the coconut palm which provides food and shelter for a variety of animals including man.
7. Does the area under question support or will it support significant commercial fisheries ? Is fish production an important factor in the local economy ? Could it become important in the future ?
8. If the carrying capacity of either humans or animals is to be increased significantly, the potential is to be increased significantly, the potential consequences should be well-understood. Will basic need such as water, food and shelter be sufficient to meet the demand ? Will the quality of life or the health of Individuals be seriously lowered ?
9. Does the area to be developed contain sites or ruins of historical significance? Will preservation and, perhaps renovation of these sites receive proper consideration ?

10 Are there existing human habitats in the region ? Will their traditional rights and needs be considered in a just and fair manner ? To what extent are they dependent upon natural populations of plants and

animals for their existence ? Will these species be affected by the proposed development ? If so, how will the people be compensated ?

11. What changes in the animal community might be expected to accompany development? Will valuable species be lost? Will pests or disease vectors such as mosquitoes become more common ?

12. Chemical herbicides and pesticides are valuable when utilized property. Guidelines for their use should include: (a) avoidance of compounds which have been demonstrated to be extremely toxic or presistent in the environment: (b) use only in situations where there is no other suitable alternative; and (c) application by trained and skilled technical experts.

13. Can the area be utilized for aquaculture operations ? Will the proposed development limit or preclude this potential ?

14. Will sufficiently large natural areas which are not dependent upon direct human management be retained? Have the political and economic consequences of this been anticipated?

15. Areas of primary productivity such as wetlands, underwater grass beds and well-developed luxuriant forests should receive priority for preservation or management. Wherever destruction or serious alteration is contemplated, benefits and costs should be carefully compared.

B: Prevention of Adverse Alterations of Air and Water Quality

1. The release into waterways or the air of pathogenic bacteria and viruses must be prevented. These originate most commonly from improperly treated human sewage, but may also be derived from farm industrial wastes.

2. Release of excess organic compounds (sewage, sugarcane wastes, etc.) into streams, lakes and coastal waters can quickly deplete dissolved oxygen concentrations which may, in turn, cause large scale mortality of fishes and invertebrates. Organic wastes should either be oxidized in a controlled manner before discharge or else released in such dilute quantities that no damage will occur.

3. Fine particulate materials such as crushed ore when dumped into bodies of water can cause extensive damage to aquatic animals and plants due to suffocation, irritation and clogging of delicate membranes. These problems can be avoided by disposing of slurries and fine particulates on the land.

4. Anything which increased water turbidity to unnaturally high levels for extended periods of time will destroy aquatic animals and plants. Damage from carefully controlled dredging for channels may be kept at

minimal levels, but extensive dredging and filling of underwater sediments or erodable above water sediments can lead to permanent eco-system degradation.

5. Unnatural salinity alterations should not be allowed to occur in coastal waters. They may result from increased or decreased release of fresh-water from the land due to water diversion projects (i.e. dams, irrigation projects) or from the dumping of saline brine or interference with underground aquifer flows.

6. Extensive and significant water temperature increase from release of heated effluents from electrical power generating stations or industrial plants can cause widespread damage to aquatic eco-systems and should be avoided.

7. Acceptable air quality is essential for good human health and should be maintained. Badly degraded air can lead to respiratory diseases and reduced visibility.

8. Will heavy metals, toxic chemicals and other industrial by-products be disposed of properly? Generally, this will mean some type of containment disposal and no releases into the environment. If dilute effluent release is contemplated, all potential mechanisms of biological concentration should be carefully investigated.

9. Accidental oil spills from ships, wells, pipelines or holding facilities are, highly destructive. Careful planning can soften the impact of damaging spills through locating industrial facilities and ship channels at as great distances as possible from vulnerable areas (i.e. mangrove forest and coral reefs).

C. Physical Planning and Development

1. A basic consideration during the preliminary stages of planning concerns potential vulnerability to strong physical processes. Generally, permanent structures should not be planned for locations such as sand-dunes, slopes subject to mud slides or low-lying areas which might be inundated by storm surges. In situations where structures are absolutely necessary, they, should be properly engineered by being elevated and reinforced so as to minimise the effects of destructive events in spite of being an expensive undertaking.

2. Will the proposed development cause accelerated soil erosion ? This is likely to occur on construction sites, farming land, stripmined tracks, on steep slopes or any other location where the protective vegetative cover has been removed. Several tons per year of valuable soil can be lost from a single hectare. This eroded soil, in turn, creates a multitude of new problems in the streams, lakes, estuaries and coastal waters into which it is deposited. Eroded sites should be repaired as well as possible by

preparing the soil with fertilizers and mulches and replanting with species which are capable of controlling erosion.

3. Wherever surface drainage patterns or run-off rates will be altered, the consequences must be anticipated. For example when large areas are paved with asphalt, infiltration rates are greatly reduced and the run-off rate accelerated.
4. Natural beach erosion patterns should be understood before development is attempted; this is particularly true near high wave energy beaches. In locations where this occurs the vulnerable zone should be set aside as an undeveloped buffer area and used for activities such as passive recreation which may require little or no permanent structures.
5. Certain types development can lead to climatic change both on a local and macro scale. Change in temperature extremes and rainfall patterns over small geographical areas caused by such factors as vegetation removal, increases in large paved areas or release of particulate material from smoke stacks, are well-documented, partially understood and may be avoided in some cases with careful planning.
6. Inshore currents and patterns of sediment deposition in coastal and estuarine waters can be seriously affected by the construction of jetties, causeways, certain type of fish traps, piers and similar structures. This can lead to beach erosion and filling in and stagnation of lagoons and shipping channels. Where these structures are absolutely can often be designed to allow better water movement so that little resistance to currents is offered.
7. Wise management of subsurface water resources is essential for most coastal areas. Many coastal cities are dependent on subsurface fresh water aquifers which, if misused, may become depleted or contaminated with saltwater or pollutants. The recharge areas for aquifers may be hundreds of kilometres inland and also must be protected.

VI. CONCLUSION

6.1 The unique environmental and ecological values of the coastal areas require their conservation, improvement and effective controls on causes that imply environmental deterioration. The trend to use coastal areas for diverse and often conflicting activities will continue in the future. However, the growing concern for environmental management would readily suggest maintenance of environmental quality by such impact assessments as suggested in these guidelines.

6.2 There can be several guidelines for promotion of environmentally sustainable development along coastal areas. The approach and treatment of activity categories in this guidelines, although selective, could readily suggest well over a few scores of combination of activities and sub-activities to assess impact assessments. This may leave an impression that environmental management could be achieved by piecemeal treatment of each problem area. However the illustrative matrices make it clear that the underlying environmental deterioration result from cumulative impacts of several activities and not in isolation. This will imply that if environmental management is to be effective in coastal areas, the guidelines should be a pointer to assess impacts and form an integral part of overall development, planning and decision-making.

6.3 The State Governments should prepare a status report on the obtaining situation of the coastal areas as a prerequisite to environmental management of the area. Such a status report should be followed by a master plan clearly identifying the areas required for conservation, preservation and development and others. Such a master plan would ensure a scientific assessment and development of the coastline. It will also help State Government/Union Territories to formulate long-term plans for coastal developments spread over several five year plan periods. A regulated growth based on scientific assessment would ultimately ensure the preservation and enhancement of the coastal ecosystem.

6.4 The desirability of carrying out scientifically based EIA for developmental activities along the coastal areas has been emphasised in the report. For this purpose a nodal agency in the governmental system to conduct such assessment is essential. The Department of Environment wherever their has been created, could act as the nodal agency for such pruposes. The Central Department of Environment could oversee the specific needs of the various States/Union Territories in this matter.

6.5 Preparation of Environmental Impact Assessment (EIA) generally involves considerable expertise from a number of specialised fields such as physical and social sciences, ecology and engineering etc. Thus the EIA technology is inter-disciplinary in nature. It would, therefore, be desirable to obtain expert consultants from the public and private sectors to assist in preparing the EIA and the EIS (Environmental Impact Statements). With a view to promoting capabilities of consultants in the area of EIA technology and to prevent and control proliferation of pseudo-experts in the area, the Development of Environmental, both at the Centre and States, may undertake measures to promote case studies both in the form of post-mortem examination of existing developments and new development preparation of Panel of experts and their periodic review etc. The Departments may recognise or derecognise expert consultants(s) based on such reviews.

ANNEXURE A

Format for Environmental Impact Statement

The environmental impact assessment is to be followed by the preparation of an Environmental Impact Statement (EIS). An EIS is a final analysis of an environmental impact assessment. The EIS indicates numerically the magnitude of impact of the development project on the various components of the environment. The EIS provides the brief for decision makers about the project. A general methodology to prepare an EIS is to review item by item, effects on individual environmental parameters (resources or values) as presented in Table A, including both identification of the resources (or values) and description and quantification of the effect to the extent possible. Environmental parameters have been arranged in four groups in Table A for making the evaluation. These four groups are:

(a) physcial resources

(b) ecological (or biological) resources

(c) human use values

(d) quality of life values.

Alteration in group (a) will affect group (b); and both group (c) and (d) will be affected by alteration in (a) and (b). Actually, any change in any environmental parameter will to some degree affect all other environmental parameters, in that they are all interrelated. However for the purpose of discussion and analysis each can be evaluated on its own, with suitable evaluations.

While the majority of projects will tend to affect most of the parameters, in particular projects some of the parameters will be of key importance and others of minor importance or insignificant, depending upon the nature of the project and upon the region in which it is located. For purpose of guidance Table B has been presented to show which environmental parameters will generally be of primary importance to the listed projects.

Table 1

Col. I	Col.II	Col. III
A. Tourism development	1. Residental	1. Structures, constructions
B. Industrial development	2. Highways and roads	2. Demolition of structures, neglected maintenance
C. Urban development	3. Infrastructural services	3. Embankments, cutting
D. Fishing villages	4. Communication network	4. Fences, barries
E. Special areas	5. Ports, Terminals	5. Vegetation clearing
F. Communication and Transport network	6. Airports	6. Paving, imperious surfaces
	7. Industries	7. Landfills, garbage, solid waste
	8. Oil refining, storage, petro-chemicals	8. Dumps, effluents and liquid waste
	9. Commercial	9. Sewage discharges, outfalls
	10. Pipelines-terrestrial and marine	10. Sewerage-septic tanks
	11. Power generation, Trasmission lines	11. Waste water
	12. Mining terrestrial	12. Fuel and oil spills and discharges
	13. Mining marine	13. Ships, tankers
	14. Made/Reclaimed land	14. Fishing vessels, fishing gear, cold storage and processing
	15. Logging/Forestry	15. Vehicles and emissions
	16. Fishing - Deep sea, others	16. Noise, vibration
	17. Scenic areas	17. Stack emission, open burning
	18. Special areas (mangroves, sanctuaries, etc.)	18. Channels, cuts, fills
	19. Land-oriented recreation	19. Wetland and submrged landfill
	20. Marine-oriented recreation	20. Bleasting-terrestrial and underwater

21. Waste disposal soild/liquid	21. Rock crushing and ore treatment
22. Sea/Ocean dumping	22. Sand/coral mining
23. Productive farming	23. Collecting marine flora and fauna
24. Crop pattern	24. Collecting artistic and historic objects
25. Horticulture/Cash crops	25. Collecting terristrial fauna and flora
26. Pesticides/Fertilizers	26. Leachtes from pesticides fertilizers
27. Irrigation and water source management	27. Preservation of historic/ancient monuments
	28. Salinity intrusion into subsoil water
	29. Fishing vessels, offals/waste disposal
	30. Crop harvesting and waste mateial disposal
	31. Excavation and earth moving
	32. Brick making/kilns
	33. Introduction and earth moving
	34. Airplanes, helicoptors
	35. Runways and aprons, helipads
	36. Reserve forests, sanctuaries
	37. Beach resorts, hotels, hostels
	38. Utilities
	39. Dredging
	40. Population increase overcrowding, insanitary conditions

TABLE A

Environmental Parameters involved in analysis of Development Projects

Environmental Parameters	Degree of Impact					
	1	2	3	I	R	P
Physical Resources						
Air resources/quality						
Climate						
Mineral resources						
Soils (including beach sands)						
Topography/geology/seismology						
Water quality						
Water quantity (hydrology)						
Ecological/Biological Resources						
Aquatic biology						
Fisheries						
Forest habitat						
Wildlife (terrestrial)						
Human Use Values						
Farming/irrigation						
Flood control/drainage						
Highways/streets						
Housing						
Industry						
Landuse patterns						
Navigation						
Sewage treatment						
Solid treatment						
Solid waste management						
Water supply						

Quality of Life Values

Archaeological values
Community cleanliness
Cultural values
Employment patterns
Noise problems
Population density
Public health
Public safety
Scio-economic

Notes: The impact may be identified in terms of 1, 2 and 3 which represent:

1 = Slight impact on environment

2 = Moderate impact on environment

3 = Heavy impact on environment

— The project may cause irreversible use of environmental resources or termination of important potential use of any of the environmental parameters in which case identify the same under IR.

— The project may be impacted significantly by any of the environmental parameters in which case identify the same under P.

TABLE B
Matrix of Environmental Resources/Values of VS Type of Project

Example of Environmental Resource/Value	Example of Types of Project														
	Manufacturing plant	Hotel	Beach resort	Dam/Reservoir	Water supply system	Shopping centre	Harbour	Fossil fuel power plant	Agro-industry	Highway	Sugar refinery	Oil refinery	Mining	Logging
Physical Resources														
Air resources														
Geology/Seismology														
Ground water														
Mineral resources														
Power														
Sediments/Erosion														
Soils														
Surface water														
Water quality														

Ecological/Biological Resources	
Aquatic biology	
Fisheries	
Forests/Watershed	
Wildlife	
Human Use Values	
Agriculture	
Flood control/Drainage	
Industrial development	
Landuses	
Navigation	
Recreation	
Resettlement	
Transportation (Land)	
Water supply	
Quality of Life Values	
Aesthetic	
Archaeological	
Cultural	
Public health	
Publis safety	
Socio-economic	

ANNEXURE XI

ENVIRONMENTAL GUIDELINES FOR THERMAL POWER PLANTS DEPARTMENT OF ENVIRONMENT

The following note attempts to highlight the parameters that have to be considered for ensuring that thermal power plants are planned, constructed and operated in a manner as to minimize the potential impact on the environment. The note mentions in checklist form some factors that have a bearing upon thermal power plant siting and operations. But only those parameters of the factors mentioned that are directly relevant to the preservation and protection of environmental quality are elaborated on. The recommendations are addressed to the present and potential power plant authorities as well as State Environment Committees of various States.

0. Factors to be considered

1. Plant parameters and infrastructure
2. Waste characteristics
3. Environmental conditions
4. Cost benefit analysis
5. Research and development.

1. Plant parameters and infrastructure

1.1 *Resources:*

1.1.1 *Fuel:*

Since coal is the fuel predominently in use, the establishment of reliable coal linkages of proper quality are important from the environmental point of view. If Grade II coal (20-24% ash) is not available coal washing facilities must be sought. The quality of coal being received must be monitored periodically. Facilities for such monitoring must be established within the plant. The use of oil for start-upflame stabilization purposes can lead to e.g. release of sulphur dioxide.

1.1.2 *Water availability and quality:*

In the interests of water conservation recyling should be practised wherever possible. The principal air should be to manage water use between process, cooling and sanitary needs, to achieve optimal consumption from available supplies of varying quality.

1.1.3 *Personnel and services:*

The training of plant personnel in the maintenance and use of pollution monitoring and abatement equipment is crucial to environment protection. If possible, inplant training should be a continuous programme.

1.2 *Technology*

1.2.1 *Pollution abatement technology:*

For preventing pollution, it should be mandatory for all proposed thermal power plants to include a combination of mechanical collectored and electrostatic precipitators to achieve a total collection efficiency for particulates of between 95% and 99%.

Specially trained personnel, equipment and spare parts for the adequate maintenance of these equipment must be built up within the plant.

The units must be taken down periodically for 4 to 5 days after every 3 months to clear the dust collection plant, repair/replace the worn out parts and make all adjustments necessary in the E.P. control equipment for tuning up the system.

It is also strongly recommended that periodic performance tests be conducted on dust collection plants to take remedial measure in time to improve the performance.

Similar attention should be given to the ash vacuation and handling system which otherwise can develop into serious bottleneck in efficient functioning of the pollution abatement equipment.

It is desirable as far as possible to reduce the number of sources of emission from a particular thermal power station since a 'point source' of emission will result in lesser pollution than a 'line source'. Therefore a number of units may be provided later in this note the use of tall stacks can become a legitimate and cost effective means of 'pollution control'. Experience indicates that an exit gas velocity of around 25 m/sec characteristics.

1.2.2 *Raw materials handling technology:*

The transportation and handling of coal at plant sites can cause severe air pollution problems. Dust suppression/extraction procedures should be employed especially at transfer points, at the location of wagon tipplers, etc. where coal fines could create pollution problems.

1.2.3 *Cooling techniques:*

These should be selected to achieve the most efficient cooling but at the same time ensuring that thermal pollution in surrounding water courses does not become a major problem.

1.2.4 *Transporation* — for construction materials and raw materials. Care should be taken in establishment of roads, rail links, communication networks, construction facilities, etc. to minimize damage to the environment.

2. Waste characteristics and standards

2.1 *Air pollution*

2.1.1 As air emission (especially particulates) are the most severe form of pollution with regard to thermal power plants, its characteristics, quantities and relationships to load patterns should be monitored as frequently as possible. Periodic monitoring or the levels of particulates at selected points in the area (cities, towns, villages, agricultural lands, etc.), surrounding the power plant should be done. Together with this an assessment of the contribution to air pollution damage by the power plant must be made. In this connection, it is also recommended that monitoring of background dust levels be made for about a year before a particular plant goes into operation so that reliable estimates can be made as to the contribution to air pollution from the plant concerned. For thermal power plants located in isolated areas away from residential areas with no foreseable significant environmental impact, particulate emission levels up to 0.5 mg/cm could be allowed. For plants which are located in crowded suburban areas or which would add significantly to an already high existing background level the State Environmental Committees or Pollution Boards Control Boards must set the appropriate standards based on studies conducted in the area.

2.1.2 *Other emissions:*

Where it is expected that SO_2 or other emissions could give to problems measures like the use of stacks be considered since use of abatement technology may be prohibitively expensive at this stage.

2.2 *Water Pollution*

2.2.1 *Ash Slurry :*

In the concern about mitigating air pollution especially from particulates the possibility of significant water or 'land pollution' is often forgotton. Appropriate steps for disposal/reuse of ash slurry must be made so that adjoining surface or groundwater supplies are not polluted.

2.2.2 The possibility of thermal pollution from ultimate of 'coolant water' has been mentioned before. It is desirable to make studies on the potential impact on the aquatic life of nearby water sources from discharge of heated water. The rise in ambient water temperature from the discharge should be periodically monitored.

2.3 *Solid Wastes*

2.3.1 *Ash:*

Economic uses for fly ash and bottom ash must be incorporated within thermal power plant configurations. Only when the economics of reuse are very unfavourable for any particular location should the ash be used as landfill or disposed off in some other manner. A list of possible uses in the construction industry would include use as a constituent in cement concrete, for soil stabilization in load buildings, load bearing fill in many types of construction work, raw materials for preparation of hollow brick etc.

2.3.2 Mention has been made before of the potential air pollution problem from handling of coal fines. Economic reuse for this 'waste' must also be explored.

3. Environmental Conditions

There are a number of conditions and components of the environment that could add to or be victims of environmental impact from thermal plants siting.

3.1 *Alternative sites*

The location criteria for thermal power plants must also incorporate considerations other than normal techno-economic ones. Siting is the single most crucial factor for mitigating environmental impact. During the feasibility report preparation stage consultants (private, State Enviornmental Boards, India Meteorological Department, NCEPC, etc.) should be called upon to suggest how environmental aspects of topography, geology, hydrology, seismology and meteorology can be incorporated in site selection criteria.

Some of the components of the environment that could suffer environmental damage and would, therefore, have to be kept in mind during site selection and subsequent plant operation would include—

3.1.1 Human population in surrounding villages, townships, cities.

3.1.2 Ecology—flora and fauna (wildlife) in the vicinity.

3.1.3 Amenity—property, historical monuments, etc.

3.1.4 Activity—agriculture, fishery, recreation etc.

3.2 *Meteorology*

Climatic conditions can considerably accentate the damage to health and amenity from thermal power plant emissions. In this connection, power plant must maintain, or have access to data for their area in wild direction and speeds (Wind Rose), temperature profiles and inversion frequencies. Study of such data can at times also suggest useful modification to operating procedures for minimising environmental impact.

4. Cost-benefit analysis

4.1 *Expenditure on pollution control*

Power plant managements should keep detailed records of the cost (capital and operating) incurred on account of pollution control as well as the efficiencies of control achieved. Such data should be submitted to the State Environmental Boards and NCEPC to help in policy formulation with regard to development of abatements technology and standards of control that are realistically achievable.

5. Research and Development

5.1 *Environment related research*

Facilities for R and D should be established by State Electricity Boards. A few areas for work are suggested below :

5.1.1 The effect of variation of gas temperature , gas velocity, power input, etc. on the performance of precipitators.

5.1.2 The effect of gas conditioning on the performance of precipitators.

5.1.3 Model studies on the effectiveness of tall chimneys in reducing ambient fly ash levels under various wind and climatic conditions.

5.1.4 Studies on wear rates, outage hours and incremental generation costs as a function of ash content in coal and composition of ash.

5.1.5 Studies on the use of quality of fuel. e.g. use of agglomerates.

5.1.6 Studies on the use of alternate (renewable) fuels for power generation.

5.1.7 Preparation of comprehensive cost-benefit analysis on cooperation with Electricity Authorities, State Environment Boards, NCEPC and other relevant institutions that attempt to quantify and take into account environmental perceptions hitherto considered as intangible benefits or disbenefits.

Questionnaire

Environment Appraisal of Thermal Power Projects

Information Regarding Questionnaire

This Questionnaire seeks to elicit information necessary for evaluation potential impacts on the environment from new thermal power projects. It forms part of the requirement for preparing project reports for thermal power schemes. It is designed to gather preliminary information which will aid the agency that examines such schemes to assess whether adequate steps are being taken to ensure environmental protection. It is expected that the exercise of collecting and consolidating the information required herewith will itself enable project authorities to be aware of factors related to the environmentally sound operation of the plot. The data related to meteorological parameters will have to be gathered from offices of the Indian Meteorological Department or collected a fresh during studies for establishing techo-economic feasibility.

The completed questionnaire together with the Feasibility Report may be forwarded through the Central Electricity Authority to:

The Director (Environmental Planning)
Department of Environment
Technology Bhawan
New Mehrauli Road
New Delhi-110 029

Basic Information for Environmental Appraisal

1. Name and Location

1.1 Name/Title of proposed thermal power plant.

1.2 Name of project authority and contact address.

1.3 Site where proposed plant is to be located.

1.4 Capacity of project under consideration.

1.5 Is this an extension ? If so, indicate capacity of existing plant.

1.6 What is the ultimate capacity envisaged ?

2. General Environmental Information

2.1 What major pollution generating establishments exist within a radius of ten kilometres of your plant ? Give details.

2.2 What is the total human population within a radus of 10 km. of the plant site ?

2.3 Give a broad description of the site including plan, physiography, topography and nature of soil.

2.4 Give a general description of the vetegation within 10 km. of your plant site (give names of species).

Crops
Forest
Scrub
Grassland
Other (specify)

2.5 List any important of wildlife (animal or plant) that exist within the same radius.

2.6 List the sites of cultural, historic or other touristic interest 20 km. of your plant.

3. Fuel Use

3.1 Type, quantity and characteristics of fuel used

	Tonnes/ day	% Ash	% Sulphur	Source of supply
Coal				
Oil				
Other (specify)				

3.2 Please furnish a fuel analysis report from a recognised laboratory.

3.3 Indicate type of coal firing to be adopted.

4. Water-use and Liquid Waste Discharge

4.1 What is your source of water ? Will it be adequate for your use ? Do you propose any measure to augment water supply ?

4.2 Quantity required for :

	Kl/day
(a) Process	
(b) Cooling	
(c) Sanitary	

4.3 What type of cooling system is proposed ? Give details including temperature difference between inlet and outlet.

4.4 Total quantity and treatment proposed to be discharged water per day.

4.5 Type of waste treatment proposed to be adopted (if any) and standards to be adhered to.

4.6 Mode of final discharge

Open channel/pipeline/other

4.7 Point of final discharge : fallow land/agricultural land/sewer/river/lake/ wetland/bay/estuary/sea.

4.8 Is any proportion of the waste water to be recycled ? If so give details.

5. Air Emission

5.1 Please furnish for your location :

(a) Wind rose

(b) mean maximum and near minimum temperature for every month of the year

(c) mean wind speed at maximum temperature

(d) man cloud amount

(e) percentage frequency occurrence of inversion

5.2 Please specify the following :

(a) Number and type of stacks

(b) Inter-stack distance

(c) Height of each stack

(d) Diameter of each stack

(e) Exit gas velocity

(f) Fine gas characteristics

(i) Volume (ii) Temperature (iii) Density (iv) Size distribution of particulates (v) Gas composition.

5.3 (a) What kind of stack emission monitoring is proposed?

(b) What equipment is proposed to be acquired for this purpose ?

5.4 Give details of air pollution control equipment you propose to instal.

5.5 Give details of the organisational set-up for maintenance of pollution control equipment and level of expertise and authority of person incharge.

5.6 What quantities of particulates and sulphur dioxide are expected to be released when control equipment is;

(a) Functioning normally,

(b) Not functioning.

5.7 What special procedures do you propose to lay down for air pollution control during periods when emission exceeds prescribed limits for any reason including malfunctioning of equipment.

6. Coal and Ash Handling

6.1 (a) What is the procedure for coal handling at the plant site ?

(b) Give details of procedures if any, for reducing pollution from coal fines and other "fugitive emission" from the plant.

6.2 What quantities of fly ash and bottom ash will be produced per day ?

6.3 Indicate the method of collection, transport and disposal of the ash and point of final disposal.

6.4 Have you considered the reuse of ask ? If so, give details.

6.5 What precautions are to be taken to prevent pollution of water courses from solid waste disposal, especially, with regard to ash slurry ?

6.6 What land area is available for fly ash disposal ? Include site plan.

7. Economics of Pollution Control

7.1 (a) What is the total project cost ?

(b) What is the capital cost of the plant ?

7.2 Indicate costs of pollution control under the following head.

Capital *Recurring (annual)*

(a) Air

(b) Water

(c) Solid waste

(d) Other (Specify)

(e) Total

ANNEXURE XII

GUIDELINES FOR ENVIRONMENTAL IMPACT ASSESSMENT OF SHIPPING AND HARBOUR PROJECTS

INTRODUCTION

The shipping and harbour activities by their very nature, interact extensively with the environment resulting in short-term and long-term physical, chemical and biological changes. The multitude of facilities such as for loading and unloading, storage and dispersal of cargoes in the port itself, navigation and berthing of ships approaching in the port, midstream anchorage, communication facilities and their supporting structures, repair facilities of a dockyard, etc. give rise to several issues having impact on air, water and land quality. In addition, several social considerations such as cultural, aesthetic and historical bear upon environmental impact of the shipping and harbour activities. These issues have to be closely examined and legislation and guidelines have to be evolved for the planned development of shipping and harbour activities in order to limit and combat their deleterious impact on the environment.

The land-sea interface and the adjoining area of our coastline and archipelagoes, namely, the coastal zone, constitute very high population density areas— it is certainly true for Bombay, Calcutta and Madras and some coastal areas for instance, from Calicut to Trivandrum. The well-being of the coastal population is directly linked with the ecological balance of the land-sea system. The major coastal cities are also the gateways for the bulk of our exports and imports. The rapid increase in the volume of seaborne traffic has been the most important factor which has influenced the development of ports and harbours in India. Like almost all other developmental projects, the experience in coastal and harbour development also shows that the cost of remedial measures would outweigh the cost of preventive measures if they were instituted during the planning and implementation stage itself. Therefore, it is essential that the environmental consequences are projected well in advance, their impact is assessed properly and suitable control measures are incorporated right in the planning, designing and execution phases of all shipping and harbour projects.

To formulate the guidelines, the basic objectives and policies to be implemented and enforced in respect of shipping and harbour projects, it is essential to define the area under the control of shipping and harbour authorities and their responsibilities; and co-operation with the local, regional and State bodies to maintain a healthy environment. The guiding principles to be followed for pollution control and acceptable environmental impact are:

- The shipping and harbour activities should not lead to the transfer of pollution from the controlled area resulting in impermissible environmental impact in the public domain;
- Within the controlled area, the acceptable environmental impact should be based on the limits of permissible levels of pollutants and deleterious materials, and preservation of the social, cultural, aesthetic and historical characteristics.

II. POLICY FORMULATION FOR PROTECTION OF THE ENVIRONMENT

1. Objectives

1.1 microbiological activity in the waters of harbours and adjoining coastal waters in the public domain should remain as hygienic as it would be in the absence of the shipping and harbour activities. Microbiological activity of significance to marine and estuarine life and man using the coastal waters should be fully protected;

1.2 (a) release of oils, chemicals and other materials should be controlled so that it does not disturb the marine flora and fauna outside the controlled harbour area;

(b) release or emission in the harbour area by the air route shall conform to regulations in respect of air quality criteria set for the public domain; and

(c) releases containing viruses, pathogenic bacteria and parasites which survive in marine life should be precluded;

1.3 (a) productivity of the marine environment adjoining the harbour and resources of the coastal waters shall remain unaffected by shipping and harbour activities;

(b) the potential for marine resources such as production of shell fish, salt, commercial fish, etc. should be maintained; and

(c) indicator organism required for the study of environmental impact should be identified and preserved.

1.4 adjoining coast and coastal marine area shall not be subjected to unintended or unplanned changes in siltation, erosion, flow pattern and coastal contours due to shipping and harbour activities;

1.5 aesthetic, cultural and social patterns and historical characteristics should not be unduly disturbed due to the shipping and harbour activities;

1.6 work environment in the controlled area should be conductive to safe and healthy working conditions; and

1.7 electromagnetic pollution and noise pollution in the controlled area should always be maintained well within the limits acceptable in the public domain.

2. Parameters

For planned development and monitoring of the environmental consequences of shipping and harbour activities, baseline information on the following parameters is essential. This data should be collected and made available for planning harbour construction/extensions. These will further serve as benchmark in the assessment of the environmental impact during the development and operation of the ports and harbour.

2.1 *Physical*

- coastal current patterns, littoral drifts, local currents due to influx of fresh water, tidal currents, wind currents, oceanic currents of the nearby regions;
- marine bed topography, siltation and silt movement, silt deposition at mouth of estuaries, natural patterns of erosion and deposition, seasonal changes of influx of silt due to influx of fresh water;
- shore and beach profile and engineering features and properties of the shore and bed materials;
- wave height, periods and distribution, breaker zones and wave refraction, diffraction during different seasons;
- wind speed and direction, their distribution frequencies, rainfall, other climate parameters and extreme meteorological conditions obtained at the coastal site under consideration;
- seismic characteristics of the region;
- fresh water resources in the region;
- temperature and salinity of the coastal waters.

2.2 *Chemical*

- dissolved oxygen, nitrates and phosphates
- COD and BOD;
- total inventory of pollutants already entering the marine environment from public domain;

- concentration of various elements and compounds entering the harbour waters from industrial and municipal discharges;
- colour, smell, turbidity and their seasonal variations;
- concentration of various and their seasonal variations;
- concentration of various halogenated hydro-carbons, hydrocarbon products from petro-chemical and other industries;
- assessment of existing air pollution levels in the harbour area from the stack emissions of the adjoining industries.

2.3 *Biological*

- microbiological activity, primary productivity, plankton distribution;
- flora and fauna in the marine and estuarine environment, fish, shell fish, algae;
- fish spawning grounds;
- commercial fisheries potential;
- vegetation including inter tidal and forestry.

2.4 *Cultural, Social and Aesthetic*

- Industries and projected industrial growth;
- population distribution;
- recreational uses of the coastal environment;
- historical monuments of significance;
- places of tourist importance.

3. Environmental Impact Studies

The following parameters should be studied continuously for monitoring environmental impact of the shipping and harbour activities:

- changes in siltation and erosion patterns, silt loads, currents, dispersal characteristics of the coastal water;
- estimated dredging sites for disposal of dredge spoils (if the dredge spoils are used for land reclamation, afforestation efforts should be simultaneously enforced for soil conservation and containing the silt load due to run off waters);
- displacement of biological communities (significant and commercial), fish spawning grounds and their eventual impact on the environment and productivity;
- corrosion of structures by sea water;
- leaching rates of pollutants from materials used for structures and floating vessels, their resident times, bioaccumulation, levels of toxicity and their capability of changing into more or equally toxic chemicals form, their eventual fate in water and sediments;

- rates of possible leakages of bulk commodities (imported or exported) handled in the port and subsequent impact on the environment.
- impact of electromagnetic radiation due to the communication systems and acoustic disturbance;
- storage facilities for handling of toxic and dangerous goods will have to be examined closely for adequacy to protect the environment, shelter for ships against extreme meteorological conditions, storage capacity, safety features of handling of these cargoes,
- insecticides used in the harbour and eventual fate in the marine environment;
- sewage treatment and management and its effectiveness on ship board and for shore based facilities;
- epidemiological studies on the population interacting with port activities.

All the existing shipping and harbour activities should be examined in detail on the points stipulated above with a view to assessing the adequacy or otherwise from pollution prevention angle. The extension activities would require conformance with the stipulations made in this document.

III. ACCIDENTS IN THE MARINE ENVIRONMENT

The two categories of accidents in the shipping and harbour operations are, viz:

- accidents involving shore based facilities; and
- accidents on and/or involving floating vessels.

It is necessary to prepare projections enveloping as complete a spectrum of accidents and incidents as possible, starting from minor incidents to the maximum credible or design basis accidents. These accidents should be evaluated and should be studied in detail with regard to their impact on the workers and the environment in the controlled area as well as impact on the environment and the population in the public domain.

It is a normal practice to design engineered safety features into the facilities to prevent accidents, specifically the ones having large consequences. The engineered safety features should also be provided to limit the consequences of such accidents and incidents. It is also essential to prepare emergency plans and provide for equipment and organisation to deal with emergency situations arising from accidents and incidents and also to undertake post-accident rehabilitation measures. Such emergency plans should be periodically tested, evaluated and improved upon by performing mock drills. It is important to plan these exercises in a manner such that each ligament of the plan is exercised during these drills.

Some examples of the types of accidents that could be considered for engineering environmental safety and for organising contingency plans are as follows:

- explosion on floating vessels or on shore;
- fire on floating vessels or on shore;
- listing or sinking of floating vessels. The floating vessels in addition to interfering with harbour movements may also contain hazardous substances, toxic and corrosive materials;
- collisions of floating vessels or impacts of floating vessels on shore structures or vessels running aground;
- failure of power supply in shore installations or on board the floating vessels;
- effluent treatment plants mal-operation either on shore or on floating vessels;
- failure of oil storage facilities on shore or on floating vessels;
- sabotage, failure of harbour security and protection measures.

A review of the national/world wide experience in this regard and built-in engineered safety features and organisational provisions provided for would be invaluable guidance for the purpose.

IV. OFFENCES AND PENALTIES

Violations of environmental rules and regulations shall attract commensurate penalty provisions against the violator(s). The guiding principles for ascertaining/estimating penalties for violation shall be:

(i) to at least offset any financial gain that may accrue to the perpetrator(s) of the offence and/or

(ii) commensurate with the damage financial or otherwise to other party or parties (estimated or established) inclusive of cost of rehabilitation of the harbour and adjoining environs to its normal state; and

(iii) extent of public hazards or nuisance arising out of the offence committed and financial compensation therefor.

V. LEGAL REQUIREMENTS

While formulating the requirements for limiting the environmental impact from shipping and harbour activities

- the organisations concerned should take into account the national legislation, rules and regulations and stipulations of various international conventions held from time to time;
- machinery should be developed to incorporate the stipulations of the international conventions without undue delay so that it is possible to ensure cleaner environment and ensure prompt implementation in international rules and regulations.

VI. INDEPENDENT TECHNICAL AND ADMINISTRATIVE SET-UP

A technical and administration set-up should be operative at all times to study the environmental impact of the shipping and harbour activities during construction, normal operations as well as during abnormal/accident situations. This organisation should be a quick responsive one and be responsible for studying impact both within the controlled area and in the neighbourhood so that the impact on the environment is continuously monitored, assessed, predictive methodology developed and corrective actions are recommended to the appropriate authorities to initiate or take actions to ensure environmental protection and improvement.

This organisation should be independent of the operating port or harbour organisation and should not be involved in any of the profit motivated activities. The organisation should be vested with responsibility and authority to enforce the regulations under the relevant provisions of the applicable legislations.

With a view to building up a viable organisation for the purpose, it has to be manned by well trained, technically and administratively qualified personnel properly equipped with adequate technical field and laboratory facilities for undertaking investigative work. The organisations should also undertake training and relevant research responsibilities.

In order to bring into force the enabling legal provisions for the enforcement of the above stipulations, an appropriate enactment by the Parliament would be needed at an early date.

VII. ENVIRONMENTAL IMPACT ASSESSMENT

A questionnaire on shipping and harbour development projects has been designed not only to elicit information about the harbour but also to draw attention of concerned designers, managers, engineers and the like to the kind of environmental parameters and considerations that must be taken cognisance of both during developmental and operational phases. A large part of the questionnaire could possibly be answered from the information already available with the port authorities. There is, however, a part environmentally very significant, which calls for special skill and experience which may not be readily available to all the port authorities. The need to employ hire such skills may not be over-emphasized. The questionnaire is intended to be comprehensive and it is not necessarily exhaustive. A more extensive project specific data base may be required for an indepth environmental impact analysis. The questionnaire has been evolved on the basis of objectives and guidelines laid out above, and is placed at Annexure-I. This particular format has been approved by concerned authorities of some of the major Port Trusts.

Annexure 1
QUESTIONNAIRE

1. General Information

1.1 Name of the Port/Harbour

1.2 Classification:

Major

Intermediate

Minor

Fishing

1.3 Location

Latitude

Longitude

1.4 Authority/Authorities:

Area under direct control (defined as controlled area)

Name of the official to whom correspondence may be addressed.

Attach organisational chart and give details of the total staff in action for day to day execution of the work. (Note: Make a special mention of the Environmental Officers, if any, and their duties.)

1.5 Approach and Charts

Is the port connected with a river/canal system? (If yes, give details)

Enclose a detailed layout map for transportation system for approach to and from the harbour.

Describe any other means of transportation including railway system with marshalling yard, etc.

List hydrographic charts in use for operational purposes and any other charts applicable.

1.6 Please indicate minimum and maximum water depth in:

Adjoining coastal waters

Approach channel to harbour waters

In harbour area

1.7 Give the list of in-house publications/reports (enclose one copy of each)

Force on the 4th June, 1974. As for reception facilities, notification No. GSR 1033 dated June 10th September, 1974 declared the ports of Bombay, Madras and Visakhapatnam as ports having reception facilities in accordance with the provisions of the Convention.

4. In 1969, the Inter-Governmental Maritime Consultative Organisation (IMCO) adopted an amendment to the aforesaid Convention. This amendment, *inter alia*, provided as follows:

(1) A ship of 500 tons gross or more, other than a tanker, shall not discharge oil or oily mixture anywhere into the sea except when one and all of the following conditions are satisfied, namely:

(a) the ship is proceeding en-route;

(b) the instantaneous rate of discharge of oil contents does not exceed 60 litres per mile;

(c) the oil content of the discharge is less than 100 parts per one million parts of the mixture; and

(d) the discharge is made as far as practicable from the nearest land.

(2) A tanker of 150 tons or more shall not discharge oil or oily mixture anywhere into the sea except when one and all of the following conditions are satisfied, namely:

(a) the tanker is proceeding en-route;

(b) the instantaneous rate of discharge of oil content does not exceed 60 litres per mile;

(c) the total quantity of oil discharged on a ballast voyage does not exceed 1/15000 of the total cargo carrying capacity; and

(d) the tanker is more than 50 miles away from the nearest land.

5. In this context it may be stressed that while the Convention as amended in 1962 permitted discharge of oil residues and oily mixture beyond prohibited zones, the 1969 amendments to it prohibit such discharge except at the instantaneous rate of discharge of 60 litres per mile subject to other conditions specified in the preceding paragraph. The instantaneous rate of discharge has been defined as the rate of discharge in litres per hour at any instant divided by the speed of the ship in knots at the same instant. With the limitation on discharge of oil or oily

mixture into the sea except at the instantaneous rate of discharge and subject to other conditions specified by the 1969 amendments to the Convention, tankers of 150 tons or more and ships of 500 tons or more will be obliged to retain on board oil residues and oily mixture in greater quantities than hithertofore, and conversely look forward to port administrations to provide reception facilities for receiving them without undue delay. Further, it was sufficient for the contracting parties to the Convention amended in 1962 to provide reception facilities only at selected ports. Under the 1969 amendments such facilities would need to be provided at all ports used by international shipping.

6. In the light of the foregoing considerations it has become imperative that the port administrations review the facilities that may be required to be provided by them at their respective ports for meeting Government's obligations as a contracting party to the Convention as amended in 1969 and prepare a phased programme for provision of such facilities with cost assessment.

MATTERS RELATED TO IMPLEMENTATION OF THE 1969 AMENDMENTS TO THE 1954 OIL POLLUTION CONVENTION : DISPOSAL OF SLUDGE FROM THE PURIFICATION OF FUEL OIL AND LUBRICATING OIL

Note by the International Chamber of Shipping to Inter-governmental Maritime Consultive Organisation: March 1977

During the sixth session of the MEPC, ICS reported that it was conducting a survey into procedures for the disposal of sludge from the purification of fuel oil and lubricating oil on diesel ships, and offered to consider making the results available to the seventh session (MEPC VI/17, paragraph 81).

A summary of the replies is attached. The survey covered 1,136 ships from 12 different countries. While in no way comprehensive, therefore, the replies may be regarded as indicative of current procedures for dealing with sludge accumulation.

The survey which was confined to diesel-propelled ships on the grounds that it is these vessels which have to purify bunker fuel oil onboard—suggests that more than one-third of such ships have some means of on board disposal. The worldwide average seems likely to be considerably lower, however, because:

(i) Paragraph 3 of the summary obscures the fact that some vessels are not only fitted with an incinerator or homogeniser, but also have the facility to burn sludge in boilers; these vessels are therefore accounted for twice in the figures;

(ii) The majority of the ships for which information was provided are fair modern and are therefore more likely to be fitted with equipment of this nature;

(iii) One major contributing country to the survey had a far greater than average number of vessels equipped with onboard means of sludge disposal, and this has influenced the total figure.

It is evident, therefore, that storage of sludge on board for subsequent disposal ashore is still by far the most common solution, and is likely to remain so. The replies also illustrated that a considerable number of ships, from countries which have not yet implemented the 1969 amendments, have not been confronted with difficulties of disposal because they have been at liberty to discharge such sludge outside "prohibited zones" at sea. Where the 1969 amendments have been applied, however, ships have often had problems both of storage capacity and of disposal ashore. Although some ships have minimal storage capacity, and on others it is almost unlimited, the average appears to be between 20 and 60 days. With the entry into force of the 1969 amendments in January 1978, therefore, it is probable that many vessels will encounter difficulties if reception facilities are not available in the ports to which they are trading within the time-limits imposed by storage capacity.

ANNEXURE XIII

CABINET SECRETARIAT'S (GOVERNMENT OF INDIA) INSTRUCTIONS ON PREVENTION OF HAZARDS FROM INDUSTRIAL UNITS

The Government are anxious that prompt action is taken for control and prevention of hazards from industrial units to their workers and to the community in the vicinity of their location. To achieve this task, it is essential that the concerned Administrative Ministries/Departments identify and prescribe necessary safety measures and regulations for hazardous industrial units and ensure that no lapses are allowed to take place in their observation and adherence.

2. A broad action plan for this purpose is outlined below:

I. Identification of hazardous Industries

A list of hazardous industries has been identified (Appendix I) by the Department of Environment, Forests and Wild Life (DOEn). DOEn would modify/up-to-date this list from time to time. Govt. also propose to set up a Hazardous Substances Control Board in due course for guiding and overseeing the implementation of various measures required for control of hazardous substances/industrial units by different Ministries/State agencies.

II. Identification of hazardous units and specification of safety standards

For identified hazardous industries, action on the following lines needs to be taken:

(a) In respect of new units, based on processes identified to be hazardous, suitable stipulations may be made in the Letters of Intent/Industrial Licences/DGTD registrations to the effect that adequate steps will be taken in regard to process hazards for ensuring safety in plants and that before going into trial production, adequacy of steps taken will be established to the satisfaction of the appropriate authorities. This will imply the need for inspection, to establish the adequacy of the safety measures, before a new unit goes into trial production.

(b) In respect of units licensed under the Industries (Development and Regulation) Act, or registered with DGTD, every administrative Ministry/

Department should identify individual units causing a high degree of hazards to the workers or to the community in the vicinity of their location. Following this identification, expert groups may be constituted by the concerned administrative Ministry/Department for undertaking, in respect of selected hazardous units, special studies of technologies, manufacturing practices and also to consider the measures required to be taken for control of hazards. On the basis of these special studies, it should be possible to suggest appropriate safeguards by way of improvements in design and equipment, maintenance practices and also to identify potential hazards from normal operating conditions and need for special measures. Stipulations for implementation of these safety measures should also be incorporated into the existing licences/registrations and/or prescribe under the provisions of specific enactments like Factories Act, Explosives Act, etc.

(c) The administrative Ministry/Department should set up an Inter-Ministerial Group (including representatives from Ministry of Labour and DOEn) to oversee and guide this work.

(d) For hazardous units in the small scale sector, the Development Commissioner (SSI) will be nodal point for making an inventory of hazardous small scale units and monitor the safety of these units through appropriate State Government authorities. For any technical assistance, appropriate expert agencies could be involved in consultation with the administrative Ministry/Department concerned.

III. Enforcement of safety standards

(a) Responsibility and the machinery for enforcement of provisions of the relevant enactments such as Factories Act, Explosives Act, Boilers Act, Water (Prevention and Control of Pollution) Act, Air (Prevention and Control of Pollution) Act, lies largely with State Governments and their agencies. State Governments are also in immediate contact with local conditions and developments. Alertness at the field level and prompt action in case of violation of safety measures would be essential for prevention of accidents and disasters. In the context, it would be advisable to coordinate the different agencies responsible for enforcement of the concerned enactments by constituting appropriate multi-disciplinary Task Forces to survey and inspect hazardous units. Some State Governments have set up such Task Forces but it will be necessary to ensure that this is done on a continuing basis and follow up measures are monitored carefully.

(b) The State Governments could also take the concerned Industries Associations into confidence and suggest that apart from internal safety audit, which should be vigorously done in any case, the management should also engage expert outside agencies to conduct safety audits. This will be, particularly, relevant in respect of units based on sophisticated hazardous technologies.

(c) Appropriate care will also have to be exercised by the State Government to ensure that in the event of closure of any unit, all hazardous chemicals, whether in bulk storage or in process, are safely disposed. Action taken for such units in this regard will also require to be very closely monitored.

(d) Safety in transportation and storage of hazardous chemicals may also be monitored by the Expert Committee/Task Forces mentioned at Para 111(a) above.

3. It is enjoined upon all Ministries/Departments that the action outlined above is implemented in a time-bound manner with the objective of eliminating the risk of major accidents and disasters from hazardous industrial units. An activitywise time schedule should be drawn up immediately. DOEn, Ministry of Labour and the concerned State Governments should be kept fully involved so as to ensure effective implementation of the action plan.

Secretaries to the Government of India (as per list).

Copy to Chief Secretaries of all States/UTs. It is requested that concerned Departments, State Pollution Control Boards and other agencies may be directed to take suitable and prompt action to ensure control and prevention of risks from hazardous industrial units.

List of Hazardous/Highly Polluted Industries

(i) Primary Metallurgical industries viz., zinc, lead, copper, aluminium and steel

(ii) Paper, Pulp and Newsprint

(iii) Pesticides/Insecticides

(iv) Refineries

(v) Fertilizers

(vi) Paints

(vii) Dyes

(viii) Leather Tanning

(ix) Rayon

(x) Sodium/Potassium Cyanide

(xi) Basic Drugs

(xii) Foundry

(xiii) Storage Batteries (lead acid type)

(xiv) Acids/Alkalies

(xv) Plasters

(xvi) Rubber-Synthetic

(xvii) Cement

(xviii) Asbestos

(xix) Fermentation industry

(xx) Electroplating industry.

ANNEXURE XIV

PRESS NOTE NO. 17

(1984 series)

ENVIRONMENTAL CLEARANCE OF INDUSTRIAL LICENCE—CONDITIONS OF LETTER OF INTENT/ INDUSTRIAL LICENCE

With a view to check and prevent air, water and soil pollution, arising out of industrial projects, certain conditions to be fulfilled are already being incorporated in the letters of intent. Subsequently, it was decided that in respect of certain industries of the highly polluting nature, it would not only be necessary to instal suitable pollution control equipments but also to identify the site and location of the project where a particular industrial unit would be set up. In order to provide concrete shape to this requirement, Government had announced, vide press note No. 9 (1984 series) dated 21st June, 1984, a list of 18 industries causing high pollution and it was stated in respect of these industries, the letter of intent would be converted into an industrial licence only after the following conditions were fulfilled:

(i) The State Director of Industries confirms that the site of the project has been approved from the environmental angle in the competent State authority.

(ii) The entrepreneur commits both to the State Government and the Central Government that he will instal the appropriate equipments and implement the prescribed measures for the prevention and control pollution.

(iii) The concerned State Pollution Control Board has certified that the proposal meets with the environmental requirements and that the equipments installed or proposed to be installed are adequate and appropriate to the requirements.

2. On further consideration of the matter the list of industries has been slightly revised and the same is indicated below:

(i) Primary metallurgical producing industries viz., zinc, lead, copper, aluminium and steel

(ii) Paper, Pulp, and Newsprints

(iii) Pesticides/Insecticides

(iv) Refineries

(v) Fertilizers

(vi) Paints

(vii) Dyes

(viii) Leather Tanning

(ix) Rayon

(x) Sodium/Potassium Cyanide

(xi) Basic Drugs

(xii) Foundry

(xiii) Storage Batteries (lead acid type)

(xiv) Acids/Alkalies

(xv) Plasters

(xvi) Rubber—Synthetic

(xvii) Cement

(xviii) Asbestos

(xix) Fermentation industry

(xx) Electroplating industry.

3. It is, therefore, notified for information of all concerned that in respect of the abovementioned 20 industries, the conversion of letter of intent into industrial licence will like place only if, apart from other prescribed conditions the environmental conditions as set-out above have been fully satisfied.

New Delhi, the 10th Dec. 1984

ANNEXURE XV

SAFETY AND HEALTH ACCIDENT REDUCTION ACTION PLAN (SAHARA)

1. The Bhopal accident has raised the need for enforcing effectively safety and occupational health measures in the chemical industry because the use of toxic substances which can give rise to a number of risks and occupational hazards to the workers and people in general. Soon after the Bhopal accident, we have been in touch with the State Governments and Union Territory Administrations and have also suggested a number of steps with a view to revamping the existing approach to enforcement of safety and prevention of accident in industries. Safety and occupational health in the chemical industry and other hazardous industries was putforth as a vital issue in the meetings of the Labour Secretaries on the 10th May, 1985, in the Labour Ministers' Conference on the 11th May, 1985 and in the Tripartite Industrial Committee on Chemical Industry held on the 30th May, 1985. There was complete unanimity on the need for undertaking a coordinated approach to tackle the problem of safety and occupational health hazardous industries. On the basis of the consensus reached in these Conferences, the Government has formulated the National Plan for Control of Hazards and Occupational Health and Safety in Hazardous industries. The national plan envisages specific and coordinated action to be taken by the Central Government, State Governments and Union Territories, industrial establishments, employers' and trade union organisations, with a view to laying greater stress on safety and to improve working environment in the chemical and other hazardous industries. The different elements of this plan will be found in the minutes and recommendations of the three Conferences referred above. However, in the light of the urgency of the matter Government would like that the action may be initiated in respect of the more important elements of the plan as stated below.

2A. Action at the State level

(1) *Constitution of Committees/Task Forces or Expert Groups:*

Constitution of Task Forces/Committees was recommended to the State Governments/Union Territory Administration in December, 1984. Most of the

State Governments have constituted the Task Forces/Committees on hazardous chemical industries. Data should be built with the help of the reports of these Committees on the state of existing safety measures followed in the hazardous and chemical industries, and in identifying additional measures necessary for safety and control of accidents in these industries.

(2) *Framing of Rules/Regulation on the Model Rules Recommended by the DGFASLI:*

The State Governments may revise rules/regulations prescribed in the Model Rules and Schedules as updated by the DGFASLI in respect of dangerous manufacturing processes. In order to enable early action on this, the period of inviting comments/suggestions would be reduced from the existing 90 days to 45 days. Each State Government/Union Territory may constitute study group for the purpose of updating Rules and Schedules and to complete the work within the next six months.

(3) *Appointment of Safety Officers:*

The States/Union Territories may take an immediate review of the progress regarding the appointment of Safety Officers by the industries which are required to do so under the notification issued by the State Governments/Union Territories. Time limit should be prescribed for the industry for appointment of the Safety Officers and action should be taken where defaults occur, after the specified period. The existing Rules may also be reviewed to ensure that the Safety Officers appointed meet the prescribed requisite qualifications and are given functions and responsibilities as are necessary for enforcement of safety conditions and standards in the industry.

(4) *Assessing Training Requirements:*

States/Union Territories may assess the requirement of training of safety personnel for the industry on the basis of the number of factories identified by the Task Forces/Expert Committees as hazardous and furnish the requirement to DGFASLI for planning additional training courses and reserving seats for the States for diploma and other training courses.

(5) *Preparation of List of Hazardous Industries:*

List of hazardous industries has been prepared by the Department of Environment. A copy of this may be seen at Annexure A-1. This would help the State Governments in preparing the list of hazardous industries and also information regarding known or suspected risks or dangers from such hazardous industries to the workers, on the basis of the reports or surveys made by the Task Forces/Expert Committees.

(6) *Setting up of Special Safety and Monitoring Cell:*

The Monitoring and Safety Cell should conform to the extent possible to the common objectives in dealing with the problems of enforcing safety and control measures in the hazardous industry. With this end in view, broad guidelines on the objectives and requirements of safety system are given in the Annexure A-11.

For monitoring the implementation of safety measures data will have to be collected according to the hazardous industries identified, known dangers associated with them, safety measures followed, and improvements in the existing safety measures desired. This information should be furnished to the DGFASLI with a copy to the Ministry of Labour. A specimen copy of proforma for furnishing this information is given in Annexure A-III.

(7) *Setting up of Review Committee on Safety & Occupational Health:*

A high-powered committee should be set up at the State level to review the progress of implementation regarding control of hazards, safety and occupational health of workers. In the initial stage, the State Level Committee may review the problems arising from location, siting of hazardous industries, dangers associated from these processes, enforcement of safety measures and introducing disaster control system by the industry.

(8) *Strengthening of Factory Inspectorates:*

As the chemicals and the other hazardous industries have to be given priority in view of the dangers/risks associated with them, the State Governments may increase first the strength of the specialist Inspectors and make arrangements for their training so that frequency and quality of inspections in case of chemicals and other hazardous industries is improved.

(9) *Priority Inspection System:*

Since it will not be possible for the State Government to maintain a list of hazardous industries and inventory of dangerous and known risks from such industry, the system of inspection should be streamlined. The State Government should set priorities for inspection and enforcement. It should be ensured that priority inspection covered more than just seeding the records in the industry. It should cover many other things, the application of standards and regulations relating to safety and control measures, observance of tolerance limits for exposure to hazardous substances and materials for the workers, monitoring arrangement for the tolerance levels of toxic agents in workplace, safety conditions in high exposure areas and attention to points of toxic release in leaks, workers breathing zones, etc.

(10) *Setting up of Industrial Hygiene Laboratories in the States:*

Keeping in view the limitations of the State Factory Inspectorates in monitoring the environmental pollutants which is a must for evaluation of the environmental conditions inside the plant, the Government have drawn up a scheme in collaboration with ILO/UNDP for setting up full-fledged Industrial Hygiene Laboratories in all the States.

The State Governments/Union Territory Administrations may complete action for providing staff and other inputs as laid down in the Project and also the officials selected should be made responsible for monitoring the environmental conditions in the selected hazardous industries.

3B. Action for the Managements of Hazardous Units

It is obligatory that the employers should take steps to provide total safety and control system in the hazardous industries. In the case of chemical and hazardous industries, the safety system established should be only ensure compliance with the general standards of safety as incorporated in the different Rules and Special Schedules mentioned in the Annexure B-1, but it should also be capable of ensuring protection against occupational diseases to the workers and control of dangers to the population in the neighbourhood. For the success of safety programmes, it is essential that the State Government should take up with the industries the formulation of programmes with the object of setting up total safety and hazard control system in the factories. In this connection, measures suggested for the industry may include programmes as indicated below.

(1) *Follow up of the National Seminar on Safety Management in Industry:*

It may be recalled that the National Seminar on Safety Management in Industry held in February, 1984 made recommendations which require specific action by the industrial managements/employers. The recommendations calling upon the employers to undertake safety and health programmes are given in Annexure B-II.

(2) *Safety and Health Accident Reduction Action Plan (SAHARA):*

A scheme has been formulated requiring the industry to establish total safety control system in respect of chemical and hazardous industries. The important elements of this scheme are given in Annexure B-III. While formulating this scheme by the management, the safety administration establishment in the factory should be given clear authority and responsibility for the observance of safety and health programmes.

(3) *Formulation of Corporate Safety Policy:*

In the industries the corporate policy on the safety and hazard control system should be adopted and its performance should find place in the annual report of the company.

(4) *Compulsory Declaration of Information on Risks and Hazards Involved in the Processes used in the Industry:*

Employers should be asked to supply information on the risks involved in the processes used in the industry and in the availability of engineering and control measures for safety and accident prevention incorporated and implemented in the industry.

(5) *Setting up of Safety Committees:*

For comprehensive safety programmes in the hazardous industries, it would be essential to set up a system of consultation and cooperation with the workers in the implementation of SAHARA scheme. This can be achieved by entrusting the scheme of workers' participation in safety by setting up Safety Committees. The objectives of the scheme for setting up of the Safety Committee in the industry are given in the Annexure B-IV.

(b) *Role of Employers' Organisation in Chemical Industry:*

4. It is necessary to lay special emphasis on the safety in chemical industry in which the rate of accidents and fatal injuries is the highest. Risks from the hazardous and dangerous process in chemical industry go beyond the limits of the workplaces and can cause irreversible damage to the population and the general environment. Therefore, accident prevention and disaster control has assumed greater importance for the chemical industry in the light of series dangers which arise from these processes not only in the work place but also in the general environment.

5. Chemical industry should, therefore, be given first priority in the matter of extending the scheme for establishing safety control system (SAHARA) in the industry, details of which have been discussed above. The scheme should be circulated among the various chemical industries and progress of its implementation should be reviewed with the association of the industry and the State to ensure that comprehensive safety system is established in these industries. A copy of letter addressed to different to employers organisations in chemical industry may be seen at Annexure B-V.

C. Role of Workers Organisations

6. The national programme recognises the important role which the workers' organisation can play in the safety and occupational health programmes in the industry. While the management has the primary responsibility for the safety and health of the workers, but the implementation of the safety system will depend on the extent of cooperation from and participation of the workers and their organisation or trade unions. It is, therefore, necessary that the workers' organisations should be aware of the needs and demands of the total safety control system and should be able to play an effective role in its implementation at the industry/plant level. The purposeful approach on the part of the workers' organisation will involve specific action to be taken in respect of some of the important areas as indicated below:

(i) To ensure management lays down clear policy regarding hazard control, safety and occupational health.

(ii) To ensure that the safety policy clearly indicates responsibilities in the line management.

(iii) To ensure that the safety organisation is established with properly qualified personnel.

(iv) To participate in the arrangements for implementing objectives of the safety policy.

(v) To ensure cooperation of individual workers in the success of safety programmes.

(vi) To create awareness among the workers and to educate them in the safety practices.

(vii) To effectively make available information to the workers on the safety and occupational health through all available resources such as safety booklets, posters, safety films, seminars, etc.

(viii) In order that the workers' organisations are able to play effective role in promoting safety and in the implementation of hazard control programmes as envisaged by the Government, it would be desirable to enter into a Memorandum of Understanding or formal agreement on the details of the safety and health programmes on which the workers and management agree. For the joint efforts to achieve these objectives, it would be necessary that any Memorandum of Understanding or Agreement must clearly stipulate that establishment of the safety organisation in the industry which must be accompanied by clear allocation of responsibilities within the Management structure (Annexure C-1). A set of guidelines for the plant managers and supervisors are given in Annexure C-11 which may serve as an illustration for the responsibilities of different functioneries involved in the programme for safety and occupational health in the industry.

D. Community Hazard Control

Risks from the hazardous industries arise to areas and population beyond the confines of the unit in which the process is carried out. Pollution occurs from the effluents discharged into the drainage system of the local area, leakage or discharge of fumes and gases into the environment. It is also seen that the risk from hazardous industries, particularly chemical industry are enormous for the general population. It causes irreparable damage to the general environment. It is, therefore, necessary that safety and hazard control in the industry, particularly in the hazardous industry should include plan for emergency controls and minimising hazards to the general public in the event of any major accident. A site emergency plan should be prepared which should give adequate information to the population living in the neighbourhood of the industry or the unit about the risk and dangers from the industry in the event of accident or emergency circumstances. It should also include provision for training of people to operate safety devices and adequate supply of equipment for protection and for control of any major accident. These plans should be prepared by the industry in consultation with the Civil Defence Organisation and the local administration and should be periodically tested for its efficiency in dealing with emergency situations.

E. Action by Central Government

(1) In the context of the industrial accident in Bhopal, the Ministry of Labour has directed the Director General, Factory Advice Service & Labour Institutes, to undertake a thorough review of the Rules and Regulations under the Factories Act and the Model Rules in order to make them more effective and adequate to deal with accident prevention, safety and health protection of the workers in hazardous industries.

(2) *Centrally Sponsored Scheme:*

For strengthening the efforts of the State Government for monitoring and enforcement of safety and health requirements in the hazardous industries, a Centrally sponsored scheme has been formulated and submitted to the Planning Commission. It is proposed to provide assistance on matching basis to the State Governments for strengthening of enforcement machinery and supply of additional equipment for environmental monitoring in the hazardous industries.

(3) DGFASLI has been asked to plan special safety and environmental studies regarding occupational hazards faced by the workers in certain selected industries. Director General would inform the State Governments the programme of undertaking special safety and environmental monitoring studies in the centres selected during 1985-86 and 1986-87 and thereafter, and keep State Governments informed about the progress of the studies.

(4) *Special Training Programmes in the Chemical Industries:*

DGFASLI has been asked to plan special training programmes for the line management and other personnel in the safety control measures in the chemical industry. Similar programmes would also be organised by the DGFASLI for the workers. These programmes will be specially designed to meet the training and education of managerial, supervisory and shopfloor personnel.

(5) *Amendment to the Factories Act, 1948:*

For laying down strict and adequate safety standards in the hazardous industries, amendments to the Factories Act are being considered. Changes in the Factories Act would be effected to provide for more deterrent punishment against defaults and violations.

(6) Government of India has approached the ILO to provide assistance with a view to strengthening the existing capabilities of the National and State level agencies dealing with safety and occupational health in hazardous industries. A two-man mission consisting of Dr. A.F. Ellis and Dr. Sedlak had already identified areas in which assistance is required and has submitted the report which include:

(a) The revision and extension of the UNDP/ILO project IND/84/021—Strengthening of Factory Inspection and Advice Service in the light of

Bhopal's major accident (inclusion of additional States—Madhya Pradesh and others, strengthening of the CLI component, provision of additional special equipment for detection and evaluation of toxic chemicals in the working environment).

(b) Assistance in the collection and evaluation of information on particular hazardous chemicals in Indian plants and in training and information on major hazard control, including:

— preparation of a manual on major hazard control system;

— organisation of two national courses on the system and prevention of accidents caused by hazardous chemicals;

— fellowships to participate in major hazard control groups in industrialised countries.

(c) Assistance in drafting of a project proposal on major hazard control systems.

(d) Assistance in the establishment of a nationwide documentation system in the Central and Regional Labour Institutes.

(e) Assistance in the preparation of a project on prevention, diagnosis, reporting, evaluation and treatment of occupational diseases mainly for medium and small scale industry.

It would help in achieving improvement in the existing facilities at the Central Government level and of the States and Union Territories in dealing with safety and occupational health in the hazardous industries.

F. Follow up of the Decisions of the Labour Secretaries and Labour Ministers' Conference

A number of important decisions have been taken to strengthen the enforcement of safety and occupational health measures in the industry and particularly in the case of chemical and hazardous industries. Extracts giving details of decisions taken at the Labour Secretaries and the Labour Ministers' Conference are enclosed as Annexure E-1 and E-11 respectively. Follow up action will be taken by the Ministry of Labour with a view to ensuring that various decisions taken are implemented to improve the measures suggested for prevention of accidents, safety and health of the workers, particularly in respect of hazardous industries.

Annexure A-1

LIST OF HAZARDOUS HIGHLY POLLUTED INDUSTRIES

(i) Primary Metallurgical producing industries viz., zinc, lead, copper, aluminium and steel;

(ii) Paper, Pulp and Newsprint;

(iii) Pesticides/Insecticides;

(iv) Refineries;

(v) Fertilizers;

(vi) Paints;

(vii) Dyes;

(viii) Leather Tanning;

(ix) Rayon;

(x) Sodium/Potassium Cyanide;

(xi) Basic Drugs;

(xii) Foundry

(xiii) Storage Batteries (lead acid type)

(xiv) Acids/Alkalies;

(xv) Plasters;

(xvi) Rubber — Synthetics;

(xvii) Cement;

(xviii) Asbestos;

(xix) Fermentation industry;

(xx) Electroplating industry.

Annexure A-11

A MODEL FOR SETTING UP FULL SAFETY CONTROL SYSTEM CELL IN HAZARDOUS INDUSTRIES IN STATES/UNION TERRITORIES

Introduction

After the Bhopal disaster, Ministry of Labour, Government of India convened a meeting of the Labour Secretaries of the State Governments and the Union Territory Administrations some time in December, 1984. In the meeting, long-term and short-term measures for the prevention and control of hazards were suggested to be implemented by the State Governments. As an immediate measures, the State Governments were advised to constitute Expert Committee/Task Forces to carry out rapid surveys of chemicals and other hazardous industrial units with a view to making an assessment of the existing safety measures in the hazardous industries. As per the information made available most of the State Governments have constituted Expert Committee/Task Forces for hazardous chemical industries. The rapid surveys in these industries will help in collecting valuable information about the nature and type of hazardous industries, existing safety measures already implemented in the units, and need for additional measures necessary for a Full Safety and Control System.

As per the Factories Act, Safety officers in each industry employing thousand or more workers have been recommended.

In order to strengthen safety and health control measures in dangerous operations, the State Governments have been asked to expedite the adoption of Schedules as prescribed under Model Rule 116. Most of the States are in the process of adopting these Rules which prescribe preventive and control measures against the hazardous operations and processes in specified industries. Those States which are still in the process of adoption of these Rules have been advised to implement them in a phased manner within a definite time frame.

In addition to the above, it is felt that there is a necessity that each State should set up a Cell for Full Safety Control System in Hazardous Industries which would catalyse, promote and support the activities of the State for maximising prevention and control of hazards in high risk identified industries. The Cell will be responsible for follow-up measures in the industries identified through the rapid survey for formulating Special Action Programme to deal with typical hazards and dangers associated with these processes. It would also be responsible for monitoring safety measures introduced by the identified hazardous industries and for preparing such guidelines/instructions as may be necessary to achieve full safety in the hazardous industries.

Objectives

Some of the broad objectives of the Cell are indicated below:

— preparing the list of hazardous industries;
— recognising major accidents/hazards in these industries;
— measures they have taken;
— additional measures required to prevent accidents and to control and to minimise the consequences of those hazards;
— specific evidence to analyse dangers, to establish safe procedures and practices;
— controlling and monitoring of operations to prevent and to minimise accidents;
— furnishing information about the accidents and dangers from the processes to the workers and general population living close to the industry; and
— imparting training in safety and accident control in emergency situations.

Identification and Requirements of system

The criteria for identifying the hazardous industries and requirements for Full Safety System are given in Appendix.

Model Plan

In order to maintain uniformity and to achieve a Full Safety System, a Model Plan for the Cell is given below.

Manpower Pattern

The Cell will be provided with Technical Officers with post-graduate degree chemistry/degree in chemical engineering/technology having a minimum of 3 years experience in chemical industry. He should be fully aware of the hazardous chemical process, reactions and the preventive and control measures. Special knowledge on the identification, assessment and control and prevention of major hazards will be an asset with the Technical Officer(s) of the Cell to maximise safety in hazardous chemical industries and processes. He should have capabilities to organise, develop and implement new methods and technology for achieving results. One such officer for a maximum of 100 hazardous industries will be provided. Each Technical Officer will be supported with a maximum of two Technical Assistants with graduation in science, chemistry as one of the subjects.

Duties and Functions

The duties and functions of the Technical Officers appointed for the Cell shall be defined by the State Governments in a manner which helps to achieve the objectives of the system mentioned above. The same may include the following activities:

— based on the above, to prepare a list of hazardous chemical industries;

— analysis and recording of operations, reactions and processes that can lead to high degree hazard and accident due to toxicity, flammability and explosion;

— to identify such reactions which under abnormal conditions of temperature, pressure and reactivity with water, air, metals, and other organic substances can result in onsite/offsite accident hazard;

— to examine the adequacy of existing safety and control measures that existed in each hazardous industry, and based on the findings to suggest to the management, additional measures that can reduce the eventuality of a high risk;

— to evaluate the type and extent of protective and emergency measures required;

— to conduct follow up surveys to assess the extent of implementations of the measures suggested and determine their adequacy through a well designed monitoring system;

— to advise the management for setting up an efficient and fail proof information system.

Laboratory

The Industrial Hygiene Laboratory which is being set up with the help of ILO/UNDP shall be equipped with the additional equipments which may be required for the recognition, evaluation and control of major hazards in the identified industries.

Identification of Hazardous Industries

Hazards may have to be identified with reference .o potential dangers from substances and processes involved, potential to give rise serious injury to the workers, damage beyond the vicinity of workplace and general environment. It will also mean major accident fires, explosions and other uncontrolled developments associated with dangerous substances. Therefore the industrial hazardous units may be identified in major groups, e.g. Toxic, Highly Reactive, Flammable or Explosive Substances.

Requirement for Full Safety System

On the basis of identified major hazards, full safety control system may require to:

— remove defects in the preliminary preventive measures (such as design, construction, installation, maintenance, etc.)

— assess the desirability of reducing the storage facilities and operation and maintenance of storage tanks and vessels;

— prevent potential hazards from normal operative conditions, e.g. leakages from valves, trips;

— take measures appropriate to control major accident arising from the processes;

— ask the hazardous units to give full account of the arrangements for safe operation, for control of serious development which may lead to major accidents, control plans in emergency situation, and warning system and their operations in emergency situations;

— furnish information on the types and the serious consequences of major accidents on the general environment, in the general public and action plan to minimise risks in the event of such accidents;

— to make arrangements to ensure that necessary information, training and equipment for major accidents given to the persons working onsite by specific steps taken to ensure that;

(a) persons working on the site have been informed of the major accident hazards of the activity and have been informed of and received training about the relevant emergency procedures;

(b) operators with particular responsibility for the activities that present a major accident hazard have been trained to a level appropriate to those responsibilities; and

(c) any special equipment necessary for use in an emergency (e.g. breathing apparatus, or fire fighting equipment provided to ensure that integrity of a means of escape has been provided).

Annexure A-111

Name of the States	Whether task Force/ Expert Group constituted*	No. of hazardous industries identified through surveys	No. of hazardous chemicals identified**	No. of units handling each of the identified hazardous chemicals**
1	2	3	4	5

Total No. of workers in hazardous industries	No. of units inspected as on 30.4.1985	No. of prosecutions made for non-compliance as on 30.4.1985	Progress of action plan for hazardous industries
6	7	8	9

* Details to be furnished.

** List to be furnished.

Annexure B-I

GENERAL STANDARDS OF SAFETY AS INCORPORATED IN SCHEDULE XII ON CHEMICALS

In the Schedule XII under the Model Rule, pertaining to chemical works framed under Section 87 of the Factories Act, Paragraph 7 requires that before commencing any large scale experimental work, or any new manufacture, all possible steps shall be taken to ascertain definitely the hazards involved both from the actual operations and the chemical reactions. The properties of the raw materials used, the final products to be made and any bye-products arising during manufacture shall be carefully studied and provisions shall be made for dealing with any hazards including effects on workers which may arise during manufacture. Paragraph 9 requires that all instruments such as pressure gauges, etc. shall be tested at regular intervals by a competent person. Paragraph 10 requires that suitable valves shall be provided in all service lines at sufficiently short intervals for convenience in blanking off, etc. Further all cocks and valves shall be operated at least once a month and tested periodically by a competent person. Paragraph 12 requires emergency instructions to be framed to ensure that effective measures will be taken in case of emergency to deal with escape of flammable, poisonous or deleterious gases, vapour, liquid or dust. These instructions shall further be displayed in bold letters in prominent places and workers shall be trained and instructed in the action to be taken in such emergencies and in the general hazards of the employment. Paragraph 13 requires that suitable arrangement shall be made to ensure that no foreign matter of any sort can fall into reaction mixtures. Paragraph 31 requires that effective steps shall be taken to prevent the escape of dangerous gases, vapours, fumes or dust from any part of the plant and effective arrangement shall be made to ensure that in the event of failure of control measures, the process shall stop immediately. Further in the event of any such escape, provisions shall be made to trap the materials and render them safe. Paragraph 45 requires adequate precautions to be taken to prevent escape of corrosive or deleterious substances and means shall be provided for rendering safe any such escape. Paragraph 51 requires that before any examination or repairs are carried out on plant and pipelines, a competent person shall issue a clearance certificate permitting such examination of repairs.

Annexure B-II

ACTION BY INDUSTRIAL MANAGEMENTS

1. The safety policy and performance of a company should find place in its Annual Report circulated to the shareholders.
2. The effectiveness of safety officers depends upon his status and that present status of safety officers in most of the factories needs to be examined.

3. Special efforts are required for ascertaining the hidden causes of accidents and highlighting the same for more effective actions.
4. Incentive schemes in industry sometimes act as negativating factor to safety and accident prevention.

Annexure - B-III

SAFETY AND HEALTH & ACCIDENT REDUCTION ACTION PLAN (SAHARA)

All Industrial Units have to adopt a total Safety Control System so as to ensure safety of the working environment, safety of the general environment and safety of the employees and the general public. State Governments and Administrations by appropriate guidelines bring this to the notice of all Registered Factories. Some of the important aspects of this are discussed below:

Total Safety Control System

2. Commitment of the industry to the safety programme means, not merely traditional approach of prevention of accidents but total safety control and management system. More and more emphasis has been laid on safety management system as the most satisfactory approach for ensuring elimination of risks, accidents and conscientious involvement in the safety and health programme leading to the well-being of the workers as well as efficiency in production. Some basic principles of Safety System are cutlined in the Appendix.

Safety and Health & Accident Reduction Action Plan

3. For the successful safety programme it is essential that industry should formulate complete safety and accident prevention policy which should clearly lay down the objectives of the safety and health programmes, obligations of the managements towards these programmes, responsibilities of the line management and cooperation and participation by the workers. In this connection the employers' organisations can give leadership in preparing model for safety and accident prevention programmes in selected industries keeping in view the dangers, hazards and risks involved to the workers and to the society. In this connection, the chemical industries and the engineering industries may be considered for taking up such programmes.

Safety Audit

4. Feedback on the performance of safety policies is as important to the management as in the case for other production departments of the industry. Each industry has to design a system of collection and analysing the accidents and injuries and performance of safety control measures at different levels. This feedback is collected by an in-company system of collection of statistics of accidents and injuries. A suitable statistical method is important step for the

performance of safety principles and practices laid down in the safety policy of the industry. It is also one of the important forms of measurement of total health and safety performance under the safety policy of the industry. Each industry has to create such a statistical information system depending upon its own organisations, size, position of workers, risks, etc. Performance of safety in the industry can also be evaluated by safety audit system. Such a system will provide improvements to evaluate the "state of the art" of the safety programme of the industry.

Monitoring

5. The last, but not the least, important element of industry's Safety and Health and Accident Reduction Plan (SAHARA), is that it will require monitoring, progress and performance of safety policies and principles. Monitoring arrangement will have to be devised by the industry. Some examples/models for the monitoring progress and measurement of safety and health programmes are available. Each industry will have to consider these models in relation to its own organisation and other interrelated factors such as processes involved, degree or risks, size of organisation, etc.

Appendix to Annexure B-III

BROAD OUTLINES OF THE FRAMEWORK OF A SAFETY SYSTEM IN THE INDUSTRY

The safety management system will have to be formulated around some basic principles of safety ; some of which are set out as under:

1. Provide active top management support

A good safety record is clear evidence of good management. Accordingly, general managers and other top divisional and plant executives will make safety their responsibility by:

— maintaining a comprehensive safety programme at all times;

— meeting with key supervisory personnel at least once a month to review safety performance;

— taking any action necessary to improve safety conditions.

This way management lends meaningful and feasible support to a continuing safety effort.

2. Maintain adequate safety personnel

Each plant should have sufficient, well-trained personnel to assure continuous careful attention to safety. A qualified person should be assigned to direct the safety programme, handle safety education and assist the supervisory force in maintaining safe working conditions. The safety should be sufficient in numbers to monitor all operations.

3. Develop safety instructions for every job

Written rules and instructions setting out safe practices for each job assignment are necessary. This material should be used as the basis for safety instruction of new employees and of employees transferred to new jobs, and then reviewed on a timely basis with all employees.

4. Instruct all new employees

All new employees should be thoroughly instructed in general safety policies, rules and procedures before being referred to their supervisor should review with them thoroughly the safety measures of the particular job, before they start to work. Subsequently, the safety performance of new employees should be reviewed regularly. This will assure that they both understand and carryout the written safety rules and instructions applicable to their jobs.

5. Operate thorough supervision

Supervisors are the key people in the safety programme because they are in constant contact with employees. Superintendent should hold meetings with their supervisors at least once a month to review safety conditions, general policies and specific situations.

6. Make every employee safety minded

The cooperation of the individual employee is vital to the success of a safety programme. Continued education is required to make certain that all concerned—management and employees alike—do their part in protecting the safety of the individual at all times. Every available medium—safety booklets, posters, signs, and plant papers—may be used to good advantage in furthering the objectives of such a programme.

7. Extend efforts beyond the plant

Special attention should be given to off-the-job safety as employees have more accidents away from work then they do on-the-job. Our objectives should include efforts to promote the safety of employees and their familities by—

— maintaining a comprehensive safety programme for employees driving company-owned vehicles;

— providing material on highway safety to aid employees driving their own cars;

— encouraging employees to develop safe practices in the home, on the farm, and in recreational activities;

— participating in community safety activities.

In the case of chemical industry which has hazards extending to the environment beyond the work place, key principles of the safety policy may include:

Safety Policy

1. We believe that all accidents are preventable and all identified health, risks are containable. This has been our guiding principle for many years.
2. The Company will comply with applicable laws and regulations.
3. The Company will try to improve on minimum legal requirements. Our responsibility and concern to our employees and neighbours and our customers does not end where the laws does.
4. Each (Company) product must be able to be made, used, processed and disposed of safely. In short, this means that our corporate responsibility does not end when our product leaves the plant gate.
5. We have a responsibility to know potential hazards and to tell others about them as needed. Whether we discover a hazard before or after the fact, we have a responsibility to tell employees, the government, our customers and other companies what we have observed.
6. Line organisation has ultimate responsibility for the health and safety of its people and products. One of (the Company's) strengths is decentralisation of operations and responsibilities, because without the penalties and rewards of responsibilities, we will simply not get the results which we need.
7. Auditing is necessary for an effective health and safety programme. The Company cannot simply say that it told the workplace. We must also get the feedback and verification that line management is meeting its responsibilities and that programmes are meeting their objectives. Auditing is simply good management and not an adversary technique.
8. Policy is to maintain safety beyond compromise. We would not hesitate to discontinue making any product if we were at any time to determine that the safe manufacture of it was either not feasible or impractical.

Environmental Policy

It is policy of this company to manufacture, handle and dispose of all substances safely and without creating unacceptable risks to human health or the environment. The industry will:

— establish and maintain programmes to assure that laws and regulations applicable to its products and operation are known and obeyed;

— adopt its own standards where laws or regulations may not be adequately protective, and adopt, where necessary, its own standards where laws do not exist; and

— stop manufacturing any product or carrying out any operations if the environmental costs are unacceptable.

To carryout this policy, the Company will:

1. Identify and control public health and environmental hazards stemming from its operations and products;
2. Conduct accident prevention and occupational health programmes to safeguard employees and the public from injuries or health hazards, to protect the company's assets and continuity of operations, and to protect the environment;
3. Conduct and support research about the health and environmental effect of potentially suspect materials handled and sold by the Company and share promptly and significant findings with others, such as employees, suppliers, customers, government agencies, and the scientific community; and
4. Work and constructively with trade associations, government agencies and others to develop equitable and realistic laws, regulations and standards to protect public health and the environment.

Every employee is expected to adhere to the spirit as well as the letter of this policy. Managers have a special obligation to keep informed about environmental risks and standards and to advice higher management promptly of any adverse situation which comes to their attention.

Annexure B-IV

WORKERS' PARTICIPATION IN INDUSTRIAL SAFETY AND OCCUPATIONAL HEALTH IN THE HAZARDOUS INDUSTRIES

For any safety programme to be successful in the industry, it is necessary that the management should lay down the objectives of the safety policies of the industry, formulate comprehensive safety programmes, set up organisation and mechanism which will implement and given support in the implementation of the safety measures systematically. It should also ensure the individual and personal responsibility at different levels in addition to the need for proper set up for giving careful attention to safety. It is also necessary to get the participation of the workers so that complete support is given to continuing safety efforts at all levels. In this connection number of methods have been adopted by the countries which give recognition to the role of workers' participation in safety measures at the plant level.

1. Safety

In the absence of statutory provisions, efforts will have to be made to select hazardous industry on the basis of specified number of workers employed to introduce the scheme of Workers' Participation in Safety by setting up Safety Committees. While it may be necessary for each hazardous industrial unit to set up Safety Committee and evolve a producer for consultation, functions and responsibilities of workers' representatives in these Committees, it will be necessary that some broad principles should be followed in setting up of these Committees. In this connection, the objectives and the functions of the Safety Committees, which are followed in United Kingdom may be of use as a model for guidance to the State Governments and the details of which are given below:

2. Objectives

— To promote cooperation between management and employees in enforcing, developing and reporting measures to ensure the health and safety at work of employees and to keep those measures under review;

— To complement efforts of the management to establish standards, codes, regulations with a view to eliminate risks and hazardous accidents in work environment;

— to achieve proper awareness by persons at managerial, supervisory and shop-floor level for observing and enforcing safety measures.

Membership of the Committees

As agreed at the management/union meetings:

Chairman	—	Workers Manager
Secretary	—	Safety Officer
		Departmental Manager
		Personnel Manager
		Chief Engineer
		Four Safety Representatives
		Other specialists such as a chemist or other technical expert may be co-opted when their expertise is necessary to assist in dealing with a particular matter.

Frequency of Meetings

Meetings should be held at intervals nor exceeding three months.

Special Meeting

Special meetings may be called by the Chairman to deal with serious events or special circumstances as required.

Records of Meetings

An agenda for each meeting will be produced by the Secretary and circulated to all members before each meeting. Items for inclusion on the agenda should be notified to the Secretary at least seven days before the meeting.

Minutes of meetings identifying action by individuals and groups will be produced by the Secretary and copies will be circulated to members after each meeting.

3. Functions

— To assess potential hazards and dangerous occurrence at the work-place and examine the effectiveness of the safety and control measures;

— To investigate complaints about risks or dangers by any employee in the area he represents relating to the employee's safety or welfare at work;

— To investigate accidents and dangerous occurrences at the work-place and examine causes of accidents;

— To suggest improvements to the management on matters arising out of above facts;

— To make representations to the employer on general matters affecting the health, safety or welfare at work of the employees at the work-place;

— To assist management in accident prevention activities, campaigns, publicity, trip, etc.

4. Terms of Office

Unless otherwise decided by agreement the normal term of office for the Members of the Committee including the Chairman should be of two years.

5. Place of Meetings

The meeting should take place on a common day fixed for this purpose. Agenda for the meeting should be supplied sufficiently before the meeting. Copies of the Minutes should be circulated to the Chief, responsible for the Safety Administration/Set Up, Trade Union, Managers and Safety Representatives and should be put up on recognised Notice Board.

6. Forum

Fixed forum should be decided depending on the total membership of the Committee.

7. Safety Committee

Safety Committee may co-opt any other person, in its opinion, would be useful to the meeting of the Committee.

8. Safety Representatives

— *Appointment of Safety Representatives*

Appointment of Safety Officers will be by nomination which should be sent by the unions.

— *Nomination*

The Unions will arrange for the nomination of suitable candidates.

— *Qualification*

A person nominated for appointment as safety representative shall have a minimum of two years experience within, where practicable the department for which he is nominated.

— *Term Office*

Safety representatives shall be appointed for a period of two years, after which they may be re-appointed for a further term.

— *Termination of appointment*

A person shall cease to be a safety representative when:

(a) the trade union which appointed him notifies management, in writing, that his appointment has been terminated;

(b) he leaves the employment of the Company;

(c) he resigns;

(d) he is transferred away from the section he represents, after the appointment of a successor.

9. Inspections

Safety representatives shall be entitled to inspect their own work-place as follows:

(a) At intervals not exceeding once every three months, after giving written notice of his intention to do so to the departmental manager of the area concerned.

(b) Where there has been a substantial change in conditions of work, plant or machinery, or new information has been published by the health and safety executive relative to hazards involved in the area.

(c) Following a notifiable accident, dangerous occurrence or notifiable disease.

During all inspections as above, the management shall be represented by a member of supervision or the safety officer.

Following all inspections as above, the safety representative should send the report to the Committee which would, in turn, send their observations to the managements. The managements should send their comments on the observations to this Safety Committee not later than one month.

10. Inspection of Documents

Safety representatives shall be entitled to inspect documents and if certain areas to be kept out on account of legal or statutory requirement these may be agreed to in writing.

Annexure B-V

COPY OF LETTER ADDRESSED TO EMPLOYERS' ORGANISATIONS, ETC. IN CHEMICAL INDUSTRY FOR TOTAL SAFETY CONTROL SYSTEM FOR HAZARDOUS INDUSTRIES

As you are aware the Ministry of Labour has been in touch with the State Governments/Union Territory Administrations since the Bhopal accident in December, 1984, with a view to make a review of the existing approach to safety and prevention of accident in industries using hazardous and toxic substances. There are serious risks and dangers from industrial units which produce or handle toxic material or substances. Therefore, safety of the work-place as well as general environment is of vitali importance so far as chemical industry is concerned. A number of measures have been suggested to the State Governments to make an assessment of the conditions of safety in chemical and other hazardous units in the State. It is necessary that all those who are responsible for running or operating hazardous industries in which chemical or toxic substances are used, they should maintain high standards of safety, control and prevention of accidents and risks from these processes. Although the Factories Act and various Schedules thereunder provide for safety measures, it has now been strongly felt that satisfactory safety standards cannot be established in the chemical and other hazardous industries unless a comprehensive and total safety measures and procedures are introduced by the employers. In the connection, a National Plan For Coordinated Action to enforce safety in chemical and other hazardous industries has been formulated on the basis of the decisions taken in the Conference of State Labour Secretaries and Labour Ministers held on the 10th and 11th May, 1985 respectively. As part of the coordinated action plan it is necessary that the employers of chemical and other hazardous industries may be asked to take action to establish comprehensive safety management system in their units. For employers, a model scheme of Safety & Health Accidents Reduction Action Plan (SAHARA) has been formulated. A copy of model SAHARA plan is enclosed herewith. This should cover all industries which are considered to be hazardous industries or industries which pose danger to health and safety of workers, public and the general environment and employ 500 or more workers, in the first instance. Later on the scheme can be extended to other units below this number. The SAHARA Plan aims at reducing accidents and health hazards in working environment and also achieving workers increasing confidence in the management by seeking cooperation and participation in the safety measures.

2. The State Governments are also required to set up a review committee, to watch the progress of the schemes in the industries covered under it. A proforma has also been devised to report the progress made and results achieved as a result of operation of SAHARA scheme in the industries.

3. It would be appreciated if immediate follow up action is taken on this and a report sent to this Ministry.

Annexure C-1

DETAILS OF MEMORANDUM OF UNDERSTANDING/FORMAL AGREEMENT ON SAFETY AND HEALTH PROGRAMMES

1. General Statement

It is the Company's policy to give and maintain a high priority to the health and safety of all its employees at work, and to avoid exposing others to risk to their health or safety. This policy will be supplemented by more detailed rules and procedures relevant to specific unit location. The policy has the following specific objectives.

2. Objectives

2.1 To provide our employees with work methods, work areas, premises and plant which are safe, thereby reducing the risk of injuries, accidents and damage to property.

2.2 To safeguard our employees from any foreseeable hazard to health or safety in existing processes and working systems and in the introduction of new substances, plant machinery and equipment, processes or premises.

2.3 To train all employees to be aware of their own responsibilities in respect of health and safety matters.

2.4 To provide general health and safety training for all new entrants and to identify training needs for all levels of our employees in the areas of health and safety, and to design training programmes to meet these needs.

2.5 To insist that health and safety instructions are carried out and that health and safety systems and procedures are followed.

2.6 To maintain proper measures for fire prevention, fire protection and fire fighting, and systems of evacuation in the event of an emergency.

2.7 To provide appropriate medical and first-aid facilities to safeguard the health and welfare of all our employees.

2.8 To maintain an analytical and statistical service to allow health and safety performance to be monitored.

2.9 To maintain an information service on legislation, codes of practice and technical developments in connection with our operations and our health and safety policy objectives.

2.10 To achieve by joint consultation the effective cooperation and involvement of all employees in attaining our health and safety objectives.

Annexure C-II

GUIDELINES FOR PLANT MANAGER/SUPERVISOR

Location Executives—Safety and Health Programme Responsibilities Policy

Plant Manager will have an awareness of rule, regulations and procedure development and dissemination. Effect corrective action when deficiencies are noted:

1. Overall responsibility for unit's safety and health programme;
2. To delegate the authority and responsibility to each supervisor to maintain a work-place free of known hazards and compliance by his employees with plant safety and health procedures;
3. Responsibility for the direction and/or assignment of personnel to act in emergencies; fires, rescue work and disasters:
4. To see that adequate provisions are made for handling accidents or fires:
5. Submit annual safety programme report:
6. To participate personally in safety programme activities:
7. To comment on and sign injury reports:
8. To act as permanent Chairman of Safety Council:
9. To enforce safety instructions and rules:
10. To advise the Safety Department and Department Head concerned on safety problems, special hazards and special situations.

Annexure E-I

GENERAL CONCLUSIONS AND RECOMMENDATIONS OF THE MEETING OF LABOUR SECRETARIES HELD ON 30.4.1985

(i) All States and Union Territory Administrations who had yet to appoint Task Forces/Expert Committees to identify hazardous and other toxic/chemical units, would do so immediately. All the States and Union Territory Administrations would send a detailed report in the enclosed proforma, to DGFASLI, the data collected and facts revealed, as an outcome of the investigations done by Task Forces/Expert Committee so that DGFASLI can build up an all-India data and also plan studies/surveys etc. on a priority basis. A report on the action taken in this regard has to be sent to the Central Government by all States.

(ii) The Safety and Health Accident Reduction Action Plan (SAHARA) which was circulated as part of the Agenda Notes (Item No. 3) was approved in principle. Central Government would be writing to all State Governments/Union Territory Administrations and Employers/Workers Organisation giving certain general guidelines in this regard so that all enterprises employing 500 or more workmen and engaged in hazardous and dangerous manufacturing processes will adopt such plans and send periodical reports to the Inspectorates of Factories of the States on the working of the Scheme. DGFASLI would also keep a watch on the progress on implementation of this scheme in all States/Union Territories.

(iii) Every State Government and Union Territory Administration, where there is a concentration of manufacturing units of chemicals and other toxic substances would set up Special Cells to monitor major hazards. To facilitate this an outline of a set up of such a Cell, its staffing pattern, its staffing pattern, its aim and objective would be circulated by Central Government to State Governments and Union Territories. The States and Union Territory Administrations should send information to Central Government about the set up created.

(iv) Central Government would amend the Factories Act, without further delay, making special provisions for checking accidents and diseases in manufacturing processes which are hazardous. The amended law would provide for stringent penalties for all types of violations and give powers to Chief Inspectors of Factories for suspension of operation of processes wherever there is evidence of danger to the lives of the employees and members of general public living in and around the working place. For continued violation of safety and health provision, the penalties would include compulsory imprisonment.

There is considerable time-lag in adopting the Schedule recommended by the DGFASLI. It was decided that the State Government should give special attention and fix a time-frame to bring up-to-date the Schedules relating to hazardous and chemical processes and also devise methods to ensure that delays are avoided in future.

(v) The Department of Industrial Development would be advised to review the provisions of the Indian Boilers Act, 1923 and take steps to make the law more effective in the light of latest developments and from the angle of safety and health of employees in Factories. The specific suggestions made at the Conference in this regard particularly by the representatives of Governments of Bihar and West Bengal would be passed on to that Department for appropriate action.

(vi) It as recognised that the machinery and equipments used in the plant should also be safe for use and manufacturers and suppliers of those items have to accept total responsibility for their safety. It is possible to achieve this by taking note of safety aspects at the designing stage itself. This matter will have to be brought to the notice of manufacturing units by the State Government through the employers' organisations.

(vii) It is to be ensured that all factories which are required to appoint safety officers should be given specified time within which they should appoint Safety Officers, with prescribed qualifications. Managements should given them proper status and entrust them exclusively with functions connected with safety and health of the industrial workers in the unit. They should not be burdened with other functions.

(viii) The policy with regard to the approval of site needs to be reviewed. The Chief Inspectors of Factories should be associated on this, right from the beginning and approval for licensing of a factory should also cover approval of site. While deciding on location it is specifically to be considered whether chemical units should work along with other units in the Industrial Estates. The Department of Environment had identified certain industries as hazardous and have also issued guidelines for location of hazardous industries. These instructions are required to be integrated with the instructions for approval of site as well as approval for giving licence to factories. This matter would be considered by the Ministry of Labour, Department of Environment, DGTD and the Department of Industrial Development and appropriate procedures laid down in this regard.

(ix) It was recognised that chemical and other hazardous units should be subjected to more frequent inspections by the State Factory Inspectorate as well as by others administering legislation connected with safety and health of workers, working environment and general environment.

(x) There was a general feeling that the State Factory Inspectorate are not adequately staffed. The need for making out a detailed case before the Planning Commission for allocation of sufficient funds for the State Governments in this area was recognised and Labour Secretary gave an assurance that on the State Governments making available details of their proposals, outcome of their discussions with the Planning Commission, etc., matter would be taken up by him with the Planning Commission.

(xi) There was a general consensus that in the area safety and health of industrial workers there should be Centrally sponsored scheme and a Working Group of the Chief Inspectors of Factories under the guidance of DGFASLI drawout details of appropriate schemes for Ministry of Labour to examine.

(xii) During discussions it was revealed that there existed 6,000-7,000 small chemical units in the country and these are sources of potential hazards otherwise. There is a need for taking special measures for awakening safety consciousness among employers and workers in these units and for helping them in identifying and combating occupational diseases. For this purpose a special committee would be constituted which would consist of representatives of the Governments of Maharashtra, West Bengal, Gujarat, Karnataka and Andhra Pradesh and a nominee of the Central Pollution Control Board. This Committee will give a Report on the nature of manufacturing/servicing activities undertaken in such units, their broad classification for purposes of safety, measures required to inculcate safety consciousness amongst those units and whether it is feasible to prescribe any rules or regulations for enforcing safety measures.

(xiii) Education and training are most vital for ensuring safety in industrial units and for preventing occupational diseases. DGFASLI, NIOH, ITRC and other specialised agencies, National Safety Council and its Chapters, supervisors and factory inspectors. It was felt that all these training programmes need to be re-oriented and special programmes should be drawn up covering all aspects of safety and health in hazardous chemical units.

(xiv) It was considered absolutely necessary that media should be made use of more liberally for purposes of educating the public in general and employers and employees in particular. Special programmes can be drawn up for publicity through Radio and T.V., Special articles on Safety could not published in various newspapers, and periodicals. The National Safety Council and its Chapters should take appropriate measures in this regard and they may also bring out proper films for education to the public by way of documentaries in T.V. as well as in cinemas.

(xv) There should be adequate literature on all aspects of safety and these should contain information on contingency plans in the event of any accident. Since various authorities are involved and conditions vary from area to area it would be preferable to have an action plan on this on a regional basis. It was felt that apart from bringing out literature, etc., the best way to achieve this is by way of holding seminars on safety and in these seminars representatives of workers and employers should actively participate. The State Governments and DGFASLI in association with employers and workers organisations should take appropriate action in this regard.

(xvi) One of the important items identified for special study and investigation related to health hazards is asbestos unit. On this it was decided that every State Government should send a report after instructing their Inspectors to visit all asbestos manufacturing and mining units. These visits should cover all aspects of safety and health, the present conditions, the facilities provided, deficiencies noticed and the like. Action on this has to be completed both by the State Governments as well as the Mines Inspectorate at the Centre and a report on this sent to the Central Government within a month's time.

Annexure E-II

RECOMMENDATIONS ON SAFETY AND HEALTH OF THE LABOUR SECRETARIES/LABOUR MINISTERS' CONFERENCE, MAY, 1985

Amendments to Factories Act, 1948

1. The Factories Act, 1948 will have a special chapter to deal with safety in hazardous industry. A process which is identified as dangerous manufacturing process, under Section 87 of the Act, would commence only after the occupier had

provided for all the safety and health protection measures, to the satisfaction of the CIFs. The CIFs will have powers to order suspension of activities in a hazardous industry, in the interest of preventing accidents and diseases. The penalty for continued violation of safety regulations in hazardous industry would be compulsory imprisonment.

Adoption of Schedules and Rules

2. The State Governments will adopt all control measures prescribed in the Model Rules and Schedules in respect of dangerous manufacturing processes by incorporating them in State Factory Rules. In order to enable early action on this the period of inviting comments/objections on draft Rules would be reduced from the existing 90 days to 45 days. Each State Government/Union Territory would constitute a study group for the purpose of updating Rules and Schedules and endeavour to complete the work within a period of six months. If any of the Model Rules and Schedules are incapable of being adopted, the Labour Secretary of the State/Union Territory would apprise the Labour Minister of the State the reasons for the same and thereafter this would be reported to the Central Government.

Appointment of Safety Officers

3. The States/Union Territories will review their rules regarding appointment of Safety Officers and ensure that these provide for prescribing requisite qualifications, functions and responsibilities of the Safety Officers. The State Government will also assess the total requirement of Safety Officers, based on the existing provisions, and also for the factories identified by the Task Forces constituted by the States/Union Territories and inform the same to the DGFASLI for planning training courses and reserving seats for the Diploma Courses for Safety Officers.

Preparation of List of Hazardous Industries

4. The State Governments would prepare a list of the hazardous industries, based on the reports of the Task Forces, and furnish the details to DGFASLI who would prepare a common list of such hazardous industries for facilitating preparation of future action plans on all-India basis for conducting studies and surveys for the benefit of all.

Strengthening of Enforcement Machinery

5. It was recognised that there is absolute need for strengthening the Factory inspectorates in all States/Union Territories and in this regard the following measures were recommended:

(a) Planning Commission would be impressed upon the need for providing sufficient funds for all the States and Union Territories in the 7th Plan for strengthening the enforcement machinery both from the angle of additional staff and additional equipment and facilities.

(b) It would be examined, based on the recommendations of the N.C. on Labour and decisions of Courts as to whether license fees could be utilised for strengthening the enforcement machinery.

(c) It would also be considered whether any special cess could be levied on factories identified as carrying on dangerous operations and hazardous processes and the proceeds of that can be utilised for augmenting the enforcement machinery of the respective States/Union Territories for safety promotional activities.

(d) There would be a Centrally Sponsored Scheme with 50 per cent contribution by the States and 50 per cent assistance by the Centre for setting up any strengthening of Industrial Hygiene Laboratories in the States with necessary manpower, equipment and facilities for monitoring the environment in hazardous chemical industries.

Reporting of Accidents

6. The Chief Inspectors of Factories would inform the DGFASLI the details of all fatal accidents, dangerous occurrences, in a prescribed proforma, within three months of such accidents/ocurrences so that the DGFASLI can maintain a national data of all the industrial fatal accidents/occurrences, for formulating necessary action plans.

Setting up Special Safety Cell

7. A special safety cell would be set up at the Department level in each State/ Union Territory and this Cell will work in coordination with all the branches in the State Labour Department. Institutions and specialists in the field of labour research.

Standing Committee of Experts on Safety

8. A Standing Committee of selected experts in various disciplines will be set up at the State level with the Chief Inspector of Factories as the Convenor. This Committee will go into the safety conditions in hazardous industries, at periodical intervals, and report on the corrective measures required to a tripartite committee at the State level.

Tripartite Safety Committee

9. There would be a high powered Tripartite Safety Committee at the State level and the Labour Minister of the State would be the Chairman of that Committee. This Committee will decide the policy matters regarding the overall safety and health situation in the factories in the States.

Safety in Small-Scale Units

10. For improving safety any working conditions in small scale sector, it was considered necessary that details of safety requirements should be given to the entrepreneurs at the time of setting up the unit. The District Industrial Centres and

big Industrial Estates will have respectively an officer of the rank of Deputy Chief Inspector of Factories and Safety Officer, for advising and coordinating on all aspects connected with maintenance of safety conditions and standards in those units.

Action for the Management of Hazardous Units

11. For achieving meaningful results, the State Factory Inspectorates would initiate the following activities:

(i) A Safety and Health Accident Reduction Action Plan will be recommended to all enterprises identified as hazardous under Section 87 for adoption.

(ii) A full Safety Control System Cell in Hazardous Industries will be set up at appropriate places in the States.

(iii) Each unit will introduce a suggestion scheme for workers involvement on safety and health hazards.

List of Equipments for Factory Inspectors

12. DGFASLI will make out a standardise list of equipments for general inspection of industries and special equipments for evaluating safety and health standards in hazardous industries and make available this list to States and Union Territories so that State Factory Inspectorates could equip themselves for carrying out proper inspections.

Special Training Programmes

13. Appropriate training courses on chemical hazards in industry would be conducted by DGFASLI in States, where there is concentration of chemical industry, after improving the content and syllabus of the courses taking note of the technology processes, new chemicals used and ascertaining the needs of the Factory Inspectors in consultation with the C.I.Fs.

Occupational Health Services

14. A cadre of Occupational Health Services in the country would be built up by taking recourse to the following measures:

(a) Appropriate programmes for training and development would draw up and operated by DGFASLI, in association with NIOH, IRTC and the Inspectorate of Factories of State Governments.

(b) The Employees' State Insurance Corporation would set up Occupational Health Diagnostic Centre in each State and these centres would work in close coordination with the DGFASLI's Occupational Health Clinic, envisaged under the Seventh Five Year Plan.

Strenthening Voluntary Organisations

15. Voluntary Safety Organisations like National Safety Council and its Chapters would be strengthened.

ANNEXURE XVI

GUIDELINES FOR DERESERVATION OF RESERVED FORESTS OR DIVERSION OF FOREST LAND TO ANY NON-FOREST USE UNDER THE FOREST (CONSERVATION) ACT, 1980 — 'COST-BENEFIT ANALYSIS'

Copy of Letter No. 11-61 / 85-Fry (Cons)
Government of India, Department of Environment, Forests & Wildlife addressed to the Chief Secretaries of all States

I am directed to inform you that it has been decided that a cost-benefit analysis needs to be carried out, to help evaluate the proposals of dereservation/ diversion of forest land to any non-forest use, under the Forest (Conservation) Act, 1980. This is considered essential to enable the Government of India to take decision after considering all aspects involved.

2. All proposals in future will need to be accompanied by a cost-benefit analysis in accordance with the proformas herewith provided in addition to the information already being furnished in accordance with guidelines previously provided.

3. Annexure I details the types of cases on which a cost-benefit analysis will be required. Annexure II lists the parameters according to which the 'cost aspect will be determined, while Annexure III gives the parameters for assessing the benefit accruing.

4. A cost-benefit analysis as above should accompany the proposals sent to the Central Government for clearance under the Forest (Conservation) Act, 1980.

5. These guidelines come into force with immediate effect.

Annexure I

Category of proposals for which cost-benefit analysis is applicable

Sl. No.	Nature of proposal	Applicable/ Not applicable	Remarks
1.	All category of proposals involving forest land less than 5 ha. in plains and less than 2 ha. in hills.	Not applicable	These proposals are to be considered on case by case basis and value judgment.
2.	Proposals for defence installation purposes and oil prospecting (prospecting only)	Not applicable	In view of National Priority accorded to these sectors, the proposals would be critically assessed to help ascertain that the utmost minimum forest land above is diverted for non-forest use.
3.	Habitation, establishment of industrial units, tourist lodges/complex and other building construction.	Not applicable	These activities being detrimental to protection and conservation of forests, as a matter of policy, such proposals would be rarely entertained.
4.	All other proposals involving forest land more than 5 ha. in plains and more than 2 ha. in hills including roads, transmission lines—minor, medium and major irrigation projects, hydel projects mining activity, railway lines—location, specific installations like microwave stations, auto repeater centres, T.V. towers etc.	Applicable	These are cases where a cost-benefit analysis is necessary to determine whether diverting the forest land to non-forest use is in the the forest land to non-forest use is in the overall public interest.

Annexure II
Parameters for evaluation of loss of forests

Sl. No.	Parameters	Nature of Proposal: Roads, Tr. lines & Railway lines	Nature of Proposal: Minor Irrigation projects, quarrying of stones/metals	Nature of Proposal: Medium & Major Irrigation, hydro-electric, large mining & other misc. projects
1	2	3	4	5
1.	Loss of value of timber, fuelwood and minor forest produce on an annual basis, including loss of man-hours per annum of people who derived livelihood and wages from the harvest of these commodities	To be quantified & expressed in monetary terms	To be quantified & expressed in monetary terms	To be quantified & expressed in monetary terms
2.	Loss of animal husbandry productivity, including loss of fodder	-do-	-do-	-do-
3.	Cost of human resettlement	-do-	-do-	-do-
4.	Loss of public facilities and administrative infrastructure (roads, buildings, schools, dispensaries, electric lines, railways etc.) on forest land, or which would require forest land if these facilities were diverted due to the project.	-do-	-do-	-do-
5.	Environmental Losses : (Soil erosion, effect on hydrological cycle, wildlife habitat, micro-climate upsetting of ecological balance.)	Though technical judgment would be primarily applied in determining the losses, as a thumb rule, the environmental value of one hectare of fully stocked forest (density 1.0) would be taken as Rs. 126.71 lakhs to accrue over a period of 50 years. The value will reduce with density, for example, if density is 0.4 the value will work out Rs. 50,696 lakhs. So if a project which requires deforestation of ha. of forest of density 0.4 gives monetary returns worth over Rs. 50,696 lakhs over a period of 50 years, may be considered to give a positive cost-benefit ratio. The figure of assumed environment at value will change if there is an increase in bank rate; the change will be proportional to percentage increase in the bank rate.		
6.	Suffering to oustees.	The social cost of rehabilitation of an oustee (in addition to the cost likely to be incurred in providing residence, occupation and social services to him) be worked out as 1.5 times of what he should have earned in two years had he been not shifted.		

Annexure III

Parameters for evaluation of benefit, notwithstanding loss of forests

Sl. No.	Parameters	Nature of proposal: Roads, Tr. lines & Railway lines	Nature of proposal: Mining projects	Nature of proposal: Irrigation/Hydel projects & others
1	2	3	4	5
1.	Increase in productivity attributable to the specific project	To be quantified & expressed in monetary terms	To be quantified & expressed in monetary terms.	To be quantified & expressed in monetary terms
2.	Benefits to economy	Value judgment	-do-	-do-
3.	No. of population benefited	-do-	Value judgment	Value judgment
4.	Employment potential	-do-	-do-	-do-
5.	Costs of acquisition of facility on non-forest land wherever feasible	To be quantified & expressed in monetary terms	To be quantified & expressed in monetary terms	To be quantified & expressed in monetary terms
6.	Loss of (a) agricultural & (b) animal husbandry production due to diversion of forest land	-do-	-do-	-do-
7.	Cost of rehabilitating the displaced persons as different from compensatory amounts given for displacement	-do-	-do-	-do-
8.	Cost of supply of free fuelwood to workers residing in or near forest area during the period of construction	-do-	-do-	-do-

ANNEXURE XVII

GUIDELINES FOR MASSIVE TREE PLANTATION FOR ABATEMENT OF AIR POLLUTION CAUSED BY INDUSTRIES

1. The species of trees to be chosen for abatement and control of air pollution should preferably have thick and rough barks, profuse branches with evergreen canopy of broad rough leaves and deep root system. The indigenous species of trees considered most suitable for the purpose may be seen at Annexure 'A'.

2. The sapplings of the abovementioned species of trees may be had on payment. Please contact the following mentioned Officers of the Forests Department of the State Government for obtaining the sapplings.

For Calcutta District

(a) Special Officer, Parks and Gardens, Eden Gardens, Calcutta

(b) Divisional Forests Officers, Howrah, 14, Nityadhan Mukherjee Road, Howrah-1.

For 24-Parganas District

(a) Range Office, 24-Parganas, Barrackpore

(b) Barasat Nurseries— Special Officer, Parks and Gardens, Eden Gardens

For Nadia District

Beat Officer, Chakda/Divisional Forests Officer, Howrah, 14, Nityadhan Mukherjee Road, Howrah-1.

For Midnapore District

(a) *Haldia*

Sutahata Range Office, Tomluk Range

Range Officer, Haldia Range, Haldia

(b) *Kharagpur*

Divisional Forests Officer, Kharagpur Social Forestry Division, Kharagpur.

For Burdwan District

Durgapur-Asansol

Divisional Forests Officer, Durgapur Social Forestry Division, Durgapur

Range Officer, Asansol Range Office, Ushagram, Asansol

For Howrah-Hooghly Districts

Divisional Forests Officer, Howrah Social Forestry Division

3. The tree-barrier should not be a mere row of trees but a number of rows to make the barrier sufficiently thick and effective like a mini-forest.

4. The plantation should agree with the general landscape of the area and it is advisable to employ the services of architects having expertise in landscaping.

5. The planners should take note of the most prevalent wind direction while preparing the scheme so as to prevent escape of the pollutants particularly into surrounding residential areas.

6. Other open spaces where tree planting is not possible should be covered with shrubs and grass for holding the soil position to minimise dust pollution and prevent soil erosion.

7. Where there is not enough space for row-planting, afforestation may be undertaken in the surrounding areas of the factory/unit. Land for this purpose may be acquired, taken on rent or with the permission of the owner. Assistance from the local authorities may be sought.

8. It is felt that a weighted emphasis should be paid to protection, maintenance and safety of the planted trees. Suitable full-timers should be employed for this purpose.

9. Planting should generally be done at the height of the monsoon in the month of July.

Department of Environment

Government of West Bengal

Dated, Calcutta, the 15th June, 1986

LIST OF THE TREES CONSIDERED SUITABLE FOR THE GREEN BELTS

Sl. No.	Botanical Name	Common Name	Ht. in metres	Colour of the flower	Flowering time
(1)	(2)	(3)	(4)	(5)	(6)
1.	Acacia arabica	Babool	8.0-10.0	Yellow	March-May
2.	Aegle Marmelos (V. Limiled)	Bel	8.0-10.0	Greenish white fruit plant	March-April
3.	Albizia lebbeck (A.Procera)	Siris	10.0-15.0	Pale-greenish yellow	April-May
4.	Artocarpus integrifolia	Kathal	6.0-8.0		Feb.-March
5.	Anogeissus latifolia 2	Dhaura	10.0-15.0	Greenish	Sept.-Jan.
6.	Anacardium occidentale	Cashew	3.0-4.0	Cream	Jan.-Feb.
7.	Anthocephalus cadamba	Kadam	10.0-15.0	Yellow	Oct.-Dec.
8.	Azadirachta indica	Neem			
9.	Bauhinia variegata	Kanchan	7.0-8.0	White-variegated with purple & white	Feb.-April
10.	Cassia javanica	Java Cassia	12.0-14.0	Deep pink	May-June
11.	Cassia fistula	Indian Laburnum Amaltas	9.0-13.0	Yellow	March-May
12.	Cassia nodosa	Pink "Mohur"	12.0-14.0	Rose pink	April-May
13.	Cassia siamea	Minjiri	10.0-13.0	Yellow	Aug.-Nov.
14.	Casuarina equisetifolia	Jhau	10.0-15.0	Flowers inconspicuous	March-May
15.	Delonix regia	Gold Mohur Gul Mohur	8.0-12.0	White-orange, Red	April-June
16.	Eucalyptus hybrid	Blue Gum tree	20.0-25.0	Cream	May-June
17.	Nyctanthes arbortristic (Priced)	Siuli	2.0-3.0	White	Oct.-Nov.
18.	Lagerstroemia floreginae	Jarul	7.0-10.0	Liliac	May-June
19.	Mangifera indica	Am	7.0-8.0	White	Feb.-March
20.	Leucaena Leucocophala	Subabul	8.0-10.0	Flowers conspicuous	July-Aug.
21.	Mimusops elengi	Bakul	4.0-5.0	White	Nov.-Dec.
22.	Nerium odorum (Priced)	Karabi	2.0-4.0	Red, white	Feb.-March
23.	Peltophorum ferruginium	Radhachura	10.0-15.0	Golden-yellow	May-Oct.
24.	Pithecolobium dulce	Jungle Jalebi	8.0-10.0	White	March-April
25.	Putranjiva roxburghii (Priced)	Indian Amulet tree	8.0-10.0	Flowers inconspicuous	March-April
26.	Polyalthea longifolia	Debdaru		Foliage	March-June

Sl. No.	Botanical Name	Common Name	Ht. in metres	Colour of the flower	Flowering time
(1)	(2)	(3)	(4)	(5)	(6)
27.	Syzygium cumminii	Jamun	10.0-12.0	Flowers inconspicuous fruit tree	March-April
	-	-	-		
28.	Tamarindus indica	Tamarind	10.0-15.0	Yellow & red	May-July
29.	Terminalia arjuna	Tamarind	10.0-15.0	Flowers inconspicuous	March-April
30.	Termanalia belerica	Bahera	10.0-15.0	Greenish-yellow	April-June

PROCEDURE FOR TRANSPLANTATION OF FULL-GROWN TREES

Method

If trees are not very old they can be transplanted easily. The percentage of survival can be hundred per cent if the work is done properly and during the rainy season. The following steps are involved:

1. The sites where the trees are to be shifted should be selected first. The sites should be free of overhead telephone or power lines. Large pits should be dug at these sites to comfortably accommodate the 'tree roots' ball of earth.

2. Distance between pits depends on the variety. In case of short varieties with a small spread, the distance should be 10 ft. to 15 ft. For tall varieties with spreads of between 15 ft. and 20 ft. on either side, the distance should not be less than 30 feet.

3. When pits are dug at the selected sites, their sizes would depend on the dimensions/age of the tree. For trees of medium size the pit size will be around 8 feet in diameter and 5 feet deep. The actual pit size for different trees can be adjusted with experience. The point to be kept sight of is that the 'tree roots' ball of earth should fit in comfortably with at least 6 to 12 inches clearance all around. Usually the pit size in feet should be directly proportional to the girth on the tree in inches.

4. Adequate quantity of soil and manure mixture @ 4 : 1 is necessary for each pit. A little bone meal can also be added. To start with only about 6" soil mixture is to be filled in each pit and watered well to form a puddle before the actual transplantation. The total quantity of soil and manure required for all the pits should be mixed and arranged before the start of the actual operation.

5. Before transplanation, the trees should be 'extensively pruned'. That is, the foliage should be completely removed and all the branches should be cut off with a pruning saw. No other implement should be

used. The cut surfaces should be painted with non-synthetic white paint to anaesthesise these portions. 'Extensive pruning' helps in easier 'replanting balance' and handling, thereby reducing the shock effect. This also aids the plant roots in recovering and adhering to the new soil and reduces transpiration and/or loss of moisture.

6. The trees are now ready for lifting or uprooting. A deep trench of at least upto 5 feet in depth is to be dug around the base of the tree at least 2 to 3 feet away from the trunk in the case of trees with a girth of up to 6". The depth of the trench and its distance from the trunk would therefore vary with the size of the tree. The trench should be dug to gradually converge towards the base of the tree so that 'tree roots' ball of earth can ultimately be detached from the ground.

7. The trees are then to be lifted with the help of a crane of suitable size. Before lifting, a piece of gunny should be wound round the trunk, with a few wooden batons secured around the gunny pack on the outside by a steel wire rope. This will facilitate lifting without injuring the bark. Immediately the 'tree roots' ball should be sprayed with potassium phosphate solution and then wrapped and tied with a piece of very wet gunny.

8. Before replanting, the soil at the base of the pit should be watered heavily after which the uprooted tree along with the 'tree roots' ball should be lowered carefully into the new pit with the help of the crane.

9. The empty space in this pit is to be filled with the previously prepared mixture of soil, bone meal and manure and thoroughly rammed in tightly, so that no air gaps are left inside the soil. Air gaps could result in fungal infection to the roots. Sand can also be added which will fill up the air gaps when watered.

10. The trunk can now be sprayed with Blytox, a copper sulphate compound whose action is anti-fungicidal in nature.

11. The transplanted tree should be watered heavily at the base.

12. Guy ropes, angle iron or bamboos should be used for a few days to secure the tree till the soil hardens around the transplanted tree to hold it erect.

13. Four to five days after transplantation the trunk can be sprayed with potassium nitrate solution for facilitating the initiation of new shoots.

14. If rains are inadequate watering should continue for three months.

The heavily pruned transplanted tree is not a pretty sight, but this should not deter the optimist, as the chances of survival are maximum without the branches and foliage.

ANNEXURE XVIII

DECISION OF THE CABINET DATED 30.6.1986 ON AMENDMENT OF THE RULES OF BUSINESS FOR EFFECTING THE GUIDELINES OF THE DEPARTMENT OF ENVIRONMENT

10A. (1) No department shall, without previous consultation with and the concurrence of the Department of Environment, authorise issue of administrative approval to any scheme or project other than such schemes or projects as may be specifically exempted for the purpose by the Department of Environment. Every order conveying the administrative approval to any scheme or project shall indicate the concurrence of the Department of Environment, where necessary.

(2) No proposal for any project/scheme which requires previous consultation of the Department of Environment under this rule, but in which the Department of Environment has not concurred, may be proceeded with unless a decision to that effect has been taken by the Cabinet.

SUPPLEMENTARY INSTRUCTIONS UNDER RULE 54 OF THE RULES OF BUSINESS

In order to ensure that Environmental Impact studies in respect of all schemes and projects are properly undertaken, the Department of Environment should have to be associated with the process of formulation of such schemes or projects by the concerned working groups, advisory bodies etc. of the relevant departments. The Department of Development and Planning should also require its advisory bodies (e.g. the State Planning Board etc.) to associate a representative of the Department of Environment who will take note of the environmental requirements of particular projects and indicate the nature of scrutiny required from the environmental angle.

ANNEXURE XIX

INCENTIVES TO INDUSTRIES FOR PREVENTION AND CONTROL OF POLLUTION AND FOR CONSERVATION OF RESOURCES

1. Exemption from Income-tax

The amounts spent for programmes of conservation of natural resources by taxpayers, private individuals and corporate sector to any association or institution will be allowed as deduction in the computation of taxable income under Section 35 ccB — Income Tax Act of 1961 with effect from June 1, 1982.

Applications for the purpose of Section 34 ccB have to be made to the Secretary, Department of Environment, Government of India.

2. Depreciation allowance

Under extra-ordinary Part-II, Section 3, sub-Section (II) No. 85 dated 23.2.1983, Central Board of Direct Taxes, Ministry of Finance, depreciation allowance at 30% will be allowed on devices and systems installed by industrial units for minimising environmental pollution or for conservation of natural resources.

A list of such devices and systems eligible for accelerated depreciation has been notified.

(a) *Air Pollution Control Equipments:*

(i) Electrostatic precipitation systems

(ii) Felt-Filter systems

(iii) Dust collector systems

(iv) Scrubber counter current/venturi/packed-bed/cyclonic scrubbers.

(b) *Water Pollution Control Equipments:*

(i) Mechanical screen systems

(ii) Aerated detritus chambers (including air compressor)

(iii) Mechanically skimmed oil and grease removal systems

(iv) Chemical feed systems and flash mixing equipment

(v) Mechanical flocculators and mechanical reactors

(vi) Diffused air/mechanically aerated activated sludge system

(vii) Aerated lagoon systems

(viii) Biofliters

(ix) Methane-recovery anaerobic Digestor systems

(x) Air floatation systems

(xi) Air/steam stripping systems

(xii) Urea hydrolysis systems

(xiii) Marine outfall systems

(xiv) Centrifuge for dewatering sludge

(xv) Rotating biological contactor or Bio-disc.

(c) *Solid Waste Control Equipments:*

"Caustic/lime/chrome/mineral/cryolite recovery system"

(No. 5101/F. No. 23/FB/8 IPL).

3. Investment allowance

Investment allowance at a higher rate of 35% of the actual cost of new machinery or plant which would assist in control of pollution or protection of environment has been granted in 1983-84 under new sub-Section (2c) in Section 32-A inserted in the Income Tax Act of 1961.

4. Exemption from tax to capital gains

To encourage industries to shift from urban areas and as a measure of decongesting the overcrowded cities and for reducing pollution, special allowances have been made to avoid capital gains tax on the sale of both land and building that fall vacant after the shifting provided that these sale proceeds are reinserted in a new industry within a period of 5 years. Previously this exemption of capital gains from tax applied to buildings or lands for the purpose of business at the new place from 1983-84, this exemption has been further extended to capital gains arising from also transfer of machinery and plant.

5. Rebate of cess levied on consumption of water under Water Cess Act of 1977

Under this Act it is provided that where any persons or local authority, liable to pay the Cess under the Cess Act, instals any plant for the treatment of sewage or trade effluent, \such person or authority, shall from such date as may be prescribed, be entitled to a rebate of 70% of the Cess payable by such industry etc. Thus any person or local authority may obtain rebate at the rate of 70% of the actual Cess on the installation of pollution abatement devices and running them efficiently to the satisfaction of the State Water Pollution Control Board.

6. In his key note address at the National Conference on Environmental Preservation and Pollution Control organised by the Federation of Indian Chamber of Commerce & Industry held on 26th & 27th March at Delhi, Sri Digvijay Sinha, Minister of Environment mentioned as follows:

(a) Special instructions have been issued by the Finance Ministry to the I.D.B.I. and other loaning institutions to give soft loans to those industries who wish to invest in installing pollution abatement equipment which would be worked out over and above the celling limit of an industry to receive such loans.

(b) The recommendations by the Department of Environment for reducing excise duties on craft paper and hard boards which can be used as substitute for timber wood in the packaging of tree, tobacco, textiles and horticultural products to enable them to be competitive has been implemented in the Finance Bill of 1984. A Similar concession may apply to ply-wood.

efficiently to the satisfaction of the State Water Pollution Control Board.

6. In his key note address at the National Conference on Environmental Preservation and Pollution Control organised by the Federation of Indian Chamber of Commerce & Industry held on 26th & 27th March at Delhi, Sri Digvijay Sinha, Minister of Environment mentioned as follows:

(a) Special instructions have been issued by the Finance Ministry to the I.D.B.I. and other loaning institutions to give soft loans to those industries who wish to invest in installing pollution abatement equipment which would be worked out over and above the celling limit of an industry to receive such loans.

(b) The recommendations by the Department of Environment for reducing excise duties on craft paper and hard boards which can be used as substitute for timber wood in the packaging of tree, tobacco, textiles and horticultural products to enable them to be competitive has been implemented in the Finance Bill of 1984. A Similar concession may apply to ply-wood.

ANNEXURE XX

ENVIRONMENTAL GUIDELINES FOR SITING OF INDUSTRY

MINISTRY OF ENVIRONMENT & FORESTS
DEPARTMENT OF ENVIRONMENT
GOVERNMENT OF INDIA
NEW DELHI
August 1985

1. Introduction

1.1 Industrial development significantly contributes towards economic growth. However, industrial progress brings along with it a host of environmental problems. Many of these problems could be avoided if industries are located on the basis of environmental considerations. Injudicious siting of industry can seriously effect the environmental features such as air, water, land, flora, fauna, human settlements and health of people. The entrepreneur should be fully aware of these implications and he should take necessary steps while setting up the industry so as to minimise the possible adverse effects on thte environmental resources and quality of life. Often, an entrepreneur finds it very costly to instal pollution control equipment and other mitigative measures after the industry is already set up. As such, preventive steps are needed at the time of siting rather than going in for curative measures at a later stage.

1.2 The Industrial Policy Statement of July 1980, recognised the need for preserving ecological balance and improving living conditions in the urban centres of the country. On the basis of this Policy, indiscriminate expansion of the existing industries and setting up of new industrial undertakings within the limits of metropolitan cities and the larger towns should not be permitted. However, the Policy has not touched upon the implications of setting up an industry in sensitive areas, both ecological or otherwise, which would have an effect on the overall development process.

1.3 At present, industries are being located on the basis of raw material availability, access to the market, transport facilities and such other techno-economic considerations without adequate attention to environmental considerations are recognised as an important criterion for setting of industry.

1.4 To prevent air, water and soil pollution arising out of industrial projects, the Industrial Licensing Procedure requires that the entrepreneurs before setting up the industry should obtain clearance from Central/State Air and Water Pollution Control Boards. The Central/State Pollution Control Boards stipulate that air (gases) and water (effluents) emanating from the industry should adhere to certain quality standards. However, these stipulations do not prevent the industry from effecting the total environment by wrong siting. Also, the cumulative effect of a number of industries at a particular place is not being studied upon, with the result that an industry or an industrial area over a period of time could cause significant damage to the surrounding environment and ecological features.

1.5 In respect of certain industrial development projects (List at Appendix 1), it is not only necessary to instal suitable pollution control equipment but also to identify appropriate sites for their location. To give a concrete shape to this requirement, a select group of 20 industries (List at Appendix II) has been notified by the Department of Industrial Development. A formalised procedure has been stipulated for site selection from environmental angle with regard to these projects.

1.6 According to this procedure for the select group of industries, the letters of intent should be converted to industrial licenses only after the following conditions have been fulfilled:

(i) The State Director of Industries confirms that the site of the project has been approved from environmental angle by the competent State Authority.

(ii) The entrepreneur commits both to the State Government and Central Government that he will instal the appropriate equipment and implement the prescribed measures for the prevention and control of pollution.

(iii) The concerned State Pollution Control Board has certified that the proposal meets with the environmental requirements and that the equipment installed or proposed to be installed are adequate and appropriate to the requirement.

1.7 The State Department of Environment will be the competent authority for approval of project sites from environmental angle. In those States where such Departments have not yet been set up, approval should be obtained from the nodal agency designated for looking after environmental matters. With regard to projects where support from the Central Government/International Agencies is envisaged and which come under the purview of Industrial Licensing, approval of the project site from environmental angle should be obtained from the

Department of Environment, Government of India. The entrepreneur should provide the details of proposed project site, pollution abatement measures and such other relevant information as required for review from environmental angle.

1.8 The entrepreneur will be required to submit half-yearly progress report on installation of pollution control devices to the respective State Pollution Control Boards.

1.9 Depending on the nature and location of the project, the entrepreneur will be required to submit comprehensive Environmental Impact Assessment Report, and Environmental Management Plans.

2. Environmental Guidelines for Industries

2.1 In order to help the concerned authorities and the entrepreneurs, it is necessary to frame certain broad guidelines for siting an industry. It is also necessary to identify the parameters that should be taken into account while setting up an industry. With this in view, the following environmental guidelines are recommended for siting of industries to ensure optimum use of natural and man-made resources in sustainable manner with minimal depletion, degradation and/or destruction of environment. Those are in addition to those directives that are already in existence under the Industries (Development and Regulation) Act.

2.1 *Areas to be avoided*

In siting industries, care should be taken to minimise the adverse impact of the industries on the immediate neighbourhood as well as distant places. Some of the natural life sustaining systems and some specific land uses are sensitive to industrial impacts because of the nature and extent of fragility. With a view to protecting such an industrial sites shall maintain the following distances from the areas listed:

(a) Ecologically and/or otherwise sensitive areas : at least 25 km; depending on the geo-climatic conditions the requisite distance shall have to be increased by the appropriate agency.

(b) Coastal Areas: at least 1/2 km. from high tide line.

(c) Flood Plain of the Riverine System: at least 1/2 km. from flood plain or modified flood plain affected by dam in the upstream or by flood control systems.

(d) Transport/Communication System: at least 1/2 km. from highway and railway.

(e) Major Settlements (3,00,000 population) : distance from settlements is difficult to maintain because of urban sprawl. At the time of siting of the industry if any major settlement's notified limit is within 50 km., the spatial direction of growth of the settlement for at least a decade must be assessed and the industry shall be sited at least 25 km. from the projected growth boundary of the settlement.

Note: Ecological and/or otherwise sensitive areas include (i) Religious and Historic Places; (ii) Archaeological Monuments (e.g. identified zone around Taj Mahal); (iii) Scenic Areas; (iv) Hill Resorts; (v) Beach Resorts; (vi) Health Resorts; (vii) Coastal Areas rich in Corals, Mangroves, Breeding Grounds of Specific Species; (viii) Estuaries rich in Mangroves, Breeding Grounds of Specific Species; (ix) Gulf Areas; (x) Biosphere Reserves; (xi) National Parks and Sanctuaries; (xii) Natural Lakes, Swamps; (xiii) Seismic Zones; (xiv) Tribal Settlements; (xv) Areas of Scientific and Geological Interest; (xvi) Defence Installations, specially those of security importance and sensitive to pollution; (xvii) Border Areas (International) and (xviii) Air Ports.

Pre-requisite; State and Central Governments are required to identify such areas on a priority basis.

2.3 *Siting Criteria*

Economic and social factors are recognized and assessed while siting an industry. Environmental factors must be taken into consideration in industrial siting. Proximity of water sources, highway, major settlements, markets for products and raw material resources is desired for economy of production, but all the above listed systems must be away for environmental protection. Industries are, therefore, required to be sited, striking a balance between economic and environmental considerations. In such a selected site, the following factors mut be recognized.

— No forest land shall be converted into non-forest activity for the sustenance of the industry (Ref: Forest Conservation Act, 1980).

— No prime agricultural land shall be converted into industrial site.

— Within the acquired site the industry must locate itself at the lowest location to remain obscured from general sight.

— Land acquired shall sufficiently large to provide space for appropriate treatment of waste water still left for treatment after maximum possible reuse and recycle. Reclaimed (treated) wastewater shall be used to raise green belt and to create water body for aesthetics, recreation and if possible, for aquaculture. The green belt shall be 1/2 km. wide around the battery limit of the industry. For industry having odour problem it shall be a kilometre wide.

— The green belt between two adjoining large scale industries shall be one kilometre.

— Enough space should be provided for storage of solid wastes so that these could be available for possible reuse.

— Lay out and form of the industry that may come up in the area must conform to the landscape of the area without affecting the scenic features of that place.

— Associated township of the industry must be created at a space having physiographic barrier between the industry and the township.

— Each industry is required to maintain three ambient air quality measuring stations within 120 degree angle between stations.

3. Environmental Impact Assessment (EIA)

3.1 The purpose of Environmental Impact Assessment (EIA) is to identify and evaluate the potential impacts (beneficial and adverse) of development projects on the environmental system. It is a useful aid for decision-making based on understanding of the environmental implications including social, cultural and aesthetic concerns which could be integrated with the analysis of the project costs and benefits. This exercise should be undertaken early enough in the planning stage of projects for selection of environmentally compatible sites, process technologies and such other environmental safeguards.

3.2 While all industrial projects may have some environmental impacts all of them may not be significant enough to warrant elaborate assessment procedures. The need for such exercises will have to be decided after initial evaluation of the possible implications of a particular projects and its location. The projects which could be the candidates for detailed Environmental Impact Assessment include the following:

(i) Those which can significantly alter the landscape, land use pattern and lead to concentration of working and service population;

(ii) Those which need upstream development activity like assured mineral and forest products supply or downstream industrial process development;

(iii) Those involving manufacture, handling and use of hazardous materials;

(iv) Those which are sited near ecologically sensitive area, urban centres; hill resorts, places of scientific and religious importance; and

(v) Industrial Estates with constituent units of various types which could cumulatively cause significant environmental damage.

3.3 Environmental Impact Assessment (EIA) should be prepared on the basis of the existing background pollution levels *vis-a-via* contributions of pollutants from the proposed plant. The EIA should address to some of the basic factors listed below:

(a) Meteorology and air quality;

Ambient levels of pollutants such as sulphur dioxide, oxides of nitrogen, carbon monoxide, suspended particulate matters, should be determined at the centre and at 3 others locations on a radius of 10 km. with 120 degrees angle between stations. Additional contribution of pollutants at the locations are required to be predicted after taking into account the emission rates of the pollutants from the stacks of the proposed plant, under different meteorological conditions prevailing in the area.

(b) Hydrology and water quality;

(c) Site and its surroundings;

(d) Occupational safety and health;

(e) Details of the treatment and disposal of effluents (liquid, air and solid) and the methods of alternative uses;

(f) Transportation of raw material and details of material handling;

(g) Impact on sensitive targets;

(h) Control equipment and measures proposed to be adopted.

3.4 Preparation of environmental management plan is required for formulation, implementation and monitoring of environmental protection measures during and after commissioning of projects. The plans should indicate the details as to how various measures have been or are proposed to be taken including cost components as may be required. Cost of measures for environmental safeguards should be treated as an integral component of the project cost and environmental aspects should be taken into account at various stages of the projects:

(a) Conceptualization: preliminary environmental assessment;

(b) Planning: detailed studies of environmental impacts and design of safeguards;

(c) Execution: implementation of environmental safety measures;

(d) Operation: monitoring of effectiveness of built-in safeguards.

The management plans should be necessarily based on considerations of resource conservation and pollution abatement, some of which are enumerated as under:

3.5 *Liquid Effluents*

(i) Effluents from the industrial plants should be treated well to the standards as prescribed by the Central/State Water Pollution Control Boards.

(ii) Soil permeability studies should be made prior to effluents being discharged into holding tanks or impoundments and steps taken to prevent percolation and groundwater contamination.

(iii) Special precautions should be taken regarding flight patterns of birds in the area. Effluents containing toxic compounds, oil and grease have been known to cause extensive death of migratory birds. Location of plants should be prohibited in such type of sensitive areas.

(iv) Deep well burial of toxic effluents should not be resorted to as it can result in re-surfacing and groundwater contamination. Re-surfacing has been known to cause extensive damage to crop and livestocks.

(v) In all cases, efforts should be made for reuse of water and its conservation.

3.6 *Air Pollution*

(i) The emission levels of pollutants from the different stacks, should conform to the pollution control standards prescribed by Central or State Boards.

(ii) Adequate control equipment should be installed for minimising the emission of pollutants from the various stacks.

(iii) In-plant control measures should be taken to contain the fugitive emissions.

(iv) Infrastructural facilities should be provided for monitoring the stack emissions and measuring the ambient air quality including micro-meteorological data (wherever required) in the area.

(v) Proper stack height as prescribed by the Central/State Pollution Control Boards should be provided for better dispersion of pollutants over a wider area to minimise the effect of pollution.

(vi) Community buildings and townships should be built up—wind of plant with one-half to one kilometre green belt in addition to physiographical barrier.

3.7 *Solid Wastes*

(i) The site for waste disposal should be checked to varify permeability so that no contaminants percolate into the groundwater or river/lake.

(ii) Waste disposal areas should be planned down-wind of villages and townships.

(iii) Reactive materials should be disposed of by immobilising the reactive materials with suitable additives.

(iv) The pattern of filling disposal site should be planned to create better landscape and be approved by appropriate agency and the appropriately pretreated solid wastes should be disposed according to the approved plan.

(v) Intensive programmes of the plantation on disposal areas should be undertaken.

3.8 *Noise and Vibration*

Adequate measures should be taken for control of noise and vibrations in the industries.

3.9 *Occupational Safety and Health*

Proper precautionary measures for adopting occupational safety and health standards should be taken.

3.10 *Prevention maintenance and operation of environmental Control Systems*

(i) Adequate safety precautions should be taken during preventive maintenance and shut down of the control systems.

(ii) A system of inter-locking with the production equipment should be implemented where highly toxic compounds are involved.

3.11 *House-Keeping*

Proper house-keeping and cleanliness should be maintained both inside and outside the industry.

3.12 *Human settlements*

(i) Residential colonies should be located away from the solid and liquid waste dumping areas. Meteorological and environmental conditions should be studied properly before selecting the site for residential areas in order to aviod air pollution problems.

(ii) Persons who are displaced or have lost agricultural lands as a result of locating the industries in the area, should be properly rehabilitated.

3.13 *Transport Systems*

(i) Proper parking places should be provided for the trucks and other vehicles by the industries to avoid any congestion or blocking of roads.

(ii) Siting of industries on the highway should be avioded as it may add to more road accidents because of substantial increase in the movements of heavy vehicles and unauthorised shops and settlements coming up around the industrial complex.

(iii) Spillage of chemicals/substances on roads inside the plant may lead to accidents. Proper road safety signs both inside and outside the plant should be displayed for avoiding road accidents.

3.14 *Recovery—reuse of waste products*

Efforts should be made to recycle or recover the waste materials to the extent possible. The treated liquid effluents can be conveniently and safety used for irrigation of lands, plants and fields for growing non-edible crops.

3.15 *Vegetal Cover*

Industries should plant trees and ensure vegetal cover in their premises. This is particularly advisable for those industries having more than 10 acres of land.

3.16 *Disaster Planning*

Proper disaster planning should be done to meeting any emergency situation arising due to fire, explosion, sudden leakage of gas etc. Fire-fighting equipment and other safety appliances should be kept ready for use during disaster/ emergency situation including natural calamities like earthquake/flood.

3.17 *Environmental Management Cell*

Each industry should identify within its set-up a Department/Section/Cell with trained personnel to take up the model responsibility of environmental management as required for planning and implementation of the projects.

Appendix I

LIST OF POLLUTING INDUSTRIES

1. Ferrous Metallurgical Industries
   - Integrated Iron and Steel (metal)
   - Ferrow-alloys
   - Special Steels
   - Iron and Steel Castings and Forgings
2. Non-Ferrous Metallurgical Industries
   - Primary Metallurgical Producing Industries, namely, zinc, lead, copper and aluminium
   - Non-Ferrous Castings and Forgings
3. Mining Industries
   - Coal Washeries
   - Hydraulic Mining
   - Hydraulic Transport
4. Ores/Mineral Processing Industries
   - Beneficiation and/or Pelletization
5. Coal (including coke) Industries
   - Coal, Lignite, Coke etc.
   - Fuel Gases (Coal Gas, Producer Gas, Water Gas and the like)
6. Power Generating Industries
7. Paper and Pulp (including paper products) Industries
   - Paper writing, Printing and Wrapping (to include security paper also)

— Newsprint

— Paper Board and Straw Board

— Paper for Packaging (corrugated papers, crafts paper, paper bags, paper containers and the like)

— Pulp—Wood Pulp, Mechanical, Chemical (including dissolving pulp)

— Sanitary Paper

— Cigarette Paper

— Insulation and Other Coated Papers

8. Fertilizer Industries

— Nitrogenous

— Phosphatic

— Mixed

9. Cement (including cement asbestos products) Industries

— Portland Cement (including slag Cement, puzzolona cement and their products)

— Asbestos Cement Products

10. Petroleum Industries

— Oil production

— Oil Refining

— Lubricating Oils and Greases

— Oil Exploration

11. Petrochemicals Industries

12. Drugs and Pharmaceuticals Industries

— Narcotics, Drugs, and Phamaceuticals including Vitamins (Antibiotics and Indigenous Systems of Medicines covered)

13. Fermentation Industries

— Alcohol (industries and potable)

14. Rubber (natural & synthetic) including Rubber Products Industries

— Natural and Synthetic Rubber

— Tyres and Tubes

— Surgical and Medical products including Prophylactics and Latex Products

— Footwear

— Other Rubber Goods

15. Paints Industries
16. Leather Tanning Industries
17. Electro-Plating Industries
18. Chemical Industries

— Coke Oven By-Products and Coaltar Distillation Products

— Industrial Gases (nitrogen, oxygen, acetylene argon, carbon dioxide, hydrogen, sulphurdioxide, nitrous oxide, halogenated hydrocarbon, ozone etc.)

— Industrial Carbon

— Alkalies

— Electrochemicals (metallic sodium, potassium and magnesium, chlorates, perchlorates, and peroxides)

— Electrothermal Products (artificial abrasive, calcium carbide)

— Electrothermal Products (artificial abrasive, calcium carbide)

— Phosphorous and its Compounds

— Nitrogenous Compounds (cyanides, cyanamides, and other nitrogenous compounds)

— Halogens and Halogenated Compounds (Chlorine, Fluorine, Bromine and iodine)

— Explosives (including industrial explosives and detenators and fuses)

19. Insecticides, Fungicides, Herbicides and other Pesticides Industries
20. Synthetic Resin and Plastics
21. Man-made Fibre (cellulosic and non-cellulosic industry).

Appendix II

LIST OF POLLUTING INDUSTRIES REQUIRED TO OBTAIN ENVIRONMENTAL CLEARANCE FOR SITING (VIDE PRESS NOTE NO. 10/60/83-LP, DATED 10TH DECEMBER, 1984 ISSUED BY THE DEPARTMENT OF INDUSTRIAL DEVELOPMENT, GOVERNMENT OF INDIA)

1. Primary metallurgical producing industries viz. lead, copper, aluminium and steel
2. Paper, Pulp and Newsprint

3. Pesticides/Insecticides
4. Refineries
5. Fertilizers
6. Paints
7. Dyes
8. Leather Tanning
9. Rayon
10. Sodium/Potassium Cyanide
11. Basic drugs
12. Foundry
13. Storage Batteries (lead acid type)
14. Acids/Alkalies
15. Elastics
16. Rubber—Synthetic
17. Cement
18. Asbestos
19. Fermentation industry
20. Electro-plating industry

APPENDIX I

EXTRACTS FROM VARIOUS LEGISLATIONS RELATING TO ENVIRONMENT PROTECTION

EXTRACTS FROM INDIAN PENAL CODE, 1860 (45 OF 1860)

The Indian Penal Code, 1860 is enacted because it is expedient to provide a general Penal Code for India. The polluter of environment can be punished, under this code for certain types of pollution. These types of pollution may be broadly categorised under the following heads:

1. Water pollution
2. Pollution of atmosphere
3. General pollution.

1. Water pollution

If a person voluntarily corrupts or fouls the water of any public spring or reservoir so as to render it less fit for the purpose for which it is ordinarily used he may be punished under Section 277.

2. Pollution of atmosphere

If a person vitialy the atmosphere in any place so as to make it noxious to the health of person in generally dwelling or carrying on business in the neighbourhood or passing along a public way, he may be punished under Section 278.

3. General pollution

If a person does any act or omits to do any act which causes any common injury, danger or annoyance to the public or to the people in general who dwell or occupy property in the vicinity or which must cause injury, obstruction, danger or annoyance to persons who may, have occasion to use any public right, this act or omission may amount to public nuisance as defined under Section 268. Such offender may be punished under Sections 290 and 291. If a person, unlawfully or negligently does any act which is, and which he knows or has reason to believe to be, likely to spread the infection of any disease dangerous to life may be punished under Section 269. If a person causes wrongful loss or damage to the public or any person, causes the destruction of any property or any such change in any property or in the situation thereof which destroys of diminishes its value or utility or affects it injuriously, he may be punished under Sections 426, 430, 431 and 432.

268. Public nuisance

A person is guilty of a public nuisance who does any act or is guilty of an illegal omission which causes any common injury, danger or annoyance to the public or to the people in general who dwell or occupy property in the vicinity, or which must necessarily cause injury, obstruction, danger or annoyance to persons who may have occasion to use any public right.

A common nuisance is not excused on the ground that it causes some convenience or advantage.

269. Negligent act likely to spread infection of disease dangerous to likely

Whoever unlawfully or negligently does any act which is, and which he knows or has reason to believe to be, likely to spread the infection of any disease dangerous to life, shall be punished with imprisonment of either description for a term which may extend to six months, or with fine, or with both.

277. Fouling water of public spring or reservoir

Whoever voluntarily corrupts or fouls the water of any public spring or reservoir, so as to render it less fit for the purpose for which it in ordinarily used shall be punished with imprisonment of either description for a term which may extend to five hundred rupees, or with both.

278. Making atmosphere noxious to health

Whoever voluntarily vitiates the atmosphere in any place so as to make it noxious to the health of persons in general dwelling or carrying on business in the neighbourhood or passing along a public way, shall be punished with fine which may extend to five hundred rupees.

290. Punishment for public nuisances in cases not otherwise provide for

Whoever commits a public nuisance in any case not otherwise punishable by this code, shall be punished with fine which may extend to two hundred rupees.

291. Continuance of nuisance after injunction to discontinue

Whoever repeats or continues a public nuisance, having been enjoined by any public servant who had lawful authority to issue such injunction not to repeat or continue such nuisance, shall be punished with simple imprisonment for a term which may extend to six months, or with fine, or with both.

425. Mischief

Whoever, with intent to cause, or knowing that he is likely to cause, wrongful loss or damage to the public or to any person causes the destruction of any property, or any such change in any property or in the situation thereof as destroys, or diminishes its value or utility, or affects it injuriously, commits "mischief".

426. Punishment for mischief

Whoever commits mischief shall be punished with imprisonment of either description for a term which may extend to three months, or with fine, or with both.

430. Mischief by injury to works of irrigation or by wrongfully diverting water

Whoever commits mischief by doing any act which causes, or which he knows to be likely to cause, a diminution of the supply of water for agricultural purposes, or for food or drink for human beings or for animals which are property, or for cleanliness or for carrying on any manufacture, shall be punished with imprisonment of either description for a term which may extend to five years or with fine, or with both.

431. Mischief by injury to public road, bridge, river or channel

Whoever commits mischief by doing any act which renders or to which he knows to be likely render any public road, bridge navigable channel natural or artificial, impassable or less safe for travelling or conveying property, shall be punished with imprisonment of either description for a term which may extend to five years, or with fine or with both.

432. Mischief by causing inundation or obstruction to public drainage attended with damage

Whoever commits mischief by doing any act which causes or which he knows to be likely to cause an inundation or an obstruction to any public drainage attended with injury or damage, shall be punished with imprisonment of either description for a term which may extend to five years, or with fine, or with both.

EXTRACTS FROM THE CODE OF CRIMINAL PROCEDURE, 1973 (2 OF 1974)

The Code of Criminal Procedure Act, 1973 is enacted by the Parliament to consolidate any amend the law relating to Criminal Procedure.

The Code of Criminal Procedure 1973

Almost all types of Pollution can be controlled or removed by District and Sub-divisional Magistrate by exercising powers under Sections 133, 143 and 144 of Criminal Procedure Code. Under Section 133 conditional injunction order may be passed against a particular person. Under Section 144, absolute orders may be passed against general public. In urgent cases of nuisance of apprehended danger, orders passed under Section 144 may be fully effective.

133. Conditional order for removal of nuisance

(1) Whenever a District Magistrate or a Sub-divisional Magistrate specially empowered in this behalf by the State Government, on receiving the report of a police officer or other information and on taking such evidence (if any) as he thinks fit, considers—

(a) that any unlawful obstruction or nuisance should be removed from any public place or from any way river or channel which is or may be lawfully used by the public; or

(b) that the conduct of any trade or occupation, or the keeping of any goods or merchandise, it injurious to the health or physical comfort of the community, and that in consequence such trade or occupation should be prohibited or regulated or such goods on merchandise should be removed or the keeping thereof regulated; or

(c) that the construction of any building, or the disposal of any substance, as is likely to occasion conflagration of explosion, should be prevented or stopped: or

(d) that any building, tent or structure, or any tree is in such a condition that it is likely to fall and thereby cause injury to persons living or carrying on business in the neighbourhood or passing by, and that in consequence the removal repair or support of such building, tent or structure, or the removal or support of such tree, is necessary; or

(e) that any tank, well or excavation adjacent to any such way or public place should be fenced in such manner as to prevent danger arising to the public; or

(f) that any dangerous animal should be destroyed, confined or otherwise disposed of;

such Magistrate may make a conditional order requiring the person causing such obstruction or nuisance, or carring on such trade or occupation, or keeping any such goods or merchandise or owning, possessing or controlling such building, tent, structure, substance, tank, well or excavation; or owning or possessing such animal or tree, within a time to be fixed in the order—

(i) to remove such obstruction or nuisance; or

(ii) to desist from carring on, or to remove or regulate in such manner any may be directed, such trade or occupation, to remove such goods or merchandise, or to regulate the keeping thereof in such manner as may be directed; or

(iii) to prevent or stop the construction of such building, or alter the disposal of such substance; or

(iv) to remove, repair or support such building, tent or structure, or to remove or support such trees; or

(v) to fence such tank, well or excavation; or

(vi) to destroy, confine or dispose of such dangerous animal in the manner provided in the said order;

if he objects so to do, to appear before himself or some other Executive Magistrate subordinate to him at a time and place to be fixed by the order and show cause, in the manner hereinafter provided, why the order should not be made absolute.

(2) No order duly made by a Magistrate under this section shall be called in question in any Civil Court.

Explanation—A "public place" includes also property belong to the State, camping grounds left unoccupied for sanitary or recreative purposes.

143. Magistrate may prohibit repetition or continuance of public nuisance

A District Magistrate or Sub-divisional Magistrate, or any other Executive Magistrate empowered by the State Government or the District Magistrate in this behalf may order any person not to repeat or continue a public nuisance, as defined in the Indian Penal Code (45 of 1860), or any special or Local Law.

144. Power to issue order in urgent cases of nuisance or apprehended danger

(1) In cases where, in the opinion of a District Magistrate, a Sub-divisional Magistrate or any other Executive Magistrate specially empowered by the State Government in this behalf, there is sufficient ground for proceeding under this section and immediate prevention or speedy remedy is desirable, such Magistrate may, by a written order stating the material facts of the case and served in the manner provided by Section 134, direct any person to abstain from a certain act or take certain order with respect to certain property in his possession or under his management such Magistrate considers that such direction is likely to prevent, or tend to prevent, obstruction, annoyance or injury to any person lawfully employed, or danger to human life, health or safety or a disturbance of the public tranquillity, or a riot or an affray.

(2) An order under this section may, in cases of emergency or in cases where the circumstances do not admit of the serving in due time of a notice upon the person against whom the order is directed be passed exparts.

(3) An order under this section may be directed to a particular individual, or to persons residing in a particular place or area, or to the public generally when frequenting or visiting a particular place or area.

(4) No order under this section shall remain in force for more than two months from the making thereof:

Provided that, if the State Government considers it necessary so to do for preventing danger to human life, health or safety or for preventing a riot or any affray, it may, by notification, or an order made by a Magistrate under this section shall remain in force for such further period not exceeding six months from the date on which the order made by the Magistrate would have, but for such order, expired, as it may specify in the said notification.

(5) Any Magistrate may, either on his own motion or on the application of any person aggrieved, rescind or alter any order made under this section by himself or any Magistrate subordinate to him or by his predecessor in office.

(6) The State Government may, either on its own motion or on the application of any person aggrieved, rescind or alter any order made by it under the proviso to sub-section (4).

(7) Where an application under sub-section (5) or sub-section (6) is received, the Magistrate, or the State Goverment, as the case may be shall afford to the applicant an early opportunity of appearing before him or it, either in person or by pleader and showing cause against the order, and if the Magistrate or the State Government, as the case may be, reject the application wholly or in part, he or it shall record in writing the reasons for so doing.

THE FACTORIES ACT, 1948

The Factories Act, 1948 is enacted primary to regulate labour in factories, specially the disposal of wastes from the factories can be regulated under this Act.

2. Section 12 of the Factories Act, 1948 provides for the regulation of disposal of wastes and effluents from the factories. It authorises the State Government to make rules for this purpose.

THE EXTRACT OF THE FACTORIES ACT, 1948

12. Disposal of wastes and effluents. (1) Effective arrangement shall be made in every factory for the treatment of wastes and effluents due to the manufacturing process carried on therein, so as to render them innocuous, and for their disposal.

(2) The State Government may make rules prescribing the arrangements to be made under sub-section (1) or requiring that the arrangements made in accordance with sub-section (1) shall be approved by such authority as may be prescribed.

THE EXPLOSIVES ACT, 1884 (IV OF 1884)

4. *Definitions*: In this Act, unless the context otherwise requires:

(c) "District Magistrate", in relation to any area for which a Commissioner of Police has been appointed, means the Commissioner of Police thereof and includes:

(i) any such Deputy Commissioner of Police, exercising jurisdiction over the whole or any part of such area, as may be specified by the State Government in this behalf in relation to such area or part; and

(ii) an Additional District Magistrate;

(d) "explosive" means gunpowder, nitroglycerine, nitroglycol, guncotton, dinitro-toluene, tri-nitro-toluene, picric acid, di-nitrophenol, tri-nitro-resorcinol (styphnic acid), cyclto-trimethylene trinitramine, penta-erythritol-tetranitrate, totryl, nir o-gannidine, lead azide, lead styphynatef ulminate of mercury of any other metal diazo-di-nitro-phenol, coloured fires or any other substances whether a single chemical compound or a mixture of substances, whether solid or liquid or gaseous used or manufactured with a view to producing a practical effect by exposionor pyrotechnic effect; and includes fog-signals, fireworks, fuses, rockets, percussion-caps, detonators, cartridges, ammunition of all description and every adaptation or preparation of an explosive as defined in this clause;

6. *Power for Central Government to prohibit the manufacture, possession or importation of specially dangerous explosives.* (1) Notwithstanding anything in the rules under the last foregoing section, the Central Government may, from time to time, by notification in the Offficer Gazette,—

prohibit, either absolutely or subject to conditions, the manufacture, possession or importation of any explosive which is of so dangerous a character that, in the opinion of the Central Government, it is expedient for the public safety to issue the notification.

[1][x x y]

(2) The officers of sea customs at every port shall have the same power in respect of any explosive with regard to the importation of which a notification has been issued under this section and the vessel containing the explosive, as they have for the time being in respect of any article, the importation of which is prohibited or regulated by the law relating to sea customs and the vessel containing the same ; and the enactments for the time being in force relating to sea customs or any such article or vessel shall apply accordingly.

(3) Any person manufacturing, possessing or importing an explosive in contravention of a notification issued under this section shall be punishable with imprisonment for a term which may extend to three years or with fine which may extend to five thousand rupees or with both and, in the case of importation by

1. Clause (b) omitted by Act 10 of 1914.
2. Inserted by Act No. 32 of 1978.

water, the owner and master of the vessel in which the explosive is imported shall, in the absence of reasonable excuse, each be punishable with fine which may extend to five thousand rupees.

6-A. Prohibition of manufacture, possession, sale, or transport of explosives by young persons and certain other persons. Notwithstanding anything in the foregoing provisions of this Act,—

(a) no person,—

(i) who has not completed the age of eighteen years, or

(ii) who has been sentenced on conviction of any offence involving violence or moral turpitude for a term of not less than six month, at any time during a period of five years after the expiration of the sentence, or

(iii) who has been ordered to execute under Chapter VIII of the Code of Criminal Procedure, 1973 (2 of 1974), a bond for keeping the peace or for good behaviour, at any time during the term of the bond, or

(iv) whose licence under this Act has been cancelled, whether before or after the commencement of the Indian Explosive (Amendment) Act, 1978, for contravention of the provision of this Act or of the rules made thereunder, at any time during a period of five years from the date of cancellation of such licence;

shall,—

(1) manufacture, sell, transport, import or export any explosive, or

(2) possess any such explosive as the Central Government may, having regard to the nature thereof, by notification in the Official Gazette, specify;

(b) no person shall sell, deliver or despatch any explosive to a person whom he knows or has reason to believe at the time of such sale, delivery or despatch, —

(i) to be prohibited under clause (a) to manufacture, sell, transport, import, export or possess such explosive, or

(ii) to be of unsound mind.

6-B. *Grant of licences.* (1) Where a person makes an application for licence under Section 5, the authority prescribed in the rules made under that section for grant of licences (hereinafter referred to in this Act as the licensing authority), after making such inquiry, if any, as it may consider necessary, shall, subject to the other provisions of this Act, by order in writing either grant the licence or refuse to grant the same.

(2) The licensing authority shall grant a licence—

(a) where it is required for the purpose of manufacture of explosives if the licensing authority is satisfied that the person by whom licence is required—

(i) possesses technical know-how and experience in the manufacture of explosives; or

(ii) has in his employment or undertakes to employ a person or persons possessing such technical know-how and experience; or

(b) where it is required for any other purpose, if the licensing authority is satisfied that the person by whom licence is required has a good reason for obtaining the same.

6-C. *Refusal of licences.* (1) Notwithstanding anything contained in section 6-B, the licensing authority shall refuse to grant a licence—

(a) where such licence is required in respect of any prohibited explosive; or

(b) where such licence is required by a person whom the licensing authority has reason to believe—

(i) to be prohibited by this Act or by any other law for the time being in force in manufacture, possess, sell, transport, import or export any explosive, or

(ii) to be of unsound mind, or

(iii) to be for any reason unfit for a licence under this Act; or

(c) where the licensing authority deems it necessary for the security of the public peace or for public safety to refuse to grant such licence.

(2) Where the licensing authority refuses to grant a licence to any person, shall record in writing the reasons for such refusal and furnish to that person on demand a brief statement of the same unless in any case the licensing authority is of opinion that it will not be in the public interest to furnish such statement.

6-D. *Licensing authority competent to impose conditions in addition to prescribed condition.* A licence granted under Section 6-B may contain in addition to prescribed conditions such other conditions as may be considered necessary by the licensing authority in any particular case.

6-E. *Variation, suspension and revocation of licences.* (1) The licensing authority may vary the conditions subject to which a licence has been granted except such of them as have been prescribed and may for that purpose require the holder of licence by notice in writing to deliver-up the licence to it within such time as may be specified in the notice.

(2) The licensing authority may, on the application of the holder of a licence, also vary the conditions of the licence except such of them as have been prescribed.

(3) The licensing authority may, by order in writing, suspend a licence for such period as it thinks fit or revoke a licence.

(a) if the licensing authority is satisfied that the holder of the licence is prohibited by this Act or by any other law for the time being in force to manufacture, possess, sell, transport, import or export any explosive, or is of unsound mind, or is for any reason unfit for a licence under this Act; or

(b) if the licensing authority deems it necessary for the security of the public peace or for public safety to suspend or revoke the licence; or

(c) if the licence was obtained by the suppression of material information or on the basis of wrong information provided by the holder of the licence or any other person on his behalf at the time of applying for the licence; or

(d) if any of the conditions of the licence has been contravened; or

(e) if the holder of the licence has failed to comply with a notice under sub-section (1) requiring him to deliver-up the licence.

(4) The licensing authority may also revoke a licence on the application of the holder thereof.

(5) Where the licensing authority makes an order varying the conditions of a licence under sub-section (1) or an order suspending or revoking a licence under sub-section (3), it shall record in writing the reasons therefor and furnish to the holder of the licence on demand a brief statement of the same unless in any case the licensing authority is of the opinion that it will not be in the public interest to furnish such statement.

(6) A court convicting the holder of a licence of any offence under this Act or the rules made thereunder may also suspend or revoke a licence:

Provided that if the conviction is set aside on appeal or otherwise, the suspension or revocation shall become void.

(7) An order of suspension or revocation under sub-section (6), may also be made by an Appellate Court or by the High Court when exercising its powers of revision.

(8) The Central Government may, by order in the Official Gasette, suspend or revoke, or direct any licensing authority to suspend or revoke, all or any licences granted under this Act throughout India or any part thereof.

(9) On the suspension or revocation of a licence under this section, the holder thereof shall without delay surrender the licence to the authority by whom

it has been suspended or revoked or to such other authority as may be specified in this behalf in the order of suspension or revocation.

6-F. *Appeals.* (1) Any person aggrieved by an order of the licensing authority refusing to grant a licence or varying the conditions of a licence or by an order of the licensing authority suspending or revoking a licence may prefer an appeal against that order to such authority (hereinafter referred to as the appellate authority) and within such period as may be prescribed:

Provided that no appeal shall lie against an order made by, or under the direction of the Central Government.

(2) No appeal shall be admitted if it is preferred after the expiry of the period prescribed therefor:

Provided that an appeal may be admitted after the expiry of the period prescribed therefor if the appellant satisfies the appellate authority that he had sufficient cause for not preferring the appeal within that period.

(3) The period prescribed for an appeal shall be computed in accordance with the provisions of the Limitation Act, 1963 (36 of 1963), with respect to the computation of periods of limitation thereunder.

(4) Every appeal under this section shall be made by a petition in writing and shall be accompanied by a brief statement of the reasons for the order appealed against where such statement has been furnished to the appellant and by such fee as may be prescribed.

(5) In disposing of an appeal the appellate authority shall follow such procedure as may be prescribed:

Provided that no appeal shall be disposed of unless the appellant has been given a reasonable opportunity of being heard.

(6) The order appealed against shall, unless the appellate authority conditionally or unconditionally directs otherwise, be in force pending the disposal of the appeal against such order.

(7) Every order of the appellate authority confirming, modifying or reversing the order appealed against shall be final.

8. *Notice of accidents.* (1) Whenever there occurs in or about, or in connection with, any place in which an explosive is manufactured, possessed or used, or[4](any aircraft, carriage or vessel) either conveying an explosive or on or from which an explosive is being loaded or unloaded, any accident by explosion or by fire attended with loss of human life or serious injury to person or property, or of a description usually attended with such loss or injury, the occupier of the place, or the [4](master of the aircraft or vessel) or the person in charge of the

3. Subs. by Act No. 32 of 1978.
4. Subs. by ibid.

carriage, as the case may be, shall within such time and in such manner as may be by rule prescribed give notice thereof and of the attendant loss of human life or personal injury, if any, to the [5](Chief Controller of Explosives) in India and to the officer-in-charge of the nearest police station.

[6](x x x)

9. *Inquiry into accidents.* (1) Where any accident such as is referred to in section 8 occurs in or about or in connection with [5](any place, aircraft, carriage or vessel) under the control of any of [5](Armed forces of the Union) an inquiry into the causes of the accident shall be held by the naval, military or air force authority concerned, and where any such accident occurs in any other circumstances, the District Magistrate [6](x x x) shall, in cases attended by loss of human life, or may, in any other case, hold or direct a Magistrate subordinate to him to hold, such an inquiry.

(2) Any person holding an inquiry under this section shall have all the powers of a Magistrate in holding an inquiry into an offence under the [5][Code of Criminal Procedure, 1973 (2 of 1974)] and may exercise each of the powers conferred on any officer by rules under Section 7 as he may think it necessary or expedient to exercise for the purposes of the inquiry.

(3) The person holding an inquiry under this section shall make a report to the Central Government stating the causes of the accident and its circumstances.

(4) The Central Government may make rules—

(a) to regulate the procedure at inquiries under this section;

(b) to enable the [7](Chief Controller of Explosives) in India to be present or represented at any such inquiry;

(c) to permit the [7](Chief Controller of Explosives) in India or his representative to examine any witnesses at the inquiry;

(d) to provide that where the [7](Chief Controller of Explosives) in India is not present or represented at any such inquiry a report of the proceedings thereof shall be sent to him;

(e) to prescribe the manner in which and the time within which notices referred to in Section 8 shall be given.

9-A. *Inquiry into more serious accidents.* (1) The Central Government may, where it is of opinion, whether or not it has received the report of an inquiry under Section 9, that an inquiry of more formal character should be held into the causes of an accident such as is referred to in Section 8, appoint the [7](Chief Controller

5. Subs. by Act No. 32 of 1978.
6. Omitted by Act No. 32 of 1978.
7. Substituted by Act No. 32 of 1978.

of Explosives) or any other competent person to hold such inquiry, and may also appoint one or more persons possessing legal or special knowledge to act as assessors in such inquiry.

(2) Where the Central Government orders an inquiry under this section, it may also direct that any inquiry under Section 9 pending at the time shall be discontinued.

(3) The person appointed to hold an inquiry under this section, shall have all the powers of a Civil Court under the Code of Civil Procedure, 1908 (V of 1908), for the purposes of enforcing the attendance of witnesses and compelling the production of documents and material objects; and every person required by such person as aforesaid to furnish any information shall be deemed to be legally bound so to do within the meaning of section 176 of the Indian Penal Code (XLV of 1860).

(4) Any person holding an inquiry under this section may exercise such of the powers conferred on any officer by rules under section 7 as he may think it necessary or expedient to exercise for the purposes of the inquiry.

(5) The person holding an inquiry under this section shall make a report to the Central Government stating the causes of the accident and its circumstance, and adding any observations which he or any of the assessors may think fit to make; and the Central Government shall cause every report so made to be published at such time and in such manner as it may think fit.

(6) The Central Government may make rules for regulating the procedure of inquiries under this section.

[8][9-B. *Punishment of certain offences.* (1) Whoever, in contravention of rules made under section 5 or of the conditions of a licence granted under the said rules—

(a) manufactures, imports or exports any explosive shall be punishable with imprisonment for a term which may extend to three years, or with fine which may extend to five thousand rupees, or with both;

(b) possesses, uses, sells or transports any explosive shall be punishable with imprisonment for a term which may extend to two years or with fine which may extend to three thousand rupees or with both; and

(c) in any other case, with fine which may extend to one thousand rupees.

(2) Whoever in contravention of a notification issued under section 6, manufactures, possesses or imports any explosive shall be punishable with imprisonment for a term which may extend to three years or with fine which may extend to five thousand rupees or with both; and in the case of importation by water, the owner and master of the vessel or in the case of importation by air, the owner and the master of the aircaft, in which the explosive is imported shall, in

8. Inserted by Act No. 32 of 1978.

the absence of reasonable excuse, each to be punishable with fine which may extend to five thousand rupees.

(3) Whoever,—

(a) manufactures, sells, transports, imports or possesses any explosive in contravention of the provisions of clause (a) of section 6; or

(b) sells, delivers or despatches any explosive in contravention of the provisions of clause (b) of that section,

shall be punishable with imprisonment for a term which may extend to three years or with fine or with both; or

(c) in contravention of the provisions of Section 8 fails to give notice of any accident shall be punishable—

(i) with fine which may extend to five hundred rupees, or

(ii) if the accident is attended by loss of human life, with imprisonment for a term which may extend to three months or fine or with both.

9-C. *Offences by companies.* (1) Whenever an offence under this Act has been committed by a company, every person who at the time the offence was committed was in charge of, or was responsible to the company for the conduct of the business of the company, as well as the company, shall be deemed to be guilty of the offence and shall be liable to be proceeded against and punished accordingly:

Provided that nothing contained in this sub-section shall render any such person liable to any punishment under this Act if he proves that the offence was committed without his knowledge and that he exercised all due diligence to prevent the commission of such offence.

(2) Notwithstanding anything contained in sub-section (1), where an offence under this Act has been committed by a company and it is proved that the offence has been committed with the consent or connivance of, or is attributable to any neglect on the part of, any director, manager, secretary or other officer of the company, such director, manager, secretary or other officer shall also be deemed to be guilty of that offence and shall be liable to be proceeded against and punished accordingly.

Explanation—For the purposes of this section—

(a) "company" means any body corporate, and incudes a firm or other association of individuals; and

(b) "director", in relation to a firm, means a partner in the firm.

17. *Extension of definition of "explosive" to other explosive substances.* The Central Government may, from time to time by notification in the Official Gazette, declare that any substance which appears to the Central Government to

be specially dangerous to life or property, by reason either of its explosive properties or of any process in the manufacture thereof being liable to explosion, shall be deemed to be an explosive within the meaning of this Act, and the provisions of this Act (subject to such exceptions, limitations and restrictions as may be specified in the notification) shall accordingly extend to that substance in like manner as if it were included in the definition of the term "explosive" in this Act.

MERCHANT SHIPPING ACT 1956 — PROVISIONS REGARDING PREVENTION OF POLLUTION OF THE SEA BY OIL

Commencement and application

356A. (1) The provisions of this Part shall take effect from such date as the Central Government may, by Notification in the Official Gazette, appoint and different dates may be appointed for different provision in respect of tankers and ships other than tankers.

Definition

(2) They shall apply to and in relation to—

(a) tankers of one hundred and fifty tons gross or more; and

(b) other ships of five hundred tons gross or more.

356B. In this Part, unless the context otherwise requires—

(a) "Convention" means the International Convention for the Prevention of Pollution of the Sea by Oil, 1954, signed in London on the 12th day of May, 1954, as amended from time to time;

(b) "discharge" in relation to oil or oily mixture, means any discharge or escape howsoever caused;

(c) "miles" means a nautical mile of 1,852 metres;

(d) "oil" means—

(i) crude oil,

(ii) fuel oil,

(iii) marine diesel oil conforming to such specifications as may be prescribed,

(iv) lubricating oil;

(e) "oily mixture" means a mixture with an oil content of hundred part or more in a million parts of the mixture;

(f) "Oil reception facilities" in relation to a port means facilities for enabling vessels using the port of discharge or deposit oil residues;

(g) "prohibited zone" means any such sea area as may be specified in the rules made under section 356J to be a prohibited zone for the purpose of this Part;

(h) "ship" means any sea-going vessel of any type whatsoever, including floating craft, whether self-propelled or towed by another vessel, making a sea voyage;

(i) "tanker" means a ship in which the greater part of the cargo space is constructed or adopted for the carriage of liquid cargoes in bulk and which is not for the time being, carrying a cargo other than oil in that part of its cargo space.

Prohibitions as to discharge of oil or oily mixture

356C. (1) No oil or oily mixture shall be discharged from an Indian tanker or other ship within any of the prohibited zones or from a foreign tanker or other ship within the prohibited zone adjoining the territories of India.

(2) The discharge of oil or oily mixture from an Indian ship, other than a tanker or from a foreign ship other than a tanker while such foreign ship is proceeding to any place or port in India, shall, during the period of three years immediately following the commencement of this sub-section be made as far as practicable from land:

Provided that this sub-section shall not apply to a ship which is proceeding to a port where oil reception facilities are not available.

(3) No oil or oily mixture shall be discharged anywhere at sea from an Indian ship, being a ship of twenty thousand tons gross tonnage or more for which the building contract was entered into on or after the coming into force of this sub-section:

Provided that this sub-section shall not apply in any case where by reason of special circumstances it is impracticable or unreasonable to retain the oil or oily mixture in the ship and the master of the ship reports, as soon as may be after such discharge, the fact in the prescribed form the manner to the Director-General.

Prohibition not to apply in certain cases

356D. Nothing in section 356C shall apply to:

(a) the discharge of oil or oily mixture from a ship for the purpose of securing the safety of a ship, preventing damage to a ship of cargo or saving life at sea;

(b) the escape of oil or of oily mixture resulting from a damage to a ship or unavoidable leakage, if all reasonable precautions have been taken after the occurrence of the damage or discovery of the leakage for the purpose of preventing or minimising the escape;

(c) the discharge of residue arising from the purification or clarification of fuel oil or lubricating oil when such discharge is made as far from land as is practicable;

(d) the discharge from the bilges of ship of a oil mixture during the period of twelve months following the date on which this class comes into force and after the expiration of such period of oily mixture containing no oil other than lubricating oil which has drained or leaked from the machinery spaces in the ship.

Equipment in ships to prevent oil pollution

356E. For the purpose of preventing or reducing discharges of oil and oily mixtures into the sea, the Central Government may make rules requiring Indian ships to be fitted with such equipment and to comply with such other requirement (including requirement for preventing the escape of fuel oil or heavy diesel oil into bilges) as may be prescribed.

Oil record book

356F. (1) Every Indian tanker and every other Indian ship which uses oil as fuel shall maintain on board the tanker or such other ship, an oil record book.

(2) The form and manner in which the oil record book shall be maintained, the nature of the entries to be made therein, the time and circumstances in which such entries shall be made, the custody and disposal thereof and all other matters relating there to shall be such as may be prescribed having regard to the provisions of the Convention.

356G. (1) A surveyor or any person appointed in this behalf may, at reasonable time, go on board a ship to which any of the provisions of this part apply, for the purpose of—

Inspection and control of ships to which the Convention applies

(a) ensuring that the prohibitions, restrictions and obligations imposed by or under this Part are complied with;

(b) satisfying himself about the adequacy of the measures taken to prevent the escape of oil or oily mixture from the ship;

(c) ascertaining the circumstances relating to an alleged discharge of oil or oily mixture from the ship in contravention of the provisions of this Part; and

(d) inspecting the oil record book.

(2) The surveyor or any such person may, if necessary, make without unduly delaying the ship, a true copy of the entry in the oil record book of the ship and may require the master of the ship to certify the copy to be a true copy and such copy shall be admissible as evidence of the facts stated therein.

Information regarding contravention of the provisions of the Convention

356H. (1) If, on report from a surveyor or other person authorised to inspect a vessel under section 356G, Central Government is satisfied that any provision of the Convention has been contravened anywhere by a foreign ship being a ship to which the provisions of the Convention apply, it shall transmit particulars of the alleged contravention to the Government of the country to which the ship belongs.

(2) On receipt of information from the Government of any country which has ratified the Convention that an Indian ship has contravened any provision of the Convention, the Central Government shall investigate the matter and if satisfied that any provision of this Part or any rule made thereunder has been contravened, take appropriate action against the owner or master and intimate such Government of the action so taken.

RECEPTION FACILITIES AT INDIAN PORTS FOR RECEIVING OIL RESIDUES FROM TANKERS AND OTHER SHIPS—PREVENTION OF POLLUTION CONVENTION 1954: AMENDMENTS 1962 AND 1969

The International Convention for the Prevention of Pollution of the Sea by Oil, 1954, as amended in 1962, *inter alia* places following restraints on discharge of oil or oily mixture into the sea from ships, namely:

(1) A tanker of 150 tons or more shall not discharge oil or oily mixture anywhere within the prohibited zones established by the Convention around the coasts of its contracting States;

(2) A ship other than a tanker of 500 tons gross or more shall discharge oil or oily mixture as far from land as practicable. After lapse of a period of three years from the date of entry into force of the Convention, any such ship shall not discharge oil or oily mixture within any prohibited zone except when it is proceeding to a port where no reception facilities have been provided.

(3) A ship of 20,000 tons gross or over, the building contract of which was placed on or after the date of coming into force of the Convention, shall not discharge oil or oily water anywhere into the sea except that it may discharge oil or oily mixture outside any prohibited zone if, in the opinion of its master, the circumstances are such that retention of oil or oily mixture on board is neither reasonable nor practicable.

2. In order to facilities discharge of oil or oily mixture retained on board by such ships at ports visited by them, Convention places the following obligations on its contracting States, namely:

(1) Each contracting Government shall take appropriate steps to promote the provision of facilities as follows:

(a) According to the needs of ships using them, ports shall be provided with facilities adequate for the reception without causing undue delay to ships, or such residues and oily mixtures as would remain for disposal from ships other than tankers if the bulk of water had been separated from the mixture;

(b) Oil loading terminals should be provided with facilities adequate for the reception of such residues and oily mixtures as would similarly remain for disposal by tanker;

(c) Ship repair berths shall be provided with facilities adequate for the reception of such residues and oily mixtures as would similarly remain for disposal by all ships entering for repairs.

(2) Each contracting Government shall determine which are the ports and oil loading terminals in its territories suitable for the purpose of provision of facilities referred to in (1) above.

3. Above provisions of the International Convention for the Prevention of the Pollution of the Sea by Oil, 1954 (as amended in 1962) have been translated into our national law by incorporating Part XIA in the Merchant Shipping Act, 1958. This Part came into force on the 4th June, 1974. As for reception facilities, notification No. GSR 1033 dated the 10th September, 1974 declared the ports of Bombay, Madras and Visakhapatnam as ports having reception facilities in accordance with the provisions of the Convention.

4. In 1969, the Inter-Governmental Maritime Consultative Organisation (IMCO) adopted an amendment to the aforesaid Convention. This amendment, *inter alia*, provided as follows:

(1) A ship of 500 tons gross or more, other than a tanker, shall not discharge oil or oily mixture anywhere into the sea except when one and all of the following conditions are satisfied, namely:

(a) the ship is proceeding en-route;

(b) the instantaneous rate of discharge of oil contents does not exceed 60 litres per mile;

(c) the oil content of the discharge is less that 100 parts per one million parts of the mixture; and

(d) the discharge is made as far as practicable from the nearest land.

(2) A tanker of 150 tons or more shall not discharge oil or oily mixture anywhere into the sea except when one and all of the following conditions are satisfied, namely;

(a) the tanker is proceeding en-route;

(b) the instantaneous rate of discharge of oil content does not exceed 60 litres per mile;

(c) the total quantity of oil discharged on a ballast voyage does not exceed 1/15000 of the total cargo carrying capacity; and

(d) the tanker is more than 50 miles away from the nearest land.

5. In this context it may be stressed that while the Convention as amended in 1962 permitted discharge of oil residues and oily mixture beyond prohibited zones, the 1969 amendments to it prohibit such discharge except at the instantaneous rate of discharge of 60 litres per mile subject to other conditions specified in the preceding paragraph. The instantaneous rate of discharge has been defined as the rate of discharge in litres per hour at any instant divided by the speed of the ship in knots at the same instant. With the limitation on discharge of oil or oily mixture into the sea except at the instantaneous rate of discharge and subject to other conditions specified by the 1969 amendments to the Convention, tankers of 150 tons or more and ships of 500 tons or more will be obliged to retain on board oil residues and oily mixture in greater quantities than higthertofore, and conversely look forward to port administrations to provide reception facilities for receiving them without undue delay. Further, it was sufficient for the contracting parties to the Convention amended in 1962 to provide reception facilities only at selected ports. Under the 1969 amendments such facilities would need to be provided at all ports used by international shipping.

6. In the light of the foregoing considerations it has become imperative that the port administrations review the facilities that may be required to be provided by them at their respective ports for meeting Government's obligations as a contracting party to the Convention as amended in 1969 and prepare a phased programme for provision of such facilities with cost assessment.

MATTERS RELATED TO IMPLEMENTATION OF THE 1969 AMENDMENTS TO THE 1954 OIL POLLUTION CONVENTION : DISPOSAL OF SLUDGE FROM THE PURIFICATION OF FUEL OIL AND LUBRICATING OIL

Note by the International Chamber of Shipping to Inter-governmental Maritime Consultive Organisation : March 1977

During the sixth session of the MEPC, ICS reported that it was conducting a survey into procedures for the disposal of sludge from the purification of fuel oil and lubricating oil on diesel ships, and offered to consider making the results available to the seventh session (MEPC VI/17, paragraph 81).

A summary of the replied is attached. The survey covered 1,136 ships from 12 different countries. While in no way comprehensive, therefore, the replies may be regarded as indicative of current procedures for dealing with sludge accumulation.

The survey which was confined to diesel-propelled ships on the grounds that it is these vessels which have to purify banker fuel oil on board—suggests that more than one-third of such ships have some means of onboard disposal. The worldwide average seems likely to be considerably lower, however, because:

(i) Paragrap 3 of the summary obscures the fact that some vessels are not only fitted with an incinerator or homogeniser, but also have the facility to burn sludge in boilers : these vessels are therefore accounted for twice in the figures;

(ii) The majority of the ships for which information was provided are fairly modern and are therefore more likely to be fitted with equipment of this nature;

(iii) One major contributing country to the survey had a far greater than average number of vessels equipped with onboard means of sludge disposal, and this has influenced the total figures.

It is evident, therefore, that storage of sludge on board for subsequent disposal ashore is still by far the most common solution, and is likely to remain so. The replies also illustrated that a considerable number of ships, from countries which have not yet implemented the 1969 amendments, have not been confronted with difficulties of disposal because they have been at liberty to discharge such sludge outside "prohibited zones" at sea. Where the 1969 amendments have been applied, however, ships have often had problems both of storage capacity and of disposal ashore. Although some ships have minimal storage capacity, and on others it is almost unlimited, the average appears to be between 20 and 60 days. With the entry into force of the 1969 amendments in January 1978, therefore, it is probable that many vessels will encounter difficulties if reception facilities are not available in the ports to which they are trading within the time-limits imposed by their storage capacity.

EXTRACTS FROM THE CALCUTTA MUNICIPAL CORPORATION ACT, 1980

301. Subject to the provisions of this Act and the regulations made thereunder and of any other law for the time being in force, the occupier of any trade premises may, with the consent of the Municipal Commissioner or, so far as may be permitted by this Act or the regulations made thereunder or any other law for the time being in force, without such consent, discharge into the municipal drains any trade effluent proceeding from those premises.

302. Notwithstanding anything contained in this Act or the regulations made thereunder or any usage, custom or agreement, where in the opinion of the Municipal Commissioner any trade premises are without sufficient means of effectual drainage of trade effluent or the drains thereof, though otherwise unobjectionable, are not adopted to the general drainage system or Calcutta, the

Municipal Commissioner may be written notice require the owner or occupier of such premises—

(a) to discharge the trade effluent in such manner, at such times, though such drains and subject to such conditions as may be specified in the notice and to cease to discharge the trade effluent otherwise than in accordance with the notice;

(b) to purify the trade effluent before its discharge into a municipal drain and to set up for purifying the trade effluent such appliances, apparatus, fittings and plant as may be specified in the notice;

(c) to construct a drain of such material, size and description and laid at such level and according to such alignment and with such fall and outlet as may be specified in the notice;

(d) to alter, amend, repair or renovate any purification plant, existing drains, apparatus, plant-fitting or article used in connection with any municipal or house-drain.

303. No person shall throw, empty, or turn into any municipal drain or into any drain communicating with a municipal drain—

(a) any matter likely to injure the drain or to interfere with the free flow of its contents or to affect prejudicially the treatment and disposal of its contents; or

(b) any chemical, refuse or waste steam, or any liquid of a temperature higher than forty-five degrees centigrade, being refuse or waste steam which, or liquid which when so heated, is either alone or, in combination with the contents of the drain, dangerous, or the cause of a nuisance, or prejudicial to health; or

(c) any dangerous petroleum.

Explanation—For the purpose of this section, the expression "dangerous petroleum" shall have the same meaning as in the Petroleum Act, 1934.

419. (1) No person shall, without the previous permission in writing of the Municipal Commissioner or otherwise than in conformity with the conditions, if any, of such permission, establish in any premises, or materially alter, enlarge or extend, any factory, workshop or trade premises in which it is intended to employ steam, electricity, water or other mechanical power:

Provided that no such permission shall be granted in contravention of the provisions of section 425.

(2) The Municipal Commissioner may refuse to give such permission if he is of the opinion that the establishment, alteration, enlargement or extension of such factory, workshop or trade premises in the proposed position—

(a) would be objectionable by reason of density of population in the neighbourhood thereof, or

(b) would be a nuisance to the inhabitants of the neighbourhood, or

(c) would be in contravention of any land use control under this Act or any other law for the time being in force.

425. (1) In the case of any premises for the use of which a licence or permission is required from Government or any statutory body under any law for the time being in force, the Municipal Commissioner shall not grant any permission under this Act to any person until such person produces before the Municipal Commissioner the licence or the permission from Government or statutory body, as the case may be, and submits duly authenticated copies thereof to him:

Provided that in the case where production of a municipal permission is a precondition for the grant of a licence or permission under any other law for the time being in force, the Municipal Commissioner may grant a provisional permission which shall become final only upon production of a licence or permission under the said law:

Provided further that such provisional permission shall have validity only for purpose of fulfilling any precondition for the licence or the permission under any other law as aforesaid.

(2) Notwithstanding anything contained in this Act, the Municipal Commissioner may, while granting permission under this Chapter, specify such special conditions, relevant to each case, regarding disposal of solid, liquid or gaseous wastes or for parkling of vehicles or for loading or unloading of goods or for abatement of nuisance of any kind whatsover as he deems fit.

EXTRACTS FROM THE HOWRAH MUNICIPAL CORPORATION ACT, 1980

148. (1) No person shall throw, empty or otherwise discharge into any water source, channel or municipal drain within or outside Howrah any matter, refuse, trade effluent or waste so as to cause pollution, health hazard or nuisance prejudicial to environment.

(2) Subject to the provisions of any other law for the time being in force, the corporation may by regulation provide for treatment standard to be maintained before discharge of any industrial waste or foul water or refuse into any river, water source, channel or municipal drainage and sewerage system.

191. (1) No person shall, without the previous written permission of the Commissioner, establish in any premises, or materially alter, enlarge or extend, any factory or workshop or work-place in which it is intended to employ steam, electricity, water or other mechanical power.

(2) The Commissioner may, in accordance with such regulations as may be made by the Corporation, refuse to give permission under sub-section (1) if he is

of opinion that the establishment, alteration, enlargement or extenstion of such factory, workshop or work-place in the proposed position would be objectionable by reason of the density of the population in the neighbourhood thereof or would be nuisance to the inhabitants of the neighbourhood.

SECTION 371A OF BENGAL MUNICIPAL ACT

Factory, etc., not to be established, etc., without permission of the Commissioners and the State Government: (1) No person shall, without the previous permission of the Commissioners and also of the State Government to be obtained in such manner as may be prescribed, establish in any place within the municipality or materially alter, enlarge or extend any factory or workshop established in any such place, in which it is intended to employ steam, electricity, water or other mechanical power.

(2) The Commissioners may, in accordance with such rules as may be made in this behalf by the Commissioners at a meeting, refuse to grant such permission, if they are of opinion that the establishment, alteration, enlargement or extension of such factory or workshop in the proposed position would be objectionable by reason of the density of the population in the neighbourhood thereof, or would be a nuisance to the inhabitants of the neighbourhood.

Notes

This section prohibits the establishment or material alteration and extension of any factory or workshop where steam, electricity, water or mechanical power is intended to be used in the process of manufacture. Sub-section (2) empowers the Commissioners to refuse such permission on certain grounds. But after once having given the permission the Commissioners cannot revoke or cancel the same on those grounds. This is the result of a decision in a case, under City of Bombay Municipal Act of 1888. In that case, the *State* v. *Ismailkhan Ahmedkhan,* A.I.R. 1955 NUC (Bom.) 2055 a Division Bench of the Bombay High Court held on an interpretation of section 479 of that Act that while the Commissioner (of the municipality) can refuse to grant permission for the establishment of a factory on the ground that it will be a nuisance to the inhabitants of the neighbourhood, he cannot revoke or cancel the permission on these grounds. It is however open to the Commissioner to impose suitable restrictions and conditions at the time of granting permission, under sub-section (1) of section 479 in order to secure that the factory will be worked in such manner that it will not become a nuisance to the residents of the locality. On breach of any of these conditions it would be possible to revoke the permission under sub-section (3) of section 479. But where no such restrictions or conditions have been imposed at the time of granting permission to the opposite party to work a flour mill, the Commissioner is not competent to revoke the permission granted to the opposite party subsequently on the ground that it will be a nuisance to the inhabitants of the neighbourhood.

APPENDIX II

THE WATER (PREVENTION AND CONTROL OF POLLUTION) ACT, 1974
(6 OF 1974)

(As modified up to the 1st November, 1990)

List of Amending Acts

1. The Water (Prevention and Control of Pollution) Amendment Act, 1978 (44 of 1978).
2. The Water (Prevention and Control of Pollution) Amendment Act, 1988 (53 of 1988).

List of Abbreviations Used

Cl.	for Clause
Ins.	for Inserted.
P.	for Page.
S. / Sec.	for Section.
Ss.	for Sections
Subs.	for Substituted.

THE WATER (PREVENTION AND CONTROL OF POLLUTION) ACT, 1974

ARRANGEMENT OF SECTIONS

Chapter I

SECTIONS PRELIMINARY

Chapter II

THE CENTRAL AND STATE BOARDS FOR PREVENTION AND CONTROL OF WATER POLLUTION

Chapter III

JOINT BOARDS

Chapter IV

POWERS AND FUNCTIONS OF BOARDS

SECTIONS

Chapter V

PREVENTION AND CONTROL OF WATER POLLUTION

19. Power of State Government to restrict the application of the Act to certain areas.
20. Power to obtain information.
21. Power to take samples of effluents and procedure to be followed in connection therewith.
22. Reports of the result of analysis on samples taken under section 21.
23. Power of entry and inspection.
24. Prohibition on use of stream or well for disposal of polluting matter, etc.
25. Restrictions on new outlets and new discharges.
26. Provision regarding existing discharge of sewage or trade effluent.
27. Refusal or withdrawal of consent by State Board.
28. Appeals.
29. Revision
30. Power of State Board to carry out certain works.
31. Furnishing of information to State Board and other agencies in certain cases.
32. Emergency measures in case of pollution of stream or well.
33. Power of Board to make application to courts for restraining apprehended pollution of water in streams or wells.

33A. Power to give directions.

Chapter VI

FUNDS, ACCOUNTS AND AUDIT

34. Contributions by Central Government.
35. Contributions by State Government.
36. Fund of Central Board.
37. Fund of State Board.

37A. Borrowing powers of Board.

38. Budget.
39. Annual report.
40. Accounts and audit.

Chapter VII

PENALTIES AND PROCEDURE

41. Failure to comply with directions under sub-section (2) or sub-section (3) of section 20, or orders issued under clause (c) of sub-section (1) of section 32 or directions issued under sub-section (2) of section 33 or section 33A.
42. Penalty for certain acts.
43. Penalty for contravention of provisions of section 24.
44. Penalty for contravention of section 25 or section 26.
45. Enhanced penalty after previous conviction.

45A. Penalty for contravention of certain provisions of the Act.

46. Publication of names of offenders.
47. Offences by companies.
48. Offences by Government departments.
49. Cognizance of offences.
50. Members, officers and servants of Board to be public servants.

Chapter VIII

MISCELLANEOUS

51. Central Water Laboratory.
52. State Water Laboratory.
53. Analysts.
54. Reports of analysts.
55. Local authorities to assist.
56. Compulsory acquisition of land for the State Board.
57. Returns and reports.
58. Bar of jurisdiction.
59. Protection of action taken in good faith.
60. Overriding effect.
61. Power of Central Government to supersede the Central Board and Joint Boards.
62. Power of State Government to supersede State Board.
63. Power of Central Government to make rules.
64. Power of State Government to make rules.

THE WATER (PREVENTION AND CONTROL OF POLLUTION) ACT, 1974

No. 6 of 1974

[23rd March, 1974.]

An Act to provide for the prevention and control of water pollution and the maintaining or restoring of wholesomeness of water, for the establishment, with a view to carrying out the purposes aforesaid, of Boards for the prevention and control of water pollution, for conferring on and assigning to such Boards powers and functions relating thereto and for matters connected therewith.

Whereas it is expedient to provide for the prevention and control of water pollution and the maintaining or restoring of wholesomeness of water, for the establishment, with a view to carrying out the purposes aforesaid, of Boards for the prevention and control of water, pollution and for conferring on and assigning to such Boards power and functions relating thereto:

And whereas Parliament has no power to make laws for the States with respect to any of the matters aforesaid except as provided in articles 249 and 250 of the Constitution;

And whereas in pursuance of clause (1) of article 252 of the Constitution resolutions have been passed by all the Houses of the Legislatures of the State of Assam, Bihar, Gujarat, Haryana, Himachal Pradesh, Jammu and Kashmir, Karnataka, Kerala, Madhya Pradesh, Rajasthan, Tripura and West Bengal to the effect that the matters aforesaid should be regulated in those states by parliament by law;

Be it enacted by parliament in the twenty-fifth year of the Republic of India as follows :-

Chapter I

PRELIMINARY

Short title, application and commencement.

1. (1) This Act, may be called the Water (Prevention and Control of Pollution) Act, 1974.

(2) It applies in the first instance to the whole of the States of Assam, Bihar, Gujarat, Haryana, Himachal Pradesh, Jammu and Kashmir, Karnataka, Kerala, Madhya Pradesh, Rajasthan, Tripura and West Bengal and the Union territories; and it shall apply to such other State which adopts this Act by resolution passed in that behalf under clause (1) of article 252 of the Constitution.

(3) It shall come into force, at once in the States of Assam, Bihar, Gujarat, Haryana, Himachal Pradesh, Jammu and Kashmir, Karnataka, Kerala, Madhya

Pradesh, Rajasthan, Tripura and West Bengal and in the Union territories and in any other State of which adopts this Act under clause (1) of article 252 of the Constitution on the date of such adoption and any reference in this Act to the commencement of this Act shall, in relation to any State or Union Territory, mean the date on which this Act comes into force in such State or Union territory.

Definition

2. In this Act, unless the context otherwise requires.

(a) "Board" means the Central Board or a State Board;

[1] [(b) "Central Board" means the Central Pollution Control Board constituted under section 3;]

(c) "member" means a member of a Board and includes the chairman thereof;

[2] [(d) "Occupier" in relation to any factory or premises, means the person who has control over the affairs of the factory or the premises, and includes, in relation to any substance, the person in possession of the substance;]

[3][(dd) "outlet" includes any conduit pipe of channel, open or closed, carrying sewage or trade effluent or any other holding arrangement which causes or is likely to cause pollution;]

(e) "pollution" means such contamination of water or such alteration of the physical, chemical or biological properties of water or such discharge of any sewage or trade effluent or of any other liquid, gaseous or solid substance into water (whether directly or indirectly) as may, or is likely to, create a nuisance or render such water harmful or injurious to public health or safety, or to domestic, commercial, industrial, agricultural or other legitimate uses, or to the life and health of animals or plants or to acquatic organisms;

(f) "prescribed" means prescribed by rules made under this Act by the Central Government or, as the case may be the State Government;

(g) "sewage effluent" means effluent from any sewerage system or sewage disposal work and includes sullage from open drains;

[2] [(gg) "sewer" means any conduit pipe or channel, open or closed, carrying sewage or trade effluent;]

[1][(h) "State Board" means a State Pollution Control Board constituted under section 4;]

(i) "State Government" in relation to a Union territory means the Administrator thereof appointed under article 239 of the Constitution;

1. Subs. by Act 53 of 1988, s. 2, for cls, (b) , (d) and (h).
2. Ins. by Act 44 of 1978, s. 2.
3. Subs. by Act 53 of 1988, s. 2, for "trade or industry."

(j) "stream" includes—

(i) river;

(ii) water course (whether flowing or for the time being dry);

(iii) inland water (whether natural or artificial);

(iv) sub-terranean waters;

(v) sea or tidal waters to such extent or, as the case may be to such point as the State Government may, by notification in the Official Gazette, specify in this behalf.

(k) "trade effluent" includes any liquid, gaseous or solid substance which is discharged from any premises used for carrying on any [8][industry, operation or process, or treatment and disposal system], other than domestic sewage.

Chapter II

THE CENTRAL AND STATE BOARDS FOR PREVENTION AND CONTROL OF WATER POLLUTION

Constitution of Central Board

3. (1) The Central Government shall, with effect from such date (being a date not later than six months of the commencement of this Act in the States of Assam, Bihar, Gujarat, Haryana, Himachal Pradesh, Jammu and Kashmir, Karnataka, Kerala, Madhya Pradesh, Rajasthan, Tripura and West Bengal and in the Union territories) as it may, by notification in the Official Gazette, appoint, constitute a Central Board to be called the [4][Central Pollution Board] to exercise the powers conferred on and perform the functions assigned to that Board under this Act.

(2) The Central Board shall consist of the following members, namely :—

(a) a full-time chairman being a person having special knowledge of practical experience in respect of [5] [matters relating to environmental protection] or a person having knowledge and experience in administering institutions dealing with the matters aforesaid, to be nominated by the Central Government:

(b) [6][such number of officials, not exceeding five to be nominated by the Central Government to represent that Government:

(c) such number of persons, not exceeding five to be nominated by the Central Government, from amongst the members of the State

4. Subs. by Act 53 of 1988 s.3, for certain words.
5. Subs. by Act 44 of 1978, s. 3, for certain words.
6. Subs. by s.3, *ibid.*, for "live officials"

Boards, of whom not exceeding two shall be from those referred to in clause (c) of sub-section (2) of section 4;

(d) [7]such number of non-officials, not exceeding three, to be nominated by the Central Government to represent the interests of agriculture, fishery or industry or trade or any other interest which in the opinion of the Central Government ought to be represented;

(e) two persons to represent the companies or corporations owned, controlled or managed by the Central Government, to be nominated by that Government;

(f) [a full time member-secretary, possessing qualifications, knowledge and experience of scientific, engineering or management aspects of pollution control, to be appointed by the Central Government.]

(3) The Central Board shall be a body corporate with the name aforesaid having perpetual succession and a common seal with power, subject to the provisions of this Act, to acquire, hold and dispose of property and to contract and may, by the aforesaid name, sue or be sued.

Constitution of Central Board.

4. (1) The State Government shall, with effect from such date[9] as it may by notification in the Official Gazette, appoint, constitute a [10][State Pollution Control Board] under such name as may be specified in the notification to exercise the powers conferred on and perform the functions assigned to that Board under this Act.

(2) A State Board shall consist of the following members namely:—

(a) a [11][chairman being a person having special knowledge or practical experience in respect of [12][matter relating to environmental protection] or a person having knowledge and experience in administering institutions dealing with the matters aforesaid, to be nominated by the State Government:

[13] [Provided that the chairman may be either whole time or part-time as the State Government may think fit:]

7. Subs. by s. 3, *ibid.*, for "three non-officials"
8. Subs. by Act 53 of 1988, s. 3, forel. (f).
9. Certain words omitted by Act 44 of 1978, s. 4.
10. Subs. by Act 53 of 1988, s.4, for "State Board"
11. The word "full-time" omitted by Act 44 of 1978, s. 4.
12. Subs. by s.4, *ibid.*, for certain words.
13. Ins. by s. 4, ibid.

(b) [14][such number of official not exceeding five] to be nominated by the State Government to represent that Government.

(c) [15][such number of persons not exceeding five,] to be nominated by the State Government amongst the members of the local authorities functioning within the State;

(d) [16][such number of non-officials, not exceeding three] to be nominated the State Government to represent the interests of agriculture, fishery or industry or trade or any other interest which, in the opinion of the State Government, ought to be represented;

(e) two persons to represent, the companies or corporations owned, controlled or managed by the State Government to be nominated by that Government;

(f) [17][a full time member-secretary, possessing qualifications, knowledge and experience of scientific, engineering or management aspects of pollution control, to be appointed by the State Government.]

(3) Every State Board shall be a body corporate with the name specified by the State Government in the notification under sub-section (1), having perpetual succession and a common seal with power, subject to the provisions of this Act, to acquire hold and dispose of property and to contract, and may, by the said name, sue or be sued.

(4) Notwithstanding anything contained in this section, no State Board shall be constituted for a Union territory and in relation to a Union territory, the Central Board shall exercise the powers and perform the functions of a State Board for that Union territory:

Provided that in relation to any Union territory the Central Board may delegate all or any of its powers and functions under this sub-section to such person or body of persons as the Central Government may specify.

Terms and conditions of service of members.

5.(1) Save as otherwise provided by or under this Act, a member of a Board, other than a member-secretary, shall hold office for a term of three years from the date of his nomination:

Provided that a member shall, notwithstanding the expiration of his term, continue to hold office until his successor enters upon his office.

---

14. Subs. by s. 4, *ibid.*, for "five officials".
15. Subs by s. 4, *ibid.*, for "five persons".
16. Subs. by Act 44 of 1978, s. 4, for "three non-officials".
17. Subs. by Act 53 of 1988, s. 4, for cl. (f).

[18][(2) The term of office of a member of a Board nominated under clause (b) or clause (e) of sub-section (2) of section 3 or clause (b) or clause (e) of sub-section (2) of section 4 shall come to an end as soon as he ceases to hold the office under the Central Government or the State Government or, as the case may be, the company or corporation owned, controlled or managed by the Central Government or the State Government, by virtue of which he was nominated.]

(3) The Central Government or, as the case may be, the State Government may, if it thinks fit, remove any member of a Board before the expiry of his term of office, after giving him reasonable opportunity of showing cause against the same.

(4) A member of a Board, other than the member-secretary, may at any time resign his office by writing under his hand addressed—

(a) in the case of the chairman, to the Central Government or, as the case may be, the State Government; and

(b) in any other case, to the chairman of the Board;

and the seat of the chairman or such other member shall thereupon become vacant.

(5) A member of a Board, other than the member-secretary, shall be deemed to have vacated his seat if he is absent without reason, sufficient in the opinion of the Board, from three consecutive meetings of the Board [19][or where he is nominated under clause (c) or clause (e) of sub-section (2) of section 3 or under clause (c) or clause (e) of sub-section (2) of section 4, if he ceases to be a member of the State Board or of the local authority or, as the case may be, of the company or corporation owned, controlled or managed by the Central Government or the State Government and such vacation of seat shall, in either case. take effect from such date as the Central Government, or, as the case may be the State Government may, by notification in the official Gazette, specify.]

(6) A casual vacancy in a Board shall be filled by a fresh nomination and the person nominated to fill the vacancy shall hold office only for the remainder of the term for which the member in whose place he was nominated.

(7) A member of a Board [20][shall be eligible for renomination].

(8) The other terms and conditions of service of a member of a Board, other than the chairman and member secretary, shall be such as may be prescribed.

(9) The other terms and conditions of service of the chairman shall be such as may be prescribed.

Disqualifications

6. (1) No person shall be a member of a Board, who —

18. Subs. by Act 44 of 1978, s. 5, for sub-section (2).
19. Subs. by s. 5, ibid for certain words.
20. Subs. by Act 53 of 1988, s. 5, for "shall not be eligible for renomination for more than two terms".

(a) is, or at any time has been adjudged insolvent or has suspended payment of his debts or has compounded with his creditors, or

(b) is of unsound mind and stands so declared by a competent court, or

(c) is, or has been convicted of an offence which, in the opinion of the Central Government or, as the case may be, of the State Government, involves moral turpitude, or

(d) is, or at any time has been, convicted of an offence under this Act, or

(e) has directly or indirectly by himself or by any partner, any share or interest in any firm or company carrying on the business of manufacture, sale or hire of machinery, plant, equipment, apparatus or fitting for the treatment of a sewage or trade effluents, or

(f) is a director or a secretary, manager or other salaried officer or employee of any company of firm having any contract with the Board, or with the Government constituting the Board or with a local authority in the State, or with a company or corporation owned, controlled or managed by the Government, for the carrying out of sewerage schemes or for the installation of plants for the treatment of sewage or trade effluents, or

(g) has so abused in the opinion of the Central Government or as the case may be of the state Government, his position as a member, as to render his continuance on the Board detrimental to the interest of the general public.

(2) No order of removal shall be made by the Central Government or State Government, as the case may be, under this section unless the member concerned has been given a reasonable opportunity of showing cause against the same.

(3) Notwithstanding anything contained in sub-sections (1) and (7) of section 5, a member who has been removed under this section shall not be eligible for renovation as a member.

Vacation of seat by members

7. If a member of a Board becomes subject to any of the disqualification specified in section 6, his seat shall become vacant.

Meetings of Boards

8. A Board shall meet at least once in every three months and shall observe such rules of procedure in regard to the transaction of business at its meetings as may be prescribed.

Provided that if, in the opinion of the chairman, any business of an urgent nature is to be transacted, he may convene a meeting of the Board at such time as he thinks fit for the aforesaid purpose.

Constitution of committees

9. (1) A Board may constitute as many committees consisting wholly of members or wholly of other persons or partly of members and partly of other persons, and for such purpose or purposes as it may think fit.

(2) A committee constituted under this section shall meet at such time and at such place, and shall observe such rules of procedure in regard to the transaction of business at its meetings, as may be prescribed.

(3) The members of a committee (other than the members of the Board) shall be paid such fees and allowances, for attending its meetings and for attending to any other work of the Board as may be prescribed.

Temporary association of persons with Board for particular purposes

10. (1) A Board may associate with itself in such manner, and for such purposes, as may be prescribed any person whose assistance or advice it may desire to obtain in performing any of its functions under this Act.

(2) A person associated with the Board under sub-section (1) for any purpose shall have a right to take part in the discussions of the Board relevant to that purpose, but shall not have a right to vote at a meeting of the Board, and shall not be a member for any other purpose.

[21] [(3) A person associated with the Board under sub-section (1) for any purpose shall be paid such fees and allowances, for attending its meetings and for attending to any other work of the Board, as may be prescribed.]

Vacancy in Board not to invalidate acts or proceedings

11. No act or proceeding of a Board or any committee thereof shall be called in question on the ground merely of the existence of any vacancy in, or any defect in the constitution of, the Board or such committee, as the case may be .

Delegation of powers to Chairman

[22][11A. The chairman of a Board shall exercise such powers and perform such duties as may be prescribed or as may, from time to time, be delegated to him by the Board.]

Member-secretary and officers and other employees of Board

12. (1) The terms and conditions of service of the member-secretary shall be such as may be prescribed.

(2) The member-secretary shall exercise such powers and perform such

21. Ins. by Act 44 of 1978, s. 6.
22. Ins. by s. 7, *ibid.*

duties as may be prescribed or as may, from time to time, be delegated to him by the Board or its chairman.

(3) Subject to such rules as may be made by the Central Government or, as the case may be, the State Government, in this behalf, a Board may appoint such officers and employees as it considers necessary for the efficient performance of its functions

[23] [****

[24] [(3A) The method of recruitment and terms and conditions of service (including the scales of pay) of the officers (other than the member-secretary) and other employees of the Central Board or a State Board shall be such as may be determined by regulations made by the Central Board or, as the case may be, by the State Board:

Provided that no regulation made under this sub-section shall take effect unless,—

(a) in the case of a regulation made by the Central Board, it is approved by the Central Government; and

(b) in the case of a regulation made by a State Board, it is approved by the State Government.]

[25][(3B) The Board may, by general or special order, and subject to such conditions and limitations, if any, as may be specified in the order, delegate to any officer of the Board such of its powers and functions under this Act as it may deem necessary.]

(4) Subject to such conditions as may be prescribed, a Board may from time to time appoint any qualified person to be a consulting engineer to the Board and pay him such salaries and allowances and subject him to such other terms and conditions of service as it thinks fit.

Chapter III
JOINT BOARDS

Constitution of Joint Board

13.(1) Notwithstanding anything contained in this Act, an agreement may be entered into —

(a) by two or more Government of contiguous States, or

---

23. Certain words omitted by s. 8, *ibid.*
24. Ins. by s. 8, *ibid.*
25. Ins. by Act 53 of 1988, s. 6.

(b) by the Central Government (in respect of one or more Union territories) and one or more Government of States contiguous to such Union territory or Union territories,

to be in force for such period and to be subject to renewal for such further period, if any, as may be specified in the agreement to provide for the constitution of a Joint Board,—

(i) in a case referred to a clause (a), for all the participating States, and

(ii) in a case referred to in a clause, (b), for the participating Union territory or Union territories and the State or States.

(2) An agreement under this section may—

(a) provide, in a case referred to in clause (a) of subsection (1), for the apportionment between the participating States and in a case referred to in clause (b) of that sub-section, for the apportionments between the Central Government and the participating State Government or State Governments, of the expenditure in connection with the Joint Board;

(b) determine in a case referred to in a clause (a) of sub-section (1), which of the participating State Governments and in a case referred to in clause (b) of that sub-section whether the Central Government or the participating State Government (if there are more than one participating State, also which of the participating State Governments) shall exercise and perform the several powers and functions of the State Government under this act and the references in this Act to the State Government shall be construed accordingly;

(c) provide for consolation in a case referred to in clause (a) of sub-section (1), between the participating State Government and in a case referred to in clause (b) of that sub-section between the Central Government and the participating State Government or State Governments either generally or with reference to particular matters arising under this Act;

(d) make such incidental and ancillary provisions, not inconsistent with this Act, as may be deemed necessary or expedient for giving effect to the agreement.

(3) An agreement under this section shall be published in a case referred to in clause (a) of sub-section (1), in the Official Gazette of the participating States and in a case referred to in clause (b) of that sub-section in the Official Gazette of the participating Union territory or Union territories and the participating State or States.

Composition of Joint Boards

14. (1) A Joint Board constituted in pursuance of an agreement entered into under clause (a) of sub-section 13 shall consist of the following members namely:—

(a) a full-time chairman being a person having special knowledge or practical experience in respect of [26] [matters relating to environmental protection] or a person having knowledge and experience in administering institutions dealing with the matters aforesaid, to be nominated by the Central Government;

(b) two officials from each of the participating States to be nominated by the concerned participating State Government to present that Government;

(c) one person to be nominated by each of the participating State Government from amongst the members of the local authorities functioning within the State concerned;

(d) one non-official to be nominated by each of the participating State Governments to represent the interests of agriculture, fishery, or industry or trade in the State concerned or any other interest which, in the opinion of the participating State Government is to be represented;

(e) two persons to be nominated by the Central Government to represent the companies or corporations owned, controlled or managed by the participating State Governments;

(f) [27] [a full-time member-secretary, possessing qualifications, knowledge and experience of scientific, engineering or management aspects of pollution control, to be appointed by the Central Government.]

(2) A Joint Board constituted in pursuance of an agreement entered into under clause (b) of sub-section (1) of section 13 shall consist of the following members, namely:—

(a) a full-time chairman being a person having special knowledge or practical experience in respect of [28][matters relating to environmental protection] or a person having knowledge and experience in administering institutions dealing with the matters aforesaid, to be nominated by the Central Government;

(b) two officials to be nominated by the Central Government from the participating Union territory or each of the participating Union territories, as the case may be, and two officials to be nominated, from the participating state or each of the participating States, as the case may be, by the concerned participating State Government;

(c) one person to be nominated by the Central Government from amongst the members of the local authorities functioning within the participating Union territory or each of the participating Union territories, as the

26. Subs. by Act 44 of 1978, s. 9, for certain words.
27. Subs by Act 53 of 1988, s. 7, for cl. (f).
28. Subs. by Act 44 of 1978, s. 9, for certain words.

case may be, and one person to be nominated, from amongst the members of the local authorities functioning within the participating State or each of the participating States as the case may be, by the concerned participating State Government;

(d) one non-official to be nominated by the Central Government and one person to be nominated by the participating State Government or State Governments to represent the interests of agriculture, fishery or industry on trade in the Union territory or in each of the Union territories or the State in each of the States, as the case may be or any other interest which in the opinion of the Central Government or, as the case may be, of the State Government is to be represented;

(e) two persons to be nominated by the Central Government to represent the companies or corporations owned, controlled or managed by the Central Government and situate in the participating Union territory or territories and two persons to be nominated by the Central Government to represent the companies or corporations owned, controlled or managed by the participating State Governments;

(f) [27][a full-time member-secretary, possessing qualifications, knowledge and experience of scientific, engineering aspects of pollutions control, to be appointed by the Central Government.]

(3) When a Joint Board is constituted in pursuance of an agreement clause (b) of sub-section, (1) of section 13, the provisions of sub-section (4) of section 4 shall cease to apply in relation to the Union territory for which the Joint Board is constituted.

(4) Subject to the provisions of sub-section (3), the provisions of sub-section (3) of section 4 and sections 5 to 12 (inclusive) shall apply in relation to the Joint Board and its member-secretary as they apply in relation to a State Board and its member-secretary.

(5) Any reference in this Act to the State Board shall, unless the context otherwise requires, be construed as including a Joint Board.

Special provision relating to giving of directions.

15. Notwithstanding anything contained in this Act, where any Joint Board is constituted under section 13,—

(a) the Government of the State for which the Joint Board is constituted shall be competent to give any direction under this act only in cases where such direction relates to a matter within the exclusive territorial jurisdiction of the State;

(b) the Central Government alone shall be competent to give any direction under this Act where such direction relates to a matter within the territorial jurisdiction of two or more States or pertaining to a Union territory.

Chapter IV
POWERS AND FUNCTIONS OF BOARDS

Functions of Central Board

16. (1) Subject to the provisions of this Act, the main functions of the Central Board shall be to promote cleanliness of streams and wells in different areas of the States.

(2) In particular and without prejudice to the generality of the foregoing function, the Central Board may perform all or any of the following functions, namely:—

(a) advise the Central Government on any matter concerning the prevention and control of water pollution;

(b) co-ordinate the activities of the State Boards and resolve disputes among them;

(c) provide technical and guidance to the State Boards, carry out and sponsor investigations and research relating to problems of water pollution and prevention, control or abatement of water pollution;

(d) plan and organise the training of persons engaged or to be engaged in programmes for the prevention, control or abatement of water pollution on such terms and conditions as the Central Board may specify;

(e) organise through mass media a comprehensive programme regarding the prevention and control of water pollution;

(ee) [29] [perform such of the functions of any State Board as may be specified in an order made under sub-section (2) of Section 18];

(f) collect, compile and publish technical and statistical data relating to water pollution and the measures devised for its effective prevention and control and prepare manuals, codes or guides relating to treatment and disposal of sewage and trade effluents and disseminate information connected therewith;

(g) lay down, modify or annual, in consultation with the State Government concerned, the standards for a stream or well:

Provided that different standards may be laid down for the same stream or well or for different streams or wells, having regard to the quality of water, flow

29. Ins. by Act 53 of 1988, s. 8.

characteristics of the stream or well and the nature of the use of the water in such stream or well or streams or wells;

(h) plan and cause to be executed a nation-wide programme for the prevention control or abatement of water pollution;

(i) perform such other functions as may be prescribed.

(3) The Board may establish or recognise a laboratory or laboratories to enable the Board to perform its functions under this section efficiently, including the analysis of samples of water from any stream or well or of samples of any sewage of trade effluents.

Functions of State Board

17. (1) Subject to the provisions of this Act, the functions of a State Board shall be—

(a) to plan a comprehensive programme for the prevention, control or abatement of pollution of streams and in the State and to secure the execution thereof;

(b) to advise the State Government on any matter concerning the prevention, control or abatement of water pollution;

(c) to collect and disseminate information relating to water pollution and the prevention, control or abatement thereof;

(d) to encourage, conduct and participate in investigations and research relating to problems of water pollution and prevention, control or abatement of water pollution;

(e) to collaborate with the Central Board in organising the training of persons engaged or to be engaged in programmes relating to prevention, control or abatement of water pollution and to organise mass education programmes relied thereto.

(f) to inspect sewage or trade effluents works and plants for the treatment of sewage and trade effluents and to review plans, specifications or other data relating to plants set up for the treatment of water, works for the purification thereof and the system for the disposal of sewage or trade effluents on in connection with the grant of any consent as required by this Act.

(g) to lay down, modify or annual effluent standards for the sewage and trade effluents and for the quality for receiving waters (not being water in an inter-state stream) resulting from the discharge of effluents and to classify waters of the State;

(h) to evolve economical and reliable methods of treatment of sewage and trade effluents, having regard to the peculiar conditions of soils, climate and water resources of different regions and more especially the prevailing flow characteristics of water in streams and wells which render it impossible to attain even the minimum degree of dilution.

(i) to evolve methods of utilisation of sewage and suitable trade effluents in agriculture;

(j) to evolve efficient method of disposal of sewage and trade effluents on land, as are necessary on account of the predominant conditions of scant stream flows that do not provide for major part of the year the minimum degree of dilution;

(k) to lay down standards of treatment of sewage and trade effluents to be discharged into any particular stream taking into account the minimum fair weather dilution in that stream and the tolerance limits of pollution permissible in the water of the stream, after the discharge of such effluents;

(l) to make vary or revoke any order —

(i) for the prevention control or abatement of discharges of waste into streams or wells;

(ii) requiring any person concerned to construct new systems for the dispose of sewage and trade effluents or to modify, alter or extend any such existing system or to adopt such remedial measures as are necessary to prevent control or abate water pollution;

(m) to lay down effluent standards to be complied with by persons while causing discharge of sewage or sullage or both and to lay down, modify or annual effluent standards for the sewage and trade effluents.

(n) to advise the State Government with respect to the location of any industry the carrying on of which is likely to pollute a stream or well;

(o) to perform such other functions as may be prescribed or as may, from time to time, be entrusted to it by the Central Board or the State Government.

(2) The Board may establish or recognise a laboratory or laboratories to enable the Board to perform its functions under this section efficiently, including the analysis of samples of water from any stream or well or of samples of any sewage or trade effluents.

Powers to give directions

18. [30][(1)] In the performance of its functions under this Act —

(a) the Central Board shall be bound by such directions in writing as the Central Government may give to it; and

30. S. 18 renumbered as sub-section (1) thereof by Act 53 of 1988, s. 9.

(b) every State Board shall be bound by such directions in writing as the Central Board or the State Government may give to it:

Provided that where a direction given by the State Government is inconsistent with the direction given by the Central Board, the matter shall be referred to the Central Government for its decision.

[31][(2) Where the Central Government is of the opinion that any State Board has defaulted in complying with any directions given by the Central Board under sub-section (1) and as a result of such default a grave emergency has arisen and it is necessary or expedient so to do in the public interest, it may, by order, direct the Central Board to perform any of the functions of the State Board in relation to such area for such period and for such purposes, as may be specified in the order.

(3) Where the Central Board performs any of the functions of the State Board in pursuance of a direction under sub-section (2), the expenses, if any incurred by the Central Board with respect to the performance of such functions may, if the State Board is empowered to recover such expenses, be recovered by the Central Board with interest (at such reasonable rate as the Central Government may, by order fix) from the date when a demand for such expenses is made until it is paid from the person or persons concerned as arears of land revenue or of public demand.

(4) For the removal of doubts, it is hereby declared that any directions to perform the functions of any State Board given under sub-section (2) in respect of any area would not preclude the State Board from performing such functions in any other area in the State or any of its other functions in that area.]

Chapter V

PREVENTION AND CONTROL OF WATER POLLUTION

Power of State Government to restrict the application of the Act to certain areas

19. (1) Notwithstanding anything contained in this Act, if the State Government after consultation with, or on the recommendation of, the State Board is of opinion that the provisions of this Act need not apply to the entire, State, it may, by notification in the Official Gazette, restrict the application of this Act, to such area or areas as may be declared therein as water pollution, prevention and control area or areas and thereupon the provisions of this Act shall apply only to such area or areas.

(2) Each water pollution, prevention and control area may be declared either by reference to a map or any reference to the line of any watershed or the boundary of any district or partly by one method and partly by another.

31. Ins. by s. 9, *ibid.*

(3) The State Government may, by notification in the Official Gazette,—

(a) alter any water pollution, prevention and control area whether by way of extension or reduction; or

(b) define a new water pollution, prevention and control area in which may be merged one or more water pollution, prevention and control, areas or any part or parts thereof.

Powers to obtain information.

20. (1) For the purpose of enabling a State Board to perform the function conferred on it by or under this Act, the State Board of any officer empowered by it in that behalf, may make surveys of any area and gauge and keep records of flow or volume and other characteristics of any stream or well in such area, and may take steps for measurement and recording of the rainfall in such area or any part thereof and for the installation and maintenance for those purposes of gauges or other apparatus and works connected therewith, and carry out stream surveys and may take such steps as may be necessary in order to obtain any information required for the purposes aforesaid.

(2) A State Board may give directions requiring any person who in its opinion is abstracting water from any such stream or well in the area in quantities which are substantial in relation to the flow or volume of that stream, or well or is discharging sewage or trade effluent into any such stream or well, to give such information as to the abstraction or the discharge at such times and in such form as may be specified in the directions.

(3) Without prejudice to the provisions of sub-section (2), a State Board may, with a view to preventing or controlling pollution of water, give directions requiring any person in charge of any establishment where any [32][industry, operation or process, or treatment and disposal system] is carried on, to furnish to it information regarding the construction, installation or operation of such establishment or of any disposal system or of any extension or addition thereto in such establishment and such other particulars as may be prescribed.

Power to take samples of effluents and procedure to be followed in connection therewith.

21. (1) A State Board or any officer empowered by it in this behalf shall have power to take for the purpose of analysis samples of water from any stream or well or samples of any sewage or trade effluents which is passing from any plant or vessel or from or over any place into any such stream or well.

(2) The result of any analysis of a sample of any sewage or trade effluent taken under sub-section (l) shall not be admissible in evidence in any legal proceeding unless the provisions of sub-sections (3), (4) and (5) are complied with.

32. Subs. by Act 53 of 1988, s. 10, for "industry or trade".

(3) Subject to the provisions of sub-sections (4) and (5) when a sample (composite or otherwise as may be warranted by the process used)) of any sewage or trade effluent is taken for analysis under sub-section (l), the person taking the sample shall—

(a) serve on the person in charge of, or having control over, the plant or vessel or in occupation of the place (which person is hereinafter referred to as the occupier) or any agent of such occupier, a notice then and there in such form as may be prescribed of his intention to have it so analysed;

(b) in the presence of the occupier or his agent, divide the sample into two parts;

(c) cause each part to be placed in a container which shall be marked and sealed and shall also be signed both by the taking the sample and the occupier or his agent;

(d) send one container forthwith,—

(i) in a case where such sample is taken from any area situated in a Union territory, to the laboratory established or recognised by the Central Board under Section 16; and

(ii) in any other case, to the laboratory established or recognised by the State Board under section 17;

(e) on the request of the occupier or his agent, send the second container,—

(i) in a case where such sample is taken from any area situated in a Union Territory to the laboratory established or specified under sub section (l) of section 51; and

(ii) in any other case to the laboratory established or specified under sub-section (l) of section 52.

[33](4) When a sample of any sewage or trade affluent is taken for analysis under sub-section (l) and the person taking the sample serves on the occupier or his agent, a notice under clause (a) of sub-section (3) and the occupier or his agent willfully absent himself, then,—

(a) the sample so taken shall be placed in a container which shall be marked and sealed and shall also be signed by the person taking the sample and the same shall be sent forthwith by such person for analysis to the laboratory referred to in sub-clause (i) or sub-clause (ii), as the case may be, of clause (e) of sub-section (3) and such person shall inform the Government analyst appointed under sub-section (1) or sub-section (2), as the case may be, of section 53, in writing about the absence of the occupier or his agent; and

33. Subs. by Act 44 of 1978, s. 10, for sub-section (4).

(b) the cost incurred in getting such sample analysed shall be payable by the occupier or his agent and in case of default of such payment the same shall be recovered from the occupier or his agent, as the case may be, as an arrear of land revenue or public demand:

Provided that no such recovery shall be made unless the occupier or, as the case may be, his agent has been given a reasonable opportunity of being heard in the matter.

(5) When a sample of any sewage or trade effluent is taken for analysis under sub-section (l) and the person taking the sample serves on the occupier or his agent a notice under clause (a) of sub-section (3) and the occupier or his agent who is present at the time of taking the sample does not make a request for dividing the sample into two parts as provided in clause (b) of sub-section (3), then, the sample so taken shall be placed in a container which shall be marked and sealed and shall also be signed by the person taking the sample and the same shall be sent forthwith by such person for analysis to the laboratory referred to in sub-clause (i) or sub-clause (ii), as the case may be, of clause (d) of sub section (3).

Reports of the result of analysis on samples taken under section 21.

22. (1) Where a sample of any sewage or trade effluent has been sent for analysis to the laboratory established or recognised by the Central Board or, as the case may be, the State Board, the concerned Board analyst appointed under sub-section (3) of section 53 shall analyse the sample and submit a report in the prescribed form of the result of such analysis in triplicate to the Central Board or the State Board as the case may be.

(2) On receipt of the report under sub-section (l), one copy of the report shall be sent by the Central Board or the State Board, as the case may be, to the occupier or his agent referred to in section 21, another copy shall be preserved for production before the courts in case any legal proceedings are taken against him and the other copy shall be kept by the concerned Board.

(3) Where a sample has been sent for analysis under clause (e) of sub-section (3) or sub-section (4) of section 21 to any laboratory mentioned therein, the Government analysis referred to in that sub-section shall analyse the sample and submit a report in the prescribed form of the result of the analysis in triplicate to the Central Board or, as the case may be, the State Board which shall comply with the provisions of sub-section (2).

(4) If there is any inconsistency or discrepancy between or variation in the results of the analysis carried out by the laboratory established or recognised by the Central Board or the State Board, as the case may be, and that of the laboratory established or specified under section 51 or section 52, as the case may be, the report of the latter shall prevail.

(5) Any cost incurred in getting any sample analysed at the request of the occupier or his agent shall be payable by such occupier or his agent and in case of default the same shall be recoverable from him as arrears of land revenue or of public demand.

Power of entry and inspection.

23. (1) Subject to the provisions of this section, any person empowered by a State Board in this behalf shall have a right at any time to enter, with such assistance as he considers necessary, any place—

(a) for the purpose of performing any of the functions of the Board entrusted to him;

(b) for the purpose of determining whether and if so in what manner, any such functions are to be performed or whether any provisions of this Act, or the rules made thereunder of any notice, order, direction or authorisation served, made, given, or granted under this Act is being or has been complied with;

(c) for the purpose of examining any plant, record, register, document or any other material object or for conducting a search of any place in which he has reason to believe that an offence under this Act or the rules made thereunder has been or is being or is about to be committed and for seizing any such plant, record, register document or other material object, if he has reason to believe that it may furnish evidence of the commission of an offence punishable under this Act or the rules made thereunder:

Provided that the right to enter under this sub-section for the inspection of a well shall be exercised only at reasonable hours in a case where such well is situated in any premises used for residential purposes and the water thereof is used exclusively for domestic purposes.

(2) The provisions of [34][the Code of Criminal Procedure, 1973] or, in relation to the State of Jammu and Kashmir, the provisions of any corresponding law in force in that State, shall, so far as may be, apply to any search or seizure under this section as they apply to any search or seizure made under the authority of a warrant issued under [35][section 94] of the said Code, or, as the case may be, under the corresponding provisions of the said law.

Explanation — For the purposes of this section, "place" includes vessel.

Prohibition on use of stream or well for disposal of polluting matter, etc.

24. (1) Subject to the provisions of this section, —

34. Subs. by Act 44 of 1978, s. 11, for "Code of Criminal procedure, 1898 5 of 1898)"
35. Subs. by s. 11, *ibid,* for "section 98".

(a) no person shall knowingly cause or permit any poisonous, noxious, or polluting matter determined in accordance with such standards as may be laid down by the State Board to enter (whether directly or indirectly) into any [36][stream or well or sewer or on land]; or

(b) no person shall knowingly cause on permit to enter into any stream any other matter which may tend, either directly, or in combination with similar matters, to impede the proper flow of the water of the stream in a manner leading or likely to lead to a substantial aggravation of pollution due to other causes or of its consequences.

(2) A person shall not be guilty of an offence under sub-section (1), by reason only of having done or caused to be done any of the following acts, namely:—

(a) constructing, improving or maintaining in or across or on the bank or bed of any stream, any building, bridge, weir, dam, sluice, dock, pier, drain or sewer, or other permanent works which he has a right to construct, improve or maintain;

(b) depositing any materials on the bank or in the bed of any stream for the purposes of reclaiming land or for supporting, repairing or protecting the bank or bed of such stream provided such materials are not capable of polluting such stream.

(c) putting into any stream any sand or gravel or other natural deposit which has flowed from or been deposited by the current of such stream;

(d) causing or permitting with the consent of the State Board, the deposit accumulated in a well, pond or reservoir to enter into any stream.

(3) The State Government may, after consultation, with or on the recommendation of the State Board, exempt, by notification in the Official Gazette, any person from the operation of sub-section (1) subject to such conditions, if any, as may be specified in the notification and any condition so specified may by a like notification and be altered, varied or amended.

Restrictions on new outlets and new discharges.

25. [37][(1) Subject to the provisions of this section, no person shall, without the previous consent of the State Board,—

(a) establish or take any steps to establish any industry, operation or process, or any treatment and disposal system or any extension or addition thereto, which is likely to discharge sewage or trade effluent into a stream or well or sewer or on land (such discharge being hereafter in this section referred to as discharge of sewage); or

36. Subs. by Act 53 of 1988, s. 11, for "stream or well".
37. Subs. by s. 12, *ibid*, for sub-section (1) and (2).

(b) bring into use any new or altered outlet for the discharge of sewage; or

(c) begin to make any new discharge of sewage:

Provided that a person in the process of taking any steps to establish any industry, operation or process immediately before the commencement of the Water (Prevention and Control of Pollution) Amendment Act, 1988, for which no consent was necessary prior to such commencement, may continue to do so for a period of three months from such commencement or, if he has made an application for such consent, within the said period of three months, till the disposal of such application.

(2) An application for consent of the State Board under sub-section (1) shall be made in such form, contain such particulars and shall be accompanied by such fees as may be prescribed.]

(3) The State Board may take such inquiry as it may deem fit in respect of the application for consent referred to in sub-section (1) and in making any such inquiry shall follow such procedure as may be prescribed.

[38][(4) The State Board may—

(a) grant its consent referred to in sub-section (1), subject to such conditions as it may impose being—

(i) in cases referred to in clauses (a) and (b) of sub-section (1) of section 25, conditions as to the point of discharge of sewage or as to the use of that outlet or any other outlet for discharge of sewage;

(ii) in the case of a new discharge, conditions as to the nature and composition, temperature, volume or rate of discharge of the effluent from the land or premises from which the discharge or new discharge is to be made; and

(iii) that the consent will be valid for such period as may be specified in the order.

and any such conditions imposed shall be binding on any person establishing or taking any steps to establish any industry, operation or process, or treatment and disposal system or extension or addition thereto, or using the new or altered outlet, or discharging the effluent from the land or premises aforesaid; or

(b) refuse such consent for reason to be recorded in writing.

(5) Where, without the consent of the State Board, any industry, operation or process or any treatment and disposal system or any extension or addition thereto, is established or any steps for such establishment have been taken or a new or altered outlet is brought into use for the discharge of sewage or a new

38. Subs. by Act 53 of 1988, s. 12, for sub-section (4), (5) and (6).

discharge of sewage is made, the State Board may serve on the person who has established or taken steps to establish any industry, operation or process, or any treatment and disposal systems or any extension or addition thereto, or using the outlet, or making the discharge as the case may be, a notice imposing any such conditions as it might have imposed on an application for its consent in respect of such establishment, such outlet or discharge.

(6) Every State Board shall maintain a register containing particulars of the conditions imposed under this section and so much of the register as relates to any outlet or any effluent, from any land or premises shall be open to inspection at all reasonable hours by any person interested in, or affected by such outlet, land or promises, as the case may be, or by any person authorised by him in this behalf and the conditions so contained in such registered shall be conclusive proof that the consent was granted subject to such conditions.]

(7) The consent referred to in sub-section (1) shall, unless given or refused earlier, be deemed to have been given unconditionally on the expiry of a period of four months of the making of an application in this behalf complete in all respects to the State Board.

(8) For the purposes of this section and sections 27 and 30,—

(a) the expression "new or altered outlet" means any outlet which is wholly or partly constructed on or after the commencement of this Act or which (whether so constructed or not) is substantially altered after such commencement;

(b) the expression "new discharge" means a discharge which is not, as respects the nature and composition temperature volume and rate of discharge of the effluent substantially a continuation of a discharge made within the preceding twelve months (whether by the same or a different outlet), so however that a discharge which is in other respects a continuation of previous discharge made as aforesaid shall not be deemed to be a new discharge by reason of any reduction of the temperature or volume or rate of discharge of the effluent as compared with the previous discharge.

Provision regarding existing discharge of sewage or trade effluent.

26. Where immediately before the commencement if this Act any person was discharging any sewage or trade effluent into a [39] [stream or well or sewer or on land], the provisions of Section 25 shall, so far as may be apply in relation to such person as they apply in relation to the person referred to in that section subject to the modification that the application for consent to be made under sub-section (2) of that section [40][shall be made on or before such date as may be specified by the State Government notification in this behalf in the Official Gazette].

39. Subs by Act 44 of 1978, s. 13, for "stream or well".

40. Subs. by s. 13, *ibid*, for certain words.

Refusal or withdrawal of consent by State Board.

27. [41][(1) A State Board shall not grant its consent under sub-section (4) of section 25 for the establishment of any industry, operation or process or treatment and disposal system or extension or addition thereto, or to the bringing into use of a new or altered outlet unless the industry, operation or process of treatment and disposal system or extension or addition thereto, or the outlet is so established as to comply with any conditions imposed by the Board to enable it to exercise its right to take samples of the effluent.]

[42][(2) A State Board may from time to time review—

[43][(a) any condition imposed under section 25 or section 26 and may serve on the person to whom a consent under section 25 or section 26 is granted a notice making any reasonable variation of or revoking any such condition.]

(b) the refusal of any consent referred to in sub-section (1) of section 25 or section 26 or the grant of such consent without any condition, and may make such orders as it deemed fit.]

(3) Any condition imposed under section 25 or section 26 shall be subject to any variation made under sub-section (2) and shall continue in force until revoked under that sub-section.

Appeals

28.(1) Any person aggrieved by an order made by the State Board under section 25, Section 26 or section 27 may, within thirty days from the date on which the order is communicated to him, prefer an appeal to such authority (hereinafter) referred to as the appellate authority as the State Government may think fit to constitute:

Provided that the appellate authority may entertain the appeal after the expiry of the said period of thirty days if such authority is satisfied that the appellant was prevented by sufficient cause from filing the appeal in time.

[44][(2) An appellate authority shall consist of a single person or three person as the State Government may think fit, to be appointed by that Government.]

(3) The form and manner in which an appeal may be preferred under sub-section (1), the fees payable for such appeal and the procedure to be followed by the appellate authority shall be such as may be prescribed.

(4) On receipt of an appeal preferred under sub-section (1), the appellate

---

41. Subs. by Act 53 of 1988, s. 13, for sub-section (1).
42. Subs. by Act 44 of 1978, s. 14, for sub-section (2).
43. Subs. by Act 53 of 1988, s. 13, for cl.(a).
44. Subs. by Act of 1978, s. 15, for sub-section (b).

authority shall, after giving the appellant and the State Board an opportunity of being heard, dispose of the appeal as expeditiously as possible.

(5) If the appellate authority determines that any condition imposed, or the variation of any condition, as the case may be, was unreasonable, then—

(a) where the appeal is in respect of the unreasonableness of any condition imposed, such authority may direct either that the condition shall be treated as annulled or that there shall be substituted for it such condition as appears to it to be reasonable;

(b) where the appeal is in respect of the unreasonableness of any variation of a condition, such authority may direct either that the condition shall be treated as continuing in force unvaried or that it shall be varied in such manner as appears to it to be reasonable.

Revisions

29. (1) The State Government may at any time either of its own motion or on an application made to it in this behalf, call for the records of any case where an order has been made by the State Board under section 25, section 26 or section 27 for the purpose of satisfying itself as to the legality or propriety of any such order and may pass such order in relation thereto as it may think fit;

Provided that the State Government shall not pass any order under this sub-section without affording the State Board and the person who may be affected by such order a reasonable opportunity of being heard in the matter.

(2) The State Government shall not revise any order made under section 25, section 26 or 27 where an appeal against that order lies to the appellate authority, but has not been preferred or where an appeal has been preferred, such appeal is pending before the appellate authority.

Power of State Board to carry out certain works.

30. [45][(1) Where under this Act, conditions have been imposed on any person while granting consent under Section 25 or section 26 and such conditions require such person to execute any work in connection therewith and such work has not been executed within such time as may be specified in this behalf, the State Board may serve on the person concerned a notice requiring him within such time (not being less than thirty days) as may be specified in the notice to execute the work specified therein.]

(2) If the person concerned fails to execute the work as required in the notice referred to in sub-section (1), then, after the expiration of the time specified in the said notice, the State Board may itself execute or cause to be executed such work.

45. Subs. by Act 53 of 1988, s. 14, for sub-section (1).

(3) All expenses incurred by the State Board for the execution of the aforesaid work, together with interest, at such rate as the State Government may, by order, fix from the date when a demand for the expenses is made until it is paid, may be recovered by that Board from the person concerned as arrears of land revenue, or of public demand.

Furnishing of information to State Board and other agencies in certain cases.

31. [46][(1) If at any place where any industry operation or process or any treatment and disposal system or any extension or addition thereto is being carried on, due to accident or other unforeseen act or event, any poisonous, noxious or polluting matter is being discharged, or is likely to be discharged into stream or well or sewer or a land and, as a result of such discharge, the water in any stream, or well is being polluted, or is likely to be polluted, then the person incharge of such place shall forthwith intimate the occurrence of such accident, act or event the State Board and such other authorities or agencies as may be prescribed.]

(2) Where any local authority operates any sewerage system or works, the provisions of sub-section (1) shall apply to such local authority as they apply in relation to the person in charge of the place where any industry or trade is being carried on.

Emergency measures in case of pollution of stream or well.

32. (1) Where it appears to the State Board that any poisonous, noxious or polluting matter is present in [47][any stream or well or on land by reason of the discharge of such matter in such stream or well or on such land] or has entered to that stream or well due to any accident or other unforeseen act or event, and if the Board is of opinion that it is necessary or expedient to take immediate action, it may for reasons to be recorded in writing, carry out such operations as it may consider necessary for all or any of the following purposes, that is to say,—

(a) removing that matter from the [48][stream or well or on land] and disposing it of in such manner as the Board considers appropriate;

(b) remedying or mitigating any pollution caused by its presence in the stream or well;

(c) issuing orders immediately restraining or prohibiting the person concerned from discharging any poisonous, noxious or polluting matter [49][into the stream or well or on land] or from making insanitary use of the stream or well.

(2) The power conferred by sub-section (1) does not include the power to construct any works other than works of a temporary character which are removed on or before the completion of the operations.

46. Subs. by s. 15, *ibid,* for sub-section (l).
47. Subs. by s. 16, *ibid.,* for "any stream or well".
48. Subs. by s. 16, *ibid.,* for "stream or well".
49. Subs. by s. 16, *ibid.,* for "into the stream or well".

Power of Board to make application to courts for restraining apprehended pollution of water in streams or wells.

33. [50][(1) Where it is apprehended by a Board that the water in any stream or well is likely to be polluted by reason of the disposal or likely disposal of any matter in such stream or well or in any sewer or on any land, or otherwise, the Board may make an application to a court, not inferior to that of a Metropolitan Magistrate or a Judicial Magistrate of the first class, for restraining the person who is likely to cause such pollution from so causing.]

(2) On receipt of an application under sub-section (1) the court may make such order as it deems fit.

(3) Where under sub-section (2) the court makes an order restraining any person from polluting the water in any stream or well, it may in that order—

(i) direct the person who is likely to cause or has caused the pollution of the water in the stream or well, to desist from taking such action as is likely to cause pollution or, as the case may be, to remove from such stream or well, such matter, and

(ii) authorise the Board, if the direction under clause (i) (being a direction for the removal of any matter from such stream or well) is not complied with by the person to whom such direction is issued, to undertake the removal and disposal of the matter in such manner as may be specified by the Court.

(4) All expenses incurred by the Board in removing any matter in pursuance of the authorisation under clause (ii) of sub-section (3) or in the disposal of any such matter may be defrayed out of any money obtained by the Board from such disposal and any balance outstanding shall be recoverable from the person concerned as arears of land revenue or of public demand.

Power to give directions.

[51][33A. Notwithstanding anything contained in any other law, but subject to the provisions of this act, and to any directions that the Central Government may give in this behalf, a Board may, in the exercise of its powers and performance of its functions under this Act, issue any directions in writing to any person, officer or authority, and such person, officer or authority shall be bound to comply with such directions.

Explanation.— For the avoidance of doubts it is hereby declared that the power to issue directions under this section includes the power to direct—

(a) the closure, prohibition or regulation of any industry, operation or process; or

50. Subs. by Act 53 of 1988 s. 17, for sub-section (l).
51. Ins. by s. 18, *ibid.*

(b) the stoppage or regulation of supply of electricity, water or any other service.]

Chapter VI
FUNDS, ACCOUNTS AND AUDIT

Contributions by Central Government.

34. The Central Government may, after due appropriation made by Parliament by law in this behalf, make in each financial year such contributions to be Central Board as it may think necessary to enable the Board to perform its functions under this Act.

Contributions by State Government.

35. The State Government may, after due appropriation made by the Legislature of the State by law in this behalf, make in each financial year such contributions to the State Board as it may think necessary to enable that Board to perform its functions under this Act.

Fund of Central Board

36. (1) The Central Board shall have its own fund, and all sums which may, from time to time, be paid to it by the Central Government and all other receipts (by way of gifts, grants, donations, benefactions [52] [fees] or (otherwise) of that Board shall be carried to the fund of the Board and all payment by the Board shall be made there from.

(2) The Central Board may expend such sums as it thinks fit performing its functions under this Act, [52][and, where any law for the time being in force relating to the prevention, control of abatement or air pollution provides for the performance of any function under such law by the Central Board also for performing its functions under such law] and such sums shall be treated as expenditure payable out of fund of the Board.

Fund of State Board

37. (1) The State Board shall have its own fund, and the sums which may, from time to time, be paid to it by the State Government and all other receipts (by way of gifts, grants, donations, benefactions [53][fees] or other) of that Board shall be carried to the fund of the Board and all payments by the Board shall be made therefrom.

(2) The State Board may expend such sums as it thinks fit for performing its functions under this Act, [53][and, where any law for the time being in force relating to the prevention, control or abatement of air pollution provides for the.

52. Ins. by Act 44 of 1978, s. 16.
53. Ins. by s. 17, *ibid.*

performance of any function under such law by the State Board also for performing its functions under such law] and such sums shall be treated as expenditure payable out of the fund of that Board.

Borrowing powers of Board.

[54][37A. A Board may, with the consent of, or in accordance with, the terms of any general or special authority given to it by the Central Government as the case may be, the State Government, borrow money from source by way of loans or issue of bonds, debentures or such other instruments, as it may deem fit, for the performance of all or any of its functions under this Act].

Budget

38. The Central Board or, as the case may be, the State Board shall, during each financial year, prepare, in such form and at such time as may be prescribed, a budget in respect of the financial year next ensuing showing the estimated receipt and expenditure and copies thereof shall be forwarded to the Central Government or, as the case may be, the State Government.

Annual report.

[55][39, (1) The Central Board shall, during each financial year, prepare, in such form as may be prescribed, an annual report giving full account of its activities under this Act during the previous financial year and copies thereof shall be forward to the Central Government within four months from the last date of the previous financial year and that Government shall cause every such report to be laid before both Houses of Parliament within nine months from the last date of the previous financial year.

(2) Every State Board shall, during each financial year, prepare, in such form as may be prescribed an annual report giving full account of its activities under this Act during the previous financial year and copies thereof shall be forwarded to the State Government within four months from the last date of the previous financial year and that Government shall cause every such report to be laid before the State legislature within a period of nine months from the last date of the previous financial year.]

Accounts and audit.

40. (1) Every Board shall maintain proper accounts and other relevant records and prepare an annual statement of accounts in such form as may be prescribed by the Central Government or, as the case may be, the State Government.

(2) The accounts of the Board shall be audited by an auditor duly qualified to act as an auditor of companies under section 226 of the Companies Act, 1956.

54. Ins. by Act 53 of 1988, s. 19.
55. Subs. by *ibid* s. 20, for s. 39.

(3) The said auditor shall be appointed by the Central Government or, as the case may be, the State Government on the advice of the Comptroller and Auditor-General of India.

(4) Every auditor appointed to audit the accounts of the Board under this Act shall have the right to demand the productions of books, accounts, connected vouchers and other documents and papers and to inspect any of the office of the Board.

(5) Every such auditor shall send a copy of his report together with an audited copy of the accounts to the Central Government or, as the case may be, the State Government.

(6) The Central Government shall, as soon as may be after the receipt of the audit report under sub-section (5), cause the same to be laid before both Houses of Parliament.

(7) The State Government shall, as soon as may be after the receipt of the audit report under sub-section (5), cause the same to be laid before the State Legislature.

Chapter VII

PENALTIES AND PROCEDURE

Failure to comply with directions under sub-section (2) or sub-section (3) of section 20, or orders issued under clause (c) of sub-section (1) of 32 or directions issued under sub-section (2) of section 33 or section 33. A.n

[56] ["41. (1). Whoever fails to comply with any direction given under sub-section (2) or sub-section (3) of section 20 within such time as may be specified in the direction shall, on conviction be punishable with imprisonment for a term which may extend to three months or with fine which may extend to ten thousand rupees or with both and in case the failure continues, with an additional fine which may extend to five thousand rupees for every day during which such failure continues after the conviction for the first such failure.

(2) Whoever fails to comply with any order issued clause (c) of sub-section (1) of section 32 or any direction issued by a court under sub-section (2) of section 33 or any direction issued under section 33A shall, in respect of each such failure and on conviction, be punishable with imprisonment for a term which shall not be less than one year and six months but which may extend to six years and with fine, and in case the failure continues, with an additional fine which may extend to five thousand rupees for every day during which such failure continues after the conviction for the first such failure.

56. Subs. by Act 53 of 1988, s. 21, for s. 41.

(3) If the failure referred to in sub-section (2) continues beyond a period of one year after the date of conviction, the offender shall on conviction, be punishable with imprisonment for a term which shall not be less than two years but which may extend to seven years and with fine.]

Penalty for certain acts.

42. (1) Whoever—

(a) destroys, pulls down, removes, injuries or defaces any pillar, post or stake fixed in the ground or any notice or other matter put up, inscribed or placed, by or under the authority of the Board, or

(b) obstructs any person acting under the orders or directions of the Board from exercising his powers and performing his functions under this Act, or

(c) damages any works or property belonging to the Board, or

(d) fails to furnish to any officer or other employee of the Board any information required by him for the purpose of this Act, or

(e) fails to intimate the occurrence of any accident or other unforeseen act or event under section 31 to the Board and other authorities or agencies as required by that section, or

(f) in giving any information which he is required to give under this Act, knowingly or willfully makes a statement which is false in any material particular, or

(g) for the purpose of obtaining any consent under section 25 or section 26, knowingly or willfully makes a statement which is false in any material particular,

shall be punishable with imprisonment for a term which may extend to three months or with fine which may extend to [57][ten thousand rupees] or with both.

(2) Where for the grant of a consent in pursuance of the provisions of section 25 or section 26 the use of a matter or gauge or other measure or monitoring device is required and such device is used for the purposes of those provision, any person who knowingly or willfully alters or interferes with that device so as to prevent it from monitoring or measuring correctly shall be punishable with imprisonment for a term which may extend to three months or with fine which may extend to [58][ten thousand rupees] or with both.

Penalty for contravention of provisions of section of 24.

43. Whoever contravenes the provisions of section 24 shall be punishable

57. Subs. by s. 22, *ibid*, for "one thousand rupees".
58. Subs. by Act 53 of 1988, s. 22, for "one thousand rupees".

with imprisonment for a term which shall not be less than [60][one year and six months] but which may extend to six years and with fine.

Penalty for contravention of section 25 or section 26.

44. Whoever contravenes the provisions of section 25 or section 26 shall be punishable with imprisonment for a term which shall not be less than [59][one year and six months] but which may extend to six years and with fine.

Enhanced penalty after previous conviction.

45. If any person who has been convicted of any offence under section 24 or section 25 or section 26 is again found guilty of an offence involving a contravention of the same provisions, he shall, on the second and on every subsequent conviction be punishable with imprisonment for a term which shall not be less than [60][two years] but which may extend to seven years and with fine:

Provided that for the purpose of this section no cognizance shall be taken of any conviction made more than two years before the commission of the offence which is being punished.

Penalty for contravention of certain provisions of the Act.

[61][45A. Whoever contravenes any of the provisions of this Act or fails to comply with any order or direction given under this Act, for which no penalty has been elsewhere provided in this Act, shall be punishable with imprisonment which may extend to three months or with fine which may extend to ten thousand rupees or with both and in the case of a continuing contravention or failure, with an additional fine which may extend to five thousand rupees for every day during which such contravention or failure continues after conviction for the first such contravention or failure.]

Publication of names of offenders.

46. If any person convicted of an offence under this Act commits a like offence afterwards it shall be lawful for the court before which the second or subsequent conviction takes place to cause the offender's name and place of residence, the offence and the penalty imposed to be published at the offender's expense in such newspapers or in such other manner as the court may direct and the expenses of such publication shall be deemed to be part of the cost attending the conviction and shall be recoverable in the same manner as a fine.

Offences by companies.

47. (1) Where an offence under this Act has been committed by a company, every person who at the time the offence was committed was in charge of, and was responsible to the company for the conduct of, the business of the company, as well

59. Subs. by *ibid.*, s. 23, for "six months".
60. Subs. by s. 24, *ibid*, for "one year".
61. Ins. by s. 25, *ibid.*

as the company, shall be deemed to be guilty of the offence and shall be liable to be proceeded against and punished accordingly:

Provided that nothing contained in this sub-section shall render any such person liable to any punishment provided in this Act if he proves that the offence was committed without his knowledge for that he exercised all due diligence to prevent the commission of such offence.

(2) Notwithstanding anything contained in sub-section (1), where an offence, under this Act has been committed by a company and it is proved that the offence has been committed with the consent or connivance of, or is attributable to any neglect on the part of, any director, manager, secretary or other officer of the company, such director, manager, secretary or other officer shall also be deemed to be guilty of that offence and shall be liable to be proceeded against and punished accordingly.

Explanation—For the purposes of this section—

(a) "company" means any body corporate and includes a firm or other association of individuals; and

(b) "director" in relation to a firm means a partner in the firm.

Offences by Government Departments.

48. Where an offence under this Act has been committed by the Department of Government, the Head of the Department shall be deemed to be guilty of the offence and shall be liable to be proceeded against and punished accordingly:

Provided that nothing contained in this section shall render such Head of the Department liable to any punishment if he proves that the offence was committed without his knowledge or that he exercised all due diligence to prevent the commission of such offence.

Cognizance of offences.

49. [62][(1) No court shall take cognizance of any offence under this Act except on a complaint made by—

(a) a Board or any officer authorised in this behalf by it; or

(b) any person who has given notice of not less than sixty days, in the manner prescribed, of the alleged offence and of his intention to make a complaint, to the Board or officer authorised as aforesaid,

and no court inferior to that a Metropolitan Magistrate or a Judicial Magistrate of the first class shall try any offence punishable under this Act.]

[63][(2) Where a complaint has been made under clause (b) of sub-section (1),

62. Subs. by Act 53 of 1988, s. 26, for sa sub-section (1)
63. Ins. by s. 26, *ibid.*

the Board shall, on demand by such person, make available the relevant reports in its possession to that person:

Provided that the Board may refuse to make any such report available to such person if the same is, in its opinion against the public interest.]

[64][(3) Notwithstanding anything contained in section 29 of the Code of Criminal Procedure 1973] it shall be lawful for any [65] [Judicial Magistrate of the first class or for any Metropolitan Magistrate] to pass a sentence of imprisonment for a term exceeding two years or of fine exceeding two thousand rupees on any person convicted of an offence punishable under this Act.

Members, officers and servants of Board to be public servants.

50. All members, officers and servants of a Board when acting or purporting to act in pursuance of any of the provisions of this Act and the rules made thereunder shall be deemed to be public servants within the meaning of section 21 of the Indian Penal Code.

Chapter VIII

MISCELLANEOUS

Central Water Laboratory.

51. (1) The Central Government may, by notification in the official Gazette,—

(a) establish a Central Water Laboratory; or

(b) specify any laboratory or institute as a Central Water Laboratory, to carry out the functions entrusted to the Central Water Laboratory under this Act.

(2) The Central Government may, after consultation with the Central Board, make rules prescribing—

(a) the functions of the Central Water Laboratory;

(b) the procedure for the submission to the said laboratory of samples of water or of sewage or trade effluent for analysis or tests, the form of the laboratory's report there under and the fees payable in respect of such report;

(c) such other matters as may be necessary or expedient to enable that laboratory to carry out its functions.

State Water Laboratory.

52. (1) The State Government may, by notification in the Official Gazette,—

(a) establish a State Water Laboratory; or

64. Sub-section (2) renumbered as sub-section (3) by s. 26, *ibid.*
65. Subs. by Act 44 of 1978, s. 19, for certain words.

(b) specify any laboratory or institute as a State Water Laboratory, to carry out the functions entrusted to the State Water Laboratory under this Act.

(2) The State Government may, after consultation with the State Board, make rules prescribing—

(a) the functions of the State Water Laboratory;

(b) the procedure for the submission to the said laboratory of samples of water or of sewage or trade effluent for analysis or tests, the form of the laboratory's report thereon and the fees payable in respect of such report;

(c) such other matters as may be necessary or expedient to enable that laboratory to carry out its functions.

Analysts

53. (1) The Central Government may, by notification in the Official Gazette appoint such persons as it thinks fit and having the prescribed qualifications to be Government analysts for the purpose of analysis of samples of water or of sewage or trade effluent sent for analysis to any laboratory established or specified under sub-section (1) of section 51.

(2) The State Government may, by notification in the Official Gazette, appoint such persons as it thinks fit and having the prescribed qualifications to be Government analysts for the purpose of analysis of samples of water or of sewage or trade effluent sent analysis to any laboratory established or specified under sub-section (1) of section 52.

(3) Without prejudice to the provisions of sub-section (3) of section 12, the Central Board or as the case may be the State Board may, by notification in the Official Gazette, and with the approval of the Central Government or the State Government as the case may be, appoint such persons as it thinks fit and having the prescribed qualifications to be Board analysts for the purpose of analysis of samples of water or of sewage or trade effluent sent for analysis to any laboratory established or recognised under section 16, or as the case may be, under section 17.

Reports of analysts

54. Any document purporting to be a report signed by a Government analysts or, as the case may be, a Board analysis may be used as evidence of the facts stated therein in any proceeding under this Act.

Local authorities to assist.

55. All local authorities shall render such help and assistance and furnish such information to the Board as it may require for the discharge of its functions, and shall make available to the Board for inspection and examination such

records, maps, plans and other documents as may be necessary for the discharge of its functions.

Compulsory acquisition of land for the State Board.

56. Any land required by a State Board for the efficient performance of its functions under this Act shall be deemed to be needed for a public purpose and such land shall be required for the State Board under the provisions of the Land Acquisition Act, 1894, or under any other corresponding law for the time being in force.

Returns and reports.

57. The Central Board shall furnish to the Central Government and a State Board shall furnish to the State Government and to the Central Board such reports, returns, statistics, accounts and other information with respect to its fund or activities as that Government, or, as the case may be, the Central Board may, from time to time, require.

Bar of jurisdiction.

58. No civil court shall have jurisdiction to entertain any suit or proceeding in respect of any matter which an appellate authority constituted under this Act is empowered by or under this Act to determine, and no injunction shall be granted by any court or other authority in respect of any action taken or to be taken in pursuance of any power conferred by or under this Act.

Protection of action taken in good faith.

59. No suit or other legal proceedings shall lie against the Government or any officer of Government or any member or officer of a Board in respect of anything which is in good faith done or intended to be done in pursuance of this Act or the rules made thereunder.

Over-riding effect.

60. The provisions of this Act shall have effect notwithstanding anything in consistent therewith contained in any enactment other than this Act.

Power of Central Government to supersede the Central Board and Joint Boards.

61.(1) If at any time the Central Government is of opinion—

(a) that the Central Board or any Joint Board has persistently made default in the performance of the functions imposed on it by or under this Act; or

(b) that circumstances exist which render it necessary in the public interest so to do,

the Central Government may, by notification in the Official Gazette, supersede the Central Board or such Joint Board, as the case may be, for such period, not exceeding on year, as may be specified in the notification:

Provided that before issuing a notification under this sub-section for the reasons mentioned in clause (a), the Central Government shall give a reasonable opportunity to the Central Board, or such Joint Board, as the case may be, to show cause why it should not be superseded and shall consider the explanations and objects if any, of the Central Board or such Joint Board, as the case may be.

(2) Upon the publication of a notification under sub-section (1) superseding the Central Board or any Joint Board,—

(a) all the members shall, as from the date of supersession vacate their offices as such;

(b) all the powers, functions and duties which may, by or under this Act, be exercised, performed or discharged by the Central Board or such Joint Board shall, until the Central Board or the Joint Board, as the case may be, is reconstituted under sub-section (3) be exercised, performed or discharged by such or persons as the Central Government may direct;

(c) all property owned or controlled by the Central Board or such Joint Board shall, until the Central Board, or Joint Board as the case may be, is reconstituted under sub-section (3) vest in the Central Government.

(3) On the expiration of the period of supersession specified in the notification issued under sub-section (1), the Central Government may—

(a) extend the period of supersession for such further term, not exceeding six months, as it may consider necessary; or

(b) reconstitute the Central Board or the Joint Board, as the case may be, by fresh nomination or appointment, as the case be, and in such case any person who vacated his office under clause (a) of sub-section (2) shall not be deemed disqualified for nomination or appointment:

Provided that the Central Board may at any time before the expiration of the period of supersession, whether originally specified under sub-section (1) or as extended under this sub-section, take action under clause (b) of this sub-section.

Power of State Government to supersede State Board.

62. (1) If at any time the State Government is of opinion—

(a) that the State Board has persistently made default in the performance of the functions imposed on it by or under this Act; or

(b) that circumstances exist which render it necessary in the public interest so to do, the State Government may, by notification in the Official Gazette, supersede the State Board for such period, not exceeding one year, as may be specified in the notification:

Provided that before issuing a notification under this sub-section for the reasons mentioned in clause (a), the State Government shall give a reasonable opportunity to the State Board to show cause why it should not be superseded and shall consider the explanations and objections, if any, of the State Board.

(2) Upon the publication of a notification under sub-section (1) superseding the State Board, the provisions of sub-sections (2) and (3) of section 61 shall apply in relation to the supersession of the State Board as they apply in relation to the supersession of the Central Board or a Joint Board by the Central Government.

Power of Central Government to make rules.

63. (1) The Central Government may, simultaneously with the constitution of the Central Board, make rules in respect of the matters specified in sub-section (2);

Provided that when the Central Board has been constituted no such rule shall be made, varied amended or repealed without consulting the Board.

(2) In particular, and without prejudice to the generality of the foregoing power, such rules may provide for all or any of the following matters, namely :—

(a) the terms and conditions of service of the members (other than the chairman and member-secretary) of the Central Board under sub-section (8) of section 5;

(b) the intervals and the time and place at which meetings of the Central Board or of any committee thereof constituted under this Act, shall be held and the procedure to be followed at such meetings including the quorum necessary for the transaction of business under section 8, and under sub-section (2) of section 9;

(c) the fees and allowances to be paid to such members of a committee of the Central Board as are not members of the Board under sub-section (3) of section 9;

(d) [66][the manner in which and the purposes for which persons may be associated with the Central Board under sub-section (1) of section 10 and the fees and allowances payable to such persons;]

(e) the terms and conditions of service of the chairman and the member-secretary of the Central Board under sub-section (9) of section 5 and sub-section (1) of section 12.

66. Subs. by Act 44 of 1978, s. 20, for cl. (d).

(f) conditions subject to which a person may be appointed as a consulting engineer to the Central Board under sub-section (4) of section 12;

(g) the powers and duties to be exercised and performed by the chairman and the member-secretary of the Central Board;

[67] * * * *

(j) the form of the report of the Central Board analyst under sub-section (1) of section 22;

(k) the form of the report of the Government analyst under sub-section (3) of section 22;

(l) [68][the form in which and the time within which the budget of the Central Board may be prepared and forwarded to the Central Government under section 38;

(ll) the form in which the annual report of the Central Board may be prepared under section 39;]

(m) the form in which the accounts of the Central Board may be maintained under section 40;

(mm) [69] [the manner in which notice of intention to make a complaint shall be given to the Central Board or officer authorised by it under section 49;]

(n) any other matter relating to the Central Board, including the powers and functions of that Board in relation to Union territories;

(o) any other matter which has to be, or may be, prescribed.

(3) Every rule made by the Central Government under this Act shall be laid, as soon as may after it is made, before each House of Parliament while it is in session for a total period of thirty days which may be comprised in one session or in two or more successive sessions, and if, [70] [before the expiry of the session immediately following the session or the successive sessions aforesaid], both Houses agree in making any modification in the rule or both Houses agree that the rule should not be made, the rule shall thereafter have effect only in such modified form or be of no effect, as the case may be; so however that any such modification or annulment shall be without prejudice to the validity of anything previously done under that rule.

Power State Government to make rules.

64. (1) The State Government may, simultaneously with the constitution of

67. Cls. *(h)* and *(i)* omitted by s. 20, *ibid*.
68. Subs. by Act 53 of 1988, s. 27.
69. Ins. by Act, *ibid.* s. 27.
70. Subs. by Act 44 of 1978, s. 20, for certain words.

the State Board, make rules to carry out the purposes of this Act in respect of matters not falling within the purview of section 63:

Provided that when the State Board has been constituted, no such rule shall be made, varied, amended or repealed without consulting that Board.

(2) In particular, and without prejudice to the generality of the foregoing power, such rules may provide for all or any of the following matters, namely:—

(a) the terms and conditions of service of the members (other than the chairman and the member-secretary of the State Board under sub-section (8) of section 5;

(b) the time and place of meetings of the State Board of any committee of that Board constituted under this Act and the procedure to be followed at such meeting including to quorum necessary for the transaction of business under section 8 and under sub-section (2) of section 9;

(c) the fees and allowances to be paid to such members of a committee of the State Board as are not members of the Board under sub-section (3) of section 9;

(d) the manner in which and the purposes for which persons may be associated with the State Board under sub-section (1) of section 10 [71][and the fees and allowances payable to such persons].

(e) the terms and conditions of service of the chairman and the member-secretary of the State Board under sub-section (9) of section 5 and under sub section (1) of section 12;

(f) the conditions subject to which a person may be appointed as a consulting engineer to the State Board under sub-section (4) of section 12;

(g) the powers and duties to be exercised and discharged by the chairman and the member-secretary of the State Board;

(h) the form of the notice referred to in section 21;

(i) the form of the report of the State Board analyst under sub-section (1) of section 22;

(j) the form of the report of the Government analyst under sub-section (3) of section 22;

(k) the form of application for the consent of the State Board under sub-section (2) of section 25, and the particulars it may contain;

(l) the manner in which inquiry under sub-section (3) of section 25 may be made in respect of an application for obtaining of the State Board and the matter to be taken into accounts in granting or refusing such consent;

71. Ins. by s. 21, *ibid.*

(m) the form and manner in which appeals may be filed, the fees payable in respect of such appeals and the procedure to be followed by the appellate authority in disposing of the appeals under sub-section (3) of section 28;

(n) [72] [the form in which and the time within which the budget of the State Board may be prepared and forwarded to the State Government under section 38;

(nn) the form in which the annual report of the State Board may be prepared under section 39;]

(o) the form in which the accounts of the State Board may be maintained under sub-section (1) of section 40;

(oo) [73][the manner in which notice of intention to make a complaint shall be given to the State Board or officer authorised by it under section 49;]

(p) any other matter which has to be, or may be, prescribed.

---

72. Subs. by Act 53 of 1988, s. 28, for cl. *(n)*.
73. Ins. by s. 28, *ibid.*

APPENDIX III

WATER (PREVENTION AND CONTROL OF POLLUTION) RULES, 1975

Form of Report of the Result of the Analysis by Board Analyst

No. PH/2206/2R-3/75 Dated, the 18th August, 1975.

In exercise of the power conferred by sub-section (1) and, in particular by clause (i) of sub-section (2) of section 64, read with sub-section (1) of section 22 of the Water (Prevention and Control of Pollution) Act, 1974 (6 of 1974), the Governor is pleased hereby to make, in consultation with the West Bengal Prevention and Control of Water Pollution Board, the following rules namely—

1. *Short title and commencement*—(1) These rules may be called the West Bengal Prevention and Control of Water Pollution (Form of Report of the Result of the Analysis by Board Analyst) Rules, 1975.

(2) They shall come into force with effect from the date of their publication in the *Calcutta Gazette*.

2. *Definition* — In these rules, unless there is anything repugnant in the subject or context, —

(a) 'Act' means the Water (Prevention and Control of Pollution) Act, 1974;

(b) 'section' means a section of the Act;

(c) 'Board' means the West Bengal Prevention and Control of Water Pollution Board constituted under sub-section (1) of section 4;

(d) 'Board Analyst' means a person appointed as such by the Board under sub-section (3) of section 53.

3. *Report of the Board Analyst* — The report of the Board Analyst under sub-section (1) of section of the Act shall be in Form A.

FORM A

(See rule 3)

Report by the Board Analyst

Report No. ....

Dated the ....

I hereby certify that I, ... Board Analyst duly appointed by the West Bengal Prevention and Control of Water Pollution Board under sub-section (3) of section 53 of the Water (Prevention and Control of Pollution) Act, 1974 received on the .... day of .... 19........ from .... a sample for analysis, properly sealed and fastened and that I found the seal intact and unbroken. The seal fixed on the container of the sample tallied with the specimen impression of the seal separately sent by the said officer/person and the sample was in a condition fit for analysis reported below:—

I further certify that I have/had cause to be analysed the aforementioned sample, on .... and declare the result of the analysis to be as follows:—

....

....

....

signed this......................... day of ....19.......

(Signature)

Board Analyst

Address..............................

....

To

....

....

Form of Report of the Result of the Analysis by Government Analyst

No. PH/2284/2R-4/75 Calcutta, the 22nd August, 1975

In exercise of the power conferred by sub-section (1) and, in particular, by clause (1) of sub-section (2) of section 64, read with sub-section (3) of section 22, of the Water (Prevention and Control of Pollution) Act, 1974 (6 of 1974), the Governor is pleased hereby to make, in consultation with the West Bengal Prevention and Control of Water Pollution Board, the following rules namely —

1. *Short title and commencement* — (1) These rules may be called the West Bengal Prevention and Control of Water Pollution (Form of Report of the Result of the Analysis by Government Analyst) Rules, 1975.

(2) They shall come into force with effect from the date of their publication in the *Calcutta Gazette*.

2. *Definition* — In these rules unless there is anything repugnant in the subject or context, —

(a) "Act" means the Water (Prevention and Control of Pollution) Act, 1974;

(b) "section" means a section of the Act;

(c) "Government Analyst" means a person appointed as such by the State Government under sub-section (2) of section 53.

3. *Report of the Government Analyst* — Report of the Government Analyst under sub-section (3) of section 22 of the Act shall be in Form A.

FORM

(See rule 3)

Report by the Government Analyst

Report No...............................

Dated the ....

I hereby certify that I,............................ Government Analyst duly appointed by the Government of West Bengal under sub-section (2) of Section 53 of the Water (Prevention and Control of Pollution) Act, 1974 received on the................ day of...............19.............from.................a sample for analysis, properly sealed and fastened and that I found the seal in-tact and unbroken. The seal fixed on the container of the sample tallied with the specimen impression of the seal separately sent by the said officer/person and the sample was in a condition fit for analysis reported below:—

I further certify that I have/had caused to be analysed the aforementioned sample, on......... and declare the result of the analysis to be as follows:—

....

....

....

signed this......... day of........19.....

(Signature)

Government Analyst

Address...........................

....

To

....

....

Form of Application for Consent of the State Board

No. PH/3020/2R-18/74 —17th December, 1974—In exercise of the power conferred by sub-section (1) and, in particular by clause (k) of sub-section (2) of section 64 read with sub-section (2) of section 25 of the Water (Prevention and Control of Pollution) Act, 1974 (6 of 1974), the Governor is pleased hereby to make the following rules, namely —

1. *Short title and commencement*—(1) These rules may be called the West Bengal Prevention and Control of Water Pollution (Fonn of Application for Consent of the State Board) Rules, 1974.

(2) They shall come into force on and from the date of their publication with *Official Gazette.*

2. *Form of application*—Application for consent of the State Board under sub-section (2) of section 25 of the Water (Prevention and Control of Pollution) Act, 1974, shall be in Form A.

(To be submitted in triplicate)

FORM A

Application for Consent for Discharge

Under sub-section (2) of section 25 and section 26 of the Act Application for consent for discharge in Water Pollution Prevention and Control Area.

From: Date: ....

....

....

....

To

The Member-Secretary, West Bengal Prevention and Control of Water Pollution Board.

....

....

Sir,

I/We hereby apply for CONSENT as required under the Water (Prevention and Control of Pollution) Act, 1974, in the prescribed form as laid down by the State Government to make discharge from land/premises owned by .... for a period upto ....

(a) Sewage/sullage via drains/outfall sewers/treatment works

(b) Trade effluent via drains/outfall sewers/treatment works

(c) Solid wastes into

(i) Stream....../river OR

(ii) on land for irrigation, bearing survey no..... adjoining/at a distance of ..... stream/river OR

(iii) lake, pond adjoining/at a distance of...... stream/river OR

(iv) directly on land for open percolation into sub-terrain strata of survey No..... adjoining/at a distance..... stream/river or

(v) tidal waters/estuarine waters known as ...... OR

(vi) sea along/off the shore known as......

2. The annexures, appendices, other particulars and plans each in triplicate are attached herewith.

3. I/We further declare that the information furnished in the annexures, appendices, and plans is correct to the best of my/our knowledge.

4. I/We hereby submit that in case of change either of the point or the quantity of discharge of its quality, a fresh application for CONSENT shall be made and until such CONSENT is granted no change shall be made.

5. I/We hereby agree to submit to the State Board an application for renewal of CONSENT one month in advance of the date of expiry of the consented period for outlet/discharge, if to be continued thereafter.

6. I/We undertake to furnish any other information within one month of its being called for by the State Board.

Yours faithfully,

Signature(s)

Name(s) of Applicant(s)..................................

Address of Applicant(s)..................................

....

Accompaniments:

(NOTE — Strike out entries not relevant)

ANNEXURE TO FORM A

Extisting

Outlet/Discharge

New/Altered

Note—Any applicant knowingly giving incorrect information or suppressing any information pertaining thereto shall be liable to be punishable under the Act.

While filling this Annexure the applicant not concerned with any of the items shall state "not concerned" against the relevant one.

1.	Full name of applicant with address	.... (Tele. No..................................)
2.	Full description of land / premises/institute/factory/ industry / local body with address	.... (Tele. No..................................)
3.	Give revenue / city survey number of land / premises for which the application is made stating district, taluka and village.	District .... Taluka .... Town .... Village .... City Survey No. Area in hectares .... Revenue Survey No. .... Area in hectares ....
4.	State the month and the year in which the land / premises / institute / factory / industry was actually put into commission or is proposed to be put into commission or the month and the year from which the local body is fuctioning.	
5.	State the Civil / Military / Defence Industrial Estate, etc., under whose administrative jurisdiction the applicant's land / premises is situated.	Collectorate .... Corporation .... Municipality .... Village Panchayat .... Cantonment .... Defence Department .... Port Trust.................................. State Government .... Prohibited Area ....

6. (a) State whether the land / premises / factory / industry / has been declared as prohibited area.	Yes/No		
(b) If yes, state the name of the authority and furnish a certified copy of the order under which the area has been declared as prohibited area.			
7. Is the industry/factory for which application is made closed on Sunday / holiday?	Yes/No		
8. State working season per year for the industry/factory.	Full year		
	From	To	
	From	To	
	From	To	
	From	To	
	.... every year		
	Sift No.	Sift No. 2	Sift No. 3
	hrs.	hrs.	hrs.
9. (a) No. of workers attending the factory	....		
(b) No. of workers residing in the premises.	....		
10. (For local Bodies only) —			
(a) Present population;	....		
(b) Population covered under regular sewerage facilities;	....		
(c) Population covered by conservancy latrines;	....		
(d) Population having septic tank / pit privy facilities.	....		

11. (a) Give the list of raw materials such as metals, alloys, chemicals, oils, fuel etc., used per month in Metric Tonnes :-

	Metal and Alloy			Name Weight
	Chemicals	Inorganic Organic	Dyes Pesticides	Name Weight
Fuels:		(a) Wood		Name Weight
		(b) Coal		Name Weight
		(c) Oil		Name Weight
		(d) Gases		Name Weight
		(e) Other		Name Weight

(b) Give the list of names of products and by-products manufactured per month in (MT)	Serial No.	Name of product	Quantity in Metric Tonne per month

12. State daily quantity of water in litres utilised.

Uses

Domestic Industrial Agriculture Others

13. (A) State the hourly maximum and daily maximum quantity of effluents arising from land/premises for which the application is made :

	In Litres	
	Hourly Maximum	Daily Maximum
(a) Domestic...		
(b) Industrial...		
(c) Agriculture		
(d) Other use...		
(e) Total quantity of effluent ...		

(B) State how measurements of rate and quantity are carried out:

14. State whether storm water drains are kept separate from Industrial/Domestic effluent drains.	Yes/No	
15. (a) Is domestic effluent allowed to get mixed in Industrial effluent?	Yes/No	
(b) If yes, state the ratio	Domestic/ Industrial	
16. (a) Describe if any treatment for industrial or domestic effluent or one for combined effluent is made.	Yes/No	

If yes, state the process of treatment in brief (separately)

(b) Is the quality of effluent emanating either without or after treatment approved by any authority?	Yes/No	
(c) If approved, furnish the authority (two certified copies to be sent).		
17. Is there any provision for disposal of:	Already made	Proposed to be made
(a) Domestic effluent in public underground sewer.	Yes/No	Yes/No
(b) Industrial effluent in public underground sewer	Yes/No	Yes/No
(c) Give the name of public authority owing the sewer.		
18. Is there any provision for disposal of:	Already made	Proposed to be made
(a) Domestic effluent over land for irrigation.	Yes/No	Yes/No
(b) Industrial effluent over land for irrigation.	Yes/No	Yes/No

(c) Domestic effluent in the underground strata.	Yes/No	Yes/No

(d) State the area of land used for (a) above in hectares.

(e) State the area of land used for (a) above in hectares.

19. Give quantitative disposal of effluent in litres provided for the places mentioned below :

	Domestic	Industrial	Mixed
(i) Stream/River.			
(ii) On lands for irrigation.			
(iii) On lands for percolation.			
(iv) Lake/Pond.			
(v) Tidal waters.			
(vi) Estuarine waters.			
(vii) Open sea.			

20. Is there any provision for equalizing or holding lagoons for tanks to store the effluent during unfavourable stream or tidal conditions?

	Already made	Proposed to be made
(i) Domestic.		
(ii) Industrial effluent.		
(iii) Combined effluent.		

21. Is sufficient land available/can be made available in case pumping effluent on lands have to be considered? Yes/No

22. (a) Give details of composition of domestic Industrial/Combined effluents in respect of the following :

		Effluent before treatment			Effluent after treatment		
		At Max. Dis	At Min. Dis.	At Ave. Dis.	At Max. Dis.	At Min. Dis.	At Ave. Dis.
		1	2	3	1	2	3
(i)	pH						
(ii)	Colour						
(iii)	Temperature						
(iv)	Total suspended solids, mg/1						
(v)	Total dissolved, solids, mg/1, Fixed/Volatile.						
(vi)	Total volatile solids, mg/1						
(vii)	B.O.D. 5 days 20°C, mg/1						
(viii)	Dissolved Oxygen, mg/1						
(ix)	C.O.D. mg/1						
(x)	Oils and Greases mg/1						
(xi)	Chloride (as Cl), mg/1						
(xii)	Phenolic compounds, mg/1						
(xiii)	Cyanides (as CN), mg/1						
(xiv)	Sulphides (as S), mg/1						
(xv)	Sulphides (SO_4), mg/1						
(xvi)	Insecticides, mg/1						
(xvii)	Total residual chlorine						
(xviii)	Flouride (as F), mg/1						
(xix)	Born (as B), mg/1						
(xx)	Arsenic (as As), mg/1						
(xxi)	Barium (as Ba), mg/1						
(xxii)	Percent Sodium						
(xxiii)	Cadmium (as Cd), mg/1						
(xxiv)	Copper (as Cu), mg/1						
(xxv)	Lead (as Pb), mg/1						
(xxvi)	Chromium (as Cr), mg/1						

(xxvii) Mercury (as Hg), mg/1
(xxviii) Nickel (as Ni), mg/1
(xxix) Salenium (as Se), mg/1
(xxx) Silver (as Ag), mg/1
(xxxi) Zinc (as Zn), mg/1
(xxxii) Any other metals, mg/1
(xxxiii) Coliform organisms MPN per 100 M1 (monthly average)

Notes: (1) Furnish a copy of the analysis report of representative samples carried out by a competent laboratory.

(2) Excepting where such methods of determination are not available in ISI, the standard methods as laid down in the book Standard Method for the examination of water and waste water 13th Edition 1971 (APHA), will be followed for determination of above mentioned parameters.

22. (b) Is the effluent toxic? Yes/No

(c) State if the Industrial effluent is having —

(i) Unpleasant smell Yes/No

(ii) Irritating and/or harmful Yes/No

(iii) Corrosive Yes/No

(iv) With colour Yes/No

(d) Is there any sudden change of temperature exceeding 10°C at any time? Yes/No

23. (a) Are facilities available with the applicant for carrying out the following tests of waste waters?

	Existing	Proposed
(i) Physical	Yes/No	Yes/No
(ii) Chemical	Yes/No	Yes/No
(iii) Bacteriological	Yes/No	Yes/No
(iv) Toxicological	Yes/No	Yes/No

(b) If yes, give details of equipment ....

....

....

24. Is the land/premises etc., for which application is made, open?

Highly Boiling matter			
Toxic	Organic	Inorganic	Micro biological

(a) Colling Tanks
(b) Mixing Tanks
(c) Missing ponds
(d) Recirculation Wells

Which contains

25. State details for solid wastes:

	Description	Quantity	Method of Collection	Method of Disposal
(i) Seasonal waste				
(ii) Spillage				
(iii) Rejected materials				

Signature ....
Name and address of the ....
Applicant on behalf of ....
....
Name and address of the firm
....

Accompaniments :

1. Site plan.
2. Detailed layout plan of the factory premises, showing structures, water supply lines, stoom, drain, sewers for domestic effluents, for trade effluent, location of effluent treatment and its disposal and any other useful information, drawing, tables, etc.

Explanatory Notes for filing in Form A and the Annexure.

The notes are given only for those items for which explanation is considered desirable. Other items are self explanatory.

FORM A

(1) Here mention the name of the declared area.

(2) Here mention the name of the owner of the land/premises or owned by other than the applicant industry or factory. If the land/premises belong to the factory/industry, say, 'self'.

(3) Here mention the date upto which the consent is sought for.

(4) Here mention the local name of the river/stream tidal waters/sea, as may be applicable.

ANNEXURE TO FORM A

Outlet—means the arrangement for discharge of the effluent for which the consent is sought for.

Discharge—means the effluent going out of the outlet.

Existing—means that which is in operation at the time of applying for the consent.

New—means that which will be brought into operation in future.

Altered—means that which has been modified due to changes in quantity and/or quality of discharge, arrangement and/or point of discharge, etc.

Item 1—Here give the names of the person who is authorised by the Institution/Industry/Factory/Local Body, etc., to transact their legal business.

Item 2—Here give the registered name of the Institution/Factory/Industry, etc., under which the business is carried out.

Item 5—Here state the concerned institution such as MIDC, CIDCO, etc., under whose administrative control the Factory/Industry, etc., is set up.

Item 6—Applicable only to those areas which are prohibited areas, such as the ordinance Factories, Mint, etc.

Item 13(B)—State the method of measurement of hourly/daily maximum quantity of effluent i.e. by flow metres, venturi metres, V. notch sump measurements, or approximately estimated, etc.

Item 16(a)—If the effluent is treated, give separately the method of treatment and flow diagram of the treatment process.

Item 16(b)—Here, mention 'yes' if any other authority such as the Local Body, MIDC or State Department has already approved the discharge of effluent, either with or without treatment, at the time of establishment of the Factory/Industry.

Item 19—Here give the quantity of effluent of difference of types such as domestic, Industrial or mixed etc. proposed to be or is let into the stream/river, lands, lakes, sea, etc., as may be applicable.

Item 22(a)—Analysis to be furnished shall cover as many parameters as are expected to be found, in the effluent. If some of the parameters are not expected to be found, say not applicable. If some other parameters than those listed under the items are expected the same may be mentioned at the end. The analysis shall be separately furnished for domestic, industrial and combined effluent.

Item 22(b)—Here toxicity means that which is established by bioassay studies on fish, as per procedure given in the Standard Methods.

GOVERNMENT OF WEST BENGAL
DEPARTMENT OF ENVIRONMENT
NOTIFICATION

No. Env/337/2W-4/83—14th April, 1983.—Whereas by the Government of West Bengal, Department of Health and Family Welfare, notification No. PH/2395/2A-7/74, dated the 20th September, 1974, a State Board, namely, West Bengal Prevention and Control of Water Pollution Board (hereinafter referred to as the said Board) was constituted.

And whereas the said Board at its meeting held on the 7th February, 1983 decided that the name of the said Board should be West Bengal Pollution Control Board.

Now, therefore, in exercise of the power conferred by sub-section (1) of section 4 of the Water (Prevention and Control of Pollution) Act, 1974 (6 of 1974), the Governor is pleased hereby to re-name the said Board as West Bengal Pollution Control Board with immediate effect.

By order of the Governor,
Secy. to the Government of West Bengal.

GOVERNMENT OF WEST BENGAL
DEPARTMENT OF ENVIRONMENT
NOTIFICATION

No. Env. 260/1 W-/83—Ist March, 1984.—In exercise of the power conferred by sub-section (1), and in particular by clause (k) of sub-section (2) of section 64 read with sub-section (2) of section 25 of the Water (Prevention and Control of Pollution) Act, 1974 (6 of 1974), the Governor is pleased hereby to make, in consultation with the West Bengal Pollution Control Board, the following amendments in the West Bengal Prevention and Control of Water Pollution (Form of Application for Consent of the State Board) Rules, 1974, published with the Department of Health and Family Planning notification No. PH/3020/2R-18/74, dated the 17th December, 1974, in Part I of the "Calcutta Gazette, Extraordinary", dated the 6th January, 1974 (hereinafter referred to as the said rules) :—

In the said rules, after rule 2, add the following rules :—

"3. *Fees for grant of consent.*—(1) Each application for consent shall be accomplished by a fee which shall be payable in advance according to the following table :—

Table

Order of slab (Kilometre of average water consumption per day)		Fee in Rs.
1.	10 or below	200
2.	more than 10 to 50	300
3.	more than 50 to 100	400
4.	more than 100 to 500	600
5.	more than 500 to 1,000	800
6.	more than 1,000 to 5,000	1,200
7.	more than 5,000 to 10,000	1,600
8.	more than 10,000 to 50,000	2,400
9.	more than 50,000 to 1,00,000	3,200
10.	more than 1,00,000 to 5,00,000	4,800
11.	more than 5,00,000 to 10,00,000	6,400

4. *Period of validity of consent.*—The consent shall remain valid for one year from the date of grant of the same or for such period as may be fixed by the State Board, whichever is less."

By order of the Governor

Dy. Secy. to the Govt. of West Bengal

GOVERNMENT OF WEST BENGAL
DEPARTMENT OF ENVIRONMENT
NOTIFICATION

No. ENV/335/IW-6/86 Calcutta, the 25th February, 1986

In exercise of the power conferred by sub-section (1), and in particular, by clause (k) of sub-section (2), of section 64, read with sub-section (2) of section 25, of the Water (Prevention and Control of Pollution) Act, 1974 (6 of 1974), the Governor is pleased hereby to make, in consultation with the West Bengal Pollution Control Board, the following amendments in the West Bengal Prevention and Control of Water Pollution (Form of Application for Consent of the State Board) Rules, 1974, published with the Department of Health and Family

Planning Notification No. PH/3020/2R-18/74, dated the 17th December, 1974, in part-I of the *Calcutta Gazette, Extraordinary,* dated the 6th January, 1975, as subsequently amended hereinafter referred to as the said rule :—

In the table below rule 3 of the said rules, in the entry against serial 11 under the heading "Order of slab (Kilometre of average water consumption per day)", *omit* the word and figures "to 10,00,000."

By order of the Governor

Dy. Secy. of the Govt. of West Bengal

INDIAN STANDARD

TOLERANCE LIMITED FOR

A. Industrial Effluents discharged into Inland Surface Waters.

IS : 2490 (Par-I)—1974

B. Industrial Effluents discharged on Land for Irrigation purpose.

IS : 3307—1965

C. Industrial Effluents discharged into Public Sewers.

IS : 3306—1974

D. Inland Surface Waters subject to pollution.

IS : 2296—1974

E. Sewage Effluents discharged into Inland Surface Waters.

IS : 4764—1973

[This standard prescribes the tolerance limits for inland surface waters (rivers), estuaries streams, lakes and reservoirs, including rivers liable to seasonal drying] subject to pollution which are used for the following purposes:—

(a) Raw water for public water supply;

(b) Bathing Ghats;

(c) Fish culture; and

(d) Irrigation.

This tolerance limits are shown in Table-1

These requirements shall apply only when, after treatment, the sewage effluent is disposed of for irrigation and on land.

Not required.

Table 1

Sl.No.	Characteristic	Tolerance Limits for							
		A	B	C	D				E
					(a)	(b)	(c)	(d)	
(i)	Total suspended solids, mg/1, Max	100	—	600, relaxable to 750 by the local authority	—	—	—	—	30
(ii)	Particle size of total suspended solids	shall pass 850 micron IS Sieve	—	—	—	—	—	—	—
(iii)	Total dissolved solids (inorganic), mg/1, Max	—	2100	2100	—	—	—	2100	—
(iv)	pH	5.5 to 9.0	5.5 to 9.0	5.5 to 9.0	6.0 to 9.0	6.0 to 9.0	6.0 to 9.0	5.5 to 9.0	—
(v)	Electrical conductance at 25°C, Max.	—	—	—	—	—	1000 x 10^{-6} mhos	3000 x 10^{-6} mhos	—
(vi)	Temperature	shall not exceed 40°C in any section of the stream within 15 metres down stream from the effluent outlet	—	45°C Max	—	—	—	—	—

Table 1

Sl.No.	Characteristic	Tolerance Limits for							
		A	B	C	D				E
					(a)	(b)	(c)	(d)	
(vii)	B.O.D. (5 days at 20°C) mg/1, Max	30	500	500, subject to relaxation or tight ending by the local authority	3	3	—	—	29
(viii)	C.O.D., mg/1, Max	250	—	—	—	—	—	—	—
(ix)	Dissolved Oxygen, Min	—	—	—	40% Saturation value or 3 mg/1 whichever is higher	40% Saturation value of 3 mg/1 whichever is higher	40% Saturation value of 3 mg/1 whichever is higher	—	—
(x)	Oils and grease, mg/1, Max	10	30	100	0.1	0.1	0.1	—	—
(xi)	Phenolic Compounds, mg/1, Max (as C_6H_5OH)	1.0	—	5, relaxable to 50 by the local authority when secondary treatment of the sewage is carried out	0.005	0.005	—	—	—

Table 1

Sl.No.	Characteristic	Tolerance Limits for							
		A	B	C	D				E
					(a)	(b)	(c)	(d)	
(xii)	Fluorides (as F), mg/1, Max	2.0	—	—	1.5	1.5	—	—	—
(xiii)	Chlorides (as Cl), mg/1, Max	—	600	600	600	600	—	600	—
(xiv)	Total residual Chlorine, mg/1	1.0	—	—	—	—	—	—	—
(xv)	Cyanides (as CN), mg/1, Max	0.2	—	2.0	0.01	0.01	—	—	—
(xvi)	Sulphides (as S), mg/1, Max	2.0	—	—	—	—	—	—	—
(xvii)	Sulphates (as SO_4), mg/1, Max	—	1000	1000	—	—	—	1000	—
(xviii)	Nitrates (as NO_3), mg/1, Max	—	—	—	50	50	—	—	—
(xix)	Ammonical nitrogen, mg/1, Max	50	—	50	—	—	1.2	—	—
(xx)	Arsenic (as As), mg/1, Max	0.2	—	—	0.2	0.2	—	—	—
(xxi)	Lead (as Pb), mg/1, Max	0.1	—	1.0	0.1	0.1	—	—	—
(xxii)	Mercury (as Hg), mg/1, Max	0.01	—	—	—	—	—	—	—
(xxiii)	Copper (as Cu), mg/1, Max	3.0	—	3.0	—	—	—	—	—
(xxiv)	Cadmium (as Cd), mg/1, Max	2.0	—	—	—	—	—	—	—
(xxv)	Zinc (as Zn), mg/1, Max	5.0	—	15	—	—	—	—	—
(xxvi)	Total Chromium (as Cr), mg/1, Max.	—	—	—	0.05	0.05	—	—	—

Table 1

Sl.No.	Characteristic	Tolerance Limits for A	B	C	D (a)	D (b)	D (c)	D (d)	E
(xxvii)	Hesavalent Chromium (as Cr)	0.1	—	2.0	—	—	—	—	—
(xxviii)	Nickel (as Ni), mg/1, Max	3.0	—	2.0	—	—	—	—	—
(xxix)	Selenium (as Se), mg/1, Max	0.05	—	—	0.05	0.05	—	—	—
(xxx)	Percent Sodium, Max	—	60	60	—	—	—	60	—
(xxxi)	Boron (as B), mg/1, Max	—	2.0	2.0	—	—	—	2.0	—
(xxxii)	Free Carbon dioxide (as CO_2), mg/1, Max	—	—	—	—	—	6.0	—	—
(xxxiii)	Insecticides	absent	—	—	absent	absent	—	—	—
(xxiv)	Radioactive materials:								
	(a) Alpha emitters, /μC/ml, Max	10^{-7}	10^{-7}	10^{-9}	10^{-9}	10^{-9}	10^{-9}	10^{-9}	—
	(b) Beta emitters, /μC/ml, Max	10^{-6}	10^{-8}	10^{-6}	10^{-8}	10^{-8}	10^{-8}	10^{-8}	—
(xxv)	Coliform organisms (Monthly average MON per 100 ml.)	—	—	—	Not 5 x 10^3 with 5% of the samples with value 20 x 10^3 and 20% of the samples with value 5 x 10^3	—	—	—	—

Note:

(a) Tolerance limits for colour and odour of 'A' have not been prescribed in this Standard but it is recommended that as far as practicable, colour and unpleasant odours should not be present in the industrial effluent.

(b) Tolerance limits for odour of 'E' have not been prescribed but it is recommended that as far as practicable, unpleasant odours should not be present in the sewage effluent. Further, while no limits have been laid down in this standard for pathogenic bacteria it is expected that adherence to limits for total suspended solid and BOD will reduce the bacterial load of the effluent.

When the sewage also carries industrial effluent the sewage effluents also satisfy the tolerance limit for industrial effluents as given in 'A'.

(c) The disposal of solids, such as ash, cinder, and tar, hair, rag, metal shavings and garbage into public sewer from industries is also considered inadmissible.

Published by Authority

Part I — Orders and Notifications by the Governor of West Bengal, the High Court, Government Treasury, etc.

GOVERNMENT OF WEST BENGAL
DEPARTMENT OF ENVIRONMENT

NOTIFICATION

No. ENV/1163/1W-10/84—7th August, 1984.—In exercise of the power conferred by section 26 of the Water (Prevention and Control of Pollution) Act, 1974 (6 of 1974) (hereinafter referred to as the said Act), the Governor is pleased hereby to specify the 31st day of October, 1984 as the date on or before which the application for consent to be made under sub-section (3) of section 25 of the said Act shall be made by any person who immediately before the commencement of the said Act was discharging any sewage or trade effluent into a stream or well or sewer or on land.

By order of the Governor,

Dy. Secy. to the Govt. of West Bengal

Published by Authority

Part I — Orders and Notifications by the Governor of West Bengal, the High Court, Government Treasury, etc.

GOVERNMENT OF WEST BENGAL
DEPARTMENT OF ENVIRONMENT

NOTIFICATION

No. ENV/1192/2R-6/83—12th December, 1983.—In exercise of the power conferred by sub-section (1) and in particular by sub-section (2) of section 64 of the Water (Prevention and Control of Pollution) Act, 1974 (6 of 1974) (hereinafter referred to as the said Act), the Governor is pleased hereby to make the following rule prescribing the qualifications for appointment of Government Analyst under sub-section (2) and Board Analyst under sub-section (3) of section 53 of the Act with effect from the date of its publication in the Official Gazette :—

Rule

The qualifications for appointment of a Government Analyst under sub-section (2) and a Board Analyst under sub-section (3) of section 53 of the said Act shall be as follows :—

(a) a Master Degree in Chemistry or Bio-chemistry or Chemical Engineering or Public Health Engineering or Environmental Engineering; and

(b) not less than three years' practical experience in Environmental Quality Management.

By order of the Governor,
Dy. Secy. to the Govt. of West Bengal

Published by Authority

Part I — Orders and Notifications by the Governor of West Bengal, the High Court, Government Treasury, etc.

GOVERNMENT OF WEST BENGAL
DEPARTMENT OF ENVIRONMENT

NOTIFICATION

No. ENV/458/2R-4/82.—12th May, 1983.—In exercise of the power conferred by sub-section (1) and in particular by clause (d) of sub-section (2) of section 64, read with sub-section (1) of section 10 of the Water (Prevention and Control of Pollution) Act, 1974 (6 of 1974), the Governor is pleased hereby to make, in consultation with the West Bengal Pollution Control Board, the following rules, namely :

1. *Short title and commencement*—(1) These rules may be called the West Bengal Prevention and Control of Water Pollution (Manner and Purposes for Associating Persons with the Board) Rules, 1983.

(2) They shall come into force at once.

2. *Definitions*—In these rules unless there is anything repugnant in the subject of context, —

(a) "The Act" means the Water (Prevention and Control of Pollution) Act, 1974 (6 of 1974);

(b) "Board" means the West Bengal Pollution Control Board constituted under sub-section (1) of section 4 of the Act;

(c) "Chairman" means the Chairman of the Board.

3. *Manner in which and purposes for which persons may be temporarily associated with the Board and fees and allowances payable to such persons.*—(1) The Board or the Chairman may invite any person whose assistance or advice is considered useful in performing any of its functions, to be associated with the Board and to participate in the deliberations of its meetings or to attend to any other work of the Board.

(2) If such person is a non-official, he shall be entitled to a fee of rupees fifty for each day of attendance in the meeting of the Board (at which business is transacted and at which he is present from the beginning to the end thereof) and for each day of actual work for any work of the Board and to travelling allowances at a rate admissible to a Group A employee of the State Government.

(3) If such person is a Government employee or an employee in a Government undertaking, he shall be entitled to travelling allowances at the rate admissible to him under the relevant rules governing his employment.

By order of the Governor,

[Illegible]

Deputy Secretary to the Government of West Bengal.

GOVERNMENT OF WEST BENGAL
DEPARTMENT OF ENVIRONMENT

NOTIFICATION

No. Env/284/2R-7/83 Calcutta, the 6th March, 1984

In exercise of the power conferred by section 64, read with sub-section (2) of section 52, of the Water (Prevention and Control of Pollution) Act, 1974 (6 of 1974) (hereinafter referred to as the said Act), the Governor is pleased to make after consultation with the West Bengal Pollution Control Board (hereinafter referred to as the Board), the following rules prescribing the functions of the State

Water Laboratory, the procedure for the submission to the said laboratory of sample of water or of sewage or trade effluent for analysis or tests and the fees payable in respect of the said laboratory's report thereon, with effect from the date of this notification:

Rules

1. *Functions of the State Water Laboratory*—The State Water Laboratory shall cause to be analysed any samples of water or of sewage or trade effluent received by it from any officer empowered by the Board in this behalf and shall submit report of the result of analysis by the Government Analyst, in triplicate, in the form prescribed under notification No. PH/2284/2R-4/75, dated the 22nd August, 1975.

2. *Procedure for submission of sample of the State Water* Laboratory.—The Officer taking the samples of water from any stream or well or samples of any sewage or trade effluent according to the provisions of section 21 of the said Act shall submit the samples to the State Water Laboratory along with a forwarding letter in Form I.

3. *Fees for report.*—A fee at the rate of Rs. 40.00 for each constituent, subject to a minimum of Rs. 200.00 for a single sample, shall be payable to the State Water Laboratory for each report of analysis.

FORM I

(See rule 2)

Form of letter for submission of samples to the State Water Laboratory

To

The Government Analyst
State Water Laboratory

Sir,

I am submitting sample No./Nos. .... of water/sewage/trade effluent taken from M/s. .... on ...... according to the provisions of section 21 of Water (Prevention and Control of Pollution) Act, 1974 (6 of 1974).

Sample No.....	Point of collection	Parameter to be analysed
		....
....	....	....
....	....	....
....	....	....

Yours faithfully,

....

(Signature of the officer taking sample)
Designation:

Copy forwarded to the Member-Secretary, West Bengal Pollution Control Board.

....

(Name and Signature of the officer taking sample)

By order of the Governor

Secy. to the Govt. of West Bengal

No. Env/284/2R-7/83/1(1)

Copy forwarded for information and necessary action to the Member-Secretary, West Bengal Pollution Control Board.

No. 630(1-8)-1/WPB-D/74 Dt. 9.4.84
Dated the 6/12th March, 1984

Sd/- A.B. Basu

Deputy Secretary

Copy to : (1) S.E., (2) E.E.-I, (3) E.E.-II, (4) E.E.-III, (5) E.E.-IV, (6) A.E-I, (7) A.E.-II, (8) A.E.-III, (9) Scientist.

GOVERNMENT OF WEST BENGAL
DEPARTMENT OF ENVIRONMENT
NOTIFICATION

No. Env/459/2R-4/82 Dated 12th May, 1983.

In exercise of the power conferred by sub-section (1) and, in particular by clause (h) of sub-section (2) of section 64, read with clause (a) of sub-section (3) of section 21, of the Water (Prevention and Control of Pollution) Act, 1974 (6 of 1974), the Governor is pleased hereby to make, in consultation with the West Bengal Pollution Control Board, the following rules, namely :—

1. *Short title and commencement.*—(1) The rules may be called the West Bengal Prevention and Control of Water Pollution (Form of Notice for Taking Samples of Effluents for Analysis) Rules, 1983.

(2) They shall come into force at once.

2. *Definitions.*—In these rules, unless there is anything repugnant in the subject or context,—

(a) "The Act" means the Water (Prevention and Control of Pollution) Act, 1974 (6 of 1974);

(b) "Board" means the West Bengal Pollution Control Board constituted under sub-section (1) of section 4 of the Act;

(c) "Section" means a section of the Act.

3. *Form of notice for taking samples of effluents for analysis.*—When a sample of effluents is taken for analysis, the person taking the sample shall serve, as required under clause (a) of sub-section (6) of section 21 a notice in Form I.

Dated ....

By order of the Governor,

Dy. Secy. to the Govt. of West Bengal

FORM I

WEST BENGAL POLLUTION CONTROL BOARD

Notice of intention to have sample analysed

To

....

....

Take notice that it is intended to have analysed the sample of water/sewage/ trade effluent which is being taken today the .... day of .... 19................ From (1) ....

....

Name and designation of the person who takes the sample.

(1) Here specify the stream, well, plant, vessel or place from where the sample is taken.

By order of the Governor

[Illegible]

Dy. Secy. to the Govt. of West Bengal

GOVERNMENT OF WEST BENGAL
DEPARTMENT OF ENVIRONMENT
NOTIFICATION

No. Env/460/2R-4/82 Dated, the 12th May, 1983.

In exercise of the power conferred by sub-section (1) and in particular, by clause (1) of sub-section (2) of section 64, read with sub-section (3) of section 25, of the Water (Prevention and Control of Pollution) Act, 1974 (6 of 1974), the Governor is pleased hereby to make, in consultation with the West Bengal Pollution Control Board, the following rules, namely:—

Rules

1. *Short title and commencement.*—(1) These rules may be called the West Bengal Prevention and Control of Water Pollution (Procedure to be followed in Inquiry in respect of Application for Consent of the Board) Rules, 1983.

(2) They shall come into force at once.

2. *Definitions* —-In these rules unless there is anything repugnant in the subject or context,—

(a) "The Act" means the Water (Prevention and Control of Pollution) Act, 1974 (6 of 1974);

(b) "Board" means the West Bengal Pollution Control Board constituted under sub-section (1) of section 4;

(c) "Section" means a section of the Act.

3. *Procedure to be followed in inquiry in respect of application for consent of the Board.*—(1) On receipt of an application for consent under section 25 or section 26, the Board may depute any of its officers accompanied by as many assistants as may be necessary, to visit the premises of the applicant, to which such application related, for the purpose of verifying the correctness or otherwise of the particulars furnished in the application or for obtaining such further particulars or information as such officer may consider necessary. Such officer may, for that purpose, inspect any place where water or sewage or trade effluent is discharged by the applicant, or treatment plants, purification works or disposal systems of the applicant and may require the applicant to furnish to him any plan specification and other data relating to such treatment plants, purification works of disposal systems or any part thereof, he considers necessary.

(2) The officer shall before visiting any premises of the applicant for the purpose of inspection under sub-rule (1), give notice to the applicant of his intention to do so in Form II. The applicant shall furnish to such officer all facilities that such officer may legitimately require for the purpose.

(3) Such officer may, before or after making the inspection under sub-rule (1), require the applicant to furnish to him, orally or in writing, such additional information or clarification, or to produce before him such documents, as he may consider necessary for the purpose of inquiry and may, for that purpose, summon the applicant or his authorised agent to the officer of the Board.

By order of the Governor,

Dy. Secy to the Govt. of West Bengal

FORM II

(See rule 3)

WEST BENGAL POLLUTION CONTROL BOARD

NOTICE OF INSPECTION

Chairman	Member-Secretary
Shri	Shri ....
....	....
....	....
	No. ....
	Dated ....

To

....

....

Take Notice that for the purpose of enquiry under section 25/26 the following officers of the Board, namely :—

(i) Shri ....

(ii) Shri ....

(iii) Shri ....

and the persons authorised by the Board to assist them shall inspect the —

(a) Water Works;

(b) Sewage Works;

(c) Waste Treatment Plant;

(d) Factory;

(e) Disposal System;

(f) Any other parts thereof or pertaining thereto under your management/control on date(s) .... between .... hours when all facilities requested by them for such inspection should be made available for them on the site. Take notice that refusal or denial to above stated demand made for performing the functions of the Board will amount to obstruction punishable under section 42 of the Act.

By order of the Board

Member-Secretary

GOVERNMENT OF WEST BENGAL
DEPARTMENT OF ENVIRONMENT
NOTIFICATION

No. Env/773/2C-2/83-II Calcutta, the 13th May, 1985.

In exercise of the power conferred by sub-section (1) and, in particular, by clause (m) of sub-section (2) of section 64, read with sub-section (3) of section 28, of the Water (Prevention and Control of Pollution) Act, 1974 (6 of 1974), the Governor is pleased to make, in consultation with the West Bengal Prevention and Control of Water Pollution Board, the following rules, namely :—

Rules

1. *Short title and commencement.*—(1) These rules may be called the West Bengal Prevention and Control of Water Pollution (Appellant Authority) Rules, 1985.

(2) They shall come into force on the date of their publication in the *Official Gazette.*

2. *Definitions.*—In these rules, unless there is anything repugnant in the subject or context,—

(a) "Act" means the Water (Prevention and Control of Pollution) Act, 1974 (6 of 1974);

(b) "Appellate Authority" means the appellate authority constituted under sub-section (1) of section 28;

(c) "Board" means the West Bengal Prevention and Control of Water Pollution Board constituted under sub-section (1) of section 4;

(d) "Form" means the form appended to these rules;

(e) "investment" means the laying out of money on capital works including land, building, machinery and other equipments;

(f) "Member-secretary" means the Member-Secretary of the Board;

(g) "Section" means a section of the Act.

3. *Fees for appeal.*—The fees payable for an appeal under section 28 shall be at the following rates :—

A. *Industries:*

(a) Industries having an investment of Rs. 5 crores and above	Rs. 5,000.00
(b) Industries having an investment of Rs. 1 crore but less than Rs. 5 crores	Rs. 2,500.00
(c) Industries having an investment of Rs. 50 lakhs but less than Rs. 1 crore	Rs. 1,000.00

(d) Industries having an investment of Rs. 10 lakhs but less than Rs. 50 lakhs — Rs. 500.00

(e) Industries having an investment of more than Rs. 1 lakh but less than Rs. 10 lakhs — Rs. 250.00

(f) Industries having an investment up to Rs. 1 lakh — Rs. 100.00

B. *Local Bodies:*

(a) Municipalities/Corporations having a population of more than 10 lakhs — Rs. 5,000.00

(b) Municipalities/Corporations having a population of more than 5 lakhs but less than 10 lakhs — Rs. 2,500.00

(c) Municipalities/Corporations having a population of more than 1 lakh but less than 5 lakhs — Rs. 1,000.00

(d) Municipalities/Corporations having a population up to 1 lakh and any other local bodies such as Notified Area Authority — Rs. 250.00

4. *Memorandum of appeal.*—(1) An appeal shall be presented in person by the appellant or by his duly authorised agent to the appellate authority during office hours or may be sent by registered post addressed to the appellate authority within the period referred to in sub-section (1) of section 28.

(2) Every such appeal shall, —

(a) either be type-written or written in ink clearly in legible hand-writing;

(b) specify the name and address of the appellant;

(c) specify the date of the order against which it is made;

(d) specify the date on which the order was communicated to the appellant;

(e) contain a clear statement of facts;

(f) specify the grounds on which the appeal is preferred;

(g) state precisely the relief prayed for; and

(h) bear the signature of the appellant or his advocate.

(3) If an appeal is presented after the expiry of the prescribed period, it shall state the reasons for the delay, provided that where the appellant wants the delay to be condoned, he shall file separate application along with the form of appeal

for the purpose together with an affidavit explaining the circumstances relied upon, failing which the appeal shall be dismissed.

(4) Every appeal shall be accompanied by,—

(a) an authenticated copy of the order against which the appeal is preferred and four typed copies thereof with four copies of the memorandum of appeal;

(b) a copy of the application made under section 25 or section 26, as the case may be;

(c) any document relevant to the appeal; and

(d) a satisfactory proof of payment of the fee prescribed under rule 3.

(5) The memorandum of appeal shall be,—

(a) in Form I where the appeal relates to matters covered by section 25 or section 26.

(b) In Form II, where the appeal relates to matters covered by section 27.

5. *Registration of appeals.*—(1) On receipt of the memorandum of appeal the appellate authority shall endorse on it the date of its receipt and shall acknowledge its receipt.

(2) On receipt of the appeal the appellate authority shall examine and note whether the appeal is made within the prescribed period and conforms to the provisions of the Acts and these rules. If the appellate authority is satisfied that the appeal conforms to the provisions of the Act and these rules, it shall cause such appeal to be registered in the appropriate register. If it finds that it does not conform to any of the provisions of the Act and these rules, it may thereupon by a notice require the appellant to remedy the defects within a period of seven days from the date of notice:

Provided that the appellate authority may, for sufficient cause, extend the period for the purpose of remedying the defects.

(3) (a) If the defects are remedied within period allowed under sub-rule (2) the appellate authority shall cause the appeal to be registered in the appropriate register.

(b) If the defects are not remedied by the appellant or his authorised agent within the period allowed under sub-rule (2), the appellate authority shall pass orders rejecting the appeal.

6. *Hearing of appeal and power to call for record.*—(1) The appellate authority shall, as soon as may be after registration of the appeal, fix a date for hearing of the appeal and give intimation of the same to the appellant and the Member-Secretary in such manner as it deems fit. A copy of the Memorandum of appeal along with its enclosures shall also be sent to the Member-Secretary.

(2) The appellate authority shall have power to call for the record of the case from the Member-Secretary, if necessary.

(3) Where the material on record is insufficient to enable the appellate authority to have a definite conclusion, it may take additional evidence or call for such further material from the appellant or the Member-Secretary as it thinks fit. Such material shall form part of the record.

(4) Where, on the date fixed for hearing or any subsequent date to which the hearing may be adjourned, the appellant or his duly authorised agent does not appear in person, the appellate authority may either dismiss the appeal or may decide *ex parte*.

(5) Where an appeal is dismissed under sub-rule (4), the appellant may, within 15 days from the date of dismissal of the appeal, apply to the appellate authority for restoration of the appeal and if the appellant shows to the satisfaction of the appellate authority that the appellant had not received intimation of the date of hearing of the appeal or was prevented by any sufficient cause from appearing when the appeal was called for hearing, the appellate authority may restore the appeal on such terms as it thinks fit.

(6) When an appeal is taken for hearing, ordinarily the appellant or his advocate shall be heard first in support of his appeal. The respondent or his advocate shall, if necessary, be heard next and in such case the appellant or his advocate shall be entitled to reply.

7. *Adjournment*.—The appellate authority may, on such terms as it thinks fit and at any stage of the proceedings, adjourn the hearing of any appeal.

8. *Stay of execution orders*.—The appellate authority may, pending disposal of any appeal and at any stage of the proceedings, stay the execution of the order appealed against:

Provided that the appellate authority shall not stay the execution of the order appealed against without giving the Board a reasonable opportunity of being heard in the matter.

9. *Order to be writing*.—The order of the appellate authority on any appeal shall be in writing and shall state the points ~~for~~ determination, the decision thereon, and the reasons for the decision.

10. *Supply of copy of order*.—A copy of the order passed in an appeal shall be supplied free of cost to the appellant. A copy of the order shall also be sent to the Member-Secretary.

FORM I

[See rule 4(5)(a)]

Form of appeal under section 28 of the Water (Prevention and Control of Pollution) Act, 1974 (6 of 1974)

To

The Appellate Authority,

The appeal of .... resident of .... Ward No. .... Tahasil .... District .... sheweth as follows :

(1) Under section 25/26 of the Water (Prevention and Control of Pollution) Act, 1974 (6 of 1974), the appellant has been granted consent by the West Bengal Pollution Control Board subject to the conditions mentioned in the consent order in respect of the Plant/Corporation/Municipality/Notified Area Authority noted below :

(a) Name of Plant/Corporation/Municipality/Notified Area Authority—

(b) Place —

(c) Ward No. —

(d) Name of the Street —

(e) Urban Area —

(f) District —

A copy of the consent order in question is attached hereto.

(II) The grounds on which the appellant relies for the purpose of this appeal are as follows :

(III) The appellant, therefore, prays that :

*The unreasonable condition No./Nos. .... imposed should be treated as annulled of it/they should be substituted by such other condition/conditions as appear/appears to be reasonable.

*The unreasonable condition No./Nos. .... should be varied in the following manner.

*The order of refusal be set aside and the Board be directed to grant consent.

*Strike out which is not applicable.

Signature ....

Occupation ....

Address ....

....

Dated ....

FORM II

[See rule 4(5)(b)]

Form of appeal under section 28 of the Water (Prevention and Control of Pollution) Act, 1974 (6 of 1974)

To

The Appellate Authority,

The appeal of .... resident of .... Ward No. .... Tahasil .... District .... sheweth as follows:

(I) Under section 27 of the Water (Prevention and Control of Pollution) Act, 1974 (6 of 1974).

*The appellant has been refused consent.

*The consent has been withdrawn by the Board in respect of Plant/Corporation/Municipality/Notified Area Authority noted below :

(a) Name of Plant/Corporation/Municipality/Notified Area Authority—

(b) Place—

(c) Ward No.—

(d) Name of the Street—

(e) Urban Area—

(f) District—

*Condition No. .... has been unreasonably varied/revoked.

A copy of the order in question is attached herewith.

(II) The appellant being aggrieved by the aforesaid order prays that the said order be set aside on, amongst others, the following ground/grounds, namely:

*Strike out which is not applicable.

Signature ....

Occupation ....

Address ....

....

Dated ....

Form of Verification

I .... the appellant/authorised agent of the appellant named in the above memorandum of appeal do hereby declare that what is stated therein is true to the best of my knowledge and belief.

Signature ....

By order of the Governor

Dy. Secy. to the Govt. of West Bengal

Dated ....

APPENDIX IV

Government of India

MINISTRY OF LAW, JUSTICE AND COMPANY AFFAIRS

(Legislative Department)

New Delhi, the 7th December, 1977/Agrahayana 16, 1899 (Saka)

The following Act of Parliament received the assent of the President on the 7th December, 1977, and is hereby published for general information—

THE WATER (PREVENTION AND CONTROL OF POLLUTION) CESS ACT, 1977

No. 36 of 1977

[7th December, 1977]

An Act to provide for the levy and collection of a cess on water consumed by persons carrying on certain industries and by local authorities, with a view to augmenting the resources of the Central Board and the State Boards for the prevention and control of water pollution constituted under the Water (Prevention and Control of Pollution) Act, 1974.

Be it enacted by Parliament in the Twenty-eighth year of the Republic of India as follows:—

1. (1) This Act may be called the Water (Prevention and Control of Pollution) Cess Act, 1977.

(2) It extends to the whole of India except the State of Jammu and Kashmir.

(3) Subject to the provisions of the sub-section (2), it applies to all the States to which the Water (Prevention and Control of Pollution) Act, 1974 applies and the Union Territories.

(4) It shall come into force on such date as the Central Government may, by notification in the Official Gazette, appoint.

2. In this Act, unless the context otherwise requires,—

(a) "local authority" means a municipal corporation or a municipal council (by whatever name called) or a cantonment board or any other body, entrusted with the duty of supplying water under the law by or under which it is constituted;

(b) "prescribed" means prescribed by rules made under this Act;

(c) "specified industry" means any industry specified in Schedule I;

(d) words and expressions used but not defined in this Act and defined in the Water (Prevention and Control of Pollution) Act, 1974, shall have the meanings respectively assigned to them in that Act.

3. (1) There shall be levied and collected a cess for the purposes of the Water (Prevention and Control of Pollution) Act, 1974, and utilisation thereunder.

(2) The cess under sub-section (1) shall be payable by —

(a) every person carrying on any specified industry; and

(b) every local authority;

and shall be calculated on the basis of the water consumed by such person or local authority, as the case may be, for any of the purposes specified in column, (1) of Schedule II, at such rate, not exceeding the rate specified in the corresponding entry in column, (2) thereof, as the Central Government may, by notification in the Official Gazette from time to time specify.

(3) Where any local authority supplies water to any person carrying on any specified industry or to any other local authority and such person on other local authority is liable to pay cess under sub-section (2) in respect of the water so supplied, then, notwithstanding anything contained in that sub-section, the local authority first mentioned shall not be liable to pay such cess in respect of such water.

Explanation.— For the purposes of this Section and section 4, consumption of water includes supply of water.

4. (1) For the purpose of measuring and recording the quantity of water consumed, every person carrying on any specified industry and every local authority shall affix meters of such standards and at such places as may be prescribed and it shall be presumed that the quantity indicated by the meter has been consumed by such person or local authority, as the case may be, until the contrary is proved.

(2) Where any person or local authority fails to affix any meter as required by sub-section (1), the Central Government shall, after notice to such person or local authority, as the case may be, cause such meter to affixed and the cost of such meter together with the cost for affixing the meter may be recovered from, such

person or local authority by the Central Government in the same manner as an arrear of land revenue.

5. Every person carrying on any specified industry and every local authority, liable to pay the cess under section 3, shall furnish such returns, in such form, at such intervals and containing such particulars to such officer or authority, as may be prescribed.

6. (1) The officer or authority to whom or which the return has been furnished under section 5 shall, after making or causing to be made such inquiry as he or it thinks fit and after statisfying himself or itself that the particulars stated in the return are correct, by order, assess the amount of cess payable by the concerned person carrying on any specified industry or local authority, as the case may be.

(2) An order or assessment made under sub-section (1) shall specify the date within which the cess shall be paid to the State Government.

(3) A copy each of the order of assessment made under sub-section (1) shall be sent to the person or, as the case may be, to the local authority concerned and to the State Government.

(4) The State Government shall, through such of its officers or authorities as may be specified by it in this behalf by notification in the Official Gazette collect the cess from the person or local authority liable to pay the same and pay the amount so collected to the Central Government in such manner and within such time as may be prescribed.

7. Where any person, or local authority, liable to pay the cess under this Act, instals any plant for the treatment of sewage or trade effluent, such person or local authority shall, from such date as may be prescribed, be entitled to a rebate of seventy per cent of the cess payable by such person or, as the case may be, local authority.

8. The proceeds of the cess levied under section 3 shall first be credited to the Consolidated Fund of India and the Central Government may, if Parliament, by appropriation made by law in this behalf, so provides, pay to the Central Board and every State Board, from time to time, from out of such proceeds, after deducting the expenses on collection, such sums of money as it may think fit for being utilised under the Water (Prevention and Control of Pollution) Act, 1974:

Provided that while determining the sum of money to be paid to any State Board under this section, the Central Government shall have regard to the amount of cess collected by the State Government concerned under sub-section (4) of section 6.

Explanation.— For the purposes of this section "State Board" includes a Joint Board, if any, constituted under section 13 of the Water (Prevention and Control of Pollution) Act, 1974.

9. Any office or authority of the State Government specially empowered in this behalf by that Government may,—

(a) with such assistance, if any, as he or it may think fit, enter at any reasonable time any place which he or it considers it necessary to enter for carrying out the purposes of this Act including the testing of the correctness of the meters affixed section 4:

(b) do within such place anything necessary for the proper discharge of his or its duties under this Act; and

(c) exercise such other powers as may be prescribed.

10. If any person carrying on any specified industry or any local authority fails to pay any amount of cess payable under section 3 to the State Government within the date specified in the order of assessment made under section 6, such person or local authority, as the case may be shall be liable to pay interest at twelve per cent annum on the amount to be paid from the date on which such payment is due till such amount is actually paid.

11. If any amount of cess payable by any person carrying on any specified industry or any local authority under section 3 is not paid to the State Government within the date specified in the order of assessment may under section 6, it shall be deemed to be in arrears and the authority prescribed in this behalf may, after such inquiry as it deems fit, impose on such person or, as the case may be, local authority, a penalty not exceeding the amount of cess in arrears :

Provided that before imposing any such penalty, such person or, as the case may be the local authority shall be given a reasonable opportunity of being heard and if after such hearing the said authority is satisfied that the default was for any good and sufficient reason, no penalty shall be imposed under this section.

12. Any amount due under this Act (including any interest or penalty payable under section 10 or section 11, as the case may be) from any person carrying on any specified industry or from any local authority may be recovered by the Central Government in the same manner as an arrear of land revenue.

13. (1) Any person or local authority aggrieved by an order of assessment made, under section 6 or by an order imposing penalty made under section 11 may within such time as may be prescribed, appeal to such authority in such form and in such manner as may be prescribed.

(2) Every appeal preferred under sub-section (1) shall be accompanied by such fee may be prescribed.

(3) After the receipt of an appeal under sub-section (1), the appellate authority shall, after giving the appellant an opportunity of being heard in the matter, dispose of the appeal as expeditiously as possible.

(4) Every order passed in appeal under this section shall be final and shall not be called in question in any court of law.

14. (1) Whoever, being under an obligation to furnish a return under this Act, furnishes any return knowing, or having reason to believe, the same to be false shall be punishable with imprisonment which may extend to six months or with fine which may extend to one thousand rupees or with both.

(2) Whoever, being liable to pay cess under this Act, wilfully or intentionally evades or attempts to evade the payment of such cess shall be punishable with imprisonment which may extend to six months or with fine which may extend to one thousand rupees or with both.

(3) No Court shall take cognizance of an offence punishable under this section save on a complaint made by or under the authority of the Central Government.

15. (1) Where an offence under this Act has been committed by a company, every person who, at the time the offence was committed, was in charge of, and was responsible to, the company for the conduct of the business of the company, as well as the company, shall be deemed to be guilty of the offence and shall be liable to be proceeded against and punished accordingly.

Provided that nothing contained in this sub-section shall render any such person liable to any punishment, if he proves that the offence was committed without his knowledge or that he exercised all due diligence to prevent the commission of such offence.

(2) Notwithstanding anything contained in sub-section (1), where an offence under this Act has been committed by a company and it is proved that the offence has been committed by a company with the consent or connivance of, or is attributable to any neglect on the part of, any director, manager, secretary or other officer of the company, such director, manager, secretary or other officer shall also be deemed to be guilty of that offence and shall be liable to be proceeded against and punished accordingly.

Explanation. — For the purposes of this section,—

(a) "company" means any body corporate and includes a firm or other association of individuals; and

(b) "director", in relation to a firm, means a partner in the firm.

16. (1) The Central Government may, by notification in the Official Gazette, add to Schedule I any industry having regard to the consumption of water in the carrying on of such industry and the consequent discharge thereof resulting in pollution of any stream and thereupon Schedule I shall, subject to the provisions of sub-section (2) be deemed to be amended accordingly.

(2) Every such notification shall be laid before each House of Parliament, if it is sitting, as soon as may be after the issue of the notification, and if it is not sitting, within seven days of its re-assembly and the Central Government shall

seek the approval of Parliament to the notification by a resolution moved within a period of fifteen days beginning with the day on which the notification is so laid before the House of the People, and if Parliament makes any modification in the notification or directs that the notification should cease to have effect, the notification shall thereafter have effect only in such modified form or to be of no effect, as the case may be, but without prejudice to the validity of anything previously done thereunder.

17. (1) The Central Government may make rules for carrying out the purposes of this Act.

(2) Without prejudice to the generality of the foregoing power, such rules may provide for all or any of the following matters, namely:—

(a) the standards of the meters to be affixed and the places at which such meters are to be affixed under sub-section (1) of section 4;

(b) the returns to be furnished under section 5, the form in which and the intervals at which such returns are to be furnished, the particulars which such returns shall contain and the officer or authority to whom or which such returns shall be furnished;

(c) the manner in which and the time within which the cess collected shall be paid to the Central Government under sub-section (4) of section 6;

(d) the date from which any person or local authority liable to pay cess shall be entitled to the rebate under section 7;

(e) the powers which may be exercised by the officer or authority under section 9;

(f) the authority which may impose penalty under section 11;

(g) the authority to which an appeal may be filed under sub-section (1) of section 13 and the time within which and the form and manner in which such appeal may be filed.

(h) the fees which shall accompany an appeal under sub-section (2) of section 13; and

(i) any other matter which has or may be prescribed.

(3) Every rule made under this Act shall be laid, as soon as may be after it is made, before each House of Parliament while it is in session for a total period of thirty days which may be comprised in one session or in two or more successive sessions and if, before the expiry of the session immediately following the session or the successive sessions aforesaid, both Houses agree in making any modification in the rule or both Houses agree that the rule should not be made, the rule shall thereafter have effect only in such modified form or be of no effect, as the case may be; so however, that any such modification or annulment shall be without prejudice to the validity of anything previously done under that rule.

SCHEDULE I

[See section 2(c)]

1. Ferrous metallurgical industry.
2. Non-Ferrous metallurgical industry.
3. Mining industry.
4. Ore processing industry.
5. Petroleum industry.
6. Petro-chemical industry.
7. Chemical industry.
8. Ceramic industry.
9. Cement industry.
10. Textile industry.
11. Paper industry.
12. Fertilizer industry.
13. Coal (including coke) industry.
14. Power (thermal and diesel) generating industry.
15. Processing of animal or vegetable products industry.

SCHEDULE II

(See section 3)

Purpose for which water is consumed	maximum rate
(1)	(2)
1. Industrial cooling, spraying in mine pits or boiler feed.	Three-fourths of a paisa, per kilo litre.
2. Domestic purpose.	One paisa, per kilo litre.
3. Processing whereby water gets polluted and the pollutants are easily bio-degradable.	Two paise, per kilo litre.
4. Processing whereby water gets polluted and the pollutants are not easily bio-degradable and are toxic.	Two and a half paise, per kilo litre.

Government of India

EXTRAORDINARY

Part II — Section 3 — Sub-section (i)

PUBLISHED BY AUTHORITY

No. 93] NEW DELHI, MONDAY, MARCH 27, 1978,

CHAITRA 6, 1900

MINISTRY OF WORKS AND HOUSING

NOTIFICATIONS

New Delhi, the 23rd March, 1978

G.S.R. 190(E).— In exercise of the powers conferred by sub-section (2) of 3 of the Water (Prevention and Control of Pollution) Cess Act, 1977 (36 of 1977), the Central Government hereby specifies that the rates of cess payable on the water consumed by—

(a) any person carrying so any industry specified in Schedule I to the said Act; or

(b) any local authority;

for the purposes specified in column (1) of the Table appended hereto shall be the rates specified in column (2) thereof.

Table

Purpose for which water is consumed	Rates of cess
1. Industrial cooling, spraying in mine pits of boiler feed.	Three-fourths of a paisa per kilo litre.
2. Domestic purpose.	One paisa per kilo litre.
3. Processing whereby water gets polluted and the pollutants are easily bio-degradable.	Two paisa per kilo litre
4. Processing whereby water gets polluted the pollutants are not easily bio-degradable and are toxic.	Two and a half paise, per kilo litre.

EXTRAORDINARY

Part II — Section 3 — Sub-section (i)

PUBLISHED BY AUTHORITY

No. 92] NEW DELHI, MONDAY, MARCH 27, 1978,

CHAITRA 6, 1900

MINISTRY OF WORKS AND HOUSING

NOTIFICATION

New Delhi, the 23rd March, 1978

G.S.R. 199(E) — In exercise of the powers conferred by sub-section (4) of section 1 of the Water (Prevention and Control of Pollution) Cess Act, 1977 (36 of 1977), the Central Government hereby appoints the 1st day of April, 1978, as the day on which the said Act shall come into force.

[No. Q-17013/2/78-EPCI]

MIR NASRULLAH

Jt. Secy. to the Govt. of India.

APPENDIX V

Government of India

EXTRAORDINARY

Part II — Section 3 — Sub-section (i)

PUBLISHED BY AUTHORITY

No. 215 NEW DELHI, MONDAY, JULY 24, 1978,

SRAVANA 2, 1900

MINISTRY OF WORKS AND HOUSING

NOTIFICATION

New Delhi, the 24th July, 1978

G.S.R. 378(E).— In exercise of the powers conferred by section 17 of the Water (Prevention and Control of Pollution) Cess Act, 1977 (36 of 1977), the Central Government hereby makes the following rules, namely:—

1. Short title and commencement — (a) These rules may be called the Water (Prevention and Control of Pollution) Cess Rules, 1978;

(b) They shall come into force on the date of their publication in the official Gazette.

2. *Definitions* — In these rules, unless the context otherwise requires:—

(a) "Act" means the Water (Prevention and Control of Pollution) Cess Act, 1977 (36 of 1977);

(b) "assessing authority" means—

(i) in relation to Union Territory, the Member-Secretary of the Central Board; and

(ii) in relation to a State, the Member-Secretary of the State Board;

(c) "consumer" means a person or local authority by whom the cess under sub-section (1) of section 3 is payable under sub-section (2) of that section;

(d) "form" means a form annexed to these rules;

(e) "section" means a section of the Act.

(f) "State Government" in relation to a Union Territory means the Administrator thereof appointed under article 239 of the Constitution.

3. *Standards of meters and places where they are to be affixed*— (1) For the purposes of measuring and recording the quantity of water consumed, every consumer shall affix water meters, venturi meters or orifice meters with integrators and recorders in conformity with the standards laid down by the Indian Standards Institution and where no standards have been laid down by that institution in conformity with such standards as may be specified by the Board.

(2) Wherever the meters referred to in sub-section (1) are not available, the consumer shall instal vee notches or rectangular notches, with indicators and recorders or pressure gauges and pumping installations after obtaining the permission of the assessing authority.

(3) Every consumer shall provide a separate meter of assessing the quantity of water used for each of the four purposes mentioned in column (1) of Schedule II to the Act.

(4) The meters shall be affixed at the entrance of the Water supply connections within the premises of the consumer of at any other place to be approved by the assessing authority, so that such meters are easily accessible for inspection and maintenance and for other purposes of the Act;

Provided that the place where is affixed shall, in no case be at a point before which water has been tapped by the consumer for utilisation for any purposes whosoever.

4. *Furnishing of returns* — Every consumer shall furnish on or before the 5th of every calendar month, to the assessing authority, a return in Form I showing the quantity of water consumed in the previous month.

5. Manner of payment of the cess of the Central Government and the time within which it shall be paid.

(1) Every State Government shall remit to the Central Government, the amount of cess collected from the consumer before the 10th day of the calendar month succeeding the month in which it is collected from the consumer.

(2) The amount of cess referred to in sub-rule (I) shall be remitted to the Central Government in the form of a bank draft drawn in favour of the pay and Accounts Officer, Ministry of Works and Housing, New Delhi in whose books of accounts, the receipts would be adjusted finally.

(3) On receiving the bank draft, the Ministry of Works and Housing shall remit the same through a Challan into the Reserve Bank of India, New Delhi, for the purpose of crediting under relevant Major Head.

6. *Rebate*—Where a consumer instals any plant for the treatment of sewage or trade effluent, such consumer shall be entitled to the rebate under section 7 on and from the expiry of fifteen days from the date on which such plant is successfully commissioned and so long as it functions successfully.

7. Powers to be exercised by the Officer or the Authority of the State Government under section 9.

The officer or authority of the State Government specially empowered under section 9 shall have, in addition to the powers referred to in clauses (a) and (b) of that section, the power to—

(i) inspect the manufacturing process or plant of the consumer.

(ii) inspect the water supply systems and installations in the plant of the consumer;

(iii) inspect waste treatment system and installations in the plant of the consumer;

(iv) inspect the drainage system and installations, including storm water disposal in the plant of the consumer.

(v) call for and inspect records relating to the use and consumption of materials and water, and those relating to production, in the plant of the consumer;

(vi) call for and inspect the records relating to power consumption in the plant of the consumer; and

(vii) call for any other information or records relating to the supply, consumption and treatment of water in the plant of the consumer.

8. *Authority to impose penalty under section 11*—The authority to impose penalty under section 11 shall be the assessing authority.

9. *Appeal*—(1) Any Consumer aggrieved by an order of assessment made under section 6 or order imposing penalty made under section 11 may appeal in Form II annexed hereto, to a Committee (hereinafter referred to as the appellate committee) consisting of—

(a) where the assessing authority is the member-secretary of the Central Board, the Chairman of the Board, who shall be the Chairman of the Committee, and two members of that Board, to be nominated by the Chairman thereof;

(b) where the assessing authority is the member-secretary of the State Board, the Chairman of that Board, who shall be the Chairman of the Committee, and two members of that Board, to be nominated by the Chairman thereof;

(2) Such appeal shall state the facts of the case and the ground relied upon by the appellant for preferring the appeal and shall be accompanied by a copy of the order of assessment made under section 6 or a copy of the order imposing penalty made under section 11 as the case may be.

(3) Such appeal shall be preferred within a period of thirty days from the date of communications of the order of assessment or the order imposing penalty of the appellant:

Provided that if the Chairman of the appellate Committee is satisfied that there was good and sufficient reason for the delay in preferring the appeal, he may, for reason to the record in writing, allow the appeal to be preferred after the expiry of the aforesaid period of thirty days and before the expiry of forty-five days from the date of communication of the order of assessment, or the order imposing penalty, on the appellant.

(4) Every appeal shall be accompanied by a fee of rupees fifty.

FORM I

(See rule 4)

Return regarding Water consumed during the month of..

Name and Address of the consumer	Purpose of which water consumed	Reading at the beginning of the first day of the calendar month under report	Reading at the end of the last day of calendar month under report	Qty. of water consumed in Kilo litres	If the meter was out of order the monthly average consumption of water for the previous 3 months of the working period	Qty. of water qualifying for rebate according to the assessee	Remarks (*)
1	2	3	4	5	6	7	8
	1. Industrial cooling spraying in mine pits or boiler feed.	(i) from Municipal water supply mains					
		(ii) from well/tube well					
		(iii) from canal					
		(iv) from river					
		(v) from any other source					
	2. Domestic purpose	(i) from Municipal water supply mains					
		(ii) from well/tubewell					
		(iii) from canal					
		(iv) from river					
		(v) from any other source					

FORM I

(See rule 4)

Name and Address of the consumer	Purpose of which water consumed	Reading at the beginning of the first day of the calendar month under report	Reading at the end of the last day of calendar month under report	Qty. of water consumed in Kilo litres	If the meter was out of order the monthly average consumption of water for the previous 3 months of the working period	Qty. of water qualifying for rebate according to the assessee	Remarks (*)
1	2	3	4	5	6	7	8
	3. Processing whereby water gets polluted and the pollutants are easily bio-degradable	(i) from Municipal water supply mains (iii) from well/tube well (iii) from canal (iv) from river (v) from any other source					
	4. Processing whereby water gets polluted and the pollutants are easily bio-degradable and are Toxic	(i) from Municipal water supply mains (ii) from well/tube well (iii) from canal (iv) from river (v) from any other source					

(*) for claiming rebate under col. 7 the assessee shall indicate in this column the analytical and other reports annexed to this return in support of this claim.

Signature of the consumer
Name
Address

ANNEXURE TO FORM I

Report of Analysis of treated effluent showing performance of the treatment plant— For the month of..............................

Sample collected on ....

Sample tested on ....

By the laboratories..............................

Sl. No.	Polluting parameters as mentioned in the conditions imposed under consent granted under section 25/26 of the Water (Prevention and Control of Pollution), Act, 1974	Maximum permissible limits or ranges allowed as per consent condition	Concentration of range of parameters as per report	Dates on which	
				There was breaknown or failure of the plant	On which under-performance noticed
1	2	3	4	5	6

Encl: Original Analysis report of Laboratory.

Signature..............................

Date..............................

Name..............................

Address..............................

FROM II

(See rule 9)

(Form of Memorandum of Appeal)

Before...............(**).................

** here mention the name and designation of the authority.

Memorandum of appeal under section 13 of the Water (Prevention and Control of Pollution) Cess Act, 1977.

Appeal No............................ of 19.

....

....

....

(here furnish complete postal address)

....Appellant

Vs.

....

....

....

(here mention the name and designation of assessing authority.)

..................................Respondent

The appellant named above, begs to prefer this memorandum of appeal against the order dated .... passed by .... on the following facts and rounds.:

Facts

(here briefly mention the facts of the case)

Grounds

(here mention the grounds on which the appeal is made)

1.

2.

3.

4.

(**) here mention the name and designation of the authority.

Prayer

In the light of what is stated above, the appellant respectfully prays that he/she/it may be exempted from the payment of cess.

He/she/it may be allowed a rebate of 70 per cent as provided for in the Act and the amount of Cess reduced to Rs.......

The amount of Cess has not been correctly assessed and that it may be reduced to Rs..........

The penalty imposed on him/her/it has been wrongfully imposed and should be set aside.

The penalty imposed on him/her/it is excessive and should be suitably reduced on the basis of the facts as stated.

2. The amount of Rs................... (Rupees......................) as fee for this appeal has been paid to .... vide Receipt

No..............................dated...................

Signature of the Appellant

Place: Name

Date: Address

MINISTRY OF WORKS AND HOUSING
CORRIGENDA

New Delhi, the 4th August, 1978

G.S.R. 394(E) — In the notification of the Government of India in the Ministry of Works and Housing G.S.R. 378 (E), dated the 24th July, 1978, published at pages 653-655 in Part II, Section 3, Sub-section (i) of the Gazette of India Extraordinary, dated the 24th July, 1978—

1. at page 653—

   (a) in clause (b) (i) of rule 2 for "in relation to Union Territory". read "in relation to a Union Territory".

   (b) in sub-rule (2) of rule 3, for "assessing" read "assessing";

   (c) in provision to sub-rule (4) of rule 3, for "where is" read "where the meter is", and

   (d) in sub-rule (1) of rule 5, for "calendar" read "calendar".

2. at page 654—

   (a) in sub-rule (2) of rule 9, for "ground" read "grounds".

   (b) in sub-rule (3) of rule 9, for "communications" read "communication".

   (c) in sub-rule (4) of rule 9, for "accompanied" read "accompanied";

   (d) in Form I in heading to column 2, for "of" read "for".

3. at page 655—

(a) in Annexure to Form I, in handing to column 4, for "of" read "or"

(b) in Form II under the heading Grounds, the brackets and words "(**) here mention the name and designation of the authority" shall be omitted.

APPENDIX VI

THE FOREST (CONSERVATION) ACT, 1980

No. 69 of 1980

(27th December, 1980)

An Act to provide for the conservation of forest and for matters connected therewith or ancillary or incidental thereto

MINISTRY OF LAW, JUSTICE AND COMPANY AFFAIRS

(Legislative Department)

New Delhi, the 27th December, 1980 Pause 6, 1902 (Sake)

The following Act, of Parliament received the assent of the President on the 27th December, 1980, and is hereby published for general information:

Short title, extend and commencement:

Be it enacted by Parliament in the Thirty-first Year of the Republic of India as follows:

1. (i) This Act may be called the Forest (Conservation) Act, 1980.

(ii) It extends to the whole of India except the State of Jammu and Kashmir.

(iii) It shall be deemed to have come into force on the 25th day of October, 1980.

Restriction on the dereservation of forests or use of forest land for non-forest purpose

2. Notwithstanding anything contained in any other law for the time being in force in a State, no State Government or other authority shall make, except with the prior approval of the Central Government, any order directing —

(i) that any reserved forest (within the meaning of the expression "reserved forest" in any law for the time being in force in that State) or any portion thereof, shall cease to be reserved;

(ii) that any forest land or any portion thereof may be used for any non-forest purpose.

Explanation—For the purposes of this section non-forest means breaking up or clearing of any forest land or portion thereto for any purpose other than reafforestation.

Constitution of Advisory Committee

3. The Central Government may constitute a Committee consisting of such number of persons as it may deem fit to advise that Government with regard to —

(i) the grant of approval under section 2; and

(ii) any other matter connected with the conservation of forests purposes which may be referred to it by the Central Government.

4. (1) The Central Government may, by notification in the Official Gazette, make rules for carrying out the provisions of this Act.

(2) Every rule made under this Act, shall be laid, as soon as may be after it is made before each House of Parliament, while it is in session for a total period of thirty days which may be comprised in one session or in two or more successive sessions, and if, before the expiry of the session immediately following the section or the successive sessions aforesaid, both Houses agree in making any modification in the rule or both Houses agree that the rule should not be made, the rule shall thereafter have effect only in such modified form or be of no effect, as the case may be; so, however, that any such modification or annulment shall be without prejudice to the validity of anything previously done under that rule.

Repeal and saving — 17 of 1880

5. (1) The Forest (Conservation) Ordinance, 1980 is hereby repealed.

(2) Notwithstanding such repeal, anything done or any action taken under the provisions of the said Ordinance shall be deemed to have been done or taken under the corresponding provisions of this Act.

R.V.S. Peri Sastri

Secretary to the Govt. of India

APPENDIX VII

THE FOREST CONSERVATION RULES, 1981
GOVERNMENT OF INDIA

MINISTRY OF AGRICULTURE

(Department of Agriculture & Co-operation)

New Delhi, the 1st August, 1981

NOTIFICATION

G.S.R.819........ In exercise of the powers conferred by subsection (i) of section 4 of the Forest (Conservation) Act, 1980 (69 of 1980), the Central Government hereby makes the following rules, namely:

1. Short title, extent and commencement:

(1) These rules may called the *Forest (Conservation) Rules, 1981*.

(2) They shall extend to the whole of India except the State of Jammu and Kashmir.

(3) They shall come into force on the date of their publication in the Official Gazette.

2. Definitions:

In these rules, unless the context otherwise requires:

(a) "Act" means the Forest (Conservation) Act, 1980 (69 of 1980);

(b) "Committee" means the Committee constituted under section 3;

(c) "Chairman" means the Chairman of the Committee;

(d) "Member" means a member of the Committee;

(e) "Section" means a section of the Act.

3. Conduct of business of the Committee:

The Chairman shall call the meetings of the Committee as often as necessary.

(2) The meetings of the Committee shall, unless the Chairman in any case, otherwise directs, be held in Delhi.

(3) The Chairman shall preside over every meeting of the Committee at which he is present:

Provided that if the Chairman is absent from a meeting and it is not expedient to adjourn the meeting, the seniormost member of the Committee shall preside over the meeting.

(4) Every question upon which the Committee is required to advise shall be considered either at its meetings or, if the Chairman so directs, by sending necessary papers to members for their opinion.

4. Procedure to make proposal by a State Government or other authority.

(1) Every State Government or other authority which seeks prior approval of the Central Government under section 2 shall send its proposal to that Government along with the particulars specified in the Annexure to these rules.

(2) Every proposal referred to in sub-rule (1) shall be sent to the following address, namely, 'Secretary to the Government of India' Department of Agriculture and Cooperation, Krishi Bhavan, New Delhi.'

5. Committee to advise on proposals received by the Central Government:

(1) The Central Government may refer any proposal received by it under sub-rule (1) of rule 4 to the Committee for its advice thereon.

(2) The committee shall have due regard to all or any of the following matters while tendering its advice on the proposals referred to it under sub-rule (1), namely:

(a) Whether the forest land proposed to be used for non-forest purpose forms part of a nature reserve, national park, wildlife sanctuary, biosphere reserve or forms part of the habitat of any endangered or threatened species of flora and fauna or of an area lying in severly eroded catchment.

(b) Whether the use of any forest land is for agricultural purposes or for the rehabilitation of persons displaced from their residences by reason of any river valley of hyrdo-electric project.

(c) Whether the State Government or the other authority has certified that it has considered all other alternatives in the circumstances are feasible and that the required area is the minimum needed for the purposes; and

(d) Whether the State Government or the other authority undertakes to provide at its cost for the acquisition of land of an equivalent area and afforestation thereof.

(3) While tendering the advice, the Committee may also suggest any conditions or restrictions on the use of any forest land for any non-forest purpose which, in its opinion, would minimise adverse environmental impact.

6. Action of the Central Government on the advice of the Committee: -

The Central Government shall, after considering the advice of the Committee tendered under rule 5 and after such further as it may consider necessary, grant approval to the proposal with or without conditions or reject the same.

ANNEXURE III

(See Rule -4)

Submission of proposals by the State Governments and othe authorities regarding dereservation of reserved forests or use of forest land for non-forest purpose.

1. Short narrative of the proposal and project/scheme for which the forest land is required with maps and sketches.

2. Location of the project/scheme

(i) State/Union Territory

(ii) District

(iii) Forest Division, Forest Block, Compartment, etc.

3. Total land required for the project/scheme along with its existing land use.

4. Details for forest land involved

(i) Legal status of forest (namely reserved, unclassed, etc.);

(ii) the details of flora existing in the area including the density of vegetation;

(iii) topography of the area indicating gradient, aspect, altitude, etc.;

(iv) its vulnerability to erosion, whether it forms a part of a seriously eroded reserve area or not;

(v) whether it forms a part of national park, wildlife sanctuary, nature reserve, biosphere reserve etc., if so, details of the area involved

(vi) rare/endangered species of flora and fauna in the area;

(vii) whether it is habitat for migrating fauna or forms a breeding ground for them; and

(viii) any other feature of the area relevant to the proposal.

5. If the project for which forest land is required involves displacement of people or requires raw material from any forest area, the details of proposals for their rehabilitation and procurement of raw material, respectively should be furnished.

6. Proposed steps to be taken to compensate for the loss of the forest area, the vegetation and wildlife.

7. Detailed opinion of the Chief Conservator of Forests/Head of the Forest Department concerned covering the following aspects, namely:

(i) out-turn to timber, fuel-wood and other forest produce from the forest land involved;

(ii) whether the district is self-sufficient in timber and fuel-wood; and

(iii) the effect of the proposal on

(a) Fuel-wood supply to rural population,

(b) economy and livelihood of the tribals and backward communities;

(iv) specific recommendations of the Chief Conservator of Forests/Head of the Forests Department for acceptance or otherwise of the proposal with reasons thereof.

Certified that all other alternatives for the purposes have been explored and the demand for the required area is the minimum demand for forest land.

Signature of the authorised officers of the
State Govt. Authority

Note: While furnishing details of flora and fauna, the species should be described by their scientific names.

ANNEXURE IV

Guidelines for laying Transmission Lines through Forest Areas—Forest (Conservation) Act, 1980

1. Where routing of transmission lines through the forest area cannot be avoided, these should be aligned in such a way that it involves the least amount of tree cutting.

2. As far as possible, the route alignment through forest areas should not have any line deviation.

3. (i) The maximum width of right of way for the transmission lines on forest lands shall be as follows:

Transmission voltage (KV)	Width of right-of-way (M)
11	7
33	15
66	18
110	22
132	27
220	35
400	52

(ii) Below each conductor, width clearance of 3 mtrs. would be permitted for taking the tension stringing equipment. The trees on such strips would have to be felled but after the stringing work is completed, dwarf trees would be planted keeping in view the electrical clearances to be maintained, except in one outer-strip which shall be left clear to permit maintenance of the transmission line.

(iii) For any repair and maintenance work of the transmission line, the Power Authorities may be allowed to fell minimum number of trees for repairs below other conductors, where dwarf trees have been planted in consultation with the local forest officer.

(iv) In the remaining width within the right-of-way up to a maximum of 52 mtrs. (for 400 KV lines) trees will not be felled but to prevent electrical hazards they be loped to the extent required, to maintain the following minimum clearance from the conductor:

Voltage (KV)	Minimum clearance between conductors and Spps of trees (mtrs.)
11	2.6
33	2.8
66	3.4
110	3.7
132	4.0
220	4.6
400	5.5

(v) In the case of transmission lines to be constructed in hilly areas, where adequate clearance is already available, trees will not be cut.

4. The Forest Department shall plant dwarf trees up to ten times the number of trees removed from the right-of-way at the cost of the State Electricity Board, Electricity Department, etc.

5. Where the forest growth consists of coconut groves or similar tall trees, widths of right-of-way greater than those indicated at S. No. 3, may be permitted in consultation with the CEA.

APPENDIX VIII

THE AIR (PREVENTION AND CONTROL OF POLLUTION) ACT, 1981

(14 OF 1981)

(As modified upto 1st June, 1990)

The Act has been amended by the Air (Prevention and Control of Pollution) Amendment Act, 1987 (47 of 1987).

LIST OF ABBREVIATIONS USED

Cl.	for	Clause.
Ins.	"	Inserted.
Rep.	"	Repealed.
S.	"	Section.
Subs.	"	Substituted.
W.e.f.	"	With effect from.

THE AIR (PREVENTION AND CONTROL OF POLLUTION) ACT, 1981

ARRANGEMENT OF SECTIONS

CHAPTER I

PRELIMINARY

SECTIONS

CHAPTER II

CENTRAL AND STATE BOARDS FOR THE PREVENTION AND CONTROL OF AIR POLLUTION

CHAPTER III

POWERS AND FUNCTIONS OF BOARDS

CHAPTER IV

PREVENTION AND CONTROL OF AIR POLLUTION

22. Persons carrying on industry etc., and to allow emission of air pollutants in excess of the standards laid down by State Board.

22A. Power of Board to make application to court for restraining persons from causing air pollution.

23. Furnishing of information to State Board and other agencies in certain cases.

24. Power of entry and inspection.

25. Power to obtain information.

26. Power to take samples of air or emission and procedure to be followed in connection therewith.

27. Reports of the result of analysis on samples taken under section 26.

28. State Air Laboratory.

29. Analysts.

30. Reports of analysts.

31. Appeals.

31A. Power to give directions.

CHAPTER V

FUND, ACCOUNTS AND AUDIT

32. Contributions by Central Government.

33. Fund of Board.

33A. Borrowing powers of Board.

34. Budget.

35. Annual Report.

36. Accounts and audit.

CHAPTER VI

PENALTIES AND PROCEDURE

37. Failure to comply with the provisions of section 21 or section 22 or with the directions issued under section 31 A.

38. Penalties for certain acts.

39. Penalty for contravention of certain provisions of the Act.

40. Offences by companies

THE AIR (PREVENTION AND CONTROL OF POLLUTION) ACT, 1981

No. 14 of 1981

[29th *March,* 1981.]

An Act to provide for the prevention, control and abatement of air pollution for the establishment, with a view to carrying out the aforesaid purposes, of Boards, for conferring on and assigning to such Boards, powers and functions relating thereto and for matters connected therewith.

Whereas decisions were taken at the United Nations Conference on the Human Environment held in Stockholm, in June, 1992, in which India participated, to take appropriate steps for the preservation of the natural resources of the earth which among, other things, include the preservation of the quality of air and control of air pollution;

And whereas it is considered necessary to implement the decisions aforesaid in so far as they relate to the preservation of the quality of air and control of air pollution;

Be it enacted by Parliament in the Thirty-Second Year of the Republic of India as follows :—

CHAPTER I
PRELIMINARY

Short title, extent and commencement.

1. (1) This Act may be called the Air (Prevention and Control of Pollution) Act. 1981.

(2) It extends to the whole of India.

(3) It shall come into force on such date[1] as the Central Government may, by notification in the Official Gazette, appoint.

Definitions.

2. In this Act, unless the context otherwise requires. —

(a) "air pollutant" means any solid, liquid or gaseous substance[2] [(including noise)] present in the atmosphere in such concentration as may be or tend to be injurious to human beings or other living creatures or plants or property or environment:

(b) "air pollution" means the presence in the atmosphere of any air pollutant;

(c) "approved appliance" means any equipment or gadget used for the burning of any combustible meterial or for generating or consuming any fume, gas or particulate matter and approved by the State Board for the purposes of this Act;

(d) "approved fuel" means any fuel approved by the State Board for the purposes of this Act;

(e) "automobile" means any vehicle powered either by internal combustion engine or by any method of generating power to drive such vehicle by burning fuel;

(f) "Board" means the Central Board or a State Board;

1. 16-5-1981: Vide notification No. G.S.R. 351 (E), dated 15.5.1981, Gazette of India, Extraordinary Part II, Section 3(i), page 944.
2. Ins. by Act 47 of 1987, s. 2, (w.e.f. 1.4.1988).

(g) "Central Board" means the [3][Central Board for the Prevention and Control of Water Pollution] constituted under section 3 of the Water (Prevention and Control of Pollution) Act, 1974.

(h) "chimney" includes any structure with an opening or outlet from or through which may air pollutant may be emitted;

(i) "Control equipment" means any apparatus device, equipment or system to control the quality and manner of emission of any air pollutant and includes any device used for securing the efficient operation of any industrial plant;

(j) "emission" means any solid or liquid or gaseous substance coming out of any chimney, duct or flue or any other outlet;

(k) "industrial plant" means any plant used for any industrial or trade purposes and emitting any air pollutant into atmosphere;

(l) "member" means a member of the Central Board or a State Board, as the case may be, and includes the Chairman thereof; .

(m) [4]["occupier" in relation to any factory or premises, means the person who has control over the affairs of the factory or the premises, and includes, in relation to any substance, the person in possession of the substance;]

(n) "prescribed" means prescribed by rules made under this Act by the Central Government or, as the case may be, the State Government;

(o) "State Board" means —

(i) in relation to a State in which the Water (Prevention and Control of Pollution) Act, 1974, is in force and the State Government has constituted for the State a [5][State Board for the Prevention and Control of Water Pollution] under section 4 of that Act, the said State Board, and

(ii) in relation to any other State Board for the Prevention and Control of Air Pollution constituted by the State Government under section 5 of this Act.

---

3. The words in brackets "Central Board for the Prevention and Control of Water Pollution" shall be subs as "Central Pollution Control Board" by Act 47 of 1987, s. 2, (date to be notified).
4. Subs. by s. 2, *ibid.* for cl, (m) (w.e.f. 1.4.1988).
5. The words in brackets "State Board for the Prevention and Control of Water Pollution" shall be subs, as "State Pollution Central Board" by S. 2. *ibid,* (date to be notified).

CHAPTER II

CENTRAL AND STATE BOARDS FOR THE PREVENTION AND CONTROL OF AIR POLLUTION

Central Board for the Prevention and Control of air Pollution.

[6][3. The Central Board for the Prevention and Control of Water Pollution constituted under section 3 of the Water (Prevention and Control of Pollution) Act, 1974, shall, without prejudice to exercise and performance of its powers and functions under that Act, exercise the powers and perform the functions of the Central Board for the Prevention and Control of Air Pollution under this Act.

State Boards for the Prevention and Control of Water Pollution to be State Boards for the Prevention and Control of Air Pollution.

4. In any State in which the Water (Prevention and Control of Pollution) Act, 1974, is in force and the State Government has constituted for that State a State Board for the Prevention and Control of Water Pollution under section 4 of that Act such State Board shall be deemed to be the State Board for the Prevention and Control of Air Pollution constituted under section 5 of this Act and accordingly that State Board for the Prevention and Control of Water Pollution shall, without prejudice to the exercise and performance of its powers and functions under that Act, exercise the powers and perform the functions of the State Board for the Prevention and Control of Air Pollution under this Act.]

Constitution of State Boards.

5. (1) In any State in which the Water (Prevention and Control of Pollution) Act, 1974 is not in force, or that Act is in force but the State Government has not

---

6. For sections 3 and 4 the following sections shall stand subs, by s. 3, *ibid,* (date to be notified), namely :—

Central Pollution Control Board,— The Central Board constituted under section 3 of the Water (Prevention and Control of Pollution), Act, 1974 (6 of 1974), shall, without prejudice to the exercise and performance of its powers and functions under that Act, exercise the powers and perform the functions of the Central Pollution Control Board for the Prevention and control of air pollution under this Act.

State Pollution Control Boards constituted under section 4 of Act 6 of 1974 to be State Boards under this Act,— In any State in which the Water (Prevention and Control of Pollution) Act, 1974, is in force and the State Government has constituted for that state a State Pollution Control Board under section 4 of that Act, such State Board shall be deemed to be the State Board for the Prevention and Control of Air Pollution constituted under section 5 of this Act, and accordingly that State Pollution Board shall without prejudice to the exercise and performance of its powers and functions under that Act, exercise the powers and perform the functions of the State Board for the prevention and control of air pollution under this Act.

constituted a [7][State Board for Prevention and Control of Water Pollution) under that Act, the State Government shall with effect from such date as it may, by notification in the Official Gazette, appoint, constitute a State Board for the Prevention and Control of Air Pollution under such name as may be specified in the notification, to exercise the powers conferred on, and perform the functions assigned to, that Board under this Act.

(2) A State Board constituted under this Act shall consist of the following members, namely :—

(a) a Chairman being a person having special knowledge or practical experience in respect of matters relating to environmental protection to be nominated by the State Government:

Provided that the Chairman may be either whole-time or part-time as the State Government may think fit;

(b) such number of officials not exceeding five, as the State Government may think fit, to be nominated by the State Government to represent that Government:

(c) such number of persons, not exceeding five, as the State Government may think fit, to be nominated by the State Government from amongst the members of the local authorities functioning within the State;

(d) such number of non-officials, not exceeding three as the State Government may think fit, to be nominated by the State Government to represent the interests of agriculture, fishery or industry or trade or labour or any other interest, which in the opinion of that Government, ought to be represented;

(e) two persons to represent the companies or corporations owned, controlled or managed by the State Government, to be nominated by that Government;

(f) [8][a full-time member-secretary having such qualifications, knowledge and experience of scientific, engineering or management aspects of pollution control as may be prescribed, to be appointed by the State Government:]

Provided that the State Government shall ensure that not less than two of the members are persons having special knowledge or practical experience in respect of matters relating to the improvement of the quality of air or the prevention, control or abatement of air pollution.

---

7. The words in brackets "State Board for the Prevention and Control of Water Pollution" shall be substituted as "State Pollution Control Board" by Act 47 of 1987, s. 4, (date to be notified).
8. Subs by s. 4, *ibid,* for cl. (f) (w.e.f. 1.4.1988).

(3) Every State Board constituted under this Act shall be a body corporate with the name specified by the State Government in the notification issued under sub-section (1), having perpetual succession and a common seal with power, subject to the provisions of this Act, to acquire and dispose of property and to contract and may by the said name sue or be sued.

Central Board to exercise the powers and perform the functions of a State Board of a State Board in the Union territories.

6. No State Board shall be constituted for a Union territory and in relation to a Union territory the Central Board shall exercise the powers and perform the functions of a State Board under this Act for that Union territory:

Provided that in a relation to any Union territory the Central Board may delegate all or any of its powers and functions under this section to such person or body of persons as the Central Government may specify.

Terms and conditions of service of members.

7. (1) Save as otherwise provided by or under this Act, a member of a State Board constituted under this Act, other than the member-secretary, shall hold office for a term of three years from the date on which his nomination is notified in the Official Gazette:

Provided that a member shall, notwithstanding the expiration of his term, continue to hold office until his successor enters upon his office.

(2) The term of office of a member of a State Board constituted under his Act and nominated under clause (b) or clause (e) of sub-section (2) of section 5 shall come to an end as soon as he ceases to hold the office under the State Government or, as the case may be, the company or corporation owned, controlled or managed by the State Government, by virtue of which he was nominated.

(3) A member of a State Board constituted under this act, other than the member-secretary, may at any time resign his office by writing under his hand addressed,—

(a) in the case of the Chairman, to the State Government; and

(b) in any other case, to the Chairman of the State Board, and the seat of the Chairman or such other member shall thereupon become vacant.

(4) A member of a State Board constituted under this Act, other than the member-secretary, shall be deemed to have vacated his seat, if he is absent without reason, sufficient in the opinion of the State Board from three consecutive meetings of the State Board or where he is nominated under clause (c) of sub-section (2) of section 5, he ceases to be member of the local authority and such vacation of seat shall, in either case, take effect from such date as the State Government may, by notification in the Official Gazette, specify.

(5) A casual vacancy in a State Board constituted under this Act shall be filed by a fresh nomination and the person nominated to fill the vacancy shall hold office only for the remainder of the term for which the member whose place he takes was nominated.

(6) A member of a State Board constituted under this Act shall be eligible for re-nomination[9]* * * *

(7) The other terms and conditions of service of the Chairman and other members (except the member-secretary) of a State Board constituted under this Act shall be such as may be prescribed.

Disqualifications

8. (1) No person shall be a member of a State Board constituted under this Act, who—

(a) is, or at any time has been, adjudged insolvent, or

(b) is of unsound mind and has been so declared by a competent court, or

(c) is, or has been convicted of an offence which in the opinion of the State Government, involves moral turpitude, or

(d) is, or at any time has been, convicted of an offence under this Act, or

(e) has directly or indirectly by himself or by any partner, any share or interest in any firm or company carrying on the business of manufacture, sale or hire of machinery industrial plant, control equipment or any other apparatus for the improvement of the quality of air or for the prevention, control or abatement of air pollution, or

(f) is a director or a secretary, manager or other salaried officer or employee of any company or firm having any contract with the Board, or with the Government constituting the Board or with a local authority in the State, or with a company or corporation owned, controlled or managed by the Government, for the carrying out of programmes for the improvement of the quality of air or for the prevention, control or abatement of air pollution, or

(g) has so abused, in the opinion of the State Government, his position as a member, as to render his continuance on the State Board detrimental to the interests of the general public.

9. The words "but not for more than two terms" omitted by Act 47 of 1987, s. 5 (w.e.f. 1.4.1988).

(2) The State Government shall, by order in writing remove any member who is or has become, subject to any disqualification mentioned in sub-section (1):

Provided that no order of removal shall be made by the State Government under this section unless the member concerned has been given a reasonable opportunity of showing cause against the same.

(3) Notwithstanding anything contained in sub-section (1) or sub-section (6) of section 7, a member who has been removed under this section shall not be eligible to continue to hold office until his successor enters upon his office, or as the case may be, for re-nomination as a member.

Vacation of seats by members.

9. If a member of a State Board constituted under this Act becomes subject to any of the disqualification specified in section 8, his seat shall become vacant.

Meetings of Board.

10. (1) For the purposes of this Act, a Board shall meet at least once in every three months and shall observe such rules of procedure in regard to the transaction of business at its meetings as may be prescribed:

Provided that if, in the opinion of the Chairman any business of an urgent nature is to be transacted he may convene a meeting of the Board as such time as he thinks fit for the aforesaid purpose.

(2) Copies of the minutes of the meetings under sub-section (1) shall be forwarded to the Central Board and to the State Government concerned.

Constitution of committees.

11. (1) A Board may constitute as many committee consisting wholly of members or partly of members and partly of other persons and for such purpose or purposes as it may think fit.

(2) A committee constituted under this section shall meet at such time and at such place, and shall observe such rules of procedure in regard to the transaction of business at its meetings as may be prescribed.

(3) The members of a committee other than the members of the Board shall be paid such fees and allowances for attending its meetings and for attending to any other work of the Board as may be prescribed.

Temporary association of persons with Board for particular purposes.

12. A Board may associate with itself in such manner, and for such purposes, as may be prescribed any person whose assistance or advice it may desire to obtain in performing any of its functions under this Act.

(2) A person associated with the Board under sub-section (1) for any purpose shall have a right to take part in the discussions of the Board relevant to that

purpose but shall not have a right to vote at a meeting of the Board and shall not be a member of the Board for any other purpose.

(3) A person associated with a Board under sub-section (1) shall be entitled to receive such fees and allowances as may be prescribed.

Vacancy in Board not to invalidate acts or proceedings.

13. No act or proceeding of a Board or any committee thereof shall be called in question on the ground merely of the existence of any vacancy in or any defect in the constitution of, the Board or such committee as the case may be.

Members-secretary and officers and other employees of State Boards.

14. (1) The terms and conditions of service of the member-secretary of a State Board constituted under this Act shall be such as may be prescribed.

[10][(2) The member-secretary of a State Board, whether constituted under this Act or not, shall exercise such powers and perform such duties as may be prescribed, or as may, from time to time, be delegated to him by the State Board or its Chairman,]

(3) Subject to such rules as may be made by the State Government in this behalf a State Board, whether constituted under this Act or not, may appoint such officers and other employees as it considers necessary for the efficient performance of its functions under this Act.

(4) The method of appointment the conditions of service and the scales of pay of the officers (other than the member-secretary) and other employees of a State Board appointed under sub-section (3) shall be such as may be determined by regulations made by the State Board under this Act.

(5) Subject to such conditions as may be prescribed a State Board constituted under this Act may from time to time appoint any qualified person to be a consultant to the Board and pay him such salary and allowances or fees, as it thinks fit.

Delegation powers.

15. A State Board may by general or special order, delegate to the Chairman or the member-secretary or any other officer of the Board subject to such conditions and limitations, if any as may be specified in the order, such of its powers and functions under this Act as it may deem necessary.

10. Subs by Act 47 of 1987, s. 6, for sub-section (2) (w.e.f. 1.4.1988).

CHAPTER III

POWERS AND FUNCTIONS OF BOARDS

Functions of Central Board.

16. (1) Subject to the provisions of this Act, and without prejudice to the performance of its functions under the Water (Prevention and Control of Pollution) Act, 1974, the main functions of the Central Board shall be to improve the quality of air and to prevent, control or abate air pollution in the Country.

(2) In particular and without prejudice to the generality of the forgoing functions, the Central Board may—

(a) advice the Central Government on any matter concerning the improvement of the quality of air and the prevention, control or abatement of air pollution;

(b) plan and cause to be executed a nation-wide programme for the prevention, control or abatement, of air pollution;

(c) co-ordinate to the activities of the State Boards resolve disputes among them;

(d) provide technical assistance and guidance to the State Boards, carry out and sponsor investigations and research relating to problems of air pollution and prevention, control or abatement of air pollution;

(dd) [11][perform such of the function of any State Board as may be specified in and made under sub-section (2) of section 18;]

(e) plan and organise the training of persons engaged or to be engaged in programmes for the prevention, control or abatement of air pollution on such terms and conditions as the Central Board may specify;

(f) organise through mass media a comprehensive programme regarding the prevention, control or abatement of air pollution;

(g) collect, compile and publish technical and statistical data relating to air pollution and the measures devised for its effective prevention control or abatement and prepare manuals, codes or guides relating to prevention, control or abatement of air pollution;

(h) lay down standards for the quality of air;

(i) collect and disseminate information in respect of matters relating to air pollution;

---

11. Ins. by Act 47 of 1987, s. 7, (w.e.f. 1.4.1988).

(j) perform such other functions as may be prescribed.

(3) The Central Board may be establish or recognise a laboratory or laboratories to enable the Central Board to perform its functions under this section efficiently.

(4) The Central Board may—

(a) delegate of its functions under this Act generally or specially to any of the committees appointed by it;

(b) do such other things and perform such other acts as it may think necessary for the proper discharge of its function and generally for the purpose of carrying into effect the purposes of this Act.

Functions of State Boards.

17. (1) Subject to the provisions of this Act, and without prejudice to the performance of its functions, if any under the Water (Prevention and Control of Pollution) Act, 1974 the functions of a State Board shall be—

(a) to plan a comprehensive programme for the prevention, control or abatement of air pollution and to secure the execution thereof;

(b) to advise the State Government on any matter concerning the prevention, control or abatement of air pollution;

(c) to collect and disseminate information relating to air pollution;

(d) to collaborate with the Central Board in organising the training of persons engaged or to be engaged in programmes relating to prevention, control or abatement of air pollution and to organise mass-education programme relating thereto;

(e) to inspect, at all reasonable times, any control equipment industrial plant or manufacturing process and to give, by order, such directions to such persons as it may consider necessary to take steps for the prevention, control or abatement of air pollution;

(f) to inspect air pollution control areas at such intervals as it may think necessary assess the quality of air therein and take steps for the prevention, control or abatement of air pollution in such areas;

(g) to lay down, in consultation with the Central Board and having regard to the standards for the quality of air laid down by the Central Board, standards for emission of air pollutants into the atmosphere from industrial plants and automobiles or for the discharge of any air pollutant into the atmosphere from any other source whatsoever not being a ship or an aircraft:

Provided that different standards for emission may be laid down under this clause for different industrial plants having regard to the quantity and composition of emission of air pollutants into the atmosphere from such industrial plants;

(h) to advice the State Government with respect to the suitability of any premises or location for carrying on any industry which is likely to cause air pollution;

(i) to perform such other functions as may be prescribed or as may, from time to time be entrusted to it by the Central Board or the State Government.

(j) to do such other things and to perform such other acts as it may think necessary for the proper discharge of its functions and generally for the purpose of carrying into effect the purposes of this Act.

(2) A State Board may establish or recognise a laboratory or laboratories to enable the State Board to perform its functions under this section efficiently.

Power to give directions.

18. [12][(1)] In the performance of its functions under this Act—

(a) the Central Board shall be bound by such directions in writing as the Central Government may give to it; and

(b) every State Board shall be bound by such directions in writing as the Central Board, the matter shall be referred to the Central Government for its decision.

(2) [13][Where the Central Government is of the opinion that any State Board has defaulted in complying with any directions given by the Central Board under subsection (1) and as a result of such a grave emergency has arisen and it is necessary or expedient so to do in the public interest, it may by order, direct the Central Board to perform any of the functions of the State Board in relation to such area, for such period and for such purposes, as may be specified in the order.

(3) Where the Central Board performs any of the functions of State Board in pursuance of a direction under sub-section (2) the expenses, if any, incurred by the Central Board with respect to the performance of such functions may, if the State Board is empowered to recover such expenses be recovered by the Central Board with the date when a demand for such expenses is made until it is paid from the person or persons concerned as arrears of land revenue or of public demand.

(4) For the removal of doubts, it is hereby declared that any directions to perform the functions of any State Board given under sub-section (2) in respect of any area would not preclude the State Board from performing such functions in any other area in the State or any of its other functions in that area.]

12. S. 18 renumbered as sub-section (1) thereof by Act 47 of 1987, s. 8 (w.e.f. 1.4.1988).
13. Ins. by s. 8, (w.e.f. 1.4.1988).

CHAPTER IV

PREVENTION AND CONTROL OF AIR POLLUTION

Power to declare air pollution control areas.

19. (1) The State Government may, after consultation with the State Board, by notification in the Official Gazette, declare in such manner as may be prescribed any area or areas within the State as air pollution control area or areas for the purposes of this Act.

(2) The State Government may, after consultation with the State Board, by notification in the Official Gazette,—

(a) alter any air pollution control area whether by way of extension or reduction;

(b) declare new air pollution control area in which may be merged one or more existing air pollution control areas or any part or parts thereof.

(3) If the State Government after, consultation with the State Board, is of opinion that the use of any fuel, other than an approved fuel, in any air pollution control area or part thereof may cause or is likely to cause air pollution, it may by notification in the Official Gazette, prohibit the use of such fuel in such area or part, thereof with effect such date (being not less than three months from the date of publication of the notification) as may be specified in the notification.

(4) The State Government may after consultation with the State Board by notification in the Official Gazette, direct that with effect from such date as may be specified therein, no appliance, other than an approved appliance, shall be used in the premises, situated in an air pollution control area:

Provided that different dates may be specified for different parts of an air pollution control area or for the use of different appliances.

(5) If the State Government after consultation with the State Board, is of opinion that the burning of any material (not being fuel) in any air pollution control area or part thereof may cause is likely to cause air pollution it may, by notification in the Official Gazette, prohibit the burning of such material in such area or part thereof.

Power to give instructions for ensuring standards for emission from automobiles.

20. With a view to ensuring that the standards for emission of air pollutants from automobiles laid down by the State Board under clause (g) of sub-section (1) of section 17 are complied with, the state Government shall, in consultation with the State Board, give such instructions as may be deemed necessary to the

concerned authority in charge of registration of motor vehicles under the Motor Vehicles At, 1939, and such authority shall, notwithstanding anything contained in that Act or the rules made thereunder be bound to comply such instructions.

Restrictions on use of certain industrial plants.

21. [14][(1) Subject to the provisions of this section, no person shall, without the previous consent of the State Board, establish or operate any industrial plant in an air pollution control area:

Provided that a person operating any industrial plant in any air pollution control area immediately before the commencement of section 9 of the Air (Prevention and Control of Pollution) Amendment Act, 1987 for which no consent was necessary prior to such commencement, may continue to do so for a period of three months from such commencement or, if he has made an application for such consent within the said period of three months, till the disposal of such application.]

(2) An application for consent of the State Board under sub-section (1) shall be accompanied by such fees as may be prescribed and shall be made in the prescribed form and shall contain the particulars of the industrial plant and such other particulars may be prescribed.

Provided that where any person, immediately before the declaration of any area as an air pollution control area, operates in such area any industrial plant, [15]* * * * such person shall make the application under this sub-section within such period (being not less than three months from the date of such declaration) as may be prescribed and where such person makes such application, he shall be deemed to be operating such industrial plant with the consent of the State Board until the consent applied for has been refused.

(3) The State Board may make such inquiry as it may deem fit in respect of the application for consent referred to in sub-section (1) and in making any such inquiry, shall follow such procedure as may be prescribed.

(4) Within a period of four months after the receipt of the application for consent referred to in sub-section (1), State Board shall, by order in writing, [16][and for reasons to be recorded in the order, grant the consent applied for subject to such conditions and for such period as may be specified in the order, or refuse such consent:]

[17][Provided that it shall be open to the State Board to cancel such consent before the expiry of the period for which it is granted or refuse further consent after

14. Subs. by Act 47 of 1987, s. 9, for sub-section (l) (w.e.f. 1-4-1988).
15. Certain words omitted by s. 9, *ibid,* (w.e.f. 1.4.1988).
16. Subs, by Act 47 of 1987, for certain words (w.e.f. 1.4.1988).
17. Ins. by s. 9, *ibid.* (w.e.f. 1.4.1988).

such expiry if the conditions subject to which such consent has been granted are not fulfilled:

Provided further that before cancelling a consent or refusing a further consent under the first proviso, a reasonably opportunity of being heard shall be given in the person concerned.]

(5) Every person to whom consent has been granted by the State Board under sub-section (4), shall comply with the following conditions namely:—

(i) the control equipment of such specifications as the State Board may approve in this behalf shall be installed and operated in the premises where the industry is carried on or proposed to be carried on;

(ii) the existing control equipment if any, shall be altered or replaced in accordance with the directions of the State Board;

(iii) the control equipment referred to in clause (i) or clause (ii) shall be kept at all times in good running conditions;

(iv) chimney, wherever necessary, of such specifications as the State Board may approve in this behalf shall be erected or re-erected in such premises;

(v) such other conditions as the State Board may specify in this behalf; and

(vi) the conditions referred to in clauses (i), (ii), and (iv) shall be complied with within such period as the State Board may specify in this behalf:

Provided that in the case of a person operating any industrial plant [18]* * * * in an air pollution control area immediate before the date of declaration of such area as an air pollution control area, the period so specified shall not be less than six months:

Provided further that—

(a) after the installation of any control equipment in accordance with the specifications under clause (i), or

(b) after the alteration or replacement of any control equipment in accordance with the directions of the State Board under clause (ii), or

(c) after the erection of re-erection of any chimney under clause (iv), no control equipment or chimney shall be altered or replaced or, as the case may be, erected or re-erected except with the previous approval of the State Board.

(6) If due to any technological improvement or otherwise the State Board is of opinion that all or any of the conditions referred to in sub-section (5) require or requires variation (including the change of any control equipment, either in whole or in part), the State Board shall, after giving the person to whom consent

18. Certain words omitted by s. 9, *ibid.* (w.e.f. 1.4.1988).

has been granted an opportunity of being heard, vary all or any of such conditions and thereupon such person shall be bound to comply with the conditions as so varied.

(7) Where a person to whom consent has been granted by the State Board under sub-section (4) transfers his interest in the industry to any other person, such consent shall be deemed to have been granted to such other person and he shall be bound to comply with all the conditions subject to which it was granted as if the consent was granted to him originally.

Persons carrying on industry etc., not to allow emission of air pollutants in excess of the standards laid down by Board.

22. No person [19]* * * * operating any industrial plant, in any air pollution control area shall discharge or cause or permit to be discharged the emission of any air pollutant excess of the standards laid down by the State Board under clause (g) of sub-section (1) of section 17.

Power of Board to make application make to court for restraining persons from causing air pollution.

22 A. [20][(1) Where it is apprehended by a Board that emission of any air pollutant, in excess of the standards laid down by the State Board under clause (g) of sub-section (1) of section 17, is likely to occur by reason of any person operating an industrial plant or otherwise in any air pollution control area, the Board may make an application to a court, not inferior to that a Metropolitan Magistrate or a Judicial Magistrate of the first class for restraining such person from emitting such air pollutant.

(2) On receipt of the application under sub-section (1) the court may make such order as it deems fit.

(3) Where under sub-section (2), the court makes an order restraining any person from discharging or causing or permitting to be discharged the emission of any air pollutant, it may in that order,—

(a) direct such person to desist from taking such action as is likely to cause emission;

(b) authorise the Board if the direction under clause (a) is no complied with by the person to whom such direction is issued, to implement the direction in such manner as may be specified by the court.

(4) All expenses incurred by the Board in implementing the directions of the court under clause (b) of sub-section (3) shall be recoverable from the person concerned arrears of land revenue or of public demand].

19. Certain words omitted by Act 47 of 1987, s. 10. *ibid.* (w.e.f. 1.4.1988).
20. Ins. by s. 11, *ibid.* (w.e.f. 1.4.1988).

Furnishing of information to State Board and other agencies in certain cases.

23. (1) Where in any[21] * * * * area the emission of any air pollutant into the atmosphere in excess of the standards laid down by the State Board occurs or is apprehended to occur due to accident or other unforeseen act or even, the person in charge of the premises from where such emission occurs or is apprehended to occur shall forthwith intimate the fact of such occurrence or the apprehension of such occurrence to the State Board and to such authorities or agencies as may be prescribed.

(2) On receipt of information with respect to the fact or the apprehension of any occurrence of the nature referred to in sub-section (1), whether through intimation under that sub-section or otherwise, the State Board and the authorities or agencies shall, as early as practicable, cause such remedial measures to be taken as are necessary to mitigate the emission of such air pollutants.

(3) Expenses, if any, incurred by the State Board, authority or agency with respect to the remedial measures referred to in sub-section (2) together with interest (at such reasonable rate, as the State Government may by order, fix) from the date when a demand for the expenses is made until it is paid, may be recovered by that Board, authority or agency from the person concerned, as arrears of land revenue or of public demand.

Power of entry and inspection.

24. (1) Subject to the provisions of this section, any person empowered by a State Board in this behalf shall have a right to enter, at all reasonable times with such assistance as he considers necessary any place—

(a) for the purpose of performing any of the functions of the State Board entrusted to him:

(b) for the purpose of determining whether and if so in what manner, any such functions are to be performed whether any provisions of this Act or the rules made thereunder or any notice order, direction or authorisation served made, given or granted under this Act is being or has been complied with:

(c) for the purpose of examining and testing any control equipment industrial plant, record register document or any other material object or for conducting a search of any place in which he has reason to believe that an offence under this Act or the rule made thereunder has been or is being or is about to be committed and for seizing any such control equipment, industrial plant, record, register, document or other material object if he has reasons to believe that it may furnish evidence of the commission of an offence punishable under this Act or the rules made thereunder.

21. The words "air pollution control omitted by s. 12, *ibid*, (w.e.f. 1.4.1988).

(2) Every person [22]* * * operating any control equipment or any industrial plant, in an air pollution control area shall be bound to render all assistance to the person empowered by the State Board under sub-section (1) for carrying out the functions under that sub-section and if he fails to do so without any reasonable cause or excuse he shall be guilty of an offence under this Act.

(3) If any person willfully delays or obstructs any person empowered by the State Board under sub-section (1) in the discharge of his duties, he shall be guilty of an offence under this Act.

(4) The provisions of the Code of Criminal Procedure, 1973, or in relation to the State of Jammu and Kashmir, or any area in which that Code is not in force, the provisions of any corresponding in enforce in that State or area, shall, so far, as may be apply to any search or seizure under this section as they apply to any search or seizure made under the authority of a warrant issued under section 94 of the said Code or, as the case may be, under the corresponding provisions of the said law.

Power to obtain information

25. For the purposes of carrying out the functions entrusted to it, the State Board or any officer empowered by it in that behalf may call for any information (including information regarding the types of air pollutants emitted into the atmosphere and the level of the emission of such air pollutants) from the occupier or any other person carrying on any industry or operating any control equipment or industrial plant and for the purpose of verifying the correctness of such information the State Board or such officer shall have the right to inspect the premises where such industry. Control equipment or industrial plant is being carried on or operated.

Power to take samples of air or emission and procedure to be followed in connection therewith.

26. (1) A State Board or any officer empowered by it in this behalf shall have power to take, for the purpose of analysis samples, of air or emission from any chimney, flue or duct or any other outlet in such manner as may be prescribed.

(2) The result of any analysis of a sample of emission take under sub-section (1) shall not be admissible in evidence in any legal proceeding unless the provisions of sub-sections (3) and (4) are complied with.

(3) Subject to the occupier of sub-section (4), when a sample of emission is taken for analysis under sub-section (1), the person taking the sample shall—

(a) serve on the provisions or his agent a notice, then and there, in such form as may be prescribed, of his intention to have it so analysed;

(b) in the presence of the occupier or his agent, collect a sample of emission for analysis;

22. Certain words omitted by Act 47 of 1987, s. 13, (w.e.f. 1.4.1988).

(c) cause the sample to be placed in container or containers which shall be marked and sealed and shall also be signed both by person taking the sample and the occupier or his agent;

(d) send, without delay, the container or containers to the laboratory established or recognised by the State Board section 17, or , if a request in that behalf is made by the occupier or his agent when the notice is served on him under clause (a), to the laboratory established or specified under sub-section (1) section 28.

(4) When a sample of emission is taken for analysis under sub section (1) and the person taking the sample serve on the occupier or his agent, a notice under clause (a) of sub-section (3), then —

(a) in a case where the occupier or his agent willfully absents himself, the person taking the sample shall collect the sample of emission for analysis to be placed in a container or containers which shall be marked and sealed and shall also be signed by the person taking the sample, and

(b) in a case where the occupier or his agent is present at the time of taking the sample but refuse to sign the market and sealed container or containers of the sample of emission as required under clause (c) of sub-section (3), the marked and sealed container or containers shall be signed by the person taking the sample,

and the container or containers shall be sent without delay by the person taking the sample for analysis to the laboratory established or specified under sub-section (1) of section 28 and such person shall inform the Government analyst appointed under sub-section (1) of section 29, in writing about the willful absence of the occupier or his agent or, as the case may be, his refusal to sign the container or containers.

Reports of result of analysis on samples taken under section 26.

27. (1) Where a sample of emission has been sent for analysis to the laboratory established or recognised by the State Board, the Board analyst appointed under sub-section (2) of section 29 shall analyse the sample and submit a report in the prescribed form of such analysis in triplicate to the State Board.

(2) On receipt of the report under sub-section (1), one copy of the report shall be sent by the State Board to the occupier or his agent referred to in section 26, another copy shall be preserved for production before the court in case any legal proceedings are taken against him and the other copy shall be kept by the State Board.

(3) Where a sample has been sent for analysis under clause (d) of sub-section (3) or sub-section (4) of section 26 to any laboratory mentioned therein, the Government analyst referred to in the said sub-section (4) shall analyse the sample and submit a report in the prescribed form of the result of the analysis in triplicate to the State Board which shall comply with the provisions of sub-section (2).

(4) Any cost incurred in getting any sample analysed at the request of the occupier or his agent as provided in clause (d) of sub-section (3) of section 26 or when he willfully absents himself or refuses to sign the marked and sealed container or containers of sample of emission under sub-section (4) of that section shall be payable by such occupier or his agent and in case of default the same shall be recoverable from him as arrears of land revenue or of public demand.

State Air Laboratory.

28. (1) The State Government may, by notification in the Official Gazette,—

(a) establish one or more State Air Laboratories, or

(b) specify one or more laboratories or institutes as State Air Laboratories to carry out the functions entrusted to the State Air Laboratory under this Act.

(2) The State Government may, after consultations with the State Board, make rules prescribing —

(a) the functions of the State Air Laboratory;

(b) the procedure for the submission to the said Laboratory of samples of air or emission for analysis or tests, the form of the Laboratory's report thereon and the fees payable in respect of such report.

(c) such other matters as may be necessary or expedient to enable that Laboratory to carry out its functions.

Analysts.

29. (1) The State Government may, by notification in the Official Gazette, appoint such persons as it thinks fit and having the prescribed qualifications to be Government analysts for the purpose of analysis of samples of air or emission sent for analysis to any laboratory established or specified under sub-section (1) of section 28.

(2) Without prejudice to the provisions of section 14, the State Board may, by notification in the Official Gazette, and with the approval of the State Government appoint such persons as it thinks fit and having the prescribed qualifications to be Board analysts for the purpose of analysis of samples of air or emission sent for analysis to any laboratory established or recognised under section 17.

Reports of analysts.

30. Any document purporting to be a report signed by a Government analyst or, as the case may be, a State Board analyst may be used as evidence of the facts stated therein in any proceedings under this Act.

Appeals.

31. (1) Any person aggrieved by an order made by the State Board under this Act may, within thirty days from the date on which the order is communicated

to him, prefer an appeal to such authority (hereinafter referred to as the appellate authority) as the State Government may think fit to constitute :

Provided that the Appellate authority may entertain the appeal after the expiry of the said period of thirty days if such authority is satisfied that to appellant was prevented by sufficient cause from filing the appeal in time.

(2) The appellate authority shall consist of a single person or three persons as the State Government may think fit to be appointed by the State Government.

(3) The form and the manner in which an appeal may be preferred under sub-section (1) the fees payable for such appeal and the procedure to be followed by the appellate authority shall be such as may be prescribed.

(4) On receipt of an appeal preferred under sub-section (1), the appellate Authority shall after giving the appellant and the State Board an opportunity of being heard, dispose of the appeal as expeditiously as possible.

Power to give directions.

[23][31 A. Notwithstanding anything contained in any law, but subject to the provisions of this act and to any directions that the Central Government may give in this behalf, a Board may in this behalf a Board may in the exercise of its powers and performance of its functions under this Act, issue any directions in writing to any persons, officer or authority and such person. Officer or authority shall be bound to comply with such direction.

Explanation. — For the avoidance of doubts it is hereby declared that the power is issue directions under this section include the power to direct.—

(a) the closure, prohibition or regulation of any industry, operation or process; or

(b) the stoppage or regulation of supply of electricity water or any other service.]

CHAPTER V
FUND, ACCOUNTS AND AUDIT

Constitutions by Central Government.

32. The Central Government may, after due appropriation made by Parliament by law in this behalf, make in each financial year such contributions to the State Boards as it may think necessary to enable the State Boards to perform their functions under this Act:

Provided that nothing in this section shall apply to any [25] [State Board for the Prevention and Control of Water Pollution] constituted under section 4 of the Water (Prevention and Control of Pollution) Act, 1974, which is empowered by

23. Ins. by Act 47 of 1987, s.14, (w.e.f. 1.4.1988).

that Act to expend money from its fund thereunder also for performing its functions, under any law for the time being in force relating to the prevention, control or abatement of air pollution.

Fund of Boards.

33. (1) Every State Board shall have its own fund for the purposes of this Act and all sums which may, from time to time, be paid to it by the Central Government all other receipts (by way of contributions, if any, from the State Government, fees, gifts grants, donations, benefactions or otherwise) of that Board shall be carried to the fund of the Board and all payment by the Board shall be made therefrom.

(2) Every State Board may expend such sums as it thinks fit for performing its functions under this Act and such sums shall be treated as expenditure payable out of the fund of that Board.

(3) Nothing in this section shall apply to any [24][State Board for the Prevention and Control of Water Pollution] constituted under section 4 of the Water (Prevention and Control of Pollution) Act, 1974, which is empowered by that Act to expend money from its fund thereunder also for performing its functions, under any law for the time being in force relating to the prevention, control or abatement of air pollution.

Borrowing powers of Board.

[25][33A. A Board may, with the consent of, or in accordance with the terms of any general or special authority given to it, by the Central Government or, as the case may be the State Government, borrow money from any source by way of loans or issue of bonds, debentures or such other instrument as it may deem fit for discharging all or any of its functions under this Act.]

Budget

34. The Central Board or, as the case may be the State Board shall, during each financial year, prepare, in such form and at such time as may be prescribed, a budget in respect of the financial year next ensuring showing the estimated receipt and expenditure under this Act, and copies thereof shall be forwarded to the Central Government or, as the case may be the State Government.

Annual report.

[26][35. (1) The Central Board shall, during each financial year, prepare, in such form as may be prescribed, an annual report giving full account of its activities under this Act during the previous financial year and copies thereof shall be forwarded to the Central Government within four months from the last date of

24. The words in brackets "State Board for the Prevention and Control of Water Pollution" shall be submitted as "State Pollution Control Board" by Act 47 of 1987, s. 15, (date to be notified).
25. Ins. by Act s. 16. *ibid.* (w.e.f. 1.4.1988).
26. Subs by s. 17, *ibid,* s. 35 (w.e.f. 1.4.1988).

the previous financial year and that Government shall cause every such report to be laid before both Houses of Parliament within nine months of the last date of the previous financial year.

(2) Every State Board shall during each financial year, prepare in such form as may be prescribed, an annual report giving full account of its activities under this Act during the previous financial year and copies thereof shall be forwarded to the State Government within four months from the last date of the previous financial year did that Government shall cause every such report to be laid before the State Legislature within a period of nine months from the last date of the previous financial year.]

Accounts and audit.

36. (1) Every Board shall in relation to its functions under this act, maintain proper accounts and other relevant records and prepare an annual statement of accounts in such form as may be prescribed by the Central Government or, as the case may be the State Government.

(2) The accounts of the Board shall be audited by an auditor duly qualified to act as an auditor of companies under section 226 of the Companies Act 1956.

(3) The said auditor shall be appointed by Central Government or, as the case may be, the State Government on the advice of the Comptroller and Auditor General of India.

(4) Every auditor appointed to audit the accounts of the Board under this Act shall have the right to demand the production of books, accounts, vouchers and other documents and papers and to inspect any of the offices of the Board.

(5) Every such auditor shall send a copy of his report together with an audited copy of the accounts to the Central Government or, as the case may be, the State Government.

(6) The Central Government shall, as soon as may be after the receipt of the audit report under sub-section (5), cause the same to be laid before Houses of Parliament.

(7) The State Government shall, as soon as may be after the receipt of the audit report under the sub-section (5), cause the same to be laid before the State Legislature.

CHAPTER VI
PENALTIES AND PROCEDURE

Failure to comply with the provisions of section 21 or section 22 or with the directions issued under section 31A.

37. [27][(1) Whoever fails to comply with the provisions of section 21 or section

27. Subs. by Act 47 of 1987, s. 18, for s. 37 (w.e.f. 1.4.1988).

22 of directions issued under section 31A, shall in respect of each such failure, be punishable with imprisonment for a term which shall not be less than one year and six months but which may extend to six years and with fine, and in case the failure continues, with an additional fine which may extend to five thousand rupees for every day during which such failure continues after the conviction for the first such failure.

(2) If the failure referred to in sub-section (1) continues beyond a period of one year after the date of conviction, the offender shall be punishable with imprisonment for a term which shall not be less than two years but which may extend to seven years and with fine.]

Penalties for certain acts.

38. Whoever—

(a) destroys pulls down, removes, injures or defaces any pillar, post or stake fixed in the ground or any notice or other matter put up, inscribed or placed, by or under the authority of the Board, or

(b) obstructs any person acting under the orders or directions of the Board from exercising his powers and performing his functions under this Act,

(c) damages any works or property belonging to the Board, or

(d) fails to furnish to the Board or any officer or other employee of the Board any information required by the Board or such officer or other employee for the purpose of this Act, or

(e) fails to intimate the occurrence of the emission of air pollutants into the atmosphere in excess of the standards laid down by the State Board or the apprehension of such occurrence, to the State Board and other prescribed authorities or agencies as required under sub-section (1) of section 23, or

(f) in giving any information which he is required to give under this Act, makes a statement which is false in any material particular, or

(g) for the purpose of obtaining any consent under section 21, makes a statement which is false in any material particular.

shall be punishable with imprisonment for a term which may extend to three months or with fine which may extend to [28][ten thousand rupees] or with both.

28. Subs. by Act 47 of 1987, s. 19. for "five hundred rupees", (w.e.f. 1.4.1988).

Penalty for contravention of certain provisions of the Act.

[29][39. Whoever contravenes any of the provisions of this Act or any order or direction issued, thereunder, for which no penalty has been elsewhere provided in this Act, shall be punishable with imprisonment for a term which may extend to three months or with fine which may extend to ten thousand rupees or with both, and in the case of continuing contravention, with an additional fine which may extend to five thousand rupees for every day during which such contravention continues after conviction for the first such contravention.]

Offences by companies.

40. (1) Where an offence under this Act has been committed by a company, every person, who at the time the offence was committed, was directly in charge of, and was responsible to, the company for the conduct of the business of the company, as well as the company, shall be deemed to be guilty of the offence and shall be liable be proceeded against and punished accordingly:

Provided that nothing contained in this sub-section shall render any such person liable to any punishment provided in this Act, if he proves that the offence was committed without his knowledge or that he exercised all due diligence to prevent the commission of such offence.

(2) Notwithstanding anything contained in sub-section (1), where an offence under this Act has been committed by a company and it is proved that the offence has been committed with the consent or connivance of, or attributable to any neglect on the part of any director, manager, secretary or other officer of the company, such director, manager, secretary or other officer shall also be deemed to be guilty of that offence and shall be liable to be proceeded against and punished accordingly.

Explanation.—For the puposes of this section.—

(a) "company" means any body corporate, and includes a firm or other association of individuals; and

(b) "director", in relation to a firm, means a partner in the firm.

Offences by Government Departments.

41. (1) Where an offence under this Act has been committed by any Department of Government, the Head of the Department shall be deemed to be guilty of the offence and shall be liable to be proceeded against and punished accordingly:

Provided that nothing contained in this section shall render such Head of the Department liable to any punishment if he proves that the offence was committed without his knowledge or that he exercised all due diligence to prevent the commission of such offence.

29. Subs. by s. 20, *ibid*, for s. 39 (w.e.f. 1.4.1988).

(2) Notwithstanding anything contained in sub-section (1), where an offence under this Act has been committed by a Department of Government and it is proved that the offence has been committed with the consent or connivance of, or is attributable to any neglect on the part of any officer, other than the Head of the Department, such office shall also be deemed to be guilty of that offence and shall be liable to be proceeded against and punished accordingly.

Protection of action taken in good faith.

42. No suit, prosecution or other legal proceeding shall lie against the Government or any office of the Government or any member or any officer or other employee of the Board in respect of anything which is done or intended to be done in good faith in pursuance of this act or the rules made thereunder.

Cognizance of offences.

43. [30][(1) No Court shall take cognizance of any offence under this Act except on a complaint made by—

(a) a Board or any officer authorised in this behalf by it; or

(b) any person who has given notice of not less than sixty days, in the manner prescribed of the alleged offence and of his intention to make a complaint to the Board or officer authorised as aforesaid,

and no court inferior to that of a Metropolitan Magistrate or a Judicial Magistrate of the first class shall try any offence punishable under this Act.

(2) Where a complaint has been made under clause (b) of sub-section (1), the Board shall, on demand by such person, make available the relevant reports in its possession to that person:

Provided that the Board may refuse to make any such report available to such person if the same is, in its opinion, against the public interest.]

Members, officers and employees of Board to be public servants.

44. All the members and all officers and other employees of a Board when acting or purporting to act in pursuance of any of the provisions of this Act or the rules made thereunder shall be deemed to be public servants within the meaning of section 21 of the Indian Penal Code.

Reports and return.

45. The Central Board shall, in relation to its functions under this Act, furnish to the Central Government, and to the State Board shall, in relation to its functions under this Act, furnish to the State Government and to the Central Board such reports, returns, statistics, accounts and other information as that Government or as the case may be the Central Board may, from time to time, require.

30. Subs. by Act 47 of 1987, s. 21, for s. 43 (w.e.f. 1.4.1988).

Bar of jurisdiction.

46. No civil court shall have jurisdiction to entertain any suit or proceeding in respect of any matter which an Appellate Authority constituted under this Act is empowered by or under this Act to determine, and no injunction shall be granted by any court or other authority in respect of any action taken or to be taken in pursuance of any power conferred by or under this Act.

CHAPTER VII
MISCELLANEOUS

Power of State Government to supersede State Board.

47. (1) If at any time the State Government is of opinion —

(a) that a state Board constituted under this Act has persistently made default in the performance of the functions imposed on it or under this Act, or

(b that circumstances exist which render it necessary in the public interest so to do,

the State Government may, by notification in the Official Gazette, supersede the State Board for such period, not exceeding six months as may be specified in the notification:

Provided that before issuing a notification under this sub-section for the reasons mentioned in clause (a), the State Government shall give a reasonable opportunity to the State Board to show cause why it should not be superseded and shall consider the explanations and objections, if any, of the State Board.

(2) Upon the publication of a notification under sub-section (1) superseding the State Board,—

(a) all the members shall, as from the date of supersession, vacate their offices as such;

(b) all the powers, functions and duties which may, by or under this Act, be exercised, performed or discharged by the State Board shall, until the State Board is reconstituted under sub-section (3), be exercised, performed or discharged by such person or persons as the State Government may direct:

(c) all property owned or controlled by the State Board shall, until the Board is reconstituted under sub-section (3), vest in the State Government.

(3) On the expiration of the period of supersession specified in the notification issued under sub-section (1), the State Government may —

(a) extend the period of supersession for such further term, not exceeding six months, as it may consider necessary: or

(b) reconstitute the State Board by a fresh nomination or appointment as the case may be and in such case any person who vacated his office under clause (a) of sub-section (2) shall also be eligible for nomination or appointment.

Provided that the State Government may at any time before the expiration of the period of supersession, whether or originally specified under sub-section (1) or as extended under this sub-section, take action under clause (b) of this sub-section.

Special provision in the case of supersession of the Central Board or the State Boards constituted under the Water (Prevention and Control of Pollution) Act, 1974.

48. Where the Central Board or any State Board constituted under the Water (Prevention and Control of Pollution) Act, 1974, is superseded by the Central Government or the State Government, as the case may be, under that Act, all the powers, functions and duties of the Central Board or such State Board under this Act shall be exercised, performed or discharged during the period of such supersession by the person or persons, exercising, preforming or discharging the powers, functions and duties of the Central Board or such State Board under the Water (Prevention and Control of Pollution) Act, 1974, during such period.

Dissolution of State Boards constituted under the Act.

49. (1) As and when the Water (Prevention and Control of Pollution) Act, 1974, comes into force in any State and the State Government constitutes a [31][State Board for the Prevention and Control of Water Pollution] under that Act, the State Board constituted by the State Government under this Act shall stand dissolved and the Board first-mentioned shall exercise the powers and perform the functions of the Board second-mentioned in that State.

(2) On the dissolution of the State Board constituted under this Act,—

(a) all the members shall vacate their offices as such;

(b) all moneys and other property of whatever kind (including the fund of the State Board) owned by, or vested in, the State Board, immediately before such dissolution, shall stand transferred to and vest in the [31][State Board for the Prevention and Control of Water Pollution];

(c) every officer and other employee serving under the State Board immediately before such dissolution shall be transferred to and

31. The words in brackets "State Board for the Prevention and Control of Water Pollution" shall be substituted as "State Pollution Control Board" by Act 47 of 1987, s. 15 (date to be notified).

become an officer or other employee of the [31][State Board for the Prevention and Control of Water Pollution] and hold office by the same tenure and at the same remuneration and on the same terms and conditions of service as he would have held the same if the State Board constituted under this Act had not been dissolved and shall continue to do so unless and until such tenure, remuneration and terms and conditions of service are duly altered by the [31][State Board for the prevention and Control Water Pollution]:

Provided that the tenure, remuneration and terms and conditions of service of any such officer or other employee shall not be altered to his disadvantage without the previous sanction of the State Government;

(d) all liabilities and obligations of the State Board of whatever kind, immediately before such dissolution shall be deemed to be the liabilities or obligations, as the case may be, of the [32][State Board for the Prevention and Control of Water Pollution] and any proceedings or cause of action, pending or existing immediately before such dissolution by or against the State Board constituted under this Act in relation to such liability or obligation may be continued and enforced by or against the [32][State Board for the Prevention and Control of Water Pollution]

50. *[Power to amend the Schedule.] Rep. by the Air (Prevention and Control of Pollution) Amendment Act, 1987 (47 of 1987), s. 22. (w.e.f. 1.4.1988).*

Maintenance of register.

51. (1) Every State Board shall maintain a register containing particulars of the persons to whom consent has been granted under section 21, the standards for emission laid down by it in relation to each such consent and such other particulars as may be prescribed.

(2) The register maintained under sub-section (1) shall be open to inspection at all reasonable hours by any person interested in or affected by such standards for emission or by any other person authorised by such person in this behalf.

Effect of other laws.

52. Save as otherwise provided by or under the Atomic Energy Act, 1962, in relation to radioactive air pollution the provisions of this Act shall have effect notwithstanding anything inconsistent therewith contained in any enactment other than this Act.

---

32. The words in brackets "State Board for the Prevention and Control of Water Pollution" shall be substituted as "State Pollution Control Board" by Act 47 of 1987, s.15 (date to be notified).

Power of Central Government to make rules.

53. (1) The Central Government may, in consultation with the Central Board by notification in the Official Gazette make rules in respect of the following matters namely:—

(a) the intervals and the time and place at which meetings of the Central Board or any committee thereof shall be held and the procedure to be followed at such meetings, including the quorum necessary for the transaction of business thereat, under sub-section (1) of section 10 and under sub-section (2) of section 11;

(b) the fees and allowances to be paid to the members of a committee of the Central Board, not being members of the Board, under sub-section (3) of section 11;

(c) the manner in which and the purposes for which persons may be associated with the Central Board under sub-section (1) of section 12;

(d) the fees and allowances to be paid under sub-section (3) of section 12 to persons associated with the Central Board under sub-section (1) of section 12;

(e) the functions to be performed by the Central Board under clause (j) of sub-section (2) of section 16;

(f) [33][the form in which and the time within which the budget of the Central Board may be prepared and forwarded to the Central Government under section 34;

(ff) the form in which the annual report of the Central Board may be prepared under section 35;]

(g) the form in which the accounts of the Central Board may be maintained under sub-section (1) of section 36.

(2) Every rule by the Central Government under this Act shall be laid, as soon as may be after it is made, before each House of Parliament while it is in session, for a total period of thirty days which may be comprised in one session or in two or more successive sessions, and if, before the expiry of the session immediately following the session or the successive sessions aforesaid, both Houses agree in making any modification in the rule or both Houses agree that the rule should not be made the rule shall thereafter have effect only in such modified form or be of no effect, as the case may be; so however, that any such modification or annulment shall be without prejudice to the validity of anything previously done under that rule.

---

33. Subs. by Act 47 of 1987, s. 23, for cl. (f) (w.e.f. 1.4.1988).

Power of State Government to make rules.

54. (1) Subject to the provisions of sub-section (3), the State Government may by notification in the Official Gazette, make rules to carry out the purposes of this Act in respect of matters not falling within the purview of section 53.

(2) In particular, and without prejudice to the generality of the foregoing power, such rules may provide for all or any of the following matters, namely:—

(a) [34][the qualifications, knowledge and experience of scientific, engineering or management aspects of pollution control required for appointment as member-secretary of a State Board constituted under the Act;]

(aa) [35][the term and conditions of service of the Chairman and other members (other than the member-secretary) of the State Board constituted under this Act under sub-section (7) of section 7;

(b) the intervals and the time and place at which meetings of the Central Board or any committee thereof shall be held and the procedure to be followed at such meetings, including the quorum necessary for the transaction of business thereat, under sub-section (1) of section 10 and the under sub-section (2) of section 11;

(c) the fees and allowances to be paid to the members of a committee of the State Board, not being members of the Board, under sub-section (3) of section 11;

(d) the manner in which and the purposes for which persons may be associated with the State Board under sub-section (1) of section 12;

(e) the fees and allowances to be paid under sub-section (3) of section 12 to persons associated with the State Board under sub-section (1) of section 12;

(f) the terms and conditions of service of the member-secretary of a State Board constituted under this Act under sub-section (1) of section 14;

(g) the powers and dates to be exercised and discharged by the member-secretary of a State Board under sub-section (2) of section 14;

(h) the conditions subject to which a State Board may appoint such officers and other employees as it considers necessary for the

34. Ins. by Act 47 of 1987, s. 24, (w.e.f. 1.4.1988).

35. Act. (a) renumbered as cl. (aa) s. 24, *ibid,* (w.e.f. 1.4.1988).

efficient performance of its functions under sub-section (3) of section 14;

(i) the conditions subject to which a State Board may appoint a consultant under sub-section (5) of section 14;

(j) the functions to be performed by the State Board under clause (i) of sub-section (i) of section 17;

(k) the manner in which any area or areas may be declared as air pollution control area or areas under sub-section (1) of section 19;

(l) the form of application for the consent of the State Board, the fees payable therefor, the period within such application shall be made and the particulars it may contain under sub-section (2) of section 21;

(m) the procedure to be followed in respect of an inquiry under sub-section (3) of section 21;

(n) the authorities or agencies to whom information under sub-section (1) of section 23 shall be furnished:

(o) the manner in which samples of air or emission may be taken under sub-section (1) of section 26;

(p) the form of the notice referred to in sub-section (3) of section 26;

(q) the form of the report of the State Board analyst under sub-section (1) of section 27;

(r) the form of the report of the Government analyst under sub-section (3) of section 27;

(s) the functions of the State Air Laboratory, the procedure for the submission to the said Laboratory of samples of air or emission for analysis or test, the form of Laboratory report thereon, the fees payable in respect of such report and other matters as may be necessary or expedient to enable that Laboratory to carry out its functions, under sub-section (2) of section 28;

(t) the qualifications required for Government analyst under sub-section (1) of section 29;

(u) the qualifications required for State Board analysts under sub-section (2) of section 29;

(v) the form and the manner in which appeals may be preferred the fees payable in respect of such appeals and the procedure to be followed by the Appellate Authority in disposing of the appeals under sub-section (3) of section 31;

(w) [36][the form in which and the time within which the budget of the State Board may be prepared and forwarded to the State Government under section 34;

(ww) the form in which the annual report of the State Board may be prepared under section 35;

(x) the form in which the accounts of the State Board may be maintained under sub-section (l) of section 36;

(xx) [37][the manner in which notice of intention to make a complaint shall be given under section 43;]

(y) the particulars which the register maintained under section 51 may contain;

(z) any other matter which has to be, or may be, prescribed.

(3) After the first constitution of the State Board, no rule with respect to any of the matters referred to in sub-section (2) other than those referred to [38][in clause (aa) thereof], shall be made, varied, amended or repealed without consulting that Board.

[The Schedule.] Omitted by the Air (Prevention and Control Pollution) Amendment Act, 1987, s. 25, (w.e.f. 1.4.1988).

36. Subs. by Act 47 of 1987, s. 24, for cl. (w) (w.e.f. 1.4.1988).
37. Ins. by s. 24, *ibid,* (w.e.f. 1.4.1988).
38. Subs by s. 24. *ibid,* for "in clause (a)" (w.e.f. 1.4.1989).

APPENDIX IX

GOVERNMENT OF WEST BENGAL
DEPARTMENT OF ENVIRONMENT
NOTIFICATION

No. ENV/1031/2R-5/83.— 29th October, 1983.— In exercise of the powers conferred by section 14 of the Air (Prevention and Control of Pollution) Act, 1981 (14 of 1981), the Governor, after consultation with the West Bengal Pollution Control Board, hereby makes the following rules:—

CHAPTER I

Preliminary

1. *Short title and commencement.*—(1) These rules may be called the Air (Prevention and Control of Pollution) Rules, 1983.

(2) They shall come into force on the date of their publication in the Official Gazette.

2. *Definitions.*— In these rules, unless there in anything repugnant in the subject or context,—

(a) "Act" means the Air (Prevention and Control) Act, 1981;

(b) "Appellant" means any person aggrieved by the appealing against an order made by West Bengal Pollution Control Board under section 20, section 21 or section 22;

(c) "Appellate Authority" means the Appellate Authority constituted by the Government of West Bengal under sub-section (1) of section 31:

(d) "Board" or "State Board" means the West Bengal Pollution Control Board constituted under section 4 of the Water (Prevention and Control of Pollution, Act, 1974;

(e) "Chairman" means the Chairman of the State Board;

(f) "Central Board" means the Central Board for the Prevention and Control of Water Pollution constituted under section 3 of the Water (Prevention and Control of Pollution) Act, 1974;

(g) "consultants" means and includes any person whose services, technical or otherwise may be obtained by the Chairman to conduct the affairs of the Board.

(h) "emission" means any solid or liquid or gaseous substance coming out of any chimney, duct or flue or any other outlet;

(i) "Form" means a form appended to these rules;

(j) "furnace" means any structure or installation where any form or type of fuel is burnt or otherwise a high temperature higher than ambient is maintained;

(k) "industrial plant" means any plant used for any industrial or trade purposes and emitting any air pollutant into the atmosphere;

(l) "member" means a member of the State Board and includes the Chairman thereof;

(m) "Member-Secretary" means the Member-Secretary of the Board;

(n) "occupier", in relation to any factory or promises, means the person who has control over the affairs of the factory or the premises and where the said affairs are entrusted to a managing agent, such agent shall be deemed to be the occupier of the factory or the premises;

(o) "premises" means any building, structure or property used for industrial or trade purpose where pollution occurs;

(p) "State Air Laboratory" means a laboratory established or specified as such under sub-section (1) of section 28;

(q) "section" means a section of the Act;

(r) "State Board Laboratory" means a laboratory established or recognised as such under sub-section (2) of section 17 of the Act;

(s) "year" means the financial year commencing of the 1st day of April.

CHAPTER II

Appointment of Consultants

3. *Conditions for appointment of consultants.*— For the purposes of assisting the Board in the performance of its functions, the Chairman may appoint a consultant to the Board for a specific period not exceeding six months:

Provided that the Chairman may with the prior approval of the Board extend the period of appointment of the consultant from time to time up to one year:

Provided further that the Chairman may with the prior approval of State Government make appointment of consultants for a period beyond one year.

4. *Power to terminate appointment.*— Notwithstanding the appointment of consultants under rule 3, the Chairman shall have the right to terminate appointment of the consultants before the expiry of the period of their appointment, if in the opinion of the Chairman this becomes desirable.

5. *Salary and allowances or fees of the consultants.*— The Chairman may pay to the consultant suitable salary and allowances or fees depending on the nature of the work and qualifications of the consultant, provided that he shall not appoint any person as consultant if the salary and allowances or fees payable exceed Rs. 2,000 per month. If the salary and allowances or fees payable exceed Rs. 2,000 per month but do not exceed Rs. 2,500 per month, he may appoint a person as consultant with the prior approval of the Board. If the salary and allowances or fees exceed Rs. 2,500 per month approval of the State Government must be obtained before he appoints a person as consultant. If the appointment is for less than one month, prorata payment to the consultants shall be made.

6. *Tours by consultant.*— The consultant may undertake tours within the country for the performance of duties entrusted to him by the Board and in respect of such tours, he shall be entitled to travelling and daily allowance at the rate applicable to Grade - I Officers of the State Government. He will, however, get the prior approval of the Chairman or member-Secretary for his tour programme.

7. *Consultant not to disclose information.*— The consultant shall not be disclose any information either given by the Board or obtained during the performance of the duties assigned to him, either by the Board or otherwise to any person other than the Board without written permission of the Board.

8. *Duties and functions of the consultants.*— The consultant shall discharge such duties and perform such functions are assigned to him by the Board/ Chairman.

CHAPTER III

The manner in which any area or areas may be declared as Air Pollution Control Area or areas under sub-section (1) of section 19

9. *Air Pollution Control and manner of declaration of such areas.* — (1) The area bounded by the respective boundaries of the industries specified in schedule appended to the Act are hereby declared as Air Pollution Control Areas under sub-section (1) or section 19.

(2) In addition to the provisions of sub-rule (i) the State Government may declare any specific area as pollution control area/areas on the recommendation of the Board after it is satisfied for the need of action to control air pollution on the basis of the status of the air quality of that area by notification in the Official Gazette.

CHAPTER IV

The form of application for the consent of the State Board, the fees payable therefor, the period within which such application shall be made and the particulars it may contain.

10. *Application for consent.*—(1) An application for obtaining the consent of the Board for bringing into use any new or altered chimney for emission into, or for continuing an existing emission from chimney under section 21 shall be made to the Board in From I.

(2) Such applications shall be accompanied by fees to be specified by the Board.

(3) Any application not accompanied by the specified fees shall not be entertained by the Board.

(4) The specified fees shall be paid Bank Draft in favour of the Board.

CHAPTER V

Procedures for making enquiry into application for consent.

11. *Procedure for making enquiry into application for consent*— (1) On receipt of an application for consent under section 21 the Board may depute any of its officers accompanied by as many assistants as may be necessary to visit and inspect any place or premises under the control of the applicant or the occupier to which such application relates for the purpose of verifying the correctness or otherwise of the particulars furnished in the application or for obtaining such further particulars or information as such officer may consider necessary. Such officer may for that purpose inspect any place or premises. Where emission from the chimney or fugitive emission from any location with the premises of the

industry as also any control devices installed in the said premises. Such officer may for that purpose, inspect any place or premises under the control of the applicant or occupier, and may require the applicant to furnish to him any plans, specifications or other data relating to control equipment or systems or any part thereof that he considers necessary.

(2) Such officer shall before visiting any premises of the applicant for the purpose of inspection under sub-rule (1) give notices to the applicant of his intention to do so in Form II. The applicant shall furnish to such officer all information and provide all facilities to conduct the inspection.

(3) An officer of the Board may, before or after carrying out an inspection under sub-rule, (1) require the applicant to furnish to him orally or in writing such additional information or clarification, or to produce before him such documents as he may consider necessary for the purpose of investigation of the application and may for that purpose summon the applicant or authorised agent to the office of the Board.

CHAPTER VI

The authorities or agencies to whom information under sub-section (1) of section 23 is to be provided

12. *Submission of information by the occupier under sub-section (1) of section 23.*— An officer-in-charge of industrial plant or occupier of the premises from where due to an accidental breakdown of some processes or installations or otherwise, an emission occurs or is apprehended to occur in excess of the standards laid down by the Board shall forthwith intimate the fact of such occurrence or of the apprehension of such occurrence to the Collector, Sub-divisional Magistrate, nearest police authority, the nearest officer of the local authority including Department of Panchayat, Environment, Health and Family Welfare and industry in addition to the State Board.

CHAPTER VII

The manner in which samples of air and emission may be taken under sub-section (1) of section 26

13. *Power to take samples.*— (1) The Board, or any officer empowered by it in this behalf shall have the power to take, for the purpose of analysis samples of air or emission from any chimney, flue or duct, plant or vessel or any other sources and outlets, stationary or mobile under sub-section (1) of section 26. The occupier of the premises shall provide all necessary facilities for sampling of air or emission from any chimney, flue or duct, plant or vessel or any other sources and outlets, stationary or mobile, as may be specified by the Board or any officer empowered by it in this behalf. The occupier of the premises shall provide all

necessary facilities for access to the sampling places as may be specified by the Board or any officer empowered by it in this behalf.

(2) The procedures used for sampling air or emission from any chimney, flue or duct, plant or vessel or any other sources and outlet, stationary or mobile, the instruments used for sampling and the methods of measuring air pollutants shall be such as may be specified by the Board to suit the situation.

CHAPTER VIII

The form of the notice referred to in sub-section (3) of section 26

14. *Form of notice.*—A notice under sub-section (3) of section 26 shall be in Form III.

CHAPTER IX

Report of Board Analyst

15. *Form of report of Board Analyst.*— When a sample of any air or emission has been sent for analysis to a laboratory established or recognised by the Board, the Board Analyst appointed under sub-section (2) of section 29 shall analyse the sample and submit to the Board a report of the result of such analysis in triplicate in Form IV.

CHAPTER X

State Air Laboratory

16. *Functions of the State Air Laboratory.*— The State Air Laboratory shall cause to be analysed any sample of air or emission received by it from any officer authorised by the Board, for the purpose, and the finding shall be recorded in triplicate in Form V.

17. *Fees for reports.*— The fees for each such report shall be such as may be notified by the Board from time to time.

CHAPTER XI

The qualifications required for Government Analyst

18. *Qualifications of Government Analyst and Board Analyst.*— The qualifications for the Government Analyst and Board Analyst under sub-section (1) and (2) of section 29 shall be as follows:

At least 2nd Class M.Sc. in Chemistry, Biochemistry or Physics with three years experience in Environmental Quality Management.

CHAPTER XII

Appeals

19. *Memorandum of Appeal*.— (1) Every appeal against an order passed by the State Board under section 20, section 21, or section 22 shall be filed by the aggrieved party in Form VII.

(2) Every aggrieved person preferring an appeal shall do so separately in his own name and no joint appeal made on behalf of more than one person shall be entertained by the appellate authority.

(3) (a) Every appeal shall—

(i) be in writing

(ii) specify the name and address of the appellant and the date of the order appealed against,

(iii) specify the date on which the order appealed against was communicated to the appellant,

(iv) contain a clear statement of facts of the case and grounds relied upon by the aggrieved person in support of the appeal,

(v) state precisely the relief prayed for, and

(vi) be signed and verified by the appellant or an agent duly authorised by the appellant in writing in this behalf.

(b) Every appeal shall be accompanied by—

(i) an authenticated copy of the order against which appeal is made,

(ii) a copy of the application made under sections 20, 21 or under section 22 as the case may be,

(iii) any document relative to the appeal, and

(iv) a satisfactory proof of the payment of the specified fee.

(c) A fee as specified by the Board shall be deposited by every appellant in the office of the appellant authority and

an authenticated copy of the receipts obtained therefore shall be annexed to every appeal. No appeal which is not accompanied by the aforesaid copy of the receipt shall be entertained by the appellate authority.

(d) Every memorandum of appeal shall be submitted in quadruplicate and shall either be presented to the appellate authority by the appellant or his authorised agent in person or sent to such authority by registered post. When the memorandum of appeal is presented by an agent duly authorised by the appellant, it shall be accompanied by a letter of authority written on a stamped paper of the value as required by law, appointing him as such an agent.

(e) On receipt of the memorandum of appeal, the appellate authority shall endorse thereon the date of its presentation or receipt by post and the name of the appellant or his duly authorised agent proceeding it, as the case may be.

20. *Procedure to be followed by the appellate authority in dealing with the disposal of the appeal.*— (1) The appellate authority shall, as soon as may be after the memorandum of appeal is filed before it, fix a date for hearing of the appeal and give intimation of the same to the appellant and the Member-Secretary in Form VIII. While giving such intimation to the Member-Secretary, a copy of the memorandum of appeal together with its enclosures shall also be sent to the Member-Secretary and he shall be called upon to send to the appellate authority, all the relevant records connected with the matter relating to the appeal.

(2) Where the material on record is insufficient to enable the appellate authority to come to a decision, it may take additional evidence and call for such further material from the appellant or the Member-Secretary as it deems fit. Such material shall form part of the record but not before the party other than that from whom such record has been received has been given an opportunity to pursue such record, itself anything contained therein which is detrimental to the interest of the party.

(3) Where on the date fixed for hearing or any date to which the hearing of the appeal may be adjourned, the appellant or his duly authorised agent does not appear when the appeal is called for hearing, the appeal shall be liable, to be dismissed.

(4) Where an appeal is dismissed under sub-rule (3) the appellant may within 30 days from the dismissal of the appeal apply to the appellate authority for the restoration of the appeal and if it is shown to the satisfaction of the appellate authority that the appellant had not received intimation of the date of hearing of the appeal or was prevented by any cause, sufficient, in the opinion of the appellate authority, from appearing when the appeal was called for hearing, the appellate authority may restore the appeal on such terms as it thinks fit.

(5) *Order to be in writing.*— The order passed the appellate authority on the appeal shall be in writing and shall state clearly the points before it was for determination, the decision thereon, and the reasons for the decision.

(6) *Supply of copy of order to the appellant and the Board.*— A copy of the order passed in appeal shall be supplied by the appellate authority free of cost to the appellant and a copy thereof shall also be sent to the Member-Secretary.

CHAPTER XIII

The particulars to be contained in the Consent Register

21. *Consent register*— The Board shall maintain a register in Form VI containing particulars of industrial plant to which consent has been granted under section 21.

CHAPTER XIV

Temporary association of persons

22. *Manner and purpose of association of persons and fees and allowances to be paid for such association*—Manner in which and purpose for which any person may be temporary associated with the Board in performing any of its functions under the Act will be as provided in the rule notified (vide notification No. Env/458/2R-4/82, dated the 12th May, 1983) under section 10 of the Water (Prevention and Control of Pollution) Act, 1974.

CHAPTER XV

Functions to be performed by the Board

23. *Functions of the Board.*— The Board shall perform such functions as may be specified by the State Government, in consultation with the State Board in writing from time to time.

CHAPTER XVI

Miscellaneous

24. *Miscellaneous.*— In respect of matters relating to the

(i) terms and conditions of service of the Chairman, Member-Secretary and Members of the Board;

(ii) Procedure for transaction of business of the Board;

(iii) temporary association of persons with the Board;

(iv) powers and duties of the Member-Secretary of the Board;

(v) budget and accounts of the Board;

(vi) annual report on the activities of the Board; and

(vii) any other matter which has not been specifically mentioned,

the Board shall follow the provisions of the relevant rules made under the Water (Prevention and Control of Pollution) Act, 1974.

FORM I

(See rule 10)

To be submitted in triplicate

Application for consent for emission/continuation of emission under section 21 of (Prevention and Control of Pollution) Act, 1981

From: Dated:

To

The Member-Secretary

West Bengal Pollution Control Board.

Sir,

I/We hereby apply for CONSENT under section 21 of the Air (Prevention and Control of Pollution) Act, 1981 (14 of 1981) to make emission from industrial plant owned by (1).................................. for a period up to (2).......................

2. The annexure, appendices, other particulars and plans are attached herewith in triplicate.

3. I/We further declare that the information furnished in the annexure/ appendices, and plans in correct to the best of my/our knowledge.

4. I/We hereby submit that in case of a change either of the point or the quantity of emission or of its quality a fresh application for CONSENT shall be made and until such consent is granted, no change shall be made.

5. I/We hereby agree to submit to the Board, application for renewal of CONSENT one month in advance of the date of the consented period for emission, or to be continued thereafter.

6. I/We undertake to furnish any other information within one month of its being called for by the Board.

Yours faithfully,

Signature...

Name of Applicant:

Address of Applicant

Accompaniments:

(i) Index/Site Plant

(ii) Topographical map

(iii) Detailed layout plan or different processes and point sources of emissions and position of stacks and chimneys

(iv) Process flow sheet

(v) Latest Analysis Report

(vi) Details of Air Pollution control devices provided or proposed to be provided

(vii) Ambient air quality report, if available

(vii) Draft No. ...., dated .... for Rs. .... drawn on .... as consent fee.

ANNEXURE TO FORM

Chimney

Existing
New
Altered

Note.— Any applicant knowingly giving incorrect information or suppressing any information pertaining thereto shall be liable to any actions under the provisions of the Act.

While filling this annexure the applicant shall for such of the items not pertaining to his activity shall state "not applicable" against the relevant one and not leave blank.

1. Full Name of the Applicant: ....

(a) Address ....

Tel. No. ....

(b) Is the firm registered ? ....

(c) If yes, give the number and date of registration and the authority with whom registered: ....

(d) Full address of the registered office: ....
....

(e) Names, designations and full address of persons like, Partners/Managing Director/Director/Manager etc.: ....
....
....

(f) Under which category does the industry fall Major/Medium/Small Scale: ....

2.	Full name of the Land/ Premises/Institute/Factory/ Industry/Local Body with address :	.... Tel. No. .... Telegraphic address ....
3.	Give Revenue / City Survey No. of the land / premises for which the application is made:	District: Town: Village: City Survey No.: Revenue Survey No.: Area in hectares:
4.	State month and year in which the plant was actually put into commission or is proposed to be put into commission :	
5.	State the Civil/Military/ Defence/Industrial Estate etc. under whose administrative jurisdiction the occupiers industrial plant is situated :	District: Corporation: Municipality: Village Panchayat/Cantonment/ Defence Deptt.: Port Trust: State Govt.: Prohibited Areas: Central Govt.: Air port Authority:
6.	(a) State whether plant site has been declared as prohibited area:	Yes/No
	(b) If yes, state the name of the authority and furnish certified copy if the order under which the area has been declared as area :	
7.	State Working season per year of the Plant.	Full Year From to From to Every year
	Continuous/Batchwise	

8. (a) No. of persons attending the factory per day:

   (b) No. of persons residing in the premises:

9. Indicate the present use of the land in the vicinity (5 Km. radius) of the plant site.
   (i) Human settlement of more than 1000 population (specify population and distance from the plants):
   (ii) Commercial:
   (iii) Industrial:
   (iv) Fisheries:
   (v) Sanctuary/National Parks/Hills Mountains:
   (vi) Ancient Monuments:

10. Climatological and meteorological details (if available):
    (a) Indicate the climate conditions at the site (e.g. arid, semi-arid etc.):
    (b) Ranifall, yearly average range:
    (c) Temperature, seasonal ranges:
    (d) Information on speed and direction of wind:
    (e) Humidity:

11. Give list of all materials used in the process in metric tonnes/day.

List of raw materials	Principle use	Amount in T/day

A process flow diagram must be included with this statement showing entry and exist points of all raw materials, intermediate products, by-products and finished products, label process and control equipment.

12. Fuel consumption in T/day.

	Coal	Oil	Wood	Natural Gas	Others (specify)
1. Daily consumption in tonnes					
2. Calorofic value					
3. Ash content %					
4. Sulphur content %					
5. Others (specify)					

13. Atmospheric emission for each stack:

(i) Stack No.

(ii) Material of construction of stack:

(iii) Stack attached to:

(iv) Stack height:

(a) above the roof Mts.
(b) above the ground level Mts.

(v) Stack top:

(a) round or circle
(b) inside dimensions of at top

(vi) Gas quantity — M^3/hr.

(vii) Flue gas tem. — ^{0}C.

(viii) Exit velocity of the gas—m/sec.

(a) Flue gas emissions:

Analysis of flue gas in mg/m^3 of stack and/or in Kg/tonnes Product

Stack No.	Type of fuel	Qty. of fuel/ hr.	Type of fi- ring	SO_2	HC	CO	Partic- ulars	Others (specify)

(b) Process emission:

Quality of gas in m^3/hr.	SO_2	CO	CO_2	NO	Analysis of Hydrocar- bons	Vent gas in mg/ng/ particulate	Others (specify)

(c) (i) Particulates analysis (if available) size-distribution.
50 ....%
10 ....%
50 ....%

(ii) Chemical composition (if available).
30 ....%
10 ....%

14. Give details of flue gas sampling arrangements :

15. Give details of laboratory facilities available for analysis of emission :

16. Is there sufficient space available for installing air pollution control equipment ?

17. Details of air pollution control system :

(a) Existing :

Give detailed specification (collectors, precipitators)

(b) Proposed :

18. State the total quantity of air handled by ventilation equipment. Specify size and number of equipment installed or to be installed :

19. Give the following details :

(a) Total investment in the factory and the year of investment :

(b) The estimated expenditure for implementing the scheme to control air pollution :

(c) Expenditure incurred to date and progress achieved (physical) for air pollution control, if any, and the year/years of investment along with physical progress achieved :

(d) Annual operation and maintenance cost of air pollution plant, if any :

(e) Further action that is being taken by the firm to control air pollution :

20. Other relevant information if any :

Signature :
Name and Address of the applicant on behalf of :
Name and Address of the firm :

Explanatory note for filling in the form and the annexure

The notes are given only for those items for which explanation is considered desirable.

FORM

(1) Here mention the name of the owner of the land/premises if other than the applicant industry or factory in continuation of legal business as per Air (Prevention and Control of Pollution) Act, 1981. If land/premises belong to the factory/industry, say self.

The industries are categorised based on the capital investment, as follows :

Major industry — more than 2 crore rupees capital.

Medium industry — lakh to 2 crores.

Small scale industry — less than 10 lakh rupees.

(2) Here mention the date up to which the consent is sought for.

ANNEXURE TO FORM

Existing means that which is in operation at the time of applying for the consent.

Now means that which will be brought into operation in future.

Altered means that which has been modified due to change in quantity and/ or quality of emission, arrangement and / or point of emission, etc.

Item No. 1. Here mention the name of the owner of the land/premises of other than the applicant industry or factory in continuation of legal business as per Air (Prevention and Control of Pollution) Act, 1981. If land/premises belong to the factory/industry, say self.

Item No. 2. Here give the registered name of the industry /institution/factory/ local bodies etc. under which the business is carried out.

Item No. 6. Applicable to only areas which are prohibited areas such as the ordance factories, mint, etc.

Item No. 10(c). Here state the temperature in °C in summer, monsoon and post-monsoon seasons.

Item No.10 (d) & (e) Here state the seasonal average wind direction and speed in and around the site of the plant. The above information can be had from representative Meteorological Centre.

Item No. 13. Analysis of the flue gas emission, process emission and particulates analysis should be done for each stack emission. Wherever stacks are not provided the shop floor specific pollutants should be reported.

Chemical analysis of the particulates matter in the emission should be furnished giving details such as organic matter, metals, non-metals, radioactive substances, asbestos, silicates, etc.

Item No. 17. Here state the detailed specifications of control system used or proposed to be used with efficiency. Also furnish the layout of the control system with dimensions.

Item No. 19. Here state the total quantity of ventilation air handled by equipments such as roof extractors, evaporative coolers, etc.

FORM II

WEST BENGAL POLLUTION CONTROL BOARD

Notice of Inspection

[See rule 11 (2)]

No. ....

Dated ....

To

....

....

TAKE NOTICE that for the purpose of enquiry under section 21 of the Air (Prevention and Control of Pollution) Act, 1981, the following officers of the State Board, namely :

(i) Shri...

(ii) Shri...

(iii) Shri...

and the persons authorised by the Board to assist them shall inspect—

any systems of your industrial plant;

any other parts thereof or pertaining thereto;

under management control of date

(a) .... between .... hours when all facilities requested by them for such inspection should be made available to them on the site. Take notice that refusal or denial to above-stated demand made under the functions of this Board shall amount to obstruction punished under section 37 (1) of the Air (Prevention and Control of Pollution) Act, 1981.

By order of the Board

Member-Secretary

Copy to :

1. ....
2. ....
3. ....

FORM III

WEST BENGAL POLLUTION CONTROL BOARD

Notice of intention to have sample analysed

(See rule 14)

To

TAKE NOTICE that it is intended to have analysed the sample of air or emission from your premises which is being taken today the .... day of .... 19 .... from ....

Name and designation of the person who has taken the sample.

* Here specify the stack, chimney or any other emission outlets.

To

....

....

FORM IV

Report by the State Board Analyst

(See rule 15)

Report No. ....

Dated, the ....

I hereby certify that I, (I) .... Board Analyst duly appointed under sub-section (2) of section 29 of the Air (Prevention and Control of Pollution) Act, 1981 received on the (II) .... day of ....19 .... from

(III) .... a sample of .... for analysis. The sample was in a condition fit for analysis reported below.

I further certify that I have analysed the aforementioned sample on (IV) .... and declare the result of the analysis to be follows :

(V) ....

The conditions of the seals, fastening and container on receipt was as follows:

....

Signed this .... day of ....19 ....

Address .... Signature, Board Analyst

....

To

....

....

(I) Here write the full name of the Board Analyst.

(II) Here write the date of receipt of the sample.

(III) Here write the name of the Board or person or body of persons or officer from whom the sample was received.

(IV) Here write the date of analysis.

(V) Here write the details of the analysis and refer to the method of analysis. If the space is not adequate the details may be given on a separate sheet of paper.

FORM V

Report by the Government Analyst

(See rule 19)

Report No. ....

Dated, the ....

I hereby certify that I, (I) .... Government Analyst duly appointed under sub-section (1) of section 29 of the Air (Prevention and Control of Pollution) Act, 1981 received on the

(II) ....day of..........................19............from

(III) .... sample of .... for analysis. The sample was in a condition fit for analysis reported below.

I further certify that I have analysed the aforementioned sample on (IV) ....and declare the result of the analysis to be as follows :

(V)...

Signed, this ....day of .... 19...............

Address .... Signature, Government Analyst

....

To

....

....

(I) Here write the full name of the Board Analyst.

(II) Here write the date of receipt of the sample.

(III) Here write the name of the Board or person or body of persons or officer from whom the sample was received.

(IV) Here write the date of analysis.

(V) Here write the details of the analysis and refer to the method of analysis. If the space is not adequate the details may be given on a separate sheet paper.

FORM VI

(See rule 21)

Under rule 21 the following shall be the form of the register to be maintained in respect of consents to be issued under section 21 of the Act.

I. General —

(a) Consent is issued to :

....

(Corporation, Company, Government, Agency, Firm, etc.)

(b) Postal Address..

(II) Location of plant or facilities (latitude and longitude must be to the nearest of 15 seconds)—

(a) Nearest city .... District............................

(b) Latitude ....Longitude............................

(c) Is it located in air pollution control area ? — Yes/No

If Yes, identification of air pollution control area :........................

III. Type of operation or process—

(a) Name of operation or process

(b) Schedule identification number

IV. Consents classification— Yes No

(a) Proposed

(b) Now operating

(c) Modification of existing emission source

(d) Location change

(e) Ownership change

(f) Present consent order number, if any

V. Implementation dates—

(a) In the case of Proposed industries operation expected to begin. .... (day) (month) (year)

(b) Air Pollution control equipment and emission to be installed standards achieved by .... (day) (month) (year)

VI. Emission standards—

Emission source Number (from plot plan)	Air pollutant emitted	Emission rate kg./hour or standard/sec.
1	2	3

VII. Consent conditions, if any —

FORM VII

Form or appeal under section 31 of the Air (Prevention and Control of Pollution) Act, 1981 (14 of 1981)

*[See rule 19 (1) (a)]

Before .... Appellate Authority constituted under section 31 of the Air (Prevention and Control of Pollution) Act, 1981 (14 of 1981) Memorandum of appeal of Shri ....

(Appellant)

West Bengal Pollution Control Board ....

(respondent).

The appeal of Shri .... Resident of .... District .... against the order .... dated .... passed by the West Bengal Pollution Control under sections 20/21/22 of the Air (Prevention and Control of Pollution) Act, 1981, showeth as follows:

(1) Under sections 20/21/22 of the Air (Prevention and Control of Pollution) Act, 1981 (14 of 1981), the appellant has been granted consent subject to the condition mentioned in the consent order in respect of the .... company / corporation / municipality / notified area committee etc., noted below:

(a) Name of plant/company/corporation/municipality/notified area committee (Here mention the grounds on which appeal is made)

(b) Place..

(c) Card No. ....

(d) Name of the street .... and

(e) District ....

A copy of the consent order in question is attached hereto.

(2) The facts of the case are as under : (Here briefly mention the facts of the case)

*Here mention the name and designation of the authority.

(3) The grounds on which the appellant relies for the purpose of this appeal are as below (Here mention the grounds on which appeal is made):

1.

2.

3.

(4) In the light of what is stated above, the appellant respectfully prayeth that —

(a) the unreasonable conditions .... imposed should be treated as annulled or it/they should be constituted for such other conditions it appears to be reasonable, or

(b) the unreasonable condition(s) .... should be varied in the following manner:

[Here mention the manner in which the condition (s) are objected to]

An amount of Rs. .... as fee for this appeal has been paid vide receipt No. .... dated .... an authorised copy of which is attached in proof of payment.

Signature of the Appellant

(Name in Block Letters)

Occuption ....

Address...............................

Dated:

Verification

I .... (appellant's name) in the above memorandum of appeal/or duly authorised agent do/does hereby declare that what is stated therein is true to the best of my knowledge and belief and nothing has been hidden thereunder.

Signature ....

Name...

(Block Letter)

Occuption.......................................

Address..

Dated:

Strike out which is not applicable.

FORM VIII

[See rule 20(1)]

Before *..................................Appellate Authority as constituted under section 31(1) of the Air (Prevention and Control of Pollution) Act, 1981 (14 of 1981).

In the matter of appeal No. .... 19.................filed under section 31 of the Air (Prevention and Control of Pollution) Act, 1981 (14 of 1981), by Shri..........................(here mention the name and address of the appellant).

Whereas Shri.............................(here mention the name and address of the appellant) has filed before this Authority a memorandum of appeal against order No..................................dated.........................passed by West Bengal Pollution Control Board under sections 20/21/22 of the Act.

And whereas under sub-section (4) of section 31 of the Act this authority is required to give the parties an opportunity of being heard;

Now, therefore, please take notice that this authority has fixed..................as the date of hearing of the aforesaid appeal. The hearing shall take place at...........a.m./p.m. on that date in the office of the Board at Calcutta. You are hereby called upon to appear before this authority at the appointed time and date and place, either in person or through a duly authorised agent, and explain your case. Please take notice that failure on your part to appear on the day of hearing either in person or through a duly authorised agent, without showing sufficient cause to the satisfaction of this authority will make your appeal liable to be dismissed or decided exparte.

Given under the hand and seal of the Appellate Authority at .... this .... day ....

By order of the Governor,

A.B. Basu

Dy. Secy. to the Govt. of West Bengal

*Here mention the name and designation of the authority. Delete whether is not applicable.

Published by authority

Part I — Orders and Notifications by the Governor of West Bengal, the High Court, Government Treasury, etc.

GOVERNMENT OF WEST BENGAL
DEPARTMENT OF ENVIRONMENT
NOTIFICATION

No. ENV/1262/2S-7/85.—16th August, 1985. — In exercise of the power conferred by section 54 of the Air (Prevention and Control of Pollution) Act, 1981 (14 of 1981), the Governor is pleased hereby to make, in consultation with the West Bengal Pollution Control Board the following amendment in the Air (Prevention and Control of Pollution) Rules, 1983, published with this department notification No. ENV/1031/2R-5/85, dated the 29th October, 1983 in Part I of the 'Calcutta' Gazette, Extraordinary", dated the 29th October 1983 (hereinafter referred to as the said rules):—

Amendment

In the said rules, after sub-rule (1) of rule 10, insert the following sub-rule:—

"(1A) Where any person immediately before the declaration of any area as an air pollution control area, operates in such area any industrial plant for the purpose of any industry specified in the Schedules to the Act, such person shall make the application under sub-section (2), for consent of the Board under sub-section (1) of section 21 within 180 days from the date of publication of this sub-rule in the Official Gazette (being not less than three months from the date of such declaration)."

By order of the Governor,
A.B. Basu.
Dy. Secy. to the Govt. of West Bengal

EMISSION STANDARD AS PER SECTION 17(1) (G) OF THE AIR (PREVENTION & CONTROL OF POLLUTION) ACT 1981

1. Cement Industry

A. Particulate matter:—

(a) 200 metric tons per day and less capacity
- i) Protected area — 250 mg/Nm^3
- ii) Other area — 400 mg/Nm^3

(b) Greated than 200 metric tons per day capacity
- i) Protected area — 150 mg/Nm^3
- ii) Other area — 15 mg/Nm^3

2. Thermal Power Industry

A. Particulate matter:—

(a) Boiler size less than 200 MW
- i) Protected area — 150 mg/Nm^3
- ii) Other area — 150 mg/Nm^3

(b) Boiler size 200 MW — i) Protected area — 150 mg/Nm^3
ii) Other area — 150 mg/Nm^3

Sulphur dioxide in terms of stack height.

(a) Boiler size less than 200 MW	i) $H = 14 (Q)^{0.3}$
(b) Boiler size 200 MW and less than 500 MW	ii) H = 220 m
(c) Boiler size 500 MW and above	iii) H = 275 m

Where Q = Sulphur dioxide emission in kg/hr. calculated by the Board using suitable emission factors.

H = Stack height in metres.

Note:— Protected area is one which is already polluted from being in a metropolitant/industrial location or the area is sensitive because of its proximity to national park, forests, historical monuments and health resorts.

3. Iron & Steel Industry

A. Particulate matter.

(a) Sintering plant	150 mg/Nm^3
(b) Steel making during normal operation	150 mg/Nm^3
(c) Steel making during oxygen lancing	400 mg/Nm^3
(d) Coke oven	150 mg/Nm^3
(e) Blast furnace	150 mg/Nm^3
(f) Cupola furnace	400 mg/Nm^3
(g) Electric Arc furnace	400mg/Nm^3

4. Calcium Carbide manufacture

A. Particulate matter.

(a) Kiln	250 mg/Nm^3
(b) Arc furnace	150 mg/Nm^3
(c) Kiln and Arc furnace combined	250 mg/Nm^3
B. Carbon monoxide	500 mg/Nm^3

5. Copper, Lead and Zinc Smelting/Refining industry

a) Particulate matter

Concentrator	150 mg/Nm^3
Refining	150 mg/Nm^3

b)	Sulphur dioxide Smelters concentrator	off gases must go for H_2SO_4 manufacture. No release of SO_2/SO shall be permitted.

6. Carbon Black industry

a)	Particulate matter	150 mg/Nm³
b)	Carbon monoxide	500 mg/Nm³
c)	Hydrogen sulphide	5 mg/Nm³

7. Fertilizer industry.

a)	Particulate matter	
	Grannulate matter	150 mg/Nm³
	Nitrogenous	150 mg/Nm³
b)	Fluoride	
	Acidification of rock phosphate	25 mg/Nm³
c)	Fluorine	
	Phosphoric acid manufacture	10 mg/Nm³
	Superphosphate and Di-ammonium Phosphate manufacture	10 mg/Nm³
d)	Hydrogen fluoride	
	Phosphate fertilizer acidification & rock phosphate	1 mg/Nm³
(e)	Fluoride (as F)	
	Phosphatic fertilizer acidification of rock phosphate	25 mg/Nm³
(f)	Ammonia Nitrogenous fertilizer plant	360 mg/Nm³
(g)	Oxide of Nitrogen	60 mg/Nm³

8. Aluminium manufacturing industry/Aluminium and its allied products and processing industry.

a)	Particulate matter	
	Calcination	250 mg/Nm³
	Aluminium Production	150 mg/Nm³
	Aluminium Processing	150 mg/Nm³
(b)	Fluorine	
	Aluminium manufacture	50 mg/Nm³
c)	Hydrogen/fluoride	
	Aluminium manufacture	3 mg/Nm³

9. Oil Refineries

a) Hydrogen sulphate	10 mg/Nm^3
b) Particulate matters	
Furnaces	120 mg/Nm^3
Catalyst Regeneration	50 mg/Nm^3

10. Industrial Boilers for electrical energy or steam

a) Suphurdioxide	
Liquid fuel burning	1200 mg/Nm^3
Solid fuel burning	1200 mg/Nm^3
b) Carbon monoxide	
Solid fuel burning	250 mg/Nm^3
Liquid fuel burning	175 mg/Nm^3
c) Particulate matter	
Protected area	150 mg/Nm^3
Other	350 mg/Nm^3

11. Paper and pulp industry

a) Sulphate pulp liquor combustion	
Particulate matter	250 mg/Nm^3
b) Craft pulp mill recovery furnace	
Particulate matter	250 mg/Nm^3

12. Sulphur dioxide manufacture

Sulphur dioxide	30 mg/Nm^3

13. Sulphuric acid manufacture

a) Sulphur dioxide	1500 mg/Nm^3
Single conversion—single absorption	10 Kg/Ton of concentrated (100%) acid produced
Double conversion—double absorption	4 Kg/Ton of concentrated (100%) acid produced

14. Nitric acid manufacture

a) Oxide of nitrogen (NO_x)	3Kg. of NO_x per ton of weak acid (before concentration) Produced

15. Glass manufacture

a) Fluorine	10 mg/Nm^3
b) Hydrogen Fluoride	1 mg/Nm^3

16. General standards for emission wherever applicable from any industries.

a)	Particulate matter	250 mg/Nm³
b)	Fluorine compounds	50 mg/Nm³
c)	Chlorine and chlorine compounds	200 mg/Nm³
d)	Carbon monoxide	500 mg/Nm³
e)	Hydrogen sulphide	5 mg/Nm³
f)	Mercury and its compounds	3 mg/Nm³

17. Minimum Stack Height

a) Plant Type	Stack Height
For all plants except thermal Power Plant	30 Meters

b) For plants where the sulphur dioxide emission is estimated as Q (Kg/hr) the stack height, H in metres is given by

$$H = 14\ (Q)^{0.3}$$

c) For plants where the particulate matter emission is estimated as Q (Tonnes/hr) the stack height, H in metres is given by

$$H = 70\ (Q)^{0.27}$$

d) If by using the formula given in (b) & (c) above, the stack height arrived at, is more than 30 M then this higher stack height should be used.

AMBIENT AIR QUALITY STANDARDS IN RESPECT OF NOISE

Section 16(2) (h) of the Air (Prevention and Control of Pollution) Act, 1981

The Central Pollution Control Board in exercise of its powers under Section 16(2) (h) of the Air (Prevention and Control of Pollution) Act, 1981 hereby notify the Ambient Air Quality Standards in respect of Noise as follows :

Area Code	Category of Area	Limits in dB (A) Leq	
		Day Time	Night Time
A)	Industrial Area	75	70
B)	Commercial Area	65	55
C)	Residential Area	55	45
D)	Silence Zone	50	40

Definition:

1.	Day Time	:	is reckoned in between 6 AM and 9 P.M.
2.	Night Time	:	is reckoned in between 9 PM to 6 A.M.
3.	Silence Zone	:	is defined as areas upto 100 metres around such premises as hospitals, educational institutions and courts. The Silence Zones are to be declared by the Competent Authority. Use of vehicular horns, loudspeakers and bursting of crackers shall be banned in these zones.

Note-1 Mixed categories of areas should be declared as one of the four above mentioned categories by the Competent Authority and the corresponding standards shall apply.

PERMISSIBLE NOISE EXPOSURE FOR INDUSTRIAL WORKERS

Exposure Time (in hr/day)	Limit in dB (A)
8	90
4	93
2	96
1	99
1/2	102
1/4	105
1/8	108
1/16	111
1/32 (2 minutes) or less	114

NOISE LIMITS FOR AUTOMOBILES AT MANUFACTURING STAGE

(To be achieved by the Year 1992)

	Categories of automobiles	Limits in dB(A)
a)	Motorcycle, Scooters & Three Wheelers	80
b)	Passengers Cars	82
c)	Passenger or Commercial vehicles of upto 4 MT	85
d)	Passenger or commercial vehicles of above 4 MT and upto 12 MT	89
e)	Passenger or Commercial vehicles exceeding 12 MT	91

NOISE LIMITS FOR DOMESTIC APPLIANCES

Domestic appliances	Limits in dB(A) Sound Pressure level at the meter distance from the operating appliance
a) Window Air Conditioners of 1 Ton to 1.5 Ton	68
b) Air Coolers	60
c) Refrigerators	46

MINISTRY OF ENVIRONMENT AND FORESTS

(Department of Environment Forests and Wildlife)

NOTIFICATION

New Delhi, the 26th December, 1989

G.S.R. 1963(E): In exercise of the powers conferred by section 6 and 25 of the Environment (Protection) Act, 1986 (29 of 1986), Central Government hereby makes the following rules further to amend the Environment (Protection) Rules; 1986, namely :—

1. (1) These rules may be called the Environment (Protection) Third Amendment Rules, 1989.

(2) They shall come into force on the date of their publication in the Official Gazette.

2. In the Environment (Protection) Rules; 1986, after Schedule 11, the following Schedule shall be inserted, namely :—

SCHEDULE III

(See rule 3)

AMBIENT AIR QUALITY STANDARDS IN RESPECT OF NOISE

Area Code	Category of area	Limits in dB(A)	Leq
		Day Time	Night Time
(A)	Industrial area	75	70
(B)	Commercial area	65	55
(C)	Residential area	55	45
(D)	Silence Zone	50	40

Note-1 Day Time is reckoned in between 6 a.m. and 9 p.m.

Note-2 Night Time is reckoned in between 9 p.m. to 6 a.m.

Note-3 Silence Zone is defined as areas upto 100 metres around such premises as hospitals, educational institutions and courts. The Silence Zones are to be declared by the Competent Authority. Use of vehicular horns, loudspeakers and burning of crackers shall be banned in these zones.

Note-4 Mixed categories of areas should be declared as one of the four above mentioned categories by the Competent Authority and the corresponding standards shall apply.

APPENDIX X

THE ENVIRONMENTAL (PROTECTION) ACT, 1986

MINISTRY OF LAW AND JUSTICE

(Legislative Department)

New Delhi, the 26th May, 1986/Jyaistha 5, 1908 (Saka)

The following Act of Parliament received the assent of the President on the 23rd May, 1986, and is hereby published for general information:—

No. 29 of 1986 (23rd May, 1986)

An Act to provide for the protection and improvement of environment and for matters connected therewith

Whereas decisions were taken at the United Nations Conference on the Human Environment held at Stockholm in June, 1972, in which India participated, to take appropriate steps for the protection and improvement of human environment;

And whereas it is considered necessary further to implement the decisions aforesaid in so far as they relate to the protection and improvement of environment and the prevention of hazards to human beings, other living creatures, plants and property;

Be it enacted by Parliament in the Thirty-Seventh Year of the Republic of India as follows:

Chapter 1

PRELIMINARY

Short title, extent and commencement

1. (1) This Act may be called the Environment (Protection) Act, 1986.

(2) It extends to the whole of India.

(3) It shall come into force on such date as the Central Government may, be

notification in the Official Gazette, appoint and different dates may be appointed for different provisions of this Act and for different areas.

Definitions

2. In this Act, unless the context otherwise requires, —

(a) "environment" includes water, air and land and the interrelationship which exists among and between water, air and land, and human beings, other living creatures, plants, micro-organism and property;

(b) "environmental pollutant" means any solid, liquid or gaseous substance present in such concentration as may be, or tend to be injurious to environment;

(c) "environmental pollution" means the presence in the environment of any environmental pollutant;

(d) "handling", in relation to any substance, means the manufacture, processing, treatment, package, storage, transportation, use, collection, destruction, conversion, offering for sale, transfer or the like of such substance;

(e) "hazardous substance" means any substance or preparation which, by reason of its chemical or physico-chemical properties or handling is liable to cause harm to human beings, other living creatures, plants, micro-organism property or the environment.

(f) "occupier" in relation to any factory or premises means a person who has control over the affairs of the factory or the premises and includes, in relation to any substance, the person in possession of the substance;

(g) "prescribed" means prescribed by rules made under this Act.

Chapter II

GENERAL POWERS OF THE CENTRAL GOVERNMENT

Power of Central Government to take measures to protect and improve environment

3. (1) Subject to the provisions of this Act, the Central Government shall have the power to take all such measures as it deems necessary or expedient for the purpose of protecting and improving the quality of the environment and preventing, controlling and abating environmental pollution.

(2) In particular, and without prejudice to the generality of the provisions of sub-section (1), such measures may include measures with respect to all or any of the following matters, namely:

(i) co-ordination of actions by the State Governments, officers and other authorities —

(a) under this Act, or the rules made thereunder; or

(b) under any other law for the time being in force which is relatable to the objects of this Act;

(ii) planning and execution of a nation-wide programme for the prevention, control and abatement of environmental pollution;

(iii) laying down standards for the quality of environment in its various aspects;

(iv) laying down standards for emission or discharge of environmental pollutants from various sources whatsoever:

Provided that different standards for emission or discharge may be laid down under this clause from different source having regard to the quality or composition of the emission or discharge of environmental pollutants from such sources;

(v) restriction of areas in which any industries, operations or processes or class of industries, operations or processes shall not be carried out or shall be carried out subject to certain safeguards;

(vi) laying down procedures and safeguards for the prevention of accidents which may cause environmental pollution and remedial measures for such accidents;

(vii) laying down procedures and safeguards for the handling of hazardous substances;

(viii) examination of such manufacturing processes, materials and substance as are likely to cause environmental pollution;

(ix) carrying out and sponsoring investigations and research relating to programme of environmental pollution;

(x) inspection of any premise, plant equipment, machinery, manufacturing or other processes, materials or substances and giving, by order, of such direction to such authorities, officers or persons as it may consider necessary to take steps for the prevention, control and abatement of environmental pollution.

(xi) establishment or recognition of environmental laboratories and institutes to carry out the functions entrusted to such environmental laboratories and institutes under this Act.

(xii) collection and dissemination of information in respect of matters relating to environmental pollution;

(xiii) preparation of manuals, codes or guides relating to the prevention control and abatement of environmental pollution;

(xiv) such other matters as the Central Government deems necessary or expedient for the purpose of securing the effective implementation of the provisions of this Act.

(3) The Central Government may, if it considers it necessary or expedient so to do for the purposes of this Act, by order published in the Official Gazette, constitute an authority or authorities by such name or names as may be specified in the order for the purpose of exercising and performing such of the powers and functions (including the power to issue directions under section 5) of the Central Government under this Act and for taking measures with respect to such of the matters referred to in sub-section (2) as may be mentioned in the order and subject to the supervision and control of the Central Government and the provisions of such order, such authority or authorities may exercise the powers or perform the functions or take the measures so mentioned in the order as if such authority or authorities had been empowered by this Act to exercise those powers or perform those functions or take such measures.

Appointment of officers and their powers and functions

4. (1) Without prejudice to the provisions of sub-section (3) of section 3, the Central Government may appoint officers with such designations as it thinks fit for the purposes of this Act and may entrust to them such of the powers and functions under this Act as it may deem fit.

(2) The officers appointed under sub-section (1) shall be subject to the general control and direction of the Central Government, or, if so directed by that Government also of the authority or authorities, if any, constituted under sub-section (3) of section 3 or of any other authority or officer.

Power to give directions

5. Notwithstanding anything contained in any other law but subject to the provisions of this Act, the Central Government may, in the exercise of its powers and performance of its functions under this Act, issue directions in writing to any person, officer or any authority and such person, officer or authority shall be bound to comply with such directions.

Explanation — For the avoidance of doubts it is hereby declared that the power to issue directions under this section includes the power to direct —

(a) the closure, prohibition or regulation of any industry operation, or process or

(b) stoppage or regulation of the supply of electricity or water or any other service.

Rules to regulate environmental pollution

6. (1) The Central Government may, by notification in the Official Gazette make rules in respect of all or any of the matters referred to in section 3.

(2) In particular and without prejudice to the generality of the foregoing power, such rules may provide for all or any of the following matters, namely:

(a) the standards of quality of air, water or soil for various areas and purposes;

(b) the maximum allowable limits of concentration of various environmental pollutants (including noise) for different areas;

(c) the procedures and safeguards for the handling of hazardous substances;

(d) the prohibition and restrictions on the handling of hazardous substance in different areas;

(e) the prohibition and restrictions on the location of industries and the carrying on of process and operations in different areas;

(f) the procedures and safeguards for the prevention of accidents which may cause environmental pollution and for providing for remedial measures for such accidents.

Chapter III

PREVENTION, CONTROL AND ABATEMENT OF ENVIRONMENTAL POLLUTION

Persons carrying on industry, operation, etc., not to allow emission or discharge of environmental pollutants in excess of the standards

7. No person carrying on any industry, operation or process shall discharge or emit or permit to be discharged or emitted any environmental pollutant in excess of such standards as may be prescribed.

Persons handling hazardous substances to comply with procedural safeguards

8. No person shall handle or cause to be handled any hazardous substance except in accordance with such procedure and after complying with such safeguards as may be prescribed.

Furnishing of information to authorities and agencies in certain cases

9. (1) Where the discharge of any environmental pollutant in excess of the prescribed standards occurs or is apprehended to occur due to any accident or other unforeseen act or event, the person responsible for such discharge and the person in charge of the place at which such discharge occurs or is apprehended to occur shall be bound to prevent or mitigate the environmental pollution caused as a result of such discharge and shall also forthwith —

(a) intimate the fact of such occurrence or apprehension of such occurrence; and

(b) be bound, if called upon, to render all assistance, to such authorities or agencies as may be prescribed.

(2) On receipt of information with respect to the fact or apprehension of any occurrence of the nature referred to in sub-section (1), whether through intimation under that sub-section or otherwise, the authorities or agencies referred to in sub-section (1) shall, as early as practicable, cause such remedial measures to be taken as are necessary to prevent or mitigate the environmental pollution.

(3) The expenses, if any, incurred by any authority or agency with respect to the remedial measures referred to in sub-section (2), together with interest (at such reasonable rate as the Government may, by order fix) from the date when a demand for the expenses is made until it is paid, may be recovered by such authority or agency from the person concerned as arrears of land revenue or of public demand.

Power of entry and inspection

10. (1) Subject to the provisions of this section, any person empowered by the Central Government in this behalf shall have a right to enter, at all reasonable times with such assistances as he considers necessary any place —

(a) for the purpose of performing any of the functions of the Central Government entrusted to him;

(b) for the purpose of determining whether if so in what manner, any such functions are to be performed or whether any provisions of this Act or the rules made thereunder or any notice, order, direction or authorisation served, made, given or granted under this Act is being or has been complied with;

(c) for the purpose of examining and testing any equipment, industrial plant, record, register, document or any other material object or for conducting a search of any building in which he has reason to believe that an offence under this Act or the rules made thereunder has been or is being or is about to be committed and for seizing any such equipment, industrial plant, record, register, document or other material object if he has reasons to believe that it may furnish evidence of the commission of an offence punishable under this Act or the rules made thereunder or that such seizure is necessary to prevent or mitigate environmental pollution.

(2) Every person carrying on any industry, operation or process or handling any hazardous substance shall be bound to render all assistance to the person empowered by the Central Government under sub-section (1) for carrying out the functions under that sub-section and if he fails to do so without any reasonable cause or excuse, he shall be guilty of an offence under this Act.

(3) If any person wilfully delays or obstructs any person empowered by the Central Government under sub-section (1) in the performance of his functions, he shall be guilty of an offence under this Act.

(4) The provisions of the Code of Criminal Procedure, 1973, (2 of 1974) or, in relation to the State of Jammu and Kashmir, or any area in which that Code is not in force, the provisions of any corresponding law in force in that State of area shall, so far as may be, apply to any search or seizure under this section as they apply to any search or seizure made under the authority of a warrant issued under section 94 of the said Code or, as the case be, under the corresponding provision of the said law.

Power to take sample and procedure to be followed in connection therewith

11. (1) The Central Government of any officer empowered by it in this behalf, shall have power to take, for the purpose of analysis, samples of air, water soil or other substance from any factory, premises or other in such manner as may be prescribed.

(2) The result of any analysis of a sample taken under sub-section (1) shall not be admissible in evidence in any legal proceeding unless the provisions of sub-sections (3) and (4) are complied with.

(3) Subject to the provisions of sub-section (4), the person taking the sample under sub-section (1) shal —

(a) serve on the occupier or his agent or person in charge of the place, a notice, then and there, in such form as may be prescribed of his intention to have it so analysed;

(b) in the presence of the occupier or his agent or person, collect a sample for analysis;

(c) cause the sample to be placed in a container or containers which shall be marked and sealed and shall also be signed both by the person taking the sample and the occupier or his agent or person.

(d) send without delay, the container or the containers to the laboratory established or recognised by the Central Government under section 12.

(4) When a sample is taken for analysis under sub-section (1) and the person taking the sample serves on the occupier or his agent or person, a notice under clause (a) of sub-section (3), then,—

(a) in a case where the occupier, his agent or person wilfully absents himself, the person taking the sample shall collect the sample for analysis to be placed in a container or containers which shall be marked and sealed and shall also be signed by the person taking the sample, and

(b) in a case where the occupier or his agent or person present at the time taking the sample refuses to sign the marked and sealed container or containers of the sample as required under clause (c) of sub-section (3), the marked and sealed container or containers shall be signed by the person taking the samples, and the container or containers shall be sent without delay by the person taking the sample for analysis to the laboratory established or recognised under section 12 and such person shall inform the Government Analyst appointed or recognised under section 13 in writing, about the wilful absence of the occupier or his agent or person, or, as the case may be, his refusal to sign the container or containers.

Environmental laboratories

12. (1) The Central Government may, by notification in his Official Gazette,—

(a) establish one or more environmental laboratories;

(b) recognise one or more laboratories or institutes as environmental laboratories to carry out the functions entrusted to an environmental laboratory under this Act.

(2) The Central Government may be, notification in the Official Gazette, make rules specifying—

(a) the functions of the environmental laboratory;

(b) the procedure for the submission to the said laboratory of samples of air, water, soil, or other substance for analysis or tests the form of the laboratory report thereon and the fees payable for such report;

(c) such other matters may be necessary or expedient to enable that laboratory to carry out its functions.

Government Analysts

13. The Central Government may by notification in the Official Gazette, appoint or recognise such persons as it thinks fit and having the prescribed qualifications to be Government analysts for the purpose of analysis of samples of air, water soil or other substance sent for analysis to any environmental laboratory established or recognised under sub-section (1) of Section 12.

Reports of Government Analysts

14. Any document purporting to be a report signed by a Government analyst may be used as evidence of the facts stated therein in any proceedings under this Act.

Penalty for contravention of the provisions of the Act and the rules, orders and directions

15. (1) Whoever fails to comply with or contravenes any of the provisions of this Act, or the rules made or orders or directions issued thereunder, shall in respect of each such failure or contravention, be punishable with imprisonment for a term which may extend to five years or with fine which may extend to one lakh rupees, or with both, and in case the failure or contravention continues, with

additional fine which may extend to five thousand rupees for every day during which such failure or contravention continues after the conviction for the first such failure or contravention.

(2) If the failure or contravention referred to in sub-section (1) continues beyond a period of one year after the date of conviction, the offender shall be punishable with the imprisonment for a term which may extend to seven years.

Offences by companies

16. (1) Where any offence under this Act has been committed by a company every person who, at the time the offence was committed, was directly in charge of and was responsible, to the company for the conduct of the business of the company, as well as the company, shall be deemed to be quilty of the offence and shall be liable to be proceeded against and punished accordingly:

Provided that nothing contained in this sub-section shall render any such person liable to any punishment provided in this Act, if he proves that the offence was committed without his knowledge or that he exercised all due diligence to prevent the commission of such offence.

(2) Notwithstanding anything contained in sub-section (1), where an offence under this Act, has been committed by a company and it is proved that the offence has been committed with the consent or connivance of, or is attributable to any neglect on the part, of any director manager, secretary or other officer of the company, such director, manager, secretary or other officer shall also deemed to be guilty of the offence and shall be liable to be proceeded against and punished accordingly.

Explanation — For the purpose of this section,—

(a) "company means any body corporate and includes a firm or other association of individuals;

(b) "director", in relation to a firm means, a partner in the firm.

Offences by Government Departments

17. (1) Where an offences under this Act has been committed by any Department of Government, the Head of the Department shall be deemed to be guilty of the offence and shall be liable to be proceeded against and punished accordingly:

Provided that nothing contained in this section shall render such Head of the Department liable to any punishment if he proves that the offences was committed without his knowledge or that he exercise all due to prevent the commission of such offence.

(2) Notwithstanding anything contained in sub-section (1), where an offence under this Act has been committed by a Department of Government and it is

proved that the offence has been committed with the consent or connivance of, or is attributable to any neglect on the part of, any officer, other than the Head of the Department, such officer shall also be deemed to be guilty of that offence and shall be liable to be proceeded against and punished accordingly.

Chapter IV

MISCELLANEOUS

Protection of action taken in good faith

18. No suit, prosecution or other legal proceeding shall lie against the Government or any officer or other employee of the Government or any authority constituted under this Act or any member, officer or other employee of such authority in respect of anything which is done or intended to be done in good faith in pursuance of this Act or the rules made or orders or directions thereunder.

Cognizance of offences

19. No court shall take cognizance of any offence under this Act except on a complaint made by —

(a) the Central Government or any authority or officer authorised in this behalf by that Government; or

(b) any person who has given notice of not less than sixty days, in the manner prescribed, of the alleged offence and of his intention to make a complaint, to the Central Government or the authority or officer authorised as aforesaid.

Information, reports or returns

20. The Central Government, may, in relation to its functions under this Act, from time to time, require any person, officer, State Government or other authority to furnish to it or any prescribed authority or officer, any reports, returns, statistics, accounts and other information and such person, officer, State Government or other authority shall be bound to do so.

Members, officers and employees of the authority constituted under section 3 to be public servants.

21. All the members of the authority, constituted, if any, under section 3 and all officers and other employees of such authority when acting or purporting to act in pursuance of any provisions of this Act or the rules made or orders or directions issued thereunder shall be deemed to be public servants within the meaning the section 21 of the Indian Penal Code. (45 of 1860)

Bar of jurisdiction

22. No civil court shall have jurisdiction to entertain any suit or proceedings in respect of anything done, action taken or order or direction issued by the Central Government or any other authority or officer in pursuance of any power conferred by or in relation to its or his functions under this Act.

Power to delegate

23. Without prejudice to the provisions of sub-section (3) of section 3, the Central Government may, by notification, in the Official Gazette delegate, subject to such conditions and limitations as may be specified in the notification, such of its power and functions under this Act [except the power to constitute an authority under sub-section (3) of section 3 and to make rules under section 25] as it may deem necessary or expedient, to any officer, State Government or other authority.

Effect of other laws

24. (1) Subject to the provisions of sub-section (2), the provisions of this Act and the rules or orders made therein shall have effect notwithstanding anything inconsistent therewith contained in any enactment other than this Act.

(2) Where any act or omission constitutes an offence punishable under this Act and also under any other Act then the offender found guilty of such offence shall be liable to be punished under the other Act and not under this Act.

Power to make rules

25. (1) The Central Government may by, notification in the Official Gazette, make rules for carrying out the process of this Act.

(2) In particular, and without prejudice to the generality of the foregoing power, such rules may provide for all or any of the following matters, namely:—

(a) the standards in excess of which environmental pollutants shall not be discharged or emitted under section 7;

(b) the procedure in accordance with and the safeguards in compliance with which hazardous substances shall be handled or cause to be handled under section 8;

(c) the authorities or agencies to which intimation of the fact of occurrence or apprehension of occurrence of the discharge of any environmental pollutant in excess of the prescribed standards shall be given and to whom all assistance shall be bound to be rendered under sub-section (1) of section 9;

(d) the manner in which samples of air, water, soil or other substances for the purpose of analysis shall be taken under sub-section (1) of section 11,

(e) the form in which notice of intention to have a simple analysed shall be served under clause (a) of sub-section (3) of section 11;

(f) the functions of the environmental laboratories, the procedure for the submission to such laboratories of samples, soil and other substances for analysis or test; the form of laboratory report; the fees payable for such report and other matters to enable such laboratories to carry out their functions under sub-section (2) of section 12;

(g) the qualifications of Government Analyst appointed or recognised for the purpose of analysis of samples of air, water, soil or other substances under section 13;

(h) the manner in which notice of the offence and of the intention to make a complaint to the Central Government shall be given under clause (b) of section 19;

(i) the authority or officer to whom any reports, returns, statistics, accounts and other information shall be furnished under section 20;

(j) any other matter which is required to be, or may be prescribed.

Rules made under this Act to be laid before Parliament

26. Every rule made under this Act shall be laid, as soon as may be after it is made, before each House of Parliament while it is in session, for a total period of thirty days which may be comprised in one session or in two or more successive sessions, and if, before the expiry of the sessions immediately following the session or the successive sessions aforesaid, both Houses agree in making any modification in the rule or both Houses agree that the rule should not be made, the rule shall thereafter have effect only in such modification form or be of no effect, as the case may be, so, however that any such modification or annulment shall be without prejudice to the validity of anything previously done under that rule.

APPENDIX XI

THE ENVIRONMENT (PROTECTION) RULES, 1986

MINISTRY OF ENVIRONMENT & FORESTS

(Department of Environment, Forests & Wildlife)

New Delhi, the 19th November, 1986

Notification

S.C. 844(E) — In exercise of the powers conferred by sections 6 and 25 of the Environmental (Protection) Act, 1986 (29 of 1986), the Central Government hereby makes the following rules, namely:

1. **Short title and commencement:**

   (i) These rules may be called the Environment (Protection) Rules, 1986.

   (ii) They shall come into force on the date of their publication in the Official Gazette.

2. **Definitions :** In these rules, unless the context otherwise requires,—

   (a) "Act" means the Environmental (Protection) Act, 1986 (29 of 1986);

   (b) "Central Board" means the Central Board for the Prevention and Control of Water Pollution constituted under section 3 of the Water (Prevention and Control of Pollution) Act, 1974 (6 of 1974);

   (c) "Form" means a form set forth in Appendix A to these rules;

   (d) "Government Analyst" means a person appointed or recognized as such under section 13;

   (e) "person" in relation to any factory or premises means a person or occupier or his agent who has control to any factory or premises and includes in relation to any substance, the person in possession of the substance;

   (f) "recipient system" means the part of the environment such as soil, water, air or other which receives the pollutants;

   (g) "section" means a section of the Act;

(h) "Schedule" means a Schedule appended to these rules;

(i) "Standards" means standards prescribed under these rules;

(j) "State Board" means a State Board for the Prevention and Control of Water Pollution constituted under section 4 of the Water (Prevention and Control of Water Pollution) Act, 1974 (6 of 1974) or a State Board for the Prevention and Control of Pollution) Act, 1981 (14 of 1981);

3. Standards for emission or discharge of environmental pollutants:

(i) For the purpose of protecting and improving the quality of the environment and preventing and abating environmental pollution, the Standards for emission or discharge of environmental pollutants from the industries, operations or processes shall be as specified in the Schedule:

Provided where an industry, operation or process has been granted time by the Central Board or a State Board to implement a time bound programme to treat the environment pollutants so as to bring them to the standards prescribed under these rules after specifying certain conditions and where such an industry, operation, or process by adhering strictly to such stipulations specified by the Central or the State Board discharges environmental pollutants is excess of the prescribed standards during such period of such time-bound programme, such discharge shall not be considered as an offence under the Act.

(2) Notwithstanding anything contained in sub-rules (1), the Central Board or a State Board may specify more stringent standards from those provided in the Schedule in respect of any specific industry, operation or process depending upon the quality of the recipient system and after recording therefor in writing.

4. Directions:

(1) Any direction issued under section 5 shall be in writing.

(2) The direction shall specify the nature of action to be taken and the time within which it shall be complied with by the person, officer or the authority to whom such direction is given.

(3) The person, officer or authority to whom any direction is sought to be issued shall be served with a copy of the proposed direction and shall be given an opportunity of not less than fifteen days from the date of service of a notice to file with an officer designated in this behalf the objections, if any, to the issue of the proposed direction.

(4) The Central Government shall within a period of 45 days from the days from the date of receipt of the objections, if any, or form the date up to which an opportunity is given to the person, officer or authority to file objections whichever is earlier after considering the objections, if any,

received from the person, officer or authority to be directed and for reasons to be recorded in writing, confirm, modify or decide not to issue the proposed direction.

(5) In a case where the Central Government is of the opinion likelihood of a grave injury to the environment it is not expedient to provide an opportunity to file objections against the proposed direction, it may, for reasons, to be recorded in writing, issue directions without providing such an opportunity.

(6) Every notice or direction required to be issued under this rule shall be deemed to be duly served —

(a) where the person to be served is a company if the document is addressed in the name of the company at its registered office or at its principal office or place of business and is either

(i) sent by registered post, or

(ii) delivered at its registered office or at the principal office or place of business;

(b) where the person to be served is an officer serving Government, if the document is addressed to the person and a copy thereof is endorsed to this Head of the Department and also to the Secretary to the Government as the case may be, incharge of the Department in which for the time being the business relating to the Department in which the officer is employed is transacted and is either

(i) sent by registered post, or

(ii) is given or tendered to him;

(c) in any other case if the document is addressed to the person to be served; and

(i) is given or tendered to him, or

(ii) if such person cannot be found is affixed on some conspicuous part of his last known place of resident or business or is given or tendered to some adult member of his family or is affixed on some conspicuous part of the land or building, if any, to which it relates, or

(iii) is sent by registered post to that person.

Explanation: For the purposes of this sub-rule:

(a) "company" means any body corporate and includes a firm or other association of individuals;

(b) "a servant" is not a member of the family.

5. Prohibition and restriction on the location of industries and the carrying on process and operation in different areas.

(1) The Central Government may take into consideration the following laid factors while prohibiting or restricting the location of industries and carrying on of processes and operations in different areas:

(i) Standards for quality of environment in its various aspects laid down for an area.

(ii) The maximum allowable limits of concentration of various environmental pollutants (including noise) for an area.

(iii) The likely emission or discharge of environmental pollutants from an industry, process or operation proposed to be prohibited or restricted.

(iv) The topographic and climatic features of an area.

(v) The biological diversity of the area which, in the opinion of the Central Government needs to be preserved.

(vi) Environmentally compatible land use.

(vii) Net adverse environmental impact likely to be caused by an industry, process or operation proposed to be prohibited or restricted.

(viii) Proximity to a protected area under the Ancient Monuments and Archaeological Sites and Remains Act, 1958 or a sanctuary, National Park, game reserve or closed area notified as such under the Wild Life (Protection) Act, 1972 or places protected under any treaty, agreement or convention with any other country or countries or in pursuance of any decision made in any international conference, association or other body.

(ix) Proximity to human settlements.

(x) Any other factor as may be considered by the Central Government to be relevant to the protection for the environmental in an area.

(2) While prohibiting or restricting the location of industries and carrying on of processes and operation in an area, the Central Government shall follow the procedure hereinafter laid down.

(3) (a) Whenever it appears to the Central Government that it is expedient to impose prohibition or restrictions on the location of an industry or the carrying on of processes and operations in an area, it may, by notification in the Official Gazette and in such other manner as the Central Government may deem necessary from time to time give notice of its intention to do so.

(b) Every notification under clause (a) shall give a brief description of the area, the industries operations, processes in that area about which such notification pertains and also specify the reasons for the imposition of prohibition or restrictions on the location of the industries and carrying on of process of operations in that area.

(c) Any person interested in filing an objection against the imposition of prohibition or restrictions on carrying on of processes or operations as notified under clause (a) may do so in writing to the Central Government within sixty days from the date of publication of the notification in the Official Gazette.

(d) The Central Government shall with in a period of one hundred and twenty days from the date of publication of the notification in the Official Gazette consider all the objections received against such notification and may impose prohibition or restrictions on location of such industries and the carrying on of any process or operation in an area.

6. **Procedure for taking samples:** The Central Government or the officer empowered to take samples under section 11 shall collect the sample in sufficient quantity to be divided into three uniform parts and effectively seal and suitably mark the same and permit the person from whom the sample is taken to add his own seal or mark the same and any of the portions so sealed and marked. In case where the sample is made up in containers of small volumes and is likely to deteriorate or be otherwise damaged if exposed, the Central Government, or the officer empowered shall take three of the said samples without opening the containers and suitably seal and mark the same. The Central Government or the officer empowered shall dispose of the samples so collected as follows:

(i) one portion shall be handed over to the person from whom the sample taken under acknowledgement;

(ii) the other portion shall be sent forthwith to the environmental laboratory for analysis; and

(iii) the last portion shall be retained by him to be produced in the court before which proceedings, if any, are instituted.

7. **Service of notice:** The Central Government or the officer empowered shall serve on the occupier or his agent or person in charge of the place a notice then and there in Form 1 of his intention to have the sample analysed.

8. Procedure for submission of samples for analysis and the form of laboratory report thereon:

(1) Sample taken for analysis shall be sent by the Central Government or the officer empowered to the environmental laboratory by registered post or through special messenger with Form II.

(2) Another copy of Form II together with specimen impression of seals of the officer empowered to take samples along with the seals/marks, if any, of the person from whom the sample is taken shall be sent separately in a sealed cover by registered post or through a special messenger to the environmental laboratory.

(3) The findings shall be recorded in Form III in triplicate and signed by the Government Analyst and sent to the office from whom the sample is received for analysis.

(4) On receipt of the report of the finding of the government Analyst, the officer shall send one copy of the report to the person from whom the sample was taken for analysis, the second copy shall be retained by him for his records and the third copy shall be kept by him for his records and the third copy shall be kept by him to be produced in the Court before which proceedings, if any, are instituted.

9. **Functions of environmental laboratories:** The following shall be functions of environmental laboratories:

(i) to evolve standardised methods for sampling and analysis of various types of environmental pollutants;

(ii) to analyse samples sent by the Central Government or the officers empowered under sub-section (1) of section 11.

(iii) to carry out such investigations as may be directed by the Central Government to lay down standards for the quality of environment and discharge of environmental pollutants, to monitor and to enforce the standards laid down;

(iv) to send periodical reports regarding its activities to the Central Government,

(v) to carry out such other functions as may be entrusted to it by the Central Government from time to time.

10. **Qualifications of Government Analyst:** A person shall not be qualified for appointment or recognised as a Government Analyst unless he is a:

(a) graduate in science from a recognized university with five years experience in laboratory engaged in environmental investigations, testing or analysis; or

(b) post-graduate in science or a graduate in engineering or a graduate in medicine or equivalent with two years experience in a laboratory engaged in environmental investigations, testing or analysis; or

(c) post-graduate in environmental science from a recognised university with two years experience in a laboratory engaged in environmental investigations, testing or analysis.

11. **Manner of giving notice:** The manner of giving under clause (b) of section 19 shall be as follows, namely:

(1) The notice shall be in Writing in form IV;

(2) The person giving notice may send notice to —

(a) if the alleged offence has taken place in a Union territory:

(i) the Central Board ; and

(ii) Ministry of Environment and Forests (represented by the Secretary to the Government of India);

(b) if the alleged offence has taken place in a State—

(i) the State Board; and

(ii) the Government of the State (represented by the Secretary to the State Government in charge of Environment); and

(iii) the Ministry of Environment and Forests (represented by the secretary to the Government of India);

(3) The notice shall be sent by registered post acknowledgement due; and

(4) The period of sixty days mentioned in clause (b) section 19 of the Environment (Protection) Act, 1986 shall be recked from the date it is first received by one of the authorities mentioned above.

Schedule

(See rule 3)

Sl. No.	Industry	Parameter	Standards
1	2	3	4
1.	Caustic Soda industry		Concentration not to exceed milligramme per litre (except for pH and flow)
		Total concentration of mercury in the final effluent*	0.01
		Mercury bearing waste-water generation (flow)	10 kilolitres/tonne of caustic soda produced
		pH	5.5 to 9.0
		*Final effluent is the combined effluent from (a) cell house (b) brine plant (c) chlorine handling (d) hydrogen handling (e) hydrochloric acid plant	
2.	Man-made fibres (synthetic)		Concentration not to exceed milligramme per litre (except for pH)
		Suspended solids	100
		Bio-chemical oxygen demand, 5 day 20^0 C	30
		pH	5.5 to 9.0

1	2	3	4
3.	Oil refinery industry	Concentration not to exceed milligramme per litre (except for pH)	Quantum, kg/1,000 tonnes crude processed
		Oil and grease	10 7
		Phenol	1 0.7
		Sulphide	0.5 0.35
		Bio-chemical oxygen demand, 5 day 20°C	15 10.5
		Suspended solids	20 14
		pH	6 to 8.5
4.	Sugar industry		Concentration not exceed milligrame per litre
		Bio-chemical oxygen demand, 5 day 20°C	100 for disposal on land 30 for disposal in surface waters
5.	Thermal power plants		Maximum limiting concentration milligramme per litre (except for pH and temperature)
	Condenser cooling waters (once through cooling system)	pH	6.5 to 8.5
		Temperature	Not more than 5°C higher than the intake water temperature
		Free available chlorine	0.5
	Boiler blowdowns	Suspended solids	100
		Oil and grease	20
		Copper (total)	1.0
		Iron (total)	1.0
	Cooling tower blowdown	Free available chlorine	0.5
		Zinc	1.0
		Chromium (total)	0.2
		Phosphate	5.0
		Other corrosion inhibiting material	Limit to be established on case by case basis by Central Board in case of Union territories and

1	2	3	4
			State Boards in case of States
	Ash pond effluent	pH	6.5 to 8.5
		Suspended solids	100
		Oil and grease	20
6.	Cotton textile industries (composite and processing)		Concentration not to exceed milligramme per litre
	Common:		
		pH	5.5 to 9.0
		Suspended solids	100
		Bio-chemical oxygen demand, 5 day 20⁰C	150
		Oil and Grease	10
		Bio-assey test	90% survival of fish of after 96 hours
	Special:	Total chromium (as Cr)	2
		Sulphide (as S)	2
		Phenolic compounds (as $C_6 C_5 OH$)	5

The special parameters are to be stipulated by the Central Board in case of Union territories and State Board in case of States depending upon the dye used in the Industry. Where the industry uses chrome dyes, sulphur dyes and/or phenolic compounds in the dyeing/prining process, the limits on chromium of 2 mg/litre, sulphides of 2 mg/litre and phenolic compounds of 5 mg/litre respectively shall be imposed.

Where the quality requirement of the recipient system so warrants the limit of BOD should be lowered up to 30 according to the requirement by the State Boards for the States and the Central Board for the Union territories.

A limit on sodium absorption ratio of 26s should be imposed by the State Boards for the States and the Central Board for the Union territories if the disposal of effluent is to be made on land.

7.	Composite woollen mills		Concentration not to exceed milligramme per litre (except for pH and bio-assay)
	Common:		
		Suspended solids	100
		pH	5.5 to 9.0

1	2	3	4
		Bio-chemical oxygen demands, 5 day 20°C	100
		Oil and grease	10
		Bio-assay	90% survival of fish after 96 hours
	Special:		
		Total chromium	2
		Sulphide (as S)	2
		Phenolic compounds (as C_6H_5OH)	5

The special parameters are to be stipulated by the Central Board in case of Union territories and State Boards in case of State depending upon the dye used in the industry. Where the industry uses chrome dyes, sulphur dyes and/or phenolic compounds in the dying/printing process, the limits on chromium of 2 mg/litre, sulphide of 2 mg/litre and phenolic compounds of 5 mg/litre respectively shall be imposed.

Where the quality requirement of the recipient system so warrants, the limit of BOD should be lowered up to 30 according to the requirement by the State Boards for the States and the Central Board for the Union territories.

A limit on sodium absorption ratio of 26 should be imposed by the State Board for the States and the Central Board for the Union territories if the disposal of effluent is to be made on land.

APPENDIX A
FORM 1

(See rule 7)

Notice of intention to have sampie analysed

To

....

....

Take notice that it is intended to have analysed the sample of....................which has been taken today, the ....day of....................
19....................from..
(Name and designation of the person who takes the sample)

*Specify the place from where the sample is taken.

(SEAL)

Date..........................

FORM II

(See rule 8)

Memorandum to Government Analyst

From

....

....

To

The Government Analyst

....

....

The portion of sample described below is sent herewith for analysis [under rule 6 of the Environment (Protection) Rules, 1986]. The portion of the sample has been marked by me with the following mark:

Details of the portion of sample taken

Name and designation of person who sends sample

(SEAL)

Date..................

FORM III

(See rule 8)

Report by Government Analyst

Report No. ....

Date ....

I hereby certify that I ....

Government Analyst duly appointed under section 13 of the Environment (Protection) Act, 1986 received on the ....day

*..

of........................19...................from...a sample of..................................for analysis.

The sample was in a condition fit for analysis as reported below.

I further certify that I have analysed the aforementioned sample on ....and declare

**...

....

The condition of seals, fastening of sample on receipt was as follows:

....

Signed this...............................day of.......................19.......................

Signature

Address.........................

(Government Analyst)

To

....

....

....

---

*Here write the name of the officer/authority from whom sample was obtained.

** Here write full details of analysis and refer to method of analysis.

FORM IV

(See rule 11)

Form of Notice

By registered post acknowledgement due

From (1)

Shri...

....

....

To

....

....

....

Notice under section 19(b) of the Environmental (Protection) Act, 1986

Whereas an offence under the Environment (Protection) Act, 1986 has been committed/is being committed by ....(2) I/we hereby give notice of 60 days under section 19(b) of the Environment (Protection) Act, 1986 of my/our intention to file a complaint in the Court against...(2) for violation of section of the Environment (Protection) Act, 1986.

Signature (s)

Place...

Date...

Explanation:

(1) In case the notice is given in the name of a company, documentary evidence authorising the person to sign the notice on behalf of the company shall be enclosed to this notice.

Company for this purpose means a company defined in explanation to sub-rule (6) of rule 4.

(2) Here give the name and address of the alleged offender. In case of a manufacturing/processing/operating unit, indicate the name/location/ nature of activity, etc.

(3) Documentary evidence shall include photographs/technical/reports/ health reports of the area, etc., for enabling enquiry into the alleged violation/offence.

APPENDIX XII(A)

MANUFACTURE, USE, IMPORT, EXPORT AND STORAGE AND HAZARDOUS MICRO-ORGANISMS, GENETICALLY ENGINEERED ORGANISMS OR CELLS RULES, 1989

The Gazette of India

EXTRAORDINARY

PART II — Section 3 — Sub-section (i)

Published by Authority

No. 621 New Delhi, Tuesday, December 5, 1989/Agrahayana 14, 1911

Ministry of Environment & Forests

Notification

New Delhi, the 5th December, 1989

Rules for the Manufacture, Use, Import, Export and Storage of Hazardous Micro Organisms/Genetically Engineered Organisms or Cells

(To be notified under the EP Act, 1986)

G.S.R. 1037 (E) — In exercise of the powers conferred by sections 6, 8 and 25 of the Environment (Prevention) Act, 1986 (29 of 1986) and with a view to protecting the environment, nature and health, in connection with the application of gene-technology and micro-organisms, the Central Government hereby makes the following rules, namely :—

1. *Short title, extent and commencement* :— (1) These rules may be called the Rules for the Manufacture, Use, Import, Export and Storage of Hazardous micro-organisms/Genetically engineered organisms or cells.

(2) These rules shall come into operation on the date to be notified for this purpose in the Official Gazette.

2. *Application*:—(1) These rules are applicable to the manufacture, import and storage of micro-organisms and Gene-Technological products.

(2) These rules shall apply to genetically engineered organisms/micro-organisms and cells and correspondingly to any substances and products and foodstuffs, etc., of which such cells, organisms or tissues hereof form part.

(3) These rules shall also apply to new gene-technologies apart from those referred to in clauses (ii) and (iv) of rule 3 and these rules shall apply to organisms/micro-organisms and cells generated by the utilisation of such other gene-technologies and to substances and products of which such organism and cells form part.

(4) These rules shall be applicable in the following specific cases:

(a) sale, offers for sale, storage for the purpose of sale, offers and any kind of handling over with or without a consideration;

(b) exportation and importation of genetically engineered cells or organisms;

(c) production, manufacturing, processing, storage, import, drawing off, packaging and repackaging of the Genetically Engineered Products;

(d) production, manufacture etc. of drugs and pharmaceuticals and foodstuffs distilleries and tanneries, etc. which make use of micro-organisms/genetically engineered micro-organisms one way or the other.

(5) These rules shall be applicable to the whole of India.

3. *Definitions* :— In these rules unless the context requires;

(i) "Biotechnology" means the application of scientific and engineering principles to the processing of materials by biological agents to produce goods and services;

(ii) "Cells hybridisation" means the formation of live cells with new combination of genetic material through the fusion of two or more cells by means of methods which do not occur naturally;

(iii) "Gene Technology" means the application of the gene technique called genetic engineering, include self-cloning and deletion as well as hybridisation;

(iv) "Genetic Engineering" means the technique by which heritable material, which does not usually occur or will not occur naturally in the organism or cell concerned, generated outside the organism or the cell is inserted into said cell or organism. It shall also mean the formation of new combinations of genetic material by incorporation of cell into a host cell, where they occur naturally (self-cloning) as well as modification of an organism or in a cell by deletion and removal of parts of the heritable material;

(v) "microorganisms" shall include all the bacteria, viruses, fungi, mycoplasma, cell lines, algae, protodoans and nematotes indicated in the schedule and those that have not been presently known to exist in the country or not have been discovered so far.

4. *Competent Authorities* :— (1) Recombinant DNA Advisory Committee (RDAC)

This committee shall review developments in Biotechnology at national and international levels and shall recommend suitable and appropriate safety regulations for India in recombinant research, use and applications from time to time. The Committee shall functions in the Department of Biotechnology.

(2) Review Committee on Genetic Manipulation (RCGM)

This committee shall function in the Department of Biotechnology to monitor the safety related aspects in respects of on-going research projects and activities involving genetically engineered organisms/hazardous microorganisms. The Review Committee on Genetic Manipulation shall include representatives of (a) Department of Biotechnology (b) Indian Council of Medical Research (c) Indian Council of Agricultural Research (d) Council of Scientific and Industrial Research (e) other experts in their individual capacity. Review Committee on Genetic Manipulation may appoint sub groups.

It shall bring out Manuals of guidelines specifying procedure for regulatory process with respect to activities involving genetically engineered organisms in research, use and applications including industry with a view to ensure environmental safety. All ongoing projects involving high risk category and controlled field experiments shall be reviewed to ensure that adequate precautions and containment conditions are followed as per the guidelines.

The Review Committee on Genetic Manipulation shall lay down procedures restricting or prohibiting production, sale, importation and use of such genetically engineered organisms of cells as are mentioned in the schedule.

(3) Institutional Biosafety Committee (IBSC)

This Committee shall be constituted by an occupier or any person including research institutions handling micro-organism/genetically engineered organisms. The committee shall comprise the Head of the Institution, Scientists engaged in DNA work, a medical expert and a nominee of the Department of Biotechnology. The occupier or any person including research institutions handling micro-organisms/genetically engineered organisms shall prepare, with the assistance of the Institutional Biosafety Committee (IBSC) an uptodate on site emergency plan according to the manuals/guidelines of the RCGM and make available copies to the District Level Committee/State Biotechnology Co-ordination Committee and the Genetic Engineering Approval Committee.

(4) Genetic Engineering Approval Committee (GEAC)

This committee shall function as a body under the Department of Environment, Forest and Wildlife for approval of activities involving large scale use of hazardous micro-organisms and recombinants in research and industrial production from the environmental angle. The Committee shall also be responsible for approval of proposals relating to release of genetically engineered organisms and products into the environment including experimental field trials.

The composition of the Committee shall be

(i) Chairman — Additional Secretary, Department of Environment, Forests and Wild life.

Co-Chairman — Representative of Department of Bio-technology.

(ii) Members: Representative of concerned Agencies and Department, namely, Ministry of Industrial Development, Department of Atomic Energy.

(iii) Expert member : Director General — Indian Council of Agricultural Research, Director General — Indian Council of Medical Research, Director General — Council of Scientific and Industrial Research, Director General — Health Services, Plant Protection Adviser, Directorate of Plant Protection, Quarantine and storage, Chairman, Central Pollution Control Board and three outside experts in individual capacity.

(iv) Member Secretary: An official of the Department or Environmental, Forest and Wildlife.

The committee may co-opt other members/experts as necessary.

The committee or any person/s authorised by it shall have powers to take punitive action under the Environment (Protection) Act.

(5) State Biotechnology Co-ordination Committee (SBCC).

There shall be a State Biotechnology Coordination Committee in the States wherever necessary. It shall have powers to inspect, investigate and take punitive action in case of violations of statutory provisions through the Nodal Department and the State Pollution Control Board/Directorate of Health/Medical Services. The Committee shall review periodically the safety and control measures in the various industries/institutions handling genetically engineered Organisms/Hazardous microorganisms. The composition of the Co-ordination Committee shall be:

(i) Chief Secretary — Chairman

(ii) Secretary, Department of Environment — Member Secretary

(iii) Secretary, Department of Health — Member

(iv) Secretary, Department of Agriculture — Member

(v) Secretary, Department of Industries and Commerce — Member

(vi) Secretary, Department of Forests

(vii) Secretary, Department of Public Works/Chief Engineer, Department of Public Health Engineering — Member

(viii) State Microbiologists and Pathologists — Member

(ix) Chairman of State Pollution Control Board

The committee may co-opt other members/experts as necessary.

(6) District Level Committee (DLC).

There shall be a District Level Biotechnology Committee (DLC) in the districts wherever necessary under the District Collectors to monitor the safety regulations in installations engaged in the use of genetically modified organisms hazardous micro-organisms and its application in the environment.

The District Level Committee/or any other person/s authorised in this behalf shall visit the installation engaged in activity involving genetically engineered organisms, hazardous micro-organisms formulate information chart, find out hazardous and risks associated with each of these installations and co-ordinate activities with a view to meeting any emergency. They shall also prepare an off-site emergency plan. The District Level Committee shall regularly submits its report to the State Biotechnology Co-ordination Committee/Genetic Engineering Approval Committee.

The District Level Committee shall comprise of:—

(i) District Collector — Chairman

(ii) Factory Inspector — Member

(iii) A representative of the Pollution Control Board — Member

(iv) Chief Medical Officer (District Health Officer) — Member (Convenor)

(v) District Agricultural Officer — Member

(vi) A representative of the Public Health Engineering Department — Member

(vii) District Microbiologists Pathologist (technical expert) — Member

(viii) Commissioner Municipal Corporation — Member

The Committee may co-opt other members/experts as necessary.

5. Classification of micro-organisms or genetically engineered product (i) For the purpose of these rules, micro-organisms or genetically engineered organisms, products or cells shall dealt with under major heads; animal pathogens and plant pests and these shall be classified in the manner specified in the Schedule.

(2) If any of the micro-organism, genetically engineered organism or cell falls within the limits of more than one risk class as specified in the Schedule, it shall be deemed to belong exclusively to the last in number of such classes.

6. Micro-organisms laid down in the Schedule are divided into the following:—

(i) Bacterial Agents;

(ii) Fungal Agents;

(iii) Parasitic Agents;

(iv) Viral, Rickettsial and Chlamydial Agents;

(v) Special Category.

7. *Approval and Prohibition, etc* :— (1) No person shall import, export, transport, manufacture, process, use or sell any hazardous micro-organisms or genetically engineered organisms, substances or cells except with the approval of the Genetic Engineering Approval Committee.

(2) Use of pathogenic micro-organism or any genetically engineered organisms or cell for the purpose of research shall only be allowed in laboratories or inside laboratory areas notified by the Ministry of Environment and Forests for this purpose under the Environment (Protection) Act, 1986.

(3) The Genetic Engineering Approval Committee shall give directions to the occupier to determine or take measures concerning the discharge of micro-organisms/genetically engineered organisms or cells mentioned in the schedule from the laboratories, hospitals and other areas including prohibition of such discharges and laying down measures to be taken to prevent such discharges.

(4) Any person operating or using genetically engineered organisms/micro-organisms mentioned in the schedule for scale up or pilot operations shall have to obtain licence issued by the Genetic Engineering Approval Committee for any such activity. The possessor shall have to apply for licence in prescribed proforma.

(5) Certain experiments for the purpose of education within the field of gene technology or micro-organism may be carried out outside the laboratories and laboratory areas mentioned in sub-rule (2) and will be looked after the Institutional Biosafety Committee.

8. *Production*:— Production in which genetically engineered organisms or cells or micro-organism are generated or used shall not be commenced except with

the consent of Genetic Engineering Approval Committee with respect of discharge of genetically engineered organisms or cells into the environment. This shall also apply to production taking place in connection with development, testing, and experiments where such production, etc., is not subject to rule 7.

9. *Deliberate or unintentional release*:— (1) Deliberate or unintentional release of genetically engineered organisms/hazardous micro-organisms or cells, including deliberate release for the purpose of experiment shall not be allowed.

Note: Deliberate release shall mean any intentional transfer of genetically engineered organisms/hazardous micro-organisms or cells to the environment or nature, irrespective of the way in which it is done.

(2) The Genetic Engineering Approval Committee may in special cases give approval of deliberate release.

10. *Permission and approval for certain substances*:— Substances and products, which contain genetically engineered organisms or cells or micro-organisms shall not be produced, sold, imported or used except with the approval of Genetic Engineering Approval Committee.

11. *Permission and approval for foodstuffs*:— Foodstuffs, ingredients in food stuffs and additives including processing aids containing or consisting of genetically engineered organisms or cells, shall not be produced, sold, imported or used except with the approval of the Genetic Engineering Approval Committee.

12. *Guidelines*:— (1) Any person who applies for approval under rules 8-11 shall, as determined by the Genetic Engineering Approval Committee submit information and make examinations or cause examinations to be made to elucidate the case, including examinations according to specific directions and at specific laboratories. He shall also make available an on-site emergency plan to GEAC before obtaining the approval. If the authority makes examination itself, it may order the applicant to defray the expenses incurred by it in so doing.

(2) Any person to whom an approval has been granted under rules, 8-11 above shall notify the Genetic Engineering Approval Committee of any change in or addition to the information already submitted.

13. *Grant of approval* :— (1) In connection with the granting of approval under rules 8 to 11 above, terms and conditions shall be stipulated, including terms and conditions to the control to be exercised by the applicant, supervision, restriction on use, the layout of the enterprise and as to the submission of information to the State Biotechnology Co-ordination Committee or to the District Level Committee.

(2) All approvals of the Genetic Engineering Approval committee shall be for a specified period not exceeding four years at the first instance renewable for

2 years at a time. The Genetic Engineering Approval Committee shall have powers to revoke such approval in the following situations:—

(a) If there is any new information as to the harmful effects of the genetically engineered organisms or cells.

(b) If the genetically engineered organisms or cells cause such damage to the environment, nature or health as could not be envisaged when the approval was given, or.

(c) Non compliance of any condition stipulated by Genetic Engineering Approval Committee.

14. *Supervision* :— (1) The Genetic Engineering Approval Committee may supervise the implementation of the terms and conditions laid down in connection with the approval accorded by it.

(2) The Genetic Engineering Approval Committee may carry out this supervisions through State Biotechnology Co-ordination Committee or the State Pollution Control Boards/District Level Committee or through any person authorised in this behalf.

15. *Penalties*:— (1) If an order is not complied with the District Level Committee or State Biotechnology Co-ordination Committee may take measures at the expense of the person who is responsible.

(2) In cases where immediate interventions is required in order to prevent any damage to the environment, nature or health, the District Level Committee or State Biotechnology Co-ordination Committee may take the necessary steps without issuing any orders or notice. The expenses incurred for this purpose will be repayable by the person responsible for such damage.

(3) The State Biotechnology Co-ordination Committee/District level may take samples for a more detailed examination of organisms and cells.

(4) The State Biotechnology Co-ordination Committee/District Level Committee shall be competent to ask for assistance from any other government authority to carry out its instructions.

16. *Responsibility to notify interruptions or accidents*:— (1) Any person who under rule 7-11 is responsible for conditions or arrangements shall immediately notify the District Level Committee/State Biotechnology Co-ordination Committee and the state medical officer of any interruption of operations or accidents that may lead to discharge of genetically engineered organisms or cells which may be harmful to the environment, nature or health, or involve any danger thereto.

(2) Any notice given under sub-rule (1) above shall not lessen the duty of the person who is responsible to try effectively to minimise or prevent the effect of interruptions of operation or accidents.

17. Preparation of Off-site emergency plan by the DIC—

(1) It shall be the duty of the DLC to prepare an off-site emergency plan detailing how emergencies relating to a possible major accident at a site will be dealt with and in preparing the plan, the DLC shall consult the occupier and such other person as it may deem necessary.

(2) For the purpose of enabling the DLC to prepare the emergency plan required under sub-rule (1), the occupier shall provide the DLC with such information relating to the handling of hazardous micro-organisms/genetically engineered organisms under his control as the DLC may require including the nature, extend and likely off-site affects of a possible major accident and the DLC shall provide the occupier with any information from the off-site emergency plan which relates to this duties under rule 16.

18. *Inspections and information regarding finance*:— (1) The State Biotechnology Co-ordination Committee or the Genetic Engineering Approval Committee the DLC or any person with special knowledge duly authorised by the State Biotechnology Co-ordination Committee or the Genetic Engineering Approval Committee or the DLC where it is the deemed necessary, at any time on due production of identity be admitted to public as well as to private premises and localities for the purpose of carrying out supervision.

(2) Any person who is responsible for the activities subject to rules 7-11 above shall at the request of District Level Committee or State Biotechnology Co-ordination Committee or the GEAC submit all such information including information relating to financial conditions and accounts, as is essential to the authority's administration under these rules. He shall also allow supervision or inspection by the authorities or person indicated in sub-rule (1).

(3) The Genetic Engineering Approval Committee may fix fees to cover, in whole or in part, the expenses incurred by the authorities in connection with approvals, examinations, supervisions and control.

19. *Appeal*:— (1) Any person aggrieved by a decision made by Genetic Engineering Approval Committee/State Biotechnology Co-ordination Committee in pursuance of these rules may within thirty days from the date on which the decision is communicated to him, prefer an appeal to such authority as may be appointed by Ministry of Environment and Forests provided that the appellate authority may entertain the appeal after the expiry of the said period of thirty days if such authority is satisfied that the appellant was prevented by sufficient cause from filing the appeal in time.

20. *Exemption*:—The Ministry of Environment and Forests shall, wherever necessary, exempt an occupier handling a particular micro-organism/genetically engineered organism from rule 7-11.

ANIMAL AND HUMAN PATHOGENS

Schedule

BACTERIAL

Risk Group II

Acinetobactor calcoacetieus

Actinobacillus — all species except A mallei, which is in Risk Group III

Aeromonoas hydrophila

Arizona hinshawii—all seotypes

Bacillus anthracis

Bordetella—all species

Borrelia recurrentis B. vincentt

Camphylobacter fetus

Campylobacter jejuni

Chalamydia psittaci

Cheamydia trachomatis

Clostridium chauvoei, Cl. difficile Cl. fallax, Clhaemolyticum Cl. histolyticum, C. novyi, (Cl. perfringes), Cl. speticum, Cl. sordelli

Corynebacterium diptheriae, C. equi, C. haemolyticum, C. pseudotuberculosis, Cl. pyogenes, C. renale

Diplococcus (Streptococcus) pneumoniae Edwardsiila tarda

Erysipelothix insidiosa

Escherichia Coli—all enteropathogenic serotypes, enterotoxigenci

Haemophilus ducrevi, H. influenzae, H. pneumoniae

Herellea vaginicola

Klebsiella—all species and all serotypes

Legionlla pneumophila

Letionella

Leptospira interrogans—all serotypes reported in India

Listeria, all species

Mima polymorpha

Moraxella—all species

Mycobacteria—all species including Mycobacterium avium

M. bovis, M. tuberculosis, M. lepra

Mycoplasma—all species except M. mycodies and M. angalactiae

Neisseric gonorrhoea, N. meningitis

Pasteurella—all species except those listed in Risk Group III

Salmonella—all species and all serotypes

Shigella—all species and all serotypes

Sphaerophorus necrophorus

Staphylococcus aureusm

Streptobacillus moniliformis

Streptococcus pneumoniae

Streptococcus pyogenes, S. equi

Streptomyees madurae, s. pelleteri, s. somaliensts

Treponema carateum, T. pallidum and T. pertenue

Vibrio foetus, V. comma including biotype EET or and

V. parahemolyticus

Vibrio cholerae

Risk Group III

Actinobacillus mallei

Bartonella—all species

Brucella—all species

Clostridium botulium, Cl. tetani

Francisella tularensis

Mycobacterium avium, M. bovis, M. tuberculosis, M. leprae

Pasteurella multocida type B ("buffalo" and other foreign virulent strains)

Pseudomonas Pseudomallai

Yersinia pestis

FUNGAL

Risk Group II

Actinomycetes (including Nocardia SP, Actinomyces species and Arachina propinica)

Aspergillus fumigatus

Blastomyces dermatitis

Cryptococcus neoformans C. fersiminosos

Epidermophyton madurella, microsporon

Paracoccidioides brasiliensis

Sporothrix

Trichoderma

Trichophyton

Risk Group III

Coccidioides immitis Histoplasma capulatum

Histoplasma capsulatum var duboissl

PARASITIC

Risk Group II

Entahoeba histolytica

Leishmania species

Naegleria gruberia

Plasmodium theilera, P. babesia, P. falcoparum

Plasmodium babesia

Schistosoma

Toxoplasma gondii

Toxocara canis

Trichinella spiralis

Trichomanas

Trypanosoma cruzi

Risk Group III

Schisistosoma mansoni

VIRAL RICKETTSIAL AND CHALMYDIAL

Risk Group II

Adenoviruses — Human, all types

Avian loukosis

Cache Valley virus

CELO (avain adenovirus)

Coxsackie A and B Viruses

Corona viruses

Cytomegalo viruses

Dengue virus, when used for transmission experiments

Echo viruses—all types

Encephalomyocarditis virus (EMC)

Flanders virus

Hart Part virus

Hepatitis — associated material — hepatitis A and B viruses, non A and non B, HDV

Herpes viruses—except herpesvirus simiae (monkey B virus) which is in Risk Group IV.

Infectious Bovine Rhinotraechitis virus (IBR)

Infectious Bursal diseases of poultry and Infectious Bronchitus

Infectious Laryngotraechitis (ILT)

Influenza virus—all types, except A/PR8/34 which is in Risk Group I

Langat virus Leucosis Complex

Lymphogranuloma venereum agent

Marek's Disease virus

Measles virus

Mumps virus

Newcastle disease virus (other than licensed strain for vaccine use)

Parainfluenza virus—all types except parainfluenza virus 3, SF4 strain, which is in Risk Group I

Polio viruses—all types, wild and attenuated

Poxviruses—all types except Alastrim, monkey pox, sheep pox and white pox, which depending on experiments are in Risk Group III and IV

Rabies virus—all strains except rabies stret virus, which should be classified in Risk Group III when inoculated into cornivores

Reoviruses—all types

Respiratory syncytial virus

Rhinoviruses—all types

Rinderpest (other than vaccine strain in use)

Rubella virus

Stimian viruses—all types except herpeavirus simlae (Monkey Virus) which is in risk Group IV

Simian virus 40—

Ad7 SV40 (defective)

Sindbis virus

Tensaw virus

Turlock virus

Vaccinia virus

Varicella virus

Vole rickettsia

Yellow fever virus, 17D vaccine strarn

Risk Group III

African House Sickness (attenuated strain except animal passage)

Alastrim, monkey pox and White pox, when used in vitro

Arboviruses—All strains except those in Risk Group II and IV

Blue tongue virus (only serotypes reported in India)

Ebola fever Virus

Epstein—Barr virus

Feline Leukemia

Feline sarcoma

Foot and Mouth Disease virus (all serotypes and subtypes)

Gibbon Ape Lymphosarcoma

Herpesvirus ateles

Herpesvirus saimiri

Herpes simplex 2

HIV-I, & HIV-2, and strains of SIV

Infectious Equine Anaemia

Lymphocytic choriomeningitis virus (LCM)

Monkey pox, when used in vitro

Non-defective Adeno -2, SV-40 hybrids

Psittacosis-ornithosi-trachoma group of agents Pseudorabies virus

Rabies street virus, when used inoculations of carnivores

Rickettsia—all species except Vole rickettsia and Coxiell burnetti when used for vector transmission or animal inoculation experiments

Sheep pox (filed strain)

Swine Fever Virus

Vesicular stomatitis virus

Woolly monkey fibrosarcoma

Yaba pox virus

Risk Group IV

Alastrim, monkey pox, white pox, when used for transmission or animal inoculation experiments

Hemorrhagic fever agents, including Crimean hemorrhagic fever (congo)

Korean hemorrhagic fever and others as yet undefined

Herpesvirus simlae (monkey B virus)

Tick-borne encephalitis virus complex, including— Russia Spring Summer Encephalitis, Kyasanur Forest Diseast, omsk hemorrhagic fever and Control European encephalitis viruses.

SPECIAL CATEGORY

BACTERIAL

Contagious Equine Metritis (H. equigentialis) Pestis petit de ruminantium

VIRAL RICKETTSIAL AND CHLAMYDIAL.

African Horse Sickness virus (serotypes not reported in India and Challenge strains)

African Swine Fever

Bat rabies virus

Blue tongue virus (Secrotypes not reported in India)

Exoitic FMD virus types and sub-types

Junin and Machupo viruses

Lassa virus

Marburg virus

Murrey valley encephalitis virus

Rift Valley Fever virus

Smallpox virus—Archieval storage and propagation Swine Vesicular Disease

Veneseulan equine encephalities virus—epidemic strains

Western Equine encephalities virus

Yellow fever virus—Wild strain

Other Arboviruses causing epizootics and so far not recorded in India.

B: PLANT PESTS

Any living stage (including active and dormant forms) of insects, mites, nematodes, slugs, snails, bacteria, fungi, protozoa, other parasitic plants or reproductive parts therof, viruses; or any organisms similar to or allied with any of the foregoing; or any infectious agents or substances, which can directly or indirectly injure or cause disease or damage in/or to any plant or parts thereof or any processed, manufactured, or other products of plants are considered plant pests.

Organisms belonging to all lower Taxa contained within the group listed are also included.

1. Viruses

All Viroids

All bacterial, fungal, algal, plant, insect and nematode viruses, special care should be taken for —

(i) Geminiviruses,

(ii) Caulimoviruses,

(iii) Nuclear Polyhedrosis viruses

(iv) Granulosis viruses, and

(v) Cytoplastic polyhedrosis viruses

Genus Phyllobacterium

Genus Erwinia

Genus Enterobacter

Genus Klebzieller

Family Spirollacea

Genus Azospirillum

Genus Acquspirillum

Genus Oceonospirillum

Family Streptomycetaceae

Genus Streptomyces

Genus Noeardia

2. Bacteria

Family Pseudomonadaceae

Genus Pseudomonas

Genus Xanthomonas

Genus Azotobacter

Family Rhizobiaceae

Genus Rhizobium/Azorhizo-bium

Genus Bradyrhizobium

Genus Agrobacterium

Gram-negative phloem-limited bacteria associated with plant disease

Gram-negative xylem-limited bacteria associated with plant diseases

Cyanobacteria — All members of blue-green algae

Mollicutes

Family Spiroplasmataceae

Mycoplasma—like organisms associated with plant diseases

Mycoplasma—like organisms associated with insect diseases

Algae

Family Chlorophyceae

Family Euglenophyceae

Family Pyrophyceae

Family Chrysophyceae

Family Phaephyceae

Family Rhodophyceae

Fungi

Family Plasmodiophoraceae

Family Chytridiaceae

Family Olpidiopsidaceae

Family Actinomyceaceae

Genus Actinomyces

Coryneform Group

Genus Clavibactor

Genus Arthrobacter

Genus Curtobacterium

Genus Bdellovibro

Family Rickettsiaceae

Rickettsial—like organisms associated with insect diseases

Family Synchytriaceae

Family Catenariaceae

Family Coelomomycetaceae

Family Saprolegniaceae

Family Zoopagaceae

Family Albuginaceae

Family Peronosporaceae

Family Pythiaceae

Family Mucoraceae

Family Choaephoraceae

Family Mortiercllaceae

Family Endogonaceae

Family Syncephalastraceae

Family Dimargaritaceae

Family Kickxellaceae

Family Saksenaeaceae

Family Entomophthoraceae

Family Ecerinaceae

Family Taphrinaceae

Family Endomycetaceae

Family Saccharomycetaceae

Family Eurotiaceae

Family Gymnoascaceae

Family Aseophaeriaceae
Family Onygenaceae
Family Microascaceae
Family Protomycetaceae
Family Elsinoeaceae
Family Myriangiaceae
Family Dothidiaceae
Family Chaetothyriaceae
Family Parmulariaceae
Family Phillipsiellaceae
Family Hysteriaceae
Family Pleosporaceae
Family Melamomataceae
Family Ophiostomataceae
Family Aseosphaeriaceae
Family Erysiphaceae
Family Meliolaceae
Family Xylariaceae
Family Diaporthaceae
Family Hypoereaceae
Family Clavicipataceae
Family Phacidiaceae
Family Ascocorticiaceae
Family Hemiphacidiaceae
Family Dermataceae
Family Sclerotiniaceae
Family Cyttariaceae
Family Helosiaceae
Family Sarcostomataceae
Family Auricolariaceae
Family Ceratobasidiaceae
Family Corticiaceae
Family Hymenochaetaceae
Family Echinodintiaceae
Family Eistuliniaceae
Family Clavariaceae
Family Polyporaceae
Family Tricholomataceae
Family Ustilaginaceae
Family Sporobolomycetaceae
Family Uredinaceae
Family Agariacaceae
Family Graphiolaceae
Family Pucciniaceae
Family Melampsoraceae
Family Gandodermataceae
Family Labonlbeniaceae
Family Sphaeropsidaceae
Family Melabconiaceae
Family Tuberculariaceae
Family Dematiaceae
Family Moniliaceae
Family Aganomucetaceae

Parasitic Weeds

Family Balanophoraceae—parasitic species
Family Cuscutaceae—parasitic species
Family Ttydonoraceae—parasitic species
Family Lauraceae—parasitic species
Genus Cassytha
Family Lennoaceae—parasitic species
Family Loranthaceae—parasitic species
Family Myzodendraceae—parasitic species
Family Olacaceae—parasitic species
Family Orobanchaceae—parasitic species

Family Rafflesiaceae—parasitic species

Family Santalaceae—parasitic species

Family Scrophulariaceae-parasitic species

Protoza

Genus Phytomonas

And all Protozoa associated with insect diseases

Nematodes

Family Anguinidae

Family Belonolaimidae

Family Caloosiidae

Family Criconematidae

Family Dolichodoridae

Family Fergusobiidae

Family Hemicycliophoridae

Family Heteroderidae

Family Hoplolaimidae

Family Meloidogynidae

Family Neotylenchidae

Family Nothotylenchidae

Family Paratylenchidae

Family Pratylenchidae

Family Tylendchidae

Family Tylenchulidae

Family Aphelenchoidiae

Family Longidoridae

Family Trichodoridae

Mollusca

Superfamily Planorbacea

Superfamily Achatinacea

Superfamily Arionacea

Superfamily Limacacea

Superfamily Helicacea

Superfamily Veronicellacea

Arthropoda

Superfamily Ascoidea

Superfamily Dermanyssoidea

Superfamily Erjophyoidea

Superfamily Tetranychoidea

Superfamily Eupodoidea

Superfamily Tydeoidea

Superfamily Erythraenoidea

Superfamily Trombidioidea

Superfamily Hydryphantoidea

Superfamily Tarasonemoidea

Superfamily Pyemotoidea

Superfamily Hemisarooptoidea

Superfamily Acaroidea

Order Polydesraidea

Family Sminthoridae

Family Forfieulidea

Order Isoptera

Order Thysanoptera

Family Acrididea

Family Gryllidae

Family Gryllacrididae

Family Gryllotalpidea

Family Phasmatidae

Family Ronaleidae

Family Tettigoniidae

Family Tetragidae

Family Thaumastocoridae

Superfamily Piesmatoidea

Superfamily Lygaeoidea

Family Otitidae

Family Syrphidae

Family Tephritidae

Family Tipulidae

Family Apidae

Family Caphidae

Family Chalcidae

Family Cynipidae

Superfamily Idiostoloidea
Superfamily Careoidea
Superfamily Pentatomoidea
Superfamily Pyrrhocoroidea
Superfamily Tingoidea
Superfamily Miroidea
Order Homoptera
Family Anobiidae
Family Apionidae
Family Anthribidae
Family Bostrichidae
Family Brentidae
Family Bruchidae
Family Buprestodae
Family Byturidae
Family Cantharidae
Family Carabidae
Family Ceambycidae
Family Chrysomelidae
Family Coecinellidae
Family Curculionidae
Family Dermestidae
Family Elateridae
Family Hydrophilidae
Family Lyctidae
Family Meloidae
Family Mordellidae
Family Platypodidae
Family Scarabaelidae
Family Scolytidae
Family Selbytidae
Family Lepidoptera
Family Agromyzidae
Family Anthomiidae
Family Cecidomiidae
Family Chioropidae
Family Ephydridae
Family Lonchaeidae
Family Muscidae
Family Eurytomidae
Family Formicidae
Family Psilidae
Family Sircidae
Family Tenthredinidae
Family Torymidae
Family Xyloiopidae

and

Also unclassified organisms and/or organisations whose classifications is unknown and all other organisms associated with plant and insect diseases.

APPENDIX XII(B)

HAZARDOUS WASTES (MANAGEMENT & HANDLING) RULES, 1989

MINISTRY OF ENVIRONMENT AND FORESTS

(Department of Environment, Forests and Wildlife)

NOTIFICATION

New Delhi, the 28th July, 1989

S.O. 594(E) — In exercise of the powers conferred by sections 6, 8 and 25 of the Environment (Protection) Act, 1986 (29 of 1986), the Central Government hereby makes the following rules, namely —

1. *Short title and commencement*—(1) These rules may be called Hazardous Wastes (Management and Handling) Rules, 1989.

(2) They shall come into force on the date of their publication in the Official Gazette.

2. *Application*—These rules shall apply to hazardous wastes as specified in Schedule and shall not apply to —

(a) waste and exhaust gases as covered under the provisions of the Water (Prevention and Control of Pollution) Act, 1974 (6 of 1974) and the Air (Prevention and Control of Pollution) Act, 1981 (14 of 1981) and rules made thereunder;

(b) wastes arising out of the operation from ships beyond five kilometers as covered under the provision of the Merchant Shipping Act, 1958 (44 of 1958) and the rules made thereunder;

(c) radio-active wastes as covered under the provisions of the Atomic Energy Act, 1962 (33 of 1962) and rules made thereunder;

3. *Definitions*—In these rules, unless the context otherwise requires,—

(a) "Act" means the Environment (Protection) Act, 1986 (29 of 1986);

(b) "applicant" means a person or an organisation that applies, in Form 1, for granting of authorisation to perform specific activities connected with handling of hazardous wastes;

(c) "authorisation" means permission for collection, reception, treatment, transport, storage and disposal of hazardous wastes, granted by the competent authority in Form 2;

(d) "authorised person" means a person or an organisation authorised by the competent authority to collect, treat, transport, store or dispose of hazardous wastes in accordance with the guidelines to be issued by the competent authority from time to time;

(e) "export" with its grammatical variations and cognate expression, means taking out of India to a place outside India;

(f) "exporter" means any person under the jurisdiction of the exporting country who exports hazardous wastes and the exporting country itself, who exports hazardous wastes;

(g) "facility" means any location wherein the processes incidental to the waste generation, collection, reception, treatment, storage and disposal are carried out;

(h) "Form" means Form appended to these rules;

(i) "hazardous wastes" means categories on wastes specified in the Schedule;

(j) "hazardous wastes site" means a place for collection, reception, treatment, storage and disposal of hazardous wastes which has been duly approved by the competent authority;

(k) "import" with its grammatical variations and cognate expression, means bringing into India from a place outside India;

(l) "importer" means on occupier or any person who imports hazardous wastes;

(m) "operator of a facility" means a person who owns or operates a facility for collection, reception, treatment, storage and disposal of hazardous wastes;

(n) "Schedule" means Schedule appended to these rules;

(o) "State Pollution Control Board" means the Board appointed under sub-section (1) of section 4 of the Water (Prevention and Control of Pollution) Act, 1974 (6 of 1974); and under Section 4 of the Air (Prevention and Control of Pollution) Act, 1981 (14 of 1981);

(p) "transboundary movement" means any movement of hazardous wastes or other wastes from an area under the national jurisdiction of one country to or through an area under the national jurisdiction of another country or to or through an area not under the national jurisdiction of any country, provided at least two countries are involved in the movement;

(q) the words and expressions used in these rules and not defined but defined in the Act, shall have the meanings respectively assigned to them in the Act.

4. *Responsibility of the occupier for handling of wastes.*—(1) The occupier generating hazardous wastes listed in column (2) of the Schedule in quantities equal to or exceeding the limits given in column (3) of the said Schedule, shall take all practical steps to ensure that such wastes are properly handled and disposed of without any adverse effects which may result from such wastes and the occupier shall also be responsible for proper collection, reception, treatment, storage and disposal of these wastes either himself or through the operator of a facility.

(2) The occupier or any other person acting on his behalf who intends to get his hazardous waste treated by the operator of a facility under sub-rule (1), shall give, to the operator of a facility, such information as may be specified by the State Pollution Control Board.

5. *Grant of authorisation for handling hazardous wastes.*—(1) Hazardous wastes shall be collected, treated, stored and disposed of only in such facilities as may be authorised for this purpose.

(2) Every occupier generating hazardous wastes and having a facility for collection, reception, treatment, transport, storage, and disposal of such wastes shall make an application in Form 1 to the State Pollution Control Board for the grant of authorisation for any of the above activities:

Provided that the occupier not having a facility for the collection, reception, treatment, transport, storage and disposal of hazardous wastes shall make an application to the State Pollution Control Board in Form 1 for the grant of authorisation within a period of six months from the date of commencement of these rules.

(3) Any person who intends to be an operator of a facility for the collection, reception, treatment, transport, storage and disposal of hazardous wastes, shall make an application in Form 1 to the State Pollution Control Board for the grant of authorisation for any of the above activities:

Provided that the operator engaged in the business of the collection, reception, treatment, transport, storage and disposal of hazardous wastes shall make an application to the State Pollution Control Board in Form 1 for the grant of authorisation within a period of six months from the date of commencement of these rules.

(4) The State Pollution Control Board will not issue an authorisation unless it is satisfied that the operator of a facility or an occupier, as the case may be, possesses appropriate facilities, technical capabilities and equipment to handle hazardous wastes safely.

(5) The authorisation to operate a facility shall be issued in Form 2 and shall be subject to conditions laid down therein.

(6) (i) An authorisation granted under this rule shall unless sooner suspended or cancelled, be in force for a period of two years from the date of issue or from the date of renewal.

(ii) An application for the renewal of an authorisation shall be made in Form 1, before its expiry.

(iii) The authorisation shall continue to be in force until it is renewed or revoked.

(7) The State Pollution Control Board may, after giving reasonable opportunity of being heard to the applicant refuse to grant any authorisation.

6. *Power to suspend or cancel an authorisation.*— (1) The State Pollution Control Board may cancel an authorisation issued under these rules or suspend it for such period as it thinks fit, if in its opinion, the authorised person has failed to comply with any of the conditions of the authorisation or with any provisions of the Act or these rules, after giving the authorised person an opportunity to show cause and after recording reasons therefor.

(2) Upon suspension or cancellation of the authorisation and during the pendency of an appeal under rule 12, the State Pollution Control Board may give directions to the persons whose authorisation has been suspended or cancelled for the safe storage of the hazardous wastes, and such person shall comply with such directions.

7. *Packaging, labelling and transport of hazardous wastes.*— (1) Before hazardous wastes is delivered at the hazardous waste site, the occupier or operator of a facility shall ensure that the hazardous wastes is packaged in a manner suitable for storage and transport and the labelling and packaging shall be easily visible and be able to withstand physical conditions and climatic factors.

(2) Packaging, labelling and transport of hazardous wastes shall be in accordance with the provisions of the rules issued by the Central Government under the Motor Vehicles Act, 1988 and other guidelines issued from time to time.

8. *Inventory of disposal sites.*— (1) The State Government or a person authorised by it shall undertake a continuing programme to identify the sites and compile and publish periodically an inventory of disposal sites within the State for the disposal of hazardous wastes.

(2) The State Government or a person authorised by it shall undertake an environmental impact study before identifying a site as waste disposal site in the State.

(3) The State Government or a person authorised by it shall undertake a continuing programme to compile and publish an inventory of sites within the State at which hazardous wastes have at any time been stored or disposed of and such inventory shall contain, besides the location and description information relating to the amount, nature and toxicity of hazardous wastes at each such site as may be associated with such site.

9. *Records and returns.*—(1) The occupier generating hazardous waste and operator of a facility for collection, reception, treatment, transport, storage and disposal of hazardous waste shall maintain records of such operations in Form 3.

(2) The occupier and operator of a facility shall send annual returns to the State Pollution Control Board in Form 4.

10. *Accident reporting and follow-up.* — Where an accident occurs at the facility or on a hazardous waste site or during transportation of hazardous wastes, the occupier or operator of a facility shall report immediately to the State Pollution Control Board about the accident in Form 5.

11. *Import of hazardous wastes.*—(1) Import of hazardous wastes from any country to India shall not be permitted for dumping and disposal of such wastes. However, import of such wastes may be allowed for processing or reuse as raw material, after examining each case on merit by the State Pollution Control Board or by an officer authorised in this behalf.

(2) The exporting country or the exporter as the case may be of hazardous wastes shall communicate in Form 6 to the Central Government (the Ministry of Environment and Forests) of the proposed transboundary movement of hazardous wastes.

(3) The Central Government shall, after examining the communication received under sub-rule (2) and on being satisfied that the import of such hazardous wastes is to be used for processing or reuse as raw material, grant permission for the import of such wastes subject to such conditions as the Central Government may specify in this behalf and if, however, the Central Government is not satisfied with the communication received under sub-rule (2), may refuse permission to import such hazardous wastes.

(4) Any importer importing hazardous wastes shall provide necessary information as to the type of hazardous wastes he is to import, in Form 6, to the concerned State Pollution Control Board, the Central Pollution Control Board in the case of Union Territories.

(5) The State Pollution Control Board shall examine the information received under sub-rule (4) and issue such instructions to the importer as it considers necessary.

(6) The Central Government or the State Pollution Control Board, as the case may be, shall inform the concerned Port Authority to take appropriate steps regarding the safe handling of the hazardous wastes at the time of off-loading the same.

(7) Any person importing hazardous wastes shall maintain the records of the hazardous wastes imported as specified is Form 7 and the records so maintained shall be open for inspection by the State Pollution Control Board the Ministry of Environment and Forests the Central Pollution Control Boards in the case of Union territories or an officer appointed by them in this behalf.

12. *Appeal*. — (1) An appeal shall lie, against any order of suspension or cancellation or refusal of an authorisation by the State Pollution Control Board to the State Government and to the Ministry of Environment and Forests in the case of the Central Pollution Central Board.

(2) Every appeal shall be in writing and shall be accompanied by a copy of the order appealed against and shall be presented within thirty days of the order passed.

SCHEDULE

(See rules 3 (i), 3(n) and 4)

CATEGORIES OF HAZARDOUS WASTES

Waste Categories	Types of wastes	Regulatory Quantities
1	2	3
Waste Category No. 1	Cyanide Wastes	1 kilograms per year calculated as cyanide
Waste Category No. 2	Metal Finishing Wastes	10 Kilograms per year the sum of the specified substance calculated as pure metal.
Waste Category No. 3	Waste containing water soluble chemical compounds of lead, copper, zinc, chromium, nickel, selenium, barium and antimony.	10 kilogrames per year the sum of specified substance calculated as pure metal.

Waste Category No. 4	Mercury, Arsenic, Thallium and Cadmium bearing wastes.	5 kilograms per year the sum of the specified substance calculated as pure metal.
Waste Category No. 5	Non-halogenated hydro-carbons including solvents	200 kilograms per year cal-culated as non-halogenated hydrocarbons.
Waste Category No. 6	Halogenated hydro-carbon including solvents	50 kilograms per year calc-ulated as halogenated hydro carbons.
Waste Category No. 7	Wastes from paints, pig-ments, glue, varnish and printing, ink.	250 kilograms per year cal-culated as oil or oil emul-sions.
Waste Category No. 8	Wastes from Dyes and Dye intermediate conta-ining inorganic chemical compounds.	200 kilograms per year calculated as inorganic chemicals.
Waste Category No. 9	Wastes from Dyes and Dyeintermediate cont-aining organic chemical compounds.	50 kilograms per year calculated as organic chemicals.
Waste Category No. 10	Waste oil and emulsions	1000 kilograms per year calculated as oil and oil emulsions.
Waste Category No. 11	Tarry wastes from refin-ing and tar residues from distillation or prolytic treatment.	200 kilograms per year calculated as tar
Waste Category No. 12	Sludges arising from treatment of waste waters containing heavy metals, toxic organics, oils, emulsions and spend che-micals and incinerations ash	irrespective of any quantity.
Waste Category No. 13	Phenols	5 kilograms per year calculated as phenols

Waste Category No. 14	Asbestos	200 kilograms per year calculated as Asbestos.
Waste Category No. 15	Wastes from manufacturing of pesticides and herbicides and residues from pesticides and herbicides, formulation units.	5 kilograms per year calculated as pesticides and their intermediate products.
Waste Category No. 16	Acid/Alkaline/Slurry Wastes	200 kilograms per year calculated as Acids/ Alkalies.
Waste Category No. 17	Off-Specification and discarded products	Irrespective of any quantity.
Waste Category No. 18	Discarded containers and Containers linears of hazardous and toxic wastes	Irrespective of any quantity.

FORM I

[See rules 3(b), 5(2)(3) and (6)(ii)]

(Application for obtaining authorisation or for its renewal for collection/ reception/treatment/transport/storage/disposal of hazardous waste)

1. Name and address of the person applying for authorisation/renewal.
2. Authorisation required for (Please tick appropriate activity/activities)
   (i) collection.
   (ii) reception.
   (iii) treatment.
   (iv) transport.
   (v) storage.
   (vi) disposal.
3. In case of renewal of authorisation previous authorisation number and date.
4. Locational address of the site where the proposed activity/activities is/ are carried out.

5. Important Environmental features of the surrounding areas of the site (Please attach a map of the area, 2.5 kms. radius with the site at the Centre indicating therein water bodies and important human activities, sensitive features)
6. Chemical identity of hazardous waste as per the Schedule.
7. Quantity of hazardous waste handled.
8. Details of the operation system for carrying out the activity/activities.

FORM 2

[See rule 3(c) and 5(5)]

(Authorisation for operating a facility for collection, reception, treatment, storage, transport, and disposal of hazardous wastes.)

1. Number of authorisation and date of issue ....
....
2. .... of .... is hereby granted an authorisation to operate a facility for collection, reception, treatment, storage, transport and disposal of hazardous waste on the premises situated at...
3. The authorisation granted to operate a facility for collection, reception, treatment, storage, transport and disposal of hazardous wastes.
4. The authorisation shall be in force for a period of .... years from the date of issue.
5. The authorisation is subject to the conditions stated below and to such conditions as may be specified in the rules for the time being in force under the Environment (Protection) Act, 1986.

Date....................

Signature..........................

Designation......................

Terms and conditions of authorisation

1. The authorisation shall comply with the provisions of the Environment (Protection) Act, 1986, and the rules made thereunder.
2. The authorisation or its renewal shall be produced for inspection at the request of an officer authorised by the State Pollution Control Board.
3. The person authorised shall not rent, lend, sell, transfer or otherwise transport the hazardous wastes without obtaining prior permission of the State Pollution Control Board.

4. Any unauthorised change in personnel, equipment as working conditions as mentioned in the application by the person authorised shall constitute a breach of his authorisation.

5. It is the duty of the authorised person to take prior permission of the State Pollution Control Board to close down the facility.

6. An application for the renewal of an authorisation shall be made as laid down in rule 5(6)(ii).

FORM 3

[See rule 9(1)]

Format for maintaining records of hazardous wastes at the facility.

1. Name and address of the occupier or operator of a facility:
2. Date of issuance of authorisation and its reference number:
3. Description of hazardous waste:

Physical form with description	Chemical form	Total volume and weight (in kg.)

4. Description of storage and treatment of hazardous waste:

Date	Method of storage of hazardous wastes	Date	Method of treatment of hazardous wastes

5. Details of transportation of hazardous waste:

Name and address of the consignee of the package	Mode of packing/of the waste for transportation	Mode of transportation to site of disposal	Date of transportation

6. Details of disposal of hazardous waste:

Date of disposal	Concentration of hazardous material in the final waste form	Site of disposal (identify the location on the relevant layout drawing for reference)	Method of disposal	Persons involved in disposal

7. Data on environmental surveillance:

Date of measurement	Analysis of ground water		Analysis of soil samples		Analysis of air sampling		Analysis of any other samples (give-details)
	Location of sampling	Depth Data of sampling	Location sampling	Depth Data of sampling	Location of sampling	Data	

Name and signature of the Head of facility

FORM 4

[See Rule 9(2)]

Format for the submission of returns, regarding disposal of hazardous Waste

(To be submitted to the State Pollution Control Board)

1. Name and address of the Institution:

2. Details of waste disposal operations:

Sl.	Date of issuence of autho-risation for the di-sposal of hazardous waste and its refere-nce No.	Description of Hazardous Waste Physical form and contents	Chemical form	Tot. vol. of the hazar-dous waste dispo-sed with No. of packa-ges.	Mode of transpo. to site of dis-posal	Site of disposal (attach a sketch showing the lo-cation(s) of dis-posal)	Brief descri-ption of the method of dis-posal	Date of disposal	Remarks (if any)

3. Details of environmental surveillance:

Date of measu-rement	Analysis of ground water			Analysis of soil samples			Analysis of air sampling		Analysis of any other samples (give-details)
	Loc-ation of sam-pling	Depth of sam-pling	Data	Loc-ation sam-pling	Depth of sam-pling	Data	Location of sam-pling	Data	

Name and signature of the Head of facility

FORM 5

(See rule 10)

1. The date and time of the accident:
2. Sequence of events leading to accident:
3. The hazardous waste involved in accident:

4. The data for assessing the effects of the accident on health or the environment.
5. The emergency measures taken.
6. The steps taken to alleviate the effects of accidents.
7. The steps taken to prevent the recurrence of such an accident.

FORM 6

[See rule 11(2) and (4)]

(Format for notification and movement document)

A. INFORMATION TO BE PROVIDED ON NOTIFICATION

1. Reason for waste export
2. Exporter of the waste[1]
3. Generator(s) of the waste and site of generation[1]
4. Importer of wastes[1]
5. Intended carrier(s) of the waste of their agents if known[1]
6. Exporting Country's Competent authority[2]
7. Expected countries of transit Competent authority[2]
8. Importing country's Competent authority[2]
9. General or single notification.
10. Projected date(s) of shipment(s) and period of time over which waste is to be exported and itinerary (including point of entry and exist)[3]
11. Means of transport envisaged (road, rail, sea, air, inland waters)
12. Information relating to insurance[4]
13. Designation and physical description of the waste and its composition[5] and information on any special handling requirements including emergency provisions in case of accidents.
14. Type of packaging envisaged (e.g. bulk, drummed, tanker).
15. Estimated quantity in weight/volume[6]
16. Process by which the waste is generated[7]
17. Method of disposal
18. Declaration by the generator and exporter that the information is correct.
19. Information transmitted (including technical description of the plant) to the exporter or generator from the importer of the waste upon which the latter has based his assessment that there was no reason to believe that the wastes

will not be managed in an environmentally sound manner in accordance with the laws and regulations of the importing country.

B. INFORMATION TO BE PROVIDED ON THE MOVEMENT DOCUMENT

1. Exporter of the waste[8]
2. Generator(s) of the waste and site of generation[8]
3. Importer of the waste and actual site of disposal[8]
4. Carrier(s) of the waste or his agent(s)
5. Subject of general or single notification.
6. The date the transboundary movement started and date(s) and signature on receipt by each person who takes charge of the waste
7. Means of transport (road, rail, inland waterway, sea, air) including countries of export, transit and import, also point of entry and exist where these have been designated.
8. General description of the waste.
9. Information on special handling requirements including emergency provision in case of accidents.
10. Type and number of packages.
11. Quantity in weight/volume.
12. Declaration by the exporter that the information is correct.
13. Declaration by the exporter indicating no objection from the competent authorities of all States concerned which are Parties.
14. Certificate by importer of receipt at designated disposal facility and indication of method of disposal and of the approximate date of disposal.

---

1. Full name and address, telephone, telex or telefax number and the name, address, telephone, telex or telefax number of the person to be contacted.
2. Full name and address, telephone, telex and telefax number.
3. In the case of a general notification covering several shipments, either the expected dates of each shipment or, if this is not known the expected frequency of the shipments will be required.
4. Information to be provided on relevant insurance requirements and how they are met by exporter, carrier and importer.
5. The nature and the concentration of the most hazardous components, in terms of toxicity and other dangers presented by the waste both in handling and in relation to the proposed disposal method.

6. In the case of a general notification covering several shipments, both the estimated total quantity and the estimated quantities of each individual shipment will be required.
7. In so far as this is necessary to assess the hazard and determine the appropriateness of the proposed disposal operation.
8. Full name and address, telephone, telex or telefax number and the name, address, telephone, telex or telefax number of the person to be contacted in case of emergency.

FORM 7

[See Rule 11(7)]

(Format of maintaining records of hardous wastes imported)

1. Name and address of the importer :
2. Date and reference number of issuance of permission to import hazardous wastes:
3. Description of hazardous wate :
   (a) Physical form :
   (b) Chemical form :
   (c) Total volume and weight (in kilogrammes) :
4. Description of storage, treatment and reuse of hazardous wate :
   (a) Date :
   (b) Method of storage :
   (c) Method of treatment and reuse (give details) :

APPENDIX XII(C)

THE MANUFACTURE, STORAGE AND IMPORT OF HAZARDOUS CHEMICALS RULES, 1989

MINISTRY OF ENVIRONMENT AND FORESTS

(Department of Environment, Forests and Wildlife)

NOTIFICATION

New Delhi, the 27th November, 1989

S.O. 966 (E) — In exercise of the powers conferred by Sections 6, 8 and 25 of the Environment (Protection) Act, 1986 (29 of 1986), the Central Government hereby makes the following rules, namely :

1. *Short title and commencement* — (1) These Rules may be called the Manufacture, Storage and Import of Hazardous Chemicals Rules, 1989.

(2) They shall come into force on the date of their publication in the Official Gazette.

2. *Definitions* — In these rules, unless the context of their publication requires,—

(a) "Act" means the Environment (Protection) Act, 1986 (29 of 1986);

(b) "Authority" means an authority mentioned in Column 2 of Schedule 5;

(c) "export" with its grammatical variation and cognate expression, means taking out of India to a place outside India;

(d) "exporter" means any person under the jurisdiction of the exporting country and includes the exporting country, who exports hazardous chemical;

(e) "hazardous chemical" means,—

(i) any chemical which satisfies any of the criteria laid down in Part I of Schedule I and is listed in Column 2 of Part II of this Schedule;

(ii) any chemical listed in Column 2 of schedule 2;

(iii) any chemical listed in Column 2 of Schedule 3;

(f) "import" with its grammatical variations and cognate expression, means bringing into India from a place outside India;

(g) "importer" means an occupier or any person who imports hazardous chemicals;

(h) "industrial activity" means,

(i) an operation or process carried out in an industrial installation referred to in Schedule 4 involving or likely to involve one or more hazardous chemicals and includes on-site storage or on-site transport which is associated with that operation or process, as the case may be; or

(ii) isolated storage; or

(iii) pipeline;

(i) "isolated storage" means storage of hazardous chemical, other than storage associated with an installation on the same site specified in Schedule 4 where that storage involves atleast the quantities of that chemical set out in schedule 2;

(j) "major accident" means an occurrence including any particular major emission, fire or explosion involving one or more hazardous chemicals and resulting from uncontrolled developments in the course of an industrial activity or due to natural events leading to serious effects both immediate or delayed, inside or outside the installation likely to cause substantial loss of life and property including adverse effects on the environments;

(k) "pipeline" means a pipe (together with any apparatus and works associated therewith) or system of pipes (together with any apparatus and works associated therewith) for the conveyance of a hazardous chemical other than a flammable gas as set out in Column 2 of Part II of Schedule 3 at a pressure of less than 8 bars absolute; the pipeline also includes inter-state pipelines;

(l) "Schedule" means Schedule appended to these rules;

(m) "site" means any location where hazardous chemicals are manufactured or processed, stored, handled, used, disposed of and includes the whole of an area under the control of an occupier and includes pier, jetty or similar structure whether floating or not;

(n) "Threshold quantity" means,—

(i) in the case of hazardous chemical specified in Column 2 of schedule 2, the quantity of that chemical specified in the corresponding entry in Columns 3 & 4,

(ii) in the case of hazardous chemical specified in Column 2 of Part I of Schedule 3, the quantity of that chemical specified in the corresponding entry in Columns 3 & 4 of that part;

(iii) in the case of substances of a class specified in Column 2 of Part II of Schedule 3, the total quantity of all substances of that class specified in the corresponding entry in Column 3 & 4 of that part.

3. *Duties of authorities*— Subject to the other provisions of these rules, the authority shall perform duties as specified in Column 3 of Schedule 5.

4. *General responsibility of the occupier during industrial activity*—(1) This rules shall apply to,—

(a) an industrial activity in which a hazardous chemical, which satisfies any of the criteria laid down in Part I of Schedule I and is listed in Column 2 of Part II of this Schedule is or may be involved; and

(b) isolated storage in which there is involved a threshold quantity of a hazardous chemical listed in Schedule 2 in Column 2 which is equal to or more than the threshold quantity specified in the Schedule for that chemical Column 3 thereof.

(2) An occupier who has control of an industrial activity in terms of sub-rule (1) shall provide evidence to show that he has, —

(a) identified the major accident hazardous; and

(b) taken adequate steps to —

(i) prevent such major accidents and to limit their consequences to persons and the environment;

(ii) provide to the persons working on the site with the information, training and equipment including antidotes necessary to ensure their safety.

5. *Notification of Major accident*—(1) Where a major accident occurs on a site, the occupier shall forthwith notify the concerned authority as identified in Schedule 5 of that accident, and furnish thereafter to the concerned authority a report relating to the accidents in instalments, if necessary, in Schedule 6.

(2) The concerned authority shall on receipt of the report in accordance with sub-rule 1 of this rule, shall undertake a full analysis of the major accident and sent the requisite information to the Ministry of Environment and Forests appropriate channel.

(3) Where an occupier has notified accident to the concerned authority under respective legislation, he shall be deemed to have complied with the requirements as per sub-rule 1 of this rule.

6. Industrial activity to which rules 7 to 15 apply —

(1) Rules 7 to 15 shall apply to, —

(a) an industrial activity in which there is involved a quantity of a hazardous chemical listed in Column 2 of Schedule 3 which is equal to or more than the quantity specified in the entry for that chemical in Column 3 & 4 (Rules 10-12 only for Column 4) and

(b) isolated storage in which there is involved a quantity of a hazardous chemical listed in Column 2 of Schedule 2 which is equal to or more than the quantity specified in the entry for that the chemical in Column 4.

(2) For the purposes of rules 7 to 15, —

(a) "new industrial activity" means an industrial activity which —

(i) commences after the date of coming into operation of these rules; or

(ii) of commenced before that date, is an industrial activity in which a modification has been made which is likely to cover major accident hazards, and that activity shall be deemed to have commenced on the date on which the modification was made;

(b) an "existing industrial activity" means an industrial activity which is not a new industrial activity.

7. *Notification of sites* — (1) An occupier shall not undertake any industrial activity unless he has submitted a written report to the concerned authority containing the particulars specified in Schedule 7 at least 3 months before commencing that activity or before such shorter time as the concerned authority may agree and for the purposes of this paragraph, an activity in which subsequently there is or is liable to be a threshold quantity or more of an additional hazardous chemical shall be deemed to be a different activity and shall be notified accordingly.

(2) No report under sub-rule (1) need to be submitted by the occupier if he submits a report under rule 10 (1).

8. *Updating of the site notification following changes in the threshold quantity*— Where an activity has been reported in accordance with rule 7 (1) and the occupier makes a change in it (including an increase or decrease in the maximum threshold quantity of a hazardous chemical to which this rule applies which is or is liable to be at the site or in the pipelines or at the cessation of the

activity) which is affects the particulars specified in that report or any subsequent report made under this rule. The occupier shall forthwith furnish a further report to the concerned authority.

9. Transitional provisions — where —

(a) at the date of coming into operation of these rules, an occupier is in control of an existing industrial activity which is required to be reported under rule 7 (1); or

(b) within 6 months after that date an occupier commences any such new industrial activity;

if shall be a sufficient compliance with that rule if he reports to the concerned authority as per the particulars in Schedule 7 within 3 months after the date of coming into operation of these rules or within such longer time as the concerned authority may agree in writing.

10. *Safety reports* — (1) Subject to the following paragraphs of this rule, an occupier shall not undertake any industrial activity to which this rule applies, unless he has prepared a safety report on that industrial activity containing the information specified in Schedule 8 and has sent a copy of that report to that concerned authority at least ninety days before commencing that activity.

(2) In the case of a new industrial activity which an occupier commences, or by virtue of sub-rule (2) (a) (ii) of rule 6 is deemed commence, within 6 months after coming into operation of these rules, it shall be a sufficient compliance with sub-rules (1) of this rule if the occupier sends to the concerned authority a copy of the report required in accordance with that sub-rule within ninety days after the date of coming into operation of these rules.

(3) In the case of an existing industrial activity, until five years from the date of coming into operation of these rules, it shall be a sufficient compliance with sub-rule (1) of this rule if the occupier on or before ninety days from the date of the coming into operation of these rules sends to the concerned authority the information specified in Schedule 7 relating to that activity.

11. *Updating of reports under Rule.10* — (1) Where an occupier has made a safety report in accordance with sub-rule (1) of rule 10 he shall not make any modification to the industrial activity to which that safety report relates which could materially affect the particulars in that report, unless he has made a further report to take account of those modifications and has sent a copy that report to the concerned authority atleast 90 days before making those modifications.

(2) Where an occupier has made a report in accordance with rule 10 and sub-rule (1) of this rule and that industrial activity is continuing, the occupier shall within three years of the date of the last such report, make a further report which shall have regard in particular to new technical knowledge which has affected the

particulars in the previous report relating to safety and hazard assessment, and shall within 30 days or in such longer time as the concerned authority may agree in writing send a copy of the report to the concerned authority.

12. *Requirements for further information to be sent to the authority.*—(1) Where, in accordance with rule,10, an occupier has sent a safety report relating to an industrial activity to the concerned authority, the concerned authority may, by a notice served on the occupier, requires him to provide such additional information as is specified in the notice and the occupier shall send that information to the concerned authority within such time as is specified in the notice or within such extended time as the authority may subsequently specify.

13. Preparation of on site emergency plan by the occupier— (1) An occupier shall prepare and keep up-to-date an on-site emergency plan detailing how major accidents will be dealt with on the site on which the industrial activity is carried on and that plan shall include the name of the person who is responsible for safety on the site and the names of those who are authorised to take action in accordance with the plan in case of an emergency.

(2) The occupier shall ensure that the emergency plan prepared in accordance with sub-rule (1), takes into account any modification made in the industrial activity and that every person on the site who is affected by the plan is informed of its relevant provisions.

(3) The occupier shall prepare the emergency plan required under sub-rule (1),—

(a) in the case of a new industrial activity, before that activity is commenced;

(b) in the case of an existing industrial activity within 90 days of coming into operation of these rules.

14. *Preparation of off-site emergency plans by the authority*—(1) It shall be the duty of the concerned authority as identified in Column 2 of Schedule 5 to prepare and keep up-to-date an adequate off-site emergency plan detaining how emergencies relating to a possible major accident on that site will be dealt with and in preparing that plan the concerned authority shall consult the occupier and such other persons as it may deem necessary.

(2) For the purpose of enabling the concerned authority to prepare the emergency plan required under sub-rule (1), the occupier shall provide the concerned authority with such information relating to the industrial activity under his control as the concerned authority may require, including the nature, extent and likely effects of off-site of possible major accidents and the authority shall provide the occupier with any information from the off-site emergency plan which relates to his duties under rule 13.

(3) The concerned authority shall prepare its emergency plan required under sub-rule (1) —

(a) in the case of a new industrial activity, before that activity is commenced;

(b) in the case of an existing industrial activity, within six months of coming into operation of these rules.

15. *Information to be given to persons liable to be affected by a major accident* — (1) The occupier shall take appropriate steps to inform persons outside the site either directly or through District Emergency Authority who are likely to be in an area which may be affected by a major accident about —

(a) the nature of the major accident hazard; and

(b) the safety measures and the 'Dos' and 'Donts' which should be adopted in the event of a major accident.

(2) The occupier shall take the steps required under sub-rule (1) to inform persons about industrial activity, before that activity is commenced, except, in the case of an existing industrial activity in which case the occupier shall comply the requirements of sub-rule (1) within 90 days of coming into operation of these rules.

16. *Disclosure of information.*— (1) Where for the purpose of evaluating information notified under rule 5 or 7, 15, the concerned authority discloses that information to some other person, that other person shall not use that information for any purpose except for the purpose of the concerned authority disclosing it, and before disclosing the information the concerned authority shall inform that other person of his obligations under this paragraph.

17. *Collection, Development and Dissemination of Information*—(1) This rule shall apply to an industrial activity in which a hazardous chemical which satisfies any of the criteria laid down in Part 1 of Schedule 1 and is listed in Column 2 of Part II of this Schedule is or may be involved.

(2) An occupier, who has control of an industrial activity in term of sub-rule 1 of this rule, shall arrange to obtain or development information in the form of safety data sheet as specified in Schedule 9. The information shall be accessible upon request for reference.

(3) The occupier while obtaining or developing a safety data sheet as specified in Schedule 9 in respect of a hazardous chemical handled by him shall ensure that the information is recorded accurately and reflects the scientific evidence used in making the hazard determination. In case, any significant information regarding hazard of a chemical is available, it shall be added to the material safety data sheet as specified in Schedule 9 as soon as practicable.

(4) Every container of a hazardous chemical shall be clearly labelled or marked to identify,—

(a) the contents of the container;

(b) the name and address of the manufacturer or importer of the hazardous chemical;

(c) the physical, chemical and toxicological data as per the criteria given at Part I of Schedule I.

(5) In terms of sub-rule 4 of this rule where it is impractical to label a chemical in view of the size of the container or the nature of the package, provision should be made for other effective means like tagging or accompanying documents.

18. *Import of hazardous chemical*—(1) This rule shall apply to a chemical which satisfies any of the criteria laid down in Part I of Schedule I and is listed in Column 2 of Part II of this Schedule.

(2) Any person responsible for importing hazardous chemicals in India shall provide at the time of import or within thirty days from the date of import to the concerned authorities as identified in Column 2 of Schedule 5 the information pertaining to —

(i) the name and address of the person receiving the consignment in India;

(ii) the port of entry in India;

(iii) mode of transport from the exporting country to India;

(iv) the quantity of chemical(s) being imported; and

(v) complete product safety information.

(3) If the concerned authority at the State is satisfied that the chemical being imported is likely to cause major accident, it may direct the importer to take such steps including stoppage of such imports as the concerned authority at the State may deem it appropriate.

(4) The concerned authority at the State shall simultaneously inform the concerned Port Authority to take appropriate steps regarding state handling storage of hazardous chemicals while off-loading the consignment within the port premises.

(5) Any person importing hazardous chemicals shall maintain the records of the hazardous chemicals imported as specified in Schedule 10 and the records so maintained shall be open for inspection by the concerned authority at the State or the Ministry of Environment and Forests or any officer appointed by them in this behalf.

(6) The importer of the hazardous chemical or a person working on his behalf shall ensure that transport of hazardous chemicals from port of entry to the ultimate destination is in accordance with the Central Motor Vehicles Rules, 1989 framed under the provisions of the Motor Vehicles Act, 1988.

19. *Improvement notices*—(1) If the concerned authority is of the opinion that a person has contravened the provisions of these rules, the concerned authority shall serve on him a notice (in this para referred to as "an improvement notice") requiring that person to remedy the contravention or, as the case may be, the matters occasioning it within such period as may be specified in the notice.

(2) A notice served under sub-rule (1) shall clearly specify the measures to be taken by the occupier in remedying said contraventions.

20. *Power of the Central Government to modify the Schedules.* — The Central Government may, at any time, by notification in the Official Gazette, make suitable in the Schedules.

SCHEDULE 1

[See rule 2 (e) (ii), 4(1)(a), 4 (2)(i), 17 and 18]

Indicative Criteria and List of Chemicals

Part I

(a) Toxic Chemicals:

Chemicals having the following values of acute toxicity and which, owing to their physical and chemical properties, are capable of producing major accident hazards.

Sl. No.	Degree of Toxicity	Medium lethal dose by the oral route (oral toxicity)LD 50 (mg/kg body weight of test animals)	Medium lethal dose by the dermal route (dermal toxicity) LD50 (mg/kg body weight of test animals)	Medium lethal conecentration by inhalation route (four hours) LC50 (mg/1 inhalatior in test animals)
1.	Extremely toxic	1-50	1-200	0.1-0.5
2.	Highly toxic	51-500	201-2000	0.5-2.0

(b) Flammable chemicals:

(i) flammable gases: chemicals which in the gaseous state at normal pressure and mixed with air become flammable and the boiling point of which at normal pressure is 20°C or below;

(ii) highly flammable liquids : chemicals which have a flush point lower than 23°C and the boiling point of which at normal pressure is above 20°C.

(iii) flammable liquids: chemicals which have a flash point lower than 65°C and which remain liquids under pressure, where particular processing conditions, such as high pressure and high temperature, may create major accident hazards.

(c) Explosives:

Chemicals which may explode under the effect of flame, heat or photochemical conditions or which are more sensitive to shocks or friction than dinitrobenzene.

PART II

LIST OF HAZARDOUS AND TOXIC CHEMICALS

Sl. No.	Name of the Chemical
1	2
1.	Acetone
2.	Acetone Cyanohydrine
3.	Acetyl Chloride
4.	Acetylene (Ethyne)
5.	Acrolein (2-Propenal)
6.	Acrylonitrile
7.	Aldicarb
8.	Aldrin
9.	Alkyl Phthalate
10.	Allyl Alcohol
11.	Allylamine
12.	Alpha Naphthyl Thiourea (Antu)
13.	Aminodiphenyl, - 4
14.	Aminophenol
15.	Amiton
16.	Ammonia
17.	Ammonium Nitrate
18.	Ammonium Nitrates in fertilizers
19.	Ammonium Sulfamate
20.	Anabasine
21.	Anilinc
22.	Anisidine-p
23.	Antimony and Compounds
24.	Antimony Hydride (Stibine)
25.	Arsenic Hydride (Arsine)
26.	Arsenic Pentoxide, (Arsenic) (v) Acide and Salts
27.	Arsenic Trioxide, Arsenious (iii) Acids and Salts
28.	Asbestos
29.	Azinphos-Ethyl
30.	Azinphos-Methyl
31.	Barium Azide
32.	Benzene
33.	Benzidine
34.	Benzidine Salts
35.	Benzoquinone
36.	Benzoyl Chloride
37.	Benzoyl Peroxide
38.	Benzyl Chloride
39.	Benzyl Cyanide
40.	Beryllium (Powders, Compounds)
41.	Biphenyl

42. Bis (2-Chloromethyl) Ketone
43. Bis (2, 4, 6 - Trinitrophenyl) Amine
44. Bis (2 - Chloroethyl) Sulphide
45. Bis (Chloromethyl) Ether
46. Bis (tert-Butylperoxy) Cyclozane, 1, 1
47. Bis (tert-Butylperoxy) Butane, - 2, 2
48. Bis, 2 Tribromophenoxy - Ethane
49. Bisphenol
50. Boron and Compounds
51. Bromine
52. Bromine Pentafluoride
53. Bromoform
54. Butadiene- 1,3
55. Butane
56. Butanethiol
57. Butanone - 2
58. Butoxy Ethanol
59. Butyl Glycidal, Ether
60. Butyl Peroxyacctate, tert
61. Butyl Perxyiosobutyrate tert
62. Butyl Peroxyisopropyl Carbonate, Tert
63. Butyl Peroxymaleate, tert
64. Butyl Peroxypivalate, tert
65. Butyl Vinyl Ether
66. Butyl -n-Mercaptan
67. Butylamine
68. C 9-Aromatic Hydrocarbon Fraction
69. Cadmium and Compounds
70. Cadmium Oxide (fumes)
71. Calcium Cyanide
72. Captan
73. Captofol
74. Carbaryl (Sevin)
75. Carbofuran
76. Carbon Disulphide
77. Carbon Monoxide
78 Carbon Tetrachloride
79. Carbophenothion
80. Cellulose Nitrate
81. Chlorates (used in explosives)
82. Chlordane
83. Chlorfenvinphos
84. Chlorinated Benzenes
85. Chlorine
86. Chlorine Dioxide
87. Chlorine Oxide
88. Chlorine Triflouride
89. Chlormequat Chloride
90. Chloroacetalchloride
91. Chloroacetaldehyde
92. Chloroaniline, -2
93. Chloroaniline, -4
94. Chlorobenzene
95. Chlorodiphenyl
96. Chloroepoxypropane
97. Chloroethanol
98. Chloroethyl Chloroformate
99. Chlorofluorocarbons
100. Chloroform
101. Chloroformyl, -4, Morpholine
102. Chloromethane
103. Chloromethyl Ether
104. Chloromethyl Methyl Ether
105. Chloronitrobenzene
106. Chloroprene
107. Chlorosulphonic Acid
108. Chlorotrinitrobenzene
109. Chloroxuron

110. Chromium and Compounds
111. Cobalt and Compounds
112. Copper and Compounds
113. Coumafuryl
114. Coumaphos
115. Coumatetralyl
116. Cresols
117. Crimidine
118. Cumene
119. Cyanophos
120. Cynothoate
121. Cyanuric Fluoride
122. Cyclohexane
123. Cyclohexanol
124. Cyclohexanone
125. Cycloheximide
126. Cyclopentadiene
127. Cyclopentane
128. Cyclotetramethylene tetranitramine
129. Cyclotrimethylene Trinitramine
130. DDT
131. Decabromodiphenyl Oxide
132. Dementon
133. Di-Isobuty Peroxide
134. Din-Propyl Peroxydicarbonate
135. Di-sec-Butyl Peroxydicarbonate
136. Dialifos
137. Diazodinitrophenol
138. Diazomethane
139. Dibenzyl Peroxydicarbonate
140. Dichloroacetylene
141. Dichlorobenzene-o
142. Dichlorobenzene-p
143. Dichloroethane
144. Dichloroethyl Ether, - 2,4
145. Dichlorophenol, -2, 4
146. Dichlorophenol, - 2, 6
147. Dichlorophenoxy Acetic Acid, - 2, 4 (2, 4-D)
148. Dichloropropane, - 1, 2
149. Dichlorosalieylic Acid, - 3, 5
150. Dichlorvos (DDVP)
151. Dicrotophos
152. Dieldrin
153. Diepoxybutane
154. Diethyl Peroxydicarbonate
155. Diethylene Glyeol Dintrate
156. Diethylene Triamine
157. Diethyleneglycol Butyl Ether/ Diethyleneglycol Butyl
158. Diethylenetriamine (DETA)
159. Diglycidyl Ether
160. Dihydroperoxypropane, -2, 2
161. Disobutyryl Peroxide
162. Dimefox
163. Dimethoate
164. Dimethyl Phosphoramidocyanidic Acid
165. Dimethyl Phthalate
166. Dimethylearbomyl
167. Dimethylnitrosamine
168. Dinitrophenol, Salts
169. Dinitrotoluence
170. Dintro-o-Cresol
171. Dioxane
172. Dioxathion
173. Dioxolane
174. Diphacinone
175. Diphosphoramide Octamethyl
176. Dipropylene Glycolmethylether
177. Disulfoton

178. Endosulfan
179. Endrin
180. Epichlorohydrine
181. EPN
182. Epoxypropane, 1, 2
183. Ethion
184. Ethyl Carbamate
185. Ethyl Ether
186. Ethyl Hexanol, -2
187. Ethyl Mercaptan
188. Ethyl Methaorylate
189. Ethyl Nitrate
190. Ethylamine
191. Ethylene
192. Ethylene Chlorohydrine
193. Ethylene Diamine
194. Ethylene Dibromide
195. Ethylene Dichloride
196. Ethylene Glycol Dinitrate
197. Ethylene Oxide
198. Ethyleneimine
199. Ethylthiocyanate
200. Fensulphothion
201. Fluenetil
202. Fluoro, - 4, -2, Hydroxybutyric Acid and Salts, Esters, Amides
203. Fluoroacetic Acid and Salts, Esters, Amids
204. Fluorobutyric Acid, -4 and Salts, Esters, Amides
205. Fluorocrotonic Acid, - 4, and Salts, Esters, Amides.
206. Formaldehyde
207. Glyeonitrile (Hydroxyacetonitrile)
208. Guanyl, -1, -4, Nitrosaminoguanyl-1 Tetrazene
209. Heptachlor
210. Haxachloro Cyclopentadience
211. Hexachlorocyclohexane
212. Hexachlorocy cloamethane
213. Hexachlorodibenzo-p- Dioxin, -1, 2, 3, 7, 8, 9
214. Hexafluoropropene
215. Hexametylpho - Sphoramide
216. Hexamethyl, -3, 3, 6, 9, 9, -1, 2, 4, -5, Texbroxacyclononane
217. Hexamethylenediamine
218. Hexane
219. Hexanitrostlbene, -2, 2, 4, 4, 6, 6
220. Hexavalent Chromium
221. Hydrazine
222. Hydrazine Nitrate
223. Hydrochloric Acid
224. Hydrogen
225. Hydrogen Bromide (Hydrobromic Acid)
226. Hydrogen Chloride (Liquified Gas)
227. Hydrogen Cyanide
228. Hydrogen Flouride
229. Hydrogen Selenide
230. Hydrogen Sulphide
231. Hydroquinone
232. Iodine
233. Isobenzan
234. Isodrin
235. Isophorone Disocyanate
236. Ispropyl Ether
237. Juglone (5-Hydroxynaphthalene-1, 4, Dione)
238. Lead (inorganic fumes & dusts)
239. Lead 2, 4, 6. - Trinitroresorcinoxide (Lead Styphnate)

240. Lead Azide
241. Leptophos
242. Lindane
243. Liquified Petroleum Gas (LPG)
244. Maleic Anhydride
245. Manganese & Compounds
246. Mercapto Benzothiazole
247. Mercury Alkyl
248. Mercury Fulminate
249. Mercury Methyl
250. Methacrylic Anhydride
251. Methacryloyl Chloride
252. Methacrylonitrile
253. Methamidophos
254. Methanesuphonyl Fluoride
255. Methanethiol
256. Methoxy Ethanol (2- Methyl Cellosolve)
257. Methoxycthylmercuric Acctate
258. Methyl Acrylate
259. Methyl Alcohol
260. Methyl Amylketone
261. Methyl Bromide (Bromomethane)
262. Methyl Chloride
263. Methyl Choloroform
264. Methyl Cyclohexene
265. Methyl Ethyl Ketone Peroxide
266. Methyl Hydazine
267. Methyl Isobutyl Ketone
268. Methyl Isobutyl Ketone Peroxide
269. Methyl Isocyanate
270. Methyl Isothiocyanate
271. Methyl Mercaptan
272. Methyl Methacrylate
273. Methyl Parathion
274. Methyl Phosphonic Dichloride
275. Methyl- N, 2, 4, 6,-Tetranitroaniline
276. Methylene Chloride
277. Methylenebis, -4, 4, (2 - Chloroaniline)
278. Methyltrichlorosidane
279. Mevinphos
280. Molybdenum & Compounds
281. N-Methyl- N, 2,4,6,-N.- Tetranitroaniline
282. Naphtha (Coal Tar)
283. Napthylamine, 2
284. Nickel & Compounds
285. Nickel Petracarbonyl
286. Nitroaniline - O
287. Nitroaniline - P
288. Nitrobenzene
289. Nitrochlorobenzene - P
290. Nitrocyclohexane
291. Nitroethane
292. Nitrogen Dioxide
293. Nitrogen Oxides
294. Nitrogen Trifluoride
295. Nitroglycerine
296. Nitrophenol-P
297. Nitropropane - 1
298. Nitropropane-2
299. Nitrosodimethylamine
300. Nitrotoluene
301. Octabromophenyl Oxide
302. Oleum
303. Oleylamine
304. OO- Diethyl S- Ethylsulphonyl - methyl
305. OO-Deithyl S-Ethylsulphonyl-methyl Phosphorothleate

306. OO-Deithyl S-Ethylthiomethyl Phospherothioate
307. OO-Diethyl S-Isopropyltniomethyl Phosphoroditnloate
308. OO-Deithyl Ethylsulphonylmethyl Phosphorodithiote
309. Oxyamyl
310. Oxydisulfoton
311. Oxygen (Liquid)
312. Oxygen Dhluoride
313. Ozone
314. Paroxon (Diethyl 4 - Nitrophenyl Phosphate)
315. Paraquat
316. Parathion
317. Parathion Methyl
318. Paris green (Bis Aceto Hexametaarsenito Tetracopper)
319. Pentaborane
320. Pentabromophenol
321. Pentabromodiphenyl Oxide
322. Pentachloro Naphthalene
323. Pentachloroethane
324. Pentachlorophenol
325. Pentaerythritol Tetranitrate
326. Pentane
327. Paracetic Acid
328. Perchloroethylene
329. Perchloromethyl Mercaptan
330. Petanone, 2, 4-Methyl
331. Phenol
332. Phenyl Glycidal Ether
333. Phenylene p- Diamine
334. Phenylmercury Acetate
335. Phorate
336. Phosacetim
337. Phosalone
338. Phosfolan
339. Phosgene (Carbonyl Chloride)
340. Phosmet
341. Phosphamidon
342. Phosphine (Hydrogen Phosphide)
343. Phosphoric Acid, and Esters
344. Phosphoric Acid, Bromoethyl Bromo (2, 2-Dimethylpropyl) Bromoethyl Ester
345. Phosphoric Acid, Bromoethyl Bromo (2, 2- Dimethylpropyl) Chloroethyl Ester
346. Bhosphoric Acid, Chloroethyl Bromo (2, 2 - Dimethoxylpropyl) Chloroethylester
347. Phosphorous & Compounds
348. Phostalan
349. Picric Acid (2, 4, 6 - Trinitrophenol)
350. Polybrominated Biphenyls
351. Potassium Arsenite
352. Potassium Chlorate
353. Promurit (1-3, 4-Dichlorophenyl) -3-Triazenethiocarboxamide)
354. Propanesultone 1, 3
355. Propen, -1, -2-Chloro-1, 3-Dio 1 Diacetate
356. Propylene Dicloride
357. Propylene Oxide
358. Propyleneimine
359. Pyrazoxon
360. Selenium Hexafluoride
361. Semicarbazide Hydrochloride
362. Sodium Arsenite
363. Sodium Azide
364. Sodium Chlorate

365. Sodium Cyanide
366. Sodium Picramate
367. Sodium Selenite
368. Styrene 1, 1, 2, 2-Tetrachloroethane
369. Sulfotep
370. Sulphur Dichloride
371. Sulphur Dioxide
372. Sulphur Trioxide
373. Sulphuric Acid
374. Sulphoxide, 3-Chloroproyloctyl
375. Tellurium
376. Tellurium Hexafluoride
377. Tepp
378. Terbufos
379. Tetrabromobisphenol - A
380. Tetrachloro, 2, 2, 5, 6, 2, 5 - Cyclohexadiene -1, 4-Dione
381. Tetrachlorodibenzo-p Dioxin, 2, 3, 7, 8, (TCDD)
382. Tetraethyl Lead
383. Tetramethylenedi - Sulphotetramine
384. Tetramethyl Lead
385. Tetraflouroethane
386. Tetranitromethane
387. Thallium & Compounds
388. Thionazin
389. Thionyl Chloride
390. Tirpate
391. Toluene
392. Toluene-2-4-Diisocynate
393. Toluidine - O
394. Toluene 2, 6-Diisocynate
395. Trans-1, 4-Chlorobutene
396. Tri, -1, (Cyclohexyl) Stannyl-1H-1, 2, 4 - Trazole
397. Triamino, -1, 3, 5, 2, 4, 6-Trinitrobenzene
398. Tribromophenol, 2, 4, 6
399. Trichloro Acetyl Chloride
400. Trichloro Ethane
401. Trichloro Napthalene
402. Trichloro (chloromethyl) Silane
403. Trichlorodichloro - phenylsilane
404. Trichloroethane 1, 1, 1
405. Trichloroethyl Silane
406. Trichloroethylene
407. Trichloromethane-Sulphenyl Chloride
408. Trichlorophenol, 2, 2, 6
409. Trichlorophenol, 2, 4, 5
410. Triethylamine
411. Triethylenemelamine
412. Trimethyl Chlorosilance
413. Trimethylpropane Phosphite
414. Trinitroanline
415. Trinitroanisole 2, 2, 4, 6
416. Trinitrobenzene
417. Trinitrobenzoic Acid
418. Trinitrocresol
419. Trinitrophenetole 2, 4, 6
420. Trinitroresorcinol 2, 4, 6 (Styphnic Acid)
421. Trinitrotoluene
422. Triorthocresyl Phosphate
423. Triphenylin Chloride
424. Turpentine
425. Uranium & Compounds
426. Vanadium & Compounds
427. Vinyl Cloride
428. Vinyl Fluoride
429. Vinyl Toluene
430. Warfarin
431. Xylene
432. Xylidine
433. Zinc & Compounds
434. Zirconium & Compounds

SCHEDULE 2

[See rule 2(e), (ii), 4,(1)(b), 4(2)(1), and 6(1) (b)]

Isolated Storage at Installations other than those covered by Schedule 4.

(a) The threshold quantities set out below relate to each installation or group of installations belonging to the same occupier where the distance between installations is not sufficient to avoid, in foreseeable circumstances, any aggravation of major accident hazards. These threshold quantities apply in any case to each group of installations belonging to the same occupier where the distance between the installations is less than 500 metres.

(b) For the purpose of determining the threshold quantity of a hazardous chemical at an isolated storage, account shall also be taken of any hazardous chemical which is:—

(i) in that part of any pipeline under the control of the occupier having control of the site, which is within 500 metres of that site and connected to it;

(ii) at any other site under the control of the same occupier any part of the boundary of which is within 500 metres of the said site; and

(iii) in any vehicle, vessels aircraft or hovercraft under the control of the same occupier which is used for storage purpose either at the site or within 500 metres of it;

but no account shall be taken of any hazardous chemical which is in a vehicle, vessel, aircraftors, hovercraft used for transporting it.

Sl. No.	Chemical	Threshold Quantities (tones)	
		For application of Rules 4,5 and 7-9	For application of Rules 10 to 15
1	2	3	4
1.	Acrylonitrile	350	5,000
2.	Ammonia	60	600
3.	Ammonium nitrate (a)	350	2,500
4.	Ammonium nitrate fertilizers (b)	1,250	10,000
5.	Chlorine	10	25

1	2	3	4
6.	Flammable gases as defined in Schedule I, paragraph (b) (i)	50	300
7.	Highly flammable liquids as defined in Schedule I, paragraph (b) (ii)	10,000	10,000
8.	Liquid oxygen	200	2,000
9.	Sodium chlorate	25	250
10.	Sulphur dioxide	20	500
11.	Sulphur trioxide	15	100

(a) This applies to ammonium nitrate and mixtures of ammonium nitrate where the nitrogen contenι derived from the ammonium nitrate is greater than 28 per cent by weight and to aqueous solutions of ammonium nitrate where the concentration of ammonium nitrate is greater then 90 per cent by weight.

(b) This applies to straight ammonium nitrate fertilizers and to compound fertilizers where the nitrogen content derived from the ammonium is greater than 28 per cent by weight (a compound-fertilizer contains ammoniumnitrate together with phosphate and/or potash).

SCHEDULE 3

[See rule 2 (e)(iii), 5 and 6 (1)(a)]

List of Hazardous Chemicals for Application of Rules 5 and 7 to 15

(a) The quantities set-out below relate to each installation or group of installations belonging to the same occupier where the distance between the installations is not sufficient to avoid, in foreseeable circumstances, any aggravation of major-accident hazards. These quantities apply in any case to each group of installations belonging to the same occupier where the distance between the installations is less than 500 metres.

(b) For the purpose of determining the threshold quantity of a hazardous chemical industrial installation, account shall also be taken of any hazardous chemicals which is :—

(i) in that part of any pipeline under the control of the occupier having control of the site, which is within 500 metres of that site and connected to it;

(ii) at any other site under the control of the same occupier any part the boundary of which is within 500 metres of the said site; and

(iii) in any vehicle, vessel, aircraft or hovercraft under the control of the same occupier which is used for storage purpose either at the site or within 500 metres of it;

but no account shall be taken of any hazardous chemical which is in a vehicle, vessel, aircraft or hovercraft used for transporting it.

Part I

Named Chemicals

Sl. No.	Chemical	Threshold Quantity		CAS Number
		For application of Rules 5, 7-9 and 13-15	for application of Rules 10 to 12	
1.	2	3	4	5
Group 1 — Toxic Substances				
1.	Aldicard	100 kg		116-06-3
2.	4- Aminodiphenyl	1 kg		96-67-1
3.	Amiton	1 kg		78-53-5
4.	Anabasine	100 kg		494-52-0
5.	Arsenic peatoxide, Arsenic (V) acid & salts	500 kg		
6.	Arsenic trioxide, Arsenious (III) acid & salts	100 kg		
7.	Arsine (Arsenic hydride)	10 kg		7784-42-1
8.	Azinphos -ethyl	100kg		2642-71-9
9.	Azinphos-methyl	100 kg		86-50-0
10.	Benzidine	1 kg		92-87-5
11.	Benzidine salts	1 kg		
12.	Beryllium (powders compounds)	10 kg		
13.	Bis (2-chloroethyl) sulphide	1 kg		505-60-2
14.	Bis (chloroethyl) ether	1 kg		542-88-1
15.	Carbofuran	100 kg		1563-66-2
16.	Carbophenothion	100 kg		786-19-6
17.	Chlorfenvinphos	100 kg		470-90-6
18.	4-(Chloroformy) morpholine	1 kg		15159-40-7
19.	Chloromethyl methyl ether	1 kg		107-30-2

1	2	3	4	5
20.	Cobalt (metal, oxides, carbonates, sulphides, as powders)	1 t		
21.	Crimidine	100 kg		535-89-7
22.	Cyanthoate	100 kg		3734-95-0
23.	Cycloheximide	100 kg		66-81-9
24.	Demeton	100 kg		8065-48-3
25.	Dailifos	100 kg		10311-84-9
26.	OO-Diethyl S-ethyl-sulphinylmethyl phosphorothioate	100 kg		2588-05-8
27.	OO-Diethyl S-ethylsulphonyl-methyl phosphorothioate	100 kg		2588-06-9
28.	OO-Diethy S-ethylthiomethyl phosphorothioate	100 kg		2600-69-3
29.	OO-Diethy S-isopropylthio-methyl phosphorothioate	100 kg		78-52-4
30.	OO-Diethy S-propylthiomethyl phosphorothioate	100 kg		3309-68-0.
31.	Dimefox	100 kg		115-26-4
32.	Dimethylcarbamoyl chloride	1 kg		79-44-7
33.	Dimethylnitrosamine	1 kg		62-75-9
34.	Dimethyl phosphoramido-cynidic acid	1 t		63917-41-9
35.	Diphacinone	100 kg		82-66-6
36.	Disulfoton	100 kg		298-04-4
37.	EPN	100 kg		2104-64-5
38.	Ethion	100 kg		563-12-2
39.	Fensulfothion	100 kg		115-90-2
40.	Fluenetil	100 kg		4301-50-2
41.	Fluroacetic acid	1 kg		144-49-0
42.	Fluoroacetic acid, salts	1 kg		
43.	Fluoroacetic acid, esters	1 kg		
44.	Fluoroacetic acid, amides	1 kg		
45.	4-Fluorobutyric acid	1 kg		462-23-7

1	2	3	4	5
46.	4-Fluorobutyric acid, salts	1 kg		
47.	4-Fluorobutyric acid, esters	1 kg		
48.	4-Fluorobutyric acid, amides	1 kg		
49.	4-Fluorocrotonic acid	1 kg		37759-72-1
50.	4-Fluorocrotonic acid, salts	1 kg		
51.	4-Fluorocrotonic acid, esters	1 kg		
52.	4-Fluorocrotonic acid, amides	1 kg		
53.	4-Fluoro-2 hydroxybutyric acid	1 kg		
54.	4-Fluoro-2 hydroxybutyric acid, salts	1 kg		
55.	4-Fluoro-2 hydroxybutyric acid, esters	1 kg		
56.	4-Fluoro-hydroxybutyric acid, amides	1 kg		
57.	Glycolonitrile (Hydroyace tonitrile)	100 kg		19407-74-3
58.	1, 2, 3, 7, 8, 9 - Hexachlor odibenzo-p-dioxin	100 kg		19408-74-3
59.	Hexamethylphosphoramide	1 kg		680-31-9
60.	Hydrogen selenide	10 kg		7783-07-5
61.	Isobenzan	100 kg		297-78-9
62.	Isodrin	100 kg		465-73-6
63.	Juglone (5-Hydroxyna-phthalene 1, 4-dione)	100 kg		481-39-0
64.	4,-Methylenebis (2-chlo-roaniline)	10 kg		101-14-4
65.	Methyl isocyanate	150 kg		624-83-9
66.	Mevinphos	100 kg		7786-34-7
67.	2-Naphthylamine	1 kg		91-59-8
68.	Nickel (metal, oxides, ca-rbonates, sulphide, as powders)	1 t		
69.	Nickel tetracarbonyl	10 kg		13463-9-3
70.	Oxydisulfoton	100kg		2497-07-6
71.	Oxygen difluoride	10 kg		7783-41-7
72.	Paraoxon (Diethyl 4-nitro-phenyl phosphate)	100 kg		311-45-5

1	2	3	4	5
73.	Parathion	100 kg		56-38-2
74.	Parathion Methyl	100 kg		298-00-0
75.	Pentaborane	100 kg		19624-22-7
76.	Phorate	100 kg		298-02-2
77.	Phosacetim	100 kg		4104-14-7
78.	Phosgane (carbonyl chloride)	750 kg	750 kg	75-44-5
79.	Phosphamidon	100 kg		13171-21-6
80.	Phosphine (Hydrogen phosphide)	100 kg		7803-51-2
81.	Promurit (1-3, 4 Dichlorophenyl) -3, Trinazenethiocarboxamide)	100 kg		5836-73-7
82.	1, 3-Propanesultone	1 kg		1120-71-4
83.	1-Propen, -2-Chloro-1, 3 Diol diacetate	10 kg		10118-72-6
84.	Pyrazoxon	100 kg		108-34-9
85.	Selenium Hexafluoride	10 kg		7783-79-1
86.	Sodium Selenite	100 kg		10102-18-8
87.	Stibine (Antimony hydride)	100 kg		7803-52-3
88.	Sulfotep	100 kg		3689-24-5
89.	Sulphur Dichloride	1 t		10545-99-0
90.	Tellurium hexafluoride	100 kg		7783-80-4
91.	TEPP	100 kg		107-49-3
92.	2, 3, 7, 8-Tetrachlorodibenzo-p Dioxin, (TCDD)	1 kg		1746-01-6
93.	Tetramethylene-disulphotetramine	1 kg		80-1206
94.	Thioanizn	100 kg		297-97-2
95.	Tirpate (2, 4-Dimethyl-1, 3-dithiolane -2-carboxaldehyde O-Methylcarbomoyloxime)	100 kg		26419-73-8
96.	Trichloromethanesulphenyl chloride	100 kg		594-42-3
97.	1-Tri, (Cyclohexyl) Stannyl 1H-1, 2, 4 - Triazole	100 kg		41083-11-8
98.	Triethylenemelamine	10 kg		51-18-3
99.	Warfarin	100 kg		81-81-2

1	2	3	4	5
Group 2 — Toxic Substances				
100.	Acetone Cyanohydrine (2-Cyanopropan-2-01)	200t		75-86-5
101.	Acrolein (2-Propenal)	20t		107-02-8
102.	Acrylonitrile	20t	200t	107-13-1
103.	Allyl Alcohol (Propen-1-ol)	200t		107-18-6
104.	Allylamine	200t		107-11-9
105.	Ammonia	50t	500 t	7664-41-7
106.	Bromine	40t		7726-95-6
107.	Carbon disulphide	20t	200t	75-15-0
108.	Chlorine	10t	25 t	7782-50-5
109.	Diphenyl methane di-Isocyanate (MDI)	20 t		101-68-8
110.	Ethylene dibromide (1, 2-Dibromoethane)	5 t		106-93-4
111.	Ethyleneimine	50 t		151-56-4
112.	Formaldehyde (concentration 90%)	5 t		50-00-0
113.	Hydrogen chloride (liquified gas)	25 t	250t	7647-01-0
114.	Hydrogen Cyanide	5 t	20 t	74-90-8
115.	Hydrogen Flouride	5 t	50 t	7664-39-3
116.	Hydrogen Sulphide	5 t	50 t	7783-06-4
117.	Methyl Bromide (Bromomethane)	20 t		74-83-9
118.	Nitrogen oxides	50 t		11104-93-1
119.	Propyleneimine	50 t		75-55-8
120.	Sulphur dioxide	20 t	250 t	7446-09-5
121.	Sulphur trioxide	15 t	75 t	7446-11-9
122.	Tetaethyl Lead	5 t		78-00-2
123.	Tetramethyl lead	5 t		75-74-1
124.	Toluene di-isocyanate (TDI)	10 t		584-84-9 75-01-4
Group 3 — Highly Reactive Substances				
125.	Acetylene (ethyne)	5 t		74-86-2

1	2	3	4	5
126.	(a) Ammonium Nitrate (1)	350 t	2500t	6484-52-2
	(b) Ammonium Nitrates in form of fertiliser	1250 t		
127.	2, 2-Bis (tert-Butylperoxy) butane (concentration 70%)	5 t		2167-23-9
128.	1, 1-Bis (tert-Butylperoxy) cyclohexane (concentration—80%)	5 t		3006-86-8
129.	tert Butyl perpoxyacetate (concentration — 70%)	5 t		107-71-7
130.	tert Butyl peroxyisobutyrate (concentration — 80%)	5 t		109-13-7
131.	tert Butyl peroxyisopropyl carbonate (concentration — 70%)	5 t		2372-21-6
132.	tert-Butyl peroxymaleate (concentration — 80%)			1931-2-0
133.	tert Butyl peroxypivalate (concentration — 77%)	50 t		927-07-1
134.	Dibenzyl peroxydicarbonate (concentration — 90%)	5 t		2144-45-8
135.	Di-sec-Butyl peroxydicarbonate (concentration — 90%)	5 t		19910-5-0
136.	Diethyl peroxydicarbonate (concentration — 30%)	50 t		14666-78-5
137.	2, 2-Dihydroperoxypropane, (concentration — 30 %)	5 t		2614-76-8
138.	Di-isobutyryl peroxide (concentration — 50%)	50 t		3437-84-1
139.	Di-n-propyl peroxydicarbonate (concentration — 80%)	5 t		16066-38-9
140.	Ethylene oxide	5 t	50 t	75-21-8
141.	Ethyl nitrate	50 t		625-58-1
142.	3, 3, 6, 6, 9, 9-Hexamethyl-1, 2, 4, 5-tetrooxacyclononane (Concentration — 75%)	50 t		22397-33-7
143.	Hydrogen	2 t	50 t	1333-74-0
144.	Liquid oxygen	200 t		7782-44-7

1	2	3	4	5
145.	Methyl Ethyl Ketone Peroxide (concentration — 60 %)	5 t		1338-23-4
146.	Methyl Isobutyl Ketone Peroxide (concentration 60%)	50 t		37206-20-5
147.	Peracetic acid (concentration — 60%)	50 t		79-21-0
148.	Propylene oxide	5 t		75-56-9
149.	Sodium chlorate	25 t		7775-09-9
	Group 4 — Explosive Substances			
150.	Barium azide	50 t		18810-58-7
151.	Bis (2, 4, 6-Trinitrophenyl) Amine	50 t		131-73-7
152.	Chlorotrinitrobenzene	50 t		28260-61-9
153.	Cellulose nitrate (containing 12.6% Nitrogen)	50 t		9004-70-0
154.	Cyclotetramethylene tetranitramine	50 t		2691-41-0
155.	Cyclotrimethylene Trinitramine	50 t		121-82-4
156.	Diazodinitrophenol	10 t		7008-81-3
157.	Diethylene Glycol Dinitrate	10 t		693-21-0
158.	Dinitrophenol, salts	50 t		
159.	Ethylene Glycol Dinitrate	10 t		628-96-6
160.	1-Guanyl-4 nitrosaminoguanyl-1-tetrazene	10 t		109-27-3
161.	2, 2' 4, 4' 6, 6'-Hexanitrostilbene	50 t		20062-22-0
162.	Hydrazine nitrate	50 t		13464-97-6
163.	Lead azide	50 t		13424-46-9
164.	Lead styphnate(Lead 2, 4, 6-Trinitroresoreinoxide)	50		15245-44-0
165.	Mercury fulminate	10 t		20820-45-5
166.	N-Methyl- N, 2,4, 6-Tetranitroaniline	50 t		479-45-8
167.	Nitroglycerine	10 t	10 t	55-63-0
168.	Pentaerythritol Tetranitrate	50 t		78-11-5
169.	Picric Acid (2, 4, 6 - Trinitrophenol)	50 t		88-89-1
170.	Sodium picramate	50 t		831-52-7
171.	Styphnic acid (2, 4, 6 - Trinitroresoricinol)	50 t		82-71-3

1	2	3	4	5
172.	1, 3, 5-Triamino-2, 4, 6-Trinitrobenzene	50 t		3058-38-6
173.	Trinitroanline—	50 t		26952-42-1
174.	2, 4, 6-Trinitroanisole	50 t		606-35-6
175.	Trinitrobenzene	50 t		25377-32-6
176.	Trinitrobenzoic acid	50 t		35860-50-5 129-66-8
177.	Trinitrocresol	50 t		28905-71-7
178.	2, 4, 6-Trinitrophenitole	50 t		4732-14-3
179.	2, 4, 6 Trinitrotoluene	50 t	50 t	118-96-7

PART II

Classes of Substances not specifically named in Part - II

1	2	3	4	5
Group 5 — Flammable substances				
1.	Flammable gases : Substances which in the gaseous state at normal pressure and mixed with air become flammable and the boiling point of which at normal pressure is 20^0 C or below;	15 t	200 t	
2.	Highly flammable liquids: Substances which have a flash point lower than 21°C and the boiling point of which at normal pressure is above 20°C;	1000 t		50000 t
3.	Flammable liquids: Substances which have a flash point lower than 55°C and which remain liquid under pressure, where parti-	25 t	200 t	

cular processing conditions,
such as high pressure and
high temperature, may crea-
te major accident hazards.

(1) This applies to ammonium nitrate and mixtures of ammonium nitrate where the nitrogen content derived from the ammonium nitrate is greater than 28% by weight and aqueous solutions of ammonium nitrate where the concentration of ammonium nitrate is greater than 90% by weight.

(2) This applies to straight ammonium nitrate fertilizers and to compound fertilizers where the nitrogen content derived from the ammonium nitrate is greater than 28% by weight (a compound fertilizer contains ammonium nitrate together with phosphate and/or potash.

SCHEDULE 4

[See rule 2 (h) (i)]

1. Installations for the production, processing or treatment of organic or inorganic chemicals using for this purpose, among others:

(a) alkylation

(b) Amination by ammonolysis

(c) carbonylation

(d) condensation

(e) dehydrogenation

(f) esterification

(g) halogenation and manufacture of halogens

(h) hydrogenation

(i) hydrolysis

(j) oxidation

(k) polymerization

(l) sulphonation

(m) desulphurization, manufacture and transformation of sulphur-containing compounds

(n) nitration and manufacture of nitrogen-containing compounds

(o) manufacture of phosphorous-containing compounds

(p) formulation of pesticides and of pharmaceutical products

(q) distillation

(r) extraction

(s) solvation

(t) mixing

2. Installations for distillation, refining or other processing of petroleum products.

3. Installations for the total or partial disposal of solid or liquid substances by incineration or chemical decomposition.

4. Installations for production, processing or treatment of energy gases, for example, LPG, LNG, SNG.

5. Installation for the dry distillation of coal or lignite.

6. Installations for the production of metals or non-metals by a wet process or by means of electrical energy.

SCHEDULE 5

[See Rules 2 (b) and (3)]

Sl. No.	Authority (ies) with legal backing	Duties and corresponding Rule
1	2	3
1.	Ministry of Environment and Forests under Environment (Protection) Act, 1986.	(1) Notification of hazardous chemicals as per Rules 2 (e) (i) 2 (e) (ii) & 2 (e) (iii)
2.	Chief Controller Imports & Exports under Import & Export (Control) Act, 1947.	Import of hazardous chemicals as per Rule 18.
3.	Central Pollution Control Board or State Pollution Control Board under Environment (Protection) Act, 1986 as the case may be.	(1) Enforcement of directions and procedures in respect of isolated storage of hazardous chemicals, regarding.

1	2	3
6.	Chief Inspector of Mines appointed under the Mines Act, 1952.	Enforcement of directions and procedures in respect of industrial installations and isolated storages dealing with hazardous chemicals and pipelines including inter-state pipelines regarding,— (i) Notification of major accidents as per Rules 5 (1) and 5 (2) (ii) Notification of sites as per Rules 7 to 9 (iii) Safety reports as per Rules 10 to 12 (iv) Preparation of on-site emergency plans as per Rule 13 (v) Preparation of off-site emergency plans in consultation with District Collector or District Emergency Authority as per S. No. 9 of this Schedule.
7.	Atomic Energy Regulatory Board appointed under the Atomic Energy Act, 1972.	Enforcement of directions and procedures as per the provisions of the Atomic Energy Act, 1972.
8.	Chief Controller of Explosives appointed under the Indian Explosives Act and Rules, 1983.	Enforcement of directions and procedures as per the provisions of the Indian Explosives Act and Rules, 1983.
9.	District Collector or District Emergency Authority designated by the State Government.	Preparation of off-site emergency plans as per Rule 14.

SCHEDULE 6

[See rule 5 (1)]

INFORMATION TO BE FURNISHED REGARDING NOTIFICATION OF A MAJOR ACCIDENT

Report number..........of the particular accident.

1. General data
   (a) Name of the site
   (b) Name and address of the manufacturer
   (Also state telephone/telex number)
   (c) (i) Registration number
   (ii) Licence number
   (As may have been allotted under any statute applicable to the site, e.g., the Factories Act)
   (d) (i) Nature of industrial activity (Mention what is actually manufactured, stored, etc.)
   (ii) National Industrial Classification, 1987 at the four digit level.

2. Type of major accident
   Explosion Fire Emission of dangerous substance
   Substance(s) Emitted ....

3. Description of the major accident
   (a) Date, shift and hour of the accident
   (b) Department/Section and exact place where the accident took place
   (c) The process/operation undertaken in the Department/Section where the accident took place.
   (Attached a flow chart, if necessary)
   (d) The circumstances of the accident and the dangerous substances involved.

4. Emergency measures taken and measures envisaged to be taken to alleviate short-term effects of the accident.

5. Causes of the major accident.
   Known (to be specified)
   Not known
   Information will be supplied as soon as possible

6. Nature and extent of damage

(a) Within the establishment — casualities ....Killed

............Injured

............Poisoned

Persons exposed to the major accident.....................

material damage

danger is still present

danger no longer exists

(b) Outside the establishment — casualities ....Killed

............Injured

............Poisoned

Persons exposed to the major accident.....................

material damage

damage to environment

the danger is still present

the danger no longer exists

7. Data available for assessing the effects of the accident on persons and environment.

8. Steps already taken or envisaged

(a) to alleviate medium or long-term effects of the accident

(b) to prevent recurrence of similar major accidents

(c) Any other relevant information.

SCHEDULE 7

[See 7 (1)]

INFORMATION TO BE FURNISHED FOR THE NOTIFICATION OF SITES

Part I

Particulars to be included in a notification of a site.

1. The name and address of the employer making the notification
2. The full postal address of the site where the notifiable industrial activity will be carried on.

3. The area of the site covered by the notification and of any adjacent site which is required to be taken into account by virtue of b (ii) of Schedule 2 and 3.
4. The date of which it is anticipated that the notifiable industrial activity will commence, or if it has already commenced a statement to that effect.
5. The name and maximum quantity liable to be on the site of each dangerous substance for which notification is being made.
6. Organisation structure, namely organisation diagram for the proposed industrial activity and set up for ensuring safety and health.
7. Information relating to the potential for major accidents, namely:—
   (a) identification of major accident hazards;
   (b) the conditions or events which could be significant in bringing one about;
   (c) a brief description of the measures taken.
8. Information relating to the site namely—
   (a) a map of the site and its surrounding area to a scale large enough to show any features that may be significant in the assessment of the hazard or risk associated with the site.—
      (i) area likely to be affected by the major accident.
      (ii) population distribution in the vicinity.
   (b) a scale plan of the site showing the location and quantities of all significant inventories of the hazardous chemicals;
   (c) a description of the process or storage involving the hazardous chemicals and an indication of the conditions under which it is normally held;
   (d) the maximum number of persons likely to be present on site.
9. The arrangement for training of workers and equipment necessary to ensure safety of such work.

PART II

Particulars to be included regarding pipeline—

1. The names and the address of the person making the notification.
2. The full postal address of the place from which the pipelines activity is controlled, address of the places from which the pipeline starts and finishes and a map showing the pipeline route drawn to a scale of not less than 1 : 400000
3. The date on which it is anticipated that the notifiable activity will commence, or if it is already commenced a statement to that effect.

4. The total length of the pipeline, its diameter and normal operating pressure and the name and maximum quantity liable to be in the pipeline of each hazardous chemical for which notification is being made.

SCHEDULE 8

[See rule 10 (1)]

INFORMATION TO BE FURNISHED IN A SAFETY REPORT

1. The name and address of the person furnishing the information.
2. Description of the industrial activity, namely—
   (a) site,
   (b) construction design,
   (c) protection zones explosion protection, separation distances,
   (d) accessibility of plant,
   (e) maximum number of persons working on the site and particularly of those persons exposed to the hazard.
3. Description of the processes, namely—
   (a) technical purpose of the industrial activity,
   (b) basic principles of the technological process,
   (c) process and safety related data for the individual process stages,
   (d) process discription,
   (e) safety-related types of utilities.
4. Description of the hazardous chemicals, namely—
   (a) chemicals (quantities, substance data, safety-related data, toxicological data and threshold values)
   (b) the form in which the chemical may occur on or into which they may be transformed in the event of abnormal conditions.
   (c) the degree of purity of the hazardous chemical
5. Information on the preliminary hazard analysis, namely—
   (a) types of accident,
   (b) system, elements or events that can lead to a major accident,
   (c) hazards,
   (d) safety — relevant components.
6. Description of safety — relevant units, among others;
   (a) Special design criteria,

(b) controls and alarms,
(c) special relief systems,
(d) quick-acting valves,
(e) collecting tanks/dumps tank,
(f) sprinkler systems,
(g) fire-fighting etc.

7. Information on the hazard assessment, namely —
(a) identification of hazards,
(b) the causes of major accidents,
(c) assessment of hazards according to their occurrence frequency,
(d) assessment of accident consequences,
(e) safety systems,
(f) known accident history.

8. Description of information on organisational systems used to carry on the industrial activity safety, namely —
(a) maintenance and inspection schedules,
(b) guidelines for the training of personnel,
(c) allocation and delegation of responsibility for plant safety,
(d) implementation of safety procedures.

9. Information on assessment of the consequences of major accidents, namely—
(a) assessment of the possible release of hazardous chemicals or of energy
(b) possible dispersion of released chemical
(c) assessment of the effects of the releases (size of the affected area, health effects, property damage).

10. Information on the mitigation of major accidents, namely —
(a) fire brigade
(b) alarm systems
(c) emergency plan containing system of organisation used to fight the emergency, the alarm and the communication routes, guidelines for fighting the emergency, information about hazardous chemicals, examples of possible accident sequences.
(d) co-ordination with the District Emergency authority and its off-site emergency plan,
(e) notification of the nature and scope of the hazard in the event of an accident.
(f) antidotes in the event of a release of a hazardous chemical.

SCHEDULE 9

[See Rule 17]

SAFETY DATA SHEET

1. CHEMICAL IDENTITY

Chemical Name | Chemical Classification

Synonyms | Trade Name

Formula | C.A.S. No. | U.N. No.:

Regulated Identification | Shipping Name Codes/Label | Hazchem No.:

Hazardous No.:

I.D, No.:

Hazardous Ingredients. | C.A.S. No.: | Hazardous Ingredients | C.A.S. No.:

1. | 2.

3. | 4.

2. PHYSICAL AND CHEMICAL DATA

Boiling Range/Point °C | Physical State | Appearance

Melting/Freezing Point °C | Vapour Pressure 35°C mm Hg | Odour

Vapour Density (Air = 1) | Solubility in water 30°C | Others

Specific Gravity (Water=1) | pH

3. FIRE AND EXPLOSION HAZARD DATA

Flammability Yes/No | LEL | % Flash Point °C | Autoignition °C Temperature

TDG Flammability | UEL | % Flash Point °C

Explosion Sensitivity to Impact | Explosion Sensitivity to Static Electricity | Hardous Combustion Products

Hazardous Polymerisation

Combustible Liquid | Explosive Material | Corrosive Material

Flammable Material | Oxidiser | Others

Pyrophoric Material | Organic Peroxide

4. REACTIVITY DATA

Chemical Stability

Incompatibility with other Material

Reactivity

Hazardous Reaction Products

5. HEALTH HAZARD DATA

Routes of Entry

Effects of Exposure/Symptoms

Emergency Treatment

TLV (ACGIH)	ppm mg/m^3	STEL	ppm mg/m^3
Permissible Exposure Limit LD_{50}	ppm mg/m^3	Odour Threshold LD_{50}	ppm mg/m^3
NEPA Hazard Signals	Health Flammability		Stability Special

6. PREVENTIVE MEASURES

Personnel Protective Equipment

Handling and Storage Precautions

7. EMERGENCY AID FIRST AID MEASURE

FIRE	Fire Extinguishing media
FIRE	Special Procedures Unusual Hazards
EXPOSURE	First Aid Measures Antidotes/Dosages
SPILLS	Steps to be taken Waste Disposal Method

8. ADDITIONAL INFORMATION/REFERENCES

9 . MANUFACTURER/SUPPLIERS DATA

Name of Firm Mailing Address Telephone/Telex Nos. Telegraphic Address	Contact Person in Emergency
	Local Bodies involved
	Standard Packing
	Tremeard Details/Ref.
	Other

10. DISCLAIMER

Information contained in this material data sheet is believed to be reliable but no representation, guarantee or warranties of any kind are made as to its accuracy, suitability for a particular application or results to be obtained from them. It is upto the manufacturer/seller to ensure that the information contained in the material safety data sheet is relevant to the product manufactured/handled or sold by him as the case may be. The Government makes name warranties expressed or implied in respect of the adequacy of this document for any particular purpose.

SCHEDULE 10

[See Rule 18 (5)]

(Format for maintaining records of hazardous chemicals imported)

1. Name and address of the Importer:
2. Date and reference number of issuance of permission to import hazardous chemicals:
3. Description of hazardous chemicals:
   (a) Physical form:
   (b) Chemical form:
   (c) Total volume and weight (in Kilogrammes/tonnes)
   description of storage of hazardous chemicals:
4. Description of storage of hazardous chemicals:
   (a) Date:
   (b) Method of storage:

Index

A

B

E

J

K

L

M

N

O

P

R

S

T

U